# Family Law for Paralegals

## Fourth Edition

ASPEN PUBLISHERS

# Family Law for Paralegals

## Fourth Edition

**J. Shoshanna Ehrlich**
Associate Professor
College of Public and Community
University of Massachusetts — Boston

 Wolters Kluwer
Law & Business

AUSTIN   BOSTON   CHICAGO   NEW YORK   THE NETHERLANDS

Aspen Publishers
Attn: Permissions Department
76 Ninth Avenue, 7th Floor
New York, NY 10011-5201

To contact Customer Care, e-mail customer.care@aspenpublishers.com,
call 1-800-234-1660, fax 1-800-901-9075, or mail correspondence to:

Aspen Publishers
Attn: Order Department
PO Box 990
Frederick, MD 21705

Printed in the United States of America.

1 2 3 4 5 6 7 8 9 0

ISBN 978-0-7355-6382-7

**Library of Congress Cataloging-in-Publication Data**

Ehrlich, J. Shoshanna.
    Family law for paralegals/J. Shoshanna Ehrlich. —4th ed.
        p.cm
    Includes bibliographical refernces and index.
    ISBN 978-0-7355-6382-7
    1. Domestic relations — United States. 2. Legal assistants — United States — Handbooks,
manuals, etc. I. Title.
KF505.E35 2007
346.7301′5 — dc22
                                                        2007025960

# About Wolters Kluwer Law & Business

Wolters Kluwer Law & Business is a leading provider of research information and workflow solutions in key specialty areas. The strengths of the individual brands of Aspen Publishers, CCH, Kluwer Law International and Loislaw are aligned within Wolters Kluwer Law & Business to provide comprehensive, in-depth solutions and expert-authored content for the legal, professional and education markets.

**CCH** was founded in 1913 and has served more than four generations of business professionals and their clients. The CCH products in the Wolters Kluwer Law & Business group are highly regarded electronic and print resources for legal, securities, antitrust and trade regulation, government contracting, banking, pensions, payroll, employment and labor, and healthcare reimbursement and compliance professionals.

**Aspen Publishers** is a leading information provider for attorneys, business professionals and law students. Written by preeminent authorities, Aspen products offer analytical and practical information in a range of specialty practice areas from securities law and intellectual property to mergers and acquisitions and pension/benefits. Aspen's trusted legal education resources provide professors and students with high-quality, up-to-date and effective resources for successful instruction and study in all areas of the law.

**Kluwer Law International** supplies the global business community with comprehensive English-language international legal information. Legal practitioners, corporate counsel and business executives around the world rely on the Kluwer Law International journals, loose-leafs, books and electronic products for authoritative information in many areas of international legal practice.

**Loislaw** is a premier provider of digitized legal content to small law firm practitioners of various specializations. Loislaw provides attorneys with the ability to quickly and efficiently find the necessary legal information they need, when and where they need it, by facilitating access to primary law as well as state-specific law, records, forms and treatises.

Wolters Kluwer Law & Business, a unit of Wolters Kluwer, is headquartered in New York and Riverwoods, Illinois. Wolters Kluwer is a leading multinational publisher and information services company.

*To Alan, Emma, my father, and the memory of my mother*

# Summary of Contents

# Contents

## 2 Premarital Agreements 73

## 3 Domestic Violence 103

# 4 The Law of Divorce, Annulment, and Legal Separation     153

# 5 Child Custody

# 7  Spousal Support                                                        321

## 8 Division of Marital Property    359

## 9 Jurisdiction    401

# 10  The Divorce Process                                    429

# 11  Determining Paternity                                         527

## 12  Child Abuse and Neglect                                    569

# 13 Adoption 603

# List of Exhibits

# Preface

Welcome to the study of family law. This book is intended to provide you with a thorough working knowledge of this exciting area of the law. Along with its in-depth topical coverage, the book also addresses the important skills that a family law paralegal is likely to need in an active law office, such as client interviewing and legal drafting. However, in my view, it is not enough for a textbook simply to cover the topics and skills that a student will need in order to work effectively in a law office. Extending beyond that, a fundamental premise of this book is that paralegals are an integral part of the legal community and are entitled to a voice in the ongoing policy debates over contemporary efforts to reconfigure the legal contours of traditional family relationships. To help you enter into these discussions in an informed and engaged way, this book looks at both the historic understandings of the family and the critical legal issues facing us today regarding the future direction and definition of the family. This coverage will deepen your understanding of contemporary family law issues and enable you to think about emerging issues in a thoughtful way.

This book is divided into 13 chapters, each of which follows the same basic format. Most chapters begin with a brief historical overview of the subject matter of that chapter. By grounding your knowledge of the present in the past, you will have a more complete understanding of how the law has developed, which, in turn, will enhance your understanding of contemporary legal issues. In the text of each chapter, key terms are bolded. These terms are listed at the end of the chapter and defined in a glossary at the end of the book. At the end of the chapters, you will also find a chapter summary, review questions, discussion questions, assignments, and cases for analysis. The chapter summary provides you with a quick overview of what was covered in the chapter; it is not intended to be a substitute for the chapter content. To help orient yourself, you may find it helpful to read the summary before you read the chapter. The review questions follow the order of the chapter and are designed to help you determine how well you understood the chapter. They are a useful self-testing device. The discussion questions frame some of the more controversial and less settled aspects of the law discussed in the chapter. The assignments are designed to help you apply and further develop your understanding of the law. Last, each chapter (with the exception of Chapter 10) includes cases for analysis. These cases point to interesting and sometimes controversial aspects of the law. They are included to deepen your knowledge of the law, acquaint you with landmark decisions, and help you to develop your analytical and critical reading skills.

In using this book, you should keep a few important points in mind. First, although every effort has been made to ensure that this book is current, the law is always changing, and that which is current today may be obsolete tomorrow based on a new court decision or statute. Second, this book is written for a national audience and is not geared to the law of any particular state. In the course of your studies, you may want to learn more about the law of your state. Third, although I hope that this book will continue to be a resource for you when you leave school, it should be clear from the above two points that when working on an actual case, this book should not be your primary source of legal information. No book can substitute for the legal research required to ensure a current and comprehensive understanding of the applicable law in your jurisdiction. Good luck, and I hope you enjoy your entry into this fascinating area of the law!

July 2007                                        *J. Shoshanna Ehrlich*

# Acknowledgments

This book has benefited greatly from the contribution of many wonderful people who have given generously of both their time and their expertise. And although I certainly hope that this book is free of errors, if any do exist, I take full responsibility for them.

First, I would like to acknowledge the contribution of both my colleagues and students at the University of Massachusetts–Boston. The following students (now all graduates) provided invaluable research assistance: Janice Babcock (College of Public and Community Service), Vicki Kelleher (College of Public and Community Service), Barry Kilroy (College of Public and Community Service), John Martin (College of Public and Community Service), Darryl Palmer (College of Public and Community Service), and Sabah Uddin (College of Arts and Sciences). I would like to extend special thanks to David Kelly, also a graduate of the College of Public and Community Service, who worked tirelessly on the first three editions of this book. Through this close collaboration, David has been a constant source of both wisdom and encouragement. I also want to thank all of my family law students at UMass—you have kept me on my toes and inspired me to keep on growing as a teacher and a writer.

Many of my colleagues at UMass Boston's College of Public and Community Service have contributed to the development of this book. They have read and commented on various chapters, shared their accumulated expertise with me, and, as importantly, have been a wonderful source of support and friendship. In particular, I would like to thank Professors Brad Honoroff, David Matz, Terry McLarney, David Rubin, and Ann Withorn, and Administrative Dean Sarah Bartlett.

Thanks also to the following individuals who have helped to shape this book through their careful review of various chapters: Jacquelynne Bowman, Lynne Dahlborg, Janet L. Dolgin, Frederick M. Ehrlich, Judith Lennett, Jennifer Levi, Mary E. O'Connell, Paula Roberts, Alan Stoskopf, Stephen N. Subrin, and Joan Zora. This book has been improved immeasurably by the contribution of their expertise. I also want to extend special thanks to Jamie Ann Sabino, who has contributed more than she realizes to this book. On a more personal note, a number of special people in my life deserve mention. To my husband Alan Stoskopf and my daughter Emma Rose Stoskopf-Ehrlich, thank you for your love and support—you are my center. I could not ask for more from my partner and daughter. To my father, Fred Ehrlich, thank you for being there, and to the memory of my mother, who loved the written word. Thank you also to my siblings and dear friends for being such an important part of my life.

I would also like to thank Betsy Kenny and Kaesmene Harrison Banks of Aspen Publishers for all their hard work on this book.

# Family Law for Paralegals

## Fourth Edition

# 1 Marriage

When people think about marriage, they usually think of it as a private, intimate relationship shaped by the love, commitment, and needs of two individuals. However, this understanding of marriage as an essentially private relationship fails to account for the fact that the state also has an interest in marriage—an interest based on the belief that the exclusivity, permanence and procreative potential of the marital bond promotes social cohesion and stability. To promote this interest, states traditionally have exercised considerable control over marriage. Although state authority over the martial relationship itself has diminished over time, the rights, obligations, and entitlements of spouses are still structured by state law. States protect their interest in marriage through laws regulating marital entrances and exits. At formation, state laws permit marriages only between "qualified" individuals. At dissolution they structure the post-marital responsibilities of the parties.

As an important corollary, states also have fostered their interest in marriage by denying legal recognition to unmarried couples. Through marriage, individuals are transformed into a legally sanctioned unit, and they are automatically entitled to a host of benefits that traditionally have been denied to nonmarital couples:

- With marriage, each partner becomes formally connected to the family of the other. One literally acquires a "family-in-law." Mirror relationships are created such that the mother of one spouse becomes the mother-in-law of the other.
- Upon marriage, spouses automatically acquire the right to a wide range of entitlements, such as: social security and workers' compensation benefits, health insurance coverage, beneficial immigration status, and statutory rights of inheritance.
- With marriage, each spouse acquires a legal obligation to support the other. Historically, this obligation was imposed only upon husbands, but this obligation is now mutual.
- If a marriage ends, rights to property and support are automatically triggered, and state law provides a structured framework within which competing claims can be resolved. Although one does not usually think of divorce as a "benefit" that comes with marriage, it is important to recognize that divorce provides married couples

with a structured dissolution process that is not available to unmarried couples.

The modern trend has been away from state control over marriage in favor of greater individual autonomy with respect to shaping both the choice of a marital partner and the contours of the marital relationship. In turn, this shift has contributed to two of the most contested — and closely related — issues in the family law arena: whether same-sex couples should be permitted to marry, and whether legal recognition should be extended to non-marital couples.

## MARRIAGE: REGULATING THE RELATIONSHIP

The modern legal approach to marriage is to permit spouses to shape the contours of their own relationship, but this is a fairly recent development. Historically, the law carefully defined the mutual rights and obligations of husbands and wives based upon highly gendered notions of appropriate marital conduct.

### Common Law Origins

Our original marriage laws were based upon English **common law**.[1] As eloquently expressed by William Blackstone, a famed English legal commentator, a defining aspect of this tradition was the legal subordination of married women.

> By marriage, the husband and wife are one person in law; that is, the very being or legal existence of the woman is suspended during the marriage, or at least is incorporated and consolidated into that of the husband; under whose wing, protection, and *cover*, she performs everything . . . Upon this principle, of a union of person in husband and wife, depend almost all the legal rights, duties, and disabilities, that either one of them acquire by the marriage.[2]

It is worth noting that this doctrine of **marital unity** by which a husband and wife are regarded as a single legal person bears a striking similarity to the biblical concept of the unity of the flesh.

Outwardly manifested by the requirement that she take her husband's last name as her own, marriage altered a woman's legal status; rights that she possessed as a single woman were transferred to her husband in exchange for his support and protection. Upon marriage, a woman lost the right to own **personal property**. Property she owned at the time of marriage or subsequently acquired became her husband's. As owner, he could sell, destroy, or bequeath it, just as he could his separately acquired property. This property could also be taken by a husband's creditors in order to satisfy his debts. In short, as her person merged into her husband's so too did her property merge into his. **Real property**—land and whatever is grown on or fixed to it—was treated differently, as title did not pass to the husband. The husband did, however, acquire the exclusive right to manage and control the realty together with the right to all rents and profits derived from it. Although the nominal owner, a married woman could not convey her realty without the consent of her husband.

A married woman was regarded as unable to think for herself and thus lacked authority to act as an autonomous legal person. As a result, she lost the right to perform a variety of legal functions. Any **contracts** that she entered into were null and void. She also lost her **testamentary capacity**—the ability to make a will—and any wills she had made prior to marriage were automatically revoked. She could not sue or be sued in her own name. As the owner of her legal claims, her husband had to be joined as a party and was entitled to collect any damages.

Of profound consequence, a married woman also lost the right to her own labor. A husband acquired the right to his wife's services both at home and as performed for third parties. Because her labor belonged to him, he acquired an interest in the fruit of her labor, and monies paid to her for services she rendered became his. A husband's right to his wife's labor was characterized as a property interest. If his wife was injured by a third party, the husband was considered a victim in his own right and could sue for the loss of his wife's ability to perform her marital responsibilities. Damages frequently included compensation for the loss of her companionship, including sexual companionship, and her domestic services. Married women had no corresponding rights to their husband's services. As explained by Blackstone: "the inferior hath no kind of property in the company, care, or assistance of the superior, as the superior is held to have in those of the inferior."[3] In exchange for the loss of her legal persona, a married woman was entitled to be supported by her husband, and he became responsible for her debts, including those she came into the marriage with. This exchange of services for support lay at the heart of the common law marital relationship, and this core feature of marriage survived well into the twentieth century long after other common law marital requirements had been replaced by more modern rules.

Charged with this support duty, the husband was unquestionably considered the legal head of household with the right to make all major family decisions. Of particular significance was his unilateral right to decide where the family should live. A wife was required to follow her husband wherever he chose to go unless his choice was clearly unreasonable or intended as a punishment.

## The Civil Law Tradition

Eight states did not follow this English common law model. These states, known as **community property** or civil law states, are Arizona, California, Idaho, Louisiana, Nevada, New Mexico, Texas, and Washington. Based upon patterns of colonization and territorial acquisitions, theses states were influenced by Spanish civil law and, in the case of Louisiana, by Spanish and French law.

At least in theory, the status of married women was different in these states. Here, a wife's legal identity did not merge into her husband's. Instead, each spouse retained his or her separate identity, and marriage was viewed as a partnership. Subject to limited exceptions, property acquired during marriage was considered community property and belonged to both partners. However, the marital partners were not regarded as equals. A husband was given complete authority over the community property, including his wife's earnings; he could spend community assets freely, potentially leaving his wife with nothing to show for her contribution. Thus, in terms of her daily reality, the difference for a married woman between the common law and the civil law approaches would not have been as great as the doctrinal distinctions suggest.

## Married Women's Property Acts

Beginning in the late 1830s, states began passing laws known as the **Married Women's Property Acts**, which led to a gradual improvement in the legal status of married women.[4] Interestingly, the first such Acts were enacted in the South and appear to have been motivated by economic concerns, rather than by a desire to emancipate married women. Prompted by the economic panic of 1837, in which many southern plantation owners faced bankruptcy and loss of property — including slaves — to their creditors, legislators passed laws giving married women rights of ownership over their own property, which served to protect it from being seized by their husbands' creditors. Husbands, however, retained their common law right of management and control over their wives' property.

In other regions of the country, most notably the Northeast, the passage of these Acts responded more directly to concerns being voiced by the newly emerging women's rights movement about the legal subordination of married women. Although individual women had spoken out previously, 1848 marks the birth of the organized women's movement. That was the year women and men came together at Seneca Falls, New York, for the first women's rights convention in this country.

Although winning the right for women to vote soon became their focus, the reformers also sought legal equality for women within the domestic sphere. They attacked marriage laws as an abuse of male power, which relegated women to the status of children. As stated by Elizabeth Cady Stanton, an outspoken leader of the movement:

> . . . A man marrying gives up no right, but, a woman, every right, even the most sacred of all, the right to her own person . . . So long as our present false marriage relation continues, which in most cases is nothing more or less than legalized prostitution, women can have no self respect . . . Personal freedom is the first right to be proclaimed, and that does not and cannot now belong to the relation of wife . . . [5]

Reformers demanded: "(1) full control over their property with the powers to contract, will, and sue regarding it; (2) the right to their own wages; (3) recognition of the wife's joint right to the earnings of the co-partnership; and (4) equal guardianship of their children."[6] Striking at the heart of the traditional marital relationship and the husband's privileged position within the home, these demands were seen as radical and were often greeted with scorn and apprehension that women were seeking to rule their husbands.

However, over the last half of the nineteenth century, states responded to these demands in halting fashion. Bit by bit, laws were passed extending property rights to married women and lifting many of the common law disabilities, although no state, with the exception of Maine, gave married women full control over their property. By the turn of the century, married women had many more rights than they had previously possessed, and in some states, they could own property, enter into contracts, and sue and be sued in their own name. Some states also passed "earnings" laws, giving a married woman a property right in the labor she performed outside the domestic realm, thus entitling her, rather than her husband, to the earnings. Despite these reforms, in no state were married women considered the legal equals of married men. Significantly, despite the passage of the earnings statutes, husbands still had a property right in their wives' domestic services,[7] and they remained firmly ensconced as the legal head of the household. Thus, the essential nature of the marital relationship remained unaltered by these Acts; the reformers' vision of true legal equality between husband and wife remained but a distant dream.

## The Move to Legal Equality ————————————————————

As discussed in the previous section, historically our marriage laws reflected a highly gendered vision of the marital relationship. Rights and responsibilities were assigned based on deeply held beliefs about the proper role of women and their subordinate status. Although these underlying beliefs were challenged in the nineteenth century, leading to some legal reforms, the defining exchange of services for support continued to structure the marital relationship.

So powerful was this vision of woman as homemaker and man as provider that couples were unable to legally redistribute their roles through private, consensual agreements. By way of illustration, in 1940, a federal district court in Michigan refused to uphold an agreement between a husband and wife in which the husband agreed to quit his job and follow his wife in her travels in exchange for a monthly sum of money:

> As a result of the marriage contract . . . the husband has a duty to support and to live with his wife and the wife must contribute her services and society to the husband and follow him in his choice of domicile. The law is well settled that a private agreement between persons married or about to be married which attempts to change the essential obligations of the marriage contract as defined by the law is contrary to public policy and unenforceable.
>
> Even in the states with the most liberal emancipation statutes, . . . the law has not gone to the extent of permitting husbands and wives by agreement to change the essential incidents of the marriage contract.[8]

Beginning in the late 1960s, this gendered approach to marriage was again challenged. With the emergence of the second women's rights movement, women again began to fight against laws that limited their rights based on fixed notions of appropriate female behavior. Reformers sought to eliminate all remaining common law marital restrictions, including laws that required a woman to take her husband's last name and to follow him in his choice of domicile, and that limited a married woman's right to freely dispose of her property or carry on a trade. Additionally, as married women assumed a greater role in the workplace, reformers challenged the still powerful exchange of support for services requirement, arguing that it confined women to the home and fostered economic dependency.

Gradually, courts began striking down most of the remaining gender-specific marital laws. Based mainly on the **equal protection clause** of the fourteenth amendment to the Constitution, courts held that it was improper for states to assign rights and responsibilities based on fixed assumptions about the proper roles of men and women. Illustrative of this approach, in 1979, the United States Supreme Court invalidated Alabama's alimony law because it only imposed a support obligation on men:

> [T]he "old notion" that "generally it is the man's primary responsibility to provide a home and its essentials," can no longer justify a statute that discriminates on the basis of gender. "No longer is the female destined solely for the home and the rearing of a family, and only the male for the marketplace and world of ideas . . ."
>
> Legislative classifications which distribute benefits and burdens on the basis of gender carry the inherent risk of reinforcing stereotypes about the "proper place" of women and their need for special protection. Whereas here, the State's . . . purposes are well-served by a gender-neutral classification . . . the State cannot be permitted to classify on the basis of sex.[9]

In reviewing these marital laws that fixed the rights and obligations of spouses based on gender, courts were also influenced by the Supreme Court's decision in Griswold v. Connecticut. This 1965 case, which struck down a Connecticut statute prohibiting the use of contraceptives by married couples, enunciated a broad right of marital privacy.[10] Drawing on this right of privacy, courts limited the authority of states to structure the terms of the marital relationship. This was now regarded as a matter to be determined by individual spouses based on their own needs and desires.

Today, marriage is no longer considered a status relationship where marital roles are assigned by law without regard for individual choice, and the law no longer assigns married women a subordinate role. Legally, marriage now more closely resembles a contractual relationship in which rights and obligations are chosen according to the needs and desires of the particular couple. Of course, legal or formal equality does not necessarily result in actual equality, and many still view marriage as an institution that has not escaped the legacy of a highly gendered past.

---

### Consideration

The move toward legal equality has generated considerable discussion about the meaning of equality in the marital relationship. What do you think it means? Does it mean there is mutual respect? Does it mean equal decision-making power? Does it mean the full interchangeability of marital roles and responsibilities? Does it mean complete freedom to choose one's role and responsibilities? In thinking about these questions, also consider what social forces may be at play here. For example, does society have different expectations of husbands and wives? How might these impact individual marriages?

# ENTRANCE INTO MARRIAGE: CHOOSING A SPOUSE ─────────

Although state laws no longer define marital rights and obligations based upon gender, they continue to play an important role in shaping our understanding of the marital relationship by imposing certain restrictions on an individual's choice of marital partner. Although most of these restrictions, such as laws that prohibit close family members from marrying one another, are not controversial, one of the most heated issues of our time is whether states can prohibit marriage between same-sex partners. Before looking at the current debate over marital rights for same-sex partners, we consider several Supreme Court decisions that limit the ability of states to regulate marital partner choice.

## Marriage as a Fundamental Right ─────────────

In 1967, the United States Supreme Court, in the case of Loving v. Virginia,[11] struck down Virginia's anti-miscegenation law, which prohibited interracial marriage between white and "colored" persons. Reflective of their racist origins, anti-miscegenation laws date back to the time of slavery and were once in effect in a majority of states. When *Loving* was decided, Virginia was one of 16 states that still prohibited interracial marriage. Virginia's law was challenged by a couple who had been convicted of violating the ban on interracial marriage. They were given a one-year jail sentence, which was suspended on the condition that they leave Virginia and not return for 25 years.

On appeal, Virginia's highest court upheld the Lovings' conviction, concluding that the law was a valid exercise of state authority over marriage, and that Virginia could legitimately seek to "preserve the racial integrity of its citizens" and prevent "the corruption of blood (and) a mongrel breed of citizens."[12] The Supreme Court disagreed. Focusing on the racial hatred that had motivated passage of anti-miscegenation laws, the Court held that Virginia had violated the equal protection clause of the fourteenth amendment by restricting an individual's choice of marriage partner based on racial classifications. It also held that, under the **due process clause** of the fourteenth amendment, marriage is a *fundamental right*: "The freedom to marry has long been recognized as one of the vital personal rights essential to the orderly pursuit of happiness by free men. Marriage is one of the 'basic civil rights of man,' fundamental to our very existence and survival."[13] This case marks the first time that the Supreme Court limited the authority of a state to regulate entry into marriage.

Eleven years later, in the case of Zablocki v. Redhail,[14] the Court again invalidated a state law that restricted an individual's right to marry. In question was a law passed by the state of Wisconsin that prohibited non-custodial parents who were behind in child support payments from marrying. In support of the law, the state argued that it was necessary to ensure that noncustodial parents met existing child support obligations. In striking down the law, the Court, building upon *Loving*, held that marriage is a fundamental right and that a state may not impinge on this right in order to collect child support, especially since other collection mechanisms are available. However, it also stated that the right to marry, although fundamental, is not absolute, and that some restrictive laws would most likely withstand constitutional scrutiny. Subsequently, in the case of Turner v. Satley, the Court invalidated a Missouri law prohibiting inmates from marrying, finding that the state's interest in rehabilitation and security did not justify this limitation on an individual's fundamental right to marry.[15]

## Restrictions on Entry into Marriage

Although the right to marry is now constitutionally protected, all states still have laws in effect that restrict an individual's choice of marriage partner. These laws have been either not challenged or upheld on the grounds that they promote important state interests. Before considering the marital rights of same-sex partners, we consider some of the more common **marriage restriction laws** in effect today.

---

### Consideration

In the following section, some common marriage restriction laws are discussed. As you read, think about how these decisions about who can marry are made, what criteria seem important, and what interests are served by these restrictions.

---

### Incest

All states have criminal **incest** laws that make it a crime for family members within a certain degree of kinship to engage in sexual relationships with one another. Running along parallel lines, marriage restriction laws generally prohibit these same relatives from marrying.

These laws have religious roots, and can be traced back to the book of Leviticus. At one time, based on the view that a husband and wife were a single person, incest laws applied equally to persons related by marriage (affinity) and those related by blood (consanguinity); in effect, the blood relatives of one spouse were treated as the blood relatives of the other. Today, most states no longer prohibit marriages between persons related by affinity but retain the prohibition against marriage between stepparents and stepchildren to protect children from sexual exploitation.

In terms of specific prohibitions, all states forbid marriage between a parent and child, a grandparent and grandchild, and a brother and sister of whole or half blood. Most states treat sibling relationships created through adoption as a blood relation, and thus prohibit marriage between adopted siblings, and most, if not all, states prohibit marriage between an uncle and a niece and between an aunt and a nephew. With respect to first cousins, the trend is in favor of lifting this restriction, and fewer than half the states now bar first cousins from marrying. This trend reflects the fact that concerns about the genetic risks of "inbreeding" have turned out to be less significant than once believed, at least where first cousins are concerned. According to a report of the National Society of Genetic Counselors, studies indicate that "the increased risk for a significant birth defect in offspring of a first cousin union range between 1.7 and 2.8% above the risk of the general population."[16] However, some states permit first cousins to marry only where the parties are over procreative age or provide evidence of genetic counseling.

Although incest laws are religious in origin, other explanations have been advanced to support such restrictions, which, at least with respect to the parent/child and sibling relationship, have near universal reach. From a sociological perspective, these restrictions have been explained as necessary to preserve the family unit by preventing it from being torn apart by sexual rivalries. From a political perspective, these restrictions have been explained as necessary to early survival and community building, as they compelled families to establish alliances outside their own immediate kin group. Genetic concerns about the dangers of inbreeding and the transmission of negative recessive traits also have played a significant role in the continuation of incest restrictions. Child advocates see these rules as necessary to protect children from sexual exploitation by family members and to provide them with a safe, sexually neutral environment in which to mature. Finally, there is the "yuck" factor — most people react with disgust at the thought of crossing the incest bar, although it is hard to know if this reaction is a cause or a result of the taboo.

Given that marriage is a fundamental right, some commentators have questioned the appropriateness of state laws that prevent consenting adults from marrying one another based on family ties. As expressed by one author:

> All too often . . . society is merely trying to save the individual from conduct that society finds repulsive. State intervention into adult decision-making must be restricted to those instances where the danger of imminent bodily harm is readily demonstrable and marriage between adults related by consanguinity or affinity does not meet this requirement.[17]

Although there has been some loosening of incest-based restrictions, as in the case of first-cousin marriages, there does not appear to be a growing trend in favor of eliminating this category of marriage restriction laws.

---

### Consideration

Despite the internal logic of this argument, it is hard to imagine that states would eliminate incest prohibitions in order to enhance individual autonomy. What role do you think morality or public repugnance should play in the preservation of legal proscriptions that limit a fundamental right?

---

### Multiple Marriages

All states prohibit a person from having more than one spouse at a time. The term **bigamy** describes the situation where a person enters into a second marriage while his or her first marriage is still in effect; the term **polygamy** applies to the situation where an individual (most commonly a man) has multiple spouses at the same time. A marriage contracted in violation of the "more than one spouse at a time" prohibition is void and may subject the participants to criminal prosecution.

Like incest prohibitions, these laws have religious underpinnings: monogamy is a central tenet of the Judeo-Christian belief structure. However, unlike the incest taboo, the prohibition against multiple spouses has far less universal reach. For example, in this country, Mormon settlers in what is now Utah regarded the taking of multiple wives as a matter of divine right based on a revelation of the religion's founder, Joseph Smith. In 1890, the Mormon Church repudiated the practice as a condition of Utah's admission as a state; however, since then Mormon fundamentalists have revived the practice.

Although rooted in religious principles, the prohibition of multiple spouses has been justified on a number of other grounds. Perhaps most important, it has been regarded as essential to preserving the integrity of families by limiting an individual's financial and emotional commitments to a single spouse and their offspring. Other concerns include the potential coercion of women, the neglect of children, and the Mormon practice of older men taking girls as young as fourteen to be one of their multiple wives.

Since the Court's decision in *Zablocki*, some commentators have questioned the validity of the state's interest in prohibiting individuals from having more than one spouse at a time. For example, they point out that these laws do not really promote the state's interest in protecting the integrity of families, since the same concerns about financial and emotional instability are present with remarriage (or as it is sometimes called, sequential polygamy) and no limits are placed on the number of times a person can remarry and reproduce with each successive spouse.

### Marital Age

Complex rules govern the ability of young people to marry. Most states set a minimum age, referred to as the **age of capacity**, below which a young person may not marry. Commonly, this age is 14. Some laws contain exceptions for circumstances such as pregnancy, but the exception usually confers a conditional rather than an absolute right of marriage since most states require a minor to first obtain parental and/or judicial consent. Most states also set an age at which a person becomes eligible to consent to his or her own marriage. This is referred to as the **age of consent**, and it is usually set at 18 — the age of majority.

For young people below the age of consent and, where applicable, above the age of capacity, the right to marry is usually conditional upon obtaining parental and/or judicial consent. Generally, states allow older minors to marry with the consent of a parent, but for younger minors, the consent of a parent and a judge is necessary. In some states, if a parent withholds permission, a minor may petition the court for approval. These laws were designed to serve at least two state interests. First, by requiring parental participation and approval, they support the traditional authority of parents over their children. Second, and perhaps more important, they are thought to protect minors from making ill-advised decisions with potentially long-term harmful consequences for themselves and future offspring. Although there has been a growing trend toward granting minors greater legal autonomy, challenges to these laws have not generally been successful.[18] One important reason is that unlike other decisions, such as whether to terminate a pregnancy, the marriage decision can be postponed without any lasting, negative consequences. Moreover, unlike anti-miscegenation laws, or laws prohibiting marriage between same-sex partners, age-restriction laws are not an absolute barrier to marrying one's chosen partner; they simply require deferral of the marriage date.

---

### Consideration

It makes sense to encourage teenagers to involve their parents in a major decision such as marriage. On the other hand, as parents cannot prohibit children from forming intimate relationships and bearing offspring outside of marriage, do marital age laws accomplish their intended purposes?

---

### Same-Sex Couples

Gay men and lesbians have been fighting for the right to marry since the early 1970s, when a number of same-sex couples who were denied marriage licenses brought lawsuits challenging the fairness of restricting marriage to heterosexual couples.[19] Citing *Loving*, they argued that with marriage now firmly established as a fundamental right, states no longer had a valid basis for excluding same-sex couples who, like their heterosexual counterparts, were seeking the acceptance and benefits that derive from state recognition.

In this early round of cases, courts did not take this assertion seriously. They consistently concluded that the fundamental right to choose one's marital partner does not extend to same-sex partners because marriage has always been between a man and a woman, thus placing same-sex partners outside the reach of the due process clause. The courts similarly concluded that because same-sex couples are critically different from male-female couples, particularly with respect to procreative potential, denying same-sex couples marital rights did not violate the equal protection clause because this clause only requires like treatment of persons who are similarly situated. Courts also made clear that a number of important state interests—such as encouraging procreation and protecting the traditional family—were of sufficient magnitude to offset any potential limitation of rights. Rejecting the *Loving* analogy, courts refused to consider the possibility that the exclusion was based on anything other than legitimate differences, such as social and religious bias against gay men and lesbians.[20]

Following these defeats, gay rights activists turned to other approaches, such as domestic partnership initiatives (discussed below), to obtain recognition of their relationships and access to family benefits. They also hoped that a more gradualist approach would lead to a greater acceptance of gay couples that would eliminate social hostility to the idea of same-sex marriage. In the late 1980s, prompted in part by the AIDS epidemic and bolstered by gains in civil rights protections for gay men and lesbians, there was renewed interest in securing marital rights. This time around, the legal challenges have met with considerably greater success; these recent gains have also, however, been eroded by a national backlash against gay marriage.

**Contemporary Marriage Cases:** In the 1990s, same-sex couples in Hawaii and Alaska who were denied marriage licenses brought lawsuits arguing that the denial deprived them of the right to privacy and equal protection under their respective state constitutions.[21] Courts in both states briefly seemed ready to extend marital rights to same-sex couples. While the cases were winding their way through the courts, though, marriage-rights opponents waged successful campaigns to amend their respective state constitutions to define marriage as being between one man and one woman thus effectively bringing the court challenges to an end.[22]

Since the cases in Hawaii and Alaska, the landscape has changed considerably. Courts in three states have extended marriage or marriage-like rights to same-sex couples. Not surprisingly, these decisions have not quieted the debate over same-sex marriage; if anything, they have further galvanized activists on both sides of the great marriage divide.

*Baker v. Vermont.* In the 1999 case of Baker v. Vermont, the Supreme Court of Vermont held that depriving same-sex couples of the legal benefits and protections that flow from marriage contravenes the common benefits clause of the Vermont Constitution, which requires equal and inclusionary treatment of all Vermont citizens.[23] In reaching this conclusion, the Court rejected the state's argument that the state needed to ban marriage to preserve the historic link between procreation and child rearing, and to reinforce the importance of having both a male and a female parent as role models. Also important to the Court's common-benefits analysis was the recognition that same-sex couples would continue to have children regardless of whether they were allowed to marry, and that Vermont allows same-sex parents to adopt, thus acknowledging as a matter of state policy that gay men and lesbians can be good parents.

In evaluating the plaintiffs' claim, the *Baker* Court focused on their exclusion from the benefits and protections of marriage rather than on their exclusion from marriage itself, and it therefore sought to rectify this tangible discrimination. In fashioning a remedy, the Court directed the Vermont legislature to equalize access to the benefits and protections of marriage, making it clear that as long as this broad goal was accomplished, the extension of marital rights was not a constitutional requirement.

Responding to the Court's decision, the Vermont legislature chose to remedy the discrimination by creating a new legal relationship, known as a **civil union**, rather than by extending marital rights to same-sex partners. By entering into a civil union, a couple is entitled to the benefits and protections of marriage, and are likewise subject to the obligations of marriage, and the relationship can be dissolved only through the filing of a divorce action in family court.

*Goodridge vs. Department of Public Health (Massachusetts).* Although the *Baker* decision went significantly further than any prior decision, it stopped short of extending equal marriage rights to same-sex couples. That dramatic development first occurred in 2003, when the Massachusetts Supreme Judicial Court (SJC), in the groundbreaking case of Goodridge v. Department of Public Health, ruled that same-sex couples have a constitutional right to marry.[24] In contrast to the Vermont Court, the SJC refused to disaggregate the tangible benefits of marriage from its symbolic value. Focusing on the importance of marriage itself, the SJC stated:

> Without question, civil marriage enhances the "welfare of the community." It is a "social institution of the highest importance." Civil marriage anchors society by encouraging stable relations over transient ones . . .
>
> Marriage also bestows enormous private and social advantages on those who choose to marry. Civil marriage is at once a deeply personal commitment to another human being and a highly public celebration of the ideals of mutuality, companionship, fidelity, and family. . . . Because it fulfils yearnings for security, safe haven, and connection that express our common humanity, civil marriage is an esteemed institution, and the decision whether and whom to marry is among life's momentous acts of self-definition.[25]

In deciding for the plaintiffs, the Court rejected the state's assertion that the marriage ban is necessary to ensure a favorable setting for procreation and child rearing, concluding that there is no reasonable connection between protecting the welfare of children and barring same-sex couples from marrying. The Court also rejected the state's argument that allowing same-sex marriage would trivialize or even destroy "the institution of marriage as it has historically been fashioned." Instead, the Court stated that "[i]f anything, extending civil marriage to same-sex couples reinforces the importance of marriage to individuals and communities . . . (and) is a testament to the enduring place of marriage in our laws and in the human spirit."[26]

In order to remedy the discrimination, the court concluded that the common law definition of marriage should be modified to mean "the voluntary union of two persons, as spouses, to the exclusion of all others." It then stayed the implementation of the decision for 180 days to give the legislature time to bring the state's marital laws into conformity with the decision. Subsequently, on May 17, 2004, in a historic first, more than one thousand same-sex couples obtained marriage licenses, with many also obtaining a waiver of the three-day waiting period, so that they could actually celebrate their marriages on this historic day.

*Lewis v. Harris (New Jersey).* Most recently, the New Jersey Supreme Court ruled that under the state constitution "every statutory right and benefit conferred to heterosexual couples through civil marriage must be made available to committed same-sex couples."[28] As this language makes clear, this Court also distinguished between the right to marry and the right to the benefits and protections of marriage. And, as did its counterpart in Vermont, the New Jersey Supreme Court also concluded that it was up to the legislature to determine whether the discrimination should be remedied through the conferral of marital rights or through the creation of a "parallel statutory structure by another name, in which same-sex couples would not only enjoy the rights and benefits, but also bear the burdens and obligations of civil marriage."[29]

**Contested Meanings of Equality:** Although high courts in three states have ruled in favor of ending discrimination against same-sex couples, only one ruled that this result requires ending the marriage ban, thus raising an important question about the meaning of equality. According to the *Baker* and *Lewis* Courts, eliminating the discriminatory allocation of the benefits and privileges of marriage satisfies the constitutional guarantee of equality. In contrast, the *Goodridge* Court sees marriage as a holistic relationship that provides both tangible benefits and "fulfils yearnings for security, safe haven, and connection that expresses our common humanity," thus making "the decision whether and whom to marry . . . among life's momentous acts of self-definition."[30] Accordingly, although the extension of benefits alone is important, it cannot rectify the "deep and scarring hardship" that exclusion from this cherished institution imposes on same-sex couples; as viewed by the *Goodridge* Court, only the extension of full marital rights can rectify the harm.[31]

As the dissenting justice in *Lewis* put it in explaining why equalizing benefits was not enough to create true equality: "We must not underestimate the power of language. Labels set people apart as surely as physical separation on a bus or in school facilities . . . By excluding same-sex couples from civil marriage, the State declares that it is legitimate to distinguish between their commitments and the commitments of heterosexual couples.

Ultimately, the message is that what same-sex couples have is not as important or as significant as "real" marriage . . ."[32] So viewed, true equality requires access to both the symbolic and the tangible dimensions of marriage, and can thus only be accomplished through the full extension of marital rights.

**The Campaign to Preserve Marriage as a Heterosexual Institution:** Since the early 1990s, when same-sex marriage first seemed realistically possible in Hawaii and Alaska, marital rights opponents have waged an active and generally successful campaign to legally define marriage as the union between one man and one woman. Motivating this campaign is the fear that states will be required to recognize same-sex marriages (and possibly also civil unions) that were entered into in other states under the long-standing common law "place of celebration" rule, which requires states to honor valid out-of-state marriages and the full faith and credit clause of the United States Constitution, which requires states to honor the "public acts, records and judicial proceedings of every other state."[33]

**Efforts at the Federal Level:** In 1996, fearing the potential spread of marital rights for gay and lesbian couples from the shores of Hawaii to the mainland, Congress enacted the **Defense of Marriage Act** (DOMA). DOMA has two key provisions. One provision seeks to avoid the potential effect of the full faith and credit clause by allowing states to deny recognition to marriages between same-sex partners. In relevant part, the Act reads: No State . . . shall be required to give effect to any public act, or judicial proceeding of any other state . . . respecting a relationship between persons of the same sex that is treated as a marriage under the laws of such other State.[34] DOMA's other key provision states that, for purposes of federal law, "the word 'marriage' means only a legal union between one man and one woman as husband and wife, and the word 'spouse' refers only to a person of the opposite sex who is a husband or wife.[35] Accordingly, even if a couple is validly married under state law, pursuant to DOMA they are not married in the eyes of the federal government; as a result, they are not entitled to the many federal benefits, such as social security, that are available to married heterosexual couples.

Many doubts have been raised about the constitutionality of DOMA. One concern is that Congress exceeded the scope of its lawful authority when it authorized states to divest same-sex couples of the right to interstate recognition of their marriages under the full faith and credit clause. Another concern is that because DOMA singles out gay men and lesbians for discriminatory treatment, it may violate the equal protection clause of the fourteenth amendment.[36]

Fearful that DOMA may eventually be invalidated by the courts, opponents of same-sex marriage are hoping to amend the federal constitution to limit marriage to heterosexual couples. First introduced into Congress in 2003, the **Federal Marriage Amendment** (FMA), states that "[m]arriage in the United States shall consist only of the union of a man and a woman," and the FMA would prevent either the federal or any state constitution from being construed to require that "marriage or the legal incidents thereof be conferred upon any union other than the union of a man and a woman."[37] The FMA would be a highly unusual constitutional amendment in that it seeks to limit, rather than to expand or protect, the rights of individuals. Nonetheless, shortly after the Goodridge decision, President Bush, although recognizing "that an amendment to the Constitution is never to be taken lightly," declared that such an approach was needed in order to "prevent the meaning of marriage from forever being changed."[38]

**Efforts at the State Level:** Following the lead of the federal government, most states have expressly banned marriages between same-sex partners. As the map below illustrates, as of November 2006, twenty-six states had amended their state constitution to limit marriage to one man and one woman, and nineteen states had accomplished the same result by statute. These mini-DOMAs, as they are often referred to, generally track the federal statute. Most define marriage as being between one man and one woman, and, they withhold recognition from valid marriages between same-sex couples that were entered into in other jurisdictions.

An important question that courts are beginning to struggle with is whether, under these mini-DOMAs, a state may refuse to recognize other types of relationships between same-sex partners, such as civil unions or **domestic partnerships**. Since the 1999 *Baker* decision, the answer in a growing number of states has become "yes," as language has been included in (or added to) laws and constitutional amendments extending the nonrecognition principle to marital-like relationships. In these instances, the state statute reaches further than DOMA, which, at least at the present time, focuses on marriage itself. Where the statute or amendment refers only to the nonrecognition of marriages between same-sex partners, the answer is less clear. Some courts have extended recognition to Vermont civil unions on the theory that they are a status separate and apart from marriage and thus lie outside the law's prohibitionary reach. Other courts, while also distinguishing civil unions from marriage, have refused to recognize them on the grounds that recognition would offend the state's public policy against the formalization of same-sex relationships, with some invoking the state's mini-DOMA as the formal embodiment of this disapproval.

## Exhibit 1.1   Statewide Marriage Law

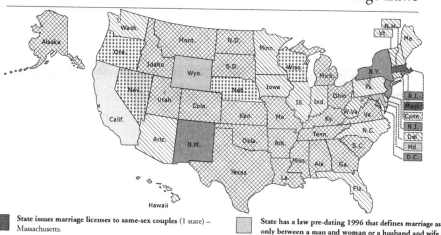

Statewide
Marriage Laws

State issues marriage licenses to same-sex couples (1 state) – Massachusetts.

State has no explicit provision prohibiting marriages between individuals of the same sex (4 states and DC) – New Jersey, New Mexico, New York, and Rhode Island and the District of Columbia.

State has passed a law in response to marriage litigation in the mid 1990s and the passage of the federal "Defense of Marriage Act" that restricts marriage to a man and woman and purports to not honor marriages between same-sex couples from other jurisdictions (16 states) – Arizona (1996), Connecticut (2005), Delaware (1996), Florida (1997), Hawaii* (1998), Illinois (1996), Indiana (1997), Iowa (1998), Maine (1997), Minnesota (1997), New Hampshire (2004), North Carolina (1996), Pennsylvania (1996), Tennessee (1996), Vermont (1999), Washington (1998) and West Virginia (2000).

State has a marriage law pre-dating 1996 that defines marriage as only between a man and woman and passed a law purporting to not honor marriages of same-sex couples from other jurisdictions (1 state) – California (1977/2000).

State has a law pre-dating 1996 that defines marriage as only between a man and woman or a husband and wife (2 states) – Maryland and Wyoming.

State has amended its state constitution to purport to declare marriages between same-sex couples void or invalid (4 states) - Nebraska (2000), Nevada (2002) Oregon (2004), and Wisconsin (2006).

State has amended its state constitution to purport to declare marriages between same-sex couples void or invalid and has passed a law in response to marriage litigation in the mid 1990s and the passage of the federal "Defense of Marriage Act" that defines marriage as between a man and woman and purports to not honor marriages between same-sex couples from other jurisdictions (22 states) – Alabama (2006/1998), Alaska (1998/1996 ), Arkansas (2004/1997), Colorado (2006/2000), Georgia (2004/1996), Kansas (2005/1996), Kentucky (2004/1998), Idaho (2006/2000), Louisiana (2004/1999), Michigan (2004/1996), Mississippi (2004/1997), Missouri (2004/2001), Montana (2004/1997), North Dakota (2004/1997) Ohio (2004/2004), Oklahoma (2004/1996), South Carolina (2006/1996), South Dakota (2006/1996), Tennessee (2006/1996), Texas (2005/2003), Virginia (2006/1997), and Utah (2004/1995).

* Hawaii is often mistaken as having a constitutional amendment prohibiting marriage for same sex couples. The state's constitution was amended in 1998 to read: "The Legislature shall have the power to reserve marriage to opposite-sex couples." It was the Hawaii Legislature that passed a law prohibiting marriage for same-sex couples.

** This information has required no update since Nov. 2006.

*Source:* Human Rights Campaign, http://www.hrc.org. Reprinted with permission.

## MARRIAGE FORMALITIES

State control over marriage, particularly in structuring the terms of the marital relationship, has diminished over time. However, as clearly evidenced by the requirement that a couple must obtain a license in order to be recognized as legally wed, marriage continues to be a state-sanctioned and regulated relationship.

Thus, although we tend to think of a marriage ceremony as a private event, it is actually compliance with state licensing procedures, rather than saying "I do," that makes one married.

### Obtaining a Marriage License

Although the requirements vary from state to state, the differences are generally minor. Allowing for variation, the following discussion provides an overview of the steps a couple must follow in order to establish a valid marriage and the rationale behind the requirements.

First, a couple must obtain a marriage license (Exhibit 1.2). Licenses are usually issued by a county or municipal officer, such as a clerk. Application is made by providing information under oath about age, prior marriages, and possibly also the legal relationship between the intended spouses. In some states, the clerk simply approves or denies the license based on the information as it appears on the face of the application. In other states, the clerk has some responsibility to assess whether the information provided is correct — for example, by requiring the production of a birth certificate or a divorce decree. This application process is a mechanism for enforcing a state's substantive restrictions on who can marry, as the information enables a clerk to determine if, for example, the applicants are underage, married to someone else, or close relatives. Disclosure of these circumstances would result in denial of the license. It also enables a state to collect vital statistics about its citizens as it does with birth and death certificates. Additionally, all states now require both parties to provide their social security numbers, which, in the event of divorce or separation, can be used to track down an absent parent for child support collection purposes.

Most states impose a waiting period, ranging from 24 hours to five days, between the time of application and the issuance of the license, although in some states, the waiting period is between issuance of the license and performance of the ceremony. It is hoped that this pause will deter couples from rushing into marriage, as it gives them time to reflect on the seriousness of their decision.

As a condition of eligibility for a marriage license, many states also require that a doctor perform a blood test and certify that neither party has

**Exhibit 1.2 Marriage License**

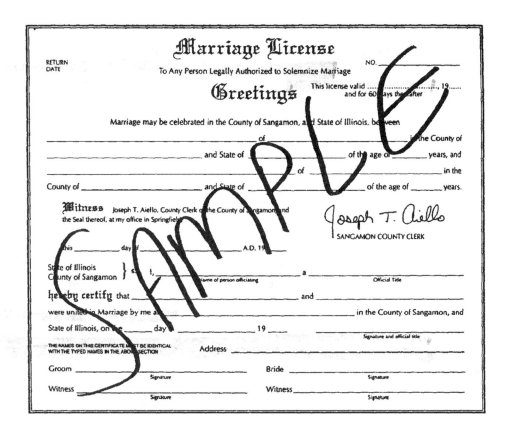

a venereal disease. The rationale of this requirement is to protect the health of the noninfected spouse and potential offspring. The measure assumes, however, that the parties have not had premarital intercourse and in recognition of changed social reality, many states have abandoned this requirement. Other less common requirements include the provision of birth control information, premarital counseling for couples under a certain age, and the distribution of information regarding the availability of AIDS and HIV testing.

Once the license is issued, a marriage ceremony must be performed by an authorized person. States usually authorize religious leaders as well as civil officers, such as justices of the peace, to perform marriage ceremonies. Beyond perhaps requiring an oath or acknowledgment of consent to become husband and wife, the presence of witnesses, and a statement by the officiator to the effect that the parties are now lawfully wed, states do not generally regulate the form, content, or manner of the ceremony. Following the ceremony, the license must be recorded in a timely manner. This is usually done by the person who officiated at the wedding.

### Consequences of Failing to Comply with Licensing Requirements

In most states, a technical failure to comply with an entry requirement (e.g., if the ceremony is performed by someone claiming to be authorized to perform weddings but who, in fact, lacked such authority) will not invalidate the marriage. The public policy in favor of marriage will usually override any such procedural flaw. In states that recognize common law marriages, a common law marriage rather than a formal marriage may be the result, but, as discussed below, this distinction has no real practical significance.

## COMMON LAW MARRIAGE

A **common law marriage** is created by the conduct of the parties in the absence of a formal ceremony. A well-established English practice, most American colonies accepted common law marriage as a practical reality in a new country whose scattered populace made access to religious and civil officials difficult. But by the close of the nineteenth century, common law marriage came under increasing attack. Reformers complained that the modern American family had lost its moral footing and that overly relaxed marriage and divorce laws were leading to social decay and promiscuity. They feared that by treating these "irregular" relationships like true marriages, the law was condoning immoral conduct, especially on the part of women, as it was mostly economically dependent wives who sought to establish the existence of a common law marriage following the death of their spouses. As a result of these challenges and increased urbanization, most, but not all, states abolished common law marriages.

### Formation Requirements and Consequences

Where still permitted, establishment of a valid common law marriage generally requires proof of three elements:

- a mutual agreement to become husband and wife,
- cohabitation, and
- reputation in the community as husband and wife. (In some states, this third element is expressed as a requirement that the parties hold themselves out as husband and wife.)

Because it can be difficult to prove that the parties agreed to become husband and wife, especially since many disputes over whether a valid common law marriage existed arise after the death of one partner, some courts will infer agreement from the fact of cohabitation and reputation, thus obviating the need for direct proof.

Once a valid common law marriage is established, the parties are considered married for all intents and purposes. They are entitled to all the benefits afforded to spouses, and dissolution of the relationship requires the filing of a divorce action. Once created, the status cannot be informally terminated. Accordingly, it is very important to distinguish common law marriage from "mere" cohabiting relationships; cohabitation may give rise to certain entitlements, but it does not lead to the creation of a spousal relationship.

## Interstate Recognition

What happens if a couple establishes a common law marriage in a state that allows them and then moves to a jurisdiction that does not allow such marriage? Will their marriage be accepted in the second state or will they be considered married in their home state and unmarried in the second state? Almost all states will recognize the marriage so long as the parties satisfied the requirements of the state in which they were originally domiciled. This comports with the general rule, subject to the above-discussed exception applicable to marriages between same-sex partners, that a validly con-tracted marriage will be recognized in all states, including a state that it could not have been entered into in the first place, unless it is in breach of that state's public policy.

The question of recognition becomes more complex when a couple from a state that does not allow common law marriage spends time in a second state that does, satisfies the requirements for establishing a common law marriage there, and then returns home. Some states will not recognize the marriage unless the parties have established a new domicile in the second state. Other states are looser and will extend recognition simply based on visits made to a jurisdiction that allows common law marriage. Other states take a middle position and will accept the marriage if the parties had sufficient contact with the second state to give rise to evidence of their relationship and reputation in that community.

## LEGAL RECOGNITION OF NONMARITAL COUPLES

As noted in the introduction to this Chapter, states traditionally have drawn a bright line between marriage and other forms of intimate association. This fixed demarcation has long been considered necessary in order to safeguard the state's interest in marriage as a vital social institution. Placed outside the realm of sanctioned family life, unwed couples thus have not been entitled to the rights and privileges of marriage. Needless to say, this exclusion has had the greatest historic impact on same-sex couples. Over the course of the past few decades, however, the law has begun moving away from a strict reliance on marriage as the exclusive marker for determining family status and the corresponding entitlement to benefits. Through a variety of approaches, the legal concept of family has gradually expanded to include nonmarital families, although these alternative approaches do not offer as comprehensive and stable a status as marriage.

Although not as controversial as same-sex marriage, the extension of legal rights to unmarried couples has nonetheless triggered considerable debate. Some commentators worry that this trend will result in a culture that takes marriage less seriously. They argue that clear boundaries are needed to preserve marriage as a privileged and unique relationship. In contrast, others welcome this increased flexibility, arguing that the law must evolve in response to reality so that outmoded concepts of what constitutes a "proper" or morally sanctioned family unit are not used to deny rights to couples who either cannot or choose not to marry.

## Cohabitation

Before 1976, courts generally refused to get involved in dissolution disputes between cohabiting partners over money and the allocation of accumulated property. Judges did not want to appear to be sanctioning nonmarital sexual relationships, and they worried that recognizing rights between cohabiting partners would diminish the importance of marriage. However, in 1976, in the landmark case of Marvin v. Marvin,[39] the door to the courthouse was opened for the first time to cohabiting partners seeking to sort out their affairs upon the dissolution of a relationship.

### The Marvin Decision

Actor Lee Marvin and Michelle Triola lived together for more than seven years, accumulating assets worth more than $1 million in the name of Marvin alone. Following their breakup, Triola sued for support and a share of accumulated assets, based on what she said was an express agreement between the parties that she would give up her musical career and provide domestic services to Marvin in exchange for his financial support and a shared interest in accumulated assets. Marvin, on the other hand, argued that any agreement between the parties was void because it was inextricably bound up with the sexual aspect of their relationship — a traditional barrier to the enforcement of these claims.

Focusing on what is seen as the inherent unfairness of Marvin's position, the California Supreme Court held that unless sexual services are the sole contribution that one party makes to the relationship (thus making the relationship akin to prostitution), the fact that cohabiting partners are engaged in a nonmarital sexual relationship should not prevent the enforcement of agreements between them: "Although we recognize the well-established public policy to foster and promote the institution of marriage, perpetuation of judicial rules which result in an inequitable distribution of property accumulated during a non-marital relationship is neither a just nor an effective way of carrying out that policy."[40]

In *Marvin*, Triola based her claim to support and a division of assets on the fact that the parties had entered into an express contract, which is an actual, articulated agreement. In holding that these agreements should be honored, the *Marvin* Court recognized that most cohabiting couples do not formalize their relational expectations, and it urged other courts to consider a variety of contractual and equitable approaches when seeking to resolve claims stemming from a failed cohabiting relationship.

Since *Marvin*, most states no longer bar suits between cohabitating partners who are seeking to resolve support and property disputes at the dissolution of their relationships; some courts, though, have hesitated to get involved in disputes between same-sex partners. In resolving these disputes, courts typically look to see if the parties had entered into some kind of agreement about property and support rights, although courts in some states have not limited themselves to a contractual remedy. For example, trust theories have been used to distribute property from one partner to the other, based on a showing that the titled partner was either actually holding it for the benefit of his or her partner or had engaged in some kind of fraud or overreaching.

Most couples do not sit down and negotiate a contract regarding the support and property rights they will have if they break up; courts therefore often infer agreements based on the conduct of the parties during their relationship, much as a court might infer an agreement to pay based on the acceptance of a paper that is delivered to one's door on a daily basis.[41] In contract parlance, an agreement that is inferred from conduct is referred to as an **implied-in-fact contract.** In the context of cohabitation, a court might find an implied agreement to share accumulated assets because a couple made purchases from a shared account or commingled their possessions. Some courts might also consider a partner's nonfinancial contribution (e.g., homemaking services) that preserves and enhances the value of the couple's property as evidence of an intent to share in the accumulation.

Courts have been more reluctant to find implied support agreements based on two traditional barriers. First, it has long been assumed that household services have no real monetary worth. Second, there is a long-standing legal presumption that household services are provided gratuitously or as a gift without expectation of compensation. These barriers, however, are breaking down. Based in part on the work of economists who have estimated what it would cost to purchase the services of a home-maker in the marketplace, courts have begun to recognize that household services have economic value and that they usually are not provided as a gift but rather, as acknowledged by the *Marvin* court, with the expectation that the parties intended a fair exchange.

### The "Marital-Status" Approach

Although courts in most states will now hear end-of-relationship dis-putes between cohabiting partners, these courts do not generally treat coha-bitation like marriage. Unlike with marriage, where the rights and obligations flow from the relationship itself, in most states a cohabitant who seeks support or a share of accumulated assets must establish that his or her claim is grounded in a prior agreement (either express or implied) of the parties. In short, rather than creating a formal legal status for cohabi-tants, what courts have done is to remove "a relationship-based impediment to their contractual freedom."[42]

Most states thus still use "contract as the conceptual underpinning for claims between intimate partners,"[43] but in 2002 the prestigious American Law Institute (ALI) recommended, in its influential *Principles of the Law of Family Dissolution* ("Principles"), that status replace contract as the domi-nant paradigm. Accordingly, upon dissolution, cohabitants who have shared a "primary residence and a life together as a couple" for a signif-icant period of time would be treated like a married couple with respect to post-relationship rights and obligations.[44] It should be noted that the Prin-ciples make no distinction between same-sex and heterosexual couples.

Family law experts are sharply divided over the ALI recommendation.[45] The recommendation's supporters argue that a status approach is a fairer way to resolve disputes because most couples simply do not think about their relationship in contractual terms: If there is no agreement to enforce, the economically more vulnerable partner may end up with nothing — a partic-ularly harsh result in the context of a long-term relationship structured along traditional gender lines. Supporters also argue that this approach advances the goal of equality by honoring a broader range of relationship choices in accordance with how people are actually living their lives, rather than simply privileging marriage above all other forms of intimate associations.

On the other side is the concern that recognizing cohabitation as a formal status will weaken the institution of marriage. There are two interwoven strands to the argument. First is the concern that recognition will blur the distinction between cohabitation and marriage, thus devaluing the unique nature of the marital commitment. Flowing from this objection is a second concern: that people will simply choose to live together because marriage will no longer seem so special. Another concern is that the imposition of post-relationship obligations may contravene the actual intentions of the parties, who, in choosing cohabitation over marriage, may have purposefully been seeking to avoid the legal consequences of marriage. Of course, this argument does not apply to same-sex couples, who, outside of Massachusetts, do not actually have this choice.

## Creating a Formal Legal Status for Unmarried Couples through Domestic Partnership and Civil Union Laws

Since the 1980s, a number of municipalities, and more recently a few states, have adopted an innovative approach that enables unmarried couples to register their relationship and obtain designated benefits. In most instances, the entitlement to benefits is far less than in marriage, although recently a few states have begun to create a quasi-marital status for same-sex couples.

### Domestic Partnerships: Creating a Status at the Local Level

Starting in the mid-1980s, a small but slowly growing number of towns and cities across the country have responded to the changing reality of family life by enacting domestic partnership ordinances.[46] These ordinances authorize the creation of a central registry at which a qualified unmarried couple can register their relationship; such registration entitles them to receive designated benefits, which are usually limited. To register, partners must complete an affidavit that requires them to attest to the following:

- that they are over the age of 18 and competent to enter into such a relationship;
- that they are cohabiting;
- that their relationship is exclusive and that neither person is married or has another domestic partner;
- that they are responsible for one another's welfare and share basic living expenses;

- that they are not related such that a marriage between them would violate state incest provisions;
- that neither has, within the preceding six months, filed a statement of domestic partnership with anyone else; and
- that if they end the relationship, they will file a certificate of dissolution.

In addition to these general qualifying factors, some locales limit eligibility to same-sex couples. Some find this approach discriminatory and think that heterosexual couples should also have the option of becoming domestic partners. On the other hand, the registration option has a profoundly different significance for gay men and lesbians because it is likely to be the only way they can formalize a relationship. Viewed this way, restrictive domestic partnership laws are not discriminatory but instead serve to remedy existing discrimination against same-sex couples.

Once registered, partners become eligible for designated benefits; however, these benefits are usually quite limited because municipalities have narrow legislative authority. A city or town cannot require private employers to extend benefits to domestic partners, nor can it compel a state to extend state benefits, such as inheritance rights if a partner dies without a will. Thus, unless one partner is a town employee, which opens up more options, registration usually only confers benefits such as jail and hospital visitation rights, protection from housing discrimination based upon status, and eligibility for family discounts at places of public accommodation. Where, however, one partner is a town employee, registration may bring more in terms of tangible gains. One of the most important potential benefits where one partner is a town employee is the ability to provide health insurance coverage for a domestic partner, just as a married employee can do for his or her spouse. Because health insurance is often a valuable component of an employee's total compensation package, the extension of coverage means that married and unmarried couples will be compensated equally for their work, which is an important goal of these laws.[47] A domestic partner may also be entitled to other equalizing benefits, such as the right to take time off to care for a domestic partner (or a member of his or her family) on the same basis that a married employee would be allowed to take time off to care for an ill spouse or a member of his or her family.

Another important dimension of registration as domestic partners is that it provides a couple with a degree of societal recognition and sanction. It is an acknowledgment that unmarried couples have important relationships that merit public affirmation and protection. This recognition is likely to be particularly important to same-sex couples who lack the access to marriage that is enjoyed by heterosexual couples.

### Domestic Partnerships and Civil Unions: Creating a Status at the State Level

Although far less controversial than same-sex marriage, domestic partnership registries are not without their detractors. Opponents worry that the registries encourage immorality and circumvent the "pro-family" principles embodied in laws prohibiting marriage between same-sex partners. Because of the anticipated difficulties in getting a statewide domestic partnership law through the legislative process, registries have been a creature of local law until quite recently. Today, however, five states — Connecticut, California, Maine, Hawaii, and New Jersey — have approved laws that create a statewide domestic partnership registry or, in Connecticut and Vermont, a statewide **civil union** registry. Because states have significantly more legislative authority than do cities and towns, they can provide many more benefits to registering couples, and in Connecticut, California, and Vermont registered couples have essentially all of the state-based rights and obligations of spouses.

Most of these states limit registration to same-sex couples, although several permit older heterosexual couples to register. Presumably, registry by older heterosexual couples is allowed to protect eligibility for benefits, such as Social Security, that might be lost if the couples were to marry. As with municipal registries, some believe that this general exclusion of heterosexual couples is discriminatory and that such couples should be entitled to choose how they wish to structure their relationships. For marital rights activists, statewide registries raise a different set of concerns. Although these activists agree that these laws clearly advance the rights of gay men and lesbians in the short term, the fear is that, over time, the laws will lock same-sex couples into a second-tier status that thwarts the possibility of ever achieving full marital rights.

## Protecting Relational Interests

Another approach that some courts have used to extend rights to cohabitants is to look beyond the lack of a formal status and instead focus on the relational interests that exist between committed cohabiting partners. At the heart of these cases is a judicial willingness to look beyond legal formalities in order to protect the integrity of a committed union. The first case to exemplify this approach is the landmark Braschi v. Stahl Associates Co.[48] decision, in which New York's highest court held that the term "family" could be defined to include same-sex life partners. In *Braschi*, a landlord sought to evict a tenant following the death of his life partner who had been the named tenant on the lease. The surviving partner sought protection under the non-eviction provisions of New York's rent control law that prevent a landlord from evicting the "surviving spouse of the deceased tenant or some other member of the deceased tenant's *family* who has been living with the tenant."[49] The court rejected the landlord's argument that the term "family" should be limited to persons related by blood, marriage, or adoption. Instead, the Court said that in defining family for purposes of the rent control statute, one must look beyond "fictitious legal distinctions or genetic history" to the "reality of family life."[50] Accordingly, where an unmarried couple's relationship partakes of the qualities that have made the traditional family a valued and protected social unit, the couple should be recognized as a family.

Since *Braschi*, courts have been particularly receptive to the "relational interest" approach in tort cases where one partner has suffered a financial or emotional loss (or both) following the injury or death of his or her partner. In the influential case of Dunphy v. Gregor,[51] the New Jersey Supreme Court allowed a woman to recover damages for the emotional distress she suffered after witnessing the man she was living with and engaged to marry die after being struck by a car while helping a friend to change a tire. Rejecting the defendant's argument that only family members who are related by marriage or blood should be allowed to recover for "bystander" injuries, the court focused on the nature of the relationship: "Central to a claim under bystander liability is the existence of an intimate familial relationship and the strength of the emotional bonds that surround that relationship. The harm . . . must be so severe that it destroys the emotional security derived from a relationship that is deep, enduring, and intimate. The quality of the relationship creates the severity of the loss."[52] So viewed, it is the quality and nature of the relationship, rather than simply the existence of a formal legal bond, that is important when determining if an individual is entitled to recover for bystander injuries.

Looking to *Dunphy*, New Mexico recently became the first state to allow a cohabiting partner to sue for loss of consortium (which generally encompasses the loss of material services, love, companionship, and sexual relations) occasioned by an injury to her life-partner, stating that "a person brings this claim to recover for damage to a relational interest, not a legal interest . . . The use of legal status necessarily excludes many persons whose loss of a significant relational interest may be just as devastating as the loss of a legal spouse."[53] Looking to *Dunphy*, the court concluded that where a cohabiting couple has a "close familiar relationship" based on factors such as "the degree of mutual dependence, the extent of common contributions to a life together . . . {and} their emotional on each other," it is as deserving of protection as a relationship between married partners.[54]

With respect to expanding the rights of nonmarital partners, the relational interest approach has two inherent limitations. First, to qualify for family status, a couple must offer up the inner workings of their private life to a court for review. This disclosure can be expensive, time-consuming, and highly intrusive. Second, unmarried couples may be held to a higher standard of family life than married couples. Married couples automatically qualify for status and benefits, regardless of how they treat one another or the degree to which their relationship conforms to a domestic norm, whereas a nonmarital couple must show that their relationship satisfies specific criteria in order to be recognized as a family unit.

## ADULT ADOPTION

In the previous sections, we looked at three approaches to establishing rights for nonmarital families. Although each approach is different, a common element is the partiality of recognition. Unlike marriage, none of these approaches provides an unmarried couple an across-the-board family status; rather, rights and recognition are contextual. Cohabitation does not create a formal status; rather, rights come into being at dissolution. With domestic partnerships, although a status is created, it lacks the social stature of marriage and entitlements are limited. Under the relational interest approach, recognition is usually only conferred within the narrow parameters of a given statutory scheme.

Some couples therefore have looked to adult adoption as a way to create a relationship that is neither partial nor contextual, but which encompasses all of the legal attributes of a fully conferred family status. To do this, one partner adopts the other, thus creating a parent-child relationship, which in turn opens the door to the full array of family benefits, including inheritance rights under state intestacy laws. Statutory inheritance rights can be particularly important if a will is successfully challenged by a family member or other person seeking to disinherit the partner of the decedent.

The benefit of adult adoption is that it creates a permanent and comprehensive family relationship; some significant drawbacks to this approach, however, have kept it from taking off as a viable option. Many states do not recognize these adoptions as valid. Moreover, even if these adoptions are allowed, another major drawback is the lack of a formal way to dissolve them—a reality that contrasts with the formal mechanisms for dissolution that accompany marriage, cohabitation, and registered relationship. The couple is thus forever bound as family. Also problematic is that unintended emotional and psychological consequences may flow from being forced to fit an adult relationship into the legal parameters of a parent-child relationship. Clearly, these two types of relationships are quite different from one another, and they embody distinct understandings of authority, responsibility, and autonomy. Because of both the legal limitations on partner adoption and the drawbacks of this approach, adult adoption is seldom used to achieve a recognizable family status.[55]

## Chapter Summary

Although we generally think of marriage as a purely private matter, states have actively sought to shape and preserve marriage as a vital social institution. Although laws no longer mandate prescribed roles based on highly gendered notions of proper marital conduct, states still regulate who can marry and the formalities that must be complied with to establish a valid marriage. However, marriage is now recognized as a fundamental right, and laws that burden an individual's right to marry will be subjected to careful judicial review.

Since the 1970s, gay men and lesbians have actively fought for the right to marry, and in 2003, in a historic first, the Massachusetts Supreme Court ruled that it was unconstitutional to bar same-sex couples from marrying. Although no other state has gone as far as Massachusetts, other high courts have ruled that it is unconstitutional to deny same-sex couples the rights and privileges of marriage. Pushing in the other direction, in 1996, Congress enacted DOMA which, for purposes of federal laws, defines marriage as being between one man and one woman, and allows states to withhold recognition from same-sex marriages from other states. Following suit, most states have enacted "mini" DOMA laws or constitutional amendments.

Most states have abolished common law marriage. However, most, if not all, states will recognize a common law marriage that was entered into in a state that still permits them.

Today marriage is no longer the only way that a couple can obtain rights and be formally recognized as a family unit. Most jurisdictions no longer deny legal access to cohabiting couples who seek to resolve property and support disputes when they dissolve their relationships. In some towns, and in a few states as well, a cohabiting couple may be able to register as domestic partners, thus acquiring a formal status and qualifying for benefits that, unless available at the state level, are usually quite limited. Under the functional family approach, the focus is on the reality of a couple's life rather than on its legal form. In carefully defined contexts, courts may protect the relational interests of cohabiting couples where their relationship partakes of many of the qualities traditionally associated with marriage. Because these approaches are partial and contextual, some couples have looked to adult adoption in order to create a fully recognized family relationship. Adult adoption remains unpopular, though, both because many states do not allow it and because of its inherent limitations.

## Key Terms

Common Law
Marital Unity
Personal Property
Real Property
Contracts
Testamentary Capacity
Community Property
Married Women's Property Acts
Equal Protection Clause
Due Process Clause
Marriage Restriction Laws
Incest
Bigamy

Polygamy
Age of Capacity
Age of Consent
Civil Unions
Defense of Marriage Act
Federal Marriage Amendment
Common Law Marriage
Cohabitation
Implied-in-Fact Contract
Domestic Partnership
Relational Interests
Adult Adoption

## Review Questions

1. What was the status of married women under common law?

2. What were a husband's legal responsibilities?

3. How was marriage seen in the community property states?

4. What prompted the passage of the Married Women's Property Acts?

5. What reforms did the Acts accomplish? What aspects of the common law marital relationship did they leave untouched?

6. When and how was the transition to gender-neutral marriage laws accomplished?

7. What did the Supreme Court decide in the case of Loving v. Virginia? Why is this case so important?

8. What kinds of marriage restriction laws are in effect today?

9. What types of arguments support these restrictions?

10. What was the outcome of the Vermont, the Massachusetts, and the New Jersey marital rights cases?

11. What is the essential difference between the Massachusetts and the other two decisions?

12. What is a civil union?

13. What is DOMA? What are its key provisions?

14. What is the Federal Marriage Amendment?

15. What steps must a couple follow to create a formal marriage? What purposes are served by these requirements?

16. What is the effect of a technical failure to comply with these requirements?

17. What is a common law marriage?

18. What elements are necessary to establish a valid common law marriage?

19. Why did courts traditionally deny relief to cohabiting couples upon dissolution of their relationship?

20. What was the result of the *Marvin* decision?

21. What is an implied-in-fact agreement, and under what circumstances might one arise in the cohabitation context?

22. What is the ALI approach to resolving dissolution disputes between cohabitants? Explain how this approach differs from the approach that most states use in resolving these disputes.

23. What is a domestic partnership?

24. Beyond tangible benefits, why else might a couple want to register as domestic partners?

25. What is the range of benefits that might be offered under a domestic partner or civil union law? Why can states offer more benefits than municipalities?

26. What is the "relational interest" approach? In what kinds of cases might this approach be used?

27. What legal relationship is created when one adult adopts another?

28. Why might an adult seek to adopt his or her partner? What concerns are raised by this approach?

## Discussion Questions

1. Since the United States Supreme Court's decision in *Zablocki,* some commentators have suggested that all restrictions on an individual's right to marry are unconstitutional. Do you think states should be able to impose restrictions on a person's choice of a marital partner? What arguments support your position?

2. Do you agree with the result of the *Goodridge* decision? Do you think civil unions provide a better approach to the extension of rights to same-sex couples? If you find neither approach persuasive, what approach do you think the law should take?

3. Do you think a state should be able to deny recognition to a same-sex marriage that was validly entered into under the laws of another state? Why or why not?

4. What does the concept of "family" mean to you? Is marriage a central aspect of your definition? Why or why not?

5. Should the law extend rights to heterosexual couples who choose not to marry, or should they be required to marry if they want legal recognition of their relationship?

## Assignments

1. Locate your state's marriage statutes and answer the following questions: a. What restrictions, such as closeness of relationship, does your state use to limit entry into marriage? b. What steps

must a couple take in order to establish a formal marriage? c. What are the consequences of failing to comply with these requirements?

2.  Identify and describe any laws (or constitutional amendments) that have been passed (or are under consideration) in your state regarding the marital rights of same-sex partners.

3.  If you are in a jurisdiction that recognizes common law marriage, what must be shown to establish the existence of such a marriage?

4.  Assume you are an appeals court judge being asked to decide whether the lower court's decision to dismiss the case of a same-sex couple who was denied a marriage license is proper. Write a legal opinion either upholding or reversing this decision. Be sure to carefully support your position.

5.  Assume that a client who is in the process of ending a long-term cohabiting relationship has come into the firm where you work. Your supervising attorney has asked you to research the law in your state regarding the rights of cohabiting partners and then write up your results in a short in-house memorandum. The purpose of the memo is to provide the attorney with an overview of the law in your jurisdiction.

6.  Select a major employer in your community. Develop a set of questions and then interview the appropriate person in human resources regarding the company's policy on providing benefits to unmarried partners. (Note: Most companies do not presently offer such benefits, so be sure to include questions regarding any future plans and the impact that extending benefits could have on the company.)

7.  A local trial judge is considering the following facts:
    Mary works as a sales clerk at Green's, which is a major department store. Green's allows employees to make purchases at a 15 percent discount. It also issues discount cards to the families of their salesclerks that entitle them to the same discount. The store defines "family" as the spouse and children of an employee.
    Mary has lived with Julie for eight years. They own a house together. They maintain a joint checking and savings account. They are committed to one another and are regarded as a family by their friends.

Mary applied for a family discount card for Julie. Green's denied the card because Julie was not a member of the family. As a result, Mary has decided to sue her employer.

Assume that you are a paralegal working in a firm that represents either Mary or Green's and that you have been asked to do the following:

a. Read Braschi v. Stahl (543 N.E.2d 49 (N.Y 1989)) in its entirety and evaluate your client's case in light of this decision.

b. Write an interoffice memo in which you explore the applicability of *Braschi* to the present facts, and develop an argument in which you urge the court (depending on whom you represent) to either accept or reject *Braschi*.

8. Determine whether any municipality in your state has a domestic partnership ordinance (or whether state law makes any provisions for domestic partners), and research what the requirements and benefits of the law are. Write up your findings in a short memorandum.

## Cases for Analysis

The following landmark decision represents the first time that the United States Supreme Court invalidated a state law restricting entry into marriage. Although now more than 30 years old, the decision still dominates legal debates over the validity of contemporary marital restriction laws, such as those prohibiting same-sex partners from marrying.

### LOVING v. VIRGINIA
#### 388 U.S. 1, 87 S.Ct. 1817, 18 L. Ed.2d 1010 (1967)

MR. CHIEF JUSTICE WARREN delivered the opinion of the Court.

This case presents a constitutional question never addressed by this Court: whether a statutory scheme adopted by the State of Virginia to prevent marriages between persons solely on the basis of racial classifications violates the Equal Protection and Due Process Clauses of the Fourteenth Amendment. . . .

In June 1958, two residents of Virginia, Mildred Jeter, a Negro woman, and Richard Loving, a white man, were married in the District of Columbia pursuant to its laws. Shortly after their marriage, the Lovings returned to Virginia . . . [A] grand jury issued an indictment charging the Lovings with violating Virginia's ban on interracial marriages. . . . [T]he Lovings pleaded guilty to the charge and were sentenced to one year in jail; however, the trial judge suspended the sentence for a period of 25 years on the condition that the Lovings leave the State and not return to Virginia together for 25 years. He stated in an opinion that:

> "Almighty God created the races white, black, yellow, malay and red, and he placed them on separate continents. And but for the interference with his arrangement there would be no cause for such marriages. The fact that he separated the races shows that he did not intend for the races to mix."

After their convictions, the Lovings took up residence in the District of Columbia. . . . [T]hey filed a motion in the state trial court to vacate the judgment and set aside the sentence on the ground that the statutes which they had violated were repugnant to the Fourteenth Amendment. . . . [T]he . . . judge denied the motion . . . and the Lovings perfected an appeal to the Supreme Court of Appeals of Virginia. . . .

The Supreme Court of Appeals upheld the constitutionality of the antimiscegenation statutes and . . . affirmed the convictions. The Lovings appealed this decision. . . . The two statutes under which appellants were convicted and sentenced are part of a comprehensive statutory scheme aimed at prohibiting and punishing interracial marriages. The Lovings were convicted of violating sect. 20-58 of the Virginia Code:

> "*Leaving State to evade law.* — If any white person and colored person shall go out of this State, for the purpose of being married, and with the intention of returning, and be married out of it, and afterwards return to and reside in it, cohabiting as man and wife, they shall be punished as provided in sect. 20-59. . . ."

Section 20-59, which defines the penalty for miscegenation, provides:

> "*Punishment for marriage.* — If any white person intermarry with a colored person, or any colored person intermarry with a white person, he shall be guilty of a felony and shall be punished by confinement in the penitentiary for not less than one nor more than five years." . . .

Virginia is now one of 16 States which prohibit and punish marriages on the basis of racial classifications. Penalties for miscegenation arose as an incident to slavery and have been common in Virginia since the colonial period. The present statutory scheme dates from the adoption of the Racial Integrity Act of 1924, passed during the period of extreme nativism which followed the end of the First World War. . . .

## I.

In upholding the constitutionality of these provisions . . . , the Supreme Court of Appeals of Virginia referred to its 1955 decision in Naim v. Naim, 197 Va. 80, 87 S.E.2d 749. . . . In *Naim*, the state court concluded that the State's legitimate purposes were "to preserve the racial integrity of its citizens," and to prevent "the corruption of blood," "a mongrel breed of citizens," and "the obliteration of racial pride," obviously an endorsement of the doctrine of White Supremacy. *Id.*, at 90, 87 S.E.2d, at 756. The court also reasoned that marriage has traditionally been subject to state regulation without federal intervention, and, consequently, the regulation of marriage should be left to exclusive state control by the Tenth Amendment.

[T]he State does not contend in its argument before this Court that its powers to regulate marriage are unlimited. . . . [T]he State contends that, because its miscegenation statutes punish equally both the white and the Negro participants in an interracial marriage, these statutes, despite their reliance on racial classifications, do not constitute an invidious discrimination based upon race. . . .

[T]he Equal Protection Clause requires the consideration of whether the classifications drawn by any statute constitute an arbitrary and invidious discrimination. The clear and central purpose of the Fourteenth Amendment was to eliminate all official state sources of invidious racial discrimination in the States. . . .

There can be no question but that Virginia's miscegenation statutes rest solely upon distinctions drawn according to race. . . . Over the years, this Court has consistently repudiated "distinctions between citizens solely because of their ancestry" as being "odious to a free people whose institutions are founded upon the doctrine of equality." Hirabayashi v. United States, 320 U.S. 81, 100 (1943). . . . [I]f they are ever to be upheld, they must be shown to be necessary to the accomplishment of some permissible state objective, independent of the racial discrimination which it was the object of the Fourteenth Amendment to eliminate. . . .

There is patently no legitimate overriding purpose independent of invidious racial discrimination which justifies this classification. The fact that Virginia prohibits only interracial marriages involving white persons demonstrates that the racial classifications must stand on their own justification, as measures designed to maintain White Supremacy. We have consistently denied the constitutionality of measures which restrict the rights of citizens on account of race. There can be no doubt that restricting the freedom to marry solely because of racial classifications violates the central meaning of the Equal Protection Clause.

**II.**

These statutes also deprive the Lovings of liberty without due process of law in violation of the Due Process Clause of the Fourteenth Amendment. The freedom to marry has long been recognized as one of the vital personal rights essential to the orderly pursuit of happiness by free men.

Marriage is one of the "basic civil rights of man," fundamental to our very existence and survival. Skinner v. Oklahoma, 316 U.S. 535, 541 (1942). See also Maynard v. Hill, 125 U.S. 190 (1888). To deny this fundamental freedom on so unsupportable a basis as the racial classifications embodied in these statutes, classifications so directly subversive of the principle of equality at the heart of the Fourteenth Amendment, is surely to deprive all the State's citizens of liberty without due process of law. The Fourteenth Amendment requires that the freedom of choice to marry not be restricted by invidious racial discriminations. Under our Constitution, the freedom to marry, or not marry, a person of another race resides with the individual and cannot be infringed by the State.

These convictions must be reversed.

### QUESTIONS

1. On what grounds did the state of Virginia seek to justify its miscegenation laws?

2. Why did Virginia claim that its miscegenation laws did not "constitute an invidious discrimination based on race"? Why did the Court disagree with Virginia on this point?

3. Based on your reading of the text, who generally has the authority to regulate the marriage?

4. In striking down Virginia's miscegenation law, the Court relies on two clauses of the fourteenth amendment. Identify these clauses and explain how the Court used them to invalidate the law.

5. How does the Court characterize the right to marry?

---

Although the Hawaii high court was clearly moving in this direction until the state constitution was amended to give the legislature the ability to limit marriage to a man and a woman, the following Massachusetts case is the first high court decision to hold that same-sex partners have a constitutional right to marry.

## GOODRIDGE v. DEPARTMENT OF PUBLIC HEALTH
### 440 Mass. 309, 798 N.E.2d 941 (2003)

. . . Marriage is a vital social institution. The exclusive commitment of two individuals to each other nurtures love and mutual support; it brings stability to our society. For those who choose to marry, and for their children, marriage provides an abundance of legal, financial, and social benefits. In return it imposes weighty legal, financial, and social obligations. The question before us is whether, consistent with the Massachusetts Constitution, the Commonwealth may deny the protections, benefits, and obligations conferred by civil marriage to two individuals of the same sex who wish to marry. We conclude that it may not. The Massachusetts Constitution affirms the dignity and equality of all individuals. It forbids the creation of second-class citizens. . . .

We are mindful that our decision marks a change in the history of our marriage law. Many people hold deep-seated religious, moral, and ethical convictions that marriage should be limited to the union of one man and one woman, and that homosexual conduct is immoral. Many hold equally strong religious, moral, and ethical convictions that same-sex couples are entitled to be married. . . . Neither view answers the question before us. Our concern is with the Massachusetts Constitution . . .

Barred access to the protections, benefits, and obligations of civil marriage, a person who enters into an intimate, exclusive union with another of the same sex is arbitrarily deprived of membership in one of our community's most rewarding and cherished institutions. That exclusion is incompatible with the constitutional principles of respect for individual autonomy and equality under law.

## I

The plaintiffs are fourteen individuals from five Massachusetts counties. As of April 11, 2001, the date they filed their complaint, the plaintiffs Gloria Bailey, sixty years old, and Linda Davies, fifty-five years old, had been in a committed relationship for thirty years; the plaintiffs Maureen Brodoff, forty-nine years old, and Ellen Wade, fifty-two years old, had been in a committed relationship for twenty years and lived with their twelve year old daughter; the plaintiffs Hillary Goodridge, forty-four years old, and Julie Goodridge, forty-three years old, had been in a committed relationship for thirteen years and lived with their five year old daughter; the plaintiffs Gary Chalmers, thirty-five years old, and Richard Linnell, thirty-seven years old, had been in a committed relationship for thirteen years and lived with their eight year old daughter and Richard's mother; the plaintiffs Heidi Norton, thirty-six years old, and Gina Smith, thirty-six years old, had been in a committed relationship for eleven years and lived with their two sons, ages five years and one year; the plaintiffs Michael Horgan, forty-one years old, and Edward Balmelli, forty-one years old, had been in a committed relationship for seven years; and the plaintiffs David Wilson, fifty-seven years old, and Robert Compton, fifty-one years old, had been in a committed relationship for four years and had cared for David's mother in their home after a serious illness until she died.

The plaintiffs include business executives, lawyers, an investment banker, educators, therapists, and a computer engineer. Many are active in church, community, and school groups. . . .

In March and April, 2001, each of the plaintiff couples attempted to obtain a marriage license from a city or town clerk's office. In each case, the clerk either refused to accept the notice of intention to marry or denied a marriage license to the couple on the ground that Massachusetts does not recognize same-sex marriage.

On April 11, 2001, the plaintiffs filed suit in the Superior Court against the department and the commissioner seeking a judgment that "the exclusion of the [p]laintiff couples and other qualified same-sex couples from access to marriage licenses, and the legal and social status of civil marriage, as well as the protections, benefits and obligations of marriage, violates Massachusetts law[,]" . . . including but not limited to their rights under . . . the Massachusetts Constitution.

A Superior Court judge . . . dismissed the plaintiffs' claim that the marriage statutes should be construed to permit marriage between persons of the same sex, holding that the plain wording of G. L. c. 207, as well as the wording of other marriage statutes, precluded that interpretation. Turning to the constitutional claims, he held that the marriage exclusion does not offend the liberty, freedom, equality, or due process provisions of the Massachusetts Constitution, and that the Massachusetts Declaration of Rights does not guarantee "the fundamental right to marry a person of the same sex." He concluded that prohibiting same-sex marriage rationally furthers the Legislature's legitimate interest in safeguarding the "primary purpose" of marriage, "procreation." The Legislature may rationally limit marriage to opposite-sex couples, he concluded, because those couples are "theoretically . . . capable of procreation," they do not rely on "inherently more cumbersome" noncoital means of reproduction, and they are more likely than same-sex couples to have children, or more children. . . .

## II

General Laws c. 207 . . . sets minimum qualifications for obtaining a marriage license and directs city and town clerks, the registrar, and the department to keep and maintain certain "vital records" of civil marriages . . .

. . . [F]or all the joy and solemnity that normally attend a marriage, G. L. c. 207, governing entrance to marriage, is a licensing law. The plaintiffs argue that because nothing in that licensing law specifically prohibits marriages between persons of the same sex, we may interpret the statute to permit "qualified same sex couples" to obtain marriage licenses, thereby avoiding the question whether the law is constitutional. See School Comm. of Greenfield v. Greenfield Educ. Ass'n, 385 Mass. 70, 79, 431 N.E.2d 180 (1982), and cases cited. This claim lacks merit.

We interpret statutes to carry out the Legislature's intent, determined by the words of a statute interpreted according to "the ordinary and approved usage of the language." Hanlon v. Rollins, 286 Mass. 444, 447, 190 N.E. 606 (1934). The everyday meaning of "marriage" is "[t]he legal union of a man and woman as husband and wife," Black's Law Dictionary 986 (7th ed. 1999), and the plaintiffs do not argue that the term "marriage" has ever had a different meaning under Massachusetts law. . . . Far from being ambiguous, the undefined word "marriage," as used in G. L. c. 207, confirms the General Court's intent to hew to the term's common-law and quotidian meaning concerning the genders of the marriage partners. . . .

. . . [T]he Legislature did not intend that same-sex couples be licensed to marry. We conclude, as did the judge, that G. L. c. 207 may not be construed to permit same-sex couples to marry.

## III

### A

The larger question is whether, as the department claims, government action that bars same-sex couples from civil marriage constitutes a legitimate exercise of the State's authority to regulate conduct, or whether, as the plaintiffs claim, this categorical marriage exclusion violates the Massachusetts Constitution. We have recognized the long-standing statutory understanding, derived from the common law, that "marriage" means the lawful union of a woman and a man. But that history cannot and does not foreclose the constitutional question.

The plaintiffs' claim that the marriage restriction violates the Massachusetts Constitution can be analyzed in two ways. Does it offend the

Constitution's guarantees of equality before the law? Or do the liberty and due process provisions of the Massachusetts Constitution secure the plaintiffs' right to marry their chosen partner? In matters implicating marriage, family life, and the upbringing of children, the two constitutional concepts frequently overlap, as they do here . . .

We begin by considering the nature of civil marriage itself. Simply put, the government creates civil marriage. In Massachusetts, civil marriage is, and since pre-Colonial days has been, precisely what its name implies: a wholly secular institution. . . .

In a real sense, there are three partners to every civil marriage: two willing spouses and an approving State. . . .

Without question, civil marriage enhances the "welfare of the community." It is a "social institution of the highest importance." French v. McAnarney, 290 Mass. 544, 546 (1935) . . . Civil marriage anchors an ordered society by encouraging stable relationships over transient ones . . .

Marriage also bestows enormous private and social advantages on those who choose to marry. Civil marriage is at once a deeply personal commitment to another human being and a highly public celebration of the ideals of mutuality, companionship, intimacy, fidelity, and family. "It is an association that promotes a way of not political faiths; a bilateral loyalty, not commercial or social projects." Griswold v. Connecticut, 381 U.S. 479, 486 (1965). Because it fulfils yearnings for security, safe haven, and connection that express our common humanity, civil marriage is an esteemed institution, and the decision whether and whom to marry is among life's momentous acts of self-definition.

Tangible as well as intangible benefits flow from marriage. The marriage license grants valuable property rights to those who meet the entry requirements, and who agree to what might otherwise be a burdensome degree of government regulation of their activities.

The benefits accessible only by way of a marriage license are enormous, touching nearly every aspect of life and death. The department states that "hundreds of statutes" are related to marriage and to marital benefits. . . .

Where a married couple has children, their children are also directly or indirectly, but no less auspiciously, the recipients of the special legal and economic protections obtained by civil marriage. Notwithstanding the Commonwealth's strong public policy to abolish legal distinctions between marital and nonmarital children in providing for the support and care of minors, . . . the fact remains that marital children reap a measure of family stability and economic security based on their parents' legally privileged status that is largely inaccessible, or not as readily accessible, to non-marital children. Some of these benefits are social, such as the enhanced approval that still attends the status of being a marital child. Others are material, such as the greater ease of access to family-based State and Federal benefits that attend the presumptions of one's parentage.

It is undoubtedly for these concrete reasons, as well as for its intimately personal significance, that civil marriage has long been termed a "civil right." . . .

Without the right to marry — or more properly, the right to choose to marry — one is excluded from the full range of human experience and denied full protection of the laws for one's "avowed commitment to an intimate and lasting human relationship." Baker v. State, 170 Vt. 194, 229 (1994). Because civil marriage is central to the lives of individuals and the welfare of the community, our laws assiduously protect the individual's right to marry against undue government incursion . . .

B

For decades, indeed centuries, in much of this country (including Massachusetts) no lawful marriage was possible between white and black Americans. That long history availed not when the Supreme Court of California held in 1948 that a legislative prohibition against interracial marriage violated the due process and equality guarantees of the Fourteenth Amendment, Perez v. Sharp, 32 Cal. 2d 711, 728 {198 P.2d 17}(1948), or when, nineteen years later, the United States Supreme Court also held that a statutory bar to interracial marriage violated the Fourteenth Amendment, Loving v. Virginia, 388 U.S. [1 (1967)]. As both *Perez* and *Loving* make clear, the right to marry means little if it does not include the right to marry the person of one's choice, subject to appropriate government restrictions in the interests of public health, safety, and welfare. See Perez v. Sharp, supra at 717 ("the essence of the right to marry is freedom to join in marriage with a person of one's choice").

The Massachusetts Constitution protects matters of personal liberty against government incursion as zealously, and often more so, than does the Federal Constitution, even where both Constitutions employ essentially the same language . . . That the Massachusetts Constitution is in some instances more protective of individual liberty interests than is the Federal Constitution is not surprising. Fundamental to the vigor of our Federal system of government is that "state courts are absolutely free to interpret state constitutional provisions to accord greater protection to individual rights than do similar provisions of the United States Constitution." Arizona v. Evans, 514 U.S. 1, 8 (1995).

The individual liberty and equality safeguards of the Massachusetts Constitution protect both "freedom from" unwarranted government intrusion into protected spheres of life and "freedom to" partake in benefits created by the State for the common good. . . . The liberty interest in choosing whether and whom to marry would be hollow if the Common-wealth could, without sufficient justification, foreclose an individual from freely choosing the person with whom to share an exclusive commitment in the unique institution of civil marriage. . . .

The plaintiffs challenge the marriage statute on both equal protec-tion and due process grounds. . . . Where a statute implicates a fundamental right or uses a suspect classification, we employ "strict judicial scrutiny." . . . For all other statutes, we employ the "'rational basis' test." . . . For the reasons we explain below, we conclude that the marriage ban does not meet the rational basis test for either due process or equal protection. Because the statute does not survive rational basis review, we do not consider the plaintiffs' arguments that this case merits strict judicial scrutiny.

The department posits three legislative rationales for prohibiting same-sex couples from marrying: (1) providing a "favorable setting for procreation"; (2) ensuring the optimal setting for child rearing, which the department defines as "a two-parent family with one parent of each sex"; and (3) preserving scarce State and private financial resources. We consider each in turn.

The judge in the Superior Court endorsed the first rationale, holding that "the state's interest in regulating marriage is based on the traditional concept that marriage's primary purpose is procreation." This is incorrect. Our laws of civil marriage do not privilege procreative heterosexual intercourse between married people above every other form of adult inti-macy and every other means of creating a family. General Laws c. 207 contains no requirement that the applicants for a marriage license attest to their ability or intention to conceive children by coitus. People who have never consummated their marriage, and never plan to, may be and stay married. . . . People who cannot stir from their deathbed may marry . . . While it is certainly true that many, perhaps most, married cou-ples have children together (assisted or unassisted), it is the exclusive and permanent commitment of the marriage partners to one another, not the begetting of children, that is the sine qua non of civil marriage.

Moreover, the Commonwealth affirmatively facilitates bringing chil-dren into a family regardless of whether the intended parent is married or unmarried, whether the child is adopted or born into a family, whether assistive technology was used to conceive the child, and whether the parent or her partner is heterosexual, homosexual, or bisexual. . . .

The "marriage is procreation" argument singles out the one unbridge-able difference between same-sex and opposite-sex couples, and trans-forms that difference into the essence of legal marriage. Like "Amendment 2" to the Constitution of Colorado, which effectively denied homosexual persons equality under the law and full access to the political process, the marriage restriction impermissibly "identifies persons by a single trait and then denies them protection across the board." Romer v. Evans, 517 U.S. 620, 633 (1996). In so doing, the State's action confers an official stamp of approval on the destructive stereotype that same-sex relationships are inherently unstable and inferior to opposite-sex relationships and are not worthy of respect.

The department's first stated rationale, equating marriage with unassisted heterosexual procreation, shades imperceptibly into its second: that confining marriage to opposite-sex couples ensures that children are raised in the "optimal" setting. Protecting the welfare of children is a paramount State policy. Restricting marriage to opposite-sex couples, however, cannot plausibly further this policy. . . .

The department has offered no evidence that forbidding marriage to people of the same sex will increase the number of couples choosing to enter into opposite-sex marriages in order to have and raise children. There is thus no rational relationship between the marriage statute and the Commonwealth's proffered goal of protecting the "optimal" child rearing unit. Moreover, the department readily concedes that people in same-sex couples may be "excellent" parents. These couples (including four of the plaintiff couples) have children for the reasons others do — to love them, to care for them, to nurture them. But the task of child rearing for same-sex couples is made infinitely harder by their status as outliers to the marriage laws. . . . Excluding same-sex couples from civil marriage will not make children of opposite-sex marriages more secure, but it does prevent children of same-sex couples from enjoying the immeasurable advantages that flow from the assurance of "a stable family structure in which children will be reared, educated, and socialized." Post at 381 (Cordy, J., dissenting).

No one disputes that the plaintiff couples are families, that many are parents, and that the children they are raising, like all children, need and should have the fullest opportunity to grow up in a secure, protected family unit. Similarly, no one disputes that, under the rubric of marriage, the State provides a cornucopia of substantial benefits to married parents and their children. The preferential treatment of civil marriage reflects the Legislature's conclusion that marriage "is the foremost setting for the education and socialization of children" precisely because it "encourages parents to remain committed to each other and to their children as they grow." Post at 383 (Cordy, J., dissenting) . . .

It cannot be rational under our laws, and indeed it is not permitted, to penalize children by depriving them of State benefits because the State disapproves of their parents' sexual orientation.

The third rationale advanced by the department is that limiting marriage to opposite-sex couples furthers the Legislature's interest in conserving scarce State and private financial resources. The marriage restriction is rational, it argues, because the General Court logically could assume that same-sex couples are more financially independent than married couples and thus less needy of public marital benefits . . .

An absolute statutory ban on same-sex marriage bears no rational relationship to the goal of economy. First, the department's conclusory generalization — that same-sex couples are less financially dependent on each other than opposite-sex couples — ignores that many same-sex couples, such as many of the plaintiffs in this case, have children and other dependents (here, aged parents) in their care. . . . Second, Massachusetts marriage laws do not condition receipt of public and private financial benefits to married individuals on a demonstration of financial dependence on each other; the benefits are available to married couples regardless of whether they mingle their finances or actually depend on each other for support.

The department suggests additional rationales for prohibiting same-sex couples from marrying. . . . It argues that broadening civil marriage to include same-sex couples will trivialize or destroy the institution of marriage as it has historically been fashioned. Certainly our decision today marks a significant change in the definition of marriage as it has been inherited from the common law, and understood by many societies for centuries. But it does not disturb the fundamental value of marriage in our society.

Here, the plaintiffs seek only to be married, not to undermine the institution of civil marriage. They do not want marriage abolished. They do not attack the binary nature of marriage, the consanguinity provisions, or any of the other gate-keeping provisions of the marriage licensing law. Recognizing the right of an individual to marry a person of the same sex will not diminish the validity or dignity of opposite-sex marriage, any more than recognizing the right of an individual to marry a person of a different race devalues the marriage of a person who marries someone of her own race. If anything, extending civil marriage to same-sex couples reinforces the importance of marriage to individuals and communities. That same-sex couples are willing to embrace marriage's solemn obligations of exclusivity, mutual support, and commitment to one another is a testament to the enduring place of marriage in our laws and in the human spirit.

It has been argued that, due to the State's strong interest in the institution of marriage as a stabilizing social structure, only the Legislature can control and define its boundaries. . . . We owe great deference to the Legislature to decide social and policy issues, but it is the traditional and settled role of courts to decide constitutional issues . . .

The marriage ban works a deep and scarring hardship on a very real segment of the community for no rational reason. The absence of any reasonable relationship between, on the one hand, an absolute disqualification of same-sex couples who wish to enter into civil marriage and, on the other, protection of public health, safety, or general welfare, suggests that the marriage restriction is rooted in persistent prejudices against persons who are (or who are believed to be) homosexual. "The Constitution cannot control such prejudices but neither can it tolerate them. Private biases may be outside the reach of the law, but the law cannot, directly or indirectly, give them effect." Palmore v. Sidoti, 466 U.S. 429, 433 (1984) . . .

## IV

Here, no one argues that striking down the marriage laws is an appropriate form of relief . . . We face a problem similar to one that recently confronted the Court of Appeal for Ontario, the highest court of that Canadian province, when it considered the constitutionality of the same-sex marriage ban . . . In holding that the limitation of civil marriage to opposite-sex couples violated the Charter, the Court of Appeal refined the common-law meaning of marriage. We concur with this remedy, which is entirely consonant with established principles of jurisprudence empowering a court to refine a common-law principle in light of evolving constitutional standards . . .

We construe civil marriage to mean the voluntary union of two persons as spouses, to the exclusion of all others. This reformulation redresses the plaintiffs' constitutional injury and furthers the aim of marriage to promote stable, exclusive relationships. It advances the two legitimate State interests the department has identified: providing a stable setting for child rearing and conserving State resources. It leaves intact the Legislature's broad discretion to regulate marriage . . .

. . . We declare that barring an individual from the protections, benefits, and obligations of civil marriage solely because that person would marry a person of the same sex violates the Massachusetts Constitution. . . . Entry of judgment shall be stayed for 180 days to permit the Legislature to take such action as it may deem appropriate in light of this opinion. . . .

So ordered.

GREANEY, J. (concurring).

A comment is in order with respect to the insistence of some that marriage is, as a matter of definition, the legal union of a man and a woman. To define the institution of marriage by the characteristics of those to whom it always has been accessible, in order to justify the exclusion of those to whom it never has been accessible, is conclusory and bypasses the core question we are asked to decide. This case calls for a higher level of legal analysis. Precisely, the case requires that we confront ingrained assumptions with respect to historically accepted roles of men and women within the institution of marriage and requires that we reexamine these assumptions. . . .

I am hopeful that our decision will be accepted by those thoughtful citizens who believe that same-sex unions should not be approved by the State. I am not referring here to acceptance in the sense of grudging acknowledgment of the court's authority to adjudicate the matter. My hope is more liberating. The plaintiffs are members of our community, our neighbors, our coworkers, our friends. As pointed out by the court, their professions include investment advisor, computer engineer, teacher, therapist, and lawyer. The plaintiffs volunteer in our schools, worship beside us in our religious houses, and have children who play with our children, to mention just a few ordinary daily contacts. We share a common humanity and participate together in the social contract that is the foundation of our Commonwealth. Simple principles of decency dictate that we extend to the plaintiffs, and to their new status, full acceptance, tolerance, and respect. We should do so because it is the right thing to do. . . .

SPINA, J. (dissenting, with whom SOSMAN and CORDY, JJ., join). What is at stake in this case is not the unequal treatment of individuals or whether individual rights have been impermissibly burdened, but the power of the Legislature to effectuate social change without interference from the courts. . . . The power to regulate marriage lies with the Legislature, not with the judiciary.

The court concludes, however, that G. L. c. 207 unconstitutionally discriminates against the individual plaintiffs because it denies them the "right to marry the person of one's choice" where that person is of the same sex . . . To reach this result the court relies on Loving v. Virginia, 388 U.S. 1, 12 (1967), and transforms "choice" into the essential element of the institution of marriage. The *Loving* case did not use the word "choice" in this manner, and it did not point to the result that the court reaches today. In *Loving*, the Supreme Court struck down as unconstitutional a statute that prohibited Caucasians from marrying non-Caucasians. It concluded that the statute was intended to preserve white supremacy and invidiously discriminated against non-Caucasians because of their race. See id. at 11-12. The "choice" to which the Supreme Court referred was the "choice to marry," and it concluded that with respect to the institution of marriage, the State had no compelling interest in limiting the choice to marry along racial lines. Id. The Supreme Court did not imply the existence of a right to marry a person of the same sex . . .

. . . The marriage statutes do not impermissibly burden a right protected by our constitutional guarantee of due process . . . There is no restriction on the right of any plaintiff to enter into marriage. Each is free to marry a willing person of the opposite sex. . . . [T]oday the court does not fashion a remedy that affords greater protection of a right. Instead, using the rubric of due process, it has redefined marriage.

## QUESTIONS

1. What was the plaintiffs' statutory argument with respect to the Commonwealth's marriage laws?

2. How did the Court respond to this claim?

3. What were the plaintiffs' constitutional arguments?

4. What arguments did the state raise in opposition to these constitutional claims?

5. What did the Court find with respect to the constitutionality of barring same-sex couples from marrying?

6. What relief did the Court order?

7. What objections did the dissent assert?

---

In the first major marital rights case after *Goodridge,* the New Jersey Supreme Court ruled that same-sex couples are entitled to the protections and benefits of marriage. Unlike the *Goodridge* Court, the New Jersey Court distinguished between the right to marry and the right to the benefits and protections of marriage.

### LEWIS v. HARRIS
#### 188 N.J. 415, 908 A.2d 196 (2006)

**A.**

Plaintiffs are seven same-sex couples who claim that New Jersey's laws, which restrict civil marriage to the union of a man and a woman, violate the liberty and equal protection guarantees of the New Jersey Constitution. Each plaintiff has been in a "permanent committed relationship" for more than ten years and each seeks to marry his or her partner and to enjoy the legal, financial, and social benefits that are afforded by marriage. . . .

Plaintiffs present a twofold argument. They first assert that same-sex couples have a fundamental right to marry that is protected by the liberty guarantee of Article I, Paragraph 1 of the State Constitution. They next assert that denying same-sex couples the right to marriage afforded to opposite-sex couples violates the equal protection guarantee of that constitutional provision.

In defending the constitutionality of its marriage laws, the State submits that same-sex marriage has no historical roots in the traditions or collective conscience of the people of New Jersey to give it the ranking of a fundamental right, and that limiting marriage to opposite-sex couples is a rational exercise of social policy by the Legislature . . .

We perceive plaintiffs' equal protection claim to have two components: whether committed same-sex couples have a constitutional right to the benefits and privileges afforded to married heterosexual couples, and, if so, whether they have the constitutional right to have their "permanent committed relationship" recognized by the name of marriage. . . .

## III.

Plaintiffs contend that the right to marry a person of the same sex is a fundamental right . . . Plaintiffs maintain that the liberty interest at stake is "the right of every adult to choose whom to marry without intervention of government." . . . In assessing their liberty claim, we must determine whether the right of a person to marry someone of the same sex is so deeply rooted in the traditions and collective conscience of our people that it must be deemed fundamental . . .

The right to marriage is recognized as fundamental by both our Federal and State Constitutions. . . . In this case, the liberty interest at stake is not some undifferentiated, abstract right to marriage, but rather the right of people of the same sex to marry. Thus, we are concerned only with the question of whether the right to same-sex marriage is deeply rooted in this State's history and its people's collective conscience. . . .

Our starting point is the State's marriage laws.

Plaintiffs do not dispute that New Jersey's civil marriage statutes . . . limit marriage to heterosexual couples. That limitation is clear from the use of gender-specific language in the text of various statutes. . . .

Although today there is a nationwide public debate raging over whether same-sex marriage should be authorized under the laws or constitutions of the various states, the framers of the 1947 New Jersey Constitution, much less the drafters of our marriage statutes, could not have imagined that the liberty right protected by Article I, Paragraph 1 embraced the right of a person to marry someone of his or her own sex. . . .

Times and attitudes have changed, and there has been a developing understanding that discrimination against gays and lesbians is no longer acceptable in this State, as is evidenced by various laws and judicial decisions prohibiting differential treatment based on sexual orientation. . . . On the federal level, moreover, the United States Supreme Court has struck down laws that have unconstitutionally targeted gays and lesbians for disparate treatment.

In Romer v. Evans, Colorado passed an amendment to its constitution that prohibited all legislative, executive, or judicial action designed to afford homosexuals protection from discrimination based on sexual orientation. 517 U.S. 620, 623-24, 116 S. Ct. 1620, 1623, 134 L. Ed. 2d 855, 860-61 (1996). The Supreme Court declared that Colorado's constitutional provision violated the Fourteenth Amendment's Equal Protection Clause because it "impos[ed] a broad and undifferentiated disability on a single named group" and appeared to be motivated by an "animus toward" gays and lesbians. Id. at 632, 116 S. Ct. at 1627, 1628, 134 L. Ed. 2d at 865-66. The Court concluded that a state could not make "a class of persons a stranger to its laws." Id. at 635, 116 S. Ct. at 1629, 134 L. Ed. 2d at 868.

More recently, in Lawrence v. Texas, the Court invalidated on Fourteenth Amendment due process grounds Texas's sodomy statute, which made it a crime for homosexuals "to engage in certain intimate sexual conduct." 539 U.S. 558, 562, 578, 123 S. Ct. 2472, 2475, 2484, 156 L. Ed. 2d 508, 515, 525-26 (2003). The Court held that the "liberty" protected by the Due Process Clause prevented Texas from controlling the destiny of homosexuals "by making their private sexual conduct a crime." Id. at 578, 123 S. Ct. at 2484, 156 L. Ed. 2d at 525 . . . .

Although those recent cases openly advance the civil rights of gays and lesbians, they fall far short of establishing a right to same-sex marriage deeply rooted in the traditions, history, and conscience of the people of this State.

Plaintiffs also rely on Loving v. Virginia, 388 U.S. 1, 87 S. Ct. 1817, 18 L. Ed. 2d 1010 (1967), to support their claim that the right to same-sex marriage is fundamental . . . . Although the Court reaffirmed the fundamental right of marriage, the heart of the case was invidious discrimination based on race, the very evil that motivated passage of the Fourteenth Amendment. Id. at 10-12, 87 S. Ct. at 1823-24, 18 L. Ed. 2d at 1017-18 . . . From the fact-specific background of that case, which dealt with intolerable racial distinctions that patently violated the Fourteenth Amendment, we cannot find support for plaintiffs claim that there is a fundamental right to same-sex marriage under our State Constitution. . . .

Despite the rich diversity of this State, the tolerance and goodness of its people, and the many recent advances made by gays and lesbians toward achieving social acceptance and equality under the law, we cannot find that a right to same-sex marriage is so deeply rooted in the traditions, history, and conscience of the people of this State that it ranks as a fundamental right. When looking for the source of our rights under the New Jersey Constitution, we need not look beyond our borders. Nevertheless, we do take note that no jurisdiction, not even Massachusetts, has declared that there is a fundamental right to same-sex marriage under the federal or its own constitution. . . .

## IV.

### A.

In conducting this equal protection analysis, we discern two distinct issues. The first is whether committed same-sex couples have the right to the statutory benefits and privileges conferred on heterosexual married couples. Next, assuming a right to equal benefits and privileges, the issue is whether committed same-sex partners have a constitutional right to define their relationship by the name of marriage, the word that historically has characterized the union of a man and a woman . . .

Today, in New Jersey, it is just as unlawful to discriminate against individuals on the basis of sexual orientation as it is to discriminate against them on the basis of race, national origin, age, or sex. See N.J.S.A. 10:5-4. Over the last three decades, through judicial decisions and comprehensive legislative enactments, this State, step by step, has protected gay and lesbian individuals from discrimination on account of their sexual orientation.

In 1974, a New Jersey court held that the parental visitation rights of a divorced homosexual father could not be denied or restricted based on his sexual orientation. In re J.S. & C., 129 N.J. Super. 486, 489, 324 A.2d 90 (Ch. Div. 1974), aff'd per curiam, 142 N.J. Super. 499, 362 A.2d 54 (App. Div. 1976). Five years later, the Appellate Division stated that the custodial rights of a mother could not be denied or impaired because she was a lesbian. M.P. v. S.P., 169 N.J. Super. 425, 427, 404 A.2d 1256 (App. Div. 1979). This State was one of the first in the nation to judicially recognize the right of an individual to adopt a same-sex partner's biological child. . . . J.M.G., supra, 267 N.J. Super. at 625, 626, 631, 632 A.2d 550 (recognizing "importance of the emotional benefit of formal recognition of the relationship between [the non-biological mother] and the child" and that there is not one correct family paradigm for creating "supportive, loving environment" for children) . . . Additionally, this Court has acknowledged that a woman can be the "psychological parent" of children born to her former same-sex partner during their committed relationship, entitling the woman to visitation with the children. V.C. v. M.J.B., 163 N.J. 200, 206-07, 230, 748 A.2d 539, cert. denied, 531 U.S. 926, 121 S. Ct. 302, 148 L. Ed. 2d 243 (2000) . . .

Perhaps more significantly, New Jersey's Legislature has been at the forefront of combating sexual orientation discrimination and advancing equality of treatment toward gays and lesbians. In 1992, through an amendment to the Law Against Discrimination (LAD), L. 1991, c. 519, New Jersey became the fifth state in the nation to prohibit discrimination on the basis of "affectional or sexual orientation." . . . See N.J.S.A. 10:5-4. In making sexual orientation a protected category, the Legislature committed New Jersey to the goal of eradicating discrimination against gays and lesbians . . .

In 2004, the Legislature passed the Domestic Partnership Act, L. 2003, c. 246, making available to committed same-sex couples "certain rights and benefits that are accorded to married couples under the laws of New Jersey." . . . N.J.S.A. 26:8A-2(d). . . .

**B.**

We next examine the extent to which New Jersey's laws continue to restrict committed same-sex couples from enjoying the full benefits and privileges available through marriage. Although under the Domestic Partnership Act same-sex couples are provided with a number of important rights, they still are denied many benefits and privileges accorded to their similarly situated heterosexual counterparts. Thus, the Act has failed to bridge the inequality gap between committed same-sex couples and married opposite-sex couples. . . .

In addition, same-sex couples certified as domestic partners receive fewer workplace protections than married couples . . .

Significantly, the economic and financial inequities that are borne by same-sex domestic partners are borne by their children too. With fewer financial benefits and protections available, those children are disadvantaged in a way that children in married households are not . . .

**C.**

We now must assess the public need for denying the full benefits and privileges that flow from marriage to committed same-sex partners. At this point, we do not consider whether committed same-sex couples should be allowed to marry, but only whether those couples are entitled to the same rights and benefits afforded to married heterosexual couples. Cast in that light, the issue is not about the transformation of the traditional definition of marriage, but about the unequal dispensation of benefits and privileges to one of two similarly situated classes of people. . . .

The Legislature has recognized that the "rights and benefits" provided in the Domestic Partnership Act are directly related "to any reasonable conception of basic human dignity and autonomy." N.J.S.A. 26:8A-2(d). It is difficult to understand how withholding the remaining "rights and benefits" from committed same-sex couples is compatible with a "reasonable conception of basic human dignity and autonomy." There is no rational basis for, on the one hand, giving gays and lesbians full civil rights in their status as individuals, and, on the other, giving them an incomplete set of rights when they follow the inclination of their sexual orientation and enter into committed same-sex relationships.

Disparate treatment of committed same-sex couples, moreover, directly disadvantages their children. . . . There is something distinctly unfair about the State recognizing the right of same-sex couples to raise natural and adopted children and placing foster children with those couples, and yet denying those children the financial and social benefits and privileges available to children in heterosexual households. . . . There is no rational basis for visiting on those children a flawed and unfair scheme directed at their parents. To the extent that families are strengthened by encouraging monogamous relationships, whether heterosexual or homosexual, we cannot discern any public need that would justify the legal disabilities that now afflict same-sex domestic partnerships . . .

**D.**

In arguing to uphold the system of disparate treatment that disfavors same-sex couples, the State offers as a justification the interest in uniformity with other states' laws. Unlike other states, however, New Jersey forbids sexual orientation discrimination, . . . Unlike New Jersey, other states have expressed open hostility toward legally recognizing committed same-sex relationships. . . .

Today, only Connecticut and Vermont, through civil union, and Massachusetts, through marriage, extend to committed same-sex couples the full rights and benefits offered to married heterosexual couples. . . .

Vermont, Massachusetts, and Connecticut represent a distinct minority view. Nevertheless, our current laws concerning same-sex couples are more in line with the legal constructs in those states than the majority of other states. In protecting the rights of citizens of this State, we have never slavishly followed the popular trends in other jurisdictions, particularly when the majority approach is incompatible with the unique interests, values, customs, and concerns of our people. . . .

We conclude that denying to committed same-sex couples the financial and social benefits and privileges given to their married heterosexual counterparts bears no substantial relationship to a legitimate governmental purpose. We now hold that under the equal protection guarantee of Article I, Paragraph 1 of the New Jersey Constitution, committed same-sex couples must be afforded on equal terms the same rights and benefits enjoyed by married opposite-sex couples.

## V.

The equal protection requirement of Article I, Paragraph 1 leaves the Legislature with two apparent options. The Legislature could simply amend the marriage statutes to include same-sex couples, or it could create a separate statutory structure, such as a civil union, as Connecticut and Vermont have done . . .

Plaintiffs argue that even equal social and financial benefits would not make them whole unless they are allowed to call their committed relationships by the name of marriage. They maintain that a parallel legal structure, called by a name other than marriage, which provides the social and financial benefits they have sought, would be a separate-but-equal classification . . . From plaintiffs' standpoint, the title of marriage is an intangible right, without which they are consigned to second-class citizenship. Plaintiffs seek not just legal standing, but also social acceptance, which in their view is the last step toward true equality. Conversely, the State asserts that it has a substantial interest in preserving the historically and almost universally accepted definition of marriage as the union of a man and a woman. . . .

Raised here is the perplexing question — "what's in a name?" — and is a name itself of constitutional magnitude after the State is required to provide full statutory rights and benefits to same-sex couples? We are mindful that in the cultural clash over same-sex marriage, the word marriage itself — independent of the rights and benefits of marriage — has an evocative and important meaning to both parties. . . .

To be clear, it is not our role to suggest whether the Legislature should either amend the marriage statutes to include same-sex couples or enact a civil union scheme. Our role here is limited to constitutional adjudication, and therefore we must steer clear of the swift and treacherous currents of social policy when we have no constitutional compass with which to navigate. . . .

Whether an issue with such far-reaching social implications as how to define marriage falls within the judicial or the democratic realm, to many, is debatable. Some may think that this Court should settle the matter, insulating it from public discussion and the political process. Nevertheless, a court must discern not only the limits of its own authority, but also when to exercise forbearance, recognizing that the legitimacy of its decisions rests on reason, not power. We will not short-circuit the democratic process from running its course. . . .

Our decision today significantly advances the civil rights of gays and lesbians. We have decided that our State Constitution guarantees that every statutory right and benefit conferred to heterosexual couples through civil marriage must be made available to committed same-sex couples. Now the Legislature must determine whether to alter the long accepted definition of marriage . . .

CHIEF JUSTICE PORITZ, concurring and dissenting.

I concur with the determination of the majority that "denying the rights and benefits to committed same-sex couples that are statutorily given to their heterosexual counterparts violates the equal protection guarantee of Article I, Paragraph 1[,]" of the New Jersey Constitution . . . I can find no principled basis, however, on which to distinguish those rights and benefits from the right to the title of marriage, . . .

I dissent also from the majority's conclusion that there is no fundamental due process right to same-sex marriage "encompassed within the concept of liberty guaranteed by Article I, Paragraph 1." . . .

In their presentation to the Court, [plaintiffs] speak of the deep and symbolic significance to them of the institution of marriage. They ask to participate, not simply in the tangible benefits that civil marriage provides — although certainly those benefits are of enormous importance — but in the intangible benefits that flow from being civilly married. . . .

We must not underestimate the power of language. Labels set people apart as surely as physical separation on a bus or in school facilities. Labels are used to perpetuate prejudice about differences that, in this case, are embedded in the law. By excluding same-sex couples from civil marriage, the State declares that it is legitimate to differentiate between their commitments and the commitments of heterosexual couples. Ultimately, the message is that what same-sex couples have is not as important or as significant as "real" marriage, that such lesser relationships cannot have the name of marriage. . . .

## II.

### A.

. . . Loving should have put to rest the notion that fundamental rights can be found only in the historical traditions and conscience of the people. . . . Had the United States Supreme Court followed the traditions of the people of Virginia, the Court would have sustained the law that barred marriage between members of racial minorities and Caucasians. . . . Most telling, the Court did not frame the issue as a right to interracial marriage but, simply, as a right to marry sought by individuals who had traditionally been denied that right. Loving teaches that the fundamental right to marry no more can be limited to same-race couples than it can be limited to those who choose a committed relationship with persons of the opposite sex.

Justices Long and Zazzali join in this opinion.

## QUESTIONS

1. Explain the Court's rationale for distinguishing between the right to marry and the right to the benefits and protection of marriage.

2. Why did the Court decide to leave the actual remedy up to the legislature?

3. The majority and dissent disagree about the symbolic importance of being able to call one's relationship "marriage."? Discuss the conflicting views on this issue.

---

As discussed in the text, the following landmark decision helped to open the doors of the court to unmarried couples seeking to untangle their interests following the dissolution of a relationship.

### MARVIN v. MARVIN
#### 18 Cal. 3d 660, 557 P.2d 106, 134 Cal. Rptr. 815 (1976)

During the past 15 years, there has been a substantial increase in the number of couples living together without marrying. Such nonmarital relationships lead to legal controversy when one partner dies or the couple separates. . . .

. . . Plaintiff avers that in October of 1964 she and defendant "entered into an oral agreement" that while "the parties lived together they would combine their efforts and earnings and would share equally any and all property accumulated as a result of their efforts whether individual or combined." Furthermore, they agreed to "hold themselves out to the general public as husband and wife" and that "plaintiff would further render her services as a companion, homemaker, housekeeper and cook to . . . defendant."

Shortly thereafter plaintiff agreed to "give up her lucrative career as an entertainer [and] singer" in order to "devote her full time to defendant . . . as a companion, homemaker, housekeeper and cook"; in return defendant agreed to "provide for all of plaintiff's financial support and needs for the rest of her life."

Plaintiff alleges that she lived with defendant from October of 1964 through May of 1970 and fulfilled her obligations under the agreement. During this period the parties as a result of their efforts and earnings acquired in defendant's name substantial real and personal property, including motion picture rights worth over $1 million. In May of 1970, however, defendant compelled plaintiff to leave his household. He continued to support plaintiff until November of 1971, but thereafter refused to provide further support. On the basis of these allegations plaintiff asserts two causes of action. The first, for declaratory relief, asks the court to determine her contract and property rights; the second seeks to impose a constructive trust upon one half of the property acquired during the course of the relationship. . . .

In the case before us plaintiff, basing her cause of action in contract . . . maintains that the trial court erred in denying her a trial on the merits of her contention. Although that court did not specify the ground for its conclusion that plaintiff's contractual allegations stated no cause of action, defendant offers some four theories to sustain the ruling. . . .

Defendant first and principally relies on the contention that the alleged contract is so closely related to the supposed "immoral" character of the relationship between plaintiff and himself that the enforcement of the contract would violate public policy. He points to cases asserting that a contract between nonmarital partners is unenforceable if it is "involved in" an illicit relationship. . . . A review of the numerous California decisions concerning contracts between nonmarital partners, however, reveals that the courts have not employed such broad and uncertain standards to strike down contracts. The decisions instead disclose a narrower and more precise standard: a contract between nonmarital partners is unenforceable only to the extent that it explicitly rests upon the immoral and illicit consideration of meretricious sexual services. . . .

Although the past decisions hover over the issue in the somewhat wispy form of the figures of a Chagall painting, we can abstract from those decisions a clear and simple rule. The fact that a man and woman live together without marriage, and engage in a sexual relationship, does not in itself invalidate agreements between them relating to their earnings, property, or expenses. Neither is such an agreement invalid merely because the parties may have contemplated the creation or continuation of a nonmarital relationship when they entered into it. Agreements between nonmarital partners fail only to the extent that they rest upon a consideration of meretricious sexual services. Thus the rule asserted by defendant, that a contract fails if it is "involved in" or made "in contemplation" of a nonmarital relationship, cannot be reconciled with the decisions.

The three cases cited by defendant which have declined to enforce contracts between nonmarital partners involved consideration that was expressly founded upon an illicit sexual services [sic]. . . .

The principle that a contract between nonmarital partners will be enforced unless expressly and inseparably based upon an illicit consideration of sexual services not only represents the distillation of the decisional law, but also offers a far more precise and workable standard than that advocated by defendant. . . .

In summary, we base our opinion on the principle that adults who voluntarily live together and engage in sexual relations are nonetheless as competent as any other persons to contract respecting their earnings and property rights. Of course, they cannot lawfully contract to pay for the performance of sexual services, for such a contract is, in essence, an agreement for prostitution and unlawful for that reason. But they may agree to pool their earnings and to hold all property acquired during the relationship in accord with the law governing community property; conversely they may agree that each partner's earnings and the property acquired from those earnings remains the separate property of the earning partner. So long as the agreement does not rest upon illicit meretricious consideration, the parties may order their economic affairs as they choose, and no policy precludes the courts from enforcing such agreements.

In the present instance, plaintiff alleges that the parties agreed to pool their earnings, that they contracted to share equally in all property acquired, and that defendant agreed to support plaintiff. The terms of the contract as alleged do not rest upon any unlawful consideration. We therefore conclude that the complaint furnishes a suitable basis upon which the trial court can render declaratory relief. . . . The trial court consequently erred in granting defendant's motion for judgment on the pleadings. . . .

As we have noted, both causes of action in plaintiff's complaint allege an express contract; neither assert any basis for relief independent from the contract. In In re Marriage of Cary, *supra*, 34 Cal. App. 3d 345, however, the Court of Appeal held that, in view of the policy of the Family Law Act, property accumulated by nonmarital partners in an actual family relationship should be divided equally. Upon examining the *Cary* opinion, the parties to the present case realized that plaintiff's alleged relationship with defendant might arguably support a cause of action independent of any express contract between the parties. . . .

Reviewing the prior decisions which had denied relief to the homemaking partner, the Court of Appeal reasoned that those decisions rested upon a policy of punishing persons guilty of cohabitation without marriage. The Family Law Act, the court observed, aimed to eliminate fault or guilt as a basis for dividing marital property. But once fault or guilt is excluded, the court reasoned, nothing distinguishes the property rights of a nonmarital "spouse" from those of a putative spouse. Since the latter is entitled to half the " 'quasi marital property' " . . . , the Court of Appeal concluded that, giving effect to the policy of the Family Law Act, a nonmarital cohabitator should also be entitled to half the property accumulated during an "actual family relationship." (34 Cal. App. 3d at p. 353.)

Cary met with a mixed reception in other appellate districts. In Estate of Atherley, supra, 44 Cal. App. 3d 758, the Fourth District agreed with Cary that under the Family Law Act a nonmarital partner in an actual family relationship enjoys the same right to an equal division of property as a putative spouse. In Beckman v. Mayhew, supra, 49 Cal. App. 3d 529, however, the Third District rejected Cary on the ground that the Family Law Act was not intended to change California law dealing with nonmarital relationships. If Cary is interpreted as holding that the Family Law Act requires an equal division of property accumulated in nonmarital "actual family relationships," then we agree with Beckman v. Mayhew that Cary distends the act. . . .

But although we reject the reasoning of Cary and Atherley, we share the perception of the Cary and Atherley courts that the application of former precedent in the factual setting of those cases would work an unfair distribution of the property accumulated by the couple. . . .

The principal reason why the pre-Cary decisions result in an unfair distribution of property inheres in the court's refusal to permit a nonmarital partner to assert rights based upon accepted principles of implied contract or equity. We have examined the reasons advanced to justify this denial of relief, and find that none have merit. . . .

First, we note that the cases denying relief do not rest their refusal upon any theory of "punishing" a "guilty" partner. Indeed, to the extent that denial of relief "punishes" one partner, it necessarily rewards the other by permitting him to retain a disproportionate amount of the property. Concepts of "guilt" thus cannot justify an unequal division of property between two equally "guilty" persons.

Other reasons advanced in the decisions fare no better. The principal argument seems to be that "[equitable] considerations arising from the reasonable expectation of . . . benefits attending the status of marriage . . . are not present [in a nonmarital relationship]." (Vallera v. Vallera, supra, 21 Cal. 2d at p. 685.) But, although parties to a nonmarital relationship obviously cannot have based any expectations upon the belief that they were married, other expectations and equitable considerations remain. The parties may well expect that property will be divided in accord with the parties' own tacit understanding and that in the absence of such understanding the courts will fairly apportion property accumulated through mutual effort. We need not treat nonmarital partners as putatively married persons in order to apply principles of implied contract, or extend equitable remedies; we need to treat them only as we do any other unmarried persons. . . .

. . . The argument that granting remedies to the nonmarital partners would discourage marriage must fail; as *Cary* pointed out, "with equal or greater force the point might be made that the pre-1970 rule was calculated to cause the income-producing partner to avoid marriage and thus retain the benefit of all of his or her accumulated earnings." 34 Cal. App. 3d at p. 353. Although we recognize the well-established public policy to foster and promote the institution of marriage . . . perpetuation of judicial rules which result in an inequitable distribution of property accumulated during a nonmarital relationship is neither a just nor an effective way of carrying out that policy.

In summary, we believe that the prevalence of nonmarital relationships in modern society and the social acceptance of them, marks this as a time when our courts should by no means apply the doctrine of the unlawfulness of the so-called meretricious relationship to the instant case. As we have explained, the nonenforceability of agreements expressly providing for meretricious conduct rested upon the fact that such conduct, as the word suggests, pertained to and encompassed prostitution. To equate the nonmarital relationship of today to such a subject matter is to do violence to an accepted and wholly different practice.

We are aware that many young couples live together without the solemnization of marriage, in order to make sure that they can successfully later undertake marriage. This trial period, preliminary to marriage, serves as some assurance that the marriage will not subsequently end in dissolution to the harm of both parties. We are aware, as we have stated, of the pervasiveness of nonmarital relationships in other situations.

The mores of the society have indeed changed so radically in regard to cohabitation that we cannot impose a standard based on alleged moral considerations that have apparently been so widely abandoned by so many. Lest we be misunderstood, however, we take this occasion to point out that the structure of society itself largely depends upon the institution of marriage, and nothing we have said in this opinion should be taken to derogate from that institution. The joining of the man and woman in marriage is at once the most socially productive and individually fulfilling relationship that one can enjoy in the course of a lifetime.

We conclude that the judicial barriers that may stand in the way of a policy based upon the fulfillment of the reasonable expectations of the parties to a nonmarital relationship should be removed. As we have explained, the courts now hold that express agreements will be enforced unless they rest on an unlawful meretricious consideration. We add that in the absence of an express agreement, the courts may look to a variety of other remedies in order to protect the parties' lawful expectations.

The courts may inquire into the conduct of the parties to determine whether that conduct demonstrates an implied contract or implied agreement of partnership or joint venture . . . or some other tacit understanding between the parties. The courts may, when appropriate, employ principles of constructive trust . . . or resulting trust. . . . Finally, a nonmarital partner may recover in quantum meruit for the reasonable value of household services rendered less the reasonable value of support received if he can show that he rendered services with the expectation of monetary reward.

Since we have determined that plaintiff's complaint states a cause of action for breach of an express contract, and, as we have explained, can be amended to state a cause of action independent of allegations of express contract, we must conclude that the trial court erred in granting defendant a judgment on the pleadings. The judgment is reversed and the cause remanded for further proceedings consistent with the views expressed herein.

## QUESTIONS

1. What was the oral agreement between the plaintiff and the defendant?

2. Why did the defendant claim that any contract entered into by him and the plaintiff would violate public policy? How does the court respond to his argument?

3. What does the court decide about the enforceability of agreements between unmarried couples regarding their economic affairs? What consideration is to be given to the sexual nature of the relationship?

4. The *Marvin* court discusses an earlier decision, *In re Marriage of Cary*. What did *Cary* hold? Why does the *Marvin* court reject that decision?

5. How does the *Marvin* court address the concern that granting rights to unmarried cohabitants will undermine the institution of marriage?

6. What role do moral considerations play in the decision?

Like *Marvin*, the following case is a landmark decision. Breaking legal ground, the Court extended the meaning of the word "family" to include nonmarital partners.

## BRASCHI v. STAHL ASSOCIATES
### 74 N.Y.2d 201, 543 N.E.2d 49, 544 N.Y.S.2d 784 (1989)

In this dispute over occupancy rights to a rent-controlled apartment, the central question to be resolved on this request for preliminary injunctive relief . . . is whether appellant has demonstrated a likelihood of success on the merits . . . by showing that, as a matter of law, he is entitled to seek protection from eviction under New York City Rent and Eviction Regulations 9 NYCRR 2204.6(d). . . . That regulation provides that upon the death of a rent-control tenant, the landlord may not dispossess "either the surviving spouse of the deceased tenant or some other member of the deceased tenant's *family* who has been living with the tenant" (emphasis supplied). Resolution of this question requires this court to determine the meaning of the term "family" as it is used in this context.

### I.

Appellant, Miguel Braschi, was living with Leslie Blanchard in a rent-controlled apartment located at 405 East 54th Street from the summer of 1975 until Blanchard's death in September of 1986. In November of 1986, respondent, Stahl Associates Company, the owner of the apartment building, served a notice to cure on appellant contending that he was a mere licensee with no right to occupy the apartment since only Blanchard was the tenant of record. In December of 1986 respondent served appellant with a notice to terminate informing appellant that he had one month to vacate the apartment and that, if the apartment was not vacated, respondent would commence summary proceedings to evict him. . . .

. . . The present dispute arises because the term "family" is not defined in the rent-control code . . .

Rent control was enacted to address a "serious public emergency" created by "an acute shortage in dwellings," which resulted in "speculative, unwarranted and abnormal increases in rents" (L 1946 ch 274, codified, as amended, at McKinney's Uncons Laws of NY §§ 8581 et seq.). . . .

To accomplish its goals, the Legislature recognized that not only would rents have to be controlled, but that evictions would have to be regulated and controlled as well (*id.*) Hence, section 2204.6 of the New York City Rent and Eviction Regulations (9 NYCRR 2204.6) . . . provides . . . noneviction protection to those occupants who are either the "surviving spouse of the deceased tenant or some other member of the deceased tenant's *family* who has been living with the tenant [of record]" (emphasis supplied). The manifest intent of this section is to restrict the landowners' ability to evict a narrow class of occupants other than the tenant of record. . . . Juxtaposed against this intent favoring the protection of tenants, is the over-all objective of a gradual "transition from regulation to a normal market of free bargaining between landlord and tenant". . . . One way in which this goal is to be achieved is "vacancy decontrol," which automatically makes rent-control units subject to the less rigorous provisions of rent stabilization upon the termination of the rent-control tenancy. . . .

Emphasizing the latter objective, respondent argues that the term "family member" . . . should be construed, consistent with this State's intestacy laws, to mean relationships of blood, consanguinity and adoption in order to effectuate the over-all goal of orderly succession to real property. Under this interpretation, only those entitled to inherit under the laws of intestacy would be afforded noneviction. . . . Further, as did the Appellate Division, respondent relies on our decision in Matter of Robert Paul P. (63 NY2d 233), arguing that since the relationship between appellant and Blanchard has not been accorded legal status by the Legislature, it is not entitled to the protections of section 2204.6(d), which, according to the Appellate Division, applies only to "family members within traditional, legally recognized familial relationships" (143 AD2d 44, 45). . . .

Contrary to all of these arguments, we conclude that the term family, as used in 9 NYCRR 2204.6(d), should not be rigidly restricted to those people who have formalized their relationship by obtaining, for instance, a marriage certificate or an adoption order. The intended protection against sudden eviction should not rest on fictitious legal distinctions or genetic history, but instead should find its foundation in the reality of family life. In the context of eviction, a more realistic, and certainly equally valid, view of a family includes two adult lifetime partners whose relationship is long term and characterized by an emotional and financial commitment and interdependence. This view comports both with our society's traditional concept of "family" and with the expectations of individuals who live in such nuclear units. . . . Hence, it is reasonable to conclude that, in using the term "family," the Legislature intended to extend protection to those who reside in households having all of the normal familial characteristics. Appellant Braschi should therefore be afforded the opportunity to prove that he and Blanchard had such a household.

This definition of "family" is consistent with both of the competing purposes of the rent-control laws: the protection of individuals from sudden dislocation and the gradual transition to a free market system. Family members, whether or not related by blood, or law who have always treated the apartment as their family home will be protected against the hardship of eviction following the death of the named tenant, thereby furthering the Legislature's goals of preventing dislocation and preserving family units which might otherwise be broken apart upon eviction. This approach will foster the transition from rent control to rent stabilization by drawing a distinction between those individuals who are, in fact, genuine family members, and those who are mere roommates . . . or newly discovered relatives hoping to inherit the rent-controlled apartment after the existing tenant's death.

The determination as to whether an individual is entitled to noneviction protection should be based upon an objective examination of the relationship of the parties. In making this assessment, the lower courts of this State have looked to a number of factors, including the exclusivity and longevity of the relationship, the level of emotional and financial commitment, the manner in which the parties have conducted their everyday lives and held themselves out to society, and the reliance placed upon one another for daily family services. . . . These factors are most helpful, although it should be emphasized that the presence or absence of one or more of them is not dispositive since it is the totality of the relationship as evidenced by the dedication, caring and self-sacrifice of the parties which should, in the final analysis, control. Appellant's situation provides an example of how the rule should be applied.

Appellant and Blanchard lived together as permanent life partners for more than 10 years. They regarded one another, and were regarded by friends and family, as spouses. The two men's families were aware of the nature of the relationship, and they regularly visited each other's families and attended family functions together, as a couple. Even today, appellant continues to maintain a relationship with Blanchard's niece, who considers him an uncle. In addition to their interwoven social lives, appellant clearly considered the apartment his home. He lists the apartment as his address on his driver's license and passport, and receives all his mail at the apartment address. Moreover, appellant's tenancy was known to the building's superintendent and doormen, who viewed the two men as a couple. Financially, the two men shared all obligations including a household budget. The two were authorized signatories of three safe-deposit boxes, they maintained joint checking and savings accounts, and joint credit cards. In fact, rent was often paid with a check from their joint checking account. Additionally, Blanchard executed a power of attorney in appellant's favor so that appellant could make necessary decisions — financial, medical and personal — for him during his illness. Finally, appellant was the named beneficiary of Blanchard's life insurance policy, as well as the primary legatee and coexecutor of Blanchard's estate. Hence, a court examining these facts could reasonably conclude that these men were much more than mere roommates.

Inasmuch as this case is before us on a certified question, we conclude only that appellant has demonstrated a likelihood of success on the merits, in that he is not excluded, as a matter of law, from seeking noneviction protection. . . .

SIMONS, J. (dissenting). I would affirm. The plurality has adopted a definition of family which extends the language of the regulation well beyond the implication of the words used in it. In doing so, it has expanded the class indefinitely to include anyone who can satisfy an administrator that he or she had an emotional and financial "commitment" to the statutory tenant. Its interpretation is inconsistent with the legislative scheme underlying rent regulation, goes well beyond the intended purposes of 9 NYCRR 2204.6(d), and produces an unworkable test that is subject to abuse. . . .

## QUESTIONS

1. What regulation was involved in this decision? What rights did it grant and to whom?

2. How did the defendant think the term "family," as used in the ordinance, should be defined?

3. Why did the court reject the defendant's argument? What meaning does the court give to the term "family"? Why, according to the court, is its meaning consistent with the purpose of the legislation?

4. In general, what factors are relevant in determining if a couple qualifies as a "family"? What factors did the court focus on in deciding that the plaintiff and his partner qualified as a family?

5. Although significant in its approach, why is this decision of limited applicability?

# Endnotes _____

1. The term *common law* refers to English case law, much of which enforced long-standing customs and traditions. Most colonies and then the newly emergent states accepted the precedential value of these English decisions. *See* Morton J. Horwitz, The Transformation of American Law 1780-1860 ch. 1 (1992).

2. 1 William Blackstone, Commentaries on the Laws of England 441-442 (15th ed. A. Strahan ed., 1809) (citations omitted).

3. 3 William Blackstone, Commentaries on the Laws of England 142 (Clarendon Press 1983).

4. This section is based mainly on the following works: Norma Basch, In the Eyes of the Law: Women, Marriage, and Property in Nineteenth Century New York (1982), and Elizabeth Bowles Warbassee, The Changing Legal Rights of Married Women 1800-1861 ch. 1 (1987).

5. Letter from Elizabeth Cady Stanton (July 25, 1857) to Susan B. Anthony, *quoted in* Elisabeth Griffith, In Her Own Right: The Life of Elizabeth Cady Stanton 103 (1984).

6. Warbassee, *supra* note 4, at 273.

7. *See* Riva Siegel, The Modernization of Marital Status Law: Adjudicating Wives' Rights to Earnings, 1860-1930, 82 Geo. L. Rev. 2127 (1994); Riva Siegel, Home as Work, 103 Yale L.J. 1073 (1994).

8. Graham v. Graham, 33 F.Supp. 936, 938-939 (E.D. Mich. 1940).

9. Orr v. Orr, 440 U.S. 268, 279-280, 283 (1979), quoting Stanton v. Stanton, 421 U.S. 7, 10, 14-15 (1975).

10. Griswold v. Connecticut, 381 U.S. 479 (1965).

11. Loving v. Virginia, 388 U.S. 1 (1967).

12. *Loving* at 7, *citing* Naim v. Naim, 197 Va. 80, 90, 87 S.E.2d 749, 756 (1955).

13. *Id.* at 13, *citing* Skinner v. Oklahoma, 316 U.S. 535, 541 (1942).

14. 434 U.S. 374 (1978).

15. Turner v. Safley, 428 U.S. 78 (1987).

16. Robin L. Bennett et al., Genetic Counseling and Screening of Consanguineous Couples and Their Offspring: Recommendations of the National Society of Genetic Counselors, 11 Journal of Genetic Counseling 97 (2002).

17. Carolyn Bratt, Is Oedipus Free to Marry?, 18 Fam. L.Q. 267, 288-289 (1984) (citations omitted).

18. *See, e.g.,* Moe v. Dinkins, 669 F.2d 67 (2d Cir. 1982).

19. This is not meant to suggest that the gay and lesbian community speaks with a single voice on this issue. In fact, there is an "intra-community" debate over whether the gay and lesbian community should devote its resources to expanding the boundaries of marriage to include same-sex couples, or whether this is an "assimilationist" goal, which threatens to undermine the vitality of the community by importing an inherently flawed heterosexual construct. *See* Evan Wolfson, Crossing the Threshold: Equal Marriage Rights for Lesbians and Gay Men and the Intra-Community Critique, 21 N.Y.U. Rev. L. & Soc. Change 576 (1994-1995); Ruthann Robson, Assimilation, Marriage, and Lesbian Liberation, 75 Temple L. Rev. 709 (2002).

20. *See, e.g.,* Jones v. Hallahan, 501 S.W.2d 588 (Ky. Ct. App. 1973), and Baker v. Nelson, 291 Minn. 310, 191 N.W.2d 185 (1971).

21. To date, plaintiffs have relied exclusively on state constitutional grounds, thus avoiding the possibility of review by the United States Supreme Court, which, were it to occur, would most certainly result in an adverse ruling.

22. In 1993, the Hawaii Supreme Court concluded that imposing a "different-sex" requirement on the choice of marriage partner violated the equal protection clause of the state constitution. It remanded the case to the trial court to give the state an opportunity to try to show that the different-sex requirement served a compelling state interest. After a hearing the trial court judge concluded that the state had not met its burden; while the case was back up on appeal, a constitutional amendment giving the legislature the authority to restrict marriage to male-female was approved. *See* Baehr v. Miike, 852 P.2d 44 (1993), and Baehr v. Miike, Civil Action No. 91-1394 (Haw. Cir. Crt. Dec. 3, 1996).

In Alaska, the constitution was amended following a trial court decision holding that the "choice of a life partner is personal, intimate, and subject to the protection of the right to privacy" for both same-sex and heterosexual couples." *See* Brause & Dugan v. Bureau of Vital Statistics (Alaska Super. Ct.; Feb. 27, 1998).

23. Baker v. Vermont, 744 A.2d 865 (Vt. 1999). The common benefits clause is Vermont's equivalent of an equal protection provision.

24. 798 N.E.2d 941 (2003).

25. *Id.* at 955-956 (internal citations omitted).

26. *Id.* at 966.

27. *Id.* at 970.

28. Lewis v. Harris, 188 N.J. 415, 908 A.2d 196, 223 (2006).

29. *Id.* at 224.

30. *Goodridge,* 798 N.E.2d at 966.

31. *Id.* at 969.

32. *Lewis,* 908 A.2d at 227-228 (Chief Justice Poritiz, joined by Justices Long and Zazzali, concurring with and dissenting from the majority opinion.)

33. U.S. Const. art. IV, § 1.

34. Defense of Marriage Act, 28 U.S.C.S. § 1738(c).

35. 1 U.S.C.S. § 7.

36. *See* Romer v. Evans, 517 U.S. 620 (1996).

37. H.J.Res.56, available on-line at: usgovinfo.about.com/cs/usconstitution/a/marriage.htm

38. White House Press Release, February 24, 2004. Available on-line at: http://www.whitehouse.gov/news/releases/2004/02/20040224-2.html.

39. 18 Cal. 3d 660, 557 P.2d 106, 134 Cal. Rptr. 815 (1976).

40. *Marvin,* 557 P.2d at 122.

41. Some couples do enter into formal cohabitation agreements in order to structure their post-dissolution rights and obligations. Some couples also execute a variety of additional legal documents, such as wills and durable powers of attorney, in order to create rights between them similar to those that the law grants to married couples.

42. Margaret M. Mahoney, Forces Shaping the Law of Cohabitation for Opposite Sex Couples, 7 J.L. Fam. Stud. 135, 161 (2005). Cohabitation is treated as a formal legal status in few states. As with marriage, then, rights and obligations flow from the existence of the relationship itself, thus eliminating the need to prove the existence of an agreement.

43. Mark Ellman, Unmarried Partners and the Legacy of Marvin v. Marvin: "Contract Thinking" Was Marvin's, 76 Notre Dame L. Rev. 1365 (2001)

44. American Law Institute, Principles of the Law of Family Dissolution: Analysis and Recommendations (2002), sec. 6.03 (1). The Principles provide detailed guidelines for "identifying those nonmarital relationships which bear a sufficient resemblance to marriage to justify and require similar post-relationship obligations between the parties, whom the Institute refers to as "domestic partners." Infra, Ellman note 43, at 1378-1379.

45. In addition to Ellman, see Nancy D. Polikoff, Making Marriage Matter Less: The ALI Domestic Partner Principles Are One Step in the Right Direction, 2004 U. Chi Legal F. 353 (2004); Marsha Garrison, Is Consent Necessary? An Evaluation of the Emerging Law of Cohabitation Obligation, 52 UCLA L. Rev. 815 (2005).

46. A growing number of private employers now provide domestic partner benefits.

47. The effort to equalize benefits between unmarried and married couples is undercut by the federal tax code. Under the code, the amount an employer contributes to a spouse's health insurance is not considered taxable income. In contrast, the amount an employer contributes to a domestic partner's health insurance coverage is considered taxable income to the employee, unless the partner qualifies as a dependent.

48. 74 N.Y.2d 201, 543 N.E.2d 49, 544 N.Y.S.2d 784 (1989).

49. *Braschi*, 543 N.E.2d at 50.

50. *Id.* at 53. *See also* In re Guardianship of Sharon Kowalski, Ward, 478 N.W.2d 790 (Minn. Ct. App. 1991), *rev. denied* (Feb. 10, 1992). Here the court described a lesbian couple as a "family by affinity."

51. 136 N.J. 99, 642 A.2d 372 (N.J. 1994).

52. *Id.* at 378-379.

53. Lozoya v. Sanchez, 133 N.M. 579, 66 P.3d 948, 956 (2003).

54. *Id.* at 958, *citing Dunphy*, 642 A.2d at 378.

55. *See* Gwendolyn L. Snodgrass, Creating Family Without Marriage: The Advantages and Disadvantages of Adult Adoption Among Gay and Lesbian Partners, 36 J. Fam. L. 75 (1997-98).

# 2 Premarital Agreements

In Chapter 1, we saw that the trend has been away from state regulation of marriage toward a legal model that emphasizes individual choice. With this increased emphasis on private ordering, **premarital agreements** have gained in both legal and social acceptance. These arrangements allow couples to control the terms of their dissolution in the event the marriage ends in divorce.[1] Typically, in a premarital agreement, one or both prospective spouses agree to waive or limit their rights to spousal support and/or a division of property as would otherwise be provided by statute upon divorce. Simply put, a premarital agreement shields a party's assets and income from the state rules of allocation in the event of a divorce. Accordingly, these agreements are often particularly attractive to wealthy individuals who are entering into a marriage with substantial income and assets. They may also be attractive to individuals who have children from a previous relationship, as they allow a parent to protect assets intended for his or her children from claims of the new spouse in the event of a divorce.

Premarital agreements have become an increasingly important dimension of the private ordering of marriage; however, they have not been accepted without controversy and some judicial ambivalence. Now valid in most, if not all, jurisdictions, courts have nonetheless typically reviewed premarital contracts much more closely and carefully than they review ordinary contracts; as discussed in this chapter, however, there is a growing trend in favor of treating premarital contracts more like any other contract.

## THE TRADITIONAL APPROACH

Until the early 1970s, premarital agreements made in contemplation of a possible divorce were generally considered **void as against public policy**. Although courts no longer disfavor such agreements, the public policy concerns that historically led states to withhold recognition from premarital agreements continue to retain some force today, and those concerns inform the debate over whether the agreements should be treated like "ordinary" contracts or whether, because of their unique nature, they should occupy a special place in the law. These concerns have also shaped the development of the rules and standards governing the enforceability of premarital agreements. Historically, the most significant fear was that premarital agreements would encourage divorce because the party who stood to benefit from the agreement would have less incentive to remain in the marriage when things got rocky. According to this way of thinking, a wealthy man whose wife had waived her right to support would be more inclined to walk away from a troubled marriage than a man who knew he would be burdened with alimony payments, thus undermining the state's interest in preserving marriage as a fundamental social unit.

A related fear was that the enforcement of premarital contracts would lead to the post-divorce impoverishment of women. In opinion after opinion, judges expressed the concern that women would be pushed into signing agreements by financially secure and sophisticated men, and they would give up future rights they did not even know they possessed. As discussed below, this protective impulse has shaped much of the present law regarding enforceability.

Nonrecognition of premarital agreements was also a logical extension of the principle that spouses lacked the authority to alter the terms of the marital relationship because defining the rights and obligations of spouses was a public, rather than a private, matter. Accordingly, since, a husband could not legally shed his duty of support during the marriage, it was considered unfair to allow him to contract out of this obligation in the event of divorce.

Another powerful apprehension was that if couples entering into a marriage were allowed to contract with one another, marriage would be reduced to a commercial enterprise. The vision of couples participating in protracted financial negotiations in contemplation of a possible divorce was an uncomfortable one that suggested the world of family was no different from the world of commerce and that spouses were more like business associates than intimate companions.

> ### *Consideration*
>
> To many, the infusion of contractual ordering into a realm of life thought to be based on ties of mutual affection and commitment would radically alter the meaning of family and make spouses more like business associates than intimate companions. Do you agree?

# THE GROWING ACCEPTANCE OF PREMARITAL AGREEMENTS

In 1970, the Florida Supreme Court, in the landmark case of Posner v. Posner,[2] held that premarital agreements made in contemplation of divorce are not per se invalid, and other states soon followed suit. This trend corresponded with changing notions about marriage and divorce. As individuals acquired greater legal freedom to structure the terms of their marriage, it was a logical development that they be permitted to structure the terms of marital dissolution. The acceptance of no-fault divorce, which eliminated many of the traditional barriers to marital dissolution, also contributed to the acceptance of premarital agreements. With the increased acceptability and availability of divorce, the argument that premarital agreements would facilitate marital dissolution no longer carried the same weight that it had when divorces were more difficult to obtain. (See Chapter 4 for more detail on "no-fault" divorce reform.) In fact, some argue that premarital agreements actually encourage marriage because they allow individuals who might otherwise be wary of getting married, based on a fear of what they might lose upon dissolution, to control the terms of any future divorce.

Another key factor underlying the acceptance of premarital agreements was the changing status of women. Today, courts no longer assume, as they once did, that women are so financially unsophisticated that they will not be able to comprehend the significance of these agreements and will be taken advantage of by prospective husbands. In a related vein, the financial dependence of married women is no longer presumed. Thus, the protective impulse behind nonrecognition is now seen as outdated—a relic of the time when women were regarded as lacking legal capacity and in need of the paternalistic protection of the law, as explained by the Pennsylvania Supreme Court in the case of Simeone v. Simeone:[3]

> Such decisions rested upon a belief that spouses are of unequal status and that women are not knowledgeable enough to understand the nature of contracts they enter. Society has advanced, however, to the point where women are no longer regarded as the "wearier" party in marriage . . . nor is there viability in the presumption that women are uninformed, uneducated, and readily subjected to unfair advantage in marital agreements . . . paternalistic presumptions and protectors that arose to shelter women . . . have, appropriately, been discarded.

> Concerns have been voiced, however, that these assumptions of equality mask the fact that in most marriages women are still the economically subordinate partner, and that enforcement of premarital agreements may reinforce the post-divorce economic disparity between husbands and wives.[4]

# LEGAL REQUIREMENTS

## Threshold Considerations

Premarital agreements are contracts. Accordingly, to be enforceable, they must, at a minimum, satisfy certain threshold requirements generally applicable to all contracts. However, as discussed below, unlike with most other contracts, satisfying these requirements may not be enough to make a premarital agreement enforceable. These threshold requirements are:

1. There must be an offer and an acceptance of the offer.
2. The contract must be supported by **consideration**. Consideration is the bargained-for exchange of something of value—here, the mutual promise of marriage.
3. The parties must have the capacity to enter into a contract.
4. The subject matter of the agreement cannot be illegal.

Additionally, in most jurisdictions, premarital contracts come within the **statute of frauds**, which is a rule specifying that certain types of contracts must be in writing in order to be enforceable. Most likely, the agreement will also need to be signed by both parties, and the signatures may need to be both witnessed and notarized.

## The Fairness Requirement

As a general rule, our legal system emphasizes **freedom of contract**—the right of each individual to freely structure his or her affairs. A corollary of this principle is that once parties have entered into a contract, they are entitled to rely upon it, and courts will protect the expectancies that arise from the terms of the agreement. Without proof of conduct that rises to the level of fraud, misrepresentation, duress, or the like, courts typically will not refuse to enforce a contract because it is more favorable to one party. Unless these more serious kinds of concerns can be established, considerations of fairness with respect to either the process by which the contract was negotiated, such as where a party felt rushed into signing it, or the resulting terms, such as where a person agrees to pay more for a painting than it is worth, are essentially irrelevant. Thus, as a general rule, adherence to the freedom-of-contract principle means that an individual cannot avoid contractual obligations because he or she realizes that the deal is unfair or more favorable to the other side. The primary exception to this rule is the doctrine of **unconscionability**, which allows a court to inquire into issues of fairness in outrageous situations; for this doctrine to apply, there usually must be gross overreaching by a party who is in a vastly superior bargaining position.

However, when a dispute involves a premarital contract, courts typically review the agreement for evidence of unfairness in either the process of negotiating the agreement, referred to as **procedural fairness,** or in the resulting terms, referred to as **substantive fairness.** This hands-on approach, as distinct from the traditional hands-off approach to contract review, flows from a number of considerations. First, by entering into a premarital contract, parties are substituting their own terms for state laws that determine rights of support and property distribution between divorcing spouses. In effect, these agreements create private law in an area long considered to be under the exclusive authority of the state because of its special interest in the marriage. Thus, the subject matter of premarital agreements is quite different from that of more ordinary contracts, such as those governing the purchase and sale of real estate.

Second, parties to a typical contract stand at "arm's-length" distance from one another — they are generally not intimately connected and each party can be assumed to be acting in his or her own self-interest. In contrast, parties to a premarital agreement are in an intimate relationship, or what the courts refer to as a "confidential relationship," and are thought to be more vulnerable to being unduly influenced by the other. This risk is compounded by the fact that the parties often are negotiating from positions of unequal bargaining power. Premarital agreements are usually proposed by the prospective spouse with greater wealth who stands to gain more from avoiding state divorce laws, and the other party may feel that she or he has no choice but to sign or face the cancellation of the wedding. Closely related, at least in the early days of recognition, were lingering concerns about the inability of prospective brides to comprehend the details of the financial terms being proposed by her future husband, particularly where differences in wealth were pronounced.

Third, the performance of contractual obligations usually begins within a reasonably short and clearly defined time period after the contract is executed. In contrast, with premarital contracts, the time of performance is uncertain or may never come to be since the triggering event is divorce. Performance of the terms could thus come several years or even several decades after execution of the contract. With the passage of time, unforeseen events may intervene that would make performance of the original terms unfair.

Finally, perhaps this heightened standard of review reflects a continued uneasiness about the contractualization of family life, rooted in a sense that the domestic realm should remain distinct from the commercial realm, courts may be reluctant to fully import legal standards developed in the realm of impersonal dealings into the realm of intimate relationships.

### Requirements of Procedural Fairness

Although the clear trend is in favor of treating premarital contracts more like ordinary agreements with a corresponding emphasis upon individual autonomy and choice,[5] most courts still look to see if the parties treated each other fairly when negotiating the terms of the agreement. If a court determines that in the course of negotiating the agreement one party did not treat the other fairly, such as by not fully disclosing assets, it may invalidate the agreement.

The requirement of full and fair disclosure is usually the most important consideration, and the general rule is that both parties have an affirmative duty to make full disclosure even where this information is not requested by the other. Although the standard for determining what constitutes adequate disclosure varies from state to state, more than a mere recitation of numbers is necessary. Thus, for example, a party may be required to determine the value of his or her property and to disclose assets that he or she is entitled to receive in the future. If disclosure is not adequate, entry into the agreement is not considered voluntary, as a party cannot freely relinquish assets or income that he or she did not know of or know the correct value of.

In some states, a limited exception to the disclosure requirement may be made where one party has actual and specific knowledge of the other potential spouse's assets. However, a general familiarity with the other's financial reputation is unlikely to justify the failure to disclose.

In preparing premarital agreements, even if not specifically required by state law, most attorneys will prepare a full schedule of their client's income and assets, which is attached to the agreement as an exhibit (see Exhibit 2.1). Frequently, paralegals will be asked to assist in this process. Great care must be taken to obtain complete and accurate information, as this may determine the subsequent enforceability of the agreement. Often a client is given a written questionnaire to complete regarding his or her income and assets. On the next page is a sample list of the information a client might be asked to provide.

In evaluating procedural fairness, some courts also consider factors such as whether the party challenging the agreement understood its provisions at the time of signing, whether she or he was made aware of the legal rights being waived (such as, e.g., to spousal support) by entry into the agreement, and whether she or he had the opportunity to review the agreement with an independent attorney. Most jurisdictions require only that a party have the opportunity to review the agreement with an attorney;

## Exhibit 2.1  Schedule of Assets for Sandra Lopez

| | Fair Market Value | Encumbrance | Net Values |
|---|---|---|---|
| **Real Estate** | | | |
| *Location:* 16 Armand Rd. | | | |
| *Recorded at:* Norfolk County, Registry of Deeds; Book No. 814, Page No. 9 | $240,000 | $170,000 | $70,000 |
| **Personal Property** | | | |
| *Household Furnishings:* | | | |
| Complete set of bedroom, living room, dining room, and kitchen furniture | $3,800 | $0 | $3,800 |
| *Other Household Items (list all worth more than $100):* | | | |
| Tiffany lamp | $600 | $0 | $600 |
| Indoor gym equipment | $1,500 | $0 | $1,500 |
| Computer | $2,500 | $0 | $2,500 |
| Kitchen appliances (including refrigerator and microwave) | $1,100 | $0 | $1,100 |
| Antique phonograph | $1,200 | $0 | $1,200 |
| *Collections:* | | | |
| Rare jazz records | $3,500 | $0 | $3,500 |
| *Jewelry (list all worth more than $100):* | | | |
| Antique diamond ring | $1,200 | $0 | $1,200 |
| Rolex watch | $1,400 | $0 | $1,400 |
| *Automobiles:* | | | |
| 2001 VW Bug | $16,000 | $4,000 | $12,000 |
| *Bank Accounts:* | | | |
| Savings account, Union Federal Bank, account no. 1743 | $4,000 | — | — |
| Individual Retirement Account, Union Federal Bank, account no. 97363 | $12,000 | — | — |
| *Stocks and Bonds:* | | | |
| 80 shares of General Utility Stock | $800 | — | — |

Note: This sample Schedule of Assets is for one party only. In actuality, both parties would complete one.

---

### Sample Questions for Compiling Schedule of Assets

1. Do you own any real estate or have an interest in any realty? If yes, please provide a detailed list, including location of the real estate, nature of your interest, purchase date, purchase amount and amount of your down payment, current fair market value, and the amount of your equity in the real estate.
2. Please provide an itemized list of all household furnishings and effects owned by you, including the fair market value of each item.
3. Please provide an itemized list of all artwork owned by you, including the fair market value of each item.
4. Please provide an itemized list of all collections owned by you, including but not limited to collection items such as stamps, coins, cards, antiques, rare books, guns, and records. Include the fair market value of each collection.
5. Please provide an itemized list of all jewelry owned by you, including the fair market value of each item.
6. Please provide a detailed list of all stocks, bonds, retirement accounts, pension plans, and profit-sharing plans, including the nature of your interest, identifying information for each item, and the current value of your interest in each.

---

actual consultation is not required. The primary objective is to prevent one partner from presenting the other with an agreement for the first time at the rehearsal dinner and telling him or her that it must be signed if the wedding is to proceed as planned. As with the requirement of financial disclosure, these elements also relate to whether entry into the agreement was free and voluntary.

In jurisdictions where freedom of contract is emphasized over considerations of procedural fairness, courts may not be concerned with the above considerations. Returning to the Pennsylvania decision, which embodies a freedom of contract over a fairness approach, the court stated:

> Absent fraud, misrepresentation, or duress, spouses should be bound by the terms of their agreements. Contracting parties are normally bound by their agreements, without regard to whether the terms thereof were read and fully understood. . . . Based upon these principles, the terms of the present prenuptial agreement must be regarded as binding, without regard to whether the terms were fully understood by appellant. *Ignorantia non excusat.* Accordingly,

we find no merit in a contention raised by appellant that the agreement should be declared void on the ground that she did not consult with independent legal counsel. To impose a *per se* requirement that parties entering a prenuptial agreement must obtain independent legal counsel would be contrary to traditional principles of contract law, and would constitute a paternalistic and unwarranted interference with the parties' freedom to enter contracts.[6]

Some courts use a somewhat flexible approach to evaluating formation fairness. They may be stricter if the parties do not stand on equal footing, such as where one partner is much wealthier or better educated than the other. However, if they stand on relatively equal footing with respect to income, assets, and education, the court may be less concerned with procedural irregularities. Also, as discussed below, if the outcome is fair, courts may be less concerned with procedural irregularities.

### Requirements of Substantive Fairness

In addition to reviewing whether the process of contract formation was fair, courts in most jurisdictions will also review the actual terms of the agreement to see if they are fair. However, the *Simeone* decision is illustrative of the growing emphasis on considerations of contractual freedom over contractual fairness. In *Simeone*, the Pennsylvania high court not only limited the scope of review for procedural fairness to considerations of adequate disclosure but also held that the terms of an agreement should not be reviewed to determine if they are fair:

> The reasonableness of a prenuptial bargain is not a proper subject for judicial review. . . . By invoking inquiries into reasonableness, . . . the functioning and reliability of prenuptial agreements is severely undermined. Parties would not have entered into such agreements, and indeed may not have entered into their marriages, if they did not expect the agreements to be strictly enforced.[7]

Fairness can be measured as it existed at the time the contract was executed, or as it exists at the time of performance, or both. Again, this kind of review is a substantial departure from the usual contract law approach that gives individuals "freedom" to make bad deals. Subject to the limited unconscionability exception, a person cannot avoid an ordinary contract because he or she subsequently realizes that it is unfair or one-sided.

**At Formation.** In jurisdictions where the terms of a premarital agreement are reviewed for fairness, a court would first evaluate them in light of the circumstances as they existed at the time the contract was executed. For example, looking back to the time of contract formation, the waiver of alimony by a two-career couple not intending to have children appears equitable, whereas a waiver by a woman planning to stay home and raise a large family would not. At this phase of the review, events taking place after execution are not considered.

States differ in the standards they use to determine if the terms were fair at the time of execution. Some will not enforce provisions that are "unreasonable," such as a waiver of support by a spouse with a good job but with a much lower earning potential than his or her partner, although something more than a mere inequality of result is generally required. Other states will strike only clauses that are unconscionable or so unfair that they "shock the consciousness." In a few jurisdictions, alimony waivers are considered per se unfair and will not be enforced, although this is a minority approach.

**At Performance.** In addition to determining if the terms were fair at the time the contract was executed, some courts will also review them to see if they are fair at the time of divorce. This is sometimes referred to as the **"second glance doctrine."** Here, traditional freedom of contract principles are clearly subordinated in favor of protecting an economically vulnerable spouse. Many courts, however, consider this too great an interference with rights of contractual freedom, adhering to the view that once parties have made an agreement that is fair at the time of execution, they are entitled to rely on it. Accordingly, the only proper role of the court is to protect legitimate expectations arising from the agreement. By way of example, let us return to our two-career couple who did not plan to have children and included an alimony waiver in their prenuptial agreement. Assuming this was fair at the time of execution, if they then changed their minds and decided to have children, the waiver might be deemed unfair at the time of performance if one parent had cut back on employment to care for them. At second glance, terms that appeared fair at the time of contract formation would now work a hardship because of changed circumstances.

Courts will usually take a second glance only at support-related clauses, and they tend to employ a very high standard of review in order to strike a balance between avoiding hardship and honoring contractual expectations. At this stage, many courts will invalidate only a term waiving or limiting support rights where enforcement would leave a party unable to meet basic needs or would force him or her onto public assistance. Other courts are less strict and will invalidate a clause if enforcement would result in a substantial reduction in a party's standard of living, even if poverty is not threatened.

### The Interdependence of Procedural and Substantive Fairness

Although the above discussion treated the requirements of procedural and substantive fairness as independent variables, many courts regard them as interdependent. Accordingly, where the substantive terms are fair, a court may choose to overlook procedural deficiencies; for example, financial disclosure will not be insisted on as a pure formality. Likewise, if the result is clearly unfair, a court may presume that the procedure was inherently flawed and proceed to review the agreement with particular care.

---

### Consideration

Do you think that premarital agreements should be treated as ordinary contracts with the traditional emphasis on individual contractual freedom, or do you think courts should scrutinize them more carefully to make sure both spouses' interests are protected?

---

## SAMPLE AGREEMENT WITH EXPLANATORY NOTES AND DRAFTING CONSIDERATIONS

Following is a relatively straightforward sample premarital agreement, with drafting suggestions and explanatory text. Keep in mind that this is only an example, and that many variations are possible. If you are asked to draft an agreement, it should be carefully tailored to meet the particular circumstances of the parties.

### Exhibit 2.2   Premarital Agreement

PREMARITAL AGREEMENT OF SANDRA LOPEZ AND MARK DANATO

**Recitals**

A. This Agreement is made this 10th day of December 2006 by and between Sandra Lopez (Sandra) and Mark Danato (Mark).

B. Mark was previously married. This marriage ended in divorce on July 12th, 2000. There is one child of this marriage, namely, Alyssa, born June 4th, 1995. Sandra has not been previously married and has no children.

C. The parties are contemplating marriage to one another, and by this agreement and consideration thereof, they desire to define and fix their respective rights and liabilities in relationship to one another in the event they do marry.

**Comment:** This section identifies the parties and makes clear that they intend for this agreement to define their rights and obligations in relationship to one another.

D. The parties agree, represent, and stipulate that they have each had the advice and representation of independent legal counsel of their choice both prior to and during the execution of this agreement. Both parties further acknowledge that they have been fully and completely informed of all their legal rights and liabilities pertaining hereto.

E. The parties further agree that they each have freely and voluntarily executed this agreement and accepted and assented to its terms, and that each of them executed this agreement without any duress, coercion, or undue influence or illegal consideration at the time of its execution.

F. The parties agree that they each have made full, complete, and accurate disclosure to the other of their financial situation, including all income, assets, and liabilities. Each party has prepared and executed a schedule of their respective assets, liabilities, and income as of the time of the execution of this agreement, which have been annexed to this agreement as Exhibits 1 and 2, and which are incorporated therein by reference. Both parties state that they have prepared these financial schedules based on information available to them at the time and with the assistance and advice of legal counsel.

**Comment:** The above three paragraphs relate to the requirement that prenuptial agreements be freely and voluntarily executed. As part of this requirement, paragraph F references the fact of the parties' financial disclosure to one another — a factor that most courts consider in deciding if an agreement is enforceable.

G. Sandra's social security number is _____. Mark's social security number is _____.

**Comment:** Disclosure of social security numbers can be useful in the event a parent defaults on a future child support obligation and cannot be located (see Chapter 7 for more detail).

H. The consideration for this agreement is based upon the mutual promises and waivers herein contained and the marriage about to be solemnized. If the marriage does not take place, this agreement shall be deemed for all purposes null and void.

NOW, THEREFORE, IT IS AGREED, in consideration of the mutual covenants herein and the proposed marriage between the parties to be celebrated hereafter, as follows:

**Comment:** This paragraph recites the consideration that supports the agreement. It also makes clear that the agreement has no effect if the parties do not marry.

### *Provisions*

### Property

1. *Sole and Separate Property:* The parties agree to keep, as their sole and separate property, all of their respective premarital property as set out in Exhibits 1 and 2 and any property subsequently acquired by inheritance or by gift from a third party, including any increase thereof or property acquired in exchange therefore. All such acquisitions, including property received in exchange for separate property, shall be recorded on an asset schedule; the schedules shall be annexed to and made part of this agreement.

2. *Marital Property:* Excepting separate property as described above in paragraph 1, the parties intend that the assets they accumulate during the marriage be considered marital property and subject to division as such.

**Comment:** These two paragraphs set out how the parties intend to characterize their property. Here, property brought into the marriage or acquired during the marriage by gift or inheritance is to be separate property belonging solely to that spouse. All other property acquired during the marriage is considered marital property and belongs to the marital entity. This distinction is critical because, as set out in the next paragraph, each spouse gives up all claims to the separate property of the other.

The definition of marital property in this agreement is fairly broad. Some couples may choose to further restrict what is considered marital property by, for example, limiting it to assets that were purchased with joint funds, leaving anything purchased with separate funds as separate property. Here, it may make sense for the parties to spell out how they will set up their bank accounts, describing which will be joint and which separate, and how each will contribute to the different accounts.

Language should be included to clarify what happens to the marital property/ separate property distinction if joint funds or the funds of one spouse are spent on the other's property. For example, what would happen if one spouse makes mortgage payments on a home belonging to the other spouse? It could be agreed that these payments do not alter the characterization of the property, or it could be agreed that the contributor acquires a share in that asset equal to the amount of his or her contribution. Additional language also might be included to spell out the impact that any nonfinancial contribution of one spouse toward the care and maintenance of the other's assets would have upon characterization of those assets.

Finally, before drafting property provisions, great care should be taken to determine how the law in your state categorizes and allocates property for divorce purposes so that the full import of the agreement is clear. For a fuller discussion of property concepts, see Chapter 9.

3. *Waivers:* In the event of divorce or an annulment, or in the event of death, the parties agree not to assert any claim of any kind to the property, assets, or estate

of the other as described in paragraph 1, above. This waiver shall not apply to marital property, as described in paragraph 2, above.

### Spousal Support

4. *Spousal Support:* In the event of divorce or an annulment, the parties agree to waive any rights to spousal support, maintenance, or separate support of any kind that either might otherwise be entitled to.

**Comment:** As discussed in the text, some courts will not enforce a waiver of alimony as provided for in the above paragraph; others will not enforce a waiver if enforcement would be unfair based on circumstances existing at the time of execution or possibly also at the time of divorce. As an alternative to a permanent waiver, modifications can be built into an agreement that is automatically triggered upon either the passage of time or the happening of certain events. For example, the parties could agree that upon the occurrence of certain events, such as the birth of a child, the disability of one spouse, or a reduction in one spouse's income, any support (and possibly also property) waivers become void. Provisions could then detail how support (and/or property rights) is to be redetermined in light of these changed circumstances, possibly using a percentage or standard of living formula. Another possibility is that the passage of time could void the waiver, and the less well-off party could be vested with increasing rights as the marriage progressed. A schedule could be drawn up linking benefits to the number of years the parties remained married. Of course, the possible risk here is that a party entitled to receive an increasing share might feel compelled to remain in a bad marriage until a certain number of years have passed. Alternatively, the financially secure party might be less motivated to remain in the marriage knowing that his or her spouse acquires additional rights with the passage of time.

Note that there are no child support provisions (in the event the parties were to have children), such as one that would allow the noncustodial parent to avoid paying child support payments or to pay less than required by the Child Support Guidelines (see Chapter 7). This is because such a provision would be unenforceable, as the right to child support belongs to the child and thus cannot be waived or limited by the custodial parent.

On a related note, there is no provision regarding custody arrangements. Such a provision would also be unenforceable, as custody must be based on the "best interests" of the child—a determination that cannot be made in advance of divorce, let alone in advance of a child's birth, because too many factors are unknown.

5. *Waiver of Estate Claims:* The parties jointly and mutually agree that each waives all rights or claims of inheritance under the laws of descent and distribution in the estate of the other party that might otherwise be asserted by either of them in the event of the death of a party intestate during the marriage.

The parties jointly and mutually agree that each waives all rights to claim a distributive share as a surviving spouse in the estate of the other, and each hereby also waives all rights to claim a forced share against the last will and testament of the other, and each further waives any claim for an advancement or allowance against the assets of the estate of the other, all of which waivers are binding and enforceable in the event of the death of either of them during the marriage.

**Comment:** This provision provides for a waiver of statutory rights that would otherwise accrue to a spouse upon the death of the other.

6. *Wills/Trusts:* In the event that the parties hereafter marry each other, nothing in this agreement shall preclude, or shall be interpreted as preventing, either party from freely executing a will or settling a trust that confers benefits, rights, titles, or interests on the other party, or from nominating the other party as executor or trustee, or from exercising any power of appointment in favor of the other party.

**Comment:** This provision makes clear that although the parties are waiving certain statutory rights (see paragraph 5 above), they may still make provisions for the other if they so choose.

### General Provisions and Arbitration

7. *General Provisions:*

A. Except as is specifically provided in this agreement, the parties hereby agree and covenant that they each accept and intend to be bound by the provisions of this agreement in full discharge and satisfaction of any and all rights and claims which they may hereafter otherwise have against each other in the event of their contemplated marriage.

B. The parties agree that this agreement represents the full and complete agreement between them. They further agree that no modification or waiver of its terms shall be valid unless it is in writing and signed by both parties.

C. No waiver of a breach or default shall be deemed a waiver of any subsequent breach or default.

D. This Agreement shall be binding upon the parties, their heirs, personal representatives, and assigns.

E. In the event that any provision of this Agreement is held to be illegal, invalid, unenforceable, or against public policy, the remaining provisions of the Agreement shall remain valid and enforceable.

**Comment:** The above severability clause is standard in almost all contracts. It ensures that the entire agreement is not invalidated in the event any provision is declared invalid. It is particularly important in the premarital agreement context, as there is a real possibility that a court could invalidate one or more provisions, particularly if there is waiver of alimony.

F. This Agreement shall be subject to the law of the State of _____ , the residence of the parties.

G. In the event a disagreement arises over any of the terms of this agreement, either party may invoke binding arbitration by notifying the American Arbitration Association of the issue to be arbitrated. She or he shall send the other side written notice of the request at her/his last known address. The notice shall provide sufficient clarity and detail regarding the issue(s) for which arbitration is being sought.

The arbitrator shall be selected and arbitration shall be conducted in accordance with the rules of the American Arbitration Association. The arbitrator shall decide the issues submitted by each party but shall be limited by the terms of this Agreement. The parties agree to share the costs of the arbitration. However, either party may request that the arbitrator make a different allocation of costs, as warranted by the circumstances. The parties agree to comply with any such determination.

**Comment:** It is important to be aware that arbitration is not the only option in the event of a disagreement. For example, the parties could agree to first try to resolve any dispute through mediation. If a mediation clause is included, the process for selecting a mediator should be spelled out. For example, if the parties cannot agree on the mediator, each could nominate a third party, such as his or her lawyer or therapist, and these individuals would select the mediator, with the parties agreeing to be bound by their selection. See Chapter 11 for a more detailed discussion of alternative dispute resolution.

### Signatures and Verifications

IN WITNESS WHEREOF, and being fully advised in the premises, the parties hereunto have subscribed their names and affixed their seals on the day and year indicated.

_____          _____
Witness                                                      (Name)

                                                                  Date: _____

_____          _____
Witness                                                      (Name)

                                                                  Date: _____

                                                                  )

                                                                  )                                 ss:

                                                                  )

Before me, a Notary Public in and for the jurisdiction aforesaid, personally appeared ___[*name of the party*]___, who made an oath that the execution of this Premarital Agreement was her free act and deed, and that the recitations contained in said Agreement and the exhibits attached hereto are true and correct.

_____
Notary Public

[SEAL]

My commission expires on _____
Date

)
)          ss:
)

Before me, a Notary Public in and for the jurisdiction aforesaid, personally appeared ___[*name of the party*]___, who made an oath that the execution of this Premarital Agreement was his free act and deed, and that the recitations contained in said Agreement and the exhibits attached hereto are true and correct.

_____
Notary Public

[SEAL]

My commission expires on _____
Date

ATTORNEYS FOR THE PARTIES:

_____          _____
Name                                                          Name
[Address]                                                   [Address]

**Comment:** In obtaining signatures, it is of critical importance that all procedural rules, such as witness requirements, be complied with.

Select provisions of this agreement are from the Massachusetts Practice Series, Family Law and Practice, Vol. 2A, pp. 548-588 (1996) authored by Kindergran and Inker. Reprinted by permission of West Group.

## Chapter Summary

Until the 1970s, premarital agreements made in contemplation of divorce were generally considered void as against public policy in large part because they were thought to encourage divorce. Nonrecognition was also thought necessary to protect women from being taken advantage of by financially savvy prospective spouses as well as from post-divorce impoverishment. However, influenced by the growing acceptance of no-fault divorce and the changing socioeconomic status of women, courts began recognizing these agreements.

Although now generally accepted, most courts still treat premarital agreements as different from ordinary contracts and, in the event of a dispute, emphasize fairness over strict adherence to freedom of contract principles. A near-universal rule is that for a premarital agreement to be enforceable, the parties must have entered into it freely and with full knowledge of the other spouse's financial circumstances. Beyond this, courts may review other procedural elements as well, such as whether the parties understood the terms of the agreement at the time of execution. Some courts will also look to see if the terms of the agreement were fair at the time of execution, and some will also take a "second glance" to determine if the terms are fair at the time of enforcement. However, the clear trend is to treat pre-marital agreements more like ordinary contracts, resulting in a growing emphasis on contractual freedom over contractual fairness.

## Key Terms

Premarital Agreements                    Unconscionability
Void as Against Public Policy            Procedural Fairness
Consideration                            Substantive Fairness
Statute of Frauds                        Second Glance Doctrine
Freedom of Contract

# Review Questions

1. What is a premarital contract?

2. Why would someone enter into a premarital agreement?

3. Why were premarital contracts made in contemplation of divorce once considered void as against public policy?

4. Why did courts gradually come to accept these agreements?

5. In what ways are premarital contracts treated differently from ordinary contracts?

6. Why are they treated differently?

7. What will a court look to in determining procedural fairness?

8. What will a court look to in determining substantive fairness?

9. How are the two concepts interrelated?

10. What direction are courts moving in with respect to reviewing premarital contracts? What considerations underlie this shift?

11. The following questions relate to the drafting of a premarital agreement:

    - Why is it so important to attach exhibits listing all of the parties' assets?
    - What is the difference between separate and marital property? What are some different ways that the parties might define these types of property?
    - Why might parties spell out how they will set up their bank accounts?
    - In the sample agreement, what rights are the parties waiving?
    - Why should one think about building in modifications, and how would one go about doing this?
    - Why would a waiver of the obligation to pay child support be unenforceable?
    - Why would an agreement regarding child custody arrangements be unenforceable?
    - Why is a severability clause important?

## Discussion Questions

1.  In the event of a dispute over the enforcement of a premarital contract, do you think the agreement should be treated like an ordinary contract or do you think courts should review them for unfairness? Identify arguments that support both positions. Additionally, in developing the arguments in favor of the fairness approach, discuss how "fair" is fair—should the courts look only at procedural fairness? Or should they also consider substantive fairness at the time of execution? At the time of execution and performance? Some combination as determined by the circumstances?

2.  If you were planning to get married, would you want to enter into a premarital contract? Why or why not? Are their any factors that would influence your decision? For example, what if you were wealthy or already had children? How would you feel if the person you were intending to marry insisted on entry into a premarital agreement? Again, would it make a difference if your spouse had children? was very wealthy? had other "concrete" reasons for his or her insistence on an agreement? In formulating your answer, think about the economic as well as the emotional issues.

3.  Do you think premarital agreements denigrate the meaning of marriage by making it more like a commercial transaction?

## Assignments

1.  Determine if premarital agreements are recognized in your state. If they are, determine the following:

    *   What is required for premarital agreements to be enforceable? For example, what kind of disclosure is required?
    *   What is the applicable standard of review? Are they treated like ordinary contracts?
    *   Do courts consider procedural fairness? Substantive fairness?
    *   Will courts take a "second glance" at any of the terms to see if they are fair at the time of execution? How is the concept of fairness defined?

(Note: If premarital agreements are not recognized in your jurisdiction, find a recent case that sets out the rationale for nonrecognition and explain the reasoning of the court.)

2. Assume that you are a paralegal working in a small law firm. A new, wealthy client has come to the office because he wants a pre-marital agreement drafted. His prospective wife, although not wealthy, has a well-paying job. He is 36, and she is 35. It is a first marriage for both of them. They do not plan to have children.

   The attorney you work for has asked you to draft a letter to the client. In the letter you are to explain how the law in your jurisdiction treats premarital agreements, * and what steps need to be taken to best ensure that the agreement will be enforced. You should also inform the client about the kinds of provisions that he should consider including in the agreement.

(*Note: If you are in a nonrecognizing jurisdiction, then assume you are in a state that is very concerned about fairness and follows the second glance approach.)

3. Assume you are a clerk working for a justice in your state's highest court. The court will soon be reviewing a case involving a dispute in which a wife is seeking to set aside a premarital agreement on the following two grounds. First, when she signed the agreement, she did not understand that she was giving up her right to alimony. Second, she believes that the alimony waiver is unfair given that her husband is extremely wealthy, and she has become disabled over the course of the marriage. She says the waiver was unfair at the time of execution and is even more so now at the time of performance.

   The justice you work for knows the trend is to treat premarital agreements more like ordinary contracts, and she wonders if it is time for your state to join this trend. She would like you to write her a short memo in which you set out some of the pros and cons of adopting this approach.

## Cases for Analysis

The following case is one of the first to hold that premarital agreements entered into to structure rights upon divorce are not void as a matter of public policy. Key to the decision is a recognition of the changing nature of marriage and the increased social acceptance of divorce.

### POSNER v. POSNER
**233 So. 2d 381 (Fla. 1970)**

This cause is before the court on rehearing, . . . the wife having appealed from those portions of the decree awarding a divorce to the husband and the sum of $600 per month as alimony to the wife pursuant to the terms of an antenuptial agreement between the parties.

The three appellate judges . . . each took a different position respecting the antenuptial agreement concerning alimony. Their respective views were (1) that the parties may validly agree upon alimony in an antenuptial agreement but that the trial court is not bound by their agreement; (2) that such an agreement is void as against public policy; and (3) that an antenuptial agreement respecting alimony is entitled to the same consideration and should be just as binding as an antenuptial agreement settling the property rights of the wife in her husband's estate upon his death. . . .

At the outset we must recognize that there is a vast difference between a contract made in the market place and one relating to the institution of marriage.

It has long been the rule in a majority of the courts of this country and in this State that contracts intended to facilitate or promote the procurement of a divorce will be declared illegal as contrary to public policy. . . . The reason for the rule lies in the nature of the marriage contract and the interest of the State therein.

. . . We have, of course, changed by statute the common-law rule respecting the indissolubility of a marriage . . . ; but the concept of marriage as a social institution that is the foundation of the family and of society remains unchanged . . . Since marriage is of vital interest to society and the state, it has frequently been said that in every divorce suit the state is a third party whose interests take precedence over the private interests of the spouses. . . .

The state's interest in the preservation of the marriage is the basis for the rule that . . . an antenuptial agreement by which a prospective wife waives or limits her right to alimony or to the property of her husband in the event of a divorce or separation, regardless of who is at fault, has been in some states held to be invalid. . . . The reason that such an agreement is said to "facilitate or promote the procurement of a divorce" was stated in Crouch v. Crouch, *supra,* as follows: —

> "Such contract could induce a mercenary husband to inflict on his wife any wrong he might desire with the knowledge his pecuniary liability would be limited. In other words, a husband could through abuse and ill treatment of his wife force her to bring an action for divorce and thereby buy a divorce for a small fee less than he would otherwise have to pay." . . .

There can be no doubt that the institution of marriage is the foundation of the familial and social structure of our Nation and, as such, continues to be of vital interest to the State; but we cannot blind ourselves to the fact that the concept of the "sanctity" of a marriage — as being practically indissoluble, once entered into — held by our ancestors only a few generations ago, has been greatly eroded in the last several decades. . . .

With divorce such a commonplace fact of life, it is fair to assume that many prospective marriage partners whose property and familial situation is such as to generate a valid antenuptial agreement settling their property rights upon the death of either, might want to consider and discuss also — and agree upon, if possible — the disposition of their property and the alimony rights of the wife in the event their marriage, despite their best efforts, should fail. . . .

We know of no community or society in which the public policy that condemned a husband and wife to a lifetime of misery as an alternative to the opprobrium of divorce still exists. And a tendency to recognize this change in public policy and to give effect to the antenuptial agreements of the parties relating to divorce is clearly discernible. . . .

We have given careful consideration to the question of whether the change in public policy towards divorce requires a change in the rule respecting antenuptial agreements settling alimony and property rights of the parties upon divorce and have concluded that such agreements should no longer be held to be void ab initio as "contrary to public policy." If such an agreement is valid . . . and if, in addition, it is made to appear that the divorce was prosecuted in good faith, on proper grounds, so that, under the rules applicable to postnuptial alimony and property settlement agreements referred to above, it could not be said to facilitate or promote the procurement of a divorce, then it should be held valid as to conditions existing at the time the agreement was made. . . .

## QUESTIONS

1. According to the court, why have premarital agreements that set out the rights of spouses in the event of divorce generally been considered void as against public policy?

2. In thinking about whether to allow premarital agreements, how is the court influenced by the changing nature of marriage and divorce?

3. Does the court hold that all premarital agreements are valid? What may an agreement not do?

---

In the following case, the Supreme Court of Pennsylvania takes a "hard-line" approach to premarital agreements. In treating them more like ordinary contracts, the court moves away from the dominant view that premarital agreements should be reviewed under a stricter standard than those applicable to contracts entered into in the business realm.

## SIMEONE v. SIMEONE
### 525 Pa. 392, 581 A.2d 162 (1990)

At issue in this appeal is the validity of a prenuptial agreement executed between the appellant, Catherine E. Walsh Simeone, and the appellee, Frederick A. Simeone. At the time of their marriage, in 1975, appellant was a twenty-three year old nurse and appellee was a thirty-nine year old neurosurgeon. Appellee had an income of approximately $90,000 per year, and appellant was unemployed. Appellee also had assets worth approximately $300,000. On the eve of the parties' wedding, appellee's attorney presented appellant with a prenuptial agreement to be signed. Appellant, without the benefit of counsel, signed the agreement. Appellee's attorney had not advised appellant regarding any legal rights that the agreement surrendered. The parties are in disagreement as to whether appellant knew in advance of that date that such an agreement would be presented for signature. Appellant denies having had such knowledge and claims to have signed under adverse circumstances, which, she contends, provide a basis for declaring it void.

The agreement limited appellant to support payments of $200 per week in the event of separation or divorce, subject to a maximum total payment of $25,000. The parties separated in 1982, and, in 1984, divorce proceedings were commenced. Between 1982 and 1984 appellee made payments which satisfied the $25,000 limit. In 1985, appellant filed a claim for alimony pendente lite. A master's report upheld the validity of the prenuptial agreement and denied this claim. . . .

We granted allowance of appeal because uncertainty was expressed by the Superior Court regarding the meaning of our plurality decision in Estate of Geyer, 516 Pa. 492, 533 A.2d 423 (1987) (Opinion Announcing Judgment of the Court). The Superior Court viewed *Geyer* as permitting a prenuptial agreement to be upheld if it either made a reasonable provision for the spouse or was entered after a full and fair disclosure of the general financial positions of the parties and the statutory rights being relinquished. Appellant contends that this interpretation of *Geyer* is in error insofar as it requires disclosure of statutory rights only in cases where there has not been made a reasonable provision for the spouse. . . .

There is no longer validity in the implicit presumption that supplied the basis for *Geyer* and similar earlier decisions. Such decisions rested upon a belief that spouses are of unequal status and that women are not knowledgeable enough to understand the nature of contracts that they enter. Society has advanced, however, to the point where women are no longer regarded as the "weaker" party in marriage, or in society generally. Indeed, the stereotype that women serve as homemakers while men work as breadwinners is no longer viable. Quite often today both spouses are income earners. Nor is there viability in the presumption that women are uninformed, uneducated, and readily subjected to unfair advantage in marital agreements. Indeed, women nowadays quite often have substantial education, financial awareness, income, and assets.

Accordingly, the law has advanced to recognize the equal status of men and women in our society. . . . Paternalistic presumptions and protections that arose to shelter women from the inferiorities and incapacities which they were perceived as having in earlier times have, appropriately, been discarded. . . . It would be inconsistent, therefore, to perpetuate the standards governing prenuptial agreements that were described in *Geyer* and similar decisions, as these reflected a paternalistic approach that is now insupportable.

Further, *Geyer* and its predecessors embodied substantial departures from traditional rules of contract law, to the extent that they allowed consideration of the knowledge of the contracting parties and reasonableness of their bargain as factors governing whether to uphold an agreement. Traditional principles of contract law provide perfectly adequate remedies where contracts are procured through fraud, misrepresentation, or duress.

. . . Prenuptial agreements are contracts, and, as such, should be evaluated under the same criteria as are applicable to other types of contracts. . . . Absent fraud, misrepresentation, or duress, spouses should be bound by the terms of their agreements.

Contracting parties are normally bound by their agreements, without regard to whether the terms thereof were read and fully understood and irrespective of whether the agreements embodied reasonable or good bargains. . . . Based upon these principles, the terms of the present prenuptial agreement must be regarded as binding, without regard to whether the terms were fully understood by appellant. Ignorantia non excusat.

Accordingly, we find no merit in a contention raised by appellant that the agreement should be declared void on the ground that she did not consult with independent legal counsel. To impose a per se requirement that parties entering a prenuptial agreement must obtain independent legal counsel would be contrary to traditional principles of contract law, and would constitute a paternalistic and unwarranted interference with the parties' freedom to enter contracts.

Further, the reasonableness of a prenuptial bargain is not a proper subject for judicial review. . . .

By invoking inquiries into reasonableness, however, the functioning and reliability of prenuptial agreements is severely undermined. Parties would not have entered such agreements, and, indeed, might not have entered their marriages, if they did not expect their agreements to be strictly enforced. If parties viewed an agreement as reasonable at the time of its inception, as evidenced by their having signed the agreement, they should be foreclosed from later trying to evade its terms by asserting that it was not in fact reasonable. . . .

Further, everyone who enters a long-term agreement knows that circumstances can change during its term, so that what initially appeared desirable might prove to be an unfavorable bargain. Such are the risks that contracting parties routinely assume. Certainly, the possibilities of illness, birth of children, reliance upon a spouse, career change, financial gain or loss, and numerous other events that can occur in the course of a marriage cannot be regarded as unforeseeable. If parties choose not to address such matters in their prenuptial agreements, they must be regarded as having contracted to bear the risk of events that alter the value of their bargains.

We are reluctant to interfere with the power of persons contemplating marriage to agree upon, and to act in reliance upon, what they regard as an acceptable distribution scheme for their property. A court should not ignore the parties' expressed intent by proceeding to determine whether a prenuptial agreement was, in the court's view, reasonable at the time of its inception or the time of divorce. . . .

In discarding the approach of *Geyer* that permitted examination of the reasonableness of prenuptial agreements and allowed inquiries into whether parties had attained informed understandings of the rights they were surrendering, we do not depart from the longstanding principle that a full and fair disclosure of the financial positions of the parties is required. Absent this disclosure, a material misrepresentation in the inducement for entering a prenuptial agreement may be asserted. *Hillegass*, 431 Pa. at 152-53, 244 A.2d at 676-77. Parties to these agreements do not quite deal at arm's length, but rather at the time the contract is entered into stand in a relation of mutual confidence and trust that calls for disclosure of their financial resources. *Id.*, 431 Pa. at 149, 244 A.2d at 675; . . .

McDermott, Justice, dissenting.

I dissent. . . . I am in full agreement with the majority's observation that "women nowadays quite often have substantial education, financial awareness, income, and assets." . . . However, the plurality decision I authored in Estate of Geyer, 516 Pa. 492, 533 A.2d 423 (1987), as well as the Dissenting Opinion I offer today, have little to do with the equality of the sexes, but everything to do with the solemnity of the matrimonial union. I am not willing to believe that our society views marriage as a mere contract for hire. . . . In this Commonwealth, we have long declared our interest in the stability of marriage and in the stability of the family unit. Our courts must seek to protect, and not to undermine, those institutions and interests which are vital to our society. . . .

. . . Thus, while I acknowledge the longstanding rule of law that prenuptial agreements are presumptively valid and binding upon the parties, I am unwilling to go as far as the majority to protect the right to contract at the expense of the institution of marriage. Were a contract of marriage, the most intimate relationship between two people, not the surrender of freedom, an offering of self in love, sacrifice, hope for better or for worse, the begetting of children and the offer of effort, labor, precious time and care for the safety and prosperity of their union, then the majority would find me among them.

In my view, one seeking to avoid the operation of an executed pre-nuptial agreement must first establish, by clear and convincing evidence, that a full and fair disclosure of the worth of the intended spouse was not made at the time of the execution of the agreement. . . . In addition to a full and fair disclosure of the general financial pictures of the parties, I would find a pre-nuptial agreement voidable where it is established that the parties were not aware, at the time of contracting, of existing statutory rights which they were relinquishing upon the signing of the agreement. . . . It is here, with a finding of full and fair disclosure, that the majority would end its analysis of the validity of a pre-nuptial agreement. I would not. An analysis of the fairness and equity of a pre-nuptial agreement has long been an important part of the law of this state. . . . I am not willing to depart from this history, which would continue to serve our public policy.

At the time of dissolution of the marriage, a spouse should be able to avoid the operation of a pre-nuptial agreement upon clear and convincing proof that, despite the existence of full and fair disclosure at the time of the execution of the agreement, the agreement is nevertheless so inequitable and unfair that it should not be enforced in a court of this state. . . .

It is also apparent that, although a pre-nuptial agreement is quite valid when drafted, the passage of time accompanied by the intervening events of a marriage may render the terms of the agreement completely unfair and inequitable. While parties to a pre-nuptial agreement may indeed foresee, generally, the events which may come to pass during their marriage, one spouse should not be made to suffer for failing to foresee all of the surrounding circumstances which may attend the dissolution of the marriage. Although it should not be the role of the courts to void pre-nuptial agreements merely because one spouse may receive a better result in an action under the Divorce Code to recover alimony or equitable distribution, it should be the role of the courts to guard against the enforcement of pre-nuptial agreements where such enforcement will bring about only inequity and hardship. It borders on cruelty to accept that after years of living together, yielding their separate opportunities in life to each other, that two individuals emerge the same as the day they began their marriage.

At the time of the dissolution of marriage, what are the circumstances which would serve to invalidate a pre-nuptial agreement? This is a question that should only be answered on a case-by-case basis. However, it is not unrealistic to imagine that in a given situation, one spouse, although trained in the workforce at the time of marriage, may, over many years, have become economically dependent upon the other spouse. In reliance upon the permanence of marriage and in order to provide a stable home for a family, a spouse may choose, even at the suggestion of the other spouse, not to work during the marriage. As a result, at the point of dissolution of the marriage, the spouse's employability has diminished to such an extent that to enforce the support provisions of the pre-nuptial agreement will cause the spouse to become a public charge, or will provide a standard of living far below that which was enjoyed before and during marriage. In such a situation, a court may properly decide to render void all or some of the provisions of the pre-nuptial agreement. . . .

The majority is concerned that parties will routinely challenge the validity of their pre-nuptial agreements. Given the paramount importance of marriage and family in our society, and the serious consequences that may accompany the dissolution of a marriage, we should not choose to close the doors of our courts merely to gain a measure of judicial economy. . . .

## QUESTIONS

1. According to the lower court's reading of the precedent case of *Estate of Geyer*, when will a premarital agreement be upheld?

2. What does the Pennsylvania Supreme Court see as the underlying presumption of the *Geyer* decision?

3. Why does the court think this presumption is no longer valid?

4. How does this lead the court to rethink the rules regarding the enforceability of prenuptial agreements?

5. According to the decision, will a party's lack of understanding of the terms of a premarital agreement invalidate the agreement? What about a party's failure to consult with legal counsel? Why does the court take the position that it does?

6. What position does the court take regarding the reasonableness of the agreement at the time of execution? at the time of enforcement? Explain the court's position.

7. What is the court's position with respect to whether full and fair disclosure is required?

8. What position does the dissent take with respect to considerations of reasonableness at the time of execution? at the time of enforcement? Why does the dissent reject the majority approach?

# Endnotes

1. This chapter will use the term "premarital agreement" or "premarital contract." Synonymous terms are "prenuptial agreement" and "antenuptial agreement." Note that the focus in this chapter is on premarital agreements, which are made in contemplation of divorce, not death. Agreements that spell out rights upon the death of one or both spouses generally have been accepted by the courts because there are no countervailing policy considerations.

2. 233 So. 2d 381 (Fla. 1970).

3. 525 Pa. 392, 581 A.2d 162 (1990).

4. *Id.* at 166.

5. *See* Gail Frommer Brod, Premarital Agreements and Gender Justice, 6 Yale J.L. & Feminism 229 (1994); Leah Guggenheimer, A Modest Proposal: The Feminomics of Drafting Premarital Agreements, 17 Women's Rights L. Rep. 147 (1996).

6. *Cf. Simeone*, 525 Pa. 392, 581 A.2d 162, 167-168.

The Uniform Premarital Agreements Act (UPAA), which was approved by the National Conference of Commissioners of Uniform State Laws in 1983, and has since been adopted in about half of the states, also has contributed to this trend. Although not going as far as the *Simeone* decision, the UPAA clearly favors enforceability of premarital agreements and limits. Regarding the UPAA, *see* Elizabeth Barker Brandt, The Uniform Premarital Agreements Act and the Reality of Premarital Agreements in Idaho, 33 Idaho L. Rev. 539 (1997).

7. *Simeone*, 581 A.2d at 167. Under the UPAA, the standard for review for substantive unfairness is unconscionability.

# 3  Domestic Violence

All states have enacted laws that enable victims of **domestic violence** (also referred to as **intimate partner violence**) to obtain civil orders of protection from abuse. These laws came about largely as a result of the women's movement that focused public attention on the extent and seriousness of violence directed toward women by their male partners. Insisting that partner violence was not simply a private matter, activists successfully campaigned for laws that would allow victims to seek legal protection from abuse.

These laws are the focus of this chapter. To put them into context, we first briefly examine the historical approach of the law to spousal abuse. This history reveals a tradition of support for a husband's right of physical authority over his wife; however, it also reveals challenges to the social acceptance of male physical dominance over their spouses. We also take a brief look at some statistics documenting the pervasiveness of intimate partner violence and its continued disproportionate impact on women.[1]

## THE TRADITIONAL APPROACH

The Roman law of marriage required that "married women . . . conform themselves entirely to the temper of their husbands and the husbands to rule their wives as necessary and inseparable possessions."[2] A husband could beat his wife to make her obey him. If a married woman drank, committed adultery, or engaged in other conduct that threatened his honor, her husband could beat her to death without inquiry or punishment, although some limits eventually were placed on a husband's right to administer unduly violent and "unjustifiable" beatings. Charged with the responsibility of maintaining domestic order, a husband with an "unruly" wife was considered derelict in his obligations.

The right of a husband to use physical force against his wife was carried forward into English common law. As the legal head of the household, a husband could physically discipline his wife to command her obedience both for its own sake and because he was legally responsible for her misconduct. He was directed to use the same moderation in physically chastising his wife as he would use when disciplining his apprentices or children.

In the United States, acceptance of the doctrine of marital unity (see Chapter 1) implied acceptance of a husband's right of "moderate chastisement"—although, as we will see, this was not without challenge. In the early days of the nation, a husband, as head of the household, was generally thought entitled to use the degree of force necessary to make his wife obey. Wives who disobeyed or displayed bad tempers were blamed for causing the violent reaction in their husbands through their disregard for his authority. This traditional understanding is captured by the following passage from an 1862 decision from North Carolina, in which the court denies the wife's divorce petition because she did not explain the circumstances giving rise to the blows administered by her husband, thus failing to prove they were not her fault:

> [W]e are of the opinion that it was necessary to state the circumstances under which the blow with the horse-whip, and the blows with the switch were given; for instance, what . . . had she done, or said to induce such violence on the part of the husband? . . .
>
> The wife must be subject to the husband. Every man must govern his household, and if by reason of an unruly temper, or an unbridled tongue, the wife persistently treats her husband with disrespect, and he submits to it, he . . . loses the respect of the other members of his family, without which he cannot expect to govern them . . . It follows that the law gives the husband power to use such a degree of force as is necessary to make the wife behave herself and know her place. . . . [S]o that there are circumstances under which a husband may strike his wife with a horse-whip or may strike her several times with a switch, so hard as to leave marks on her person, and these acts do not furnish sufficient grounds for divorce.[3]

The court here appears to draw a distinction between "justifiable" and unjustifiable beatings, thus indicating that the law did not grant husbands unlimited authority over their wives. Beatings that were "unprovoked" by the wife, or involved more force than necessary to secure her obedience, might furnish grounds for a divorce on the basis of cruelty, or possibly subject a husband to criminal prosecution.

---

### Consideration

Does any of this history continue to influence our society today?

## EARLY REFORM IMPULSES

As we saw above, there is a long history of support for a husband's right to command the obedience of his wife through the use of physical force. However, starting with the Puritans, there were some early efforts aimed at altering this traditional allocation of authority.[4]

In 1641, the Puritans passed the first law in the Western world to expressly prohibit wife beating; a few years later, this law was amended to also prohibit husband beating. For the Puritans, who hoped to establish a religious community in the New World, violence between family members was a sin that lowered the standing of the community before God. Neighbors were encouraged to watch over each other's households and report instances of abuse to the minister. Ministers preached against the evils of wife abuse, and serious cases could be brought before the church court, which sought to disgrace the sinner. The goal of this intervention was reconciliation and family preservation. Protection of the victims was not a primary concern, and where necessary to uphold their authority, husbands remained entitled to use physical force against a spouse.[5]

In the early 1800s, the temperance movement, which sought to ban the sale and consumption of alcohol, became the first reform movement to draw attention to domestic cruelty. Linking violence to excess alcohol use, women temperance reformers focused on the threat they believed male drinking posed to the well-being of women and children. Through speeches and literature, they vividly depicted images of women and children being terrorized by men who had been converted into "brutes" by liquor. Although highly critical of this male behavior, temperance reformers did not seek to protect or empower women, as these approaches would have been considered too radical. Instead, they called on women to use their moral influence to reform their husbands. They emphasized the womanly duty of self-sacrifice for the benefit of their families.

In the mid-1800s, the women's rights movement also sought to publicize the plight of abused women. However, unlike the temperance reformers, these activists did not focus on the moral obligation of women to reform men; instead, they sought to lessen women's dependence on their husbands by seeking reform of marriage laws that subordinated women and of divorce laws so as to make divorce easier in cases of violence. Seen as unwomanly radicals, these activists were accused of seeking to destroy the family. Their efforts to change the law were regarded as subversive of the moral order and met with little success.

After the Civil War, there was another attempt to address the issue of wife abuse. Members of the legal establishment, including judges and prosecutors, campaigned to bring back the whipping post to punish wife beaters, and between 1882 and 1905, three states actually passed such laws. However, the protection of abused wives was not the real focus of this effort; rather, it was part of a broader campaign to control individuals, notably newly freed slaves and immigrants, who were considered by many in the ruling elite to be a threat to the social order. This campaign came to an end at the turn of the century when Progressive Era reformers shifted the focus away from punishment toward seeking to understand and eliminate the root causes of criminal activity.[6]

As a result, the issue of domestic violence moved off the national agenda as a matter of pressing social concern. Newly established family courts were entrusted with the responsibility of resolving the problem within the confines of each family unit. Abuse complaints were handled by the family court's social service department. The goal of intervention was reconciliation. Once again, women were charged with responsibility for ending the violence, and they were frequently counseled on how to improve their homemaking skills in order to gain their husbands' respect.[7]

This focus on resolving domestic violence within the family context was reinforced by the emerging field of psychiatry, which sought to explain domestic violence as a function of interpersonal dynamics. Seen as rooted in the realm of psychological functioning, a mental health approach to domestic violence was emphasized over any kind of legal response. This remained the prevailing approach until the late 1960s, when domestic violence again emerged as a social problem that called for a public rather than a privatized solution.[8]

## PRESENT LEGAL APPROACH TO DOMESTIC VIOLENCE ————

During the 1960s, the women's rights movement again focused public attention on the issue of domestic violence. Reformers challenged the prevailing understanding that intimate violence was a private matter expressive of the interpersonal personal functioning of an individual couple and instead located its roots in the history of male authority over women in the domestic realm. As part of a broader effort to reallocate this historical imbalance of power, legal reform efforts focused on the enactment of **abuse prevention laws.**

Now in effect in all states, these laws enable victims of domestic violence to obtain **protective orders** through a simplified court procedure. More recently, these state efforts have been strengthened by the federal Violence Against Women Act (VAWA). After taking a close look at the protections available under abuse prevention laws and the general process for obtaining protective orders, we will consider some of VAWA's key provisions.

Before turning to the law, it is important to recognize that domestic violence remains a serious problem, although, on an encouraging note, the rate of "non-fatal intimate partner violence" dropped significantly between 1993 and 2004.[9] What remains unchanged, however, is the gendered impact of partner violence, with women comprising approximately 76 percent of the victims during this period. Put another way, during these years, "non-fatal intimate partner victimizations represented 22 percent of violent victimizations against females and 3 percent of those against males aged 12 and older."[10]

## OBTAINING CIVIL ORDERS OF PROTECTION UNDER ABUSE PREVENTION LAWS

To understand generally how abuse protection laws work, it is helpful to consider a number of basic questions. These questions can also be used to analyze the provisions of an individual state's law. They include the following:

- What kinds of relationships qualify for a protective order?
- What kind of harms entitles a victim to obtain a protective order?
- What kinds of protection are available?
- What is the process for obtaining an order?
- How is the order enforced?

These questions will guide our discussion, but keep in mind that the precise answers vary from state to state.

## Qualifying Relationships

Abuse prevention laws are intended to provide protection to persons who are being abused by someone with whom they have an intimate, family, or family-like relationship. When parties are in a more distant relationship, such as that of neighbor or co-worker, protection cannot usually be obtained through an abuse prevention law, although other remedies, such as a criminal action, may be available. A few states have eliminated the relationship requirement; the available protections are generally more limited, however, if the party seeking protection does not have a "qualifying" type of relationship with the abuser.

The statutes in some states are fairly comprehensive and allow someone to seek protection from abuse by a range of persons with whom they have a "special" relationship. An inclusive statute might permit someone to seek protection from:

- a spouse or former spouse;
- a cohabiting partner or former cohabiting partner (but some statutes frame this category more broadly to include all household members even if there is no family or intimate relationship);
- the parent of a child in common (though statutes in a few states now expressly permit a pregnant woman to seek an order before the birth of the "child in common," a topic discussed later in this chapter);
- family members related by blood and possibly by marriage;
- a dating partner (a topic discussed below).

Most state statutes are not this inclusive, and many impose specific eligibility qualifications on certain categories of individuals. For example, although statutes include spouses and most, if not all, include former spouses, some exclude spouses who are in the process of getting a divorce or a legal separation. (Note that similar relief may be provided through comparable provisions in the applicable divorce or separation statute.) And although virtually all statutes cover unmarried cohabiting partners, some exclude former cohabiting partners. This is an unfortunate omission because research shows that battered women are at increased risk of abuse when they leave a relationship. Some cohabitation provisions specify that a couple must live together in a spousal-like relationship, which (as discussed below) has been used to deny coverage to victims in a same-sex relationship, and many provisions exclude other householders unless they are family members.

Many states now permit an individual to seek protection from a person with whom he or she has had a child, even if they do not have any kind of ongoing relationship. These are often referred to as "child in common" provisions. In states that have such a provision, an issue that has come up is whether a woman can seek protection while she is pregnant but has not yet given birth. In recognition of the fact that where there is a history of violence, a pregnant woman may be at high risk of abuse, some "child in common" provisions expressly extend coverage to pregnant women. Where the statute is silent, case law is divided. Some courts have held that battered pregnant women come within the purpose and intent of the "child in common" provision, while other courts have denied coverage based on a narrow reading of the statutory language holding that birth is a condition precedent to eligibility.[11]

In addition to the above relationships, some states permit an individual who is assisting a victim of violence to seek an order of protection for him- or herself. In effect, this person is regarded as being in a "special" relationship with the abuser based on the connection with the victim, as this connection may place him or her in direct risk of harm.

As states have sought to determine which relationships should qualify for protection, some tension has existed around the inclusion of dating relationships and same-sex couples, which, of course, can be overlapping categories.

### Dating Relationships

At first, abuse prevention laws did not address dating violence, which was not considered to be a serious or common problem. However, it became increasingly apparent that intimate partner abuse is not limited to marital or cohabiting relationships and also occurs within the context of dating relationships. Research reveals that women are at greatest risk of being abused when they are between the ages of 16 and 24 and that approximately one in five young women in high school have been physically and/or sexually abused by someone they were dating,[12] with research indicating that within heterosexual dating relationships, young men are more likely than young women to initiate the abuse.

Presently, more than half of the states have amended their abuse protection laws to include individuals in dating or engagement relationships. Some statutes refer simply to dating relationships, while others impose specific definitional requirements. For example, in Massachusetts, one of the first states to include dating relationships in its abuse protection law, an individual must first establish the existence of a "substantial dating or engagement relationship." In evaluating substantiality, a judge is to consider the duration and type of the relationship and the frequency of the parties' interaction. If the relationship has ended, the judge must consider how much time has elapsed since termination.[13] Some statutes impose very specific qualifying requirements. For example, some define a "dating relationship" as one that is sexually intimate, thus potentially excluding relationships at an early stage of development or those between young teens. Others require that one or both parties be adults, thus again excluding teens, while others require the parties to be in a heterosexual dating relationship, which excludes same-sex dating couples.

These kinds of limitations respond to concerns that some have raised that including dating partners would open the floodgates to petitions by persons who are simply friends or acquaintances and therefore outside the intended scope of abuse prevention laws. However, experts in the field have raised a number of concerns about these limitations. First, they exclude some potential victims of dating violence, such as teens, who might need the protection offered by a restraining order. Second, some of the qualifying conditions—such as that the relationship be substantial or that the parties be sexually intimate—give judges considerable discretion to decide if a petitioner qualifies for protection. If the judge's standard is not met, the petitioner may be in even greater danger because she has brought the perpetrator into court but then leaves without a protective order in place. Third, requiring proof that the relationship has reached a certain level of intimacy or has lasted for a certain time period means that abuse cannot be addressed early on in the relationship and, since violence often escalates in frequency and severity over time, a victim of dating violence may have to wait until there is a risk of serious injury before being eligible for protection. Further, experts generally agree that the earlier the intervention in a violent relationship, the more likely it is to succeed.

**Teen Dating Relationships.** Teen dating violence raises some particular concerns. Looking outside of the law for a moment, one concern is that although it is often difficult for any victim of domestic violence to disclose their situation to others (see "Working with Victims of Domestic Violence" box), disclosure can be especially difficult for teens who are struggling to establish their autonomy and adult sense of self. In addition, if there is violence at home, a teen may assume that such treatment is the norm. Another complicating factor is that if abuse is disclosed, adults may discount the potential seriousness of the situation based on the view that romantic relationships between teenagers are not very serious, and can easily be ended.[14]

Teens also face legal barriers that adults usually do not have to contend with. First, if a statute excludes dating relationships altogether or limits them to adult dating relationships, most teens will not be able to obtain a protective order unless they are in another qualifying relationship, such as where they are seeking protection from a family member or the father of a "child in common." Second, if there is a "sexual intimacy" requirement, it is possible that a teen dating relationship will not qualify. Moreover, even if a teen is sexually active within the meaning of the statute, she may be more reluctant than an adult would be to share this with a judge. This is particularly likely to be true if a parent has accompanied her to court. This leads us to another consideration: Many statutes do not permit a minor to seek a protective order on his or her own, but require that it be filed on the minor's behalf by a parent or other responsible adult. Although the involvement of an adult can provide a minor with much-needed support, this requirement may deter some teens from seeking help.

### Same-Sex Couples

Intimate partner violence is not limited to heterosexual couples; however, the law has been slower to respond to victims who experience violence within the context of same-sex relationships. In large part, this reflects the legal system's traditional reluctance to take same-sex relationships seriously. Additional complicating factors include fear within the gay and lesbian community that disclosure of abuse within same-sex relationships will exacerbate existing negative stereotypes, and an apprehension that judges will not respond to these cases with the seriousness and sensitivity that they merit. Nonetheless, experts in the field generally agree that differential treatment of same-sex and heterosexual couples is wrong and exacerbates the isolation and shame that victims often experience.

Abuse prevention laws take a variety of approaches toward same-sex couples. In some states, it is clear from the face of the statute that protection is not available. In these jurisdictions, protection is typically limited to individuals who are related by blood or marriage and to cohabiting and possibly also to dating couples comprised of a male and a female partner. At the other end of the continuum, a few statutes expressly extend protections to same-sex couples, thus formally equalizing the treatment of same-sex and heterosexual relationships. Additionally, even if it is not expressly provided for in the abuse prevention statute, coverage clearly would be required in the handful of states in which same-sex couples are entitled to all of the benefits and protections of marriage. (See Chapter 1.)

In most states, however, the abuse prevention law does not expressly include or exclude same-sex couples, which makes the availability of protection less clear and more dependent on the presiding judge's discretion. Where a statute does not expressly limit protection to "opposite-sex" cohabiting or dating couples — and thus does not presume heterosexuality — the judicial trend has favored providing relief to abuse victims in same-sex relationships. Including such victims is often seen as being consistent with the statutory goal of providing relief to all domestic violence victims, with some judges also noting that exclusion on the basis of sexual orientation would run afoul of state equal protection requirements. Although the gradual trend has been in favor of inclusion, over the years some judges have concluded that definitional language, such as that requiring cohabiting couples to live in a "spousal-like" relationship, precludes coverage of gay men and lesbians.

The recent spate of state laws and constitutional amendments limiting marriage to heterosexual couples (see Chapter 1) raises the troubling possibility that judges will now increasingly interpret their abuse prevention laws to deny protection to same-sex couples. Take, for example, the case of Ohio. Ohio's abuse prevention law protects cohabiting partners who are living in a spousal-like relationship. Seeking to promote the legislative goal of providing protection to all victims of partner violence, Ohio courts consistently interpreted the statute to include same-sex cohabitants — until recently. Following the 2004 enactment of a constitutional amendment that both bans same-sex marriage and prevents the recognition of a "legal status for relationships of unmarried individuals that intends to approximate the design, qualities, significance or effect of marriage,"[15] a split has developed among Ohio's state courts regarding the constitutionality of providing relief to unmarried (gay or straight) litigants. Many trial courts have dismissed charges against unmarried defendants on grounds that granting of relief would be tantamount to recognizing a relationship that "approximates" marriage — a result prohibited by the state constitutional amendment. Some appellate courts have upheld the dismissals, while others have reversed them, concluding that the legislature's intent in including nonmarital cohabitants in the abuse prevention law was to extend protections to a broad class of victims, rather than to confer a marital-like status upon cohabitants.[16]

## Covered Conduct

What types of abusive behavior trigger eligibility for protection? There is not as much variability here as there is with respect to who is entitled to seek protection, but some statutes are more comprehensive than others and include types of conduct, such as the malicious destruction of property, that is usually not covered by abuse prevention laws. The following discussion focuses on the kinds of behaviors that are covered in most states.

Most often petitioners are seeking protection from physical abuse, and all states authorize the issuance of protective orders in this situation. *Physical abuse* includes acts such as slaps or pushes as well as potentially life-threatening conduct such as beatings with a baseball bat or repeated pummeling with a closed fist. Protection usually can also be sought for *attempted physical harm*, such as where someone throws a rock but misses.

Most statutes also cover *threatened physical harm*. Generally, a petitioner must show that he or she was placed in fear of imminent bodily harm — the definition of criminal assault. However, as a practical matter, some judges are reluctant to issue orders for threats of harm in the absence of a history of physical abuse. This reluctance can put a victim at great risk because threats often escalate into violence; for instance, research indicates that up to 50 percent of battered women who are murdered by their partners had previously been threatened with death.[17] Some states also authorize relief for *emotional* or *verbal abuse*, which does not involve threats of physical harm, although these provisions are not common. Courts tend to interpret these provisions narrowly, and may, for instance, grant relief only where there has been a prior history of abuse or where an intent to harm can be inferred from accompanying conduct.

Orders also may be granted based on *harassment* or *interference with an individual's liberty*, although most states do not recognize these as separate qualifying behaviors, but subsume them into another category of harm such as threatened physical harm. Harassment has been defined to include a range of conduct, such as preventing a person from leaving a room, pulling the telephone out of the wall or cutting the wires, or slashing the tires of someone's car. As with threats, harassing behavior, if left unchecked, can escalate into more serious acts of violence. Similarly, an order may be based on *stalking* (see section below entitled "Supplementing the Enforcement Process: Criminal Anti-Stalking Laws") either as a distinct behavior or as tied to some other category of recognized harm, such as threatened physical harm.

Many statutes also expressly authorize the granting of protective orders based on sexual assault. In states where sexual assault is not specifically mentioned, judges are likely to include this conduct in their working definition of physical abuse. *Sexual assault* is generally understood to involve coercing someone to engage in sexual relations against their will through force, threats of force, or, possibly, duress, such as where someone says, "If you do not have sex with me you'll never see your children again." In such cases, the consent is negated by the coercion.

## Available Remedies

Most abuse prevention laws authorize a fairly broad range of specific remedies, including a "catchall" provision that allows a judge to tailor the remedy to the circumstances of the case before him or her. In this section, we look at the generally available remedies.

### Refraining from Further Abuse

Judges in all states can enjoin the abusive party from engaging in conduct that places the victim at risk of harm. This is often expressed as a requirement that the abuser refrain from committing any further acts of abuse as defined by the applicable abuse prevention law. This provision is commonly referred to as a **restraining order**. By itself, a restraining order does not usually prohibit contact between the parties; it simply prohibits abusive behavior.

## Vacate and Stay-Away Orders

In most, if not all, states, a judge can issue a **vacate order**, which requires a batterer to vacate the parties' home. In many instances, removal of the perpetrator is an important step in securing the safety of the abuse victim, but in other cases, this remedy is worth little because it leaves the victim living in a place that is known to the abuser. Thus, despite the fact that the law may require the perpetrator to depart the premises, safety concerns may force the victim to vacate the shared premises. The issuance of a vacate order does not affect the vacated party's title to the property.

Where the parties do not live together, a judge can issue a **stay-away order**, which requires the abuser to stay away from the victim's home. This stay-away order can be supplemented by language that further requires the abuser to stay away from other places such as the victim's place of work, her parents' house, and her neighborhood. Stay-away provisions can also be used to supplement a vacate order.

## No-Contact Orders

Most abuse prevention laws expressly authorize a judge to issue a **no-contact order**. Where not expressly authorized, a no-contact order can issue under a law's "catchall" provision. When drafted with care and specificity, no-contact orders can greatly enlarge the scope of available protection because they can be used to prohibit the abusive party from seeking any contact with the victim through any means or in any place. No-contact orders also can be drafted to prevent individuals who are acting on the abuser's behalf from contacting the victim.

## Custody and Visitation

Most abuse prevention laws authorize judges to include temporary custody awards of minor children in a protective order. In some states, custody can be awarded only to the person seeking relief, while others employ a rebuttable presumption against awarding custody to the perpetrator of violence.

Some statutes permit a judge to fashion a temporary visitation order; however, recognizing that visitation often carries with it a serious risk of continued abuse, judges frequently impose specific conditions to help ensure the safety of the victim as well as the children, and in some states this is statutorily required. Accordingly, supervised visitation may be ordered, or the parties may be required to drop off and pick up the children at the home of a third party or other neutral location, such as a police station or social service agency. Such arrangements may need to be made through an intermediary. By so structuring visitation, the need for contact between the parties is minimized, which in turn reduces the risk of continued abuse. Despite the availability of these preventive measures, some judges are reluctant to interfere with a parent's visitation rights and hesitate to impose restrictions except in the most egregious circumstances.

It is important to be aware that these custody and visitation orders are temporary in nature and may be superseded by orders entered in a subsequent divorce, custody, or separation proceeding. Moreover, if such an action is pending at the time a protective order is sought, the judge in the abuse action may be required to defer to this proceeding in matters of custody and visitation. If you are assisting someone who is seeking a restraining order, it is important to be aware of how the various statutory provisions governing custody and visitation interact in your jurisdiction. The interactive patterns are often complex and can result in conflicting orders that must be properly prioritized so the controlling order can be determined. The failure to do this can leave a client unprotected and at risk of violating a court order that has been superseded by a subsequent one.

### Support and Monetary Compensation

Most states authorize the inclusion of a temporary child support and/ or a temporary spousal support award in a protective order. However, even where allowed, some judges are reluctant to make support awards, perhaps believing that financial matters are best addressed in a divorce proceeding. The failure to provide financial support, whether through a statutory exclusion or a judicial omission, can compromise a battered woman's safety. If she is unable to provide for herself and her children, she may feel that she has no choice but to return to the abuser.

Distinct from support, most statutes enable a judge to order the abuser to compensate the victim for any financial loss suffered due to the abuse. Compensation might include out-of-pocket medical expenses, the repair or replacement of damaged property, lost wages, and moving costs. However, frequently fearful that the court action will provoke retaliation, many victims are reluctant to request relief not directly related to securing their safety and the safety of their children.

### Treatment/Counseling

In most states, a judge can order an abuser to participate in a treatment or counseling program that works specifically with batterers. **Batterer**

**intervention programs**, as they are generally referred to, generally target men who abuse female intimate partners, but some now provide services to women who abuse their male partners and to gay men and lesbians. A growing number of states have adopted mandatory guidelines that batterer intervention programs must follow. These guidelines allow for state oversight of the quality and effectiveness of the program. Guidelines often relate to matters such as staff qualifications, intake and discharge procedures, and the intervention approach.

Unlike the above-discussed remedies, a judge may only have the authority to order a party into a batterer intervention program after a violation of the protective order has occurred. However, a judge may be able to *recommend* that an abuser seek help as part of the initial order. Where intervention is ordered rather than just recommended, the abuser's attendance is monitored, often by having the program send periodic reports back to the judge; if sessions are missed, the judge can impose sanctions.

Most experts in the field are at best cautiously optimistic about whether batterer intervention programs are effective in changing behavior. It appears that they may have a "small but significant" effect when part of a coordinated community anti-violence effort, rather than being relied on as the singular solution to domestic abuse. Research also indicates that intervention may be more effective with some men, for instance those without a significant mental disorder or substance abuse problem, than with others. One concern in this regard is that victims are often lulled into a false sense of security when they learn that the person who abuses them has enrolled in a batterer intervention program, as they assume that this will end the violence. To guard against this, most programs have some means for communicating with the partners of participants. Some send out a cautionary brochure explaining that intervention often does not result in changed behavior, and many programs will contact the partner of a participant if they have cause to believe that she is at risk of harm.

### Relinquishment of Firearms

The use of a firearm significantly increases the chance of a violent death. According to one study, "family and intimate assaults with firearms are 12 times more likely to result in death than non-firearm assaults."[18] In households where there is a history of domestic abuse, the presence of a gun increases the risk of murder by twenty times; this compares to the threefold increase in the risk of murder where a gun is present in a household but there is no history of abuse.[19]

Given these potentially deadly consequences, many abuse prevention laws now include gun (and other weapon) possession provisions that restrict an abuser's access to firearms and ammunition. In some states, the entry of a protective order based on specific criteria, such as that the abuser poses a credible threat to the safety of the petitioner, results in a mandatory prohibition on the possession of a firearm. More commonly, however, a judge is given the discretion to enter an order prohibiting the abuser from possessing a firearm. Additionally, some abuse prevention laws allow a judge to revoke the abuser's license to carry a firearm for the duration of the protective order.

In addition to these state law provisions, in 1994, based on a recognition of the increased risk of lethality when domestic violence involves firearms, Congress, in addition to passing the Violence Against Women Act (discussed below), amended the Federal Gun Control Act of 1968 to criminalize the possession of a firearm or ammunition by a party who is already subject to a qualifying restraining order.[20] In 1996, Congress added an additional provision to the Gun Control law to criminalize the purchase or possession of firearms or ammunition by any person who has been convicted of a qualifying misdemeanor crime of domestic violence.[21]

### Statutory Obligations of Police Officers

Although not technically a form of relief, it should be pointed out that most abuse prevention laws impose specific obligations on police officers to assist victims of domestic violence. An officer may be required to provide a victim with information about obtaining an order, to arrange or provide transportation to a hospital or shelter, to remain on the scene until the threat of immediate danger has passed, and to assist the victim to collect his or her belongings. In some states, the police may be able to seize a batterer's weapons where they have cause to believe that continued possession exposes the victim to the risk of serious injury. As discussed below under "Enforcement," the police also have a role in serving and enforcing protective orders.

## Court Procedure: Obtaining Protective Orders

Due to the urgent nature of domestic violence cases, the court process for obtaining protective orders is simpler and quicker than it is in most other kinds of cases. Filing a petition does not require a lawyer. Many petitioners successfully obtain orders on their own, but it can be helpful to have an advocate present. Unanticipated issues can arise in the course of a hearing, particularly if minor children are involved, that an advocate can help sort out. It can also be very frightening and possibly dangerous for a victim to face an abuser in court, especially where the perpetrator has threatened to take revenge if a court action is filed. An advocate can provide much needed support and help ensure that the victim is not pressured into abandoning the action. It should be noted that the scope of what an advocate is permitted to do varies from state to state and sometimes from judge to judge within an individual state.

This section provides a general step by step overview of the process for obtaining a protective order. Of course, the particulars vary from state to state, and local rules should always be consulted.

## OBTAINING A PROTECTIVE ORDER

1. The party seeking the order files a complaint with a supporting affidavit. A filing fee is usually not required.
2. In most cases, the complaint is heard on an ex parte basis.
3. A temporary protective order is issued. Depending on the jurisdiction, the date for the second hearing may be set at this time.
4. Service is made on the defendant.
5. At the second hearing, the original order may be extended, modified, or vacated. If extended, a date for its expiration is usually established.
6. Prior to the expiration of the protective order, the plaintiff may return to court to seek an extension.

The court process for obtaining a protective order usually takes place in two distinct stages. First, the person seeking protection (the petitioner) goes to the appropriate court and files a complaint for protection from abuse (Exhibit 3.1). Many jurisdictions also require a supporting affidavit. As part of the filing process, most states allow the petitioner to request that his or her address be kept confidential. The case is generally heard right away on an **ex parte** basis, which means that notice is not given to the other side. If the petitioner shows an imminent risk of danger or that there will be an imminent risk once the other side knows the action has been filed, the judge can issue a **temporary order** without notice to the other side. Some statutes limit the relief that is available at this stage to restraining and eviction orders and postpone consideration of matters such as custody, support, and counseling until the second hearing. Some judges limit the relief they will grant at this stage even if not so restricted by the applicable statute, which concerns many advocates.

## Exhibit 3.1    *Request for Protective Order*

---

**DV-100**    **Request for Order**

*Clerk stamps below when form is filed.*

**①** Your name (person asking for protection):

_____

Your address *(skip this if you have a lawyer):* *(If you want your address to be private, give a mailing address instead):*

_____

City: _____ State: _____ Zip: _____
Your phone # *(optional):* (_____) _____

Your lawyer *(If you have one): (Name, address, phone #, and State Bar #):*

_____
_____
_____

*Court name and street address:*

**Superior Court of California, County of**

**②** Name of person you want protection from (restrained person):

_____

Describe that person: Sex: ☐ M ☐ F  Ht.: _____  Wt.: _____
Race: _____ Hair Color: _____
Eye Color: _____ Age: _____ Date of Birth: _____

**Case Number:**

**③** Besides you, who needs protection? *(Family or household members)*

| Full Name | Age | Lives with you? | How are they related to you? |
|---|---|---|---|
| _____ | _____ | ☐ Yes ☐ No | _____ |
| _____ | _____ | ☐ Yes ☐ No | _____ |
| _____ | _____ | ☐ Yes ☐ No | _____ |
| _____ | _____ | ☐ Yes ☐ No | _____ |

☐ *Check here if you need more space. Attach Form MC-020 and write "DV-100, Item 3—Protected People" by your statement. NOTE: In any item that asks for Form MC-020, you can use an 8 1/2 x 11 inch sheet of paper instead.*

**④** What is your relationship to the person in **②** ? *(Check all that apply)*

a. ☐ We are now married.
b. ☐ We used to be married.
c. ☐ We live together.
d. ☐ We used to live together.
e. ☐ We are relatives, in-laws, or related by adoption *(specify relationship):* _____
f. ☐ We are dating or used to date.
g. ☐ We are engaged to be married or were engaged to be married.
h. ☐ We are the parents together of a child or children under 18:

Child's Name: _____ Date of Birth: _____
Child's Name: _____ Date of Birth: _____
Child's Name: _____ Date of Birth: _____

☐ *Check here if you need more space. Attach Form MC-020 and write "DV-100, Item 4h" by your statement.*

i. ☐ We have signed a Voluntary Declaration of Paternity for our child or children. *Attach a copy if you have one.*

**This is a not a Court Order.**

Judicial Council of California, www.courtinfo-ca.gov
Rev. January 1, 2004, Mandatory Form
Family Code, § 6200 et seq.

**Request for Order**
(Domestic Violence Prevention)

DV-100, Page 1 of 4

## Exhibit 3.1   Continued

Case Number: _____

Your name: _____

**5**  **Other Court Cases**

a.  Have you and the person in **2** been involved in another court case?  ☐ No ☐ Yes
If yes, where? County: _____ State: _____
What are the case numbers? *(If you know)* _____
What kind of case? *(Check all that apply)*
☐ Divorce/Dissolution ☐ Parentage/Paternity ☐ Legal Separation ☐ Domestic Violence ☐ Criminal
☐ Juvenile ☐ Child Support ☐ Nullity ☐ Civil Harassment
☐ Other *(specify)*: _____

b.  Are there any domestic violence restraining/protective orders now (criminal, juvenile, family)?
☐ No ☐ Yes   *If yes, attach a copy if you have one.*

**What orders do you want? Check the boxes that apply to your case ☑**

**6**  ☐ **Personal Conduct Orders**

I ask the court to order the person in **2** not to do the following things to me or any of the people listed in **3**:

a. ☐ Harass, attack, strike, threaten, assault (sexually or otherwise), hit, follow, stalk, molest, destroy
personal property, disturb the peace, keep under surveillance, or block movements
b. ☐ Contact (either directly or indirectly), or telephone, or send messages or mail or e-mail

**7**  ☐ **Stay-Away Order**

I ask the court to order the person in **2** to stay at least _____ yards away from: *(Check all that apply)*

a. ☐ Me                                    e. ☐ The children's school or child care
b. ☐ The people listed in **3**           f. ☐ My vehicle
c. ☐ My home                              g. ☐ Other *(specify)*: _____
d. ☐ My job or workplace                  _____

If the person listed in **2** is ordered to stay away from all the places listed above, will he or she still be able
to get to his or her home, school, job, or place of worship? ☐ Yes ☐ No  *(If no, explain)*: _____
_____

**8**  ☐ **Move-Out Order**

I ask the court to order the person in **2** to move out from and not return to *(address)*:
_____

I have the right to live at the above address because *(explain)*: _____
_____

**9**  ☐ **Child Custody, Visitation, and Child Support**

I ask the court to order child custody, visitation, and/or child support. *You must fill out and attach
Form DV-105.*

**This is not a Court Order.**

## Exhibit 3.1 Continued

| | Case Number: |
|---|---|
| Your name: _____ | |

### What orders do you want? Check the boxes that apply to your case ☑

**(10)** ☐ **Record Unlawful Communications**
I ask for the right to record communications made to me by the person in ❷ that violate the judge's orders.

**(11)** ☐ **Property Control**
I ask the court to give *only* me temporary use, possession, and control of the property listed here:
_____

**(12)** ☐ **Debt Payment**
I ask the court to order the person in ❷ to make these payments while the order is in effect:
☐ *Check here if you need more space. Attach Form MC-020 and write "DV-100, Item 12—Debt Payment" by your statement.*
Pay to: _____ For: _____ Amount: $ _____ Due date: _____
Pay to: _____ For: _____ Amount: $ _____ Due date: _____
Pay to: _____ For: _____ Amount: $ _____ Due date: _____

**(13)** ☐ **Property Restraint**
I am married to the person in ❷. I ask the judge to order that he or she not borrow against, sell, hide, or get rid of or destroy any possessions or property, except in the usual course of business or for necessities of life. I also ask the judge to order the restrained person to notify me of any new or big expenses and to explain them to the court.

**(14)** ☐ **Attorney Fees and Costs**
I ask that the person in ❷ pay some or all of my attorney fees and costs.
*You must complete and file Form FL-150, Income and Expense Declaration.*

**(15)** ☐ **Payments for Costs and Services**
I ask that the person in ❷ pay the following:
*You can ask for lost earnings or your costs for services caused directly by the person in ❷ (damaged property, medical care, counseling, temporary housing, etc.). You must bring proof of these expenses to your hearing.*
Pay to: _____ For: _____ Amount: $ _____
Pay to: _____ For: _____ Amount: $ _____
Pay to: _____ For: _____ Amount: $ _____

**(16)** ☐ **Batterer Intervention Program**
I ask the court to order the person listed in ❷ to go to a 52-week batterer intervention program and show proof of completion to the court.

**(17)** **No Fee to Serve (Notify) Restrained Person**
*If you want the sheriff or marshal to serve (notify) the restrained person about the orders for free, ask the court clerk if you need to file more forms. You may need Form CH-101/DV-290 and Form 982(a)(17).*

**This is not a Court Order.**

## Exhibit 3.1   Continued

---

Case Number: _____

Your name: _____

**What orders do you want? Check the boxes that apply to your case** ☑

**18** ☐ **More Time for Notice**
I need extra time to notify the person in ❷ about these papers. Because of the facts explained on this form, I want the papers served up to _____ days before the date of the hearing. *For help, read DV-210.*
*If necessary, add additional facts:* _____
_____

**19** ☐ **Other Orders**
What other orders are you asking for? _____
_____

☐ *Check here if you need more space. Attach MC-020 and write "DV-100, Item 19—Other Orders" by your statement.*

**20** **Turn in Guns or Other Firearms**
I ask the judge to order the person in ❷ to sell or turn in any guns or firearms that he or she has or controls.
If the judge approves the orders at a noticed hearing, the restrained person will be required to sell to a gun dealer or turn in to police any guns or firearms that he or she has or controls. *Describe any use or threatened use of firearms in* ㉑.

**21** **Describe the most recent abuse.**
a. Date of most recent abuse: _____
b. Who was there? _____
c. What did the person in ❷ do or say that made you afraid?
_____
_____
_____
_____
_____
_____
_____

d. Describe any use or threatened use of guns or other weapons: _____
_____

e. Describe any injuries: _____
_____

f. Did the police come? ☐ No    ☐ Yes
If yes, did they give you an Emergency Protective Order? ☐ Yes ☐ No ☐ I don't know
*Attach a copy if you have one.*
☐ *Check here if you need more space. Use Form MC-020 and write "DV-100, Item 21—Recent Abuse" by your statement.*
☐ *Check here if the person in ❷ has abused you (or your children) other times. Use Form DV-101 or Form MC-020 to describe any previous abuse.*

**22** I declare under penalty of perjury under the laws of the State of California that the information above is true and correct.

Date: _____

▶

_____          _____
*Type or print your name*                              *Sign your name*

**This is not a Court Order.**

Because abuse frequently takes place on weekends or in the evening when courts are closed, most states have a procedure in place for obtaining after-hour emergency orders. An emergency judge might be available on a 24-hour on-call basis, or an official, such as a magistrate, might be empowered to issue after-hour orders. These orders generally are good only until the next business day.

Service must be made on the other side (the respondent). This is usually accomplished by a police officer or a sheriff. As a general rule, service must be made in hand, although statutes often permit alternative means of service under specified circumstances, such as allowing the papers to be left at the last and usual address when attempts at personal service have failed. As a general rule, the ex parte orders are not considered to be in effect until service has been made. In addition to being given a copy of the complaint and any ex parte orders, the respondent must be informed of the right to be heard in court. In some states, a second hearing date is set at the ex parte hearing, usually for somewhere between 10 to 20 days later, and the initial orders are only good until then. In other states, the second hearing date is not set by the court but must be requested by the responding party, who has a right to be heard promptly. Here, the ex parte orders remain in effect until the second hearing is held; if a hearing is not requested, they remain in effect until a judicially selected or a statutory expiration date is reached.

The next stage is the second hearing at which both parties are given the opportunity to present their version of what took place. After hearing the evidence, the judge can either extend or decline to extend the original orders for an additional period of time. The judge can also address any matters that may have been left unresolved at the ex parte stage, such as support. Most states allow orders to be extended for up to at least one year, although, as noted above, the trend is in favor of longer extension periods, and a few states do not impose any mandatory durational limits. (For an example of an abuse prevention order, see Exhibit 3.2.) Most states allow the petitioner to return to court to seek an extension before the orders issued at the second hearing expire. An extension generally can be granted based on a credible fear of renewed harm — acts of violence do not need to have been committed while the order was in effect.

Although the practice has drawn considerable criticism and has been prohibited in a number of jurisdictions, some judges are inclined to grant **mutual orders of protection** at the second hearing whereby each party is ordered to refrain from harming the other, despite the fact that only one party has requested relief. By suggesting that both persons are responsible for the violence, mutual orders fail to hold abusers accountable for their behavior. They can also create enforcement problems for police responding to a call for assistance because each party can claim that he or she is the

**Exhibit 3.2   *Abuse Prevention Order***

| DV-110 | Temporary Restraining Order and Notice of Hearing |

Clerk stamps below when form is filed.

**1** Protected person's name: _____

Protected person's address *(skip this if you have a lawyer): (If you want your address to be private, give a mailing address instead):*
_____

City: _____ State: _____ Zip: _____
Phone # (optional): _____

Protected person's lawyer *(if any):(Name, address, phone # and State Bar #):*
_____
_____
_____

Court name and street address:

**Superior Court of California, County of**

**2** Restrained person's name:
_____
Description of that person: Sex: ☐ M ☐ F  Ht.: _____
Wt.: _____ Race: _____ Hair Color: _____
Eye Color: _____ Age: _____ Date of Birth: _____

**Case Number:**

**3** List the full names of all family or household members protected by this order: _____
_____

**4** **Court Hearing Date (*Fecha de la Audiencia*)**
Court will fill in box below.

The court hearing will be at:

| Hearing Date | Date: _____  Time: _____  _____ |
|              | Dept.: _____  Rm.: _____  _____ |

To the person in **2**: At the hearing, the judge can make restraining orders that last for up to 3 years. The judge can also make other orders about children, child support, money, and property. At the hearing, you can tell the judge if you do not want the orders against you. Even if you do not attend the hearing, you *must* obey the orders.

*Para la persona nombrada en* **2***: En esta audiencia el juez puede hacer que la orden de restricción sea válida hasta un máximo de 3 años. El juez puede también hacer otras órdenes acerca de niños, manutención, dinero y propiedad. Si Usted se opone a estas órdenes, vaya a la audiencia y dígaselo al juez. Aunque no vaya a la audiencia, tiene que obedecer estas órdenes.*

**5** **Temporary Orders (Ordenes Temporales)**
Any orders made in this form end on the date and time of the court hearing in **4**, unless a judge extends them. Read this form carefully. All checked boxes ☑ and item 10 are court orders.

*Todas las órdenes hechas en esta formulario terminarán en la fecha y hora de la audiencia en* **4***, al menos que un juez las extienda. Lea este formulario con cuidado. Todas las casillas marcadas* ☑ *y artículo 10 son órdenes de la corte.*

**This is a Court Order.**

Judicial Council of California, www.courtinfo.ca.gov
Rev. January 1, 2004, Mandatory Form
Family Code, §§ 6200 et seq. Approved by DOJ

**Temporary Restraining Order (CLETS)**
(Domestic Violence Prevention)

DV-110, Page 1 of 5
→

## Exhibit 3.2  Continued

Case Number: _____

Protected person's name: _____

**6**  ☐ **Personal Conduct Orders**

The person in ❷ must **not** do the following things to the protected people listed in ❶ and ❸:

a. ☐ Harass, attack, strike, threaten, assault (sexually or otherwise), hit, follow, stalk, molest, destroy personal property, disturb the peace, keep under surveillance, or block movements

b. ☐ Contact (either directly or indirectly), or telephone, or send messages or mail or e-mail

☐ Except for brief and peaceful contact as required for court-ordered visitation of children unless a criminal protective order says otherwise

Peaceful written contact through a lawyer or a process server or another person to serve legal papers is allowed and does not violate this order.

**7**  ☐ **Stay-Away Order**

The person in ❷ must stay at least _____ yards away from:

a. ☐ The person listed in ❶

b. ☐ The people listed in ❸

c. ☐ Home   ☐ Job   ☐ Vehicle of person in ❶

d. ☐ The children's school or child care

e. ☐ Other (specify): _____

_____

**8**  ☐ **Move-Out Order**

The person in ❷ must take only personal clothing and belongings needed until the hearing and move out immediately from (address): _____

**9**  ☐ **Child Custody and Visitation Order**

a. ☐ You and the other parent must make an appointment for court mediation (address and phone #):

_____

b. ☐ Follow the orders listed in Form DV-140, which is attached.

**10**  **No Guns or Other Firearms**

The person in ❷ cannot own, possess, have, buy or try to buy, receive or try to receive, or in any other way get a gun or firearm.

**11**  ☐ **Turn In or Sell Guns or Firearms**

The person in ❷:

■ Must sell to a licensed gun dealer or turn in to police any guns or firearms that he or she has or controls. This must be done within 48 hours of receiving this order. But if the person in ❷ was at a hearing on this order, it must be done within 24 hours of the hearing.

■ Must bring a receipt to the court within 72 hours of receiving this order, to prove that guns have been turned in or sold.

**12**  ☐ **Property Control**

Until the hearing, *only* the person in ❶ can use, control, and possess the following property and things:

_____

**This is a Court Order.**

## Exhibit 3.2    Continued

Protected person's name: _____

| Case Number: |
|---|

**13**  ☐ **Property Restraint**

If the people in ❶ and ❷ are married to each other, they must not transfer, borrow against, sell, hide, or get rid of or destroy any property, except in the usual course of business or for necessities of life. In addition, each person must notify the other of any new or big expenses and explain them to the court.

**14**  ☐ **Record Unlawful Communications**

The person in ❶ can record communications made by the person in ❷ that violate the judge's orders.

**15**  **No Fee to Notify Restrained Person**

If the sheriff or marshal serves this order, he or she will do it for free.

**16**  ☐ **Other Orders** *(specify):* _____
_____
_____

**17**  If the judge makes a restraining order at the hearing, which has the same orders as in this form, the person in ❷ will get a copy of that order by mail at his or her last known address. *(Write restrained person's address here):*
_____

If this address is not correct, or to know if the orders were made permanent, contact the court.

**18**  ☐ **Time for Service**

| **Ⓐ**    To: Person Asking for Order | **Ⓑ**    To:  Person Served With Order |
|---|---|
| Someone 18 or over – **not you or the other protected people** – must personally "serve" a copy of this order to the restrained person at least _____ days before the hearing. | If you want to respond in writing, someone 18 or over – **not you** – must "serve" Form DV-120 on the person in ❶, then file it with the court at least _____ days before the hearing. |

*For help with Service or Answering, read Form DV-210 or DV-540.*

Date: _____

▶ _____
    *Judge (or Judicial Officer)*

---

**Certificate of Compliance With VAWA**

This temporary protective order meets all Full Faith and Credit requirements of the Violence Against Women Act, 18 U.S.C. 2265 (1994) (VAWA) upon notice of the restrained person.  This court has jurisdiction over the parties and the subject matter; the restrained person has been or will be afforded notice and a timely opportunity to be heard as provided by the laws of this jurisdiction.  **This order is valid and entitled to enforcement in all jurisdictions throughout the 50 United States, the District of Columbia, all tribal lands, and all U.S. territories, commonwealths, and possessions and shall be enforced as if it were an order of that jurisdiction.**

---

**This is a Court Order.**

## Exhibit 3.2    Continued

Protected person's name:_____

Case Number:

**Warnings and Notices to the Restrained Person in ❷**

**19**  **If you do not obey this order, you can be arrested and charged with a crime.**

■ It is a felony to take or hide a child in violation of this order. You can go to prison and/or pay a fine.

■ If you travel to another state or to tribal lands, or make the protected person do so, with the intention of disobeying this order, you can be charged with a federal crime.

■ If you do not obey this order, you can go to prison and/or pay a fine.

**20**  **You Cannot Have Guns or Firearms**

You cannot own, have, possess, buy or try to buy, receive or try to receive, or otherwise get a gun while the order is in effect. If you do, you can go to jail and pay a $1,000 fine. If item ⑪ on this form is checked, you must sell to a gun dealer or turn in to police any guns or firearms that you have or control. The judge will ask you for proof that you did so. If you do not obey this order, you can be charged with a crime. Federal law says you cannot have guns or ammunition if you are subject to a restraining order made after a noticed hearing.

**21**  **After You Have Been Served With a Restraining Order**

■ Obey all the orders.

■ If you want to respond, fill out Form DV-120. Take it to the court clerk with the forms listed in Item ㉒.

■ File DV-120 and have all papers served on the protected person by the date listed in Item ⑱ of this form.

■ At the hearing, tell the judge if you agree to or disagree with the orders requested.

■ Even if you do not attend the hearing, the judge can make the restraining orders last for 3 years.

**22**  **Child Custody, Visitation, and Support**

■ Child Custody and Visitation: If you do not go to the hearing, the judge can make custody and visitation orders for your children without hearing your side.

■ Child Support: The judge can order child support based on the income of both parents. The judge can also have that support taken directly from your paycheck. Child support can be a lot of money, and usually you have to pay until the child is 18. File and serve a Financial Statement (FL-155) or an Income and Expense Declaration (FL-150) so the judge will have information about your finances. Otherwise, the court may make support orders without hearing your side.

**This is a Court Order.**

## Exhibit 3.2   Continued

Case Number: _____

Protected person's name: _____

**Instructions for Law Enforcement**

**23   Start Date and End Date of Orders**

The start date is the date next to the judge's signature on page 3. The orders end on the hearing date on page 1 or the hearing date on Form DV-125, if attached.

**24   Arrest Required If Order Is Violated**

If an officer has probable cause to believe that the restrained person had notice of the order and has disobeyed the order, the officer must arrest the restrained person. (Pen. Code, §§ 836 (c) (1), 13701 (b).) A violation of the order may be a violation of Penal Code section 166 or 273.6.

**25   Notice/Proof of Service**

■ Law enforcement must first determine if the restrained person had notice of the orders. If notice cannot be verified, the restrained person must be advised of the terms of the orders. If the restrained person then fails to obey the orders, the officer must enforce them. (Fam. Code, § 6383.)

Consider the restrained person "served" (noticed) if:

■ The officer sees a copy of the Proof of Service, or confirms that the Proof of Service is on file *or*

■ The restrained person was at the restraining order hearing, or was informed of the order by an officer (Fam. Code, § 6383, Pen. Code, § 836 (c) (2).)

**26   If the Protected Person Contacts the Restrained Person**

Even if the protected person invites or consents to contact with the restrained person, the orders remain in effect and must be enforced. The protected person cannot be arrested for inviting or consenting to contact with the restrained person. The orders can be changed only by another court order. (Pen. Code, § 13710(b).)

**27   Child Custody and Visitation**

■ Custody and visitation orders are on Form DV-140, Items ❸ and ❹. They are sometimes also written on additional pages or referenced in DV-140 or other orders that are not part of the restraining order.

■ **Forms DV-100 and DV-105 are not orders. Do not enforce them.**

**28   Enforcing the Restraining Order in California**

Any law enforcement officer in California who receives, sees, or verifies the orders on a paper copy, or on the California Law Enforcement Telecommunications System (CLETS), or in an NCIC Protection Order File must enforce the orders.

**29   Conflicting Orders**

If a criminal restraining order (CR-160) conflicts with a civil restraining order (DV-110 or DV-130), enforce the criminal order. Even if the criminal order is older, the officer must still enforce it over the civil order. (Pen. Code, § 136.2 (h).) Any nonconflicting terms of the civil restraining order remain in full force.

---

*Clerk's Certificate*

*[seal]*

I certify that this Temporary Restraining Order is a true and correct copy of the original on file in the court.          Date: _____

Clerk, by _____ , Deputy

**This is a Court Order.**

protected one and that the other should be arrested. Additionally, a mutual order can adversely impact the petitioner in a subsequent custody or visitation dispute in which the court is directed to consider the existence of prior protective orders when making an award because both parties will appear to be equally responsible for the violence. (See below discussion regarding VAWA and mutual restraining orders.)

Where the responding party fails to appear at the second hearing, many courts will continue the order based on the evidence presented by the petitioner, and in some states this result is mandated by statute. In other states, a bench warrant may be issued to secure the respondent's appearance. In some states, if the petitioner fails to appear, the action may be automatically dismissed. Advocates for battered women have raised serious concerns about this approach because a victim's failure to appear at the second hearing may be the result of fear or intimidation, rather than the result of a voluntary decision not to proceed.

## Enforcement of Protective Orders

If protective orders are to be worth more than the paper they are written on, effective enforcement is essential. Accordingly, although the orders themselves are civil in nature, violations can be prosecuted in the criminal justice system. Importantly, in most states, the act of violating an order is in and of itself a separate and independent crime. This is particularly valuable in situations where the violating behavior may not itself be an independent crime, such as where a party continually telephones the petitioner in violation of a no-contact order. However, most acts committed in violation of a protective order are themselves crimes (e.g., trespass, assault, battery, and false imprisonment), and a party can thus be prosecuted for any specific criminal acts as well as for violating the order.

Until fairly recently, the criminal justice system did not take domestic abuse cases as seriously as other criminal matters, seeing them primarily as private family matters. Police officers were frequently reluctant to make arrests, and prosecutors often used their discretion to drop cases, especially if the victim was at all ambivalent about proceeding, without first inquiring whether the reluctance stemmed from fear or coercion. Advocates for battered women began to press for change, demanding that intimate assaults be taken as seriously as other kinds of violence and not treated as inconsequential private spats.

Responding to these concerns, many states have adopted mandatory arrest policies that require police officers to arrest a suspect, without having to first obtain a warrant, whenever there is probable cause to believe an act of domestic violence has occurred, regardless of whether the officer witnessed the incident or not. These laws thus remove police discretion. Similarly, many states have adopted mandatory prosecution (or no-drop) policies that enable a prosecutor to pursue a domestic violence case even if the victim does not want to proceed.

Although the adoption of mandatory arrest and prosecution policies clearly signifies that domestic violence is being taken more seriously by the criminal justice system, this approach is nonetheless quite controversial. Stressing the importance of enhancing victim safety, supporters of a mandatory approach worry that the traumatic effects of abuse and the fear of reprisal can compromise the ability of victims to make appropriate decisions that maximize their well-being. They further worry that the "ongoing humiliation and assaults of personhood may encourage women to believe that they are partially responsible for their partner's violence which may compromise their ability to judge their own best interests."[22]

On the other hand, some advocates for battered women believe that mandatory policies deprive victims of the right to make decisions for themselves based upon a personal and individualized assessment of their own needs and safety concerns. Critics worry that divesting a woman of decisional authority will "perpetuate the disempowerment of the victim by sending a message that she is too helpless to survive without the controlling direction of a stronger person."[23] Another concern is that mandatory policies may actually endanger the people they were intended to protect, as anger over an arrest and prosecution may prompt an abuser to seek revenge against a victim, who, had she been given a choice, might have decided that it was too risky to seek the assistance of the criminal justice system.[24]

### Supplementing the Enforcement Process: Criminal Anti-Stalking Laws

Starting with California in 1990, all states have enacted criminal anti-stalking statutes. These laws punish a range of threatening behaviors and can be an additional source of protection for victims of intimate partner violence.[25] Researchers have established that the clear majority of stalking victims are women, while most perpetrators are male, and that most stalking is committed by former rather than current partners/spouses. Studies also indicate a "strong link between stalking and emotionally abusive and controlling behavior," and between "stalking and lethal forms of partner violence against women."[26]

**Stalking** is generally defined as harassing or threatening behavior, including following someone or making intimidating phone calls, which an individual engages in on a repeated, and often escalating, basis. Although this is the generally accepted definition of stalking, some statutes are more restrictive, and may, for example, limit stalking to situations where a victim is actually pursued or kept under surveillance. Many states now also specifically include the growing problem of **cyberstalking**—the use of the Internet or other mode of electronic communication to threaten or harass someone—in their anti-stalking law.

Perhaps more significant than definitional differences, there is considerable variability from state to state with respect to whether other elements must also be present for the conduct to rise to the level of a prosecutable crime. For example, in some states, there must be a credible threat of bodily harm; however, the majority approach is that the act of stalking itself is a crime. Some statutes also require proof that the stalker intended to induce fear in his victim. However, because it can be difficult to prove what a person's specific intent was, many states have made stalking a "general intent" crime. This means that intent to cause harm does not need to be established, but only that the defendant intentionally engaged in a prohibited act.[27]

Aiming to stop behavior before it becomes fatal, stalking laws recognize that abusive behavior often escalates in both frequency and severity. Accordingly, most statutes provide for the escalation of penalties for repeat violations. Additionally, in many states, the initial act of what is considered "aggravated" stalking, such as stalking in violation of a protective order and/or while armed with a weapon, will result in an enhanced penalty.

## Specialized Domestic Violence Courts

As we have seen, intimate partner violence is a pervasive and multidimensional problem, and, in contrast to other types of family law matters, abuse prevention cases are both civil and criminal in nature. Adding to the complexity and potential fragmentation of the legal response, families may also be involved in separate proceedings, such as a divorce or custody action, in which domestic violence is a central consideration. The various court actions are rarely coordinated despite their overlapping issues.

This lack of coordination is inefficient, and it can result in conflicting or inconsistent orders. But research points to a more serious consequence: that this "disjointed approach . . . has proven ineffective at stopping violence and protecting victims from repeated violence."[28] Even more chilling is that violence may actually escalate after a victim "has sought refuge in the law against the batterer." One study shows that 17 percent of domestic homicide victims had obtained a protective order prior to their death.[29]

Responding to this grim reality, many jurisdictions across the country have established specialized courts to solve the problems inherent in the traditionally fragmented approach to domestic violence cases. Although the models vary, most use a "comprehensive interdisciplinary system of handling domestic violence case,"[30] with a carefully coordinated approach to the handling of the civil and criminal components of these actions at its core. In many cases, this approach means that "not only do 'judges, clerks, district attorneys, police and probation officers work closely with one another, [but] they also work collaboratively with 'social services providers and community agencies,' that provide services to both the victim and the batterer." Other important innovations include the use of specially trained domestic violence clerks who can assist victims navigate the court system, and, in some jurisdictions, the assignment of the case to a single judge who assumes responsibility for all of the related legal matters.

## The Federal Response to Domestic Violence: The Violence Against Women Act

In 1994, Congress enacted the **Violence Against Women Act** (VAWA)[31] as part of a national effort to combat intimate partner violence against women. This Act was updated in 2000 (VAWA II),[32] and again in 2005 (VAWA III).[33] In addition to establishing federal protections and remedies for abuse victims, VAWA provides grants to states to enable them to better meet the needs of women who are the victims of domestic violence; funding is used to train police officers, support community anti-violence initiatives, provide victims with legal advocacy services, and assist victims with immigration matters. VAWA also established a national domestic violence hotline to provide 24-hour emergency assistance for abuse victims.

Under VAWA III, funding has increased for services directed at targeted populations who face unique challenges or experience a dispro-portionately high rate of abuse. For example, based on the Congressional finding that "youth, under the age of 18, account for 67 percent of all sexual assault victimizations reported to law enforcement officials,"[34] grants are provided to organizations, including schools, juvenile courts, and community groups for the implementation of specialized programs designed to educate youth and enhance both the safety of victims and the accountability of perpetrators. Similarly, based on findings indicating that American Indian and Alaska Native women suffer from a higher rate of intimate partner violence than any other population of women, VAWA III funds both a research study and a range of efforts designed to enhance the understanding of and response to violence against native women. One important addition is the establishment of a Deputy Director of Tribal Affairs within the federal Office on Violence Against Women who is charged with ensuring that a "portion of tribal set-aside funds from any grant awarded under ... [VAWA] is used to enhance the capacity of Indian tribes to address the safety of Indian women; and, ensure that another portion is used to hold offenders accountable."[35]

Although a detailed discussion of VAWA is beyond the scope of this text, three of the Act's provisions are particularly important:

**The Criminalization of Interstate Domestic Violence.** Under VAWA, it is a federal crime to cross a state line to violate a protective order. It is also a crime to cross a state line in order to injure, intimidate, or stalk an intimate partner. Under VAWA III, cyberstalking is now a federal crime, as is stalking through surveillance, by the use of devices, such as Global Positioning Systems and interactive computer systems.

By making these acts federal crimes, VAWA makes it easier to prosecute abusers who pursue their partners across a state line.

**The Extension of Full Faith and Credit to Abuse Prevention Orders.** VAWA fills a significant enforcement gap by requiring states to give full faith and credit to protective orders from other states that meet the basic requirements of the Act — including that the court had jurisdiction over the parties and provided the defendant with reasonable notice and an opportunity to be heard — and to enforce these orders as if they were issued by a court in that state. Prior to VAWA, states often did not recognize protective orders from other states and required domestic violence victims who had left their home states to obtain new orders.[35] VAWA III makes it clear that states must now also give full faith and credit to custody, visitation, and support provisions that are included in protective orders.

**Protections for Battered Immigrant Women.** VAWA recognizes that battered immigrant women are a vulnerable population. The fear of deportation or the dependence on a spouse for obtaining lawful permanent resident status may prevent immigrant women from seeking protection from or filing criminal charges against an abuser. VAWA therefore permits a battered immigrant to self-petition for lawful permanent resident status, which frees her from reliance on an abusive spouse to obtain this status. Under VAWA III, battered immigrant women also now are entitled to expanded opportunities to petition for relief from deportation proceedings.

If you are assisting a battered woman who is an immigrant, a variety of other protections may be available to her under VAWA and other related laws. Knowledge of these laws and of immigration law (which is a complex and highly specialized field) is essential for anyone working with immigrant women to ensure that their rights are fully protected and that no action is taken that jeopardizes their immigration status. Family law practitioners would be well advised to consult with an immigration expert in these situations.

## WORKING WITH VICTIMS OF DOMESTIC VIOLENCE

*Although there is no easy formula for how to work with victims of partner violence, the following considerations will contribute to effective and supportive interactions with clients who have been abused:*

- Victims often feel a tremendous sense of shame and may be reluctant to acknowledge the violence in their lives. Listen carefully for clues that may suggest an abusive relationship — for example, a woman who says "Well, I don't get out much; my husband doesn't approve of my friends." Inquire further in a sensitive manner. You might, for example, respond to such statements with the following questions: "Why doesn't your husband approve of your friends?" and "What might happen if you went out with someone he doesn't approve of?" With a client who is not quite ready to open up, these questions work more effectively than do more direct questions such as "So, is your husband abusive?"
- Trust the client's assessment of the danger; too often, professionals minimize the potential risks that victims face.
- Depending on the allocation of responsibilities in your office, you or the attorney for whom you work should fully inform clients about the abuse prevention laws in your state. If your office does not assist clients in obtaining protective orders, then provide referrals.
- Understand that it can be very difficult for persons to extricate themselves from an abusive relationship. For example, a client may have no money and be unable to find housing that she can afford. She may fear greater harm if she leaves. She may fear community or family disapproval, or she may worry about taking the children away from their father. It is not your job to criticize her for failing to leave or take action. She should know that your services are available if and when she does decide to leave or seek a court order.
- Make certain you have information available regarding local shelters, hotline numbers, and battered women's support groups. These are invaluable resources. Many shelters, hospitals, and police departments have developed materials on "safety plans" that help domestic violence victims think through how best to extricate themselves from a dangerous situation. You should also make these available.

- If you are assisting an abuse victim who is an immigrant to this country, you should be aware that certain protections may be available under the federal Violence Against Women Act. In this situation, it may be appropriate for the client to also meet with an immigration law specialist (see above discussion on VAWA).

## Chapter Summary

Domestic violence is a serious problem among intimate partners, including those who are in dating relationships. All states have abuse prevention laws that enable domestic violence victims to obtain civil orders of protection. In some states, the statutes are broad and cover most intimate and family relationships; in other states, the scope of coverage is narrower, and many individuals — for example, someone being abused by a dating partner or a former cohabiting partner — may not be able to obtain protection. A few states also expressly exclude same-sex couples from the reach of their statutes. Protection can be obtained from a wide range of abusive behaviors, including physical abuse, attempted physical abuse, sexual assaults, and threats of harm and harassment. Many types of relief can be included in a protective order, such as ordering the respondent to refrain from further acts of abuse, to vacate the premises, to avoid any contact with the petitioner, and to relinquish any firearms. In most jurisdictions, the courts can also make temporary support and custody awards.

A protective order is usually obtained in two stages. First, the petitioner appears before the court in an ex parte proceeding at which temporary relief may be ordered. The other party is then served with the orders and informed of the right to be heard. At the second hearing, both parties are given the opportunity to present their version of events. The judge may either extend or decline to extend the ex parte order. Specialized domestic violence courts that provide integrated legal and social services are a recent innovation designed to eliminate the disjointed approach to domestic abuse cases.

Effective enforcement procedures are essential to ensure the safety of abuse victims, and much effort has been devoted to increasing the responsiveness of the criminal justice system, including the adoption of mandatory arrest and prosecution policies. These policies are quite controversial. Some experts believe that the policies play a critical role in enhancing victim safety, while others believe that they disempower victims and put them at risk of retaliatory violence. In many states, the violation of a protection order is an independent crime. All states now have anti-stalking laws that criminalize qualifying harassing or threatening behavior.

At the federal level, VAWA has increased protections for domestic violence victims by criminalizing interstate acts of violence and requiring states to give full faith and credit to protective orders. The Act also provides relief to battered immigrants, such as by allowing them to self-petition for lawful permanent resident status, thus avoiding reliance on the batterer and expanding anti-deportation protections.

## Key Terms

Domestic Violence

Intimate Partner Violence

Abuse Prevention Laws

Protective Order

Restraining Order

Vacate Order

Stay-Away Order

Batterer Intervention Program

No-Contact Order

Ex Parte

Temporary Order

Mutual Orders of Protection

Stalking

Cyberstalking

Violence Against Women Act (VAWA)

## Review Questions

1. Why was a husband in ancient Rome permitted to beat his wife?

2. What did English common law and early U.S. law say about wife abuse?

3. What was the attitude of the Puritans toward domestic violence?

4. What did the temperance reformers see as the cause of wife abuse? How did they propose to solve the problem?

5. How did women's rights activists view the problem? How did their proposed solutions differ from those of the temperance reformers'?

6. What was the post—Civil War approach to combating domestic violence?

7. In brief, what is a civil order of protection?

8. What kinds of relationships would qualify for a protective order in an inclusive state?

9. What kinds of qualifications might a statute place on someone who is in a dating relationship? What problems might these qualifications pose?

10. What approaches do states take with respect to same-sex couples?

11. How have some judges in Ohio responded to abuse cases involving unmarried cohabitants following the enactment of the 2004 constitutional amendment limiting marriage to heterosexual couples and denying recognition to marital-like relationships?

12. What kinds of abusive behavior are covered by most abuse prevention laws?

13. What kinds of relief are generally available under an abuse prevention law?

14. Why are gun relinquishment orders important to the safety of victims? What protections are provided by federal law?

15. What kinds of obligations do police officers have toward victims of domestic violence under an abuse prevention law?

16. Explain the two-step process for obtaining a protective order.

17. How are protective orders enforced?

18. What has been the traditional attitude of the criminal justice system toward domestic abuse cases?

19. How has this changed? What new approaches have been adopted?

20. Why are mandatory arrest and prosecution policies controversial?

21. What is stalking?

22. What are the nature and function of specialized domestic violence courts?

23. What are some of the key provisions of VAWA?

## Discussion Questions

1. Many people wonder why battered women do not simply walk away from a relationship after the first incident of abuse. Why do you think this might not be so easy for someone to do?

2. What do you see as the explanation for the prevalence of domestic violence? Do you think it is an expression of anger or stress, or do you believe it says something about power relationships between men and women?

3. Do you think someone who is in a dating relationship should be allowed to seek protection under abuse prevention laws? What about same-sex couples?

4. When a court is making a decision about visitation, how should it balance a woman's right to safety with a father's interest in seeing his children?

5. Do you think that mandatory arrest and prosecution policies make sense? Why or why not?

## Assignments

1. Find the abuse prevention act for your state and determine the following:

   - What court(s) are these cases heard in?
   - Who can petition the court for relief?
   - Are dating partners eligible? If so, are there any qualifications?
   - Is a person in a same-sex relationship eligible to seek relief under the statute?
   - What kinds of protection are available?

2. Using the abuse prevention act located for question 1, trace the court procedure from start to finish. Make sure you include all relevant time frames.

3. Assume that you are doing an internship as a legal advocate at a local battered women's shelter. They have asked you to develop a brochure that sets out the basic elements of your state's abuse prevention law and explains the court process so women coming to the

shelter will know what their legal rights are. The key here is to make sure the brochure is complete, accurate, and comprehensible to the layperson.

4. A number of women are presently serving time for killing their batterers. A controversial question is whether, as part of their defense cases, expert testimony can be admitted regarding the "battered women's syndrome." Assume you are a trial judge who has been asked to rule on the admissibility of such evidence. Research and then write a legal memorandum setting out your conclusion.

5. Assume that you are a legislative aid in a state that is considering adopting a mandatory arrest and prosecution law. In an advisory memo, evaluate the arguments in favor of and against such an approach, and then develop a persuasive position in which you argue in favor of or against such a law.

## Cases for Analysis

In the following case, the court looks to two important legal trends — the increasing protection for victims of domestic violence and the expanding concept of family — in order to grant a restraining order to a grandmother who is raising her grandchild.

### TURNER v. LEWIS
#### 434 Mass. 331, 749 N.E.2d 122 (2001)

This appeal raises the question whether the paternal grandparent of a child whose parents were not married is "related by blood" to the child's mother, and thus, has a right to invoke protection from domestic abuse under G. L. c. 209A. . . . The grandmother has custody of the child, and the child resides with her. . . .

The grandmother makes the following allegations. On September 2, 1999, the mother entered the grandmother's home unannounced and without permission while the grandmother and the child were upstairs. The mother, who appeared "obviously high," yelled for the child and demanded that she come downstairs. The grandmother told her that the child was not at home. When the grandmother then attempted to descend the stairs, the mother blocked her, and punched and pushed her, saying, "You know what I want to do to you, don't you?" The mother then punched the grandmother again and pushed her up against the wall, causing the grandmother's head to hit a windowsill. After hitting the grandmother once more, the mother fled the scene in a van. The grandmother telephoned the police.

The grandmother subsequently filed a . . . complaint against the mother for protection from abuse under G. L. c. 209A. Although a Probate and Family Court judge granted the grandmother an emergency protective order, another Probate and Family Court judge declined to extend that order, because she found that the "parties are [not] related by blood, marriage or household membership" as required by the statute. . . .

In 1978, Massachusetts enacted G. L. c. 209A to address the problem of domestic violence through the provision of judicial remedies. . . . Under G. L. c. 209A, a person "suffering from abuse from an adult or minor family or household member may file a complaint in the court requesting protection from such abuse". . . .

The question in this case is whether the abuse was perpetrated by a "family or household member."[1] Under G. L. c. 209A, § 1, "family or household members" include persons who, among other categories, . . . "(c) are or were related by blood or marriage. . . ." The grandmother claims that the parties are "related by blood" and have a "child in common," and thus, she qualifies for protection under the statute. . . .

Here we conclude that the parties are "related by blood." The paternal grandmother, through her son, is "related by blood" to the child. Likewise, the child and her mother are "related by blood." Thus, the child is "related by blood" to both parties, making the mother and grandmother "related by blood" through that child.

Interpreting the term "related by blood" to include the relationship between the grandmother and the mother would be consistent with the Legislature's purpose in enacting c. 209A. We note first that, in light of the grandmother's custody of the child and the mother's visitation rights with the child, there will likely be significant, albeit unwanted, contact between the mother and the grandmother, a fact particularly evidenced by the events that precipitated this appeal. . . .

Our conclusion is supported by sound public policy. We take judicial notice of the social reality that the concept of "family" is varied and evolving and that, as a result, different types of "family" members will be forced into potentially unwanted contact with one another. The recent increases in both single parent and grandparent headed households are two examples of this trend. . . .

. . . Because of the parental hostility that may accompany grandparental custody, it is imperative that caregivers like the grandmother in this case be protected from such domestic abuse by c. 209A.

These trends require that "domestic violence statutes [such as G. L. c. 209A] offer coverage to a wide range of extended family relationships to fully reflect the reality of American family life [and] . . . the definition of 'family members' embraced by civil protection order statutes must be equally applicable to all concepts of family as they exist in the reality of our diverse family relationships." Klein, Providing Legal Protection for Battered Women: An Analysis of State Statutes and Case Law, 21 Hofstra L. Rev. 801, 818-820 (1993). The relationship here meets the definition of "family," carrying with it all the risks and problems inherent in domestic violence. It is within that familial setting that this grandmother was exposed to violence and the threat of future violence.

For these reasons, we conclude that the grandmother and the defendant are "related by blood," and that the Probate and Family Court's ruling contravenes "the Commonwealth's public policy against domestic abuse — preservation of the fundamental human right to be protected from the devastating impact of family violence." Champagne v. Champagne, *supra* at 327. Accordingly, we vacate the denial of the extension of the protective order. . . .

COWIN, J. (dissenting, with whom SOSMAN, J., joins). I respectfully dissent. In my view, the legislative history indicates that the phrase "related by blood" was not intended to encompass persons such as the paternal grandmother and mother in this case.

The court's decision ignores legislative history and bases its decision on social policy. . . .

. . . I do not believe that it is the court's function to interpret a statute in accordance with the most recent "trend" or judicial perception of what "is best" as a matter of social policy, particularly when such interpretation is not consistent with the statutory language. . . . I recognize that the violence alleged in this case would, in common parlance, be viewed as a form of "domestic" violence, and that the unique remedies of G. L. c. 209A would seem suitable to the situation. However, it is not for this court to engraft G. L. c. 209A onto any dispute that is, in some sense, a "domestic" dispute. The appropriate procedure for protecting a person such as the paternal grandmother in this case is by legislative, not judicial, amendment to G. L. c. 209A.

## QUESTIONS

1. Why did the grandmother in the case seek a restraining order and whom did she seek it against?

2. Why did the trial court deny her request for an order?

3. What was the definitional issue that the court was confronted with?

4. According to the court, how were the parties "related by blood"?

5. According to the court, how was its interpretation of the term "related by blood" consistent with the legislative purpose in enacting the abuse prevention law?

6. What public policies did the court look to in reaching its decision?

---

In the following case, the court grants a protective order based on harassment and the future risk of harm. As in the previous case, the court here is seeking to fully effectuate the protective intent of abuse prevention laws.

### IN RE MARRIAGE OF BLITSTEIN & BLITSTEIN
212 Ill. App. 3d 124, 569 N.E.2d 1357, 155 Ill. Dec. 746 (1991)

Respondent, Berle Blitstein (Berle), appeals from a protective order entered by the circuit court . . . pursuant to the Illinois Domestic Violence Act of 1986 . . . The order gave petitioner, Barbara Blitstein (Barbara), and her children exclusive possession of the marital residence and directed Berle not to abuse or harass them. . . .

Barbara and Berle resided in a 15-room house in Highland Park with their two children and Barbara's child from a prior marriage. . . .

On March 30, 1990, Barbara filed a petition for an order of protection . . . She alleged in the petition that Berle should be prohibited from remaining at the marital home because of an incident that took place on March 29, 1990, in which he allegedly harassed and physically abused her. . . .

. . . Barbara testified that Berle had physically abused her three times prior to the March 29, 1990, incident. She stated that one day in the summer months of 1988, Berle punched her in the shoulder while they were arguing in their bedroom. According to Barbara, Berle pushed her against the bedroom wall during an argument in July 1989. She further testified that during an October 1989 argument, Berle grabbed her and threw her into some kitchen cabinets, injuring her shoulder. During his testimony, Berle denied physically abusing Barbara on any of these three occasions.

With regard to the events of March 29, 1990, Barbara testified that she and Berle were in bed watching television. Barbara asked Berle to turn off the television so she could go to sleep. When Berle refused, Barbara got up and turned the set off. She then started walking down the hall. Berle grabbed her, made some remarks, and then slapped her in the face. According to Barbara, she then told Berle he would never hit her again and ran to the bedroom telephone, which was on a glass table at the side of the bed.

She intended to call the police. Berle grabbed the phone out of Barbara's hand, pushed her onto the bed, and yanked the phone out of the wall. In so doing, he knocked over the glass table and broke some of the glass.

Barbara stated that she then ran to an adjoining sitting room and again attempted to call the police. Berle grabbed the receiver out of her hand, pushed her onto a couch, and yanked that phone out of the wall. Barbara tried to exit the room, but Berle closed the door leading to the hall when she tried to open it, and he blocked the exit for a few minutes. Barbara asked Berle to let her out, but he initially refused to do so, and he called her a bitch. Barbara then yelled for the couple's 12-year-old son, David, who started yelling, "[m]ommy, mommy." Berle then opened the door, and Barbara ran to the laundry room.

Barbara testified that she picked up the laundry room phone and tried to call the police again. Berle grabbed the phone out of her hands and pulled the cord from the wall. Barbara then ran into the maid's room, and David went in with her. She called the police from a phone in the maid's room. Two police officers arrived at the home shortly thereafter. Barbara and David left the house after this incident and temporarily stayed with one of Barbara's friends. Barbara further testified that she had not been employed during the 15 years she had been married to Berle.

With regard to the events of March 29, 1990, Berle testified that he was watching television while in bed with Barbara late that evening. Barbara asked him to turn the set off at about 11:20, and he stated he wished to keep it on another 10 minutes. Barbara then got up and turned the set off. Berle testified that he then went into the adjoining sitting room to watch the television in there. While he was walking toward the sitting room, Barbara pushed him into the wall. She then hit Berle in the arms several times and screamed at him, telling him to go ahead and hit her. Barbara then picked up a bowl and threw it at him.

According to Berle, Barbara continued screaming at him, telling him to hit her so she could call the police and have him thrown out of the house. She then ran to the bedroom and said she was going to call the police. When she started to call, Berle pulled the cord from the phone box out of the wall. While doing so, he fell backwards into the nightstand but did not break any glass on it.

Barbara ran to the sitting room and tried to call the police again. Berle testified that he removed the phone jack from the wall outlet. Barbara and Berle both went to the sitting room door; Berle got there first and stood in front of it. Barbara was screaming, "David, David, daddy is beating me." Berle then heard David saying, "[m]ommy, mommy" from down the hall. Berle then opened the door, and Barbara ran down the hall. Berle tried to comfort David by telling him his parents loved him and everything would be all right. Barbara ran to the maid's room and called the police.

Berle stated that he did not slap or push Barbara at any time during the above incident. Berle also testified that Barbara appeared to be calm and calculated while the incident was taking place. . . . Highland Park police officer Michael Gilbert testified that he arrived at the Blitstein home at about 11:40 on the evening of March 29, 1990. Barbara claimed that Berle had slapped her, but she did not state that he had physically assaulted her in any other manner. Officer Gilbert saw that the nightstand in the bedroom had been overturned. He did not see any broken glass, but it did appear there had been an altercation near the nightstand. Officer Gilbert noticed that phone cords in the bedroom, sitting room, and laundry room had been pulled from the wall; Berle admitted that he had done this. . . .

The trial judge found that Berle had not physically abused Barbara but also found that he had harassed her by pulling out the phone cords which caused her to suffer emotional distress. The judge also found that a risk of future abuse existed, noting that Berle came close to abusing Barbara physically when he blocked the doors in the sitting room and would not allow her to leave. Determining that, because of his income, it would be much easier for Berle to find a new residence than it would be for Barbara, the trial judge entered a protective order directing him to remain away from the marital home and prohibiting him from abusing or harassing Barbara or the children. . . .

Berle argues that, in light of the trial court's finding that he did not physically abuse Barbara, it was error for the court to issue an order of protection excluding him from the marital residence in Highland Park. Under section 214(a) of the Act (Ill. Rev. Stat. 1989, ch. 40, par. 2312 — 14(a)), if the trial court finds that the petitioner has been abused, neglected, or exploited, the court must enter an order of protection prohibiting such abuse, neglect, or exploitation. The term "abuse" is defined to include harassment. (Ill. Rev. Stat. 1989, ch. 40, par. 2311 — 3(1).) The term "harassment" is defined as "knowing conduct which is not necessary to accomplish a purpose that is reasonable under the circumstances; would cause a reasonable person emotional distress; and does cause emotional distress to the petitioner." (Ill. Rev. Stat. 1989, ch. 40, par. 2311 — 3(6).) . . .

The trial judge found that Berle harassed Barbara, relying primarily upon the fact that he pulled three telephone cords from the walls while Barbara tried to call the police. Since, according to the Act, abuse includes harassment, this means the court found that Berle abused her. . . .

Although Berle testified that he only removed two telephone cords from the wall, Barbara testified that he removed three, and Officer Gilbert stated that Berle had admitted removing three. The evidence reveals that Berle pulled the bedroom cord out so violently that he either knocked over the nightstand or caused himself to fall into the nightstand and knock it over. Such conduct would clearly cause emotional distress to one attempting to use the phones. Berle's testimony that Barbara remained calm throughout the March 29 incident is belied by his own further testimony that she was screaming at him and running throughout the house.

Berle argues that he removed the phone cords for a proper purpose, to prevent the police from coming over and disturbing the couple's son, David. The trial court could reasonably have determined, however, that attempting to prevent a party to a domestic dispute from calling the police over to calm the dispute is not a proper purpose. According to the evidence, Berle also physically prevented Barbara from leaving the sitting room for a few minutes by blocking the door. The trial court mentioned this in determining a risk of future abuse existed. Berle had no right to stop Barbara from telephoning the police if she desired to do so, and the extreme measures he took in an effort to stop her from doing this were not justified by his alleged desire to prevent his son from waking up and being disturbed, which occurred anyway. . . .

The trial court's finding that a risk of future abuse existed was not an abuse of discretion. Although the trial judge found that no physical abuse had taken place, Berle's actions were still violent and could easily have led to physical violence between the couple. The Act is to be construed liberally to protect victims of domestic violence, help them avoid further abuse, and to expand the remedies for victims of domestic violence including, when necessary, physical separation of the parties. . . .

Although Berle argues that a lesser remedy, such as ordering him to sleep in a separate bedroom, should have been used, the trial judge could have reasonably determined in light of the tension between the parties and Berle's violent conduct on March 29 that one of them would have to leave the home to prevent potential future violence. . . .

## QUESTIONS

1. What were the findings of the trial court judge?

2. On what basis did the judge grant the protective order to the wife?

3. Why did the husband argue that the order was in error?

4. Why did the appeals court decide the trial court was correct when it issued the order?

In the following case, a woman whose children were killed by her husband sued her attorney for negligence based on his failure to seek a protective order despite her repeated requests that he do so.

## ROBERTS v. HEALEY
### 991 S.W.2d 873 (Tex. 1999)

FACTS

Karin Roberts married Daniel Charles Kennedy on July 6, 1991, and they had two children, Ashli Patriciamae, born on December 10, 1991, and Alexis Marie, born on March 20, 1994. During the marriage, Kennedy developed a drug habit and became increasingly unstable. By September 1994, Kennedy's behavior had become so erratic that Karin asked him to move out of their mobile home. On October 11, 1994, Karin contacted Healey's office to discuss representation in a divorce and scheduled an appointment for October 13.

Kennedy made harassing telephone calls and pages to Karin, including several threats which she relayed to Healey. Karin also told Healey about Kennedy's drug use. At Healey's request, Karin prepared a narrative outlining Kennedy's violent history to be used in obtaining a temporary restraining order. Healey converted the outline into an affidavit, which Karin later signed. Healey then filed an application for a restraining order with the original divorce petition, but never made any effort to obtain a signed protective order despite repeated calls from Karin and her mother, Marjorie Roberts . . .

Because of Kennedy's behavior, Karin moved to a new apartment with her daughters. On one occasion, she called the police and asked that they keep Kennedy from following her because she was afraid Kennedy would locate her new apartment.

On November 1, 1994, Kennedy attempted to commit suicide, which Karin reported to Healey. Kennedy was admitted to a psychiatric ward, but checked out two days later. A few days later, Kennedy left a note on the door of Karin's apartment. Fearful that Kennedy had learned where she lived, Karin immediately took the note to Healey's office and gave it to his secretary.

On November 16, 1994, Kennedy, while high on cocaine, confronted Karin in the parking lot outside her apartment as she was leaving for work. Kennedy forced Karin to accompany him to the apartment, where he broke in and shot and killed his two children. He also shot and wounded his mother-in-law, Marjorie, and then committed suicide.

Appellants then filed this suit, contending Healey's failure to obtain a protective order constituted negligence . . . which caused the deaths of the two children, the wounding of Marjorie, and the resulting damages ... The trial court granted Healey's motion for summary judgment ... and this appeal resulted.

## CAUSATION

... Healey argued that his failure to obtain a protective order against Kennedy was not ... the proximate or producing cause of appellants' injuries ... Proximate cause consists of cause in fact and foreseeability ... Cause in fact does not exist if the defendant's negligence does no more than furnish a condition which made the injury possible.

... Healey argued that even if he had obtained a protective order Kennedy would nevertheless have killed his daughters and shot Marjorie. Therefore, Healey contends his failure to actually obtain a protective order did not cause the injuries, and that even if a protective order had been entered, it would not have deterred Kennedy. As proof, he attached to his summary judgment motion a portion of Karin's deposition stating she lied to Kennedy on the day of the attack telling him she already had a protective order in an attempt to prevent his violent acts.

At some point in the causal chain, the defendant's conduct may be too remotely connected with the plaintiff's injury to constitute legal causation. See Union Pump, 898 S.W.2d at 775. The court in Union Pump noted the difficulty we face here, of drawing the line where legal causation may exist and where, as a matter of law, it cannot. Id. The court held that legal cause is not established if the defendant's conduct does no more than furnish the condition that makes the plaintiff's injury possible. 898 S.W.2d at 776. Viewing the evidence in the light most favorable to Karin, Healey's failure to obtain a protective order did no more than create the condition (absence of a protective order) that enabled Kennedy to kill Karin's children and wound her mother ... We hold that Healey's failure to obtain a protective order is too attenuated from Kennedy's criminal conduct to constitute a legal cause of injury to Karin, her mother, and her children.

While there may be a fact question as to foreseeability because Healey was aware of numerous threats made by Kennedy immediately prior to his attack, it is immaterial in the absence of legal cause. We hold Healey conclusively disproved cause in fact so as to entitle him to summary judgment.

## QUESTIONS

1. What legal concept does this case turn on? Why does the court decide against the plaintiff with respect to her negligence claim?

2. Why don't you think the attorney obtained a protective order on behalf of his client?

3. Do you think the attorney was responsible for what happened — why or why not?

# Endnotes ————————————————————————————

1. Please note that although much of the language in this chapter is cast in gender-neutral terms, gender-specific terminology is also used because most perpetrators of intimate partner violence are male and most victims are women.

2. R. Emerson Dobash and Russell Dobash, Violence Against Wives 35 (1979) (citing Not in God's Image: Women in History (Julia O'Faolain and Lauro Martines eds., 1974)).

3. Joyner v. Joyner, 59 N.C. 324, 325 (1862).

4. This section draws heavily on Elizabeth Pleck: Domestic Tyranny: The Making of American Social Policy Against Domestic Violence from Colonial Times to the Present (1987).

5. *Id.* at 17-31.

6. *Id.* at 108-121.

7. *Id.* at 125-126, 138-142.

8. *Id.* at 145-150.

9. Shannon Catalano, Intimate Partner Violence in the United States (2006), U.S. Department of Justice, Office of Justice Programs, Bureau of Justice Statistics, http://www.ojp.usdoj.gov/bjs/ (accessed December 29, 2006).

10. Intimate Partner Violence Declined Between 1993 and 2004, Press Release issued on December 28, 2006, Department of Justice, Office of Justice Programs, Bureau of Justice Statistics, http://www.ojp.usdoj.gov/bjs/ (accessed December 29, 2006).

11. Catherine F. Klein and Leslye E. Orloff, Providing Legal Protection for Battered Women: An Analysis of State Statutes and Case Law, 21 Hofstra L. Rev. 801, 825-829 (1993).

12. For facts on some of the gendered aspects of dating violence, see: The Facts on Teenagers and Intimate Partner Abuse, http://www.endabuse.org (accessed May 17, 2007).

13. Mass. Gen. Laws Ann. ch. 209A, § 1, http://www.mass.gov/legis/laws/ mgl/gl-209a-toc.htm (accessed September 27, 2004).

14. Christine N. Carlson, Violence Against Women: Invisible Victims: Holding the Educational System Liable for Teen Dating Violence at School, 26 Harv. Women's L.J. 351, 360 (2003).

15. Ohio Const. art. XV, sect. 11.

16. For a detailed discussion of what has transpired in Ohio, *see* C. Susie Lorden, The Law of Unintended Consequences: The Far-Reaching Effects of Same-Sex Marriage Ban Amendments, 25 Quinnipiac L. Rev. 211 (2006). As Lorden discusses, this split of authority most likely will be resolved through legislative action or a decision of the Ohio Supreme Court.

17. Klein and Orloff, *supra* note 11, at 859.

18. John Hopkins University, Center for Gun Policy and Research, Fact Sheet, "Firearms and Intimate Partner Violence." To access, go to: *http://www.jhsph. edu.* Click on Research Centers and Institutes, then click on John Hopkins Center for Gun Policy and Research. From here, click on Research and Publications, then click on Center Publications for this report.

19. *Id.*

20. This law is codified at 18 U.S.C. §§ 922 (g)(8). This provision contains an exception for certain government employees, such as police officers and military personnel, who are required to carry a weapon as part of their official duties.

21. This law is codified at 18 U.S.C. § 924(g)(9). Unlike the protective order provision (see footnote 20), the "official-use" exception does not apply to government employees who have been convicted of a misdemeanor. For further detail, *see* Lisa D. May, The Backfiring of the Domestic Violence Firearm Bans, 14 Colum. J. Gender & L. 1 (2005); Deborah Epstein, Margaret E. Bell, and Lisa A. Goodman, Transforming Aggressive Prosecution Policies: Prioritizing Victims' Long-Term Safety in the Prosecution of Domestic Violence Cases, 11 Am. U. J. Gender Soc. Poly. & L. 465 (2003); and Darren Mitchell and Susan B. Carbon, Firearms and Domestic Violence: A Primer for Judges, 39 Court Rev. 32 (2002).

22. Donna Coker, Criminal Control and Feminist Law Reform in Domestic Violence Law: A Critical Review, 4 Buff. L. Rev. 801, 823-826 (2001).

23. Erin L. Han, Mandatory Arrest and No-Drop Policies: Victim Empowerment in Domestic Violence Cases, 23 B.C. Third World L.J. 159, 176 (2003).

24. *See, e.g.,* Deborah Epstein, Margaret E. Bell, and Lisa A. Goodman, Transforming Aggressive Prosecution Policies: Prioritizing Victims' Long-Term Safety in the Prosecution of Domestic Violence Cases, 11 Am. U. J. Gender Soc. Poly. & L. 465 (2003).

25. Unlike abuse prevention laws, anti-stalking laws generally do not impose a "special" relationship qualification on the parties. This breadth of application is also true of the federal anti-stalking law, known as the Interstate Stalking Punishment and Prevention Act of 1996 (18 U.S.C. § 2261A (2004)), which prohibits persons from crossing state lines in order to injure or harass another individual.

26. *See* Patricia Tjaden and Nancy Thoennes, The Role of Stalking in Domestic Violence Crimes Reports Generated by the Colorado Springs Police Department. (2001) This article can be accessed on line at: http://www.ncjrs.gov/App/Publications/alphaList.aspx?alpha=S (accessed May 5, 2007).

27. Strengthening Anti-Stalking Statutes, Legal Series Bulletin #1. http://www.ncjrs.gov/App/Publications/alphaList.aspx?alpha=S (accessed May 5, 2007).

28. Judge Lowell D. Castleton, Bruce J. Castleton, Melissa M. Bonney, & Amber M. Moe, Ada County Family Violence Court: Shaping the Means to Better the Result, 39 Family L. Q. 27, 31 (2005).

29. Betsy Tsai, The Trend Toward Specialized Domestic Violence Courts: Improvements on an Effective Innovation, 68 Fordham L. Rev. 1285, 1292 (2000) 29. *Id.* at 1302.

30. Jennifer Thompson, Who's Afraid of Judicial Activism? Reconceptualizing a Traditional Paradigm in the Context of Specialized Domestic Violence Courts, 56 Me. L. Rev. 407, 428 (2004), *citing* Tsai, *supra* note 30, at 1298.

31. Violence Against Women Act, Pub. L. No. 103-322, 108 Stat. 1902 (1994). VAWA was enacted as Title IV of the Violent Crime Control and Enforcement Act of 1974, Pub. L. No. 103-322, 108 Stat. 1796 (1994).

32. Victims of Trafficking and Violence Protection Act of 2000, Pub. L. No. 109-162, 114 Stat. 1464 (2000) (codified in scattered sections).

33. Violence Against Women Reauthorization Act of 2005, Pub. L. No. 109-162, 119 Stat. 2960 (2006). For a comparative discussion of the provisions of the successive Acts, *see* Leila Abolfazli, Violence Against Women Act, 7 Geo. Gender and L. 863, (2006). For an excellent chart comparing the provisions of VAWA II and III, visit the web site of the National Coalition Against Domestic Violence, http://www.ncadv.org (accessed December 29, 2006).

34. As quoted in Abolfazli, *supra* note 35, at 880.

35. Implementation of the initial full faith and credit provision of the Violence Against Women Act of 1994 proved difficult; as a result, Congress made some changes when it reenacted VAWA in 2000. Additionally, in response to remaining inconsistencies and unanswered questions, the National Conference of Commissioners on Uniform State Laws (NCCUSL) in 2000 approved the Uniform Interstate Enforcement of Domestic Violence Protection Orders Act, which has since been adopted by at least 11 states.

# 4 The Law of Divorce, Annulment, and Legal Separation

Put simply, **divorce** is the legal dissolution of a marital relationship. Marriage creates a legal bond; divorce severs it. For the divorcing couple, however, divorce is not this simple; the process is multidimensional, with profound emotional, spiritual, economic, and legal consequences. Lives are profoundly reshaped — often in unanticipated ways. For some, divorce brings tremendous relief and a welcome opportunity to build a better life; for others, it brings loneliness or new relationships that recycle the difficulties of the past.[1]

This chapter focuses on the substantive law of divorce. As you read the chapter and as you work with people going through a divorce, it is important to be aware that the applicable legal principles are not mere abstractions but touch the core of people's lives. Accordingly, divorce law should not be thought of in isolation from its human context. (For a discussion on working with emotionally distraught clients, see Chapter 10 on the divorce process.)

## HISTORICAL OVERVIEW

During the final quarter of the last century, this country underwent a divorce "revolution." Starting with California in 1970, all states adopted some form of no-fault divorce law. Now an integral part of our legal landscape, many people today take the availability of no-fault divorce for granted. However, the no-fault principle is a radically new concept. To understand the significance of this change, we begin with a historical overview of divorce law. We start in premodern England, as our present system is rooted in the English experience.

## Religious Underpinnings ————————————————————————

### Marriage as an Indissoluble Bond

Throughout history, many societies practiced divorce by mutual consent of the parties. This was true in what was to become England and much of Western Europe until sometime into the tenth or eleventh century, when marriage came under the authority of the Catholic Church. As the church gained in influence, a cohesive theology emerged, and a systematic body of canon law, including laws regulating marriage, was developed.[2] According to the teachings of the Church, marriage was a sacrament. It conferred grace on a couple and was a spiritual instrument of salvation. The relationship between a husband and a wife was thought to mirror the loving bond between Christ and His Church. Like the bond between Christ and His Church, the marital bond between a husband and wife was considered to be **indissoluble**.

Since it was a sacrament, marriage was placed under the exclusive authority of the church. Divorce was strictly prohibited, but an individual could petition the ecclesiastical courts for an **annulment** or a legal separation (also known as a *divorce a mensa et thoro*—a divorce from board and bed). Neither of these procedures ran afoul of the doctrine of indissolubility. As discussed later in this chapter, an annulment is essentially a statement that due to existing impediments no valid marriage was ever created, and a divorce from board and bed allowed an innocent spouse to live apart from her or his sinful spouse without dissolving the marital bond.

### The Protestant Reformation

In the early 1500s, the Protestant Reformation challenged many of the Catholic Church's teachings, including those related to marriage. According to Reformation thinkers, marriage was not a sacrament—it was of this world and carried no promise of spiritual redemption. Having divested marriage of its holy and redemptive status, the Protestants accepted the necessity of divorce in cases involving grievous marital sins committed in violation of Christian principles.[3]

### The English Experience

Influenced by the Reformation, many western European nations became Protestant. Divorce was permitted, and both marriage and divorce came under the control of civil rather than religious authorities. However, in England, the pattern was different. Although King Henry VIII broke with the Catholic Church in 1534 and established the Church of England, the Catholic view of marriage as a sacrament was retained. As a result, divorce was not permitted, and marriage remained under Church control until 1857—far later than the rest of Western Europe. By way of historical interest, it should be noted that King Henry's decision to break from the Church was at least in part motivated by the fact that the Pope refused to annul his marriage to Catherine of Aragon when she failed to provide him with a son.

## The American Experience

### Divorce in the Colonies

Divorce generally was accepted much earlier in this country than it was in England due mainly to the influence of Protestantism. During the colonial period, the availability of divorce varied from region to region. In the New England colonies, divorce was available from the start, although in some areas, only the legislature had the authority to dissolve a marriage. Here, the colonists, mainly Pilgrims and Puritans, although profoundly religious, believed that marriage was a civil concern. For them, the family unit was the foundation on which their pious commonwealth was based. Because these two domains were so closely intertwined, family instability was thought to threaten the stability of the community. Accordingly, if a spouse maltreated his or her partner, and reconciliation was impossible, the New England colonists believed it was important for the innocent spouse to be released from the marriage so he or she could move on to form a new functional family unit. The guilty spouse was usually prohibited from remarrying and creating another dysfunctional family that would again threaten the well-being of the community.[4]

In contrast, divorce was unheard of in most of the southern colonies. Here, the teachings of the Church of England held sway, and marriage was regarded as indissoluble, although, as in England, both annulments and divorces from board and bed were permitted. The middle colonies appear to have occupied a middle position between New England, where divorce was well established, and the South, where it was prohibited.

In no region of the country did slaves have formal access to divorce, mainly because the colonists refused to honor the validity of marriages between enslaved persons. However, although their practices were not formally recognized, slaves created their own marriage rituals, and historians have located records indicating that some African American churches granted divorces to married slaves. Additionally, although again outside the formal bounds of the law, some plantation owners may have recognized and regulated marriage and divorce among their slaves.

### The Rising Tide

Following the colonies' independence from England, two trends became apparent. The divorce rate began to rise rapidly, and many states, including the once-recalcitrant southern states, amended their laws to add new divorce grounds, making divorce somewhat easier to obtain.

A number of factors contributed to this loosening of laws and attitudes. For one, revolutionary ferment found its way into the domestic sphere. Leaders such as Thomas Jefferson transposed arguments about individual rights to liberty and happiness from the struggle against England to the marital context. Divorce was needed to oust spousal tyrants and ensure that women were not trapped in domestic regimes that denied them their humanity. Thus, themes that fueled the revolution contributed to an acceptance of divorce.[5] This connection between divorce and the emancipation of women would be picked up by women's rights reformers in the next century.

Changing expectations about the marital relationship also contributed to a greater acceptance of divorce. With industrialization, production moved out of the home, and the family no longer stood at the center of economic activity. The significance of marriage as an economic arrangement diminished, and spouses increasingly looked to each other for love and companionship. As spouses came to expect more from one another, the risk of disappointment also increased, as marriage did not always provide the parties with what they were looking for. As a result, there was an increased acceptance of divorce as a necessary safety valve for spouses who were trapped in failed marriages.[6]

Despite these changes, divorce was still understood in very narrow terms. Rooted in the Puritan belief of marital wrong as sinful conduct, divorce required serious **marital fault**, and only an **innocent spouse** was entitled to a divorce. Divorce was understood as a remedy for the innocent spouse and a punishment for the guilty one. It was not regarded as a right, but as an evil made necessary by the realities of human existence.[7]

Nonetheless, the rising divorce rates and the expansion of divorce grounds, which in a few states went as far as permitting divorce whenever "just and reasonable," evoked a storm of outrage by those who feared that these trends signaled the moral disintegration of both family and society. The debate raged, and in 1885, the National Divorce Reform League, later renamed the National League for the Protection of the Family, was established to limit the spread of divorce and restore moral order.

By the turn of the century, anti-divorce activists could claim some success. They helped slow the move toward more expansive divorce grounds and secured the repeal of some liberalized divorce laws.[8] For the most part, until the no-fault divorce reform movement of the 1970s, divorce remained firmly linked — at least officially — to grievous marital wrongdoing (but see the discussion of collusive divorce below). By retaining the link to fault, divorce law supported the permanency of marriage through limiting the permissible grounds for marital exits while also acknowledging the reality of spousal cruelty and marital failure.

## FAULT DIVORCE: COMMON GROUNDS AND DEFENSES

In the wake of no-fault divorce reform, **fault divorce** tumbled from its place of preeminence. Some states abolished fault-based divorce altogether and now have only no-fault grounds; in other states, no-fault grounds were added to existing fault grounds, and fault divorce remains an option. The following discussion focuses on three of the most commonly available fault grounds and the primary defenses to charges of marital misconduct. As always, you need to check the specifics of your state's laws because other statutory options may be available. (See Chapters 7 and 8 for a discussion of the role that fault plays in determining spousal awards and the division of property.)

## Divorce Grounds

### Adultery

Historically, adultery has been regarded as the most serious marital wrong and has been the most widely accepted ground for divorce. **Adultery** is generally defined as an act of sexual intercourse by a married person with someone other than his or her spouse. In the past, the law did not treat a husband's extramarital relations as seriously as a wife's transgressions. In many states, a woman could not obtain a divorce for adultery unless she could also establish aggravating circumstances, such as cruelty, or that her husband had engaged in a course of adulterous conduct, whereas a man had to show only that his wife had committed a single adulterous act. Although no longer legally true today, some experts believe that social attitudes have not necessarily changed, and that many people continue to regard adultery by a woman, especially if she is a mother, as a greater wrong than when committed by a man.

Because there are usually no eyewitnesses, a claim of adultery, when disputed, is generally established by circumstantial evidence. A party must show that his or her spouse had both the opportunity and the disposition or inclination to commit adultery. Relevant evidence might include love letters, public displays of affection, and frequent visits to a home or hotel, or the introduction of venereal disease into the marriage.

Recently, several courts have addressed the question of whether "adultery" is limited to acts of sexual intercourse between a man and a woman, or whether it can be defined to include sexual relations between a married person and someone of the same sex. Most courts that have considered this issue have concluded that adultery is not limited to heterosexual intercourse. As one court explained: "We view appellant's definition of adultery as unduly narrow and overly dependent upon the term sexual intercourse. . . . [E]xplicit extra-marital sexual activity constitutes adultery regardless of whether it is of a homosexual or heterosexual character."[9] However, in 2003, the New Hampshire Supreme Court reached the opposite conclusion. Relying on both the dictionary meaning of *adultery* and nineteenth century case law, the court held that the "concept of adultery was premised upon a specific act. To include in that concept other acts of a sexual nature, whether between heterosexuals or homosexuals, would change beyond recognition this well established ground for divorce."[10] The dissenting justices argued that the majority was closing its eyes to "the sexual realities of our world" and that a more realistic definition of adultery would include all "extra marital intimate sexual activity with another, regardless of the specific intimate sexual acts performed, the marital status, or the gender of the third party."[11]

### Desertion/Abandonment

**Desertion** (or abandonment) has long been accepted as an appropriate ground for divorce. Prior to no-fault divorce, desertion was particularly important in states that did not recognize cruelty or construed it narrowly (see below). As a general rule, desertion requires a departure from the marital residence. Some courts have held that the refusal to have a sexual relationship with one's spouse satisfies the separation requirement even if the parties remain in the marital home; however, withdrawal from other aspects of the marital relationship is unlikely to be considered desertion.

In most jurisdictions, a spouse must prove the following elements to establish desertion:

1. That there has been a voluntary separation;
2. for the statutory period;
3. with the intent not to return;

4. without consent; and
5. without justification.

For the separation to qualify, the departing spouse must leave of his or her own will. An involuntary departure, such as where a person is drafted, jailed, or committed to a mental hospital, is not desertion. The separation must exist continuously for the statutory time period. Interruptions by, for example, a good-faith offer of reconciliation or even a single act of sexual intercourse may stop the time from running. As a general rule, the calculation of time begins again if there is a second departure — the time periods cannot be added together.

It is not desertion if the "stay-at-home" spouse consents to the departure because desertion by its very nature is a nonconsensual act. If the departure is justified, such as where a spouse flees physical abuse, it is also not classified as desertion. In fact, the spouse who has caused the departure through his or her misconduct may be considered as the deserting spouse based on the doctrine of **constructive desertion**, which imputes the act of desertion to the spouse responsible for the other's departure.[12]

### Cruelty

In most states, **cruelty** was not initially included as a ground for divorce, but by the late 1800s, most divorce statutes had been amended to add it as a ground. It soon became the most commonly used ground. Statutes employ a variety of terms such as "extreme cruelty," "cruel and inhuman treatment," and "indignities," but the meaning is generally the same. Initially, borrowing from ecclesiastical law, cruelty was narrowly defined to include only repeated acts of severe physical abuse that inflicted bodily harm. The concept has gradually expanded and in most states it now includes acts of mental as well as physical cruelty, although some jurisdictions require that the mental cruelty result in some kind of physical symptoms. Proof that the symptoms abated or improved after the parties separated may also be required. The thinking here is that by requiring "objective" evidence of physical impairment, trivial or false claims of cruelty will be weeded out. However, many courts accept fairly general and unsubstantiated statements about loss of sleep, changes in appetite, and increased anxiety as proof of physical impairment.[13]

## Defenses

When marital fault is alleged, the defendant-spouse can raise legal defenses to absolve him- or herself of marital wrongdoing. If successful, the divorce cannot be granted on the basis of the alleged fault. However, because most divorce actions are ultimately settled, these defenses are of little practical significance. Moreover, because of the availability of no-fault divorce, when cases are contested, the dispute almost always involves matters of custody, support, and the like, rather than the grounds for the divorce itself. Nonetheless, some familiarity with the major defenses is important, as a defendant-spouse may need to raise a defense in responding to a fault complaint. (See Chapter 10 on the divorce process.)

### Connivance

The essence of the defense of **connivance** is consent. This defense has primarily been used in adultery cases in which the defendant-spouse seeks to prove the party seeking the divorce consented to the adultery, such as by helping to arrange the liaison. In some states, a more passive course of action, such as a spouse's not actively seeking to prevent a known affair, constitutes connivance.

### Condonation

The essence of the defense of **condonation** is forgiveness. If a spouse forgives his or her partner's marital misconduct, this misconduct can no longer be the basis of a divorce action; condonation restores the marital innocence of the erring spouse. In some states, if a spouse reengages in wrongful activity, the condonation may be canceled and the original divorce grounds revived.

States differ as to what constitutes forgiveness. In some states, engaging in sexual relations after the plaintiff has learned of the misconduct is by itself condonation; here, the plaintiff's state of mind is irrelevant. In other states, the plaintiff's state of mind is key; the plaintiff must actually forgive the defendant—forgiveness will not be inferred from resumed intimacy.

### Recrimination

The defense of **recrimination** has been subject to much criticism and has been abolished in many jurisdictions. Here, a defendant-spouse, rather than seeking to defeat a divorce by minimizing the wrongfulness of his or her conduct, seeks to defeat it by showing that the plaintiff-spouse, rather than being an innocent victim, is also guilty of marital wrongdoing. When mutual wrongdoing is established, neither spouse is entitled to a divorce, and the couple must remain married even though each has treated the other badly. Although seemingly illogical, this defense is rooted in the view of divorce as a remedy for the innocent; accordingly, when both spouses are guilty of marital transgressions, neither qualifies as the innocent victim entitled to relief. In some states the harshness of this result has been modified by the doctrine of **comparative rectitude**, which allows a court to grant a divorce if the plaintiff-spouse's wrongdoing is adjudged to be less serious than the defendant's.

### Collusion

**Collusion** involves an agreement by a couple to obtain a divorce and the deliberate crafting of a case for presentation to the court. Collusion can occur in several ways. The parties could agree that one spouse would actually commit a marital wrong, such as adultery, in order to provide grounds for divorce (this would also be considered connivance). More likely, the parties would agree to fabricate a marital wrong, exaggerate the extent of their discontent with one another, or fail to present a valid defense. This ground runs counter to the basic assumptions of the fault system, which conceptualizes divorce as an adversarial process. The reality is that although collusion is generally classified as a defense, it is unlikely to be raised by either party because it would prevent the granting of the divorce that the parties were attempting to set up.

## NO-FAULT DIVORCE

During the 1960s, fault divorce came under increasing attack; by 1970, no-fault reform was well under way; and by 1985, **no-fault divorce** was available in virtually all states. As part of this effort to move away from the adversarial model of the past, many states also began to use the word *dissolution* instead of divorce, thus signaling a new emphasis on the state of the marriage rather than the conduct of the parties.[14]

## The Underpinnings of Reform

During the 1960s, there was a groundswell of support for divorce reform. Critics of the fault system argued that it was outmoded and ineffectual and that the time had come to give couples the option of divorcing without having to prove marital wrongdoing. The following discussion sets out some of their major criticisms.

Reformers pointed to the practice of collusion as an indication that something was not working with the fault model. In a collusive divorce, spouses who wanted out of their marriage would agree to divorce and then carefully stage the process. In most cases, the defendant would simply fail to appear at the divorce hearing, and the trial court would accept the plaintiff's pro forma recitation about fault. In other cases, fault evidence was manufactured; most commonly, acts of adultery were staged. Some lawyers even helped in the process by providing the paramour, most often the office secretary, to pose for the adulterous photographs. It has been suggested that judges may have been aware of the collusive nature of many divorce actions, but chose to ignore it.

According to historians, the practice of collusion began at the end of World War I and became increasingly frequent over the course of the following decades. It thus appears that although the law on the books was strict in terms of fault requirements, for much of the twentieth century the reality was quite different, as couples were successfully exiting marriages in the absence of proven fault.[15] Reformers hoped that the introduction of no-fault divorce would bring the law into conformity with actual practice and end the hypocrisy of collusive divorce.

Another powerful criticism was that in noncollusive cases, the focus on fault increased the anger and hostility between the parties, especially since financial awards were often influenced by considerations of fault. The legal system was blamed for heightening antagonism by forcing couples into an adversarial posture, thus destroying any hope of reconciliation and making reasoned custody negotiations impossible. Reformers hoped that by eliminating fault, the process would become less adversarial and thus less destructive to the parties and their children.

Fault divorce was further criticized as being out of keeping with the contemporary understanding of marital relationships. Reformers argued that the messy reality of people's marriages did not conform to the fault model, which naively assumed that all marital breakups involved a good spouse and a bad spouse and that this determination could be made simply by identifying who had committed the marital wrong. To reformers, it had become apparent that the named ground was often a symptom of marital distress rather than the actual cause of the breakup. For example, an affair, rather than being the singular "bad" act that brought a marriage to an end, might instead be a response to a complete withdrawal of affection on the part of the other spouse, thus making it unfair to characterize the affair as the only marital transgression.

In light of rising divorce rates, it was also clear to reformers that strict divorce laws were not forcing couples to resolve their difficulties and remain together in furtherance of the state's interest in marital permanency. Moreover, in keeping with the trend toward greater individual autonomy and privacy within the domestic realm, reformers argued that the right of an unhappy spouse to leave a marriage should not be subordinated to the state's interest in family preservation. Rather than being forced into legal pigeonholes in accordance with the state's view of what kinds of wrongs justified marital departures, reformers believed that an unhappy spouse should have greater control over when and why to leave a marriage. In effect, divorce began to be seen as more of a right than a strictly controlled remedy for a spouse aggrieved by marital wrongdoing.

In seeking to shift the balance from the historic interest of the state in family preservation toward the right of an unhappy spouse to leave a failed marriage, some reformers were influenced by the women's rights movement, which insisted that women be seen as autonomous, self-defining individuals, rather than primarily as dependent members of family units. Claiming greater educational and employment rights for women, activists encouraged women not to remain trapped in marriages that threatened their physical and emotional well-being. As with no-fault reform, here too we see a greater emphasis on the needs and aspirations of individual spouses within a marriage, rather than upon the enduring social importance of the marital unit.

## No-Fault Laws

Beginning with California in 1970, no-fault reform swept the country. Within 15 years, the legal landscape had been radically altered. When California reformed its law, it essentially opted to abolish all fault grounds and replace them with a single no-fault standard. A significant number of states followed California's lead and now have only no-fault grounds. A majority of states, however, chose to maintain their existing fault grounds and add no-fault provisions, thus creating a dual system of divorce.

### No-Fault Grounds

There are two primary no-fault grounds: **marital breakdown** and **living separate and apart**, with the former being the most common. A few states have combined these grounds and require proof of both a marital breakdown and a separation. Although both grounds will be discussed below in greater detail, keep in mind that many states have unique requirements, making familiarity with the laws of your jurisdiction essential.

**Marital Breakdown.** Marital breakdown is the principal no-fault ground. Statutes use a variety of terms to express this essential concept — such as **"irreconcilable differences"** or the **"irretrievable"** or **"irremediable breakdown"** of the marriage. Whichever term is used, the emphasis is on the failed state of the marital relationship rather than on the conduct of the spouses.

At least in theory, the judge at the divorce hearing is supposed to conduct a searching inquiry into whether the marriage is in fact broken and beyond hope of repair. (See Chapter 10 on the divorce process.) Factors relevant to this determination include the following:

- the degree to which the parties are unable to relate to one another
- the extent of any differences between them
- prior efforts to resolve their marital difficulties
- whether there is any hope of reconciliation

Many states specifically bar evidence of fault; in other states such evidence is not considered relevant, except perhaps to help establish the extent of the breakdown.

No-fault hearings were not intended to be mere rubber stamps of the parties' decision, and judges in most states have considerable discretion to decide whether or not a marriage is truly over. In fact, some reformers hoped to give judges more freedom to deny a divorce if they believed there was any hope of reconciliation than they had under the fault system, where proof of fault mandated the granting of the divorce. Accordingly, in some states, a judge can stay the proceedings until the parties have sought counseling if the judge is not convinced that the marriage is over.

In reality, however, it appears that searching inquiries into whether a marriage is really over are rare. Couples are generally taken at their word that the marriage is beyond repair, and a few states have eliminated the requirement of a hearing if there are no collateral issues to resolve.

Many states do not require both parties to agree that the marriage is over before a no-fault divorce can be granted. This raises the possibility that a spouse could seek to block the divorce by expressing his or her continued love and belief that the marriage was still intact or not beyond repair; but most judges will grant a divorce in this situation on the basis that a viable partnership does not exist where each spouse has such a radically different view of the relationship. When faced with this situation, a judge, where allowed to do so, might stay the proceedings and order the couple into counseling.

**Living Separate and Apart.** The other major no-fault ground is that the parties have lived separate and apart for a statutory period of time. Time periods range from about 18 months to three years, with most falling somewhere in between. The underlying assumption is that the separation itself is proof of marital breakdown, and judicial inquiry into the relationship's demise is not required. The term "separate and apart" has generally been construed to require separate residences, but some courts have granted a divorce when a couple remained under the same roof but had essentially ceased all interaction for the requisite time period.

Some courts impose an intent requirement and will not qualify the separation even if it lasts for the statutory period unless the parties intended for it to be a permanent one. Thus, if a separation begins as a temporary one, the statutory period will not start to run unless and until the parties decide to make the separation permanent. Some states also require that the separation be voluntary on the part of both parties. Accordingly, if the parties are living apart because of desertion, flight from abuse, or over the objection of one spouse, the separation is not voluntary and will not qualify the parties for a divorce. Similarly, a separation caused by involuntary circumstances such as the draft, hospitalization, or incarceration would not be a valid ground for divorce. Also, when one spouse is mentally incompetent, a separation initiated by the other spouse will not generally be regarded as voluntary if the noninitiating spouse lacks the ability to comprehend what is going on and to give his or her consent. In a few states, the separation need be voluntary only on the part of one spouse.

Where voluntariness is required, a separation that begins involuntarily can be converted into a voluntary one if the parties agree they wish to live apart. The running of the statutory period is calculated from the time the parties reached this agreement rather than from the time of the initial separation. Many jurisdictions, however, do not impose a voluntariness requirement; accordingly, virtually any separation for the statutory time period can ripen into a divorce action.

## The Divorce Counterrevolution

No-fault divorce has come under increasing criticism from individuals and groups who believe it is undermining the institution of marriage. In 1996, in an effort to strengthen marriage, State Representative Jesse Dahlman of Michigan introduced one of the nation's first comprehensive divorce reform bills. Asserting that no-fault divorce is tantamount to "legalized desertion,"[16] and that "[d]isposable marriage cheapens the commitment and degrades our vows of fidelity and lifelong love,"[17] she proposed eliminating "unilateral" no-fault divorce by requiring proof of fault if one spouse objected to the divorce.

Since then, a variety of divorce-reform proposals have been introduced in states across the country with the common goal of making a no-fault divorce more difficult to obtain. Also, in 2000, a grassroots national "Marriage Movement" was born for the purpose of "renewing a marriage culture."[18] As we will see, many view this trend with concern. They fear that those seeking to limit the availability of no-fault divorce aim to turn back the hands of time by reimposing outdated notions of marriage on contemporary couples. They question both the analysis of the harms of no-fault divorce as well as the proposed solutions.[19]

### The Debate over No-Fault Divorce

**Critics of No-Fault Divorce.** Critics contend that no-fault divorce has contributed to a "divorce culture" that emphasizes the pursuit of individual happiness and fulfillment over commitment to one's spouse and children. According to this view, rather than accepting that all marriages have their ebbs and flows and that it takes effort to sustain intimacy, no-fault divorce encourages spouses to walk out the door in pursuit of their own goals. No-fault divorce is thus blamed for cheapening the meaning of connection and permanence with its seductive promise of an easy way out. As one activist puts it: "No-fault divorce does not expand everyone's personal choice. It empowers the spouse who wishes to leave. . . . The spouse who chooses divorce has a liberating sense of mastery. . . . Being divorced however . . . reinforces exactly the opposite sense of life."[20]

Critics further contend that children are the primary victims of this trend toward loosened marital ties. They point to both the economic and psychological dislocation that often follows divorce, and criticize parents for placing their own needs over the needs of their children. Although generally not opposed to divorce that is truly fault based, they criticize adults whom they see as placing their own need for fulfillment over their children's need for stability and sustained connections.

**Supporters of No-Fault Divorce.** Many others, however, challenge the view that no-fault divorce is responsible for altering our understanding of marital commitment. Pointing to the widespread practice of collusive divorce during the fault era, they argue that no-fault divorce responded to rather than initiated changes that had already taken place in society's understanding of marriage. Supporting this view, no-fault supporters point out that divorce rates began to rise before no-fault reform owing to a number of factors, including increased social acceptance of divorce, the Vietnam War (studies consistently show that divorce rates increase during times of war), the women's rights movement, and changing economic conditions.[21] Accordingly, supporters argue that eliminating no-fault divorce is a misguided strategy that will not accomplish its intended goal of significantly reducing the rate of divorce.

Another concern of no-fault supporters is that eliminating no-fault divorce will recreate many of the problems of the past such as the practice of collusive divorce, trapping women in abusive marriages.

Focusing on domestic violence victims, one study concluded that no-fault divorce has led to a "striking decline" in female domestic violence rates and "a decline in females murdered by their intimates."[22] The authors suggest that this is due both to the increased availability of divorce and to the fact that "the switch to a unilateral divorce regime redistributes power in a marriage, giving power to the person who wants out, and reducing the power previously held by the partner interested in preserving the marriage."[23]

Interestingly, Barbara Defoe Whitehead, a self-described critic of contemporary divorce,[24] also raises concerns about the impact that the elimination of no-fault would have on battered women:

> Some marriages will be preserved that probably should end, including those that involve physical abuse and violence. Unfortunately, fault is likely to be most successful in deterring socially isolated and timorous women, often battered wives, from seeking divorce. It would be a cruel irony indeed if a pro-marriage policy unintentionally became a pro-bad-marriage policy.[25]

Whitehead also points to another possible unintended consequence of reform—that restricting the availability of no-fault divorce may deter people from marrying in the first place. She argues that based on life experience and cultural messages about the high rates of marital failure, young adults are already apprehensive about marital commitments. If they then hear how hard it is to get divorced they may "interpret legal restrictions on divorce as yet another reason to avoid marriage."[26] Thus, Whitehead argues that the current reform effort may backfire and may "further undermine and weaken the commitment to marriage, the very institution it intends to save. Worse, it sends a glum and dispiriting message to a generation already deeply pessimistic about the chances for a lasting marriage."[27]

Supporters of no-fault divorce are also concerned about the well-being of children. They recognize the impact that divorce can have on children but focus on the harms of growing up in a household that is rife with conflict. Again challenging the critics' understanding of causality, they point out that many of the emotional and psychological harms that are attributed to divorce may be due to long-standing problems in the family. Accordingly, efforts to compel parents to remain together may exacerbate rather than alleviate childhood distress. Moreover, no-fault supporters point out that the impact of divorce can be mitigated by carefully structured custody and visitation plans to account for the needs of the children and by support awards that are sufficient to offset the potential economic disruption of divorce.

### Legal Reforms

Based on concerns about no-fault divorce, reform measures that aim to make marital dissolution more difficult have been introduced in many states. By increasing the barriers to divorce, it is hoped that spouses will be more inclined to work out their differences, rather than opting for no-fault's promise of an "easy" escape from commitment. These measures have met with some success, but they have also been resisted based on the kinds of concerns discussed above, such as that they will entrap spouses in destructive marriages and discourage people from marrying in the first place. Another important concern is the potential intrusiveness of these measures, as they limit the ability of individuals to decide when a marriage is in fact over. Framed slightly differently, the concern is that these proposals seek to limit choice in furtherance of an idealized notion of marital life that may bear little connection to a couple's daily reality.

Not surprisingly, many of these reforms target no-fault divorce. Some measures propose eliminating no-fault as a divorce ground altogether; others seek to limit its availability to couples who do not have minor children. Another approach is to require mutual consent, thus eliminating the option of unilateral no-fault divorce—in some instances, this has been proposed only in cases where there are minor children. Other reforms include both premarital as well as predivorce counseling and extended waiting periods for divorce. Another reform measure that has generated considerable controversy is covenant marriage. Although identified in name as relating to marriage, covenant marriage laws are part of the effort to reduce divorce rates.

### Covenant Marriage

In 1997, the state of Louisiana passed the nation's first **covenant marriage** law. Since then, although covenant marriage bills have been considered in a majority of states, only Arizona and Arkansas have followed Louisiana's law and enacted such a measure into law. Moreover, few couples within these states have availed themselves of this option. To some, the failure of covenant marriage to take hold points to the inherent limitations of a two-tiered approach to marriage, while others argue that it reflects the corrosive effect of our anti-marriage culture.[28] Either way, this controversial innovation merits careful consideration because it remains an important option in the campaign to "restore the institution of marriage" by offering, to "those who belong to a religious community or those who adhere to a traditional morality, a safe haven from the post-modern dominant culture."[29]

Covenant marriage laws give couples who are contemplating marriage a choice — they can either opt for "regular" marriage or choose to enter into a "covenant" marriage. Designed to counter what some regard as the destructive effects of no-fault divorce, covenant marriage seeks to "change the dominant paradigm of marriage . . . by educating couples about the seriousness of marriage and equipping them for the inevitable 'difficulties.' "[30] The term "covenant" is biblical in origin and suggests the infusion of religious values into the marital relationship; a covenant marriage thus can be understood as involving "at least three interrelated concepts: permanence . . . unconditional love, and involvement (or witness) of God, or at a minimum, the larger community." . . . [31]

The following language from Louisiana's statute captures the essence of what covenant marriage entails:

> A covenant marriage is a marriage entered into by one male and one female who understand and agree that the marriage between them is a lifelong relationship. Parties to a covenant marriage have received counseling emphasizing the nature and purposes of marriage and the responsibilities thereto. Only when there has been a complete and total breach of the marital covenant commitment may the non-breaching party seek a declaration that the marriage is no longer recognized.[32]

Drawing on this language and thus using Louisiana's law as the prototype, we now consider some of the defining features that distinguish covenant marriage from "regular" marriage.

First, prospective spouses must take some initial steps in order to enter into a covenant marriage. They must undergo premarital counseling and then sign a Declaration of Intent attesting that they have satisfied the counseling requirement; that they understand that marriage is a lifelong commitment; and that they will take all reasonable steps to preserve their marriage, including further counseling as needed. They also must disclose to one another any information that could negatively affect their ability to enter into the marriage and must attest to the fact of full disclosure. Second, embodied in the Declaration of Intent is the obligation to take all reasonable steps, including marital counseling, to keep their marriage together. Third, and perhaps the key distinguishing factor, is that the prospective spouses in a covenant marriage agree in advance that they will not seek a no-fault divorce. By eliminating this option, they commit themselves to divorcing only if there has been a complete breach of the marital commitment, which occurs as essentially defined along traditional fault lines or if the spouses have lived separate and apart for two years.

Proponents hope that entering into a covenant marriage will cause couples to take their marital commitments more seriously. They hope that the counseling requirements and the limits on divorce will reinvigorate marriage by requiring spouses to work hard at their relationships, thus counteracting the seductiveness of easy divorce and restoring the primacy of marital commitment. Counterpoising covenant marriage to the contemporary vision of marriage, Katherine Spaht, a leading proponent of this marital approach, explains that "covenant spouses defer to marriage, an abstraction representing a third party to the marriage itself, rather than view marriage as a loose union of two radically autonomous selves . . ."[33]

Many serious concerns, however, have been raised about covenant marriage. One concern is that it infuses a biblical conception of marriage into state law, thus breaching the required boundary between church and state. In a related vein, although proponents such as Spaht herald the subordination of individual interests to the martial enterprise, critics worry that this very subordination will reinvigorate the longstanding tradition of *female* subordination within marriage, thus disrupting the modern trend towards greater spousal equality.

Also of concern is that it is impossible to predict the future, and committing one's self in advance to a particular course of action may work to a spouse's detriment. Thus, for example, if a husband turns out to be abusive, by entering into a covenant marriage, a woman has committed herself to participating in counseling with him, when the best and safest course of action may be for her to disengage from the relationship as quickly as possible. Moreover, once having committed to what some have dubbed "super-marriage," the psychological consequences of disentanglement are likely to be greater, thus making it more difficult for an at-risk spouse to extricate herself from this "lifelong" commitment.

Critics also point to the element of coercion. If one spouse wishes to enter into a covenant marriage and the other does not, the commitment of the recalcitrant spouse may be questioned, thus compelling him or her to choose covenant marriage rather than run the risk of no marriage at all. Lastly, critics have also raised concerns about the costs associated with counseling and about the inefficacy of counseling when parties are acting out of legal compulsion rather than genuine desire to work on their problems.

## THE LAW OF ANNULMENT

Marriages can also be "terminated" by the granting of an annulment. Although annulments are rare, it is nonetheless important to have a basic understanding of the law in this area. A client who comes to your office may want an annulment for religious reasons, or a client may be confused about the law, believing, for example, that an annulment is the only way to end a short-term or unconsummated marriage.

As you read this section, keep in mind that we are speaking only about the civil annulment process. A number of religious bodies also grant annulments in accordance with their own internal principles and procedures.

## Distinguished from Divorce

An annulment is a retroactive declaration that no valid marriage ever existed between the parties. The modern annulment action emerged out of ecclesiastical practice. Unlike divorce, the procedure was consistent with the religious belief in the indissolubility of the marital relationship because an annulment establishes that the parties were never validly married.

Divorce is premised on the existence of a valid marriage. It operates to dissolve the legal bond between a husband and wife based on problems that arose during the course of the marriage. It operates prospectively to terminate the bond from the date of the divorce forward. In contrast, an annulment works retrospectively to invalidate the marital bond based on a defect that existed at the time the marriage was celebrated—it is a statement that because of this defect, the marriage was flawed from its inception. Accordingly, an annulment cannot be granted for a problem that arises after a marriage is celebrated because a valid marriage would have been established, and annulment speaks to marital invalidity. Thus, although common, it is technically incorrect to speak of an annulment as terminating a marriage because it is a declaration that the parties were never in fact married.

## Grounds

Grounds for annulment vary from state to state. Most of the grounds can be grouped into two categories: (1) those involving the lack of capacity or intent and (2) those involving breaches of state marital restriction laws.

This distinction has important practical significance. Some defects make a marriage **void** from its inception, while others make it **voidable**. In general, a marriage contracted in violation of state marital laws is considered void from its inception (however, see below regarding marital age restrictions). This means that a decree of annulment is not required to invalidate the marriage—the marriage is regarded as having never taken place. However, a party may prefer to obtain a decree of annulment in order to eliminate any confusion about his or her marital status.

In contrast, a marriage premised on the **lack of capacity** or intent is generally considered voidable rather than void. A voidable marriage is considered valid until and unless it is invalidated by a decree of annulment. As a general rule, the annulment petition can be filed only by the "innocent" spouse — the one not responsible for the defect. The annulment may be denied if the spouse seeking the annulment knew about the defect at the time of celebration or ratified the marriage by cohabitation after learning of it. Prior knowledge and ratification are not defenses if the marriage is void.

## Marital Restriction Laws

An annulment can be granted if a marriage is contracted in violation of a marital restriction law. Specific grounds include bigamy, incest, and being under the age of capacity (see Marital Age Restrictions, Chapter 1). Incestuous and bigamous marriages are void and cannot be ratified by cohabitation or consent. In contrast, a marriage that is contracted when one or both parties were under age is generally voidable, and continued cohabitation beyond the age of consent will ratify the marriage.

## Lack of Capacity or Intent

An annulment may also be granted if one party lacked the capacity or the intent to contract a real marriage due to fraud, duress, mental incapacity, insanity, and, possibly, incurable impotence. Of these, considerations of fraud probably come up the most. To warrant an annulment, the fraud must go to the "essentials" of the marriage. This concept has traditionally been limited to the sexual and procreative aspects of marriage, such as concealing a pregnancy by another man, misrepresenting an intent to consummate the marriage, or misrepresenting an intent to have children where no such intent exists. Some jurisdictions have expanded the concept of fraud to include other critical aspects of the marital relationship, such as religious beliefs — for example, where one party pretends to be deeply religious in order to entice the other into marriage.

A spouse may be able to defeat an annulment action by showing that the other spouse has ratified the marriage. For instance, using the example about religious misrepresentation, if the deceived partner remains in the marriage after learning about the deception, she or he will probably be deemed to have ratified the marriage and would not be entitled to an annulment. Similarly, a court might find that the passage of years has mitigated the impact of the defect because the parties would have had the time to establish an independent relationship.

## Consequences of an Annulment Decree

As a matter of logic, if an annulment decree undoes a marriage back to the date of celebration, then any children born to the couple would be "illegitimate"; additionally, no marital rights to support or property would accrue. Although this was the common law approach, this is no longer the case in most states.

### Children

In keeping with the modern legal approach to children of unmarried parents (see Chapter 12), children of an annulled marriage are no longer considered "illegitimate." Accordingly, the law treats these children similarly to children of divorcing parents when it comes to custody, visitation, and support determinations.

### Spousal Support and the Division of Property

Because alleviating financial hardship is considered important enough to outweigh the risk that a party will have been required to support someone eventually determined not to be his or her spouse, many courts will award temporary support during the pendency of an annulment action. However, regardless of need, support will not usually be awarded to a spouse who is denying the validity of the marriage because these are regarded as mutually inconsistent claims. A number of states have enacted statutes allowing an award of permanent alimony in cases of need following an annulment, but some permit an award only if this spouse entered into the marriage with a good-faith belief in its validity. In authorizing support, these statutes eschew reliance on legal formalities and recognize that the declaration of invalidity does not mitigate the financial needs of an economically dependent partner. In the absence of express statutory authorization, a court might make an alimony-like award, such as it might do in a cohabitation case. With respect to property, many statutes expressly authorize the court to make a distribution of accumulated assets much as it would do in a divorce case (see Chapter 9).

### Revival

Following an annulment, difficult questions may arise regarding the nature of third-party obligations when such obligations turn on the recipient's marital status. Using a hypothetical, two situations will be briefly discussed.

Let's assume that the marriage of Juan and Maria ended in divorce and that Juan was to pay support until such time as Maria remarried. Now assume that Maria remarries and Juan stops paying alimony based on the fact of her remarriage. What happens if Maria's second marriage is subsequently annulled? Because annulment effectively cancels out the second marriage, Maria could logically argue that there was no remarriage and that Juan's support obligation is subject to **revival**. Moreover, she could claim that he owes her money back to the date he stopped paying. Most courts would reject Maria's claim for support on the basis that Juan had a right to rely on the marriage as it appeared, as distinct from its technical, legal status, and his support obligation would not be revived.

However, when benefits such as social security are involved, courts are much more likely to revive payments upon an annulment. For example, if before her second marriage, Juan had died, and Maria was receiving social security benefits, these payments would cease upon her remarriage, but if this second marriage were annulled, most courts would revive the payments because the payor does not rely on the remarriage in the same way as a former spouse would when planning for the future.

## LEGAL SEPARATION

The third remedy for an unhappy marriage is a **legal separation**, also known as a "judicial separation," a "limited divorce," and, historically speaking, a "*divorce a mensa et thoro*" (a divorce from board and bed).

## The Nature of the Action

A legal separation is a judicial decree formally permitting or, perhaps more accurately, requiring, a husband and wife to live apart. In some states a separation can be granted for an unlimited period of time; in others, there are durational limits. Grounds are generally similar to those found in fault-based divorce laws, although some statutes simply give a judge the discretion to decide if sufficient cause for a separation exists. The no-fault concept has not permeated this action, perhaps because, unlike with a divorce, a couple can always agree to separate without a court decree.

A legal separation does not terminate the marital relationship. Accordingly, it does not free the parties to remarry. As part of its decree, a court can determine custody and award both child and spousal support. In some states, a division of property also may be ordered; in others, the distribution of property is prohibited unless and until the parties actually divorce. One might wonder why an unhappy spouse would file for a legal separation rather than for a divorce. One reason might be religious beliefs that do not permit divorce because the marital bond is considered indissoluble but would allow a separation because this does not dissolve the marriage. A variety of personal and emotional reasons also might influence the decision to seek a separation rather than a divorce. An individual wishing to live apart from his or her spouse may not be ready to file for divorce but might need the protection of court orders — if, for example, he or she fears the other spouse might disappear with the children — or the financial support that the court could award. A spouse also might hope to send a wake-up call to his or her partner.

A number of states provide for the conversion of a separation into a divorce after the passage of a specified period of time. Where conversion is not allowed, filing for a separation and then filing for divorce (should a divorce eventually be desired) entails a significant duplication of efforts; therefore, a client's reasons for wanting to start with a legal separation rather than initiating divorce proceedings should be carefully explored. For instance, if the client knows that the marriage is over but isn't quite ready emotionally to implement the decision, it is worth exploring whether it makes sense to wait to initiate legal proceedings until he or she is ready to proceed with the divorce.

## Distinguished from an Action for Separate Maintenance

Upon separation, a party might file a complaint for **separate maintenance**. Although similar to an action for a legal separation, the essence of a complaint for separate maintenance is a claim for support. Thus, the focus is on the plaintiff's need for support, rather than on the reason for the parties' separation. The decree usually does not involve findings on the reason for separation nor does it specifically authorize the parties to live apart, although reconciliation generally terminates the support obligation. Also, in most states the court cannot order a division of property or determine custody as part of a separate maintenance action.

## Chapter Summary

Divorce is a legal action that dissolves the marital bond. Our divorce laws are rooted in the Protestant concept of marital sin. Historically, divorce law was premised on marital fault, and a divorce could be granted only to an innocent spouse based on marital wrongdoing. Many couples, however, evaded the law's strictness through the practice of collusive divorce. Beginning in the 1960s, concerns about collusion and the adversarial nature of the fault system led to no-fault reform. Some states eliminated fault grounds altogether and enacted pure no-fault systems. Others added no-fault grounds as an option. The principal no-fault grounds are marital breakdown and living separate and apart for a statutorily prescribed time period.

No-fault laws have been the subject of considerable debate, and there has been a recent backlash against them. Many proposals have been suggested to make divorce more difficult to obtain, especially when a married couple has children. Covenant marriage is a key example of such an effort. A couple entering into a covenant marriage must seek premarital and predivorce counseling, and waive the right to seek a no-fault divorce. However, concerns have been voiced about these efforts, including that they blur the line between church and state and may entrap spouses in marriages that are abusive or otherwise destructive.

An annulment is a declaration that no valid marriage ever existed between the parties due to an impediment that was present at the time of celebration. Annulments are usually based on a lack of capacity or intent, or a violation of a marital restriction law. Some defects, such as a prior existing marriage, render a marriage void from its inception, while others, such as the lack of capacity, make a marriage voidable.

A legal separation is a decree that the parties have good cause for living apart. It does not terminate the marital relationship, and the parties cannot remarry. It is distinguishable from an action for separate maintenance, which focuses on support rather than on the reason for the underlying separation.

## Key Terms

Divorce

Indissoluble

Annulment

Marital Fault

Innocent Spouse

Fault Divorce

Adultery

Desertion

Constructive Desertion

Cruelty

Connivance

Condonation

Recrimination

Comparative Rectitude

Collusion

No-Fault Divorce

Marital Breakdown

Living Separate and Apart

Irreconcilable Differences

Covenant Marriage

Void

Voidable

Lack of Capacity

Revival

Legal Separation

*Divorce a Mensa et Thoro*

Separate Maintenance

## Review Questions

1. What were the Catholic Church's views on marriage?

2. What remedies were available from the ecclesiastical courts for an unhappy marriage?

3. How did the Protestant view of marriage differ from the Catholic Church's? What impact did this have on divorce law?

4. In what way was England different from the other Protestant countries?

5. How did the Puritans view divorce?

6. Explain the relevance of guilt and innocence in a fault-based divorce system.

7. What are the key fault grounds? What are the requirements for each one?

8. What views do courts hold on the question of whether adultery can be defined to include extramarital same-sex relationships?

9. What are the key divorce defenses? What is the essence of each one?

10. What criticism did the no-fault reformers level at fault-based divorce?

11. What is the difference between a pure no-fault and a dual system?

12. Explain the no-fault ground of marital breakdown.

13. What kind of judicial inquiry is usually conducted in these hearings? How does this differ from the vision of some reformers?

14. Explain the no-fault ground of living separate and apart.

15. What concerns have been raised about the availability of no-fault divorce? What reform measures have been proposed?

16. What concerns have supporters of no-fault divorce raised about present efforts to reform/eliminate no-fault divorce?

17. What is covenant marriage? What do supporters hope to accomplish?

18. What are some of the major criticisms of covenant marriage?

19. What is an annulment, and how does it differ from a divorce?

20. What is the difference between a void marriage and one that is voidable?

21. What is a legal separation? How does an action for separate maintenance differ from a legal separation?

## Discussion Questions

1. Many people believe that no-fault divorce makes divorce too easy and has caused people to lose respect for the institution of marriage. Do you think this is true? Why or why not? If so, what do you think should be done? Do you think covenant marriage is a good response to these concerns?

2. With no-fault divorce, a spouse usually can obtain a divorce because he or she no longer loves the other spouse. Should this be permitted over the objection of a spouse who claims to still be madly in love and committed to working out the relationship? What should the court do in this situation? Should the presence of children change the picture?

3. Apart from the needs of children, do you think the state has a legitimate interest in encouraging marital permanency through its divorce laws? If so, how should the state's interest be balanced with the interests and needs of the parties to a marriage?

# Assignments

1.  Locate your state's divorce law and determine the following:

    *   Are fault grounds still used, or is your state a "pure" no-fault jurisdiction?
    *   If yes, what grounds are available? What defenses are available?
    *   What no-fault ground(s) is (or are) available in your state?
    *   What must a party show to qualify for a no-fault divorce?

    Having reviewed the statute, identify and describe any recent changes that are designed to slow down the divorce process (such as waiting periods or counseling requirements) or limit divorce options (such as limiting no-fault divorce to couples without children).

2.  Attend a court session where divorces are heard and observe several uncontested divorce hearings. Write up your observations. Note the grounds for each divorce you watch. Describe the judge's role very carefully. Evaluate the extent to which you believe she or he really inquired into the parties' circumstances.

3.  A client has come to the office where you work as a paralegal. She is unhappy in her marriage but does not know what she wants to do. The attorney you work for has asked you to draft a letter explaining her legal options. At this point, you do not have all the facts, but, based on a brief interview, you know the following:

    *   She thinks that her husband never loved her and that he married her solely to make his family happy.
    *   They have been married for three years, during which time, based on his wishes, they have lived totally separate lives, although they have had sexual intercourse on occasion.

    In your letter you should explain the general differences between divorce, annulment, and legal separation and discuss the specific requirements of the laws in your state.

4.  Assume you are a legislative aide in a state that is considering enacting a covenant marriage law along the lines of Louisiana's law. The senator you work for has asked you to prepare a "briefing" memo in which you explain the basic requirements of covenant marriage and set out the arguments in favor of and against such a law.

5.  Assume you are a law clerk for a family court judge who has recently taken a divorce case under advisement because it raises a new issue of law. The wife filed for divorce on the grounds of adultery because her husband has engaged in an intimate relationship with another man. The husband denies this is adultery, asserting that the concept only covers heterosexual intercourse. The judge has asked you to locate cases from other jurisdictions that have addressed this issue, and write an interoffice memorandum in which you first analyze the case law and then set out your thoughts to how she should rule in this matter.

## Cases for Analysis

The following case addresses the issue of whether sexual relations between two women comes within the definition of adultery as used in the New Hampshire divorce statute.

### IN THE MATTER OF BLANCHFLOWER
#### 150 N.H. 226, 834 A.2d 1010 (2003)

. . . The record supports the following facts. The petitioner filed for divorce from the respondent on grounds of irreconcilable differences. He subsequently moved to amend the petition to assert the fault ground of adultery under RSA [Revised Statutes Annotated] 458:7, II. Specifically, the petitioner alleged that the respondent has been involved in a "continuing adulterous affair" with the co-respondent, a woman . . . The co-respondent sought to dismiss the amended petition, contending that a homosexual relationship between two people, one of whom is married, does not constitute adultery. . . .

Before addressing the merits, we note this appeal is not about the status of homosexual relationships in our society or the formal recognition of homosexual unions. The narrow question before us is whether a homosexual sexual relationship between a married person and another constitutes adultery within the meaning of RSA 458:7 . . . II.

RSA 458:7 provides, in part: "A divorce from the bonds of matrimony shall be decreed in favor of the innocent party for any of the following causes:

. . . II. Adultery of either party." The statute does not define adultery. Id. Accordingly, we must discern its meaning according to our rules of statutory construction.

The plain and ordinary meaning of adultery is "voluntary sexual intercourse between a married man and someone other than his wife or between a married woman and someone other than her husband." Webster's Third New International Dictionary 30 (unabridged ed. 1961). Although the definition does not specifically state that the "someone" with whom one commits adultery must be of the opposite gender, it does require sexual intercourse.

The plain and ordinary meaning of sexual intercourse is "sexual connection esp. between humans: COITUS, COPULATION." Webster's Third New International Dictionary 2082. . . .

We note that the current criminal adultery statute still requires sexual intercourse . . . Based upon the foregoing, we conclude that adultery under RSA 458:7, II does not include homosexual relationships.

We reject the petitioner's argument that an interpretation of adultery that excludes homosexual conduct subjects homosexuals and heterosexuals to unequal treatment, "contrary to New Hampshire's public policy of equality and prohibition of discrimination based on sex and sexual orientation." Homosexuals and heterosexuals engaging in the same acts are treated the same because our interpretation of the term "adultery" excludes all non-coital sex acts, whether between persons of the same or opposite gender. The only distinction is that persons of the same gender cannot, by definition, engage in the one act that constitutes adultery under the statute.

The petitioner also argues that "public policy would be well served by applying the same law to a cheating spouse, whether the promiscuous spouse chooses a paramour of the same sex or the opposite sex." This argument is tied to the premise, as argued by the petitioner, that "the purpose underlying [the adultery] fault ground is based upon the fundamental concept of marital loyalty and public policy's disfavor of one spouse's violation of the marriage contract with another." We have not, however, seen any such purpose expressed by the legislature. As noted above, the concept of adultery was premised upon a specific act. To include in that concept other acts of a sexual nature, whether between heterosexuals or homosexuals, would change beyond recognition this well-established ground for divorce and likely lead to countless new marital cases alleging adultery, for strategic purposes. . . .

The dissent defines adultery not as a specific act of intercourse, but as "extramarital intimate sexual activity with another." This standard would permit a hundred different judges and masters to decide just what individual acts are so sexually intimate as to meet the definition. The dilemma faced by Justice Stewart and his fellow justices applying their personal standards to the issue of pornography in movies demonstrates the value of a clear objective definition of adultery in marital cases. See Jacobellis v. Ohio, 378 U.S. 184, 12 L. Ed. 2d 793, 84 S. Ct. 1676 (1964).

We are also unpersuaded by the dissent's contention that "it is improbable that the legislature intended to require an innocent spouse in a divorce action to prove the specific intimate sexual acts in which the guilty spouse engaged." . . . [T]he dissent notes that adultery usually has no eye-witnesses and therefore "ordinarily must be proved by circumstantial evidence." While this is true, it does not support the dissent's point. For over a hundred and fifty years judges, lawyers and clients have understood that adultery meant intercourse as we have defined it. It is an act determined not by the subjective test of an individual justice but by an objective determination based upon the facts. What must be proved to establish adultery and what evidence may be used to prove it are separate issues. Adultery cases have always required proof of the specific sexual act engaged in, namely, sexual intercourse. That circumstantial evidence may be used to establish the act does not negate or undermine the requirement of proof that the act actually occurred . . .

BROCK, C.J., and BRODERICK, J., dissenting . . . We respectfully dissent because we believe that the majority's narrow construction of the word "adultery" contravenes the legislature's intended purpose in sanctioning fault-based divorce for the protection of the injured spouse . . .

To strictly adhere to the primary definition of adultery in the 1961 edition of Webster's Third New International Dictionary and a corollary definition of sexual intercourse, which on its face does not require coitus, is to avert one's eyes from the sexual realities of our world . . .

New Hampshire permits both fault-based and no-fault divorces . . . The purpose of permitting fault-based divorces is to provide some measure of relief to an innocent spouse for the offending conduct of a guilty spouse . . . We should therefore view the purpose and fabric of our divorce law in a meaningful context, as the legislature presumably intended, and not so narrow our focus as to undermine its public goals.

From the perspective of the injured spouse, the very party fault-based divorce law is designed to protect, "an extramarital relationship . . . is just as devastating . . . irrespective of the specific sexual act performed by the promiscuous spouse or the sex of the new paramour." S.B. v. S.J.B., 258 N.J. Super. 151, 609 A.2d 124, 126 (N.J. Super. Ct. Ch. Div. 1992) . . . Indeed, to some, a homosexual betrayal may be more devastating. Accordingly, consistent with the overall purpose of New Hampshire's fault-based divorce law, we would interpret the word "adultery" in RSA 458:7, II to mean a spouse's extramarital intimate sexual activity with another, regardless of the specific intimate sexual acts performed, the marital status, or the gender of the third party. . . .

Defining the word "adultery" to include intimate extramarital homosexual sexual activity by a spouse is consonant . . . with the decisions of other courts that have considered this issue . . .

The majority suggests that to define "adultery" so as to include intimate extramarital homosexual sexual activity by a spouse is to propose a test so vague as to be unworkable. Apparently, a similar test has been adopted in . . . three jurisdictions. . . . Further, while such a definition is more inclusive than one reliant solely upon heterosexual sexual intercourse, we do not believe that "intimate extramarital sexual activity" either requires a more explicit description or would be subject to such a widely varying judicial view . . .

## QUESTIONS

1. According to the court, why did the wife's conduct not come within the meaning of the term "adultery"? What did the court look to in reaching its decision?

2. Why did the dissent disagree with the majority's conclusion?

---

In this era of no-fault divorce, parties typically do not go to trial over the existence of grounds for divorce. In the following case, however, the court faced the somewhat unusual question of whether the husband's lack of good faith was sufficient to defeat his condonation defense.

### LAWRENCE v. LAWRENCE
### 2006 Miss. App. LEXIS 633

April and Andy were married on May 16, 1998. They had two children. Noah Andrew was born on July 19, 1999. Emma Katherine was born on July 30, 2000. . . .

In the spring of 2003, April and Andy separated for approximately a week. When Andy returned to the marital home, April confronted him about rumors of an affair. At first, Andy denied the affair, but later admitted the affair and begged forgiveness. On April 17, 2003, April filed her initial complaint for divorce on the grounds of adultery or, in the alternative, irreconcilable differences. April and Andy, even though the complaint for divorce was filed, continued to reside together and were not legally separated. Affidavits from April and Andy indicate that Andy admitted his affair, which occurred in 2002. They attempted to reconcile, but April's complaint for divorce was never dismissed.

In the fall of 2003, April began to ask Andy to leave the marital residence, and the divorce proceedings were resumed. They continued to reside in the same household.

In December of 2003, April met Brian Sellers. The following May, April moved from the marital home into a rental home in Caledonia.

In June of 2004, the chancellor entered a temporary order that granted April custody of the two minor children and ordered Andy to pay child support. For several months prior to the temporary order, Andy did not deposit his paycheck into the couple's joint bank account and did not provide any financial support for the children.

On August 4, 2004, Andy filed a motion for summary judgment. He claimed that he was entitled to judgment on the claim of adultery because April condoned his affair. The result was that Andy's adultery could no longer support the grounds for divorce pled in April's complaint for divorce.

### Analysis

April argued that condonation was conditional on Andy's continued good behavior. In Wood v. Wood, 495 So.2d 503, 505 (Miss. 1986), the supreme court held:

> The defense of condonation is recognized in our law. Stribling v. Stribling, 215 So.2d 869, 870 (Miss. 1968); Starr v. Starr, 206 Miss. 1, 39 So.2d 520, 523 (1949). Condonation is the forgiveness of a marital wrong on the part of the wronged party. Condonation may be expressed or implied . . .
>
> The mere resumption of residence does not constitute a condonation of past marital sins and does not act as a bar . . . to a divorce being granted. Compare Miss. Code Ann. §93-5-4 (1972). Condonation, even if a true condonation exists, is conditioned on the offending spouse's continued good behavior. If the offending party does not mend his or her ways and resumes the prior course of conduct, there is a revival of the grounds for divorce. Manning v. Manning, 160 Miss. 318, 321, 133 So. 673, 674 (1931).
>
> In practical effect, condonation places the offending spouse on a form of temporary probation. Any subsequent conduct within a reasonable time after resumption of cohabitation which evidences an intent not to perform the conditions of the condonation in good faith, may be sufficient to avoid the defense of condonation, . . .

In her response to the motion for partial summary judgment, April offered her affidavit where she testified about her belief that Andy resumed the marital relationship "merely as a ploy to defeat the grounds of adultery" and that he "has continued to have an affair."

We conclude that April's affidavit presented a genuine issue of material fact and Andy was not entitled to a judgment as a matter of law. In Wood, the supreme court held that:

> [a]ny subsequent conduct within a reasonable time after resumption of cohabitation which evidences an intent not to perform the conditions of

the condonation in good faith, may be sufficient to avoid the defense of condonation, even though the conduct so complained of in and of itself may not be grounds for divorce.

Wood, 495 So.2d at 505. Based on this language, Andy's intent in the resumption of the marital relationship is indeed an issue to be determined by the chancellor. Simply engaging in the act of sex does not seal the defense of condonation. Thus, April's personal belief that Andy resumed the marital relationship "merely as a ploy to defeat the grounds of adultery" presents a genuine issue of material fact in dispute that does not entitle Andy to a judgment as a matter of law on his defense of condonation.

Accordingly, we reverse the chancellor's entry of a partial summary judgment, and we remand for further proceedings consistent therewith ...

## QUESTIONS:

1. What does the court mean when it says that "condonation places the offending spouse on a form of temporary probation?"

2. Why did the court reverse the chancellor's grant of partial summary judgment and remand the case? On remand, what must the chancellor take into account?

## Endnotes

1. *See* Judith S. Wallerstein and Sandra Blakeslee, Second Chances—Men, Women, and Children a Decade After Divorce: Who Wins, Who Loses—and Why (1989).

2. Mary E. O'Connell, Alimony After No-Fault: A Practice in Search of a Theory, 23 New Eng. L. Rev. 437, 444-447 (1988).

3. *See* John Witte, Jr., The Reformation of Marriage Law in Martin Luther's Germany: Its Significance Then and Now, 4 J. L. & Religion 295 (Summer 1986).

4. Glenda Riley, Divorce: An American Tradition 9-15 (1991).

5. Norma Basch, Framing American Divorce: From the Revolutionary Generation to the Victorians 19-30 (1999).

6. Riley, *supra* note 4, at 53-84.

7. O'Connell, *supra* note 2, at 454-455.

8. Riley, *supra* note 4, at 108-112.

9. RGM v. DGM, 410 S.E.2d 564, 566-567 (S.C. 1991).

10. In the Matter of Blanchflower, 150 N.H. 226, 230; 834 A.2d 1010, 1013 (2003).

11. *Id.* at 231-232, 1014 (dissenting opinion of Justices Brock and Broderick (citing S.B. v. S.J.B., 609 A.2d 124, 126 (N.J. Super. Ct. Ch. Div. 1992)).

12. Homer H. Clark, Jr., The Law of Domestic Relations in the United States 503-506 (Hornbook Series student ed., 1988).

13. *Id.* at 506-509.

14. It is worth noting that, before 1970, some states had amended their laws to permit divorce without proof of fault where either party had lived separate and apart for a certain period of time or where there had been an irremediable breakdown of the marriage. These earlier efforts are not generally regarded as a significant departure from the fault model because the changes were grafted piecemeal onto old laws, and considerations of fault continued to play a major role in decisions about spousal support and the division of assets.

15. *See* Lawrence M. Friedman, Rights of Passage: Divorce Laws in Historical Perspective, 63 Or. L. Rev. 649 (1984).

16. Katherine Shaw Spaht, Revolution and Counter-Revolution: The Future of Marriage in the Law, 49 Loy. L. Rev. 1, 49 (2003) and (citing Representative Dalman as quoted in 1997 Mich. Legis. Serv. 5217 (West 1997)).

17. Jesse Dalman and Susan Agar, Abolish No-Fault Divorce?, http://divorceonline.com (accessed May 12, 2004).

18. The Marriage Movement: A Statement of Principles, 2000. Center for Marriage and Families at the Institute for American Values. http://center.americanvalues.org (accessed January 10, 2007).

19. Much has been written on both sides of the divorce reform debate, including the following works: Peter Nash Swisher, Marriage and Some Troubling Issues with No-Fault Divorce, 17 Regent U.L. Rev. 243 (2004/2005); Nicholas H. Wolfinger, The Next Blessings of No-Fault Divorce, 4 Whittier J. Child & Fam. Advoc. 407 (2005); Katherine Shaw Spaht, A Proposal: Legal Re-Regulation of the Content of Marriage, 18 Notre Dame J.L. Ethics & Pub. Poly. 243 (2004); Justin Wolfers

and Betsey Stevenson, Bargaining in the Shadow of the Law: Divorce Laws and Family Distress 19 (Stanford Law and Economics Olin Working Paper No. 273; Stanford Law School, Public Law Working Paper No. 73, December 2003), http://ssrn.com/abstract3478162; Allen M. Parkman, Reforming Divorce Reform, 41 Santa Clara L. Rev. 379 (2001); James Hubie DiFonzo, Customized Marriage, 75 Ind. L. Rev. 875 (2000); Robert M. Gordon, Note, The Limits of Limits on Divorce, 107 Yale L.J. 1435 (1998); Katherine Shaw Spaht, Marriage: Why a Second Tier Called Covenant Marriage?, 12 Regent Univ. L. Rev. 1 (1999-2000); Lynn D. Wardle, No-Fault Divorce and the Divorce Conundrum, 1991 B.Y.U. L. Rev. 79; Jeanne Louise Carriere, "It's Déjà Vu All Over Again": The Covenant Marriage Act in Popular Cultural Perception and Legal Reality, 72 Tul. L. Rev. 1701 (1998).

20. Maggie Gallagher and Barbara Defoe Whitehead, End No-Fault Divorce?, FirstThings: The Journal of Religion and Public Life *2, http://www.firstthings.com/ftissues/ft9708/articles/gallagher.html (accessed October 1, 2004).

21. Donna S. Hershkowitz and Drew R. Liebert, The Direction of Divorce Reform in California: From Fault to No-Fault . . . and Back Again?, Counsel Assembly Judiciary Committee, California State Legislature, http://www.assembly.ca.gov (click on Committee Directory, and then click on Committee on Judiciary, and then click on Hearing Reports). See also Stephen Bahr, Social Science Research on Family Dissolution: What It Shows and How It Might Be of Interest to Family Law Reformers, 4 J.L. Fam. Stud. 5, 8 (2002).

22. Wolfers and Stevenson, *supra* note 19, at 19. The authors of this study also found that the introduction of no-fault divorce led to a significant decline in female suicides; no such correlation was found for males.

23. *Id.* at 2.

24. Gallagher and Whitehead, *supra* note 20 at 6.

25. Gallagher and Whitehead, *supra* note 20 at 5.

26. *Id.* at 6.

27. *Id.*

28. *See, e.g.,* Nathan Bracken, Foundational Marriage: A Counteroffer to Covenant Marriage in Utah, 7 J.L. Fam. Stud. 427 (2005); and Katherine Shaw Spaht, Covenant Marriage Seven Years Later: Its as Yet Unfilled Promise, 65 La. L. Rev. 605, 628 (2005).

29. Katherine Shaw Spaht, The Last One Hundred Years: The Incredible Retreat of Law from the Regulation of Marriage, 63 La. L. Rev. 243, 261 (2003).

30. Spaht, *supra* note 16, at 2.

31. Margaret F. Bring and Steven L. Nock, What Does Covenant Mean for Relationships?, 18 Notre Dame J.L. Ethics & Pub. Poly. 137, 140 (2004).

32. La. Rev. Stat. § 9:272 (2004).

33. Spaht, *supra* note 28 at 629.

# 5 Child Custody

In cases involving child **custody** and **visitation** disputes between divorcing parents, judges face the daunting task of allocating rights and responsibilities between two parents who are likely to have very different perceptions of the arrangement that would be best for their children.[1] Judges often have to make agonizingly difficult choices that have profound and lasting consequences for the parents and their children. Increasingly, judges are also being called on to resolve custody and/or visitation disputes between a child's legal parent and a co-parent, stepparent, or grandparent(s).

The "best interest of the child" (or "best interest") is the standard that is used to resolve custody conflicts between parents; however, important concerns have been raised about the standard's indeterminacy. The applicable standard is far less clear when the dispute is between a legal parent and a third party, such as a co-parent, stepparent, or grandparent,[2] and these cases pose a challenge to traditional understandings of the weight and meaning of parenthood. Before considering the contemporary legal framework for resolving custody disputes, we begin with a historical overview.

## EVOLVING LEGAL STANDARDS

### Paternal Preference

Our custody laws have roots in the Roman doctrine of *patria potestas*, which gave fathers the right of absolute control over their children. So complete was this authority that until the fourth century, fathers were entitled to sell their children or have them put to death. Although never vesting fathers with this degree of control over their children's lives, our early laws continued this legal tradition of paternal rights.

The colonial family was hierarchical in nature, and each member had a defined place in its internal structure. The husband/father was the "governor" of the household, and his wife and children occupied well-defined subordinate positions, subject to his unquestioned authority and control. A father had complete command over the education, training, and discipline of his children. He also owned his children's labor — a valuable right in an agrarian society where the world of work and home were essentially one and the same.

In turn, a father was charged with the responsibility of supporting his children and preparing them, particularly his sons, for passage into the world. In sharp contrast, mothers had no legal authority. As explained by William Blackstone, a mother was "entitled to no power, but only reverence and respect."[3]

During this time, custodial rights were understood in property terms: "Custody law held children to be dependent, subordinate beings, assets of estates in which fathers had a vested right."[4] During his lifetime, a father could assign the care and custody of his children to a third party regardless of the wishes of the children's mother, and he could do the same upon his death through his will. Upon family dissolution, the **paternal preference** rule gave fathers a near-absolute right to custody.

Courts and commentators advanced various theories to explain the undisputed legal supremacy of fathers. Their status was said to be divinely ordained or rooted in immutable laws of nature. As explained by one court:

> We are informed by the first elementary books we read, that the authority of the father is superior to that of the mother. It is the doctrine of all civilized nations. It is according to the revealed law and the law of nature, and it prevails even with the wandering savage who has received none of the lights of civilization.[5]

The lack of maternal rights can also be understood as a logical extension of the common law status of married women. How could a married woman, who herself was regarded as incapable of managing her own affairs and in need of male protection, be entrusted with responsibility and control over her children? In the eyes of the law, she was little more than a child herself.

## Shift to Maternal Custody

In the late eighteenth century, the patriarchal family structure began to break down as the nation moved from an agrarian to an industrial society. As production moved from the family farm into the factory, the world of work became increasingly identified with men, and the world of home with women. Home was now seen as a sanctuary from the burdens of the harsh world in which women's gentle influence could flourish. Children, who had been seen both as economically valuable assets and as needing a father's stern corrective influence, began to be seen more as innocent beings in need of protection and nurture, and mothers replaced fathers as "the most powerful agent in developing a child's character."[6]

Gradually, the favored legal status of fathers gave way to a clear maternal preference. By the end of the nineteenth century, the common law doctrine of paternal rights had been displaced by the **tender years presumption**, which embodied the belief that children, particularly young children, belonged with their mothers. This shift enhanced the status of married women and curtailed male authority over the domestic realm. It also gave legal meaning to the mother-child bond, entitling women to more than "reverence and respect."

This presumption was expressly incorporated into some statutes, while others authorized the court to award custody to either parent, sometimes specifying that the controlling factor should be in the best interest of the child. However, through judicial decisions, the term "**best interest**" became virtually synonymous with maternal custody, at least with respect to young children, unless the mother was deemed unfit. In some jurisdictions, a preference for paternal custody continued where older children, particularly boys, were involved, as it was thought that the father could better prepare them for life beyond the home. Once established, maternal custody became the unquestioned norm until the latter part of the twentieth century.

## The Modern Best Interest Test

By the 1970s, as fixed notions about proper roles for men and women began to break down, the tender years presumption lost favor. By 1990, virtually all states had eliminated the explicit use of the tender years presumption in favor of a gender-neutral best interest standard. Formally uncoupled from gender determinants, the best interest of the child standard is supposed to ensure that each case is resolved on its own merits, with neither parent being given an advantage based on assumptions about gender.

If parents reach an agreement regarding custody and visitation, a judge will review the terms at the divorce hearing (see Chapter 10) to determine whether they promote the best interest of the children. In most states, the judge conducting this review is not required to defer to the wishes of the parents as embodied in their agreement; rather, the agreement is simply viewed as expressive of their preferences and is only one of many factors in the assessment of best interest. Based, however, on the belief that parents are in a better position than the court to know what is best for their children, some states have begun to give more weight to their custodial preferences, by, for example, adopting a presumption that, without clear evidence to the contrary, the agreed-upon terms are in the best interest of the children.

Where custody is contested, the focus is supposed to be on the child rather than on the status or the rights of the parents. However, it is questionable whether the needs of children have really become stage center, as battling parents, intentionally or not, often distort the picture to maximize their own chance of "winning." This along with other concerns have led some family law experts to call for changes in both the prevailing custody standard and the process by which custody decisions are made.

---

### Consideration

In what ways do you think gender may still be a factor in custody decisions?

---

### Formulating the Test

The best interest test requires an analysis of a child's needs and an assessment of which parent can best meet those needs. It is intended to be a flexible, child-centered approach that allows a judge to take a child's individual circumstances into account when making a custody determination. The inherent flexibility of this approach allows for an individualized consideration of all relevant factors. On the flip side, the best interest standard has been criticized for being too vague and indeterminate, which means that judges have room to import their personal views into custody determinations, making results unpredictable and possibly idiosyncratic.

Some states have attempted to address this concern by adopting guidelines enumerating specific factors that a judge must consider in making a custody decision. The Michigan statute is a good example of this multifaceted approach. In determining custody, a judge must consider and enter findings of fact on each of the following:

"(B)est interests of the child" means the sum total of the following factors to be considered, evaluated, and determined by the court:

(a) The love, affection, and other emotional ties existing between the parties and the child.

(b) The capacity and disposition of the parties involved to give the child love, affection, and guidance and to continue the education and raising of the child in his or her religion or creed, if any.

(c) The capacity and disposition of the parties involved to provide the child with food, clothing, medical care or other remedial care recognized and permitted under the laws of this state in place of medical care, and other material needs.

(d) The length of time the child has lived in a stable, satisfactory environment, and the desirability of maintaining continuity.

(e) The permanence, as a family unit, of the existing or proposed custodial home or homes.

(f) The moral fitness of the parties involved.

(g) The mental and physical health of the parties involved.

(h) The home, school, and community record of the child.

(i) The reasonable preference of the child, if the court considers the child to be of sufficient age to express preference.

(j) The willingness and ability of each of the parties to facilitate and encourage a close and continuing parent-child relationship between the child and the other parent or the child and the parents.

(k) Domestic violence, regardless of whether the violence was directed against or witnessed by the child.

(l) Any other factor considered by the court to be relevant to a particular child custody dispute.[7]

Even with such guidelines in place, judges still have considerable decisional discretion. Although a judge is usually required to consider each enumerated factor, most statutes do not prioritize them. Accordingly, a judge is free to assign the weight to each factor that he or she believes it merits based on either the circumstances of an individual case or on his or her own beliefs about what considerations are most important. Accordingly, one judge might regard the preference of the child as primary while another might attach little weight to it. Moreover, the factors do not lend themselves to precise definitions. For example, what does the term "satisfactory environment" mean? One judge might emphasize the emotional environment of a parent's home, while another might consider more tangible qualities, such as dwelling size.

*Applying the Test*

In this section we will look more closely at some of the factors that judges tend to emphasize in custody determinations. These include:

- the parent-child bond
- past caretaking
- time availability

- stability of environment
- preference of the child
- domestic violence

**The Parent-Child Bond.** Important to any custody determination is the attempt to evaluate the strength and integrity of the bond that each parent has with his or her children. In some cases, such as where one parent is abusive or disengaged from the family, this task is easy. However, given that most parents have a deep attachment to their children, this assessment can be difficult and may require a multifaceted approach in which a judge weighs a variety of considerations, such as (1) the amount of time each parent spends with the children, (2) the quality and the appropriateness of the interactions, (3) the degree of emotional engagement, and (4) whom the child relies on for emotional and other kinds of essential support.

**Past Caretaking.** Past caretaking has always been an important consideration in custody determinations. Responding to concerns about the vagueness of the best interest standards, some states now give greater weight to considerations of the caretaking role of each parent during the marriage, and favor the **primary caretaker**. Some states have accomplished this by statute, while others leave it to judicial discretion.[8] (For a discussion of the primary caretaker presumption, see below section entitled "Critique of and Alternatives to the Best Interest Standard.")

A number of distinct, mutually supportive rationales support reliance on past caretaking as a critical factor in the decisional matrix. First, there is general agreement among experts that a child usually develops the strongest psychological bond with the parent who has been most involved with his or her daily care (i.e., the primary caretaker) and that preservation of this relationship is essential to a child's healthy development. This attachment theory "suggests that a strong, caring parent-child dyad leads to a strong secure attachment [and an emotionally secure child]. This same theory posits that if the care provided is unsupportive or unpredictable, then insecurity is manifested."[9] However, some commentators worry that the attachment theory is too simplistic and does not fully account for the complexity of human relations.

Predictability is another major reason that past caretaking has become an increasingly important consideration in custody determinations. Predictability is important for two distinct reasons. First is the belief that reliance on past caretaking will reduce some of the inherent uncertainty about how a child will be cared for following a divorce. A parent's prior commitment to providing primary care is seen as a reasonably reliable predictor of how he or she will respond to the child's needs in the future, whereas determining how a parent who has not been intimately involved with caretaking will respond is far more speculative. Accordingly, reliance on past caretaking patterns provides a protective buffer for children, carrying forward familiar rhythms and interactions.

A more recent consideration is that because past caretaking is a more objective criterion than other custody variables, reliance upon it makes custody outcomes more predictable. In turn, this predictability enables couples to enter into custody negotiations with a clearer sense of what they would be likely to gain or lose by going to court. This is particularly important for women because studies have shown that mothers are likely to give up some economic benefits in order to secure custody of their children. If results were more predictable, going to court would be less of a risk, and there would be less need to sacrifice financial entitlements for custodial security.[10] (See below discussion of the primary caretaker presumption.)

Lastly, reliance on past caretaking accords with the overall trend in favor of the private ordering of family relationships. By looking to the arrangements that the parties agreed on for the care of their children, greater weight is being given to what they believe (or, perhaps, more accurately, believed) makes sense for their family rather than to what a judge believes is best.

**Time Availability.** The time that a parent has available to devote to his or her children is another important consideration. This is a sensible concern that tends to favor the parent with a less demanding work schedule, who has more flexibility to respond to the needs — both routine and unanticipated — of the children. It is likely that this parent is the one who has provided most of the past caretaking and thus has a primary attachment to the children.

**Stability of Environment.** Children generally have a need for stability and continuity in the wake of divorce's dislocation. Accordingly, judges often give considerable weight to a parent's ability to maintain a stable home environment. The emphasis on stability may lead a judge to look with disfavor on a parent who has moved around a lot. This can be problematic where the frequency of moves is attributable to the economic strain occasioned by the marital breakup. In order to avoid penalizing a parent in this situation, it is important for judges to consider a number of factors, including intangible ones such as continuity of care, when assessing the stability of a child's environment.

**Preference of the Child.** Given that the undisputed focus of a best interest inquiry is the child, an important consideration is how much weight should be given to a child's stated preference. This is a difficult question that has generated considerable controversy.

Historically, the custodial preferences of children carried little, if any, weight. This disregard of children's views reflected the traditional understanding of children as lacking an independent legal identity. As we have seen, children traditionally were defined by their dependent and subordinate status within the family unit, and they had no separate voice with which to express a preference. This understanding of children has changed over time. Children, especially as they reach their teen years, are now regarded as distinct legal persons with some degree of autonomy and say about their lives, including post-divorce custodial arrangements.

Today, all states allow for consideration of a child's wishes. Generally, there are no fixed rules about minimum qualifying ages, and many states require that a child's wishes be seriously considered once she or he reaches a certain age, usually 12 or 14. A few states give children over the age of 14 the right to choose the parent with whom they wish to live, and his or her choice will be disregarded only if that parent is deemed unfit. Even where not specified by statute or judicial decision, most lawyers believe there is no point in litigating a case where a child over the age of 14 has a clear preference, as a court will almost always respect his or her wishes.

Although chronological age is an important factor in determining whether a child's views will be elicited, and if elicited, what weight they will be given, it is not the only consideration. A judge might also look to the child's maturity, including his or her decision-making ability, and the articulated reasons for any expressed preference. Family circumstances, such as whether there is a history of violence or whether a child blames one parent for ending the marriage, may also be taken into account in assessing the reliability of the child's views.

***The Debate Over the Appropriate Role of Children.*** There are conflicting views about whether children should participate in custody disputes between their parents. The discussion is often framed as if there were only two possible options—that a child either participates in a decision-making capacity or not at all. However, there are other approaches that give children a voice without requiring them to specify which parent they wish to live with. Before considering these options, we review some of the arguments that have been raised on both sides of the involvement debate, keeping in mind that these views generally assume an "all or nothing" approach.

Some experts believe that it is too stressful for children to be brought into a custody dispute. Children often have complex, shifting views regarding the nature of their relationship with each parent and, by being drawn into the conflict, may feel as if the weight of the world has been placed on their shoulders. Given that children often blame themselves for their parents' divorce, the concern is that participation will intensify their distress.

Another concern is that a child's stated preference may be shaped by considerations unrelated to best interest, such as fear of reprisal or worry about upsetting a parent perceived as sensitive. A child may also be subject to the undue influence of a parent or may choose a distant, disapproving parent as a way of winning that parent's love. A child may also identify with the parent who she or he perceives as being more powerful in order to avoid feeling powerless or like a "loser." This is of particular concern in cases involving domestic violence because a child may seek to avoid identification with the victim, who is perceived as weak and vulnerable, in order to enhance his or her own sense of security. This tendency may be more pronounced in boys, especially as they approach adolescence. A child also may be angry at the parent who initiated the divorce and may blame that parent for destroying the family. This anger, which may not be articulated, may influence the child to choose the "innocent" parent in order to get back at the other.

A further consideration is that judges, who usually are not experts in child psychology, will not be able to unearth these complex and often deeply buried motivations and may thus give too much weight to "surface" explanations. Although the use of experts can be helpful, their presence does not necessarily solve the problem. The complexity of a situation may not be fully revealed within the necessary time frame for making a decision, and experts often reach conflicting conclusions, thus still leaving a judge with the job of sorting through competing understandings of a situation.

On the other hand, experts who believe the child's preference should be seriously considered argue that children are entitled to a say in a proceeding with such significant implications for their lives and that to do otherwise is paternalistic and demonstrates a lack of respect for the ability of children to participate in important decisions. They fear that if a child is not listened to, his or her true needs might never surface, since parents, although professing concern for the child, are often seeking to vindicate their own rights and fulfill their own needs. Custody battles may become a fight for supremacy between the parents, with the child as a shadow player. Parents may thus distort, deliberately or not, the wishes of the child to suit their own position.

Although recognizing the difficulties inherent in sorting through the motivational factors, those who favor eliciting the views of children believe that judges are capable of sifting through layers of meaning. They suggest that understanding the views of a child is no more challenging than sorting through other kinds of conflicting evidence, and that making sense of the entangled strands of a family's situation is the essence of the judicial function in a custody case.

Drawing on social science research, some experts have shifted the focus away from casting children as *decision makers* to focus on the importance of incorporating them as *participants* in the decisional process. According to these studies, children who are excluded from the process "complain about feeling isolated and lonely during the divorce process, and many older youngsters express anger and frustration about being left out."[11] Providing children with a structured mechanism for giving voice to both their feelings and possible arrangements can counteract these feelings, but inclusion must be more than a symbolic gesture. Children are entitled to expect that "both their parents and the professionals involved will listen with respect to their comments. When parents indicate that they do not value and respect their children's thinking, feelings, worries, and needs, it is unlikely to be helpful, and may create cynicism and anger."[12]

There are several different ways to involve children in the proceedings. Traditionally, the judge would interview children in chambers. However, this practice is apparently not that common today and, according to a study of judges in Arizona, was the least liked method of obtaining a child's views except for that of eliciting their views in the open courtroom—an approach that none of the judges used.[13] Increasingly common is the use of a third-party professional—such as a guardian ad litem, mental health expert, mediator, or some combination thereof—who can engage the child in a meaningful discussion of what is going on and what the various options might be, without putting him or her in the difficult position of having to choose. Thus for example, if a shared custody arrangement is on the table, a child could be given a chance to express his or her views, such as that the arrangement involves too many switches between households and that fewer transfers would be less disruptive.[14]

**Domestic Violence.** Traditionally, courts did not consider interspousal violence—as distinct from physical abuse of the child—relevant to the determination of best interest. Spousal abuse was seen as connected to the marital relationship, with little or no spillover effect into the parent-child arena. However, new understandings of the dynamics of abuse have led to important changes in the law. Almost all states now take domestic violence into account when making a custody determination, a judicial practice, usually legislatively prescribed, that makes a "powerful statement that the perpetrator of violence against any family member engages in unacceptable behavior that violates his . . . obligations as a parent."[15]

Perhaps most significantly, increased attention has been paid to the fact that many children, even if not themselves direct victims of violence, are exposed to acts of parental violence. According to the research, somewhere between 70 and 87 percent of children in homes where domestic abuse is present have witnessed violence against their mothers,[16] with many of these children witnessing up to half of the incidents that take place.[17]

A growing body of social science literature clearly demonstrates that witnessing spousal violence significantly affects children. According to one early study, "Children who witness violence between their parents . . . are no less victimized than children who are direct victims of abuse. All our findings show that children from violent homes retain searing memories of violence between their parents."[18] Since then, researchers have confirmed that this victimization has serious emotional and developmental implications. Children exposed to domestic violence are at greater risk of engaging in aggressive and destructive "externally' directed behaviors, such as bullying and assaultive conduct. They also suffer from "internally" directed problems, including depression and anxiety, and they may suffer from posttraumatic stress disorder.[19]

Other negative outcomes include cognitive and behavioral delays, which can affect a child's functioning in school and ability to develop friendships. These consequences may vary with age. Thus, for example, babies and very young children may "develop fear of separation or other new fears," while preschool children "who have witnessed domestic violence have been shown to perform less well on tests of verbal intelligence . . . and to be less empathetic and less able to make accurate social inferences than children from nonviolent homes." They are also "more likely to express negative feelings, to play aggressively, to withdraw from others, and to insult or name-call than nonexposed children." Once they reach school age, exposed children "have more academic difficulties than their peers from nonviolent homes and are also compromised in their ability to judge right from wrong."[20]

Another serious concern is that children who are exposed to battering are at greater risk of both becoming abusers and being abused themselves in intimate relationships. According to one study, about one-half of the children who had witnessed violence between their parents experienced violence in their own adult intimate relationships, the boys as abusers and the girls generally as victims.[21]

In addition to directly impacting the well-being of children, partner abuse has other important implications for child custody determinations. First, men who abuse their partners are more likely to abuse their children. According to two observational studies, "fathers who were violent with their partners were also more physically and emotionally aggressive in interactions with their children."[22] There is also a positive correlation between the severity of the partner abuse and the severity of the child abuse.[23]

Also highly relevant is the fact that spousal abuse does not necessarily end upon separation and divorce; in fact, "it is well documented that separation can serve as a catalyst for increased violence" and that "escalated abuse by the batterer as a response to actual or perceived separation is so common that experts have coined the phrase 'separation assault' to describe it."[24] Accordingly, an abusive parent's right of access to the children may need to be limited in order to safeguard the well-being of the abused parent. In turn, paying attention to the safety of the custodial parent has multiple implications for the well-being of children. Not only will this vigilance shield children from continuing exposure to violence, and the associated risk of harm, the reduced threat of violence may well enhance the ability of a caretaker parent to focus on the needs of her children.

Custody statutes generally take one of two approaches with respect to domestic violence. The majority of statutes direct judges to take domestic violence into account as one of the factors that must be weighed when determining custody, with a few statutes directing judges to weigh it more heavily than other considerations. The other approach is to create a rebuttable presumption against awarding sole or joint custody to a parent who has been the perpetrator of domestic violence. To rebut the presumption, a spouse might, for example, seek to show that he has successfully completed a batterer's treatment program and no longer engages in violent behavior.

### Parental Lifestyle and Life Circumstances

The question often arises as to the weight, if any, that should be given to a parent's lifestyle or life circumstances when determining best interest, especially if this places the parent outside what can loosely be referred to as the "mainstream." Are matters of morality relevant? Is it appropriate for a judge to base decisions upon his or her own views about what constitutes a proper environment for a child? Should a judge be allowed to reflect popular community views; for example, that children should be raised by heterosexual parents? Or should judicial discretion be limited by requiring proof that the parental attributes in question bear some relationship to the well-being of the child?

Clearly, it does not make sense for judges to base custody decisions on their own subjective views of what is best for a child. In effect, this would mean that in any given case, the concept of best interest would embody the judge's own sense of morality and understanding of the world, and results would be highly idiosyncratic. To prevent this kind of subjectivity, the basic rule is that there must be a direct **nexus** (or connection) between the parental attribute in question and the well-being of the child. The rule is intended to limit judicial discretion and keep the child at the center of the decision-making process.

An important question is whether judges can really set aside their own views, or whether these views are likely to exert an unarticulated influence on custody outcomes. For example, what if a judge believes that interracial or same-sex relationships are inherently immoral and corruptive of the social order—how likely is it that he or she could set aside these views to dispassionately consider whether an award of custody to a parent in such a relationship is in the child's best interest?

> ## Consideration
>
> In this section, we will see how these lifestyle issues play out in a number of contexts. As you read, think about your own reactions. It is likely that you will feel more comfortable with some situations than with others and that each person in the class will have a unique reaction, which may or may not correspond with yours. It is also likely that each person, on some level, will feel that his or her own reaction is the correct one. Now, put yourself in the shoes of a trial judge. What role should these feelings play in your decision making? How do you reconcile your views with those of your classmates? Now consider what you would do if you were told by an appellate court that your feelings could not influence your custody rulings. Do you think that you could set them aside, or do you think that on some level they would influence your response to the parties?

**Interracial Relationships.** In the landmark case of Palmore v. Sidoti,[25] the United States Supreme Court reversed a Florida trial court decision transferring custody of a young girl from her mother to her father because the mother, who was white, married a black man subsequent to the parties' divorce. In transferring custody, the trial court focused on the possibility that the child would suffer from the stigma of living in a racially mixed household, especially once she began school. In reversing the decision, the Supreme Court made clear that social prejudice should not determine custody outcomes and that the equal protection clause prohibits giving effect to personal bias through the medium of custody adjudications. Moreover, the Court made clear that harm to a child cannot be assumed even though racial prejudice may subject him or her to "a variety of pressures and stresses not present if the child were living with parents of the same racial or ethnic origin."[26]

Although unambivalent in condemning custody decisions premised on racial prejudice, the Court left open a significant question. What should happen if the harm were no longer presumed, but became a reality, such as where a child was subjected to racial taunting? What if she were threatened with injury or actually injured? Should custody be transferred here, or would the court again be giving effect to and perhaps encouraging racial prejudice? This situation raises difficult questions as to how the twin goals of protecting children and not furthering discrimination can be accommodated—a question that is not limited to the context of interracial relationships.

**Sexual Activity: Heterosexual.** Another important question is what weight, if any, should a judge give to the sexual behavior of a parent seeking custody of a minor child? The majority view is that sexual behavior by itself or the fact that a parent is living with a partner she or he is not married to is not relevant unless a detrimental effect on the child or the parent-child relationship is clearly established. In requiring proof of a nexus between the behavior of the parent and the well-being of the child, harm to the child is not to be presumed from the fact that the parent is engaged in a non-marital relationship, as this would be tantamount to a moral pronouncement embodying the judge's subjective views rather than an assessment of the parent's actual ability to care for the child. Rather, such conduct is relevant only where detriment can be shown; for example, where sexual activity occurs in front of the children or where the parent leaves the children on their own in order to pursue a relationship.

Judges may respond somewhat differently if a parent is engaged in a series of sexual relationships, particularly if they are of the one-night-stand variety. Uneasiness about this kind of conduct may result in a judge's presuming harm rather than requiring actual proof of a detrimental impact on the child.

**Sexual Orientation: Gay and Lesbian Parents.** Although the unquestioned majority approach is that a parent's involvement in a heterosexual dating or cohabiting relationship will not impact his or her ability to obtain or maintain custody absent a clear showing that this involvement somehow harms the child, the law's approach is more varied when it comes to gay and lesbian parents. For years, the dominant approach was to presume, without requiring proof of harm, that it was bad for a child to be raised by such a parent. This is frequently referred to as the **per se approach**—in which harm is assumed to flow from the parent's conduct without requiring proof of actual detriment.

A number of concerns underlie the use of this approach in cases involving same-sex relationships. Foremost is the belief that homosexuality is immoral and unnatural and that children must be protected from its influence. Some courts also fear that children of gay parents are likely to become gay or sexually dysfunctional. The issue of stigma—that a child raised by a gay or lesbian parent will be the object of scorn and derision—is frequently raised. In the much-discussed 1995 *Bottoms* case,[27] which involved a grandmother who sought to obtain custody of her grandchild from her lesbian daughter, the Supreme Court of Virginia, although purporting to reject the per se approach, expressed one of the animating fears: "[L]iving daily under conditions stemming from active lesbianism may impose a burden upon a child by reason of the 'social condemnation' attached to such an arrangement, which will inevitably afflict the child's relationship with its 'peers and the community at large.'"[28]

However, the tide has begun to turn, and an increasing number of states have adopted the nexus standard in custody cases involving gay and lesbian parents. Using a "sexual-orientation neutral" approach, judges are to treat these cases no differently from cases involving parents who are in a heterosexual dating or cohabiting relationship. Thus, a parent cannot be denied custody based on a presumption of harm; rather, as when a parent in engaged in a heterosexual relationship, actual detriment must be proved. In adopting the nexus approach, many of these states have been influenced by social science studies that have concluded "that the family environments provided by lesbian and gay parents are as likely as those provided by heterosexual parents to foster and promote children's psychological well-being."[29]

Of course, the possibility always exists that a judge will deny custody based on anti-gay sentiment and then mask the true basis of the decision by articulating reasons unrelated to sexual identity. According to the dissenting justice, this is precisely what occurred in McGriff v. McGriff,[30] a recent case from Idaho, in which the mother (Shawn) sought to modify a joint custody arrangement because the father (Theron) was now cohabiting with his male partner. Although the majority of the justices on the Idaho Supreme Court accepted the judge magistrate's assertion that he was not transferring sole custody to the mother because of the father's sexual orientation, the dissenting justice vigorously disagreed:

> Although it is clear that Shawn's petition is based on Theron's homosexuality, the majority upholds the magistrate's decision, which clearly appears to take Theron's homosexuality into consideration. Immediately after stating that homosexuality did not play a role in its holding, the magistrate stated, "However, [Theron's] decision to openly co-habit with Nick Case, his partner, is a change in circumstances which will generate questions from the girls and their friends regarding their conservative culture and morays (sic) in which the children live."[31]

As further evidence of the pervasive influence of the father's sexual orientation on the custody outcome, the dissenting justice in McGriff also notes that the father's visitation rights are contingent upon his domestic arrangements. In a rebuke to the majority, the dissenting justice states that "[i]f Theron's sexual orientation is not a factor, it is disinguous that Theron may only exercise his visitation rights if he does not live with his male partner. The majority somewhat incredulously states that the limitation has nothing to do with Theron's homosexuality, rather it is a consequence of hang-up phone calls allegedly made by Theron's partner to {the mother}. . . . "[32]

Again, a court would be faced with a somewhat different question if a child was subjected to threats or harm because of a parent's sexual orientation; here, there is an arguable link between the child's well-being and the parent's lifestyle. Potential problems, however, would not necessarily be eliminated by denying custody to this parent. Regardless of who has custody, the child still has a gay or lesbian parent and might be less well equipped to deal with societal prejudice if living with a parent who also displayed negative attitudes toward homosexuality.

Although not common, another approach falls somewhere between the nexus and the per se approaches. In this intermediate approach, the status of being a gay man or a lesbian is not in and of itself deemed harmful, as it would be under a per se approach; rather, the focus is on associated conduct. Under this approach, a court might award a gay or lesbian parent custody but impose certain behavioral limitations. For example, a parent might have to agree, as a condition to receiving or keeping custody, that she or he will not engage in any displays of affection in front of the children or participate in any gay-identified activities. One might ask whether this approach is simply a twist on the per se rule, as it requires a parent to forgo any meaningful expressions of intimacy and personal identity in order to qualify for custody.

**Religion.** The issue of religion usually comes up in custody disputes in one of two ways. A parent may claim that he or she can best meet the religious needs of the child and should therefore be awarded custody. Alternatively, a parent may claim that the religion of the other parent is detrimental to the child or goes against the child's established identity, and should therefore disqualify that parent from custodial consideration. In the first situation, religion is presented as a positive, qualifying factor; in the second, it is presented as a negative, disqualifying one.[33]

In evaluating these claims, a court becomes involved in a delicate and sensitive task, as it must respect the first amendment rights of both parents. This amendment (which is applied to the states through the due process clause of the fourteenth amendment) prevents state interference with an individual's freedom of religion and undue state involvement with religion (e.g., expressing a preference for one religion over another). Absent a compelling interest, a state must remain neutral and uninvolved where religion is concerned.

Where a parent raises religion as a qualifying factor, it cannot be the sole custodial determinant because the judge would be expressing a preference for the religion of one parent over the religion of the other or over the lack of religious involvement. Moreover, the court would be giving preferential weight to religion, saying, in effect, that it is the most important aspect of a child's upbringing.

Must then a court disregard what a parent has to offer by way of religious education and guidance? The generally accepted view is that although a court may not make a value judgment about religion (or the lack thereof) and cannot presume that one parent is better equipped to meet a child's religious needs, it may consider a child's actual religious needs and determine which parent can best meet them. Accordingly, where religion is an established part of a child's life, matching parent to child in this regard is one aspect of determining who can best provide stability and continuity of care. Thus, for example, if a child regularly attends religious services and educational classes, the court might look at which parent has been actively involved with these activities, much as it would evaluate parental involvement in other areas of the child's life. The essential concern is determining which parent will best be able to meet the ongoing needs of the child, without making a value judgment about the kind of religious upbringing a child should have.

Where religion is raised as a disqualifying factor, the parent often belongs to a religion that is considered outside of the mainstream by the parent seeking custody. Typically, the nonmember parent argues that the other's religious beliefs or practices pose a threat of harm to the child's emotional, physical, or psychological well-being. For example, a common concern is that a child will be isolated from his or her peers by restrictions that prohibit certain activities, such as participation in school celebrations, watching television, or associating with nonmembers. The parent seeking custody may also fear that the child will be alienated from him or her if the religion of the other parent espouses that, as a nonbeliever, he or she is evil and will suffer eternal consequences.

Most courts employ a nexus approach in these cases. A parent must show actual harm before the other parent's religious practices are considered relevant. At least in theory, this avoids the risk that a court will make value judgments about a parent's religion. Other courts employ a somewhat less exacting standard and may disqualify a parent if his or her religious beliefs and practices are shown to pose a substantial or reasonable likelihood of harm. Even under this lower standard, however, general assertions about potential isolation or confusion from being raised in a "different" environment will not be given effect. A number of cases have dealt with the difficult question of how to evaluate the potential risk when the parent seeking custody belongs to a religion that prohibits certain medical practices, such as blood transfusions. Some courts have found that such a belief, in and of itself, poses a substantial risk of harm; others have held that where there is no evidence that the child is in need of the procedure, the risk is too speculative to justify a denial of custody on that ground alone. For example, in the 1995 case of Garrett v. Garret, the Nebraska

Court of Appeals stated with respect to the award of custody to a mother who was a practicing Jehovah's Witness:

> ... in order for Jeanne's religion to constitute a ground for awarding custody to Larry, we must be able to determine from the record that the Jehovah's Witness religion as practiced by Jeanne constitutes an immediate and substantial threat to the minor children's temporal well-being. ...
>
> As evidence of an immediate and substantial threat to the minor children, Larry makes reference to the fact that even in the case of a medical emergency, Jeanne would refuse to consent to any of the children's receiving a blood transfusion ...
>
> No evidence was presented showing that any of the minor children were prone to accidents or plagued with any sort of an affliction that might necessitate a blood transfusion in the near future. We cannot decide this case based on some hypothetical future accident or illness which might necessitate such treatment.[34]

**Parental Health.** In keeping with the nexus approach, the basic rule with regard to considerations of parental physical or mental health is that it is not a relevant consideration unless a direct connection between a parent's health condition and harm to the child can be established. Thus, for example, the fact that a parent is taking medication for depression is, by itself, largely irrelevant; however, if a parent is ravaged by depression, and thus unable to care for his or her child, the nexus test will be satisfied. The same rule is true if the parent has a physical disability.

As eloquently expressed by a California appeal court in a case involving a parent who had become a quadriplegic following an accident: "If a person has a physical handicap it is impermissible for the court simply to rely on that condition as prima facie evidence of the person's unfitness as a parent ... rather, in all cases the court must view the handicapped person as an individual and the family as a whole"; moreover, it is a mistake to "assume that the parent's handicap inevitably handicaps the child."[35]

Despite this stated principle, courts initially tended to view the matter differently when the health issue involved a parent's HIV status. Many of the early decisions limited the custodial (or visitation) rights of a parent who were seropositive or had AIDS based mainly on a fear that the disease would be transmitted to the child. It is also likely that some judges were negatively influenced by the underlying behavior that exposed the parent to the disease.

However, as more has become known about the AIDS virus and how it is transmitted, the trend has been away from imposing restrictions on the sole basis of infection with HIV. Utilizing the nexus approach, courts will not assume that a child will be harmed emotionally or physically because of the parent's seropositive status. Where the disease has progressed, however, a court may assess the ability of the parent to care for the child. Consistent with other situations, the court does not presume harm but instead evaluates how the parent's condition impacts the child. These cases can raise very difficult issues — such as whether a child should be protected from the impact of living with a dying parent or whether a parent can still be considered a primary caretaker based on the existing emotional bond where a home health aide provides most of the child's physical care due to the weakened condition of the parent.

## Critiques of and Alternative Approaches to the Best Interest Standard

As the above discussion suggests, the best interest standard has been subject to serious criticisms, most notably that it lends itself to gender-biased decisions and that its open nature means that results are often unpredictable and idiosyncratic. In this section, we consider these critiques and look at two possible alternative approaches: the **primary caretaker presumption** and the American Law Institute's (ALI) "approximation" rule.

### Gender Bias

Although the best interest standard is gender neutral on its face, concerns continue to be raised that judges import gender bias into their custody decisions. Fathers' rights groups argue that fathers are often less valued as parents than mothers and that judges often assume men cannot be primary caretakers. They thus argue that despite gender-neutral laws, the concept of best interest remains linked to beliefs about the natural superiority of maternal nurturing and caretaking abilities.

On the other hand, many women's groups argue that when fathers seek custody, they are often favored by judges, especially when a mother works outside the home, as women are held to a higher parenting standard than men. Accordingly, an employed mother may be regarded as unsatisfied with her role as mother and as being more concerned with gratifying her own needs than caring for her children. Exacerbating this problem, they note that fathers may get "extra credit" for the time they spend with their children, as this contribution is seen as "special" — as being over and above what is expected of them as men. This double standard thus penalizes mothers for time spent away from their children while unduly rewarding fathers for time spent with them.

## Lack of Predictability

The other key critique of the best interest standard is its unpredictability. (Note the connection between these two critiques, since it is the lack of clear standards that enables gender bias to influence custody outcomes.) On the positive side, unpredictability is a function of the standard's flexibility, which permits a judge to tailor results to the circumstances of an individual case. This can be very helpful given the complexity and variability of family relationships. On the other hand, as suggested earlier, it also means that judges have considerable room to make decisions that reflect their personal views of what is best for a child.

Consider the following situation. A couple has two grade-school age children and live in a middle-class suburb. The father is employed full time and the mother is a stay-at-home parent. Both parents are kind and loving, but the primary attachment is to the mother. Both parents want sole custody. If the father is awarded custody, he will be able to remain in the home and to offer the children the presumed advantages of a middle-class lifestyle, including keeping the children in the school they presently attend. If the mother is awarded custody, she will need to move to a less expensive community where the schools are not as good because, even with child support and possible part-time employment, she will not be able to afford the home they live in.

What is the likely outcome? Does the best interest standard compel one result over the other? The answer is hard to predict because the outcome depends on whether the judge regards continuity of caretaking or continuity of home, school, and community as more important. Given the flexibility of the standard, and the corresponding decisional discretion of judges, either outcome could be justified as serving the children's best interest.

As noted in the earlier discussion about the past caretaking factor, the indeterminacy of the best interest standard has significant implications for the settlement process (see Chapter 10). If the outcome cannot be predicted with some degree of certainty, then it means that custody negotiations are taking place in the absence of a transparent decisional framework, thus making it difficult for the parties to assess what they stand to gain or lose as they consider various proposals. In significant part, this problem has given rise to the formulation of two alternatives standards — the primary caretaker presumption and the ALI's approximation rule — that seek to make custody outcomes more predictable.

## The Primary Caretaker Presumption

Emerging out of dissatisfaction with the vagaries of the best interest standard, a number of states have considered adopting a custodial presumption in favor of the parent who has been the primary caretaker. Under this standard, primary caretaking would be the sole determinant of best interest.

In 1981, in the leading case of Garska v. McCoy[36] the state of West Virginia became the first state to adopt the primary caretaker standard (although it has since moved to the ALI approximation rule). In adopting this standard, the *Garska* court focused on the harm caused to the primary care parent by the unpredictability of the best interest test:

> The loss of children is a terrifying specter to concerned and loving parents; however, it is particularly terrifying to the primary caretaker parent, who, by virtue of the caretaking function, was closest to the child before the divorce . . . Our experience instructs us that uncertainty about the outcome of custody disputes leads to the irresistible temptation to trade the custody of the child in return for lower alimony and child support payment.[37]

In anchoring custody outcomes to a fixed standard, the court was thus seeking to prevent custody from being used as a bargaining weapon to extract economic concessions from the primary caretaker parent in order to ensure a favorable custody result.

This presumption has been praised for its recognition of the under-valued job of parenting and the importance of the bond between children and their primary caregivers. It has also been praised for introducing certainty into the process and protecting the often vulnerable economic status of primary caretaking parents. However, the presumption has also been criticized. As with past caretaking, some have critiqued the presumption as overly mechanistic and as failing to account for the complexity of parent-child relationships. Fathers' rights groups have attacked the presumption for being gender-biased, asserting that it is a thinly disguised effort to reintroduce the tender years presumption to the detriment of fathers.[38] Others disagree, noting that if a father is the primary caregiver, the presumption will favor him. Moreover, it is noted that although more mothers than fathers might end up with custody under the presumption, this would reflect the actuality of how families allocate caretaking responsibilities rather than generalized assumptions about gender-appropriate roles.

It has also been argued that the presumption can work against women as well. Although a stay-at-home mom, or one who is employed on a very part-time basis, would clearly be identified as the primary caretaker, the concern is that a judge may not recognize that a woman who works full-time may nonetheless still be the primary caregiver. The judge may assume that the world of work and home are incompatible, thus rendering invisible a woman's continued domestic and caretaking responsibilities.

Despite the considerable interest and discussion that the primary caretaker presumption has generated, states have not rushed to adopt it. Nonetheless, it has contributed to ongoing discussions and efforts to reformulate the best interest standard, including the ALI's approximation rule.

## The American Law Institute's Approximation Rule

In 2002, after more than a decade of research, the prestigious American Law Institute published the *Principles of the Law of Family Dissolution: Analysis and Recommendations* in order to bring "conceptual clarification and improved adaptation to social needs" to the dissolution process.[39] With respect to custody, the Principles recommend shifting from the best interest standard to a more objective "approximation" standard that would allocate custodial responsibilities between divorcing parents in rough proportion to the amount of time each parent spent engaged in caretaking responsibilities during the marriage. Thus, the post-divorce parenting arrangement is to *approximate* the pre-divorce arrangement.

A primary advantage of this approach is that it introduces a strong measure of predictability into the custody process. This provides a clear framework for negotiations and enables parties to make informed decisions about what they would lose or gain by seeking a judicial resolution of the dispute. With the result more predictable, primary caretakers will be less likely to bargain away economic rights in order to secure custody. Another potential advantage is that children will be provided with greater stability and continuity of care as each parent, to the extent possible, will continue to play the same role in their lives that they did prior to the divorce.

However, some important concerns have also been raised about the approximation rule. First, some commentators are concerned that it is too deferential to parents and not sufficiently child-centered. What if, for example, past caretaking arrangements were adopted to meet the need of the parents rather than to provide optimal care for the children? What if other ways of allocating custodial responsibilities would be better for the children? Absent clear problems, such as abuse or domestic violence, will these kinds of concerns get lost in the approximation process?

Another important question is whether it is overly optimistic to assume that arrangements that worked when the parents presumably got along with one another will continue to work in the aftermath of dissolution when parental cooperation and goodwill is apt to be at a minimum. (Note: This concern also applies to the more familiar joint custody context and will be developed further in that section.)[40]

## CUSTODY AND VISITATION ARRANGEMENTS ———————————

Resolution of a custody case becomes even more complex when one takes the variety of custodial and visitations arrangements that are available into account. Traditionally, custody was essentially a unitary concept—one parent, usually the mother, was responsible for raising the child and making all significant decisions affecting the child's life, and the other parent simply visited.

However, beginning in the 1970s, the wisdom of allocating parental roles along such lines was questioned, and joint custody emerged as an approach that would enable children to maintain an ongoing relationship with both parents following a divorce. By 1990, most jurisdictions had amended their custody laws to include joint custody as an option, and some created a presumption that joint custody is in the best interest of the child, although some of these laws have since been repealed. In this section we focus on the actual working out of custody and visitation arrangements.

### Physical and Legal Custody Distinguished ———————————

For the sake of clarity, the terms physical and legal custody will initially be defined in reference to one parent, but as will become apparent, either can be shared. Also, you should be aware that there has been some move away from the traditional terminology, in part to reflect the current emphasis on cooperative post-divorce parenting. Thus, for example, the ALI Principles use the term "custodial responsibility" instead of physical custody, and the term "decision-making responsibility" for legal custody. Also, physical custody is now sometimes referred to as residential custody.

**Physical custody** refers to where a child lives. A parent with physical custody maintains a primary residence for the child and is generally responsible for the child's daily care. With physical custody comes the authority to make all of the day-to-day decisions that arise in the course of caring for a child.

**Legal custody** refers to decision-making authority. Whereas physical custody incorporates the right to make routine decisions, legal custody gives a parent the right to make major decisions affecting the health, welfare, and education of a child, such as whether a child should go to private school or begin mental health counseling. As a general rule, major decisions are distinguished from day-to-day decisions by their importance and their nonrepetitive nature, although, as discussed in the following section, this distinction is often easier to state than to apply.

## Sole and Joint Custody Distinguished ———————————————

The term **sole custody** refers to the vesting of custodial rights in one parent; either legal or physical custody can be sole. With an award of *sole physical custody*, the child lives with one parent and that parent has primary caretaking responsibility. With an award of *sole legal custody*, one parent has the authority to make all of the major decisions affecting the child. Where both custodies are vested in one parent, the other parent will generally have visitation rights without significant parenting responsibilities.

**Joint custody** refers to the sharing of rights and responsibilities; both legal and physical custody can be allocated on a joint basis. *Joint legal custody* denotes the sharing of decision-making authority, and *joint physical custody* denotes the sharing of the day-to-day responsibility for raising a child.

## A Closer Look at Shared Custody Arrangements ———————————

Two shared custody arrangements are most likely: A couple may share both physical and legal custody, or one party may have sole physical custody and share legal custody with the other parent. It is also theoretically possible for a couple to share physical custody, with sole legal custody assigned to one parent, but it is hard to envision many situations where a parent who is responsible for the daily care of a child would not want or would be deemed incapable of major decision-making authority.

Where parents share legal custody, neither one is supposed to make a major decision affecting the child without the participation and consent of the other parent, absent emergency circumstances. Where parents disagree, no action can be taken until a resolution is reached. This can have serious implications for the well-being of a child, where, for example, parents disagree about whether the child needs to be evaluated by a therapist. Ultimately, these disputes may have to be submitted to a court for resolution.

In situations where one parent has sole physical custody with shared legal custody, the distinction between major and day-to-day decisions can become critical. Some decisions are easy to characterize: enrollment in a private school, elective surgery, or mental health counseling are clearly major issues. The choice between blue socks or green or whether to attend a friend's birthday party are clearly of the daily variety. But what about ear piercing? or violin versus tuba lessons? or a significant change in hairstyle? These decisions are harder to characterize and can lead to tremendous conflict over who has the right to make such decisions.

Where parents share physical custody, both are responsible, though not always equally, for the day-to-day care of the child. Here, many arrangements are possible. A child could spend roughly equal amounts of time with each parent, rotating between the households according to a fixed schedule that allocates time on a daily, weekly, monthly, or even yearly basis. Each parent would maintain a home for the child, who would in effect have two principal places of residence. It is also possible for the sharing to be less equal. A child might have one primary residence but spend a significant amount of time with the other parent, who would remain much more directly and consistently involved in the child's life than the traditional visiting parent.

## The Joint Custody Controversy

The joint custody trend began in the 1980s based on a number of considerations. First, a number of studies indicated that fathers tended to drift out of their children's lives following a divorce, causing children to feel a sense of abandonment and rejection. Rather than blaming fathers for not caring about their children, joint custody proponents saw this disengagement as stemming from the awkwardness and insignificance of being cast in a visitor's role and hoped that, given a more meaningful place in their children's lives, fathers would remain more connected to them. Second, an emerging fathers' rights movement was seeking to combat what they perceived as anti-male bias in the family courts, and joint custody became a central demand as a way of wresting custodial control from women. Third, corresponding to the no-fault goal of making divorce a less adversarial process, it was hoped that joint custody would encourage parents to stop fighting over their children and to work out a cooperative arrangement where neither emerged the victor.

Although it has become more commonplace, joint custody remains a contentious issue. Most experts agree that where parents freely choose joint custody and are committed to making it work, it can be a positive arrangement because it gives a child meaningful contact with both parents. However, making it work can be extremely difficult. Parents need to be able to set aside their anger and disappointment in the other as a spouse and respect him or her as a parent. In short, they must have the ability to distinguish between their spousal and their parenting roles. Reflective of these complexities, with time, many parents who begin their post-separation lives with joint custody, find themselves settling into more traditional patterns, with one parent, usually the mother, assuming primary care responsibility of the children.[41]

Even where parents are able to work things out between them, concerns have been raised that joint custody may overburden children, as it requires them to negotiate life in two different households. This can be particularly difficult for some children either because of their temperament or because of their developmental stage.[42] For example, when parents do not live in the same community, adolescents may resent having to be away from their friends and social network on a regular basis.

The far more contentious issue is whether courts should be able to impose joint custody where one parent objects to it. According to fathers' rights proponents, it is essential for courts to have this authority in order to counteract the bias they believe exists against fathers in the divorce courts. They argue that if joint custody were allowed only where it was agreed upon, mothers could routinely defeat the claims of fathers by objecting to joint custody. Fathers' rights groups thus have lobbied for laws that create a presumption in favor of shared custody; the groups also have brought class action lawsuits based on the argument that state laws that do not ensure each parent an equal share of parenting time violate their fundamental right to the care and custody of their children. Although these legal challenges generally have not been successful, with courts finding that the best interest of children trumps a parent's asserted right to equal custodial time, many states have amended their custody laws to include a preference or presumption in favor of joint custody.

However, serious doubts have been raised about the wisdom of giving courts the authority to compel joint custody over the objection of a parent, particularly in high-conflict families. A major concern is that the frequent interaction that joint custody demands may keep alive spousal animosity and conflict and thereby interfere with the parents' ability to disengage from the marriage. Perpetuating spousal animosity is likely to have a spillover effect on the children, who may experience serious mental health issues as a result of continuing exposure to parental anger and arguments.[43] Based on growing evidence that imposing joint custody on recalcitrant and noncooperative parents can have negative effects on children, and that "the bulk of newly divorced spouses cannot remain as positively involved with each other on an everyday basis as joint physical custody requires, [and] that the presumption is causing more litigation to already crowded dockets," states have begun to move away from joint custody presumptions in favor of making joint custody one of the options to consider when determining the best interest of children.[44]

Concerns about joint custody presumptions or preferences are paramount in cases in which there is a history of domestic violence. As many commentators have pointed out, successful shared parenting arrangements require the ability to cooperate and communicate effectively, and these characteristics are likely to be absent in a relationship that was marked by violence. Moreover, the frequency of the interaction demanded by joint custody may keep the victim at risk of continued harm, with a deleterious spillover effect on the children.[45] Recognizing the seriousness of these concerns, most statutes expressly recognize that where there is a history of violence, joint custody is not likely to be in a child's best interest, and these cases are therefore exempted from any statutory preference in favor of joint custody.

## Legal Status of the Noncustodial Parent

At the opposite end of the custodial spectrum from a shared physical and legal custody arrangement is one in which both custodies are vested in a single parent, and the other is a **noncustodial parent**. As discussed below, this parent is usually granted visitation rights; however, before considering visitation, it is important to understand this parent's legal status.

Loss of custody in the context of a divorce action does not sever the parent-child relationship; a mother or father who does not have either legal or physical custody of a child is still that child's parent. (The termination of parental rights is covered in Chapter 13.) The retention of one's legal status as a parent has the following important ramifications:

1. Because custodial determinations are not permanent, a noncustodial parent may always seek to modify the existing arrangement and thus may acquire custodial rights at some point in the future; in contrast, a termination of parental rights results in a permanent severance of the parent-child relationship.
2. Noncustodial parents retain a number of important rights. These include visitation rights; the right of access to school, medical, and other records; and the right to make medical decisions in the event of an emergency or the unavailability of the custodial parent.
3. In addition to these rights, a noncustodial parent remains subject to a support obligation.
4. With the legal relationship intact, benefits and statutory rights that depend on the existence of a parent-child relationship will most likely not be lost. For example, if a noncustodial parent dies without a will, the child will be entitled to a share of the estate under a state's intestacy laws. However, entitlements that depend on proof of actual dependency may be denied.

Thus, although loss of custody may be a devastating event in a mother or father's life, she or he is still a parent. This may seem like a legal abstraction to a noncustodial parent, who may no longer feel like a parent; however, the legal relationship carries with it a bundle of rights and an ongoing support obligation.

# Visitation Rights

The general assumption is that, following a divorce, it is in a child's best interest to have continued contact with both parents. Accordingly, in virtually all cases, a noncustodial parent (referring here to a parent without physical custody) will be granted visitation rights. Because this parent plays a less significant role in the life of a child than the custodial parent does, courts generally use a lower standard for deciding about visitation than they do for deciding about custody. Accordingly, a parent who may not be capable of providing the day-to-day care and nurture that a child needs will, in most cases, be considered capable of spending some meaningful time with the child on a regular basis.

However, as discussed in more detail below, if continued contact is deemed to pose a risk of emotional or physical harm to a child, visitation rights will be denied or subject to limitations.

## *The Visitation Schedule*

As the following discussion makes clear, working out a viable visitation schedule, including determining the appropriate nomenclature, involves the careful consideration of multiple factors.

**Amount of Time and Frequency of Visits.** Because there is so much variability in visitation arrangements, it is hard to state with any certainty how much time the "average" visiting parent spends with his or her children. However, the unquestioned trend is to increase visitation time and frequency well beyond the traditional four hours on Sunday afternoon — which gave dad just enough time to take the kids to the zoo and out for a quick dinner.

Setting aside, for the moment, those cases in which visitation may pose a threat to a child's physical or emotional well-being, visitation rights are now seen as providing the noncustodial parent with the opportunity to remain an integral part of his or her child's life as opposed to simply being the "fun" parent. When the parents live close to one another, the noncustodial parent may be able to see the child on a regular basis, which can provide a sense of continuity and familiarity. The schedule may well include some overnight time and some extended time during school and summer vacations. When the parents do not live near each other, visitation will, of course, be less frequent, and it will be harder for the noncustodial parent to remain connected to the rhythms of a child's daily life. This may be offset somewhat by extended visitation time over the summer and school vacations.

**Setting the Parameters.** Visitation arrangements, as set out in a court order, separation agreement, or parenting plan, can be open-ended, spelled out in elaborate detail, or somewhere in between. An open-ended arrangement generally provides for a right of reasonable or liberal visitation and leaves the details up to the parties. This kind of arrangement usually works best if the parties have been separated for a while and have informally worked out and implemented a mutually satisfactory schedule. Because an open-ended agreement requires frequent communication, it is not likely to succeed if the parties are angry and hostile, or have not been successful at working out an informal arrangement. The constant negotiations necessitated by an open-ended schedule may serve to keep the anger between the parties alive longer and prevent them from settling into a reasonably calm visitation pattern, to the clear detriment of the children. A visitation arrangement can be spelled out with great specificity, detailing precisely when each and every visit is to occur and who is responsible for transporting the children to and from the visits. A visitation schedule for summer and school vacations and holidays also may be detailed. Specific guidelines for when a parent may deviate from the schedule may be included as well. (See Chapter 10 for an example of a separation agreement with a very specific visitation schedule.)

A middle-ground approach is to provide a fairly set schedule, with a proviso that this does not represent the full extent of the visiting parent's rights and that he or she may also visit at mutually agreed upon times. This minimizes the negotiations inherent in a completely open-ended arrangement but also builds in a degree of flexibility that may benefit both parents — especially if it is written to accommodate both of their needs.

Parents often do not anticipate how emotionally difficult the visitation process can be for both them and the child, especially around holidays and when a former partner begins to date. Accordingly, at least in the initial period following a divorce, a good argument can be made that most parents do better with a specific visitation plan that minimizes the need for constant negotiations. Frequently, after the initial emotional intensity has dissipated, parents are better able to be more flexible in responding to the needs of the other parent.

**The Boundary Between Shared Physical Custody and Sole Custody with Visitation Rights.** The formal boundary between sole custody with visitation rights and joint physical custody cannot always be fixed with precision, although some states have set a minimum amount of time that a parent must spend with a child for the arrangement to qualify as shared custody. For example, the following arrangement could, absent specific statutory criteria, be characterized either way: a child lives with his mother during the week and spends every weekend — from Friday at 6:00 P.M. until Sunday evening — with his father. He also has dinner with his father every Wednesday night.

In negotiating an agreement, many attorneys try to avoid these terms because they carry a lot of emotional baggage. For example, if parents have negotiated an arrangement in which the children are to be with the mother 70 percent of the time and with the father 30 percent, the mother may object to calling this shared physical custody because it obscures the fact that she has the children most of the time. On the other hand, the father might object to his time being identified as visitation because this can suggest minimal involvement. Accordingly, alternative terms such as "primary care parent" and "secondary care parent" can be substituted, or the agreement may refer to shared parenting responsibilities with each parent having custody when the children are with him or her, regardless of how the total time is allocated.

### When Unrestricted Visitation Is Not in a Child's Best Interest

Despite the priority that the law gives to preserving the relationship between a child and the noncustodial parent, there are situations in which continued contact is considered not to be in a child's best interest, such as where it would place a child at risk of emotional or physical harm. Another possibility is that visitation would be allowed but would be subject to restrictions, such as that visits be supervised by a third party. The parent might also be required to be in therapy and/or attend some kind of parenting class.

Restrictions on visitation may also be imposed where a history of domestic violence places the custodial parent at risk even if the child has not been a direct victim of the abuse. Here, restrictions are generally aimed at limiting contact between the parents, such as that the child is dropped off and picked up at a neutral location (for instance, an agency that provides custody exchange services) at a timed interval so there is no contact between the parents.

Frequently, a parent who has been denied visitation rights or who has restricted visitation will return to court seeking unrestricted access to his or her child. In response, a judge must determine if the child (or the custodial parent) is still at risk of harm. If visits are being allowed for the first time, a judge is likely to impose some restrictions. Judges vary in their approach to requests for the lifting of existing restrictions. Some judges are reluctant to modify restrictions on the ground that the risk of potential harm does not outweigh the potential benefit of allowing visitation to occur in a more natural, unstructured way. Other judges take the view that if a parent has complied with the requirements of the initial restrictions, he or she is entitled to a second chance to reestablish a relationship with his or her child that is not dependent on the involvement of third parties.

## Parenting Plans and Parent Education Programs

Although, as noted above, the trend has shifted away from joint custody presumptions in favor of making joint custody an option, this shift does not signal a return to the traditional "zoo daddy" model, in which fathers had a few hours of fun with their children on Sunday afternoons and an occasional holiday, with no expectation of a sustained and meaningful role in their childrens' lives. Rather, as we have seen, the preferred approach today is to create a structure that enables both parents — Custodial and Visiting — to sustain meaningful ties with their children. Although research indicates that children fare better when they sustain a quality post-dissolution relationship with both parents, the studies also make clear that continued parental conflict and hostility, which can be exacerbated by frequent contact, has a deleterious impact on children. Accordingly, to minimize post-divorce animosity and enhance the ability of parents to coordinate caring for their children, parenting plans and parenting education programs have become increasingly popular legal options.

A growing number of states now require parents to develop and submit a "parenting plan" to the court for approval if custody is to be shared, and a few states require the submission of a plan in all cases involving minor children. Parents may be required to participate in mediation if they cannot agree upon a plan. A **parenting plan** is a written agreement in which the parents detail how they intend to care for their children following a divorce. Designed to minimize hostility and foster cooperative parenting, parenting plans generally must cover all aspects of child rearing, including how time between the two households is to be divided, how responsibilities are to be allocated, and how decisions are to be made and disputes resolved. Depending on the state, other matters, such as relocation and child support, may also be addressed.

Parenting plans appear to make a good deal of sense where parents wish to share custody. However, paralleling the criticisms of joint custody with which these plans are often associated, serious concerns have been raised about the appropriateness of requiring parenting plans in cases involving domestic violence or where there is a parental hostility. Accordingly, exemptions or special protections have been incorporated into many of these laws to cover situations where the kind of cooperative parenting envisioned by parenting plans is either not safe or feasible.

A related trend is the enactment of laws setting up parenting education programs for divorcing parents. Depending on the state or the circumstances of the family, these programs may be mandatory or offered on a voluntary basis, and, like parenting plans, they are intended to facilitate the transition to post-divorce parenting. These programs are designed to educate "parents about the potential effects of their behavior and attitudes on their children."[46] The hope is that, once they gain such awareness, parents will modulate negative behaviors so that they can respond more effectively to the needs of their children.

Again, important concerns have been raised about parent education programs where there has been a history of domestic violence; in states where participation is mandatory, judges are usually allowed to waive the attendance requirement for good cause, such as where necessary to protect a party from the risk of abuse. Other options have also been suggested that would enable a victim of domestic violence to attend a parent education class while also protecting her safety, such as by having the parents attend class on different nights or in different locations.[47]

A more recent innovation is for courts to offer educational programs for the children of divorcing parents to help them understand and cope with the changes in their lives. Children are usually grouped according to age, and the curriculum is adapted to the development needs of the targeted age. Although these programs are usually offered on a voluntary basis, they may be required in some jurisdictions. For instance, under local court rules in Kentucky, children in many parts of the state are required to attend the children's component of the state's Divorce Education program. That portion of the overall program is designed to "provide a sense of security, awareness and understanding as a beginning point for children learning to cope with dual parenting in separate households." Children in grades 1-5 attend Kids' Time, and those in grades 6-8 attend Tweens' Time.[48]

---

### Interview Checklist

Following is a list of the kinds of information you will need to learn about in cases where custody or visitation (or both) may be an issue. As discussed in greater detail in Chapter 10, it often takes a while for a client to feel comfortable enough to speak openly about the intimate details of his or her life. Thus, absent an emergency situation where an immediate custody decision must be made, all of the following information does not need to be obtained at the initial interview. In fact, you are likely to obtain a more accurate and complete picture if you do not push for all this information up front. Accordingly, the checklist below should not mechanistically be converted into a set of interview questions. Also keep in mind that parents, regardless of their particular situations, are likely to be worried and anxious about their future relationship with their children; you need to be sensitive to the volatility of child-related issues. Remember, too, that information about the other parent coming from your client is likely to be different from the information the other parent provides to his or her own attorney.

1.  What is the nature of the relationship each parent has with the child?
2.  How have responsibilities been allocated between the parents over time? More specifically:
    - Who makes the child-care arrangements?
    - Who transports the child to and from child care or school?
    - Who arranges the child's activities?
    - Who stays home with the child when he or she is sick?
    - Who supervises homework?
    - Who helps the child get off to childcare or school in the morning (e.g., getting breakfast, clothing)?
    - Who is responsible for bathing the children and putting them to bed?
    - Who makes the child-related purchases?
    - Who attends school meetings (including parent-teacher conferences)?
3.  How much time does each parent have available to be with the child?
4.  What is each parent's approach to discipline (including any potential concerns about abuse)?
5.  What activities does each parent enjoy with the child?
6.  How does each parent intend to make post-divorce adjustments in his or her schedule to accommodate the changed family structure?
7.  What are each parent's strengths and weaknesses?
8.  Does either parent have a history of alcohol or drug abuse?
9.  Does either parent have a history of mental health problems?
10. What are the available support systems, such as friends and relatives, of each parent?
11. What are each parent's commitments, in addition to work?

## POST-DIVORCE CUSTODY AND
## VISITATION DISPUTES

Following a divorce, disputes often arise regarding custody or visitation arrangements—or both—and a parent may return to court seeking to either enforce or change existing arrangements. The former is accomplished through a **complaint for contempt** and the latter through a **complaint for modification**; as a general rule, a complaint for modification must be based upon an unforeseen change in circumstances that alters the existing arrangement so that it is no longer in the best interest of the child. Courts have continuing jurisdiction over these disputes until children reach the age of majority and are no longer subject to the custodial authority of their parents. Rather than returning to court, parents also may seek to resolve these disputes through mediation or arbitration; in fact, their separation agreement may require them to try and resolve their dispute through one of these methods before they can seek court relief. (For detail on the procedural aspects of this paragraph, see Chapter 10.)

These post-divorce actions can be a double-edged sword. On the one hand, in order to make certain that a child is protected from harm and that his or her needs are being met, courts must have the authority to hear and resolve post-divorce disputes. On the other hand, this creates the possibility that parents who are engaged in an acrimonious dispute for control of a child will continuously return to court, claiming that the child is not being cared for properly. Because courts have a duty to ensure that custodial arrangements do not pose a risk of harm to a child, a court must assess the situation, even where it appears that in bringing the action, the parent was motivated by hostility rather than a genuine concern for the child. Below, we consider three common categories of post-divorce disputes, and the emerging debate over "virtual visitation."

### Disputes About Custody

Following a divorce, parents often express concern about the custodial arrangements and seek to change them. Thus, for example, in a situation of shared legal custody, it may turn out that the parents cannot make decisions without a protracted struggle, and the parent with physical custody feels this is interfering with his or her ability to meet the needs of the child. Or where parents share physical custody of a child who is now a teenager, the parent who lives in the town where the child attends school may seek sole custody because the teen resents having to spend sustained time away from his or her primary group of friends. Or a parent may realize that the other parent, who had been sober for an extended time period at the time of the parties' divorce, has relapsed and is again abusing alcohol and is thus not able to care for the child properly.

In the above examples, the desired modifications are based both on a genuine concern for the well-being of the child and on a change in circumstance that makes the existing arrangement unworkable. Of course, the other parent may not see the situation in the same way, and she or he may vehemently oppose the requested change. Some requests for modification, however, are not based on a concern for the child but stem from continued hostility toward the other parent. Thus, for example, a parent may resent the fact that his or her former spouse is cohabiting with a new partner and may seek to have that parent's custodial rights revoked, claiming that the partner is a bad influence on the child. Note that although this is clearly a change in circumstances, there must also be an adverse impact on the child. It is not always easy for the court to sort out what is going on, and modification actions that stem from parental hostility often become bitter and protracted as old antagonisms resurface.

## Disputes About Visitation

As with custody, bitter fights may occur around visitation. The visiting parent may assert that the custodial parent refuses to let him or her see the child, while the custodial parent may assert that he or she always gets the child ready and the other parent never shows up. These disputes are difficult to resolve. Often, there is not much a court can do other than admonish the parties to comply with the terms of the visitation arrangement. If, however, the custodial parent is truly interfering with the visiting parent's ability to see the child by, for example, consistently not being at home when the visiting parent is supposed to pick up the child, the visiting parent can bring a contempt action; the ultimate sanction for interference with visitation rights would be a transfer of custody to the other parent. If, on the other hand, the custodial parent has good cause for limiting access, such as where the visiting parent has shown up intoxicated to pick up the child, or there is a consistent failure of the visiting parent to adhere to the schedule, the custodial parent may be able to bring a modification action to curtail or restructure the existing arrangement. Unfortunately, there is no real remedy for a custodial parent who wishes to compel the other parent to exercise his or her visitation rights. A parent cannot be forced to visit when he or she chooses not to.

## Relocation Disputes ────────────────────────────────────────────

Following a divorce, most states do not permit a custodial parent to move out of state with the child without first obtaining the consent of the other parent or the court. As might be expected, **relocation disputes** are fraught with bitterness. A custodial parent is likely to resent the potential limitation on the ability to seek a better life, especially in light of the fact that a visiting parent can move about freely without having to secure anyone's consent, and the noncustodial parent is likely to resent the potential loss of access to the child.

States take a variety of approaches to relocation cases, but the recent trend has been to favor the right of the custodial parent to relocate with the children. Generally, the parent must show that the move is motivated by good faith—such as by a job opportunity or the desire to move closer to extended family, rather than by a desire to interfere with the rights of the noncustodial parent—and is in the child's best interest.[49]

Under this approach, the concept of best interest is usually broadened to take the needs of the custodial parent into account based on the view that the child and custodial parent are interdependent, and a move that benefits the parent, by, for example, locating him or her closer to extended family, will inure to the benefit of the child. As explained in one of the first cases to adopt this expanded view of best interest:

> The children, after the parents' divorce or separation, belong to a different family unit than they did when the parents lived together. The new family unit consists only of the children and the custodial parent, and what is advantageous to that unit as a whole, to each of its members individually and to the way they relate to each other and function together is obviously in the best interests of the children. It is in the context of what is best for that family unit that the precise nature and terms of visitation and changes in visitation by the noncustodial parent must be considered.[50]

The relationship between the child and the noncustodial parent is certainly not an irrelevant consideration in jurisdictions favoring the custodial parents in relocation disputes. However, given that the primary focus is on the importance of continuity of care within the custodial household and what is needed to make that family function effectively, the fact that visitation will occur on a less regular basis is generally not enough to prevent a move. It may be enough to defeat the move, however, when considered with other factors, such as where the move is not prompted by reasons calculated to benefit the custodial household but by, for example, a desire to change scenery.

States that favor the custodial parent generally approach the issue differently where the parents share physical custody. Here, the child has two distinct post-divorce households, and his or her best interest is not so clearly identified with one parent as it is when one parent has sole custody. In this situation, a court might decide that preserving the status quo is in the child's best interest and deny the relocation request. Another possible approach would be to modify or terminate the existing custody order, and make a de novo determination of the child's best interest, which would incorporate a determination about relocation.

The other approach is to give more weight to the interests of the non-custodial parent in preserving his or her relationship with the child. Accordingly, the custodial parent most likely will be required to prove more than simply good faith and best interest. In terms of his or her motivation for moving, he or she may need to establish that the move is compelled by "extraordinary reasons." In terms of its impact on the child, the parent may need to show that it offers a "real advantage"; although the meaning of this term is not entirely clear. At a minimum, the parent may need to prove that the child would gain a tangible benefit that is not available in the home state. Under this approach, courts generally do not take an expanded view of best interest and will thus not assume, without supporting evidence, that changes for the better in the custodial parent's life naturally benefit the child.

Recently, the trend favoring the custodial parent in relocation disputes has been questioned by some commentators who argue that this approach simply assumes that a child's well-being is tied to the custodial parent, and fails to account for the actual experiences of children. Thus, for example, one recent study suggests that children might be adversely impacted when they move more than an hour's drive from the noncustodial parent, while others suggest that relocation outcomes might vary based upon a complex array of factors, such as the age of the children, how soon the move follows the time of separation, and the nature and frequency of contact the children and the noncustodial parent have before the move.[51] Such research could well influence the future direction of relocation cases.

### Virtual Visitation

A recent issue is whether judges should consider the availability of technological innovations, such as videoconferencing and interactive Web sites, when resolving a visitation dispute. This issue has arisen mainly in the context of relocation disputes, although it could also arise at the time of the initial divorce decree if one parent had moved to a new community that was some distance from the marital residence.

In some cases, judicial orders have referred to the use of e-mail and the Internet as a way to supplement communication between a child and a noncustodial parent. In a number of relocation cases from around the country, judges have even included "**virtual visitation**" provisions in their decrees. For example, in Cleri v. Cleri, a Connecticut trial court allowed the mother's relocation request and, in addition to two weekend visits per month, granted the father two virtual visits per week:

> The Husband shall have "virtual visitation" with the children twice per week, on Tuesdays and Thursdays, from 6:00 P.M. to 7:00 P.M., and at each additional times as the parties may agree. To facilitate the virtual visitation each party shall forthwith purchase and install a video camera attachment and the related software for his or her computer.[52]

In Kaleita v. Sniderman, a Florida trial court denied the mother's relocation request and instead transferred custody of the parties' ten-year-old daughter from the mother to the father. Having made this decision, the court then ordered the parents to facilitate "virtual visitation." Each parent was ordered to install a telephone line in their daughter's bedroom in each of their homes for her exclusive use and to purchase and install a "state-of-the-art" computer in her bedroom (again in each home) with "video conferencing equipment and software, including a video camera with audio capabilities." Each parent was also ordered to purchase "appropriate computer furniture" for their daughter's bedroom.[53]

In *Kaleita* and *Cleri*, the court did not enter its "virtual visitation" order until after it had completed a separate multifactorial analysis to determine whether to allow the mother's relocation request. Thus, the availability of virtual visitation was not a consideration in the underlying relocation decision, but came into play only after this decision had been made as a way to facilitate communication with the now noncustodial mother. Given that we are in the age of the computer, looking to technology to supplement communication with a nonresidential parent seems a reasonable approach, although one might question the appropriateness of ordering parents to purchase the latest in computer equipment along with appropriate furniture.

The issue is potentially more complex, however: What if a judge considered the availability of this technology in making the relocation decision itself? Here, it would not simply be a way to supplement other avenues of communication once an independent decision had been made, but it would be a factor in the decisional matrix, to be weighed along with other considerations, such as the reason for the move and the best interests of the child. This raises profound questions about the nature of human interaction and how meaningful relationships are maintained with people who are not in physical proximity. Must connection occur in person for it to count as meaningful contact? Can one really "interact" virtually? What is lost when technological connections replace physical contact? What does it mean for human relationships when spatial proximity is no longer needed for "real time" communication? These and other related questions will only become more pressing in the coming years as the distance between virtual and actual reality continues to diminish.

## THE CUSTODIAL AND VISITATION RIGHTS OF "NONPARENTS"

Until this point, the focus of this chapter has been on custody and visitation disputes between divorcing parents. In these disputes, the rights of each party, at least in a formal legal sense, are deemed to be equal. Each is entitled to try to establish that an award of custody to him or her would further the best interest of the child. In this section, we turn to a consideration of custody and visitation disputes between parents and "nonparents"—namely, grandparents, stepparents, and co-parents, although, as we will see, the term nonparent is problematic in the co-parent context, as it assumes the lack of a parental status, which is often the issue in controversy.

Before considering these disputes, it will be helpful to review four fundamental principles that have guided the law's traditional understanding of the parent-child relationship:

1. Parenthood is achieved solely through biology or adoption.[54]
2. Parents have a fundamental right to direct the upbringing of their children, including deciding who will have access to them.
3. A child can have only one legally recognized mother and one legally recognized father, for a sum total of two different-sex parents.
4. In a dispute between a parent and a "nonparent," there is an automatic preference in favor of the parent based on the assumption that he or she is best able to meet the child's needs absent extraordinary circumstances.

In accordance with these principles, these disputes are treated differently from those between two divorcing parents. Although the approaches vary from jurisdiction to jurisdiction, the basic rule is that as a nonparent, this party must establish something more than best interest in order to maintain an ongoing relationship with a child in the face of opposition from a parent. She or he may need to prove that the parent is unfit before being able to assert her or his own rights to see the child or that severing the relationship between the child and the party would cause demonstrable harm to the child. In some instances, a "nonparent" may even be denied standing (this concept is discussed below) to assert a claim in the first instance.

## Grandparents

At common law, grandparents had no legal right of access to their grandchildren. Parents were said to have a moral but not a legal obligation to permit grandparents to see their grandchildren. In essence, this meant that a grandparent's right of access was derivative; he or she had no direct link to the child as the connection flowed through the related parent. This rule was based on a number of considerations, including the right of parents to control the upbringing of their children and the concern that a legal dispute between grandparent and parent would be destructive to the child, particularly if the child blamed him- or herself for the controversy.

This approach began to change in the 1960s, and today all states have statutes that, to varying degrees, modify the common law rule of no access. Some states have enacted specific grandparent visitation statutes, while others include grandparents within a broader third-party visitation statute. The enhanced legal status of grandparents reflects a number of developments. First, with the graying of the population, the organizational and political clout of senior citizens, an important force behind these laws, has increased. Second, as the divorce rate has risen, increased attention has focused on the importance of providing children with continued access to essential relationships in order to help buffer the dislocation of divorce. And, closely related, is an increased awareness of how important the bond between a grandparent and child can be.[55] These statutes reflect the changing reality of the U.S. family and the often vital role that nonparents play in the upbringing of children.

In looking at grandparent visitation statutes, it is helpful to ask two questions: (1) Under what circumstances may a grandparent seek visitation rights? and (2) What substantive standard will be used to resolve the dispute? The first question is often characterized as a matter of standing. **Standing** is a jurisdictional concept that requires a person to have a sufficient stake in the outcome of a controversy in order to be allowed to maintain a legal action; if a party lacks standing, his or her action is dismissed. Most statutes require that there be some kind of family disruption, such as divorce or parental death, in order for a grandparent to have standing. In other states, the statutes give grandparents a more general right to seek visitation without specifying the circumstances under which a petition can be filed. However, based on considerations of family privacy, many courts will not allow a petition to go forward where the family is "intact" and require some kind of disruption or proof of parental unfitness as a prerequisite to the maintenance of an action.

Once it is determined that a grandparent has standing to seek visitation rights, the next consideration is the standard to be used for resolving the dispute. Some states have adopted a best interest standard (see, however, the discussion of *Troxel* below), although judges generally require proof of something more than simply that the child would enjoy a continued relationship with the grandparent. Other states have adopted a higher burden of proof, most frequently by requiring the grandparent(s) to establish that the denial of visitation rights would harm the child.

As grandparents began turning to the courts to gain access to their grandchildren after contact had been denied or limited by a son or daughter (or by a daughter- or son-in-law), some parents responded by challenging the constitutionality of the grandparent visitation laws, arguing that such laws were an unwarranted intrusion into the realm of family privacy. Initially, courts tended to uphold the validity of the statutes, finding that any intrusion into a fit parent's right to direct the upbringing of his/her children was offset by the benefit to the child of a continued relationship with his or her grandparent. As expressed by the Kentucky Supreme Court in the case of King v. King, these early decisions tended to sentimentalize the grandparent-grandchild relationship:

> While the Constitution . . . does recognize the right to rear children without undue governmental interference, that right is not inviolate . . .
>
> In an era in which society has seen a general disintegration of the family, it is not unreasonable for the General Assembly to attempt to strengthen familial bonds. . . . There is no reason that a petty dispute between a father and son should be allowed to deprive a grandparent and grandchild of the unique relationship that ordinarily exists between those individuals. . . .
>
> If a grandparent is physically, mentally and morally fit, then a grandchild will ordinarily benefit from contact with the grandparent . . . Each benefits from contact with the other. The child can learn respect, a sense of responsibility and love. The grandparent can be invigorated by exposure to youth, can gain an insight into our changing society, and can avoid the loneliness which is so often a part of an aging parent's life. These considerations by the state do not go too far in intruding into the fundamental rights of the parents.[56]

In 1993, however, starting with the decision of Tennessee Supreme Court, in the case of Hawk v. Hawk, courts began to give greater consideration to the rights of parents to decide who should have access to their children:

> ... Bill and Sue Hawk argue that grandparent visitation is a "compelling state interest" that warrants use of the state's parens patriae power to impose visitation in "best interests of the children." ... We find, however, that without a substantial danger of harm to the child, a court may not constitutionally impose its own subjective notions of the "best interests of the child" when an intact, nuclear family with fit, married parents is involved.
>
> The requirement of harm is the sole protection that parents have against pervasive state interference in the parenting process.
>
> ... [I]t is not within the power of a court, ... to make significant decisions concerning the custody of children, merely because it could make a better decision or disposition. The State is parens patriae and always has been, but it has not displaced the parent in right or responsibility ... [57]

The court goes on to critique the Kentucky Supreme Court's *King* decision:

> ... the *King* majority engaged in a sentimental reflection on the "special bond" between grandparent and grandchild. ... In his dissent, however, Justice Lambert disputed the constitutionality of a statute "which has as its only standard the subjective requirement of 'best interest of the child' adding that "mere improvement in quality of life is not a compelling state interest and is insufficient to justify invasion of constitutional rights."[58]

In 2000, the United States Supreme Court, in the case of Troxel v. Granville, entered the fray. Under consideration in this case was the state of Washington's opened-ended statute that gave "any person" the right to petition the court for visitation rights at "any time" based on the best interest of the child. This case involved an unmarried couple with two children. After the relationship ended, the father moved in with his parents. He saw his children on a regular basis, with the visits often taking place at his parents' home. About two years after the separation, the father committed suicide. The grandparents continued to visit with the children. The mother then decided to limit the visits, and the grandparents sued for increased access to their granddaughters.

The Washington Supreme Court declared the law unconstitutional, stating, "It is not within the province of the state to make significant decisions concerning the custody of children merely because it could make a 'better' decision."[59] The United States Supreme Court agreed that the statute was invalid, but it did so on far narrower grounds, finding that it was invalid only *as applied* to the facts of the case before it. Of primary concern to the Court was the "sweeping breadth" of the statute, which effectively allowed a judge to substitute his or her views regarding visitation for the views of a fit parent:

> Once . . . the matter is placed before a judge, a parent's decision that visitation would not be in the child's best interest is accorded no deference . . . Instead, the Washington statute places the best-interest determination solely in the hands of the judge. Should the judge disagree with the parent's estimation of the child's best interests, the judge's view necessarily prevails. Thus, in practical effect, in the State of Washington a court can disregard and overturn any decision by a fit custodial parent concerning visitation whenever a third party affected by the decision files a visitation petition, based solely on the judge's determination of the child's best interests.[60]

As the Court explains, an exercise of such unfettered judicial discretion is precisely what happened in *Troxel*. The trial court failed to give any real weight to the mother's views, thus disregarding the usual presumption that fit parents act in the best interest of their children. Moreover, the lower court seemed to have presumed that the visitation request should be granted, thus placing "on Granville, the fit custodial parent, the burden of *disproving* that visitation would be in the best interest of her daughters."[61]

In deciding this case, the Court made clear that it was not declaring as a matter of constitutional principle that all third-party visitation laws are an impermissible encroachment on the rights of parents, or that harm must be established before allowing visitation over the wishes of a parent. Instead, the Court held only that, at a minimum, some "special weight" must be given to the stated preference of a fit parent. This result is far from definitive; as the current state of the law shows, the standard is subject to multiple interpretations. *Troxel* can be read broadly to require almost complete deference to parents, so long as they are fit; it also can be read more narrowly to, for example, place a burden on grandparents to show that something more than the child's best interest is needed in order to override the wishes of a fit parent.[62]

## Stepparents

Traditionally, if a second marriage ends in divorce, a **stepparent** (the spouse of a child's parent) has not been entitled to visitation or custody on the theory that their status derives from the marriage and thus lasts only as long as the marriage does. This result would, of course, be different if the stepparent had adopted the child because adoption creates a permanent parent-child relationship that is not dependent on the continued existence of the marriage. However, compelled by the awareness that stepparents often play a critical role in the lives of children, particularly when the noncustodial parent is uninvolved, the law has begun to give stepparents greater rights upon marital dissolution.

Some states have statutes that specifically allow a stepparent to seek visitation, and possibly also custodial rights, following a divorce. In other states, in the absence of a statute, courts have used a number of theories to extend parental-like rights to stepparents at the time of marital dissolution. For instance, a Michigan court extended parental status based on the concept of **equitable parenthood** and permitted a stepparent to be treated as a parent where:

> (1) the husband and child mutually acknowledge a relationship as father and child, or the mother of the child has cooperated in the development of such a relationship over a time prior to the filing of the complaint for divorce, (2) the husband desires to have the rights afforded to a parent, and (3) the husband is willing to take on the responsibility of paying child support.[63]

Other courts have extended rights to stepparents based on the doctrine of *"in loco parentis."*[64] Here, parental rights (and obligations, such as the duty to pay child support) may be extended to someone who has assumed the role of a parent over an extended period of time through the provision of sustained nurturance and support. To be *in loco parentis*, a stepparent must intend to participate in a child's life as a parent—a casual relationship will not give rise to this status. Although this doctrine has been used to extend a stepparent-child relationship beyond the end of a marriage to the child's parent, a limitation is that the relationship can be terminated at will by the stepparent (or the child), thus bringing the legal bond with its corresponding rights and duties to an end.

In jurisdictions where stepparents can pursue post-dissolution claims, the approach tends to be more liberal where visitation, as distinct from custody, is at issue. Where there is a meaningful connection between a stepparent and child, a court may recognize the importance of continuing this bond beyond the marriage and allow visitation based on a best interest standard. Following *Troxel*, some courts may be inclined to require more than proof of best interest, while others see a distinction between a grandparent and someone who has been in an actual parental role. Where custody is at issue, the traditional preference in favor of biological parents means that considerably more weight will be given to the expressed views of the legal parent. To prevail, a stepparent may need to establish unfitness or the presence of "extraordinary circumstances" that would merit depriving the biological parent of custody.

## Co-Parents

Like heterosexual couples, many same-sex couples decide that they wish to share in the joys of raising a child together — for the purpose of our discussion, we will assume a lesbian couple, as most of the major cases to date have involved co-mothers. Accordingly, based on their mutual intent to parent a child in common, one woman is either inseminated or adopts a child.[65] Although both women may regard the child as equally theirs, and the child may likewise regard both women as his or her mother, the traditional approach of the law has been to regard this **co-parent** as a "legal stranger" to the child.

However, this approach has begun to change as these "nonparents" have sought to establish their right to maintain an ongoing relationship with the child they helped to raise when their relationship with the legal parent ends. Seeking to be recognized as legal parents, co-parents have used a number of legal theories, such as those discussed above in relationship to stepparents. Regardless of which approach is used, at the heart of these cases is the desire to be recognized as a parent based on shared intent and the reality of their parental relationship with the child.

Many jurisdictions have denied these claims and continue to regard co-mothers as akin to a legal stranger based on her lack of a biological or adoptive connection. Here, great weight is given to traditional understandings of parenthood and the right of exclusivity that this status confers. Where denied parental status, the lesbian co-mother is then treated as a third party. In jurisdictions where third-party standing is limited to a defined class of persons, such as grandparents and stepparents, she most likely will not be able to assert any claim to the child. In jurisdictions where standing is conferred on a broader group of persons — such as all persons with a significant relationship with a child — a co-parent may be able to assert her claim, although it is also possible that a court would refuse to recognize the relationship as significant. However, having crossed this jurisdictional threshold, the dispute would still be characterized as one between a parent and a nonparent, and the parental preference would be triggered. Thus, unlike a divorcing mother and father, the two would not begin on equal footing, and the co-parent would need to show more than best interest to overcome the preference, which can be a difficult burden to overcome.

A small but growing number of courts have moved beyond this formalistic conception of what it means to be a family and have extended parental status to co-parents based on the day-to-day reality of these families and the needs of the children within them. In extending formal recognition to co-parents, the Massachusetts high court, in the 1999 case of E.N.O. v. L.M.M.,[66] recognized:

A child may be a member of a nontraditional family in which he is parented by a legal parent and a de facto parent. A de facto parent is one who has no biological relation to a child, but has participated in the child's life as a member of the child's family.[67]

The court went on to explain that to be considered a **de facto parent**, an individual must show that she resided with the child and shared caretaking responsibilities with the consent and cooperation of the legal parent. Moreover, these caretaking functions must be performed "for reasons primarily other than financial compensation,"[68] thus eliminating the concern that some have raised that a nanny or babysitter could qualify as a de facto parent.

In Holzman v. Knott[69] the Wisconsin high court set out a similar test for determining parental status. According to this court, to demonstrate the existence of a parent-like relationship, a co-parent must establish the following elements:

1. The legal parent consented to and fostered the relationship.
2. She resided with the child in the same household.
3. She assumed the responsibilities of parenthood.
4. She was in the parental role for long enough to establish meaningful connection with the child.[70]

A critical consideration in such cases is the element of consent on the part of the legal parent. In both *E.N.O.* and *Holzman*, the decision to share parental status and responsibilities was mutual. In the former case, for example, the parties sent out joint birth announcements, embodied their parenting intent in a range of legal documents including a co-parenting agreement, gave the child both of their last names, and fully shared parenting responsibilities. Similarly, in a case from Rhode Island in which the co-parent was granted visitation rights, the child was given a hyphenated name, the names of both parties appeared on the baptismal certificate and the birth announcements, and both parties fully participated in the raising of the child.[71]

Accordingly, this status is not one that courts impose on a legal parent, rather, recognition of a co-parent honors a reality that would not have existed without the consent and active cooperation of the legal parent. In a similar vein, this consent and cooperation means that the court is not encroaching upon the exclusive domain of the legal parent. As explained by the New Jersey Supreme Court:

> This opinion should not be viewed as an incursion on the general right of a fit legal parent to raise his or her child without outside interference. What we

have addressed here is . . . the volitional choice of a legal parent to cede a measure of a parental authority to a third party . . . In such circumstances the legal parent has created a family with the third party and the child, and has invited the third party into the otherwise inviolable realm of family privacy.[72]

Once recognized as a de facto parent, a party is no longer a "legal stranger." However, the question still remains as to whether a de facto parent stands on equal footing with her former partner, much as a divorcing husband and wife would. For instance, the New Jersey Supreme Court stated that "[o]nce a third party has been determined to be a psychological parent to a child, under the previously described standards, he or she stands in *parity* with the legal parent." The Court went on to emphasize, however, that "parity" does not require equality of treatment, and that because ". . . in the search for self-knowledge, the child's interest in his or her roots will emerge," if "the evidence concerning the child's best interests (as between a legal parent and psychological parent) is in equipoise," custody should be awarded to the legal parent.[73]

In contrast, in a recent co-parent custody case, the Supreme Court of Washington made clear that once a party is found to be a de facto parent, he or she is in "legal parity" with the other parent, which places them in "equivalent parental positions." In rejecting the biological mother's argument that such a determination interfered with her fundamental rights as a parent, the Court concluded that once a determination of parentage is made, both parents have a "fundamental liberty interest" in the "care, custody, and control" of their child.[74]

## Chapter Summary

Historically, fathers had an absolute right to the custody of their children. With industrialization, the rights of fathers yielded to the tender years presumption, which assumed that mothers were the best caretakers of young children. Now, virtually all statutes use a best interest of the child standard. In theory, this is a child-centered, gender-neutral approach to resolving custody disputes. Judges are directed to evaluate each case on its individual merits, focusing on the needs of the child rather than the rights of the parents. Where parental conduct or lifestyle is at issue, most jurisdictions employ the nexus approach and require proof of harm. However, this standard has been criticized for its lack of predictability and objective criteria.

Custody has both a legal and a physical component; either may be awarded on a sole or a joint basis. Although there has been an increased focus on shared custody, this approach has been subject to criticism, especially in cases involving a history of domestic violence. A noncustodial parent is presumptively entitled to visitation unless there is a risk of harm to the child. To facilitate post-divorce parenting, there has been an increased focus on parenting plans and parenting education.

Custody and visitation disputes have increasingly involved claims by "third parties," most notably grandparents, stepparents, and co-parents. Where grandparents are concerned, all states have statutorily modified the common law rule of nonaccess and permit visitation under certain circumstances, and a number of states also now recognize post-divorce claims of stepparents seeking to maintain an ongoing relationship with the child of their spouse. A small but growing number of states have extended formal recognition to co-parents. As "de facto" parents, they have visitation and custodial rights, although states may give greater weight to the interests of the "legal" parent.

## Key Terms

| | |
|---|---|
| Custody | Noncustodial Parent |
| Visitation | Parenting Plan |
| Paternal Preference | Complaint for Contempt |
| Tender Years Presumption | Complaint for Modification |
| Best Interest | Relocation Disputes |
| Primary Caretaker | Virtual Visitation |
| Nexus | Standing |
| Per Se Approach | Stepparent |
| Primary Caretaker Presumption | Equitable Parenthood |
| Physical Custody | *In Loco Parentis* |
| Legal Custody | Co-Parent |
| Sole Custody | De Facto Parent |
| Joint Custody | |

## Review Questions

1. What were the rights of fathers at common law?

2. When and why did mothers become the preferred custodial parent?

3. What is the best interest standard?

4. What factors is a judge likely to consider when determining best interest?

5. What criticisms are commonly made about the best interest standard?

6. What are the pros and cons of basing a custody decision on the stated preference of a child?

7. What impact does witnessing spousal abuse have on children? For what other reasons do courts take intra-spousal violence into account when deciding custody?

8. Under *Palmore*, what effect, if any, is given to the role of race in custody disputes?

9. Explain the difference between the nexus and the per se harm approaches to resolving custody disputes where parental lifestyle is an issue. Why doesn't the "nexus" standard always ensure that a result is free from bias?

10. How do courts approach custody cases in which one parent is involved in a heterosexual relationship? a same-sex relationship?

11. How do courts generally approach the issue of religion when it is raised as a positive factor? as a negative factor?

12. How do courts generally approach cases in which a parent seeking custody has AIDS or is HIV-positive?

13. Explain the primary caretaker presumption. How does it respond to the concerns about the best interest standard?

14. Explain the ALI approximation rule. How does it respond to the concerns about the best interest standard?

15. What is the difference between physical and legal custody? between sole and joint custody?

16. What concerns have been raised about joint custody? Under what circumstances is it most likely to be successful?

17. What is the legal status of a noncustodial parent?

18. Why will courts generally grant visitation rights to a parent who might not be an appropriate custodial parent?

19. What are the general approaches to structuring visitation?

20. What kinds of restrictions might a court impose on a visiting parent?

21. Discuss the intended functions of parenting plans and parent education programs.

22. What are the two basic approaches that states take with respect to post-divorce relocation disputes?

23. How have courts taken the possibility of "virtual visitation" into account when faced with relocation decisions?

24. What is meant by the term "natural parent preference"?

25. What was the common law status of grandparents in relationship to their grandchildren?

26. What considerations prompted the passage of grandparent visitation statutes?

27. Under what circumstances do most grandparent visitation statutes permit a grandparent to seek visitation rights? Why did the Supreme Court invalidate Washington's grandparent visitation statute?

28. Explain the concept of "standing."

29. What is the traditional legal status of stepparents? How has this begun to change?

30. What has been the law's approach to a lesbian co-parent?

31. Explain the concept of de facto parent. What considerations does a court take into account when deciding whether someone qualifies as a de facto parent?

32. Why is the element of consent so important?

# Discussion Questions

1. In determining custody, what weight do you think "moral" considerations should have? Do you think it is possible for judges to set aside their own views of morality when making decisions about custody?

2. Would you allow a grandparent to have visitation rights with a grandchild over the objections of the parent(s)? What factors do you think a court should weigh in making these determinations?

3. Much was written in the chapter about gender bias in custody determinations. Based on your reading and general knowledge, what do you think? Do you think the bias favors mothers or fathers?

4. Do you think it makes sense to extend parental status to a lesbian co-parent? What are the arguments in favor of and against the extension of rights?

5. Many fathers' rights organizations have argued that unless a court can order joint custody even where one parent is opposed, men will never be treated fairly. What do you think of this position?

6. Assuming a relocation decision is made in good faith, do you think the court should give greater weight to the desire of the custodial parent to move or to the noncustodial parent's wish to maintain the existing visitation arrangement? What factors would you weigh?

# Assignments

1. Locate the custody provisions of your state's divorce statute and answer the following questions:

   - Have any specific guidelines for determining best interest been adopted by statute or judicial decision?
   - Based on the guidelines or key court decisions, what factors are to be considered when determining custody?
   - Is domestic violence a factor to be considered? If so, how?
   - Is joint custody a permissible option? If yes, is there a presumption in favor of joint custody? Can it be ordered over the objection of a parent?

2.  Assume you are working in a law firm, and the senior partner has asked for your assistance in a custody relocation dispute in which your firm is representing the father. The father is seeking to prevent his former wife, who is the custodial parent, and children from moving out of state to another state that is about 350 miles away. Assume that the children are ages five and seven, that the father visits with them regularly and has a good relationship with both daughters, and that money is not a significant concern. The partner has asked you to prepare an in-house legal memorandum in which you analyze the relevant statutory section, if any, and controlling case law on this issue.

3.  Develop a detailed client intake questionnaire for use in all cases where custody or visitation might be an issue. Think carefully about all of the information you would want to know about your client and his or her spouse.

4.  Assume you are an appeals court judge in Florida and that the *Palmore* case is back before the court. This time, assume that the father returned to court and won custody of his daughter, whom we'll call Carrie, based on the following facts. Carrie is now school-aged and has been subjected to taunting and harassment. This has been very upsetting to Carrie. She has been experiencing difficulty eating and sleeping and cries every morning about having to go to school. The mother has filed an appeal with your court. As a judge, please decide whether the trial court decision should be affirmed or reversed, and write an opinion explaining your decision.

5.  The attorney you work for has asked you to prepare the first draft of a parenting plan for a divorce case she is working on. She represents the wife and is concerned that the parties will not be able to effectively carry out the joint custody arrangement that they want. She would like the plan to be as detailed as possible. At a minimum it should cover the allocation of time and responsibilities, how decisions are to be made, and a process for resolving any disputes that come up. Given her concerns, she would like the plan to be drafted with particular care so that it facilitates the intended custodial arrangement. Following are the relevant facts:

    •   The parties have agreed to share physical and legal custody of their daughter, Melinda, age four.

- Both parents work full-time, although the mother's schedule is more flexible, and she tends to work shorter hours than the father; however, she travels about once a month.
- The parties want to try to make this arrangement work, but communication is tense and has gotten worse since the father has begun living with his new girlfriend.
- The parties live in the same town.
- The mother worries that the father is too strict and rigid in relationship to Melinda, and the father worries that the mother is too permissive and sets no rules.

(Note: If the courts in your state have a standard parenting plan form, you should use this form for the assignment.)

6.  Assume you are a clerk for a trial judge who is facing a case that raises a new issue in your jurisdiction. He will be deciding a lesbian co-parenting case next week, and would like to know what the law from other jurisdictions says about this issue. For now, he would like you to concentrate on the various arguments on the merits and ignore the procedural issues. In short, focus on the arguments in favor of and against recognizing the co-parent as a legal parent and not on issues such as standing, jurisdiction, and the like.

## **Cases for Analysis**

The following case exemplifies how courts have begun to pay careful attention to the impact that witnessing domestic violence has on children.

### MARY ANN P. v. WILLIAM R.P., JR.
#### 197 W. Va. 1, 475 S.E.2d 1 (1996)

## I.  FACTS

The parties were married in March of 1985 and two sons were born of the marriage. William Raphael P. III (Billy) was born in May of 1985 and Mark Patrick P. was born in July of 1986. The record reflects that from the beginning the couple had a troubled marriage. The defendant was physically and mentally abusive to the plaintiff throughout their marriage. . . .

The plaintiff received custody of the children as she was determined to be the primary caretaker. The numerous proceedings held before the family law master focused primarily on the defendant's visitation rights which are at issue in this appeal. At the March 3, 1992, hearing before the family law master, the plaintiff detailed the physical and mental abuse that occurred during the marriage. She testified the defendant did not want her to have either of the boys and he urged her to have abortions both times she became pregnant. He showed little interest in the children when they were infants and openly expressed his disappointment that he had boys instead of girls. . . .

The plaintiff also testified the defendant had a violent temper and would yell and curse at her in front of the children. . . . During arguments, the defendant punched and kicked the plaintiff. He threatened her with a knife. He choked her around the neck so hard she had to wear a scarf to hide the bruises. He drug her across the floor by her hair in front of the children. The plaintiff testified that when the children would witness this abuse they would scream and cry and try to hide. The defendant would hit and kick the children's toys and broke toys in front of the children in fits of rage. The plaintiff testified that "the trauma and crying that these children have seen in their life is unreal."

During one argument, the defendant locked the plaintiff out of the house and kept the children inside. She testified she was afraid for the children's safety and put her fist through a window to enter the house. She severed three nerves in her arm and underwent surgery to correct the damage.

Billy and Mark have severe allergy problems and needed frequent medical treatments for ear infections, allergies, and colds when they were infants. The plaintiff testified the defendant was not sympathetic to the children's medical needs and, on certain occasions, blocked her attempts to get medical attention for the boys because he believed the plaintiff was overreacting to the children's symptoms. The defendant continued to smoke in front of the boys even though it caused them respiratory problems.

Despite the foregoing, the plaintiff maintains she encouraged the children's visitation with their father following the separation. However, she stated he exercised his visitation rights sporadically. . . .

The plaintiff testified Billy and Mark no longer want to have any contact with their father. It upsets them greatly when they have to visit with him. When the defendant comes to the house to visit, the boys frequently run and hide and have to be coaxed to come out to speak with their father. The plaintiff testified the visitations have had a profound effect on Billy. He has nightmares and acts out aggressively toward other children. Billy builds traps and barricades and frequently checks to see the doors and windows are locked because he is afraid the defendant will enter the house.

Several witnesses who accompanied the defendant on supervised visits testified regarding the boys' and the defendant's behavior. While the evidence is somewhat conflicting, it appears the boys do not want to visit their father and behave poorly in his presence. . . . The defendant . . . stated his visitations with the children are not as bad as the plaintiff contends. He testified that the plaintiff interferes with his relationship with his children. . . .

Christina Marie Arco, Ph.D., a psychologist . . . , testified at a hearing held in October of 1994 that she provided therapy for the children. At a hearing held in January of 1995, Dr. Arco testified she was still seeing Billy for therapy. She stated that Billy's anger and aggressiveness are at very high levels. He has fears and anxieties about his father. Billy told Dr. Arco he wished his father were dead so he would not have to worry about him anymore. Dr. Arco testified that any forced visitation with his father would cause serious regression in Billy. She also stated that the negativity the children have about their father is much more motivated by fear, anxiety, and anger than by any negative comments that may have been made by the plaintiff. . . .

After hearing the . . . evidence, the family law master rendered his recommended order. He found:

> "It is clear that . . . plaintiff does not like the defendant, and justifiably so because of the history of physical violence in their marriage, but that there can be no further justification whatsoever of any restriction of defendant's right of visitation with his children." . . .

. . . The family law master stated that, due to the history of domestic violence in the case, for six months the defendant's visitation with the boys would be restricted to the presence of a third person. . . .

The plaintiff filed exceptions to the family law master's recommended decision. . . . After hearing additional evidence on the issue of whether resumption of visitation would be harmful to the children, the circuit court ordered supervised visitation with the defendant until the boys attain an age where enforced visitation would be "meaningless." . . . The circuit court . . . found the record "only partially supports a conclusion that resumed visitation will result in serious psychiatric regression" and that no "high risk of suicide or withdrawal" should occur if visitation resumes. . . .

. . . Our decision to affirm this portion of the circuit court's order, however, is not determinative of the final disposition of this case. . . .

. . . The family law master found the plaintiff suffered from physical and emotional abuse during the marriage, but failed to address the negative consequences such abuse now has on the children's relationship to and visitation with their father. To be clear, we are not speaking of a child's general reluctance to visit with his or her noncustodial parent. What we are dealing with in this case is Mark's and Billy's documented intense fears and anxieties in visiting with their father. . . .

A fair reading of the record reveals that the boys' feelings of animosity toward their father are in large part due to their father's treatment of their mother. During counseling sessions, the boys stated their father was "mean" because he did "awful things" to their mother. The plaintiff testified that during the marriage the boys would scream and cry when she and the defendant would fight. The defendant's physical abuse of the plaintiff was witnessed by the boys, and they were terrified of their father because of this abuse.

The evidence of the negative impact the physical abuse that occurred during the marriage had in regard to the children's well-being was not rebutted. . . .

This Court joins with the majority of jurisdictions in finding that domestic violence evidence should be considered when determining parental fitness and child custody. In Syllabus Point 1, in part, of Henry v. Johnson, 192 W. Va. 82, 450 S.E.2d 779 (1994), we stated:

> "Children are often physically assaulted or witness violence against one of their parents and may suffer deep and lasting emotional harm from victimization and from exposure to family violence; consequently, a family law master should take domestic violence into account[.]"

See W. Va. Code, 48-2A-1(a)(2) (1992) (domestic violence statute states that children "may suffer deep and lasting emotional harm from victimization and from exposure to family violence"). Similarly, in the dissenting opinion in Patricia Ann S. v. James Daniel S., 190 W. Va. 6, 18, 435 S.E.2d 6, 18 (1993), Justice Workman recognized that "spousal abuse has a tremendous impact on children" regardless of whether the children were directly abused. While custody was not at issue in this case, evidence of domestic violence is still relevant in deciding the visitation issue because it appears to be the root cause for why visitation has not been successful. . . .

. . . Based on the foregoing, we agree with the plaintiff that supervised visitation should not immediately resume. . . . The record is clear that forced visitation at this time would be detrimental to the children and futile on the defendant's behalf without professional intervention. In Mary D. v. Watt, 190 W. Va. at 348, 438 S.E.2d at 528, this Court held that a "family law master or circuit court may condition . . . supervised visitation upon the offending parent seeking treatment." On remand, the circuit court should address this issue. The circuit court should also consider whether it would be beneficial for the defendant and the children to attend counseling sessions together to help build a more positive relationship. . . .

In Mary D., Chief Justice McHugh set forth guidelines to help provide children with a safe and secure atmosphere when supervised visitation is exercised. Although Mary D. dealt specifically with supervised visitation following a finding that sexual abuse occurred, we find it just as applicable in this case where the children harbor such strong feelings against their father, whatever the source of such emotional estrangement. It is in everyone's interest to see that supervised visitation goes as smoothly as possible. In Syllabus Point 3 of *Mary D.*, we held:

In Patricia Ann S., 190 W. Va. at 18, 435 S.E.2d at 18, Justice Workman quoted the following excerpt from L. Crites & D. Coker, What Therapists See That Judges May Miss, The Judges' Journal 9, 11-12 (Spring 1988):

> "'Children learn several lessons in witnessing the abuse of one of their parents. First, they learn that such behavior appears to be approved by their most important role models and that the violence toward a loved one is acceptable. Children also fail to grasp the full range of negative consequences for the violent behavior and observe, instead, the short term reinforcements, namely compliance by the victim. Thus, they learn the use of coercive power and violence as a way to influence loved ones without being exposed to other more constructive alternatives.'" In addition to the effect of the destructive modeling, children who grow up in violent homes experience damaging psychological effects. There is substantial documentation that the spouse abuser's violence causes a variety of psychological problems for children. Children raised in a home in which spouse abuse occurs experience the same fear as do battered children. . . . "'Spouse abuse results not only in direct physical and psychological injuries to the children, but, of greatest long-term importance, it breeds a culture of violence in future generations.'"
>
> "Where supervised visitation is ordered pursuant to W. Va. Code, 48-2-15(b)(1) [1991], the best interests of a child include determining that the child is safe from the fear of emotional and psychological trauma which he or she may experience. The person(s) appointed to supervise the visitation should have had some prior contact with the child so that the child is sufficiently familiar with and trusting of that person in order for the child to have secure feelings and so that the visitation is not harmful to his or her emotional well being. Such a determination should be incorporated as a finding of the family law master or circuit court."

## QUESTIONS

1. What was the recommendation of the family law master with respect to visitation?

2. Why did the circuit court order supervised visitation?

3. What critique does this court have of the family law master's findings?

4. According to the court, why is evidence of domestic violence relevant in custody and visitation determinations?

5. What was the court's ultimate decision with respect to visitation? What were the remand instructions to the trial court?

---

The following case illustrates the potential complexity and bitterness of post-divorce custody disputes. It also provides a thoughtful discussion of the "change in material circumstances" modification standard.

## BOYER v. HEIMERMANN
### 2007 Tenn. App. LEXIS 185

On December 22, 1995, the Circuit Court for Davidson County entered a decree of divorce ending the marriage of Charles William Heimermann and Cynthia Statham Heimermann. The decree provided that the parties would "share custody" of their three minor children — then between two and seven years of age. The children would reside with their mother "during the nine (9) month school year" and with their father "during the three (3) summer months." Throughout the year, the parents were given visitation on alternating weekends, and the parent with whom the children were not residing was given one day of mid-week visitation.

Both parties remarried. . . .

Mr. Boyer earns a good income, and that has enabled Ms. Boyer to work sparingly and to devote a significant amount of time to the parties' children. She home-schooled the children from 2001 through 2003. Ms. Boyer participates in many of the children's extracurricular activities and chauffeurs them to their sports events, driving tests, and doctor's visits. She also has frequent telephone conversations with them during the summer when they are residing with Mr. Heimermann. The parties' youngest daughter regards Ms. Boyer as her best friend.

Mr. Heimermann is a self-employed carpenter. His work requires him to leave home early in the morning while the children are still asleep and to return home late. He works on the weekends when business requires. His regular routine when he comes home from work includes a nap and a shower and then dinner with the family around 8:30 or 9:00 p.m. Mr. Heimermann retires shortly after dinner.

Following the divorce in 1995, Mr. Heimermann has insisted on a rigid demarcation between the time the children spend with him during the summer and the time they reside with Ms. Boyer. He has cancelled the children's appointments with doctors if Ms. Boyer made then [sic] on "his time," and he has refused to make appointments for the children during the summer. He has also refused to permit Ms. Boyer to see the children during the summer months except for the periods prescribed in the divorce decree.

The children's summer routine is vastly different from their routine during the school year, even though Mr. Heimermann's home is only twenty minutes away from Ms. Boyer's home. They are essentially house-bound. Mr. Heimermann does not permit them to see their friends or engage in their usual activities, including church events, drama clubs, and sports. He will not permit the children to have part-time jobs to earn money for school or to buy a car. After his son found a job at Kroger, Mr. Heimermann personally went to Kroger to have his son fired. When the children have asked their father to drive them to friends' houses or to church functions or other activities, he has called them "high maintenance" and "spoiled."

Mr. Heimermann also expects absolute obedience from his children during the summer and is a strict disciplinarian. After his older daughter stayed out too late, he forbade her from attending her regular church and insisted that she attend church with him. When his daughter defied him and went to her own church with her brother, Mr. Heimermann went to the church and physically removed the children during the service. Following an argument in the parking lot, Mr. Heimermann called the police and charged his daughter with unruly conduct. . . .

As the years went on, the children became increasingly hesitant about spending the entire summer with Mr. Heimermann. While they loved and respected him, they did not relish the prospect of spending the summer months with no contact with their friends, no activities or summer jobs, and with little to do other than staying at home watching television and listening to music. Ms. Boyer encouraged the children to cooperate with their father and also urged Mr. Heimermann to spend more time with the children and to provide them with more activities. Mr. Heimermann ignored her suggestions.

Eventually, in response to the children's reluctance to continue to spend the entire summer with their father, Ms. Boyer filed a petition in the Circuit Court for Davidson County in May 2005 requesting a modification in summer visitation. Mr. Heimermann moved to dismiss the request to modify the summer visitation on the ground that no material change of circumstances had occurred since the entry of the divorce decree. . . .

Mr. Heimermann moved for a directed verdict at the close of Ms. Boyer's case-in-chief. The trial court granted the motion based on its conclusion that there had been "absolutely no specific change of circumstance at all that was not foreseeable. . . ."

Ms. Boyer asserts that the trial court erred by concluding that she had failed to establish that material changes in the parties' and the children's circumstances had occurred during the ten-year period between the entry of the parties' divorce decree and the filing of her petition to modify the existing custody arrangement. . . .

The threshold issue in every case involving a modification in an existing custody or visitation arrangement is whether a material change in circumstances has occurred. Kendrick v. Shoemake, 90 S.W.3d 566, 570 (Tenn. 2002). During the past decade or so, the "material change in circumstances" standard has undergone a statutory and common-law metamorphosis. Kesterson v. Varner, 172 S.W.3d 556, 560 (Tenn. Ct. App. 2005). The standard, as it now exists, provides a flexible framework within which the courts consider a number of factors when determining whether an existing custody or visitation arrangement should be modified. Cranston v. Combs, 106 S.W.3d 641, 645 (Tenn. 2003).

The evolution of the "material change in circumstances" standard has focused on the criteria for determining whether a particular change in circumstances is "material" enough to require reconsideration of an existing custody or visitation arrangement. In 2002 and 2003, the Tennessee Supreme Court handed down three decisions that clarified the principles associated with the "material change in circumstances" standard. . . . The court emphasized that there are no bright-line rules for determining whether a material change in circumstances has occurred. Cranston v. Combs, 106 S.W.3d at 644; Kendrick v. Shoemake, 90 S.W.3d at 570; Blair v. Badenhope, 77 S.W.3d at 150. . . . The court also explained that several of the many considerations relevant to determining whether a material change in circumstances has occurred include: (1) whether the change occurred after the entry of the order sought to be modified, (2) whether the change was not known or reasonably anticipated when the order was entered, and (3) whether the change is one that affects the child's well-being in a meaningful way. Cranston v. Combs, 106 S.W.3d at 644; Kendrick v. Shoemake, 90 S.W.3d at 570; Blair v. Badenhope, 77 S.W.3d at 150.

In 2004, the Tennessee General Assembly enacted legislation directed specifically at the "material change in circumstances" standard . . . Tenn. Code Ann. § 36-6-101(a)(2)(C) provides:

If the issue before the court is a modification of the court's prior decree pertaining to a residential parenting schedule, then the petitioner must prove by a preponderance of the evidence a material change of circumstances affecting the child's best interest. A material change of circumstances does not require a showing of a substantial risk of harm to the child. A material change of circumstances for purposes of modification of a residential parenting schedule may include, but is not limited to, significant changes in the needs of the child over time, which many include changes relating to age; significant changes in the parent's living or working condition that significantly affect parenting, failure to adhere to the parenting plan; or other circumstances making a change in residential parenting time in the best interest of the child. . . .

Whether a particular change in circumstances could reasonably have been anticipated at the time of the entry of the original decree is only one of many factors to consider. It has never been outcome-determinative. Indeed, the courts and the General Assembly have recognized that material changes in circumstances can arise solely by the passage of time because children's needs change as they grow older. . . .

Not every change in the circumstances of either a child or a parent will qualify as a material change in circumstances. The change must be "significant" before it will be considered material. . . .

Using the standards required by Tenn. Code Ann. § 36-6-101(a)(2)(C), it is difficult to reach any conclusion other than that Ms. Boyer and her children have established that a material change in the children's circumstances has occurred. More than a decade has passed since the entry of the divorce decree, and during that time, the children have grown older and have developed new interests and focuses for their lives . . . They have become teenagers involved in a variety of activities, and they have developed a number a varying interests ranging from team sports and drama clubs to church groups and camps. . . . They want to spend time with their friends and get jobs to earn money for college or to purchase cars. . . .

Based on the evidence in this record, the children have not been permitted to pursue their interests, take jobs, or spend time with their friends during the summer when they are living with their father. According to the children, their activities are mostly limited to sitting around the house and doing little other than watching television and listening to music all day, every day. Mr. Heimermann works extremely hard at an exhausting job that leaves him too tired and with too little energy to spend much time with his children. He has been unable or unwilling to accommodate the children's outside activities or interests while he is working, and this lack of flexibility has clearly caused considerable strain on his relationship with his children. . . . As a result, the children no longer desire to spend the entire summer with their father.

The trial court erred by focusing solely on the foreseeability that the children would grow older and that their needs and interests would change over time. Following the enactment of Tenn. Code Ann. § 36-6-101(a)(2)(C), the court should have considered whether the changes that have occurred in the children's lives are significant. The salient consideration is not the change of age alone; it is the age-related changes in the children's needs.

By enacting Tenn. Code Ann. § 36-6-101(a)(2)(C), the General Assembly has made a policy decision to make it easier to establish that a material change in circumstances has occurred. The courts must adhere to this policy, even if it establishes a lower threshold than heretofore existed in Tennessee or that currently exists in other states. Tenn. Code Ann. § 36-6-101(a)(2)(C) establishes that significant changes in the needs of children as they grow older constitute a material change of circumstance. That is precisely what has transpired in this case.

Based on the evidence in this record, it cannot be reasonably questioned that the children's interests, involvements, and capabilities have changed significantly since the entry of their parents' divorce decree. They are no longer the young children they were in 1995. . . . Thus, a custody and visitation arrangement that was satisfactory when they were ages two, five, and seven may not, and probably does not, serve their current needs. At this stage, the unrebutted testimony of Ms. Boyer and the parties' children make out a prima facie case that a material change in circumstances has occurred. Accordingly, we find that the evidence does not support the trial court's conclusion that Ms. Boyer has failed to prove the existence of a material change in circumstances.

## IV.

### THE CHILDREN'S BEST INTERESTS

Concluding that Ms. Boyer made a prima facie showing that there has been a material change in the children's circumstances during the past ten years does not end the matter. The existing custody and visitation arrangement should not be modified unless it is in the children's best interests to do so. The trial court's hasty decision to dismiss the case following Ms. Boyer's case short-circuited the inquiry into whether altering the existing custody arrangement would be in the two remaining minor children's best interests.

These two questions—the existence of a material change in circumstances and the child's best interests—have the unfortunate tendency to not only shade the other, as is inevitable and appropriate, but to bleed to become indistinguishable. Despite this tendency, the proper inquiry into whether there has been a material change in circumstances is actually not directly tied to the substantive question regarding the best custody and visitation arrangement under the present circumstances. . . . A finding of a material change in circumstances since the entry of the visitation order does not predetermine the outcome of the best interests analysis. . . . Instead, such a finding requires the court move to the second step—best interests analysis.

Mr. Heimermann was not afforded an opportunity to present evidence of his own because of the trial court's peremptory dismissal of Ms. Boyer's case. It would be unfair to Mr. Heimermann to rule on the merits of Ms. Boyer's petition to change custody and visitation until he has been given a full and fair opportunity to present evidence refuting the evidence already in the record that a material change in circumstances has occurred or establishing that the children's interests would be best served by leaving the current custody and visitation arrangement intact. Accordingly, this appeal does not present an appropriate occasion to decide what the best interests of the children are. This decision should be made only after Mr. Heimermann has been given an opportunity to present his evidence.

## QUESTIONS

1. Why did the lower court deny the mother's motion for a change in custody?

2. Explain why the appeals court concluded that the lower court was wrong to deny the motion.

3. According to the appeals court, what is the correct approach to determining if there has been a sufficient change in materials circumstances to warrant a modification?

4. Why does the appeals court say that the father must be given an opportunity to present evidence rather than simply granting the mother's motion?

---

The following case involves a custody/visitation dispute between two co-parents. In recognizing the rights of the co-mother, this court joins a small but growing minority of jurisdictions that have extended parental rights to this class of parents.

### V.C. v. M.J.B.
**163 N.J. 200, 748 A.2d 539 (2000),** *cert. denied,*
**531 U.S. 926 (2000)**

In this case, we are called on to determine what legal standard applies to a third party's claim to joint custody and visitation of her former domestic partner's biological children, with whom she lived in a familial setting and in respect of whom she claims to have functioned as a psychological parent. Although the case arises in the context of a lesbian couple, the standard we enunciate is applicable to all persons who have willingly, and with the approval of the legal parent, undertaken the duties of a parent to a child not related by blood or adoption.

**I.**

The following facts were established at trial. V.C. and M.J.B., who are lesbians, met in 1992 and began dating on July 4, 1993. On July 9, 1993, M.J.B. went to see a fertility specialist to begin artificial insemination procedures. . . . According to M.J.B., she made the final decision to become pregnant independently and before beginning her relationship with V.C. . . .

Between November 1993 and February 1994, M.J.B. underwent several insemination procedures. V.C. attended at least two of those sessions. In December 1993, V.C. moved into M.J.B.'s apartment. Two months later, on February 7, 1994, the doctor informed M.J.B. that she was pregnant. . . . Eventually, M.J.B. was informed that she was having twins.

During M.J.B.'s pregnancy, both M.J.B. and V.C. prepared for the birth of the twins by attending pre-natal and Lamaze classes. . . .

The children were born on September 29, 1994. V.C. took M.J.B. to the hospital and she was present in the delivery room at the birth of the children. At the hospital, the nurses and staff treated V.C. as if she were a mother. . . .

The parties opened joint bank accounts for their household expenses, and prepared wills, powers of attorney, and named each other as the beneficiary for their respective life insurance policies. At some point, the parties also opened savings accounts for the children, and named V.C. as custodian for one account and M.J.B. as custodian for the other.

The parties also decided to have the children call M.J.B. "Mommy" and V.C. "Meema." M.J.B. conceded that she referred to V.C. as a "mother" of the children. In addition, M.J.B. supported the notion, both publicly and privately, that during the twenty-three months after the children were born, the parties and the children functioned as a family unit. . . .

M.J.B. agreed that both parties cared for the children but insisted that she made substantive decisions regarding their lives. . . . V.C. countered that she was equally involved in all decision-making regarding the children. . . .

M.J.B. acknowledged that V.C. assumed substantial responsibility for the children, but maintained that V.C. was a mere helper and not a co-parent. However, according to V.C., she acted as a co-parent to the children and had equal parenting responsibility. . . .

Together the parties purchased a home in February 1995. Later that year, V.C. asked M.J.B. to marry her, and M.J.B. accepted. In July 1995, the parties held a commitment ceremony where they were "married." At the ceremony, V.C., M.J.B. and the twins were blessed as a "family." . . .

During their relationship, the couple discussed both changing the twins' surname to a hyphenated form of the women's names and the possibility of V.C. adopting the children. M.J.B. testified that the parties considered adoption and in June 1996 consulted an attorney on the subject. . . . The parties never actually attempted to . . . proceed with the adoption. . . .

Just two months later, in August 1996, M.J.B. ended the relationship. The parties then took turns living in the house with the children until November 1996. In December 1996, V.C. moved out. M.J.B. permitted V.C. to visit with the children until May 1997. During that time, V.C. spent approximately every other weekend with the children, and contributed money toward the household expenses.

In May 1997, M.J.B. went away on business and left the children with V.C. for two weeks. However, later that month, M.J.B. refused to continue V.C.'s visitation with the children, and at some point M.J.B. stopped accepting V.C.'s money. M.J.B. asserted that she did not want to continue the children's contact with V.C. because she believed that V.C. was not properly caring for the children, and that the children were suffering distress from continued contact with V.C. Both parties became involved with new partners after the dissolution of their relationship. Eventually, V.C. filed this complaint for joint legal custody.

At trial, expert witnesses appeared for both parties. Dr. Allwyn J. Levine testified on behalf of V.C., and Dr. David Brodzinsky testified on behalf of M.J.B. . . .

Dr. Levine concluded that both children view V.C. as a maternal figure and that V.C. regards herself as one of the children's mothers. "Because the children were basically parented from birth" by V.C. and M.J.B. "until they physically separated," Dr. Levine concluded that the children view the parties "as inter-changeable maternal mothering objects" and "have established a maternal bond with both of the women." Dr. Levine likened the parties' relationship to a heterosexual marriage. Consequently, the children would be affected by the loss of V.C. just as if they had been denied contact with their father after a divorce. . . .

Likewise, Dr. Brodzinsky concluded that V.C. and the children enjoyed a bonded relationship that benefited both children. Dr. Brodzinsky determined that the children regarded V.C. as a member of their family. The doctor believed that it was normal for young children to feel that way about a person with whom they have spent considerable time. However, Dr. Brodzinsky noted that as children "get older, family becomes more specifically tied . . . to biological connections." The doctor's report indicated that, when asked who their mother was, the children did not immediately point to V.C., but upon further inquiry agreed that V.C. was their mother. . . .

In contrast to Dr. Levine's opinion, Dr. Brodzinsky believed that the loss of V.C. was not akin to the loss of a parent in a heterosexual divorce. The doctor explained that societal views foster the expectation that a child and a parent will continue their relationship after a divorce, but that no similar expectation would exist for the children's relationship with V.C. . . . Assuming that the parties could maintain a reasonably amicable relationship, Dr. Brodzinsky felt that the children "would probably benefit from ongoing contact [with V.C.] as they would with any person with whom they have a good solid relationship that can nurture them." The trial court denied V.C.'s applications for joint legal custody and visitation because it concluded that she failed to establish that the bonded relationship she enjoyed with the children had risen to the level of psychological or de facto parenthood. In so doing, the court gave significant weight to the fact that the decision to have children was M.J.B.'s, and not a joint decision between M.J.B. and V.C.

Finding that V.C. did not qualify as a psychological parent to the children, the trial court opined that it would "only be able to consider [V.C.'s] petition for custody if [she] was able [to] prove [M.J.B.] to be an unfit parent." Because V.C. did not allege that M.J.B. was an unfit parent, the trial court held that V.C. lacked standing to petition for joint legal custody. The court also denied V.C.'s application for visitation, determining that even a step-parent would not be granted such visitation except for equitable reasons, not present here. Further, it resolved that visitation was not in the children's best interests because M.J.B. harbored animosity toward V.C. that would "inevitably pass[ ] along to the children." . . .

## II.

On appeal, M.J.B. argues that we lack subject matter jurisdiction to consider V.C.'s custody and visitation claims because the legislative scheme and the common law do not recognize her rights; that V.C. lacks standing to claim custody and visitation because she has not asserted parental unfitness; that V.C.'s application intrudes on M.J.B.'s basic liberty interest in raising her children as she sees fit; that protection of the children from serious harm is the only basis for governmental intervention into her private life with her children; that she has an absolute right to decide with whom her children will associate; that V.C. was the equivalent of a nanny whose status deserves no special acknowledgment; that she did not give consent to V.C.'s role as a "parent". . . . V.C. counters that she qualifies as a parent under N.J.S.A. 9:2-13(f); that she is a psychological parent[3] of the twins thus justifying the invocation of the court's parens patriae power to sustain that relationship; that in such circumstances the best interests test applies; and . . . that denial of joint legal custody was erroneous because of her status as a de facto parent. . . .

## III.

We turn first to M.J.B.'s claim that we lack jurisdiction and that V.C. lacks standing to apply for joint custody and visitation because neither the statutes nor the common law acknowledge the existence of such a cause of action by a third party.

### A.

There are no statutes explicitly addressing whether a former unmarried domestic partner has standing to seek custody and visitation with her former partner's biological children. That is not to say, however, that the current statutory scheme dealing with issues of custody and visitation does not provide some guiding principles. N.J.S.A. 9:2-3 prescribes:

> When the parents of a minor child live separately, or are about to do so, the Superior Court, in an action brought by either parent, shall have the same power to make judgments or orders concerning care, custody, education and maintenance as concerning a child whose parents are divorced. . . .

Further, N.J.S.A. 9:2-4 provides, in part, that the Legislature finds and declares that it is in the public policy of this State to assure minor children of frequent and continuing contact with both parents after the parents have separated or dissolved their marriage and that it is in the public interest to encourage parents to share the rights and responsibilities of child rearing in order to effect this policy. . . .

N.J.S.A. 9:2-13(f) provides that "the word 'parent,' when not otherwise described by the context, means a natural parent or parent by previous adoption." M.J.B. argues that because V.C. is not a natural or adoptive parent, we lack jurisdiction to consider her claims. That is an incomplete interpretation of the Act. Although the statutory definition of parent focuses on natural and adoptive parents, it also includes the phrase, "when not otherwise described by the context." That language evinces a legislative intent to leave open the possibility that individuals other than natural or adoptive parents may qualify as "parents," depending on the circumstances. . . .

By including the words "when not otherwise described by the context" in the statute, the Legislature obviously envisioned a case where the specific relationship between a child and a person not specifically denominated by the statute would qualify as "parental". . . .

**B.**

Separate and apart from the statute, M.J.B. contends that there is no legal precedent for this action by V.C. She asserts, correctly, that a legal parent has a fundamental right to the care, custody and nurturance of his or her child. . . . Various constitutional provisions have been cited as the source of that right . . . In general, however, the right of a legal parent to the care and custody of his or her child derives from the notion of privacy. According to M.J.B., that right entitles her to absolute preference over V.C. in connection with custody and visitation of the twins. She argues that V.C., a stranger, has no standing to bring this action. We disagree.

The right of parents to the care and custody of their children is not absolute. For example, a legal parent's fundamental right to custody and control of a child may be infringed upon by the state if the parent endangers the health or safety of the child. Wisconsin v. Yoder, 406 U.S. 205, 233-234, 92 S. Ct. 1526, 1542, 32 L. Ed. 2d 15, 35 (1972); Prince v. Massachusetts, 321 U.S. 158, 166-167, S. Ct. 438, 442, 88 L. Ed. 645, 652-653 (1944). Likewise, if there is a showing of unfitness, abandonment or gross misconduct, a parent's right to custody of her child may be usurped. *Watkins, supra,* 163 N.J. at 246, . . .

According to M.J.B., because there is no allegation by V.C. of unfitness, abandonment or gross misconduct, there is no reason advanced to interfere with any of her constitutional prerogatives. What she elides from consideration, however, is the "exceptional circumstances" category (occasionally denominated as extraordinary circumstances) that has been recognized as an alternative basis for a third party to seek custody and visitation of another person's child. *Watkins, supra,* 163 N.J. at 247, . . .

Subsumed within that category is the subset known as the psychological parent cases in which a third party has stepped in to assume the role of the legal parent who has been unable or unwilling to undertake the obligations of parenthood. . . .

At the heart of the psychological parent cases is a recognition that children have a strong interest in maintaining the ties that connect them to adults who love and provide for them. That interest, for constitutional as well as social purposes, lies in the emotional bonds that develop between family members as a result of shared daily life. Smith v. Organization of Foster Families for Equality and Reform, 431 U.S. 816, 844, 97 S. Ct. 2094, 2109, 53 L. Ed. 2d 14, 35 (1977). That point was emphasized in Lehr v.

Robertson, 463 U.S. 248, 261, 103 S. Ct. 2985, 2993, 77 L. Ed. 2d 614, 626 (1983), where the Supreme Court held that a stepfather's actual relationship with a child was the determining factor when considering the degree of protection that the parent-child link must be afforded. The Court stressed that the importance of the familial relationship, to the individuals involved and to the society, stems from the emotional attachments that derive from the intimacy of daily association, and from the role it plays in "promoting a way of life" through the instruction of children as well as from the fact of blood relationship. [*Ibid.*] . . .

## IV.

The next issue we confront is how a party may establish that he or she has, in fact, become a psychological parent to the child of a fit and involved legal parent. That is a question which many of our sister states have attempted to answer. . . .

Several state courts have attempted to refine the concept further. . . .

The most thoughtful and inclusive definition of de facto parenthood is the test enunciated in Custody of H.S.H.-K., 193 Wis. 2d 649, 533 N.W.2d 419, 421 (Wis. 1995), . . . Under that test, to demonstrate the existence of the petitioner's parent-like relationship with the child, the petitioner must prove four elements: (1) that the biological or adoptive parent consented to, and fostered, the petitioner's formation and establishment of a parent-like relationship with the child; (2) that the petitioner and the child lived together in the same household; (3) that the petitioner assumed the obligations of parenthood by taking significant responsibility for the child's care, education and development, including contributing towards the child's support, without expectation of financial compensation [a petitioner's contribution to a child's support need not be monetary]; and (4) that the petitioner has been in a parental role for a length of time sufficient to have established with the child a bonded, dependent relationship parental in nature. [Custody of H.S.H.-K., *supra*, 533 N.W.2d at 421 (footnote omitted).]

Recapping, the legal parent must consent to and foster the relationship between the third party and the child; the third party must have lived with the child; the third party must perform parental functions for the child to a significant degree; and most important, a parent-child bond must be forged. We are satisfied that that test provides a good framework for determining psychological parenthood in cases where the third party has lived for a substantial period with the legal parent and her child.

Prong one is critical because it makes the biological or adoptive parent a participant in the creation of the psychological parent's relationship with the child. Without such a requirement, a paid nanny or babysitter could theoretically qualify for parental status. To avoid that result, in order for a third party to be deemed a psychological parent, the legal parent must have fostered the formation of the parental relationship between the third party and the child. . . .

The requirement of cooperation by the legal parent is critical because it places control within his or her hands. That parent has the absolute ability to maintain a zone of autonomous privacy for herself and her child. However, if she wishes to maintain that zone of privacy she cannot invite a third party to function as a parent to her child and cannot cede over to that third party parental authority the exercise of which may create a profound bond with the child.

Two further points concerning the consent requirement need to be clarified. First, a psychological parent-child relationship that is voluntarily created by the legally recognized parent may not be unilaterally terminated after the relationship between the adults ends. . . . Thus, the right of the legal parent [does] not extend to erasing a relationship between her partner and her child which she voluntarily created and actively fostered simply because after the party's separation she regretted having done so. [J.A.L. v. E.P.H., 453 Pa. Super. 78, 682 A.2d 1314, 1322 (Pa. Super. Ct. 1996) (footnote omitted).] . . .

The second issue that needs to be clarified is that participation in the decision to have a child is not a prerequisite to a finding that one has become a psychological parent to the child. . . . Although joint participation in the family's decision to have a child is probative evidence of the legally recognized parent's intentions, not having participated in the decision does not preclude a finding of the third party's psychological parenthood. . . .

Concerning the remaining prongs of the *H.S.H.-K.* test, we accept Wisconsin's formulation with these additional comments. The third prong, a finding that a third party assumed the obligations of parenthood, is not contingent on financial contributions made by the third party. Financial contribution may be considered but should not be given inordinate weight when determining whether a third party has assumed the obligations of parenthood. Obviously, as we have indicated, the assumption of a parental role is much more complex than mere financial support. It is determined by the nature, quality, and extent of the functions undertaken by the third party and the response of the child to that nurturance. . . .

## V.

This opinion should not be viewed as an incursion on the general right of a fit legal parent to raise his or her child without outside interference. What we have addressed here is a specific set of circumstances involving the volitional choice of a legal parent to cede a measure of parental authority to a third party; to allow that party to function as a parent in the day-to-day life of the child; and to foster the forging of a parental bond between the third party and the child. In such circumstances, the legal parent has created a family with the third party and the child, and has invited the third party into the otherwise inviolable realm of family privacy. By virtue of her own actions, the legal parent's expectation of autonomous privacy in her relationship with her child is necessarily reduced from that which would have been the case had she never invited the third party into their lives. Most important, where that invitation and its consequences have altered her child's life by essentially giving him or her another parent, the legal parent's options are constrained. . . .

## VI.

Once a third party has been determined to be a psychological parent to a child, under the previously described standards, he or she stands in parity with the legal parent. . . . Custody and visitation issues between them are to be determined on a best interests standard. . . .

That is not to suggest that a person's status as a legal parent does not play a part in custody or visitation proceedings in those circumstances. . . .

. . . The legal parent's status is a significant weight in the best interests balance because eventually, in the search for self-knowledge, the child's interest in his or her roots will emerge. Thus, under ordinary circumstances when the evidence concerning the child's best interests (as between a legal parent and psychological parent) is in equipoise, custody will be awarded to the legal parent.

Visitation, however, will be the presumptive rule, . . . as would be the case if two natural parents were in conflict.

## VII.

That said, the issue is whether V.C. should be granted joint legal custody and visitation. . . . V.C. and M.J.B. are essentially equal. Each appears to be a fully capable, loving parent committed to the safety and welfare of the twins. Although there is animosity between V.C. and M.J.B., that is not a determinant of whether V.C. can continue in the children's lives.

We note that V.C. is not seeking joint physical custody, but joint legal custody for decision making. However, due to the pendency of this case, V.C. has not been involved in the decision making for the twins for nearly four years. To interject her into the decisional realm at this point would be unnecessarily disruptive for all involved. We will not, therefore, order joint legal custody in this case.

Visitation, however, is another matter. V.C. and the twins have been visiting during nearly all of the four years since V.C. parted company from M.J.B. Continued visitation in those circumstances is presumed. Nothing suggests that V.C. should be precluded from continuing to see the children on a regular basis. Indeed, it is clear that continued regular visitation is in the twins' best interests because V.C. is their psychological parent. . . .

## QUESTIONS

1. Why did M.J.B. argue that the court lacked jurisdiction to resolve the custody/visitation dispute between the parties?

2. On what basis did the court determine that it had jurisdiction over the dispute?

3. What was the essence of M.J.B.'s argument with respect to the rights of V.C.? How did she characterize V.C.?

4. According to the court, what is a "psychological" or "de facto" parent?

5. What is the four-pronged test for determining whether a party is a psychological/de facto parent? Why is the cooperation of the legal parent so important in determining whether a party qualifies as a de facto parent?

6. Why, according to the court, does a finding that a party is a de facto parent not interfere with the privacy/parental rights of the legal parent?

7. What is the status of a party once she or he is determined to be a psychological/de facto parent? What standard is to be used in resolving custody and visitation disputes?

8. Why does the court decide that where all factors are equal, custody should be awarded to the "legal" parent over the de facto parent? Is this consistent with the discussion regarding the legal status of the de facto parent?

# Endnotes

1. For a discussion of custody disputes involving unmarried parents, *see* Chapter 11; for a discussion of custody issues in the context of abuse and neglect proceedings, *see* Chapter 12.

2. As discussed later in this chapter, the term "third party" is not accurate as applied to co-parents.

3. William Blackstone, Commentaries on the Laws of England 372-373 (19th London ed. 1857).

4. Michael Grossberg, Governing the Hearth: Law and the Family in Nineteenth Century America 235 (1985). Although rarely mentioned in works discussing the nature of paternal authority, it is important to recognize that fathers who were slaves did not have this kind of authority over their children; slave owners had complete control over the lives of their slaves without regard for their family relationships.

5. Baird v. Baird, 21 N.J. Eq. 384, 393 (1869) (dissent), *quoted in* Alan Roth, The Tender Years Presumption in Child Custody Disputes, 15 J. Fam. L. 423, 428 (1976-1977).

6. Elizabeth Pleck, Domestic Tyranny: The Making of American Social Policy from Colonial Times to the Present 39 (1987).

7. MCL § 722.23 (2006).

8. *See* Katherine T. Bartlett, U.S. Custody Law and Trends in the Context of the ALI Principles of the Law of Family Dissolution, 10 Va. J. Soc. Poly. & L. 5, 16-22 (2002).

9. Robert F. Kelly and Shawn L. Ward, Allocating Custodial Responsibilities at Divorce: Social Science Research and the American Law Institute's Approximation Rule, 40 Fam. Ct. Rev. 350, 356, 358 (2002).

10. *See* Margaret F. Bring, Feminism and Child Custody Under Chapter Two of the American Law Institute's Principles of the Law of Family Dissolution, 8 Duke J.L. & Poly. 301, 308-309 (2001). *See* note 49, *infra,* for a list of articles on this issue.

11. Joan B. Kelly, Psychological and Legal Interventions for Parents and Children in Custody and Access Disputes: Current Research and Practice, 10 Va. J. Soc. Poly. & L. 129, 150 (2003). According to Kelly, these feelings are also attributed to parents' failure to "talk with their children about even the most elementary and relevant aspects of the separation or divorce." *Id. See also* Barbara A. Atwood, Hearing Children's Voices in Custody Litigation: An Empirical Survey and Suggestions of Reform, 45 Ariz. L. Rev. 629 (2003).

12. Kelly, *supra* note 11, at 154.

13. Atwood, *supra* note 11, at 638.

14. Kelly, *supra* note 11, at 152-161.

15. Elizabeth Scott, Parental Autonomy and Children's Welfare, 11 Wm. & Mary Bill of Rts. J. 1071, 1093 (2003).

16. N. Zoe Hilton, Battered Women's Concerns About Their Children Witnessing Wife Assault, 7 J. Interspousal Violence 1 (1990); Leigh Goodmark, From Property to Personhood: What the Legal System Should Do for Children in Family

Violence Cases, 102 W. Va. L. Rev. 237 (1999). *See also* Amy Levin and Linda G. Mills, Fighting for Child Custody When Domestic Violence Is at Issue: Survey of State Laws, 48 Social Work 463 (2003).

17. Goodmark, *supra* note 16, at 245.

18. Judith S. Wallerstein and Sandra Blakeslee, Second Chances — Men, Women, and Children a Decade After Divorce 113-121 (1989). *See also* Alan J. Tomkins et al., The Plight of Children Who Witness Woman Battering: Psychological Knowledge and Policy Implications, 18 Law & Psychol. Rev. 137 (1994).

19. Hon. Donna J. Hitchens and Patricia Van Horn, Courts Responding to Domestic Violence; The Court's Role in Supporting and Protecting Children Exposed to Domestic Violence, 6 J. Center for Fam. Child. 7 Cts. 31 (2005). This article contains an excellent review of the relevant literature.

20. Hitchens and Van Horn, *supra* at note 19, at 34. As the authors note, not all children who witness parental violence experience these problems (internal citations omitted). For a brief discussion regarding childhood resiliency, *see id.* at 33-34.

21. Wallerstein and Blakeslee, *supra* note 18, at 110-121.

22. *Id.* at 38. To date, the research has focused on the connection between partner abuse committed by men and their treatment of children.

23. Cynthhia Grover Hastings, Letting Down Their Guard: What Guardians Ad Litem Should Know About Domestic Violence in Child Custody Disputes, 24 B.C. Third World L.J. 283,314 (2004).

24. Hastings, *supra* note 23, at 301-302.

25. Palmore v. Sidoti, 466 U.S. 429 (1984).

26. *Id.* at 433.

27. Bottoms v. Bottoms, 249 Va. 410, 457 S.E.2d 102 (1995) (citations omitted).

28. 457 S.E.2d at 108 (quoting Roe v. Roe, 228 Va. 772, 778, 324 S.E.2d 691, 694 (1985)).

29. For a review of many of the studies, *see* Serena Lambert, Gay and Lesbian Families: What We Know and Where to Go from Here, 13 The Family Journal: Counseling and Therapy for Couples and Families, 43, 49 (2005). For an alternate perspective on the research, *see* Lynn D. Wardle, Considering the Impacts on Children and Society of "Lesbigay" Parenting, 23 Quinnipiac L. Rev. 541 (2004).

30. McGriff v. McGriff, 140 Pd. 642, 99 P.3d 111 (2004) (dissenting opinion of Justice Kidwell). For a detailed analysis of the *McGriff* case, *see* Susan M. Moss, McGriff v. McGriff: Consdieration of a Parent's Sexual Orientation in Child Custody Disputes, 41 Idaho L. Rev. 593 (2005). The author notes that despite the trial court's assertion that it was not basing the decision on the father's homosexuality, a textual review of the decision reveals a "disproportionate judicial focus on it," with twenty-five separate references to his "lifestyle," "homosexuality" and "sexual orientation." *Id.* at 632.

31. *Id.* at 125.

32. *Id.*

33. This discussion draws on the following articles: Carol Wah, Restrictions on Religious Training and Exposure in Child Custody and Visitation Orders: Do They Protect or Harm the Child, 45 J. Church & St. 14 (2003); Carol Wah, Religion in Child Custody and Visitation Cases: Presenting the Advantage of Religious Participation, 28 Fam. L.Q. 269 (1994); Note, The Establishment Clause and Religion in Child Custody Disputes: Factoring Religion into the Best Interest Equation, 82 Mich. L. Rev. 1702 (1984); Collin R. Magnum, Exclusive Reliance on Best Interest May Be Unconstitutional: Religion as a Factor in Child Custody Cases, 15 Creighton L. Rev. (1982).

34. Garrett v. Garrett, 527 N.W.2d 213, 221-222 (Neb. Ct. App. 1995).

35. Marriage of Carney, 598 P.2d 36, 42 (Cal. Ct. App. 1979).

36. 167 W. Va. 59, 278 S.E.2d 357 (1981).

37. 278 S.E.2d at 360.

38. *See* Ronald K. Henry, "Primary Caretaker": Is It a Ruse?, 17 Fam. Advoc. 53 (1994).

39. ALI Press Release, May 15, 2002, http://www.ali.org. The American Law Institute was founded in 1923 to address the uncertainty and complexity of our legal system. In addition to publishing the renowned Restatement series, the ALI "engages in intensive examination and analysis of legal areas thought to need reform. This type of study generally culminates in a work product containing extensive recommendations or proposals for change in the law," such as the Principles of the Law of Family Dissolution, http://www.ali.org (accessed May 22, 2004).

40. The following articles discuss the ALI's approximation rule: Katherine T. Bartlett, U.S. Custody Law and Trends in the Context of the ALI Principles of the Law of Family Dissolution, 10 Va. J. Soc. Poly. & L. 5, 17-18 (2002); Margaret Bring, Feminism and Child Custody Under Chapter Two of the American Law Institute's Principles of the Law of Family Dissolution, 8 Duke J. Gender L. & Poly. 301 (2002); Robert F. Kelly and Shawn L. Ward, Allocating Custodial Responsibility at Divorce: Social Science Research and the American Law Institute's Approximation Rule, 40 Fam. Ct. Rev. 350 (2002).

41. *See, e.g.,* Eleanor Maccoby & Robert H. Mnookin, Dividing the Child: Social and Legal Dilemmas of Custody (1992).

42. *See* Judith S. Wallerstein and Sandra Blakeslee, Second Chances — Men, Women and Children a Decade After Divorce 256-273 (1989).

43. *See* Gerald W. Hardcastle, Joint Custody: A Family Court Judge's Perspective, 32 Fam. L.Q. 201 (1998); Judith S. Wallerstein and Janet R. Johnston, Children of Divorce, Recent Findings Regarding Long-Term Effects and Recent Studies of Joint and Sole Custody, 11 Pediatrics in Rev. 197 (1990).

44. Margaret F. Bring, Extending Default Rules Beyond Purely Economic Relationships: Penalty Defaults in Family Law: The Case of Child Custody, 33 Fla. St. U. L. Rev. 779, 782 (2006).

45. *See* D. Lee Khachutarian, Domestic Violence and Shared Parental Responsibility: Dangerous Bedfellows, 44 Wayne L. Rev. 1745 (1999), and articles cited therein.

46. Joan Kelly, Psychological and Legal Interventions for Parents and Children in Custody and Access Disputes: Current Research and Practice, 10 Va. J. Soc. Poly. & l. 129, 135 (2002).

47. Victoria L. Lutz and Cara E. Grady, Models of Collaboration in Family Law: Domestic Violence and Parent Education: Necessary Measures and Logistics to Maximize the Safety of Victims of Domestic Violence Attending Parent Education Programs, 42 Fam. Ct. Rev. 363 (2004).

48. For a description of Kentucky's Divorce Education programs, see: http://courts.ky.gov/courts/circuit/familycourt/divorceeducation. (accessed January 15, 2007).

49. *See generally* Lucy S. McGough, Starting Over: The Heuristics of Family Relocation Decision Making, 77 St. John's L. Rev. 291 (2003); Charles P. Kindregan, Family Interests in Competition: Relocation and Visitation, 36 Suffolk U. L. Rev. 31 (2002); Edwin J. Terry, Relocation: Moving Forward or Moving Backward?, 31 Tex. Tech. L. Rev. 983 (2000).

50. D'Onofrio v. D'Onofrio, 365 A.2d 27, 29-30 (N.J. Super. Ct. Ch. Div. 1976), *aff'd*, 365 A.2d 716 (N.J. Super. Ct. App. Div. 1976).

51. For a discussion of some of this research, *see* Kenneth Waldron, A Review of Social Science Research on Post Divorce Relocation, 19 J. Am. Acad. Matrimonial Law. 337 (2005); Eric G. Mart & Rachel M. Bedard, Child Custody and Post-Divorce Relocation in the Light of Braver et al., 31 Ver. B.J. & L. Dig. 47 (2005).

52. Cleri v. Cleri, No. 01D-0009-D1 (Conn. Prob. Ct. July 2, 2002), *cited in* Sarah L. Gottried, Virtual Visitation: The New Wave of Communication between Children and Non-Custodial Parents in Relocation Cases, 9 Cardoza Women's L.J. 567, 582-583 (2003). This article provides an excellent overview of some of the issues raised by virtual visitation. *See also* Madeline Marzano-Lesnevich and Scott Adam Laterra, The Argument Against Virtual Visitation, 164 New Jersey L.J. 27 (2001).

53. Gottried, *supra* note 52, at 42 (citing the court's decision in Kaleita v. Sniderman, No. 99-DR-4601 (Fla. Seminole County Ct., Oct. 30, 2000) (order resolving pending motions)).

54. As discussed in Chapter 11, the common law presumption of paternity under which all children born to a married woman are presumed to be offspring of the marriage even if they were conceived as a result of an extramarital affair is a longstanding exception to this rule, as it allows for fatherhood by presumption. As also discussed in Chapter 11, the rules for establishment of paternity when a child is conceived through donor insemination are a further exception to the basic rule that parenthood is accomplished by adoption or biology.

The operative principle — that legal parenthood is a function of biology or adoption — also has been challenged by the practice of assisted reproduction, such as surrogate motherhood. For further information, *see* Helene S. Shapo, Assisted Reproduction and the Law: Disharmony on a Divisive Social Issue, 100 Nw. U.L. Rev. 465 (2006); David D. Meyer, Parenthood in a Time of Transition: Tensions Between Legal, Biological, and Social Conceptions of Parenthood 54 Am. J. Comp. L. 125, (2006); Sanja Zgonjanin,What Does It Take To Be A (Lesbian) Parent? On Intent and Genetics, 16 Hastings Women's L.J. 251 (2005).

55. *See* Patricia S. Fernandez, Grandparent Access: A Model Statute, 6 Yale L. & Poly. Rev. 109 (1988).

56. 828 S.W.2d 630, 632-633 (Ky. 1992).

57. 855 S.W.2d 573, 580-583 (Tenn. 1993) (internal citations omitted).

58. *Id.* at 583.

59. *Troxel,* 530 U.S. at 64 (citing the Supreme Court of Washington's decision, Smith v. Stillwell-Smith (In re Custody of Smith), 969 P.2d 21, 31 (Wash. 1998)). The difference in the case name results from the Washington court's consolidation of three cases.

60. *Id.* at 58-59.

61. *Id.* at 68 (emphasis in original).

62. For a discussion of post-*Troxel* decisions, *see* Joan Catherine Bohl, That "Thorny" Issue, California Grandparent Visitation Law in the Wake of *Troxel v. Granville,* 36 Golden Gate U.L. Rev. 121 (2006); Kristine L. Roberts, *Troxel v. Granville* and the Courts' Reluctance to Declare Grandparent Visitation Statutes Unconstitutional, 41 Fam. Ct. Rev. 14 (2003).

63. Atkinson v. Atkinson, 160 Mich. App. 601, 608-609, 408 N.W.2d 516, 519 (1987).

64. For a discussion of this approach, *see* Bryce Levine, Divorce and the Modern Family: Providing In Loco Parentis Stepparents Standing to Sue for Custody of Their Stepchildren in a Dissolution Proceeding, 25 Hofstra L. Rev. 315 (1996).

65. We will assume that the sperm donor is unknown and thus cannot assert any claims to the child. In this regard it should be noted that although the principles discussed in this section would apply equally to a gay male couple, their situation might be complicated somewhat if a surrogate mother was involved, as she might be able to assert her own claims to the child.

66. E.N.O. v. L.M.M., 429 Mass. 824, 711 N.E.2d 886, *cert. denied,* 120 S. Ct. 500 (1999).

67. *Id.* at 891.

68. *Id.* at 891, n. 6.

69. 193 Wis. 2d 649, 533 N.W.2d 419 (1995), *cert. denied,* 516 U.S. 976 (1995).

70. *Id.* at 436-437.

71. Rubano v. DiCenzo, 759 A.2d 959 (R.I. 2000).

72. V.C. v. M.J.B., 163 N.J. 200, 748 A.2d 539 (2000).

73. *Id.* at 554-555.

74. Carvin v. Britian (In re Parentage of L.B.0, 155 Wn. 2d 679,122 P.3d 161, 178 (2005); *cert. denied* 126 S.Ct. 2021 (2006).

For further discussion of the use of parenting presumptions to formalize the status of same-sex co-parents, see Chapter 11. *See also* Jennifer L. Rosato, Children of Same-Sex Parents Deserve the Security Blanket of the Parentage Presumption, 44 Fam. Ct. Rev. 74 (2006); Deborah L. Forman, Married with Kids and Moving: Achieving Recognition for Same-Sex Parents Under the Uniform Parentage Act, 4 Whittier J. Child & Fam. Advoc. 241 (2005).

# 6 Child Support

As we have seen so far, family law is primarily a matter of state concern. However, this changes when we come to **child support**, an arena in which the federal government plays an important role.

In the 1970s, the issue of child support came under intense public scrutiny. Studies documented that in almost half of the families with absent fathers, no child support was awarded, and where awarded, amounts were generally inadequate. Highlighting the problem in a dramatic way, one study showed that two-thirds of noncustodial fathers in Denver paid more in monthly car payments than in child support payments.[1] Where orders *were* entered, there was a high rate of noncompliance. Census data consistently showed that slightly less than 50 percent of custodial parents received the full amount of child support they were entitled to, while almost 30 percent received nothing.[2]

Between 1970 and 1981, the number of people in female-headed families living below the poverty level increased significantly, and the term "feminization of poverty" was coined to underscore the fact that households made up of women and children were sliding into poverty. Underlying the concern about poverty was an increased awareness of the difference in post-divorce standards of living between men and women with children. Studies consistently showed that the financial well-being of men improved following a divorce, while that of women and children deteriorated; for instance one study found a 17 percent increase in standard of living for men compared to a 29 percent decline for women and children.[3]

At the federal level, there was a growing awareness that many women and children were being forced to turn to public assistance, namely Aid to Families with Dependent Children (AFDC, more commonly referred to as "welfare"), because they were not receiving the child support they were entitled to. The AFDC program was begun in 1935 through an amendment to the Social Security Act. Its original purpose was to provide financial assistance to widows with minor children to enable them to keep their children with them.[4] However, by the 1970s, the vast majority of families on AFDC required assistance because of paternal nonsupport rather than paternal death.

This sobering picture prompted the federal government to enter the child support field. In 1974, hoping to force absent parents to become financially responsible and thereby reduce federal welfare expenditures, Congress passed the Child Support Enforcement and Establishment of Paternity Act of 1974 (1974 Act), which added **Title IV-D** to the Social Security Act.[5] As explained by Margaret Heckler, then Secretary of the U.S. Department of Health and Human Services, in favor of this increased federal role: "Children deserve to be supported by both parents. For the sake of America's children, we must put an end to what has become a national disgrace. Our new federal legislation will help States obtain support orders quickly and pursue them vigorously."[6] This new law required states to develop comprehensive child support programs to help custodial parents obtain and enforce child support awards.

Since 1974, Congress has amended Title IV-D multiple times and passed other child support legislation intended to strengthen the ability of states to establish and collect child support awards.[7] Congress has also passed a series of laws that require states to speed up what historically has been a very slow process. Responding to this mandate, states have adopted a variety of expedited judicial and administrative processes for both issuing and enforcing support orders.[8] Before examining this joint federal-state child support system, we begin with a brief historical overview of the parental support duty.

## HISTORICAL OVERVIEW

According to English common law, fathers had a moral but not a legal duty to support their children; mothers had neither. In contrast, in this country, most states adopted the view that even in the absence of a specific statute, fathers owed their children a legal duty of support; mothers had a support duty only to the extent that fathers were unable to fulfill theirs. A father's obligation was enforceable through the common law doctrine of necessaries, which allowed wives and children to pledge a husband's/father's credit to purchase necessaries that he had failed to provide.

Eventually, this paternal duty was embodied in a variety of statutes. Civil liability was imposed through family responsibility or family expense statutes. Family responsibility laws required fathers or other relatives to support their children so they did not become a public burden; family expense statutes permitted the taking of parental property to satisfy debts incurred in meeting the family's needs. Nonsupport was also made a crime in all states.

## ADMINISTRATIVE FRAMEWORK FOR THE ESTABLISHMENT AND ENFORCEMENT OF CHILD SUPPORT ORDERS _____

### The Federal Office of Child Support Enforcement _____

The 1974 Act established the Office of Child Support Enforcement (OCSE). The OCSE is located within the Administration for Children and Families (ACF) in the United States Department of Health and Human Services (HHS). OCSE is the federal oversight agency with responsibility for helping states to develop, manage, and run their child support programs effectively and in accordance with federal law.[9] It also operates the federal Parent Locator Service, which helps custodial parents to locate absent parents.

### At the State Level: The IV-D Agency _____

The 1974 Act required each state to develop a comprehensive child support program and to designate a single state agency—known as an **IV-D agency**—to administer the program. IV-D agencies must provide the following five basic services to custodial parents:

- assistance in locating absent parents
- establishment of child support awards
- periodic review of awards
- enforcement of support awards
- where necessary, the establishment of paternity

Before looking at these components of the child support system, we will look at how custodial parents access the services of a IV-D agency. As will become clear, the process differs depending on whether or not the parent is a recipient of public assistance.

### Eligibility for IV-D Services _____

Custodial parents who apply for public assistance are automatically referred to an IV-D agency for child support services. In order to receive benefits, the parent must assign her rights to child support over to the state and agree to cooperate with the state in locating the absent parent and collecting support—unless the custodial parent can establish good cause, such as a risk of abuse, for not cooperating with the state. Once support has been assigned by the custodial parent, the noncustodial parent's support obligation runs to the state, and funds collected by the state may be used to reimburse the government for assistance payments made to the family. However, states have the option of "passing through" to the family up to $100.00 (or up to $200.00 in families with two or more children) of the collected support. If paternity has not been established, a custodial mother must cooperate with this process as well, unless good cause for non-cooperation has been established. (Paternity establishment is addressed in Chapter 11.)[10]

IV-D agencies also must provide child support assistance to families who are not applying for or receiving public assistance. Today, in contrast to the early years of the IV-D program, most of the families who receive child support services are not on public assistance, although many are former welfare recipients.[11] This represents a shift "from an emphasis on recouping Federal funds to the current mission of ensuring the support and care of America's children, without regard to receipt of government assistance."[12] A parent in this category must complete an application requesting IV-D services, and may be charged a $25.00 fee. Because public funds are not involved, the use of a IV-D agency is optional, and there is no assignment of support rights or a cooperation requirement, and all collected support payments go directly to the custodial parent. (Private child support agencies are discussed below.)

## Locating Absent Parents

A major barrier to obtaining and enforcing child support orders is that many noncustodial parents cannot be located, and some try to conceal their identity to avoid paying child support. To address this problem, the 1974 Act established the Federal **Parent Locator Service** (FPLS), which is operated by the OCSE, and required each state IV-D agency to establish its own parent locator service.

If a custodial parent does not know where the other parent is, he or she can request assistance from the state parent locator service. The locator service will check the records of other state agencies, such as the registry of motor vehicles or department of revenue, to see if it can locate the absent parent; credit-reporting agencies are also an important source of information. The locator service must also search the State Case Registry, a database with information regarding all state support cases, and the State Directory of New Hires, a database containing information submitted by employers containing information about all new hires, to determine if there is a match. If the parent cannot be located within the state, and there is cause to believe the parent is in another state, the parent locator service in the second state must initiate a search as described in this paragraph.

If the parent still cannot be located, the state locator service can ask the FPLS to assist in the search. Requests for federal assistance must come from an IV-D agency; individuals cannot file a direct request for federal assistance. Until 1996, the federal locator relied on the records of other federal agencies; however, under welfare reform, two important new search tools were added: (1) the Federal Case Registry of Child Support Orders (FCR), a comprehensive database containing information on all U.S. child support cases and (2) the National Directory of New Hires, a database including information about all new hires nationwide and persons who have applied for unemployment. As on the state level, these databases must be checked for matches. (See Enforcement below for more information on these databases.)

Although the increased focus on the centralization and sharing of information facilitates the child support collection process, it also poses risks to domestic violence victims because there is a possibility that information could be released to an abuser who is seeking to track down a former partner. Accordingly, federal law has now built in a number of safeguards to limit the disclosure of information where there is a known risk of harm. For example, a domestic violence indicator or flag may be placed on an at-risk individual's file to restrict disclosure of FPLS data.[13]

## CHILD SUPPORT GUIDELINES

To address the problem of inadequate and inconsistent awards, federal law requires each state to adopt **child support guidelines**. The guidelines must provide specific numeric criteria for the computation of support awards, and calculations must result in a presumptively correct support amount. Deviations from the guideline amount are permitted, but only where justifiable based on the circumstances of the case. Some guidelines include specific factors for a decision maker to consider when determining if a deviation is warranted, while other guidelines are general.

Guidelines are controlling with respect to both temporary and "permanent" child support awards.[14] The guidelines also control in cases in which the parents reach agreement on the support amount; to guard against the risk that a parent might bargain away support rights in exchange for something else of value, most commonly custody, any deviation must be justified to the court or reviewing agency. To assist in the computation of support amounts, many states have developed a standardized **support worksheet**. In preparing a case, a paralegal may be asked to complete a support worksheet, so it is important for you to have a complete and accurate understanding of how the guidelines work in your jurisdiction. Exhibit 6.1, a child support worksheet from the state of New Jersey, is included as a sample to give you a sense of what a worksheet looks like.

## Guideline Formulas

Although federal law requires states to adopt child support guidelines, it left the job of developing the actual guidelines up to the states. In developing their guidelines, most states have used either a percentage-of-income or an income-shares approach. These approaches — together with a hybrid approach, often referred to as the "Melson formula" after Judge Elwood F. Melson, Jr., of the Delaware Family Court — are set out below.

### Percentage of Income

The percentage-of-income (or fixed percentage) approach sets the support amount as a fixed percentage of the noncustodial parent's income. Usually, the only relevant variable is the number of children in the household, although some states permit consideration of other factors, such as shared custody arrangements. Thus, for example, the support percentage might be set at 25 percent of the noncustodial parent's income for one child; at 30 percent for two children; and at 34 percent for three children.

The advantage of this model is its simplicity. However, by not building in consideration of multiple factors, the results may be inequitable. For example, a custodial parent who is employed part-time or at home with young children would get the same amount of support as a custodial parent who is employed at a well-paying job.

### Income Shares

The income-shares approach is premised on the assumption that children are entitled to receive the same share of parental income that they would have had the family stayed together. To arrive at the support amount, the income of both parents is combined and a basic support obligation computed. This obligation is then allocated between the parents in proportion to income, with the noncustodial parent paying his or her share in support payments and the custodial parent assumed to be paying his or her share in direct expenditures on the children.

## Exhibit 6.1   Child Support Worksheet

| CHILD SUPPORT GUIDELINES - SHARED PARENTING WORKSHEET | | | |
|---|---|---|---|
| **Case Name:** *vs.*    *Plaintiff*    *Defendant* <br> PPR is the ☐ Plaintiff ☐ Defendant | **County:** <br> **Docket No.:** <br> **Number of Children:** | | |

| *All amounts must be weekly.* | **PARENT OF PRIMARY RESIDENCE (PPR)** | **PARENT OF ALTERNATE RESIDENCE (PAR)** | **COMBINED** |
|---|---|---|---|
| 1. Gross Taxable Income | $ | $ | |
| 1a. Mandatory Retirement Contributions (*non-taxable*) | –$ | –$ | |
| 1b. Alimony Paid (*Current and/or Past Relationships*) | –$ | –$ | |
| 1c. Alimony Received (*Current and/or Past Relationships*) | +$ | +$ | |
| 2. Adjusted Gross Taxable Income ((L1 - L1a-L1b)+L1c) | $ | $ | |
| 2a. Federal, State and Local Income Tax Withholding | –$ | –$ | |
| 2b. Prior Child Support Orders (*Past Relationships*) | –$ | –$ | |
| 2c. Mandatory Union Dues | –$ | –$ | |
| 2d. Other Dependent Deduction (from separate worksheet) | –$ | –$ | |
| 3. Net Taxable Income (L2-L2a-L2b-L2c-L2d) | $ | $ | |
| 4. Non-Taxable Income  (*source:*     ) | +$ | +$ | |
| 5. Net Income (L3+L4) | $ | $ | $ |
| 6. Percent Share of Income (L5 Each Parent ÷ L5 Combined) | | | 1.00 |
| 7. Number of Overnights With Each Parent | | | |
| 8. Percent of Overnights With Parent (L7 Parent ÷ L7 Combined) | | | 1.00 |
| **→ If PAR time sharing is less than the equivalent of two overnights per week (28%), use Sole Custody Worksheet ←** | | | |
| 9. Basic Child Support Amount (from Appendix IX-F Schedules) | | | $ |
| 10. PAR Shared Parenting Fixed Expenses (PAR L8×L9×0.38 ×2) | | $ | $ |
| 11. Government Benefits for the Child | | | $ |
| 12. Shared Parenting Basic Child Support Amount ((L9 + L10) - L11) | | | $ |
| 13. PAR Share of SP Basic Child Support Amount (PAR L6 × L12) | | $ | |
| 14 PAR Shared Parenting Variable Expenses (PAR L8 × L9 × 0.37) | | $ | |
| 15. PAR Adjusted SP Basic Child Support Amount (L13 - L10 - L14) | | $ | |
| 16. Net Work-Related Child Care (from Appendix IX-E Worksheet) | | | $ |
| 17. Child's Share of Health Insurance Premium | | | +$ |
| 18. Unreimbursed Health Care Expenses over $250 per child per year | | | +$ |
| 19. Court-Approved Extraordinary Expenses | | | +$ |
| 20. Total Supplemental Expenses (L16+L17+L18+L19) | | | $ |
| ☞ *Continued on Page 2* ☞ | | | |

**Exhibit 6.1    Continued**

| CHILD SUPPORT GUIDELINES - SHARED PARENTING WORKSHEET - PAGE 2 | | | |
|---|---|---|---|
| *All amounts must be weekly.* | PPR | PAR | COMBINED |
| 20. Total Supplemental Expenses (from reverse side) | | | $ |
| 21. PAR's Share of Total Supplemental Expenses (PAR L6 × L20) | | $ | |
| 22. PAR Net Work-Related Child Care PAID | | $ | |
| 23. PAR Health Insurance Premium for the Child PAID | | +$ | |
| 24. PAR Unreimbursed Health Care Expenses (>$250/child /year) PAID | | +$ | |
| 25. PAR Court-Approved Extraordinary Expenses PAID | | +$ | |
| 26. PAR Total Payments/Supplemental Expenses (L22+L23+L24+L25) | | $ | |
| 27. PAR Net Supplemental Expenses (L21 - L26) | | $ | |
| 28. PAR Net Child Support Obligation (L15 + L27) | | $ | |
| 29. Line 28 PAR CS Oblig WITH Other-Dependent Deduction | | $ | |
| 30. Line 28 PAR CS Oblig WITHOUT Other-Dependent Deduction | | $ | |
| 31. Adjusted PAR CS Obligation ((L29+L30)÷2) | | $ | |
| 32. Self-Support Reserve Test (PAR L5 - PAR L28 or L31 if any). If PAR amount is greater than 105% of the poverty guideline for one person (*pg*) *or* the PPR L32 income is less than the *pg*, enter the L28 or L31 amount on the PAR L34.  If PAR L32 amount is less than the *pg* and the PPR's L32 income is greater than the *pg*, go to Line 33.  If L28 or L31 is negative, see App. IX-B (shared-parenting worksheet) for instructions. | $ | $ | |
| 33. Maximum CS Obligation (Obligor Parent's L5 net income - 105% of the poverty guideline for one person). Enter result here and on L34. | $ | $ | |
| 34. Child Support Order (negative L28 or L31 denotes PPR obligation) to | $ | $ | |
| ➡ If the PAR is the Obligor, Continue to Line 35 | | | |
| 35. PPR Household Income Test - (L5 PPR net income from all sources + net income of other household members +L34 order)  If less than the PPR household income threshold (see App. IX-A, ¶14(c)), the SOLE-CUSTODY WORKSHEET must be used. | $ | | |
| **Comments, Rebuttals, and Justification for Deviations** | | | |

1. The child support order for this case ☐ was ☐ was not  based on the child support guidelines award.

2. If different from the child support guidelines award (Line 34), enter amount ordered: $

3. The child support guidelines were not used or the guidelines award was adjusted because:




( ☐ additional pages attached)

4. The following extraordinary expenses were added to the basic support obligation on Line 19:


| 5. Custodial Taxes: | App. IX-H | Circ. E | Other: _____ | #Allowances:_____ | Marital: S M H |
| Non-Cust Taxes: | App. IX-H | Circ. E | Other: _____ | #Allowances:_____ | Marital: S M H |

| Prepared by: | Title | Date |
|---|---|---|

Critics of this approach argue that it falls short in two ways that are particularly applicable in sole custody cases. First, it ignores the fact that following a divorce, the expenses of the custodial parent generally increase because he or she now must pay for services—such as baby-sitting, household cleaning, and repairs—to compensate for losing the contribution of the other parent would have made to the household. Second, it discounts the large non-economic contribution the custodial parent makes to the well-being of the children.

### The Melson Formula

Under this approach, a noncustodial parent is first permitted to keep a minimum level of income for his or her essential needs. This is referred to as a self-support reserve. Then, until the basic needs of the children are met, the parent cannot retain income above this minimum level; it must be allocated to child support. Once these needs are provided for, a percentage of the remaining parental income is allocated to increasing the basic support amount, thus enabling the children to benefit from a higher standard of living.

## Determining What Income Is Subject to the Child Support Obligation

In developing their guidelines, states, in addition to determining which basic approach to use, also had to decide what income would be subject to the support obligation. This determination entails two distinct considerations: (1) How is income to be defined? and (2) What support base will be used?

### Defining Income

Most guidelines define "income" broadly. All states include earned employment income in their definition, although treatment of sporadic income, such as income from occasional odd jobs or overtime, varies. In some states, sporadic income is excluded. In other states, it is averaged over time and added to regular earnings.

Most guidelines also recognize the concept of **imputed** (or **attributed**) **income**. Here, a parent who is voluntarily unemployed or underemployed is treated as if he or she has income commensurate with his or her earning capacity, and support is calculated based on this amount rather than on actual earnings. By attributing income to a parent and setting the support amount accordingly, a parent must find suitable employment or face sanctions for nonsupport. In some states, if a noncustodial parent remarries or cohabits and voluntarily stops working in reliance on the new partner's income, a portion of the household income will be attributed to that parent. In states where the income of the custodial parent is factored into the support equation, income may also be attributed to this parent where he or she is voluntarily under- or unemployed. However, most courts will not impute income if a parent has reduced his or her earnings due to child-related responsibilities, at least not until the child reaches a certain age — commonly age 6.

The ability to attribute income is important in situations where a parent deliberately reduces earnings in order to avoid a support obligation. However, what if a parent has reasons other than the avoidance of support for reducing his or her income? For example, take the situation of an attorney who after years of working in a major firm decides she is burned out and wants to open a small practice with a resulting loss of income. Should she be permitted to drastically reduce support payments? Is this fair to the children? On the other hand, is it fair to force a parent to remain in a particular career track by maintaining a support obligation based on earning potential?

Some states, either through guidelines or judicial decision, also permit income to be imputed to assets a party owns, such as jewelry or antiques, even if they are not income earning. The rationale for such a policy "is to discourage spouses from placing all of their assets into non-income yielding forms and thus shielding all of their assets from consideration in support."[15]

The definition of *income* almost always includes investment earnings, rents, profit shares, dividends, annuities, and governmental benefits, such as social security retirement and unemployment benefits. Some states also include the value of non-income producing assets — such as jewelry, antiques, and undeveloped real estate — within the meaning of the term "income."

### Setting the Income Base

In addition to defining income, the relevant income base must be determined. Here, states have three basic choices: Support can be calculated based on gross income, adjusted gross income, or net income.

**Gross Income Base.** A gross income base is used by many states. In this approach, the gross income of the support obligor is used as the base for determining the support amount. The advantage of this approach is its simplicity and the fact that income cannot be manipulated because no deductions are taken before the support amount is calculated. On the other hand, gross income may not be an accurate measure of the income that is actually available to the support obligor.

**Adjusted Gross Income Base.** Other states use an adjusted gross income base. To arrive at this amount, federal and state tax obligations, including social security, are deducted from gross earnings; nonvoluntary payroll withholdings, such as union dues and retirement payments, as well as prior support obligations also are usually deducted. Support is then based on this adjusted amount. Many believe this is the fairest approach, as it is a more accurate measure of the obligor's available income, although it does not permit the same kind of discretionary deductions that are allowable under the net income approach.

**Net Income Base.** Still other states use a net income base, which allows for further deductions than the adjusted gross income base. Gross income is reduced, for example, by voluntary payroll withholdings and job-related expenses before the support amount is calculated. The drawback of this approach is that it can be manipulated to show a reduced income, thus limiting the support base. On the other hand, it may be the most accurate indicator of actual available income.

## Consideration of Specific Factors

Most child support guidelines include a number of factors that are to be taken into account when calculating the support amount. Others fix a basic amount varied only by a limited number of factors, such as the number of children, and then identify factors that will justify a deviation from the presumptive amount. These factors are relevant in determining both the initial amount and whether a modification is warranted. Commonly considered factors include:

- income of the custodial parent
- income of a new partner
- income/resources of the child
- multiple families
- extraordinary expenses
- health insurance
- custody and visitation arrangements

### Income of the Custodial Parent

With the exception of states using the percentage-of-income approach, most guidelines take the income of the custodial parent into account. Under the income-shares approach, the income of both parents is combined to establish a basic support obligation. This amount is then allocated in proportion to income, and the noncustodial parent contributes his or her share in support payments. Another approach is to base the initial support calculation on the noncustodial parent's income and then reduce it to account for the custodial parent's income. States generally use a percentage reduction formula, rather than a dollar-for-dollar offset, as this could significantly reduce the amount of support available to the children. In some states, the custodial parent's income is disregarded until it reaches a threshold amount, and then only income above this threshold is considered.

### Income of a New Partner

If either parent remarries or cohabits with a new partner, the question often arises as to how this partner income should be treated. As a general rule, this person has no direct support obligation to the children. Accordingly, few, if any, guidelines require inclusion of this income, and some specifically exclude it from consideration. However, because it may free up parental income, some states permit consideration of partner income as a basis for deviating from the presumptive guideline amount.

### Income/Resources of the Child

Situations may arise where a minor child has independent resources; for example, he or she may receive governmental benefits, have income from a part-time job, or be the beneficiary of a trust or an inheritance. Most states do not build this into their support formulas or treat this as income to the custodial parent. Again, however, this income may be considered in determining if a deviation from guidelines is appropriate.

### Multiple Families

Almost 75 percent of people who are divorced remarry, and many then have children with their new spouses.[16] Cases involving multiple families raise difficult questions about how (often scarce) resources can be fairly allocated between two households.

A thorny question is whether a noncustodial parent should be allowed to reduce support to his or her first family upon establishing a new household, especially if he or she has additional children with this new partner. The traditional guideline approach puts "first families first" and does not permit reductions based on obligations to a subsequent family. The children from the first family are said to have a pre-existing, hence superior, claim to the income, which the parent should have considered before starting a second family. However, based on the recognition that this approach may shortchange the children in the second family, who have no control over their place in the birth order, some states will permit support adjustments based on subsequent children. In some of these jurisdictions, the presence of subsequent children can be used as a "shield" to defend against a request for an upward modification but not as a "sword" to request a downward modification.

Given the high failure rate of second marriages, another difficult issue is how support payments to a second family are to be calculated if this relationship also dissolves. If a parent is already paying child support under a court order to a prior family, most guidelines permit him or her to deduct this amount from income before the support order for the second family is calculated. This arguably favors the first family, as the income base available to them is larger; however, it is generally thought fair to protect this family's standard of living from fluctuations based on changes in the noncustodial parent's life over which the family has no control.

### Extraordinary Expenses

Guidelines are generally based on the assumption that the custodial parent is responsible for the ordinary costs of raising a child. A trickier question is whether she or he is also responsible for extraordinary expenses, or whether these should be dealt with separately. The term **extraordinary expense** has been defined as "any large, discrete, legitimate child-rearing expense that varies greatly from family to family or from child to child," as distinct from *ordinary expenses*, which tend to be "relatively small, predictable, and fairly consistent in families of the same size and income level."[17] This issue most often arises with respect to medical, child-care, and educational expenses; as far as medical expenses are concerned, some guidelines specify that unreimbursed medical expenses in excess of an identified dollar amount per occurrence or calendar year are considered extraordinary expenses, while other guidelines identify the qualifying kinds of expenditures.

States use a number of approaches when dealing with extraordinary expenses, and within a particular state, the approach may vary depending on the category of expense. One common approach is to treat extraordinary expenses as an "add-on" to the basic support amount. The expense is prorated between the parents based on their income, and the noncustodial parent's share is added to the support amount. Another possibility is to permit deviations from the guideline amount to account for extraordinary expenses. For example, a judge might be permitted to increase the basic support amount if the custodial parent were faced with significant medical bills. This deviation would most likely be temporary in nature, and the guideline amount would be reinstated once the custodial parent was no longer facing these expenditures.

### Health Insurance

Under federal regulations, child support guidelines must take a child's medical needs into account. Additionally, all child support orders obtained through a state child support enforcement agency must include a medical support provision, and the agency has a duty to try to obtain health insurance coverage for the supported children. As of October 2005, the agency may look to both the custodial parent and the noncustodial parent to provide health insurance coverage, with appropriate cost-sharing for the coverage allocated between the parents. To facilitate coverage, federal law now requires every employer group health plan to provide coverage to the children named by the court (or a qualified administrative agency) in what is known as a **qualified medical child support order (QMCSO)**.[18]

With respect to the cost of coverage, some states allow the noncustodial parent to deduct the amount of the premium that is attributable to family coverage from gross income before calculating the support amount. Correspondingly, if the custodial parent is providing the insurance, a portion of the premium amount may be added to the basic support obligation. Another approach is to prorate the cost of the insurance between the parents based on their proportion of the total income, and then add the obligor's share to the support payments. Still other states consider the provision of health insurance as a grounds for deviating from the presumed amount.

### Custody and Visitation Arrangements

Support guidelines are generally based on the assumption that one parent has physical custody and the other has visitation rights, and visitation-related expenditures do not usually impact the support calculation. However, guidelines may permit adjustments to account for situations where a parent either spends a significant amount of time with a child or, conversely, hardly sees the child at all. Some guidelines spell out what time allocation will trigger a support reduction, such as where the child spends more than a specified percentage of time or more than a certain number of overnights with the noncustodial parent, while other guidelines leave it to the decision maker to decide when a reduction is warranted. The amount of the reduction is usually left to the decision maker, although limits may be placed on his or her discretion. Some judges take a cautious approach to these reductions based on the recognition that increased visitation does not necessarily result in substantial savings in child-related expenditures, as the custodial parent usually remains responsible for them. Although less frequently addressed by guidelines, nonvisitation also may be the basis for an upward revision of support, as the custodial parent is assuming responsibility for visitation-associated expenses that the guidelines implicitly allocated to the noncustodial parent.

Turning to custodial arrangements, it is often assumed that joint physical custody and split custody (where at least one child lives with each parent) will cancel the support obligation because both parents are providing for the children on an equal basis. This assumption, however, is not accurate.

First, although an arrangement may be identified as joint custody, the time allocation between the two households may not be equal. Second, even where it is equal, one parent, typically the primary caregiver during the marriage, often continues to assume greater parenting responsibilities, including making most of the purchases for the child. Thus, although both parents maintain a home for the child, the cost of raising the child is not borne equally. Another concern is that eliminating the support award will put the lower-income parent in a worse financial situation than that parent would have been in had he or she maintained sole custody and received the guideline amount. In this regard, experts note that a disparity in the standard of living between parental households is especially confusing for a child in a joint custody situation, since both residences are the child's home.

Accordingly, although most guidelines permit consideration of these custodial arrangements in determining the support amount, they do not automatically trigger its elimination. One approach that is used is to compute a support obligation for each parent as if he or she had sole custody, offset the amounts, and order the parent with the greater obligation to pay the net amount to the other. Of course, support may be eliminated where parents earn close to the same amount and really share responsibility for raising the children.

## Financial Disclosure

As the above discussion makes clear, a proper child support order cannot be calculated unless all relevant information has been disclosed. Accordingly, most, if not all, states require each party to make full financial disclosure to the other, usually by completing and filing a **financial affidavit**. Some also require the filing of supporting documents, such as tax returns and wage stubs. Additionally, in an effort to encourage attorneys to monitor and prevent the filing of fraudulent or inaccurate financial affidavits, some states require the affidavit to be signed by the lawyer as well as by the party submitting it. Exhibit 6.2 is a sample financial affidavit.

Despite their usefulness, affidavits often do not provide a complete financial picture. The form itself may not call for full disclosure. Also, affidavits provide a snapshot of a party's current financial situation but do not give a picture of his or her financial situation over time; for instance, an affidavit probably would not reveal a reduction in income or a transfer of assets or income that took place before the affidavit was completed. In many states that require parties to update affidavits as a divorce proceeds, subsequent changes may be revealed. Accordingly, a party may need to engage in other *discovery*—the process by which a party obtains information from the other side—to gain a more complete picture of the other side's financial situation. This step is critical because the failure to obtain complete and accurate information will result in an inaccurate assessment of a parent's financial situation and thus an incorrect support calculation.

Paralegals often play a critical role in this process. It may be your job to assist the client in completing the financial affidavit. These forms can be confusing. For example, a party who is asked to itemize expenditures on a weekly basis may be inclined to ignore expenditures that are made on a less regular basis, such as for clothing. You can help a client figure out what he or she spends on clothing over the course of a year, accounting for seasonal fluctuations in order to arrive at an average weekly clothing amount.

If formal discovery is required, you may be involved in drafting documents and organizing the responses, including the supporting materials such as tax returns and bank statements that are often requested. You may also be responsible for helping your office's client respond to requests from the other side, which again may require you to sort through and organize financial data. (For more detail on discovery, see Chapter 10.)

## ENFORCING THE CHILD SUPPORT OBLIGATION

Nonpayment of support is a very serious problem. In 2000, the total national child support arrearage was $84 billion, an amount which, as one commentator noted, is "greater than the gross national product of

## Exhibit 6.2   Financial Disclosure Affidavit

**IN THE CIRCUIT COURT OF LAKE COUNTY, ILLINOIS**

IN RE The   ☐  Marriage        ☐  Custody
            ☐  Support of:

_____,
                        Petitioner,

              and

_____,
                        Respondent,

No. _____

**11.02**
**FINANCIAL AFFIDAVIT**

STATE OF ILLINOIS        )
                         ) ss
COUNTY OF LAKE           )

Affiant, _____, having been duly sworn, upon oath, states that the information contained herein is true and correct as of _____, 2_____:

Name:        _____          Telephone No.   _____
Address:     _____
                                                 Date of Birth:  _____

Date of Marriage  _____     Date of Dissolution of Marriage (if applicable)

                                                 _____

Minor and/or Dependent Children of this Marriage:

_____ age _____      residing with _____
_____ age _____      residing with _____
_____ age _____      residing with _____

Current Employer:   _____        Address:  _____
Self Employment:    _____        Address:  _____
Other Employment:   _____        Address:  _____
_____ Check if unemployed

Number of Paychecks per year (Please Circle)   12   24   26   52
Number of Exemptions claimed: _____
Number of Dependents claimed: _____

Gross Income from all sources last year: _____

Gross income from all sources this year through _____: _____
                                                          Date

## Exhibit 6.2   Continued

Case No._____

STATEMENT OF INCOME         As of _____

Gross Monthly Income
    Salary/wages/base pay                                                    $ _____
    Overtime/commission                                                      _____
    Bonus                                                                    _____
    Draw                                                                     _____
    Pension and retirement benefits                                          _____
    Annuity                                                                  _____
    Interest income                                                          _____
    Dividend income                                                          _____
    Trust income                                                             _____
    Social Security                                                          _____
    Unemployment benefits                                                    _____
    Disability payment                                                       _____
    Worker's compensation                                                    _____
    Public Aid/Food stamps                                                   _____
    Investment income                                                        _____
    Rental income                                                            _____
    Business income (including non-taxable distributions)                    _____
    Partnership income                                                       _____
    Royalty income                                                           _____
    Fellowship/stipends                                                      _____
    Other income (specify): _____                       _____

TOTAL GROSS MONTHLY INCOME                          $ _____   $ _____

Additional Cash Flow (Monthly)
    Spousal support received (specify)                              $ _____
       ____ Pursuant to a prior judgment or order in another case
       ____ Pursuant to a prior judgment or order in this case
       ____ Voluntarily paid in this case

    Child Support received (specify)                                $ _____
       ____ Pursuant to a prior judgment or order in another case
       ____ Pursuant to a prior judgment or order in this case
       ____ Voluntarily paid in this case

    Total additional cash flow                          $ _____   $ _____

Required Monthly Deductions
    Federal Tax (based on _____ exemptions)                    $ _____
    State Tax (based on _____ exemptions)                      _____
    FICA (or Social Security equivalent)                            _____
    Medicare Tax                                                    _____
    Mandatory retirement contributions required by law or as condition of
       employment                                               _____
    Union Dues (Name of Union: _____)           _____
    Health/hospitalization Premiums                                 _____
    Prior obligation(s) of support actually paid pursuant to Court order    _____
    Other (specify)                                                 _____

**Exhibit 6.2   Continued**

Case No. _____

<u>TOTAL REQUIRED DEDUCTIONS FROM INCOME</u>            $ _____   $ _____

                                    <u>NET MONTHLY INCOME</u>            $ _____   $ _____

STATEMENT OF MONTHLY LIVING EXPENSES            As of _____

1.   Household                                               $ _____
    a.   Mortgage or rent (specify):                     _____
    b.   Home equity loan payment                        _____
    c.   Real estate taxes, assessments                  _____
    d    Homeowners or renters insurance                 _____
    e.   Heat/fuel                                       _____
    f.   Electricity                                     _____
    g.   Telephone (include long distance)               _____
    h.   Water and Sewer                                 _____
    i.   Refuse removal                                  _____
    j.   Laundry/dry cleaning                            _____
    k.   Maid/cleaning service                           _____
    l.   Furniture and appliance repair/replacement      _____
    m.   Lawn and garden/snow removal                    _____
    n    Food (groceries, household supplies, etc.)      _____
    o.   Liquor, beer, wine, etc.                        _____
    p.   Other (specify): _____        _____

SUBTOTAL HOUSEHOLD EXPENSES:                    $ _____   $ _____

2.   Transportation
    a.   Gasoline                                        $ _____
    b.   Repairs                                         _____
    c.   Insurance/license/city stickers                 _____
    d.   Payments/replacement                            _____
    e.   Alternative transportation                      _____
    f.   Other (specify): _____        _____

SUBTOTAL TRANSPORTATION EXPENSES                $ _____   $ _____

3.   Personal
    a.   Clothing                                        $ _____
    b.   Grooming
    c.   Medical(after insurance proceeds/reimbursement)
        (1)   Doctor                                  _____
        (2)   Dentist                                 _____
        (3)   Optical                                 _____
        (4)   Medication                              _____
    d.   Insurance
        (1)   Life (term)                             _____
        (2)   Life (whole)                            _____
        (3)   Medical/Hospitalization                 _____
        (4)   Dental/Optical                          _____
    e.   Other (specify) _____         _____

SUBTOTAL PERSONAL EXPENSES                      $ _____   $ _____

## Exhibit 6.2   Continued

Case No. _____

4.  Miscellaneous:
    a.  Clubs/social obligations/entertainment          $ _____
    b.  Newspapers, magazines, books                      _____
    c.  Gifts                                             _____
    d.  Donations, church or religious affiliations       _____
    e.  Vacations                                         _____
    f.  Other (specify)  _____  _____

SUBTOTAL MISCELLANEOUS EXPENSES:                  $ _____  $ _____

5.  Dependent children:        Names & ages:

    _____

    _____

    _____

    a.  Clothing                                     $ _____
    b.  Grooming                                       _____
    c.  Education
        (1)  Tuition                                   _____
        (2)  Books/Fees)                               _____
        (3)  Lunches                                   _____
        (4)  Transportation                            _____
        (5)  Activities                                _____
    d.  Medical (after insurance proceeds/reimbursement)
        (1)  Doctor                                    _____
        (2)  Dentist                                   _____
        (3)  Optical                                   _____
        (4)  Medication                                _____
    e.  Allowance                                      _____
    f.  Child care/After-school care                   _____
    g.  Sitters                                        _____
    h.  Lesson and supplies                            _____
    i.  Clubs/Summer Camps                             _____
    j.  Vacation                                       _____
    k.  Entertainment                                  _____
    l.  Other (specify): _____      _____

SUBTOTAL CHILDREN'S EXPENSES:                      $ _____

                    TOTAL MONTHLY LIVING EXPENSES:  $ _____

STATEMENT OF LIABILITIES

| CREDITOR'S NAME | PAYMENT FOR | BALANCE DUE | MONTHLY PAYMENT |
|---|---|---|---|
| _____ | _____ | $ _____ | $ _____ |
| _____ | _____ | $ _____ | $ _____ |
| _____ | _____ | $ _____ | $ _____ |
| _____ | _____ | $ _____ | $ _____ |
| TOTAL LIABILITIES | | $ _____ | |
| TOTAL MONTHLY DEBT SERVICE | | | $ _____ |

## Exhibit 6.2 Continued

Case No. _____

STATEMENT OF ASSETS
CASH or CASH EQUIVALENTS:

1. Savings or interest-bearing accounts     $ _____
2. Checking Accounts     _____
3. Certificates of Deposit     _____
4. Money Market Accounts     _____
5. Cash     _____
6. Other (specify): _____     _____

TOTAL CASH OR CASH EQUIVALENTS     $ _____     $ _____

INVESTMENT ACCOUNTS and SECURITIES:

1. Stocks     $ _____
2. Bonds     _____
3. Tax exempt securities     _____
4. Other (specify): _____     _____

TOTAL INVESTMENT ACCOUNTS AND SECURITIES     $ _____     $ _____

$ _____

STATEMENT OF HEALTH INSURANCE COVERAGE
Currently effective health insurance coverage? _____ Yes _____ No
Name of insurance carrier: _____ Policy of Group No. _____
Type of insurance: _____ Medical _____ Dental _____ Optical
Deductible: Per individual _____ Per family _____
Persons covered: _____ Self _____ Spouse _____ Dependents
Type of policy: _____ HMO _____ PPO _____ Full indemnity
Provided by: _____ Employer _____ Private Policy _____ Other Group
Monthly costs: _____ Paid by Employer _____ Paid by employee: $ _____ for dependents
    $ _____ for self

NET MONTLY INCOME   $ _____
TOTAL MONTHLY LIVING EXPENSES AND EXPENSES   $ _____
LESS MONTHLY DEBT SERVICE   $ _____
TOTAL INCOME AVAILABLE PER MONTH   $ _____

The foregoing Financial Affidavit has been carefully read by the undersigned who states under oath, under penalties as provided by law pursuant to 735 ILCS 5/109, that this affidavit includes all of his/her income and expenses, he/she has knowledge of the matters stated and he/she certifies that the statements set forth in this Affidavit are true and correct, except as to matters specifically stated to be on information and belief, and as to such matters the undersigned certifies as aforesaid that he/she believes same to be true.

_____
Signature of party
_____ Petitioner     _____ Respondent

_____
Type or Print Name

**Exhibit 6.2   Continued**

---

### 11.02 FINANCIAL AFFIDAVIT
### SUPPLEMENTAL FORM

The foregoing Financial Affidavit has been carefully read by the undersigned who states

under oath, under penalties as provided by law pursuant to 735 ILCS 5/109, that this affidavit is

complete to the extent of my knowledge, but that I do not have access to sufficient information

to fully and accurately complete the affidavit because I do not have access to the necessary

financial records and information.

 

_____
                                                    Signature of Party

_____ Petitioner              _____ Respondent

_____
                                                    Type or Print Name

Ireland."[19] By the end of fiscal year 2002, the accumulated support arrearages had increased to more than $90 billion, a figure that Sherri Z. Heller, Commissioner of the Federal Office of Child Support Enforcement, characterized as "numbing," with about 60 percent of support obligors making some payment towards their accumulated debt.[20] By the end of fiscal year 2005, the amount had climbed to a staggering $107 billion, again with collections of at least some of the monies due in about 60 percent of the cases.[21]

Seeking to close this enforcement gap, federal child support laws require states to adopt specific enforcement methods and have created an extensive network of databases for the collecting and sharing of child support information. Many states have adopted enforcement mechanisms beyond those required by federal law, such as lottery winning intercepts and the use of the "Denver boot," "a steel, fifty-pound clamp that is attached to an automobile tire, effectively immobilizing the vehicle by preventing it from being driven until the offender responds to the legal system," which in this context would mean satisfaction of the support debt.[22]

In this section, we look at some of the key enforcement mechanisms required by federal law, followed by a brief discussion of the enforcement process in interstate cases. As noted in the discussion, some of these enforcement methods are available only in support cases that are handled by an IV-D agency (IV-D cases). This has contributed to a new and lively debate in the child support field over whether private child support collection agencies should be given access to the databases and enforcement tools of the IV-D agencies. We take up the issue of the role of private collection agencies in the enforcement process in the next section, followed by a discussion about state enforcement methods.

## Data Collection and Sharing

In 1996, the child support provisions of the Personal Responsibility and Work Opportunity Reconciliation Act (better known as the welfare reform law) created a "series of interconnected databases on the local, state, national and international levels" that allow for the collection and sharing of information regarding all child support cases.[23] Each state must have the following databases:

- a State Case Registry containing records on all child support orders
- a State Disbursement Unit for the centralized collection and disbursement of child support payments, including payments withheld by employers (see income withholding, below)
- a State Directory of New Hires to track job changes so wage assignments can follow the support obligor to a new job

At the federal level, the Act established a Federal Case Registry of Child Support Orders and National Directory of New Hires, which amass information from the parallel state databases. These interrelated databases permit the sharing, tracking, and matching of information on a massive scale in order to identify, locate, and seek payments from non-custodial parents who are not meeting their support obligation.

Although this system is a clear boon to the child support enforcement effort, the amassing and sharing of information on such a widespread scale has raised serious privacy concerns, including concerns that inaccurate information will be replicated in multiple databases, that information may be used for unintended purposes, or that information may be disclosed in situations, such as where there is a history of abuse, that puts family members at risk.[24]

### Income Withholding

The single most important enforcement mechanism is **wage** (or income) **withholding**, whereby support payments are deducted from the noncustodial parent's paycheck, much the way taxes are withheld. Income also can be withheld from other forms of periodic payments such as those received from a pension plan or government benefits. Where benefits are concerned, the general rule is that they must be a form of remuneration for employment, such as social security or unemployment benefits; needs-based benefits, such as Supplemental Security Income (SSI) payments, are not subject to withholding.[25]

Although all child support orders must include a wage withholding provision, only IV-D support cases are subject to an immediate withholding requirement under federal law (although state support laws may mandate this). This means that a custodial parent does not have to wait for an **arrearage** — an overdue or unpaid amount — to accrue in order for the withholding to take effect. There are only two exceptions to immediate withholding: (1) when good cause to suspend it is established and (2) when the parties enter into a written agreement providing for an alternative arrangement.

If the withholding is suspended, it must take effect once an arrearage equal to the support payable for a month has accrued. The noncustodial parent is entitled to notice that withholding is to commence. He or she may challenge the effectuation of the withholding, but may raise only mistakes of fact, such as a miscalculation of the arrearage. The validity of the underlying order cannot be challenged.

Employers are responsible for withholding the designated amount. An employer who fails to withhold child support will be responsible for the amount of support that should have been withheld. Also, fines can be levied against an employer who takes adverse action against an employee because of the withholding.

One problem has been that withholding does not keep up with a parent's job changes if the parent does not provide the information necessary to effectuate the withholding with his or her new employer. The new data-matching process addresses this problem. Information in the State or National Directory of New Hires can be matched with information in the Federal or State Case Registry, which enables the state to contact the new employer and direct it to begin withholding wages in accordance with the existing support order.

*Liens*

Under federal law, states must now have a law that creates a **lien** against the personal and real property of the noncustodial parent in the amount of unpaid support. A lien is a nonpossessory interest in property, that operates as a cloud against title, and would prevent the noncustodial parent from selling, transferring, or borrowing against the property until the arrearage is paid.

The following passage from the Office of Child Support Enforcement's Manual, Essentials for Attorneys in Child Support Enforcement, provides an excellent description of how liens operate:

> A lien is often referred to as a "slumbering" interest that allows the noncustodial parent to retain possession of the property, but which prevents transfer of clear title of affected property either directly (by prohibiting the recording agency from issuing a new title or deed) or indirectly (by providing that all subsequent interests in the property will be subject to the lien). The latter method is most common. It works because subsequent potential purchasers and lenders receive notice of the . . . lien . . . [and] reacts to this . . . by requiring the noncustodial parent to satisfy the lien, or to obtain a release from the custodial parent, before proceeding with the transfer or loan.[26]

Under federal law, the lien must arise as a matter of law, which means that it happens automatically, without any required action on the part of the custodial parent. However, under state law, the custodial parent may need to take certain steps to "perfect" the lien, such as recording a copy of the support order in the appropriate office or registry of public records, in order for it to have priority over other liens.

*Federal/State Tax Refund Intercept*

Another enforcement device is the **tax refund intercept**. Conceptually, it may be useful to think of an intercept as a withholding against a parent's tax refund. The withheld amount is then used to satisfy an outstanding child support obligation. Both federal and state refunds can be intercepted;[27] however, only IV-D cases have access to the federal tax intercept.

A noncustodial parent is entitled to notice and a hearing before his or her tax return is intercepted. Available defenses are limited. He or she can argue that no support is owed, that the arrearage calculation is incorrect, or that the refund is owed to his or her new spouse and thus not subject to the intercept, but the validity of the underlying order cannot be challenged.

### Credit Reporting

Under federal law, IV-D agencies must periodically report to **credit reporting** agencies the name of any parent whose support arrearage has reached a specific dollar amount. Before the report is made, the parent must be given notice and an opportunity to correct any inaccurate information. Although reporting does not result in an immediate transfer of income to the custodial parent, it is hoped that the threat of a negative credit report will serve as an inducement to support obligors who might otherwise be tempted to avoid paying child support.

### Licenses

Under federal law, states must adopt procedures by which they can withhold, suspend, or restrict an individual's professional or occupational license, driver's license, or recreational/sporting licenses due to the non-payment of support. As with credit reporting, these sanctions do not directly transfer money to the custodial parent. Rather, it is hoped that the threat of losing or having restrictions placed on one's license will operate as a strong deterrent to the nonpayment of support.

## Interstate Cases

About 30 percent of child support cases involve parents who live in different states.[28] These cases have been the bane of the child support system. The process of obtaining and enforcing support orders across state lines has been notoriously difficult due to the lack of coordination between states, the lack of access to information, and the low priority given to these cases.[29] To improve this system, the IV-D agency in each state must have a Central Registry that coordinates interstate cases. States also are required to give interstate cases the same priority that they give to cases involving their own residents. Additionally, two fairly recent federal laws, the Uniform Interstate Family Support Act and the Full Faith and Credit for Child Support Orders Act, address some of these concerns and are intended to streamline the interstate process.

### The Uniform Interstate Family Support Act (UIFSA) and the Full Faith and Credit for Child Support Orders Act (FFCCSOA)

In 1996, the welfare reform act (i.e., the Personal Responsibility and Work Opportunity Reconciliation Act) required states to adopt and implement UIFSA by 1998 in order to remain eligible for federal child support funds.[30] A primary purpose of UIFSA is to avoid the proliferation of competing orders as family members move to different states with the resulting confusion regarding validity and enforceability. Under UIFSA, there should only be one valid support order at any given time, which must be enforced in all states according to its original terms.

**The Initial Support Order.** UIFSA allows a custodial parent to seek the initial child support order in his or her home state, so long as the state can assert personal jurisdiction over the noncustodial parent through its "long-arm" provisions (see Chapter 10) or in the state of the noncustodial parent. In the latter case, the custodial parent initiates the action in his or her home state, and the IV-D agency then sends it on to the IV-D agency in the respondent's state, in what is referred to as a "two-state" proceeding.

**Enforcing the Order.** Once there is a support order, it can be enforced in any state where the noncustodial parent or his or her assets are located. This is usually done through the IV-D agencies in the appropriate states. However, an important innovation is the "direct income withholding" by which an IV-D agency, or the custodial parent him- or herself, sends the income withholding order directly to the noncustodial parent's employer. Assuming the order is "regular on its face," the employer must honor the order, as if it had been issued by a court in the employer's home state, and withhold wages as directed.

Of critical importance, the issuing state retains exclusive jurisdiction to modify the order so long as either parent or the child remains in that state.[31] By vesting continuing authority in the issuing state, UIFSA avoids the potential confusion of multiple orders. Only when all parties have left the issuing state will modification jurisdiction shift to a new state. Further strengthening this "one-order" system, FFCCSOA[32] requires states to give "full faith and credit" to properly issued orders from other states, thus also limiting the ability of states to modify orders from other states.

# Enforcement by Private Child Support Collection Agencies _____

Over the course of the past ten or fifteen years, a new player has entered the child support enforcement field to help custodial parents collect child support that is owed to them — the for-profit child support collection agency. These agencies promise to fill the existing gap in enforcement services that IV-D agencies seem unable to meet. Many in the child support field argue that this is an idea whose time has come — that we need to face the reality that despite considerable progress, IV-D agencies are not able to handle the high volume of existing support cases:

> [T]he government child support enforcement program simply cannot meet the needs of all families needing child support service.
>
> The most recent data (FY 2000) provided by the federal Office of Child Support Enforcement shows that the national Title IV-D program made collections in only 41.6 of the 17.4 million cases in its caseload . . .
>
> The troubling situation is not likely to change, no matter how effectively the state Title IV-D agencies use the vast information and enforcement resources available to them. The amounts of obligated, but uncollected support will continue to mount at a rate beyond the ability of the program ever to collect.[33]

Some have argued that if we are to solve the current support crises, these private agencies (as well as the private bar) need enhanced power and increased resources. To this end, a variety of legislative proposals have been introduced that would give these private entities access to the databases, the parent locator resources, and the enforcement tools, such as tax refund intercepts, of the IV-D agencies.

Yet many in the field are wary of these agencies and do not want to encourage their proliferation or their access to governmental databases and enforcement tools. Serious concerns have been raised about some of these agencies' business practices, particularly the fees they charge, which can be as high as 50 percent of the collected support, thus diverting funds intended for the support of children. Moreover, these fees often are demanded even if the money is ultimately collected and disbursed by the IV-D agencies.[34] Other criticized practices include contracts that are almost impossible to cancel, harassment of the support obligor, threats of arrest without proper authority, and the collection of fees from current, rather than past, support as required.[35]

Other concerns focus on the risks of providing access to governmental databases and enforcement tools. It is argued that access to information may lead to breaches of privacy or to the potential misuse of highly confidential information and that increasing the tools at the disposal of these agencies may exacerbate existing questionable trade practices. Again, this raises particular concerns about the safety of domestic violence victims.

## Enforcement Under State Law Procedures

In addition to the remedies discussed above, a support award can also be enforced through traditional state remedies, such as a **criminal**

**non-support** or **contempt proceeding**. These remedies can be pursued by an individual or by an IV-D agency on behalf of a custodial parent who is receiving its services.

### Criminal Nonsupport

Most, if not all, states make the failure to support minor children a crime. Generally, nonsupport is classified as a misdemeanor. As in all criminal proceedings, the goal is punishment of the offender and vindication of the public interest. However, most states will suspend the sentence if the defendant agrees to pay support, which accomplishes the civil goal of providing support to the children. If the payment is not made following the suspension, the sentence will be reimposed.

For a conviction, the failure to support must be willful. The state has the burden of proving willfulness by establishing that the defendant had the ability to provide support and deliberately failed to do so. Some states also require proof that the nonsupport left the children in "destitute or necessitous" circumstances. In these states, support from the custodial parent or a third party that keeps the children out of poverty may bar a conviction. The defendant is entitled to the procedural protections that apply in all criminal cases, including the privilege against self-incrimination. This may make proof of ability to pay difficult because the defendant cannot be forced to testify or to disclose adverse information through discovery.

For these reasons, criminal nonsupport actions generally are not the remedy of choice. However, they can be useful where the failure to pay support is flagrant or where the obligor is self-employed, thus precluding wage withholding. The willful failure to pay a past-due support obligation on behalf of a child in another state is now a federal crime. In addition, under the Deadbeat Parents Punishment Act of 1998, it is a felony to travel interstate (or internationally) in order to avoid an unpaid support order that meets specified durational and amount requirements.[36]

### Contempt

A contempt action can be brought where an obligor fails to comply with a court order of support. Contempt actions can be either civil or criminal in nature. A contempt is usually not the remedy of choice, but it can be a useful supplemental remedy, especially where a parent is self-employed and thus not amenable to a wage withholding.

**Civil Contempt.** The purpose of a civil contempt proceeding is to secure compliance with the support order, and a jail sentence may be imposed for this purpose. In most states, the obligor must have the present ability to pay the ordered support amount in order to be found in civil contempt. If found in contempt, the obligor must be given the opportunity to avoid jail or, if jailed, to secure release by purging the contempt, usually by satisfying the terms of the underlying order.

**Criminal Contempt.** The purpose of a criminal contempt proceeding is to punish the support obligor for violating the court's order. In contrast to civil contempt, if a jail sentence is imposed, its purpose is to punish the violation rather than to secure compliance with the order. Unlike in a civil contempt, an obligor cannot purchase his or her freedom by complying with the order. Accordingly, present ability to pay is not a required element; instead, the state must prove ability to pay during the time of noncompliance. As with criminal nonsupport, the procedural protections generally available to defendants in criminal cases are available here.

## MODIFICATION AND ADJUSTMENT OF SUPPORT AWARDS

Once a child support amount has been established, subsequent events may occur that warrant a change in the amount. Where this occurs, a parent may seek a **modification** of the support order. Additionally, states must implement a **review and adjustment procedure** for all support cases enforced through the IV-D agency.

## Modification Based on Changed Circumstances

Child support orders are not generally considered final judgments and are subject to modification. However, modification actions are not designed to give parents a second bite at the apple; that is, issues that have already been determined are not supposed to be relitigated.

In a "traditional" modification action, the petitioner must show that there has been a **change in circumstances** that justifies an upward or downward revision of the support amount. Most, if not all, states also require that the change was not foreseeable at the time the order was entered. Support amounts agreed on by the parties in a separation agreement are subject to modification, as the right to adequate support belongs to the child and cannot be bargained away by a parent. However, some courts give considerable weight to parties' agreement and impose a greater burden on the petitioner to prove that a modification is warranted.

Either party can seek a modification. Typically a custodial parent who is seeking an upward revision looks to changes such as increased needs of the children, an increase in the other parent's income, remarriage of the noncustodial parent, or a decrease in his or her own income. Typically a noncustodial parent who is seeking a downward revision looks to changes such as a decrease in his or her own income, responsibility for a second family, an increase in the custodial parent's income, remarriage of the custodial parent, or employment of the child.

A contentious question is whether a noncustodial parent can seek a reduction in support payments if the custodial parent is interfering with his or her visitation rights. The majority view is that visitation and support issues are independent variables and should not be linked. Exceptions to this policy of nonlinkage may occur in extreme situations—for example, where a parent falsifies employment information to avoid paying support or a custodial parent hides a child to prevent visitation from taking place.

In addition to the traditional change in circumstances standard, most states' guidelines, in accordance with federal regulations, include a modification provision authorizing a change in the amount of support "when there is a threshold difference between the current support amount and the presumptive guideline amount." This difference is usually expressed either as a dollar or a percentage of support amount.[37]

The fact that support orders can be modified has historically caused considerable confusion in the interstate arena because states have readily modified orders of other states, resulting in multiple and potentially conflicting orders. However, FFCCSOA addresses this problem by vesting exclusive and continuing jurisdiction over the order in the issuing state so long as the child or any other party continues to reside there; as long as this condition is met, other states are precluded from modifying the order.

---

### Consideration

Do you think visitation and support issues should be linked?

---

## The Review and Adjustment Procedure

In addition to modification based on changed circumstances, support orders must be reviewed every three years in all cases in which there is an assignment of support rights. In all other cases, the three-year review process is not automatic but must be requested by a parent. Where the state's child support guidelines or changes in the cost-of-living justify a modification, a support order will be adjusted either upward or downward to account for the changes.[38]

# DURATION OF THE PARENTAL SUPPORT OBLIGATION

In general, a parent has an obligation to support his or her child until the child reaches 18—the age of majority. In certain situations, however, the support obligation may be terminated before majority or extended beyond it. These durational issues are generally controlled by state law.

## Termination of Support Prior to Majority

Support can be terminated prior to majority only under very limited circumstances, such as emancipation of the minor, death of the parent paying support, or the termination of parental rights. A custodial parent does not generally have the authority to agree to a termination of support because, again, the right of support belongs to the child not to the parent.

### Emancipation

**Emancipation** extinguishes the reciprocal rights and obligations that exist between a parent and child and releases the child from the authority and control of his or her parents. Many states recognize a common law doctrine of emancipation under which certain acts, most notably marriage and entry into the armed services, are regarded as creating a status that is incompatible with parental control and thus serve to emancipate the minor. In some states, a child who is living on his or her own and is self-supporting may also be considered emancipated. Some states have a statutory emancipation procedure that permits a child, or possibly a parent, to file a court petition seeking a declaration of emancipation.

Once a child is emancipated, the support obligation will in all likelihood terminate because the child is now considered able to care for him- or herself. However, where emancipation occurs through a court proceeding, a court might decide to only partially emancipate a minor, such as for the limited purpose of consenting to medical procedures, and continue the support obligation.

### Parental Death

At common law, the death of a parent terminated the support obligation. This responsibility did not pass to the decedent's estate, but the estate was liable for arrearages that had accrued prior to death. Many states now have statutes that authorize a court to hold the parent's estate responsible for continued support payments unless the parties otherwise agreed in a separation agreement.

In the absence of a specific statute or separation agreement, many judges believe that they lack the authority to order post-death support, as this would upset the estate plan of the decedent who has a legal right to disinherit his or her children. According to this view, ordering such support would give greater rights to children of divorced parents compared to children of still-married parents. Other judges take a different view of the matter and may continue support following the death of the noncustodial parent. These judges give greater weight to providing for children than to protecting the stability of estate plans and the expectations of beneficiaries. This approach also recognizes that a noncustodial parent may be more likely to disinherit his or her children, thus creating a greater need for a remedy.

### Adoption/Termination of Parental Rights

Where parental rights are extinguished through adoption or an involuntary termination proceeding, the parental support obligation is likewise extinguished. The only issue is identifying *when* the obligation ceases. The general rule is that this occurs upon the actual cessation of the parent-child relationship rather than upon the consent to the adoption.

## Extension of Support Beyond Majority _____

### The Adult Student

With the age of majority now set at 18 in most states, questions often come up regarding whether an adult child has a right to continued support if he or she is still in high school or wishes to attend college. States take a variety of approaches in these situations.

Many states have statutory provisions permitting the continuation of support up to a certain post-majority age, usually 21 or 22, if the child is a full-time student or regularly attending school. However, a number of states have statutes that cut off support at age 18 even if a child is still in high school, as well as statutes providing that a parent cannot be required to contribute to the cost of an adult child's college education (but see "Mental and Physical Disabilities" below).

In the absence of a statute, courts generally take one of two approaches. Many judges believe it is not fair to require divorced parents to pay for their children's college education, since, had the family remained together, the parents would have been free to decide whether or not to contribute to their child's college education, and the child would have no legal claim to such support.

Other courts take the position that education is a basic parental obligation and will order support in appropriate cases. These courts often point out that had the parents remained together, it can be assumed that they would have made a reasonable effort to finance their child's education and that divorce should not work a deprivation. They are also aware that if support is not ordered, the financial burden will most likely fall on the custodial parent.

In deciding whether to order support so a child may attend college, courts generally look at a number of factors, including the reasonable expectations of the child, academic interest and ability, and the parents' financial status. Courts may also try to determine whether the family would have provided a college education had the parents remained together. Unfortunately, these factors may work against a young person who is not from a middle-class family, as a judge may decide that a college education is not necessary or within reasonable expectations.

### Mental and Physical Disabilities

Almost all states permit courts to continue support beyond age 18 where an adult child is mentally or physically disabled and is incapable of self-support. Some states require the disability to have begun during minority and will not require support where the child becomes disabled as an adult.

## TAX IMPLICATIONS OF CHILD SUPPORT AWARDS _____

There are two basic tax questions to consider with regard to the payment of child support:

- How are payments to be treated for tax purposes?
- What is the relationship between paying support and claiming the dependency exemption for the children?

## Characterization of Child Support Payments

The basic rule is that child support payments are not considered income to the custodial parent and are not subject to taxation. Because payments are not includible in income to the recipient, the noncustodial parent is not entitled to deduct the amount of the payments from his or her income. In effect, payment of child support is a tax-neutral event.

This changes, however, if child support payments are lumped together with alimony payments so that a single support payment is made without designating how much is for alimony and how much for child support. This is commonly referred to as **unallocated support**. Where support is unallocated, the entire amount will be treated as alimony. Unlike child support, alimony is regarded as taxable income to the recipient and entitles the payor spouse to deduct the payments from his or her gross income.

Given this potential tax benefit, a support obligor may be tempted to characterize the entire support amount as alimony. This could also benefit the support recipient because the tax savings realized by the obligor could be passed on, in whole or in part, as additional support payments. This would, of course, increase the recipient's taxable income but, where he or she is in a lower tax bracket, could result in a net gain.

To deter parties from disguising child support payments as spousal support, the federal tax code now includes rules regarding the treatment of unallocated support payments. Where support is unallocated, reductions that are tied to a contingency relating to a child or to a time associated with such a contingency create a refutable presumption that the amount of the reduction was in fact child support, and it will be treated as such.

Child-related contingencies include reaching majority, marriage, and completing school. For example, if the wife is to receive $500 per month with no contingencies other than remarriage or death, the full amount will be considered alimony. But if the agreement calls for payments to be reduced to $200 per month at the child's eighteenth birthday, the IRS will recharacterize the amount of the reduction as child support. Moreover, if a creative attorney tries to avoid this rule and has the reduction occur two months before the child's birthday, the IRS will consider this as occurring at a time associated with a child-related contingency and will again presume that this amount is child support. The presumption can be rebutted by proof that the timing of the reduction was selected based on independent, non–child-related considerations.

## The Dependency Exemption and Child Tax Credit

The basic rule is that the custodial parent is entitled to claim the children as dependents for federal tax purposes. However, because the noncustodial parent is usually in a higher tax bracket, the dependency exemption may be worth more to this parent. Accordingly, as part of divorce negotiations, parties often negotiate over who will take the **dependency exemption**. If the custodial parent agrees that the noncustodial parent can claim the children, the custodial parent must effectuate this by signing a written release. The release can be made permanent or for a temporary period. Parties may also agree to alternate years for claiming the exemption or to each claim the exemption for a different child.

Since 1997, decisions about which parent will claim the children as dependents have assumed an even greater importance because the parent who claims the child is now also entitled to a **child tax credit**. Unlike the dependency exemption, which permits an adjustment to gross income, the child tax credit gives a parent an actual credit against his or her tax liability.

## Chapter Summary

In 1974, Congress enacted the Child Support Enforcement and Establishment of Paternity Act, marking the entrance of the federal government into the child support arena. States must now have a comprehensive child support program in effect, which is administered by a single entity, known as an IV-D agency. Child support awards must be based on guidelines that use numeric criteria to arrive at a presumptive amount; deviations are permitted under limited circumstances. States must also have an array of enforcement mechanisms in place to help with the collection of child support. The most important of these is income withholding. To aid in the establishment and enforcement of child support, federal law has mandated the creation of an extensive interconnected set of databases, which permit the collection, sharing, and matching of information regarding child support cases.

Interstate cases have been the bane of the child support system. To address this situation, all states must now have a central registry for the coordination of interstate cases. Furthermore, all states have adopted UIFSA, which, by continuing modification jurisdiction in the issuing state for as long as a parent or child remains there, eliminates the problem of conflicting orders. Under FFCCSOA, all states must give full faith and credit to child support orders of other states.

A parent's support obligation generally lasts until a child reaches the age of majority (18) but, under limited circumstances, it can be terminated earlier or extended beyond this point. Support orders can be modified based on a change in circumstances; they are also subject to a periodic review and adjustment process.

Child support payments are not considered income to the recipient—nor are they deductible by the payor. If folded into an unallocated support award, the entire amount will be treated as alimony unless reductions are tied to child-related contingencies. Unless released, the dependency exemption belongs to the custodial parent. The parent who takes the dependency exemption is also entitled to the child tax credit.

## Key Terms

Child Support

Title IV-D

IV-D Agency

Parent Locator Service

Child Support Guidelines

Support Worksheet

Imputed/Attributed Income

Extraordinary Expense

Qualified Medical Child Support
  Order (QMCSO)

Financial Affidavit

Wage Withholding

Arrearage

Lien

Tax Refund Intercept

Credit Reporting

Criminal Nonsupport

Contempt Proceeding

Modification

Review and Adjustment
  Procedure

Change in Circumstances

Emancipation

Unallocated Support

Dependency Exemption

Child Tax Credit

## Review Questions

1. Why did the federal government decide to enter the child support field?

2. When was the federal Office of Child Support Enforcement established, and what is its function?

3. What is a IV-D agency, and what is its role in the child support field?

4. What must a custodial parent do when applying for public assistance? What is the nature of the parent's relationship with the IV-D system?

5. How does a custodial parent who is not on public assistance access the services of a IV-D agency?

6. What is a parent locator service?

7. Explain how child support guidelines work, making sure that you include an explanation of the concept of deviation.

8. Identify and explain the various guideline approaches.

9. How do states generally define income?

10. What is meant by imputed or attributed income, and when is this concept used?

11. Explain the terms "gross income," "adjusted gross income," and "net income" in the child support context.

12. How do guidelines typically treat income of the custodial parent's new partner?

13. How do guidelines treat the income of a child?

14. Where a parent is ordered to pay support for a second family, how is his or her prior support order usually accounted for?

15. How do guidelines treat the situation where an obligor wants to pay less to his first family because he now has a second family with minor children?

16. Explain the concept of extraordinary expenses and how states treat them when determining support.

17. When might visitation arrangements trigger an adjustment in support?

18. Why do courts generally not terminate support where parents have joint custody? What approaches do courts take in these situations?

19. What kinds of databases exist at the state and federal level, and what roles do they play in the child support system? What concerns have been raised about them?

20. Explain how income withholding works. When can an income withholding be bypassed?

21. What is a lien, and what role does it have in the child support context?

22. What is the concept of a tax refund intercept?

23. What is the function of the central registry in an interstate case?

24. What is the overall purpose of UIFSA? What are its key provisions?

25. What does FFCCSOA require?

26. What role do private support collection agencies seek to fill? What arguments have been raised in favor of and against such an approach?

27. What is the goal of a criminal nonsupport case? How is the civil goal of supporting children accomplished?

28. Explain the difference between criminal and civil contempt.

29. Explain the two ways in which support orders can be changed.

30. What is the relationship between support and visitation?

31. What circumstances might trigger a termination of support prior to majority?

32. What circumstances might permit a continuation of support after majority?

33. As a general matter, what tax impact does child support have?

34. Explain the tax rules regarding unallocated support awards.

35. Who is entitled to the dependency exemption? How can the other parent become entitled to it?

# **Discussion Questions**

1. Despite all the legislative changes discussed in this chapter, serious concerns still exist regarding the inadequacy of support payments and noncompliance with support orders. Why do you think child support continues to be such a social problem? Given what you have learned about divorce, what dynamics do you think might be at work?

2. Let's take a hypothetical case: A couple divorces when their child is three years old. Mom has custody, and Dad moves out of state. For the first few years, Dad sees the child regularly, but now he has remarried and his visits are infrequent. He is now happy and actively participating in the raising of his two new children.

   He wishes to reduce support to his first child because he feels resentful about providing for a child he has no relationship with and money is tight in his new household. Do you think he should be permitted to do this? What do you base your opinion on? Does your answer change if Mom has interfered with his visits without good reason? Does your answer change if Mom left him because he was abusive? Should these kinds of issues influence support determinations?

3. Here's another hypothetical: Two parents divorce. Dad has custody of the two children, ages two and four. He works half-time. Mom is a corporate executive and hates her work. She earns a good salary and pays enough child support so that Dad and the children are reasonably comfortable. It is important to Dad that the children not be in full-time day care. Mom decides to leave her job and pursue her lifelong dream of being a freelance writer. Assume that Mom is acting in good faith; in other words, she is not making this job change for the purpose of avoiding child support. Do you think the court should impute income to her based on her earning capacity and use this figure for the calculation of support? How do you balance the equities in this situation? What factors would you weigh?

4. Should judges be able to order divorced parents to contribute to their children's college education?

5. Do you think private support collection agencies are a good idea? Do you think they benefit or harm children?

# Assignments

1. Obtain a copy of your state's child support guidelines and answer the following questions:

   a. What approach is used?
   b. How is income of the custodial parent treated?
   c. How is income of the child treated?
   d. What happens when the obligor has a prior family? a subsequent family?
   e. How are extraordinary expenses treated?
   f. What other factors influence the amount?

2. Obtain a copy of the child support worksheet that is used in your state to calculate support awards. Using the worksheet and consulting the guidelines where necessary, calculate a support award based on the following facts:

   a. Mom has custody of the two children, ages four and nine.
   b. Her gross income is $22,000, her adjusted gross income is $18,700.
   c. She has yearly child-care expenses of $8,000.
   d. Dad's gross income is $46,000; his adjusted gross income is $39,000.
   e. He spends what would be considered a typical amount of time visiting with his children.
   f. Dad maintains a family health insurance policy that covers the children—the cost of this policy to him is $380 per month and the cost of maintaining an individual policy would be $190 per month.
   g. The nine-year-old child has severe learning disabilities, which require the hiring of special tutors—the monthly cost of this is $225.
   h. Neither parent has other children.

3. Determine whether your state has implemented any support enforcement tools that go beyond those that are required under federal law (if you are not certain of this, you can check the tool against the mandated remedies that are discussed in Chapter 10 of the child support manual cited in note 8).

4.  Develop a client intake questionnaire for use in cases where support is an issue. Make sure you consult the guidelines so that all relevant considerations are accounted for.

5.  Assume that a client in your office is seeking a divorce from her husband, who left the state five years ago. Since that time, she has had no contact with him, but she does know where he is living. Locate UIFSA as adopted by your state and determine whether your state can exercise personal jurisdiction over him for purposes of entering a child support order. Now, do the same but with the following change. Assume that the client and her husband never lived together in your state but that she moved here following their separation. However, the husband makes periodic visits to see the child. Under this set of facts, can your state obtain personal jurisdiction over him? Explain your answer.

## Cases for Analysis

In this "high income" case, the Pennsylvania high court ordered the custodial parent to pay child support to the noncustodial parent based on the significant disparity in their incomes. The decision provides an interesting discussion of the relationship between support and child custody, particularly when one takes the views of the dissent into account.

### COLONNA v. COLONNA
#### 581 Pa. 1, 855 A.2d 648 (2004)

Appellant, Mary M. Colonna (Mother), and Appellee Robert J. Colonna (Father), were married in 1983 and separated in 1996. . . . At the time of separation, the parties agreed to a temporary order of shared legal and physical custody, pursuant to which the children lived three and one-half days per week with each parent. They later amended the agreement to provide that the children would alternate between parental homes on a weekly basis . . .

On November 19, 1997, the trial court ordered Father to pay . . . child support and to provide health insurance for Mother and the children . . .

By Order dated May 4, 1998, the trial court awarded primary legal and physical custody to Father during the school year, and primary legal and physical custody to Mother during the summer. Mother has partial custody of one or more of the children on Tuesday and Thursday during the school year, and Father has partial custody of one or more of the children on Tuesday and Thursday during the summer. The parties alternate holidays and weekends throughout the year, and each parent has two weeks with the children for summer vacation.

On July 24, 1998, Father sought to terminate child support on the basis that he was now the children's primary custodian. . . .

The master determined that Mother had custody 27% of the year, and Father had custody 73% of the year. She was troubled by the disparities in the parties' income and the fact that Mother has certain fixed expenses incident to her alternating weekend and summer custody . . .

. . . The Superior Court concluded that for purposes of calculating child support, the custodial parent is the obligee and the non-custodial parent is the obligor. Because the children spend 73% of the time with Father and 27% with Mother, the Superior Court determined that Father, as the obligee, does not owe child support to Mother, who is the obligor. The Superior Court relied upon Pa.R.C.P. 1910.16-1, Explanatory Comment B.2., which provides:

> Each parent is required to contribute a share of the child's reasonable needs proportional to that parent's share of the combined net incomes. The custodial parent makes these contributions entirely through direct expenditures for food, shelter, clothing, transportation and other reasonable needs. In addition to any direct expenditures on the child's behalf, the non-custodial parent makes contributions through periodic support payments.

Accordingly, the Superior Court held that Mother was not entitled to child support. It concluded:

> Where primary physical custody is changed from one parent to the other parent, no valid justification remains for requiring the new custodial parent to continue payments that are intended to be purely for the support, benefit and best interest of the children. Consequently, directing support payments to a non-custodial parent . . . serves no purpose for the children after custody changes and would only confer a personal benefit upon the non-custodial parent if the payments were allowed to continue.

Colonna v. Colonna, 2001 PA Super 368, 788 A.2d 430, 442 (Pa. Super. 2001).

We adamantly disagree with this conclusion . . . we are troubled by the disparity in the parties' incomes and are concerned that the refusal to consider this as a factor when fashioning a support order may be contrary to the best interests of the children. We must always be mindful of the fact that the support laws work in conjunction with our custody laws. The General Assembly has declared:

> It is the public policy of this Commonwealth, when in the best interest of the child, to assure a reasonable and continuing contact of the child with both parents after a separation or dissolution of the marriage and a sharing of the rights and responsibilities of child rearing by both parents. . . .

23 Pa. [Cons. Stat.] § 5301.

Where the parent who does not have primary custody has a less significant income than the custodial parent, it is likely that he or she will not be able to provide an environment that resembles the one in which the children are accustomed to living with the custodial parent. While a downward adjustment in lifestyle is a frequent consequence of divorce that affects both adults and children, we would be remiss in failing to ignore the reality of what happens when children are required to live vastly different lives depending upon which parent has custody on any given day. To expect that quality of the contact between the non-custodial parent and the children will not be negatively impacted by that parent's comparative penury vis-a-vis the custodial parent is not realistic. Issuing a support order that allows such a situation to exist clearly is not in the best interests of the children.

Therefore, where the incomes of the parents differ significantly, we believe that it is an abuse of discretion for the trial court to fail to consider whether deviating from the support guidelines is appropriate, even in cases where the result would be to order child support for a parent who is not the primary custodial parent. . . .

In a case such as the instant matter, the trial court should inquire whether the non-custodial parent has sufficient assets to provide the children with appropriate housing and amenities during his or her period of partial custody. We specifically note that the term "appropriate" does not mean equal to the environment the children enjoy while in the custodial parent's care, nor does it mean "merely adequate." The determination of appropriateness is left to the discretion of the trial court, upon consideration of all relevant circumstances.

Mr. Chief Justice Cappy, dissenting.

Because I believe that a custodial parent should not be obligated to pay child support to a non-custodial parent, I must respectfully dissent.

. . . I find the majority's approach disquieting because I believe it transforms a child support action into a quasi-equitable distribution action. In my view, the majority's new rule is not so much addressing whether the needs of the children are being met . . . but rather is focused on augmenting the wealth of the non-custodial parent. While such a focus may be proper in an equitable distribution matter, it has no place in a child support action. A child support action should not be used to jerry-rig a new balance between the respective financial positions of the spouses . . .

[M]ost importantly, I am not in accord with the majority's foundational premise concerning the relationships between parents and children. The majority appears to be of the belief that if there is a disparity in income, the parent-child relationship will perforce be corrupted by the wealthier parent's desire to "buy the affection of the children. . . ." Majority slip op at

7 n.5. . . . The majority believes we should capitulate to what it perceives to be a social reality, and redistribute the wealth so that the affections of the child will not be alienated due to a parent's inability to provide the child with material advantages comparable to those provided by the wealthier parent.

I am disturbed by this approach. First, I can find no basis in the law for the proposition that a non-custodial spouse must be enabled, via payments from the custodial parent, to provide material advantages and entertain her children in the same lavish fashion as may the custodial parent. This simply has not been the law of this Commonwealth.

Furthermore, I am disturbed by the philosophy underpinning this rule. Unlike the apparent view of the majority, I do not believe that the health of any given parent-child relationship is measured by a parent's ability to provide a surfeit of expensive possessions or experiences for her child. Rather, the parent-child relationship thrives, or withers, based on the availability of intangibles such as love, attention, and affection. While it may be true that we live in a highly materialistic culture, does this fact stand in contradiction to the timeless realities of parenting? Or, to put it colloquially, can money buy love? I think not. And, more importantly, I balk at this court's implication that not only are a child's affections for sale, but also that our judiciary should be in the business of fostering the market for such a "commodity." For the foregoing reasons, I respectfully dissent.

Mr. Justice Castille joins this dissenting opinion.

## QUESTIONS

1. What is the parties' custodial arrangement?

2. Why does the court reference the custody statute given that this is a support case?

3. How does the court justify the support award?

4. What reasons does the dissent give for objecting to the decision?

5. What philosophical concerns does the dissent raise?

---

In the following case, the court addresses the question of whether a child support order should be modified or terminated when a parent is incarcerated, which, here was because the father had sexually assaulted his daughter. The opinion is thoughtful and clear and is instructive on the issue of modification/termination in general.

## YERKES v. YERKES
### 573 Pa. 294, 824 A.2d 1169 (2003)

The question presented in this case is whether incarceration, standing alone, is a "material and substantial change in circumstances" that provides sufficient grounds for modification or termination of a child support order. We hold that it is not.

Appellant Keith A. Yerkes ("Father") and Appellee Lydia A. Yerkes ("Mother") were married in November 1978 and separated in August 1992. During their marriage, the parties had two children: Amy, born in January 1983, and Richard, born in August 1988. Immediately following the parties' separation, Mother sought child support from Father. The parties eventually reached an agreement for support in November 1992.

In 1994, Father was arrested for sexually assaulting Amy, who was eleven years old at the time. He was ultimately convicted of aggravated indecent assault and has been incarcerated for that crime since August 1994. Father . . . will be released by August 2004.

In May 1997, Father petitioned the trial court for modification or termination of the November 1992 support order . . .

The thrust of Father's argument is that his support obligation should be modified or terminated because he is unable to pay due to his imprisonment and the inadequate wage he earns . . .

To give effect to the requirement of reasonable financial support, the Pennsylvania Rules of Civil Procedure provide a comprehensive set of guidelines for the appropriate amount of child support to be contributed by each parent. See generally Pa.R.C.P. No. 1910.16-1 to 1910.16-7 . . .

This Court has never directly addressed whether incarceration, standing alone, is a "material and substantial change in circumstances" that provides sufficient grounds for modification or termination of a child support order. A review of cases from other jurisdictions, however, reveals a wealth of case law that can be loosely categorized into three groups, each of which represents a different approach to assessing the effect of incarceration on support obligations. The first approach, dubbed the "no justification" rule, generally deems criminal incarceration as insufficient to justify elimination or reduction of an open obligation to pay child support. See Thurmond, 962 P.2d at 1068-70; Halliwell, 741 A.2d at 644. The second approach, known as the "complete justification" rule, generally deems incarceration for criminal conduct as sufficient to justify elimination or reduction of an existing child support obligation. See Thurmond, 962 P.2d at 1070-71; Halliwell, 741 A.2d at 644-45. Finally, the third approach is the "one factor" rule, which generally requires the trial court to simply consider the fact of criminal incarceration along with other factors in determining whether to eliminate or reduce an open obligation to pay child support. See Thurmond, 962 P.2d at 1071-72; Halliwell, 741 A.2d at 645.

The fundamental disagreement between those courts applying a "no justification" rule and those adopting one of the other two rules hinges on whether relief should ever be granted to incarcerated parents. It appears that each court's ultimate conclusion on this issue is driven by three underlying considerations: (1) whether allowing relief to an incarcerated parent serves the best interests of the child, (2) whether relief is in accord with fairness principles, and (3) whether it is appropriate to treat incarceration in the same manner as voluntary unemployment.

With regard to the first consideration, i.e., whether relief serves the best interests of the child, courts invoking the "no justification" rule often maintain that it is in the best interests of the child for the support order to remain intact because of the possibility of future reimbursement . . . On the other hand, those jurisdictions that reject the "no justification" rule often counter that such an approach to the best interests principle is unrealistic:

> [Under the "no justification" rule,] the child support judgment will not be paid during the time that the parent is incarcerated, and therefore the judgment will simply accrue with interest. Such a situation provides little or no benefit to anyone. The children do not receive the benefit of the proceeds during the time they require the funds, and the parent is simply confronted with a large, nondischargeable judgment upon release from prison, at a time when the prospect of paying a large judgment with interest is extremely unlikely. At current interest rates the judgment will double every 6 or 7 years. How this can be in the children's best interest is difficult . . . to imagine.

Pierce, 412 N.W.2d at 293 (quoting Ohler v. Ohler, 220 Neb. 272, 369 N.W.2d 615, 618-19 (Neb. 1985) (Krivosha, C.J., dissenting)). . . .

Having considered the arguments on both sides of this issue, we conclude that the best interests of the child are better served by the "no justification" rule than by a rule that would allow suspension of the support obligation during an obligor's incarceration. As the Appellate Division of the Superior Court of New Jersey has cogently explained:

> We perceive two possible scenarios. In the first, the obligor is incarcerated and the support obligation is not suspended. Payments go into arrears. Upon release, the obligor cannot pay both current support and arrears, so only the current support is paid. In the second scenario, the obligor is incarcerated and the obligation is suspended during incarceration. Upon release, the obligor resumes paying the pre-incarceration support obligation. . . .

In both situations, the child receives no support during the obligor's incarceration, and in both, the child begins to receive support upon the obligor's release. . . . [T]he scenario-one child suffers during the obligor's incarceration, but there is a possibility of compensation at some point in the future. The scenario-two child also suffers during the obligor's incarceration, but there is no realistic chance that the substantial arrearage will ever be fully paid. . . .

Thus, scenario two works to the benefit of the obligor, while scenario one works to the benefit of the child, at least theoretically. The scenario-two child essentially takes on a burden because the obligor has been relieved temporarily of the parental duty of support.

The question is which scenario is worse. Clearly, it is scenario two, in which the child has no real hope of ever seeing the missed support payments to which (s)he is entitled. . . .

Halliwell, 741 A.2d at 645-46 (footnote omitted). We agree with the New Jersey court that, although none of the three rules will provide short-term relief to the child, the "no justification" rule at least provides for the possibility that the obligor will repay the support owed to the child . . .

With regard to the second consideration, i.e., which approach is most "fair," proponents of the "no justification" rule often reason that fairness principles dictate that an obligor should not benefit from criminal conduct or be allowed to use it as a means to escape child support obligations . . . These courts often opine that because the needs of the children have not changed, their needs must prevail over the difficulties of the incarcerated parent . . . On the other hand, those rejecting the "no justification" rule argue that fairness weighs in favor of the obligor because, without relief, the obligor parent would be saddled with an onerous burden upon release from prison . . .

On balance, we believe that fairness principles also weigh in favor of the "no justification" rule, primarily because affording relief to the incarcerated parent would effectively subordinate child support payments to the parent's other financial obligations. . . . As such, we simply cannot justify relieving incarcerated parents of their child support obligations when they are not relieved of their other financial obligations . . .

Finally, with regard to the third consideration, . . . courts following the "no justification" rule often liken obligors who are sent to prison for criminal conduct to those who voluntarily assume lower paying jobs or leave their jobs . . . As the Supreme Court of Montana stated:

. . . We see no reason to offer criminals a reprieve from their child support obligations when we would not do the same for an obligor who voluntarily walks away from his job. Unlike the obligor who is unemployed or faced with a reduction in pay through no fault of his own, the incarcerated person has control over his actions and should be held to the consequences. . . . [An obligor] should not be able to escape his financial obligation to his children simply because his misdeeds have placed him behind bars. The meter should continue to run.

Mooney, 848 P.2d at 1023 (citation omitted) . . . On the other hand, the Supreme Court of Alaska has rejected the analogy to voluntary unemployment:

Although incarceration is often a foreseeable consequence of criminal misconduct and all criminal acts are in some sense voluntary, non-custodial parents who engage in criminal misconduct seldom desire the enforced unemployment that accompanies incarceration; nor can they alter their situation; and, in stark contrast to parents who consciously choose to remain unemployed, jailed parents rarely have any actual job prospects or potential income. Equating incarceration to voluntary unemployment would require us to ignore these significant, real-life distinctions.

Bendixen, 962 P.2d at 173 . . . ,

[W]e agree with the courts favoring the "no justification" rule that it is appropriate to analogize incarceration to voluntary unemployment . . .

[I]t is foreseeable that criminal conduct can lead to incarceration, a reduction in income occasioned by criminal incarceration is clearly within the control of the obligor. Thus, we conclude that an incarcerated obligor, though in somewhat different circumstances from a voluntarily unemployed obligor, has control over his or her circumstances . . .

In sum, we conclude that the "no justification" rule best serves the interests of the child and is in harmony with fairness principles and the child support laws of Pennsylvania . . . In this case, Father was incarcerated for sexually assaulting his daughter.[13] His sole argument in support of his petition for modification or termination of his child support obligation was that his incarceration made him unable to pay. Thus, Father cannot obtain relief from his child support obligations . . .

### QUESTIONS

1. What are the three approaches that jurisdictions take with respect to whether incarceration justifies relief from a child support obligation?

2. What approach does the court adopt?

3. What considerations underlie this approach?

4. As reviewed here, what views do other courts take with respect to these considerations?

5. At the end of the decision, the court notes that the result is "particularly appropriate" given that the father's incarceration stems from his sexual assault of his daughter—how significant do you think this factor is? Do you think the result would have been the same if the incarceration was for a reason unrelated to his family? Will this be a distinguishing factor in the future?

———————

This case addresses whether it is proper to impute income where it is impossible to determine a party's earnings due to deception. Although the father's candor is refreshing, this case illustrates what some parents do to avoid their support obligation.

### IN RE THE MARRIAGE OF DODD
#### 120 Wash. App. 638, 86 P.3d 801 (2004)

FACTS

In May 1998, Mr. Dodd was ordered to pay $1,018 per month in child support for his two children based upon a net monthly income at $3,419. Mr. Dodd's failure to pay child support led to a series of support enforcement contempt proceedings. . . .

In July 2001, Mr. Dodd petitioned for support modification. In its oral ruling the commissioner partly stated:

> Now, the father's situation is controversial at best. He describes himself as a heavy equipment operator and a logger. . . . He is self-employed . . . If you believe him and his tax returns, he is showing fairly minimal gross receipts, and those are either partially or entirely offset by listed expenses, so that his income returns are showing a nominal income at best.
>
> He has a rather unique financial arrangement. He apparently is living with his girlfriend, and when he does his logging business he asks the mills, who employ him on an independent contractor basis, to pay his girlfriend, not him, and she then apparently cashes the check and gives him the money. When asked in his deposition why he does that, he indicates that he can't have a checking account because whenever he does the State of Washington simply attaches it for back child support. And so, I guess he was fairly candid

about his deception with the State of Washington. But it makes for an almost impossible situation for me to try and figure out what he is actually earning. I don't — I don't know what he is earning . . .

## ANALYSIS

Where income is unknown because of voluntary underemployment or voluntary unemployment, RCW 26.19.071(6) provides, "a parent's imputed income shall be based on the median income of year-round full-time workers as derived from the United States bureau of census, current population reports, or such replacement report as published by the bureau of census." . . . It is consistent with the plain language of the statute and its underlying purpose to consider a parent who conceals income in order to escape his or her support obligation as voluntarily underemployed or voluntarily unemployed for purposes of imputing income . . .

. . . Mr. Dodd's income was impossible to compute due to his deceptions, and thus unknown. The record contains substantial evidence that Mr. Dodd's admitted dishonesty rendered his claimed income unverifiable . . . Imputing income in accordance with census tables was proper under this record because Mr. Dodd's situation was analogous to voluntary underemployment or voluntary unemployment . . . because Mr. Dodd's deceptions made his income impossible to ascertain under this record.

## QUESTIONS

1. How did the father conceal the actual amount of his income?

2. What rule did the court rely on in imputing income to the father?

3. How did the father's situation differ from that referenced in the rule?

4. Why did the court conclude that this rule was applicable in this situation?

## Endnotes

1. *See* Lucy Yee, What Really Happens in Child Support Cases: An Empirical Study of Establishment and Enforcement of Child Support Orders in the Denver District Court, 57 Denv. L.J. 21 (1979).

2. Joseph I. Lieberman, Child Support in America: Practical Advice for Negotiating and Collecting a Fair Settlement 11 (1988).

3. Lieberman, *supra* note 2, at 14.

4. In 1996, as part of a sweeping welfare reform act known as the Personal Responsibility and Work Opportunity Reconciliation Act (PRWORA), Congress abolished AFDC and replaced it with Transitional Assistance to Needy Families (TANF).

5. Pub. L. No. 93-647, 88 Stat. 2351 (codified as amended at 42 U.S.C. §§ 651-662).

6. U.S. Dept. of Health and Human Services, Child Support: An Agenda for Action (1984).

7. No systematic attempt will be made to match developments with a particular legislative enactment. For your reference, some of the more significant amendments to date include the Child Support Enforcement Amendments of 1984, Pub. L. No. 98-378, 98 Stat. 1305 (42 U.S.C. § 667); the Family Support Act of 1988, Pub. L. No. 100-485, 102 Stat. 2343 (codified in scattered sections of 42 U.S.C.); the Child Support Recovery Act of 1992, Pub. L. No. 102-521, 106 Stat. 3403 (codified as amended at 18 U.S.C. § 228 and scattered sections of 42 U.S.C.); and the Personal Responsibility and Work Opportunity Reconciliation Act of 1996, Pub. L. No. 104-193, 110 Stat. 105 (42 U.S.C. §§ 601 et seq.).

8. Office of Child Support Enforcement, Essentials for Attorneys in Child Support Enforcement ch. 6 (3rd ed. 2002) ("Essentials"). This excellent resource can be found online at http://www.acf.hhs.gov/programs/cse/pubs under the heading ACF/OCSE Reports. (Accessed May 5, 2007.)

9. A state that does not comply with federal law risks losing a percentage of its federal funding for the administration of its child support program.

10. A detailed discussion about the complex relationship between child support and public assistance is beyond the scope of this text. However, if you are working with clients who are applying for or receiving public assistance, you must become familiar with the interplay between the two. This is particularly important if your client is a victim of domestic violence, as the initiation of a child support action can trigger or escalate abuse or possibly lead to the disclosure of a victim's whereabouts. It may also trigger a retaliatory custody or visitation action

11. Vicki Turetsky, What If All the Money Came Home? Welfare Cost Recovery in the Child Support Program, 43 Fam. Ct. Rev. 402 (2005).

12. Essentials, *supra* note 8, ch. 3.

13. For more detail on these protections, *see* Susan Notar and Vicki Turetsky, Models for Safe Child Support Enforcement, 8 Am. U. J. Gender Soc. Poly & L. 657 (2000).

14. The word "permanent" does not mean forever, as support awards are modifiable. Rather, the term "permanent support" is used to distinguish awards

that are entered at the time of divorce from those that are entered during the pendency of the case and are thus interim in nature.

15. Laura W. Morgan, Imputing Income to Non-Income and Low-Income Earning Assets, 17 Am. J. Fam. L. 191 (2004).

16. Essentials, *supra* note 8, ch. 9. Although questions about multiple families usually arise in the course of a modification proceeding, the topic will be discussed here in keeping with the organizational format of many guidelines. For an excellent discussion on this topic, *see* Marianne Takas, U.S. Dept. of Health and Human Services, The Treatment of Multiple Family Cases Under State Child Support Guidelines (1991).

17. Sally F. Goldfarb, Child Support Guidelines: A Model for Fair Allocation of Child Care, Medical and Educational Expenses, 21 Fam. L.Q. 325, 331 (1987).

18. 45 C.F.R. § 302.56(c)(8).

19. Drew A. Swank, The National Child Non-Support Epidemic, 2003 Det. C.L. Rev. 357, 359 (2003).

20. FY 2002, Preliminary Data Report, April 2003, http://www.acf.hhs.gov/programs/cse/pubs.

21. FY 2002, Preliminary Data Report, April 2003, http://www.acf.hhs.gov/programs/cse/pubs.

22. Drew A. Swank, Das Boot! A National Survey of Booting Programs' Impact on Child Support Compliance, 4 J.L. Fam. Stud. 265, 268 (2002).

23. Samuel V. Schoonmaker IV, Current International and Domestic Issues Affecting Children: Consequences and Validity of Family Law Provisions in the "Welfare Reform Act," 14 J. Am. Acad. Matrimonial L. 3, 11 (1997). This article contains a comprehensive overview of the reforms made by this 1996 Act. *See also* Margaret Campbell Haynes and Peter S. Feliceangeli, Child Support in the Year 2000, 3 Del. L. Rev. 65 (2000); and Personal Responsibility and Work Opportunity Reconciliation Act of 1996, Pub. L. No. 104-193, 110 Stat. 105 (42 U.S.C. §§ 601 et seq.).

24. Regarding privacy concerns in general, *see* Schoonmaker, *supra* note 23, at 45-62. Regarding concerns in the domestic violence context, *see* Notar and Turetsy, *supra* note 13.

25. Essentials, *supra* note 8, ch. 10.

26. *Id.* at p. 9.

27. For a federal intercept, the arrearage must meet a modest threshold amount. In addition, a IV-D agency can submit a case to the IRS for its "full collection" procedure. This is a remedy of last resort, available only under limited conditions. The IRS then uses the full range of its collection procedures to collect the support.

28. Schoonmaker, *supra* note 23, at 7 (internal references omitted).

29. Interstate Child Support Remedies (Margaret Campbell Haynes with Diane G. Dodson eds., 1989).

30. UIFSA can be found at 9 (pt. 1B) U.L.A. 235 (1999). In 2000, the child support community asked the National Conference of Commissioners on Uniform State Laws (NCCUSL) to review UIFSA, and in 2001, the NCCUSL approved a number of important amendments to the act. To date, states are not required to adopt these amendments, although a number of states have done so. A critical

amendment for present purposes is that which clarifies that the act's long-arm provisions apply only to the establishment and not to the modification of support orders.

The revised version of UIFSA, together with prefatory notes and comments, can be found at http://www.law.upenn.edu/bll/ulc/uifsa/final2001.htm (accessed June 15, 2004).

31. The 2001 revisions also permit parties to consent to continuing jurisdiction in this state even if everyone has moved away.

32. FFCCSOA can be found at 28 U.S.C. § 1738B (2001). For an excellent overview of interstate issues, *see* Patricia Hatamyer, Interstate Establishment, Enforcement, and Modification of Child Support Orders, 25 Okla. City U. L. Rev. 511 (2000).

33. Laura W. Morgan, Private Attorney Access to Child Support Enforcement Tools: Recommendations of the Interstate Commission, 16 Am. J. Fam. L. 169 (2002).

34. Drew A. Swank, Note from the Field: Child Support, Private Enforcement Companies, and the Law, 2002 Army Law. 57, 58.

35. *Id.*

36. Child Support Recovery Act, *as amended by* "Deadbeat Parents Act," Pub. L. No. 105-187 § 2, 112 Stat. 618 (1998) (codified at 118 U.S.C. § 228).

37. Essentials, *supra* note 8, ch. 11.

38. In light of the fact that the review and adjustment process has been somewhat cumbersome, the federal Office of Child Support Enforcement has set up a collaborative federal-state initiative to help states automate the process. *See* Automated Systems for Child Support Enhancement: A Guide for Enhancing Review and Adjustment Automation, U.S. Department of Health and Human Services, Administration for Children and Families, Office for Child Support Enforcement, July 2006; http://www.acf.dhhs.gov/programs/cse.

# 7 Spousal Support

At the time of divorce, one spouse may be required to provide financial support to the other. This support, traditionally known as **alimony**, from the Latin *alimonia,* meaning nourishment or sustenance, is now also commonly referred to as maintenance or **spousal support**. As we will see, no-fault divorce reform triggered a major restructuring of the traditional support model that was closely linked to marital fault and grounded in a vision of permanent female economic dependence.

## HISTORICAL OVERVIEW

### English Roots: Alimony and Fault

Our spousal support laws are rooted in the English ecclesiastical practice of awarding alimony as part of a divorce from board and bed, which, as discussed in Chapter 4, enabled a couple to live apart without severing the marital bond. Alimony was considered an extension of the husband's marital duty to support his wife, who upon marriage lost most of her property rights and control over her earnings. Alimony was awarded only to "innocent" wives; if a wife was the "guilty" party, the right was lost. The amount of the support award was influenced by the degree of the husband's fault as well as by the value of the property that he had acquired from the wife during the marriage.

In continuing the practice of awarding alimony, most U.S. jurisdictions followed the rule of limiting it to innocent wives, although some seem to have abandoned this rule based on considerations of economic necessity. Courts continued to speak of alimony as a substitute for the husband's duty of support, although some questioned the logic of extending a marital duty when the relationship giving rise to it had been dissolved.[1] In any event, the practice was most likely continued based on economic reality—most married women simply did not have the means to support themselves.

In awarding alimony, courts came to explain it in terms of the role it played in a fault-based divorce system. It became the measure of damages paid to an injured wife to compensate her for the loss occasioned by her wrongdoing husband, much like damages in a tort or breach of contract action. Without alimony, a guilty husband would be benefiting from his wrongdoing—a result at odds with the prevailing view of divorce as a remedy for the grievously wronged. Thus, although compelled by economic necessity, alimony was cast as a punishment for wrongdoing and inextricably linked to fault.[2]

## Alimony on the Eve of the No-Fault Reform Era

As discussed in Chapter 4, our thinking about divorce was radically reshaped in the 1970s in the wake of no-fault reform. Because alimony was bound up with considerations of fault, this reform triggered a transformation in the nature of the spousal support obligation. Before looking at this shift, we briefly consider key characteristics of the support obligation as it existed on the eve of no-fault divorce reform:

1. Although alimony was still linked to determinations of fault, this link had become weaker as the fault premise undergirding our divorce system was increasingly being called into question. Accordingly, the idea of alimony as a form of damages was beginning to lose hold.[3]
2. The concept of alimony was highly gendered. In most states, alimony could not be awarded to husbands, as women had no duty to support their husbands. Alimony, by its very nature, was understood as a male responsibility.
3. Alimony awards were "permanent" and incorporated an assumption of continued female economic dependence.

As the underlying fault rationale for alimony was called into question, some courts began to speak disparagingly of women who sought support. In the words of one judge, alimony had ensured a "perpetual state of indolence" and had the potential to convert a "host of physically and mentally competent young women into an army of alimony drones who neither toil nor spin and become a drain on society and a menace to themselves."[4] This fear appears to have been unfounded, however, as the average alimony award was modest; for instance, in 1968, the median award was $98 per month, nowhere near the amount needed to secure a life of indolence.[5]

## IMPACT OF NO-FAULT REFORM _____

With no-fault reform, the traditional legal framing of divorce as a necessary evil justifiable only in cases of grievous marital wrongdoing gave way to a greater acceptance of divorce as a solution for unhappy marriages. The elimination of fault as an essential precondition for the granting of a divorce led many in the field to reconceptualize marriage as a partnership which, as in the business world, is terminable by either party based on dissatisfaction with the undertaking. In keeping with the partnership model, the desirability of allowing each partner to make a **clean break** from the marriage was emphasized, and, as with the dissolution of a business relationship, continuing obligations deriving from the failed marital relationship were henceforth to be kept to a minimum. As discussed in this chapter, the declining role of fault and the corresponding emergence of the partnership model of marriage prompted a profound reconceptualization of the traditional support model.

### Property Division as the Primary Distributive Event _____

With no-fault reform, many states began to emphasize property division as the preferred way to adjust the post-divorce economic rights of the parties. As the division of property is a final, unmodifiable event (see Chapter 8), it was thought to more closely correspond with the emerging partnership model of marriage than did an award of spousal support. As in a business, the assets of the failed enterprise would be distributed, leaving the former partners free to pursue other endeavors unencumbered by the past. Alimony, embodying notions of continued obligation, was to be deemphasized and awarded only in exceptional cases. Underlying the emphasis on property division was an often unstated assumption that the divorcing spouses should be equally capable of achieving **economic self-sufficiency** regardless of any differences in their labor market participation during the marriage. (Note: As discussed in Chapter 8, the partnership model also incorporates a contemporary understanding of marriage as a joint enterprise in which the whole enterprise benefits from the individual contribution of each spouse, thus creating an entitlement to a share of accumulated assets at the time of divorce.)

## Shifting the Focus from Moral to Economic Considerations

As discussed, prior to no-fault reform, alimony awards were linked to marital conduct. The court looked back into the marriage and used alimony as a way to compensate an innocent wife for past harms. With the uncoupling of alimony from fault, alimony awards have been reanchored to economic considerations and, in a blame-free manner, are supposed to respond to financial needs arising out of the marital relationship. Nonetheless, in keeping with the clean-break approach, the overall emphasis has been to move away from the idea of a continuing obligation even where need or financial inequality exists.

## Degendering the Support Obligation

The support obligation has also been uncoupled from its origins as a male-only responsibility. The Supreme Court has held that gender-specific alimony laws are unconstitutional because they carry the "inherent risk of reinforcing stereotypes about the 'proper place' of women and their need for special protection."[6] In theory, spousal support is now a gender-neutral concept and is no longer premised on an assumption that married women, as a class, are financially dependent and incapable of self-support. In practice, however, few men (at least in heterosexual unions) meet the economic criteria for a support award.

## Shifting from an Assumption of Female Economic Dependence to an Assumption of Economic Self-Sufficiency

Following no-fault reform, the idea of permanent alimony awards fell out of favor. Seen as embodying outmoded assumptions regarding female economic dependence and requiring ongoing entanglement, a clear trend developed in favor of short-term support awards intended to help a spouse acquire the skills needed to become self-supporting. (See below discussion of rehabilitative alimony.) In sharp contrast to the past, this shift embodied the assumption that all married women, regardless of the role they played during the marriage, should be self-supporting either at the time of divorce or following a brief transitional period. It thus corresponded with both the changing role of women and the partnership model of marriage, which minimizes the ongoing responsibility of a former spouse.

## Critique of the "Clean Break" Approach _____

The clean-break approach has an appealing simplicity. As with former business partners, each spouse exits with a share of the accumulated assets and is divested of other economic entanglements stemming from the failed relationship. Each spouse is thus free to build a new life for him- or herself. However, despite this surface appeal, the clean-break approach has been subject to significant criticism.

To begin with, some have argued that the analogy itself is flawed because it is based on a distortion of what actually occurs in the business realm: the decision to dissolve even an ongoing business concern, so the argument goes, does not bring all mutual obligations between partners to a screeching halt. Rather, following the actual dissolution of a partnership, such as when a partner leaves a law firm, there may be a protracted period in which the partners wind up their affairs. During this time, the partners "continue to be linked by mutual obligations and continue to share a fiduciary relationship," and no matter how " 'strained' the relationships between the partners may actually be, the UPA (Uniform Partner Act), views the process of winding up as a 'cooperative' " venture.[7]

Of primary concern, critics of the clean-break approach argue that because many heterosexual marriages embody a gendered division of labor, with the husband's career assuming primary importance even where the wife works outside the home, the assumption that a division of assets will permit both parties to begin life anew with an equal capacity for economic self-sufficiency is erroneous. It is argued that this marital division of labor has serious and long-lasting implications that endure well beyond the end of the marital relationship. In families in which wives devote considerable effort to the domestic realm, they will generally leave the marriage with a **diminished earning capacity**. In contrast, a husband who has been far less encumbered by household and child-related responsibilities is likely to exit the marriage with an **enhanced earning capacity**. By failing to recognize and account for this differential, a woman's domestic contribution—which enhances family life during the marital relationship—hinders her ability to create a secure post-marital life.

Closely related is the concern that the clean-break approach ignores the fact that a majority of divorcing couples have minor children who will continue to have needs following the divorce. The approach thus assumes a level of disengagement that does not correspond with the reality of the continued involvement that comes with having children in common. Further, the economic disparity between divorcing spouses is likely to be even more pronounced in households with children, as motherhood has a significant impact on the persistent wage gap between male and female workers; one study shows that, over the course of their lifetime, women with two children who had completed high school earned 49 percent of the wages earned by male workers.[8] In sacrificing alimony to promote the ideal of noninvolvement, the clean-break approach thus ignores the reality of this post-divorce engagement between former spouses.

Following from this, critics argue that alimony needs to be reformulated to eliminate the disadvantage that flows from this marital allocation of work and family responsibilities; since the economic consequences of marriage continue beyond its duration, critics argue, so must the financial obligations. Although the proposals vary, a common thread is that, at least for a period of time following a divorce, earnings be subject to some kind of pooling requirement so that the primary wage earner does not disproportionately gain from the marital allocation of labor. Critics have suggested several specific proposals: that income be treated as a form of marital property, which, like the accumulated assets, would be subject to the claims of the partnership based on an assumption of joint contribution to the marital enterprise as a whole; that income be distributed to ensure that each household enjoys an equal standard of living; that the husband be required to buy out the wife's interest in his enhanced earning capacity; and that income be shared to "reflect the returns flowing from efforts made while the joint marital venture was operational."[9]

Some of these concerns, coupled with concerns about the lack of theoretical coherence as to the underlying purposes of spousal support and the lack of predictability in awards, have begun to influence lawmakers. As developed below, a variety of support reforms are again being considered, including the use of alimony guidelines, and a number of courts have shown a renewed commitment to permanent support awards.

---

### Consideration

Do you think alimony should be used as a vehicle for adjusting economic inequalities rising out of a division of labor during marriage to ensure that the spouse with lower earnings is not disadvantaged by his or her marital role?

---

## SUPPORT DETERMINATIONS

In reforming their support laws, most states, whether by statute or judicial decision, adopted a multifactored approach to assist the court in determining the circumstances under which support will be awarded. Although judges are usually required to consider all of the enumerated factors, much as in custody determinations, they generally have the discretion to assign them whatever weight they believe is appropriate in any given case. Again, as with custody, this gives judges the flexibility to consider the unique circumstances of a divorcing couple's situation, but it also makes it difficult to predict the circumstances under which alimony will be awarded. This lack of certainty is compounded by the fact that when support is awarded, it is difficult to predict the support amount; unlike with child support, guidelines with numeric criteria for determining the appropriate amount are not generally employed. In this section, we first look at the kinds of factors that courts weigh in deciding about spousal support and then discuss the ways in which support awards can be structured. We then consider some of the reform proposals that are currently being considered.

## Factors to Be Considered

In most states, judges are required to consider a variety of factors when deciding if a spouse should be provided with support. These factors often include the following:

- financial need
- earning potential
- age
- duration of the marriage
- physical and mental health
- income and financial resources
- the marital standard of living
- contribution to the marriage

Additionally, although greatly diminished in importance and eliminated from consideration in a number of jurisdictions, many states still include marital fault as one of the factors that must be considered, and it continues to operate as a complete bar to a spousal support award in a handful of states. Where it is identified as a factor to be considered, marital wrongdoing is generally balanced against other factors, such as need. Also, even in states where marital fault in the traditional sense of the word is not identified as a factor, economic fault may be a permissible consideration. Thus, for example, in assessing the husband's need for support, the court might give weight to the fact that the wife had squandered the family fortune on her lover, thus placing the husband in an economically vulnerable position.

It should also be noted that "contribution to the marriage" is not limited to financial considerations but is generally intended to account for a spouse's nonmonetary contributions to a marriage in the domestic realm. This allows for the recognition that a spouse may have a diminished capacity for self-support because of a primary commitment to the home and/or child rearing.

The general rule is that a judge must consider all of the enumerated factors but can assign them whatever weight he or she believes is appropriate in light of the circumstances of each case. This provides a consistent framework for evaluating cases, while giving a judge the freedom to attach different weights to different combinations of factors based on a couple's particular situation. However, need tends to be the most important across-the-board factor, and many of the other factors often are tied in to need. Thus, for example, a spouse's need may be more acute because of age, health, or a diminished earning capacity, as these considerations often build off of one another in a cumulative way.

To get a clearer picture of how this works, let's look at how a judge might weigh different factors based on the individual circumstances of a case. For example, in a case involving a disabled spouse, a judge might give significant weight to considerations of health and need and little or no weight to the fact that the spouses were married only for a short period of time. However, in another short-term marriage case, the same judge might give considerable weight to this factor and decide that the brevity of the relationship precludes a support order. In yet another short-term marriage situation where one party — let's say a husband in his early sixties — gave up a good job to move across country to join his new spouse and has been unable to find work, the same judge might again discount duration in favor of the combined weight of need, age, earning potential, and, possibly, contribution, with respect to the sacrifice he made so the couple could be together.

## New Directions: Alimony Guidelines and the ALI Compensatory Principle

The flexibility of this multifactored approach enables judges to make individualized determinations tailored to fit each case rather than having to squeeze everyone into a one-size-fits-all support package. However, this flexibility also contributes to a lack of consistency and predictability, which, as we saw in the child custody context, means that parties lack a coherent framework within which to negotiate an agreement. As a result, it becomes difficult to assess the value of a negotiated exchange if one does not know what one is giving up or gaining in the exchange process.

Another, more abstract, concern is that this flexibility has led to doctrinal incoherence — that the essential purpose of spousal support cannot be stated with clarity because the factors point in multiple directions.[10] Thus, for instance, the fault factor looks backward into the marriage and preserves the historical association between support and punishment, while other factors, such as need, direct a judge to look ahead into the future. Still other factors, such as contribution, suggest a compensatory purpose, and some, such as earning capacity, may reflect multiple impulses — a judge might be inclined to look to the future to determine if a spouse will be capable of self-support and/or back into the marriage to determine if there has been a diminution of earning capacity due to the assumption of domestic responsibilities. As one judge wryly put it: "Modern spousal support encompasses at least . . . five separate and distinct functions. Yet we treat them as one. In short, we are calling every animal in the zoo a cat, and in doing so, we lose our ability to apply rational criteria to decision-making."[11]

As is true of the family law field as a whole, there is a tension between the need for discretion and flexibility on the one hand, and the desirability of predictability and coherence on the other. When it comes to child support, this tension has been resolved in favor of clear rules; following suit, a number of states are considering adopting computational guidelines for spousal support awards, with a few jurisdictions having already adopted this approach. Another proposed approach can be found in the ALI's Principles of the Law of Family Dissolution, which recommends shifting from a needs-based focus to a compensatory focus in order to allocate the "financial losses that arise at the dissolution of a marriage according to equitable principles that are consistent and predictable in application."[12] Central to this shift is the recognition that, especially in long-term marriages, there often is a "loss in living standard experienced at dissolution by the spouse who has less wealth or earning capacity."[13]

As articulated in the principles, loss is directly related to a spouse's contribution to the marriage, and thus rather than suggesting dependency, as support so often does, this reframes support as a necessary and coherent response to the prior allocation of marital roles and responsibilities. As one commentator put it: "In the paradigm shift that this approach follows, there is an implicit recognition of 'entitlement' rather than 'charity.' Payments are made because they are earned rather than pled for. 'Need' is more clearly defined as being an outcome of loss, rather than a reason in and off itself."[14]

## Different Approaches to Structuring Spousal Support

As developed in this section, support can be structured in a variety of ways to accomplish different objectives. Each approach has its own rules regarding the modification and termination of the support award.

### Permanent Alimony

"Permanent" alimony is probably what most people think of when they think of alimony, but since no-fault reform it has been somewhat eclipsed by rehabilitative support (discussed below). The primary purpose of **permanent alimony** is to provide financial assistance to the spouse in an economically weaker position. It is payable in regular intervals on an ongoing basis.

---

### Interview Checklist

In any case where spousal support is an issue, you will need to obtain the following kinds of information about both parties. It is unlikely that you will be able to obtain all of the necessary information about your client's spouse from an interview; discovery will probably be needed to complete the picture. (See Chapter 10.)

1. Obtain complete employment histories for each job held during the marriage and for a reasonable time before it, including the following information:

   - job titles
   - promotions
   - salaries
   - hours worked
   - general responsibilities

2. Obtain the educational histories of each spouse, including any specific career training.
3. Ask about the parties' career goals, including any educational plans.
4. Get explanations of any gaps in the parties' employment histories—especially those stemming from child rearing or other domestic responsibilities.
5. Ascertain factors that may affect the parties' employment potential, such as

   - earning capacity
   - general market outlook for each spouse's career/job
   - health considerations that may impact future employment

6. Obtain a picture of the ways in which each spouse has contributed to the marriage. Focus on both financial and non-financial contributions.

Permanent alimony can also serve a compensatory purpose. A spouse (almost always the wife) who restricts her participation in the paid labor force to care for her family experiences a loss of earning capacity over the course of the marriage. At the same time, the earning capacity of her spouse is enhanced, as he is freed up to focus on his labor market participation. Although this may be a mutually beneficial arrangement during the marriage, upon divorce the spouses stand on very different footing—in effect, there has been a transfer in earning ability from one spouse to the other. Alimony payments may be used to offset this result and compensate a spouse for the **opportunity cost** of having invested a significant portion of her time in the domestic realm to the detriment of her earning ability.[15]

Unlike rehabilitative support, the goal of permanent alimony is not to help a spouse achieve economic self-sufficiency, and there is no duty to use the money for this purpose. Accordingly, a defining aspect of a permanent support award is that it is not subject to a fixed time limitation but is continuous.

Although permanent alimony is not subject to durational limits, *permanent* does not necessarily mean forever. The term is used to distinguish support awarded at the time of divorce from support awarded during the pendency of the divorce action—known as **alimony pendente lite**, or **temporary alimony**—which is intended to assist a spouse during this interim period. Thus, although not subject to pre-established durational limits, permanent alimony is subject to reduction or termination based on a **change in circumstances**, with the near universal rule being that remarriage of the recipient spouse or the death of either one terminates the obligation. (See below on Post-Divorce Modification and Termination of Support.)

### Lump-Sum Support

Although not a frequently used option, many states authorize the award of a **lump-sum support** payment, sometimes referred to as **alimony in gross**. Unlike permanent alimony, this involves the payment of a sum certain. It is generally paid in a single installment, although it can also be made payable in periodic installments until the full amount of the order is reached. Once ordered, most states agree that the recipient acquires a vested right to the entire amount, thus making it nonmodifiable based on a change in circumstances, including remarriage of the recipient. This remains true even where the lump sum is payable in installments. If the payor dies before the full amount is paid, the balance is chargeable to his or her estate; likewise, if the recipient dies before receiving payment in full, the balance due can be collected by his or her estate. Accordingly, along the lines of the old adage "a bird in the hand is worth two in the bush," a recipient may prefer to accept a potentially smaller but definite lump-sum payment instead of running the risk that periodic payments will not always be made.

### Rehabilitative Support

As noted above, following no-fault reform, **rehabilitative support**, often called **transitional support**, became the preferred approach in many jurisdictions. Rehabilitative support is awarded on a time-limited basis for the purpose of enabling an economically dependent spouse to obtain the education or training necessary to become financially self-sufficient.

To establish the durational limit, a court will try to predict how long it will take for a spouse to become self-sufficient and then set this as the date for the expiration of the obligation; in some states, maximum time limits are set by statute. In some states, courts may retain jurisdiction and extend the time limit if a spouse can show that despite a good-faith effort he or she has not been able to achieve the degree of self-sufficiency contemplated at the time of the award. Many jurisdictions, however, do not permit extensions even where a spouse is not yet self-sufficient despite a good-faith effort. Here, rather than focusing on the economic situation of the spouse seeking to achieve self-sufficiency, the courts prioritize the expectancy interest of the payor spouse and his or her wish to plan for the future unencumbered by unexpected obligations from a previous marriage.

Although there is general agreement that the goal of rehabilitative support is self-sufficiency, there is disagreement about what this means. A few states take a bare-bones approach and consider a person self-sufficient if, at the end of the rehabilitative period, he or she is not dependent on public assistance. Other courts, particularly in situations involving a long-term marriage, define self-sufficiency by reference to the marital standard of living. Here, the goal is met when a spouse is able to obtain employment that would enable him or her to approximate the prior marital standard of living.

Rehabilitative support took hold quickly during the period of no-fault reform, as it represented a break from the traditional alimony model that was associated with outmoded assumptions about fault and the economic incapacity of divorced women. Its underlying objectives were commendable and consistent with the new approach to restructuring family obligations following divorce. Rehabilitative support sets out to accomplish the following goals:

- to enable previously economically dependent spouses to develop their earning potential and realize true independence

- to enable spouses to make a clean break and begin life anew on equal footing in keeping with the partnership view of marriage
- to release spouses from ongoing financial obligations derived from a failed relationship

Beginning in the mid-1980s, however, a countertrend emerged. Appellate judges began to set aside rehabilitative awards, denouncing them as an abuse of judicial discretion. One judge went so far as to label them a "male-oriented, sexist approach."[16] These reversals have generally come in cases of long-term marriages where a woman has forgone labor market participation or has moved in and out of the workplace based on the needs of her family. According to the courts, the goal of economic self-sufficiency is illusory in these situations because a woman who has been family-centered will not be able to recapture her lost earning potential, and a rehabilitative award would leave the spouses with a gross disparity in earning capacity — a result that undervalues her contribution to the marriage.

Accordingly, trial courts have become a bit more circumspect, particularly in cases involving long-term marriages where responsibilities have been allocated along traditional gender lines. Rather than assuming that a rehabilitative award is appropriate, a court might instead place a burden on the party seeking to limit support to show how the other spouse will be able to achieve meaningful financial independence within the proposed time frames. This may require evidence about available educational programs and labor market conditions in the spouse's area of interest that indicate a likelihood of employment at a decent wage.

## The Professional Degree Cases

Although the permanent, lump-sum, and rehabilitative approaches to spousal support are relatively easy to characterize, there has been considerable confusion regarding what to do in cases where one spouse supports the other through a professional degree program thus greatly increasing the degreed spouse's future earning capacity, but the marriage ends before these gains are realized. In this section we consider the various options.

### The Degree as Property

One option is to treat the degree as marital property and subject it to division along with the other marital assets. However, the overwhelming majority of jurisdictions have rejected this approach, deciding that a degree, or the enhanced earning capacity it represents, does not fit within the meaning of the term *property*. In deciding against this approach, courts have focused on the difficulty of valuing a degree, as this would require speculation about the course someone's career will take.[17] They have also focused on other characteristics that distinguish a degree from other forms of property such as that acquisition of a degree requires substantial personal effort and sacrifice; that it lacks an objective value in the open market; and that it is personal to the holder and cannot be sold, transferred, or left to future generations. (See Chapter 8 for property-related concepts.)

### Spousal Support Options

Although generally declining to treat the degree or the enhanced earnings it represents as marital property, courts may consider it when determining the appropriateness and amount of support. One approach is to fashion a reimbursement alimony award; another is to consider the non-degreed spouse's contribution as a relevant factor in the support calculus.

**Reimbursement Alimony.** The Supreme Court of New Jersey is generally credited with developing the concept of **reimbursement alimony** in the 1982 case of Mahoney v. Mahoney in which the husband left the marriage soon after earning an advanced degree with the wife's dedicated support:

> In this case, the supporting spouse made financial contributions towards her husband's professional education with the expectation that both parties would enjoy material benefits flowing from the professional license or degree. It is therefore patently unfair that the supporting spouse be denied the mutually anticipated benefit while the supported spouse keeps not only the degree, but also all of the financial and material rewards flowing from it. . . .
>
> . . . Also, the wife has presumably made personal financial sacrifices, resulting in a reduced or lowered standard of living. Additionally, her husband, by pursuing preparations for a future career, has forgone gainful employment and financial contributions to the marriage . . . She has postponed, as it were, present consumption and a higher standard of living, for the future prospect of greater support and material benefits . . . The unredressed sacrifices . . . coupled with the unfairness attendant upon the defeat of the supporting spouse's shared expectation of future advantages, further justify a remedial award.[18]

In fashioning the award, the court held that the supporting spouse was entitled to be reimbursed for all financial contributions made to the training of the other spouse, including "household expenses, educational costs, school travel expenses and any other contribution used by the supported spouse in obtaining his or her degree or license."[19]

Many jurisdictions have followed New Jersey's lead and will reimburse a spouse for contributions to the other's education, recognizing that the supporting spouse made significant sacrifices based on the reasonable expectation that he or she would share in the future gain represented by the degree. Through reimbursement, courts can adjust this imbalance by returning the contribution to the spouse who will not participate in the anticipated benefits because of divorce.

Consistent with their focus on dashed expectations, courts have generally disallowed reimbursement where the marriage continued for a reasonable period of time after the degree was obtained on the theory that the supporting spouse would have realized his or her expectation during the marriage. Moreover, unlike where the divorce follows on the heels of the degree, there is likely to have been an accumulation of assets that can be divided.

Some courts have broadened the concept of reimbursement alimony beyond simply providing recompense for actual expenditures to include "lost opportunity costs," such as forgone income while the degree-holding spouse was enrolled in school and possibly also for forgone educational opportunities. Alternatively, some courts have instead provided rehabilitative support so the nondegreed spouse could also obtain further education.

An important critique of the reimbursement approach is that it only repays a spouse's initial investment in the career of the other and does not provide the spouse with any return on the investment through giving him or her a share of the increased earnings attributable to the enhanced earning capacity. Simply put: "this approach treats the supporting spouse as a lender, not as an investor in the asset."[20]

**The Degree as a Relevant Factor.** A number of courts have declined to embrace the concept of reimbursement. Instead, they prefer to consider the degree as one of the factors that must be weighed in determining if support should be awarded. This is a flexible approach enabling courts to emphasize different considerations. Thus, one court might give greater weight to the contribution and sacrifice of the supporting spouse, while another might focus on the enhanced earning capacity of the degree-holding spouse relative to the stagnant or possibly even diminished earning capacity of the supporting spouse.

## MEDICAL INSURANCE

The issue of continued medical coverage frequently arises with considerable urgency at the time of divorce because one spouse, typically the primary wage earner, may have a group policy through his or her employer that provides family coverage. Many states now have laws that authorize the court to order a spouse to continue to provide health insurance coverage for his or her former spouse, at least during the time that a support order is in effect.

In addition, although there is no federal law comparable to state statutory provisions requiring the continued provision of health insurance, divorced spouses may be entitled to post-divorce coverage under COBRA (short for the Consolidated Omnibus Budget Reconciliation Act), which was passed by Congress in 1986. Under Cobra, employers with more than 20 employees must provide the spouse of a divorcing employee with a temporary extension of group health coverage if a timely request is made. However, the covered spouse is responsible for the entire amount of the premium since COBRA does not hold the employer or the employed spouse responsible for the cost of the continued coverage.[21]

## POST-DIVORCE MODIFICATION AND TERMINATION OF SUPPORT

### The General Concept

Following a divorce, as with custody or child support, either party may seek to revise the spousal support amount by filing a complaint for **modification**. This action is usually filed in the court that entered the original support order, which has continuing jurisdiction over the matter. If a support order is not entered at the time of divorce, a court may lose jurisdiction; accordingly, to protect against this, some courts will order payment of a nominal support amount, such as a dollar per month. This preserves its jurisdiction should the need for support arise in the future. The complaint for modification must be based on a change in circumstances that makes the original order unfair. States use different yardsticks to measure unfairness. Some employ a strict unconscionability standard, while others employ a more relaxed standard. Again, the general rule is that the change must have been unforeseeable. Accordingly, a future job change that was known about at the time of the original order cannot generally be the basis for a modification, as this should have been accounted for in the original order. Similarly, most jurisdictions will not base a modification upon inflation or cost-of-living increases in the obligor's salary, as these events are foreseeable and could have been addressed.

In addition to being unforeseeable, courts may require that the change be involuntary. Accordingly, an obligor who seeks to reduce payments because she has left the corporate world to become an artist will probably not be successful. Likewise, a support recipient who relocates to a luxury apartment complex and then seeks an upward revision based on the increased rent is not likely to succeed.

## Modifiability and Termination of "Permanent" Support

Remarriage, cohabitation, and a change in financial circumstances are the most common reasons for a modification action. Each is discussed below.

### Remarriage

In most states, the statutory rule is that an award of "permanent" support automatically terminates upon the remarriage of the recipient spouse. In some of these jurisdictions, termination occurs immediately upon remarriage without the need for any kind of court action, while in others the support obligor must file a modification petition, which almost certainly will be granted. The principle underlying the termination rule is that the recipient's new spouse has a support obligation, and a person is not entitled to be supported by both a spouse and a former spouse at the same time.

The basic rule—that remarriage terminates the spousal support obligation—is also firmly in place in states that do not have statutory termination provision through judicial decision. Although some of these jurisdictions follow the automatic termination approach, others are more flexible. A few treat remarriage as simply a factor to be considered in determining whether a change in circumstances justifies a modification, although the more common approach is to presume termination, absent a showing of extraordinary circumstances. The concept of "extraordinary" is typically defined narrowly, and the burden of proof is placed upon the alimony recipient, rather than, as is usually the case, on the person seeking the modification.

This termination rule raises difficult questions about what should happen if a spouse who is receiving rehabilitative support remarries during the rehabilitative period. From a recipient's perspective, the remarriage may be irrelevant, as he or she is seeking to regain economic independence. However, from the payor's perspective, it may seem unfair to continue paying support in a situation where the former spouse is remarried and now has access to other sources of income. It should thus come as no surprise that jurisdictions approach this issue differently, with some giving greater weight to the recipient's interest in completing the education he or she embarked on, while others are more focused on shifting responsibility to the new spouse.

The general rule is that remarriage by the paying spouse does not entitle him or her to a downward revision of support. Courts generally focus on the voluntary aspect of the act and the inequity to the former spouse. However, remarriage combined with other circumstances, such as the birth of children, may support a downward revision. Conversely, if the payor spouse remarries someone with substantial income or assets, the question may arise as to whether the recipient spouse can rely on this as a change in circumstances warranting an upward adjustment. While it is clear that the recipient has no direct claim on the new spouse's income, some courts may be willing to consider a modification based on the fact that this money may liberate some of the former spouse's income.

### Cohabitation

Whereas remarriage almost always terminates alimony, the result is less certain where a recipient cohabits with a new partner because, unlike marriage, cohabitation does not impose a legal duty of support. The majority approach is to focus on whether cohabitation has resulted in an improvement in the recipient's financial situation — and only where it has will support be reduced or terminated. Some states impose an initial threshold requirement: The party seeking to reduce or terminate support must show that the relationship is not merely fleeting but instead rises to a certain level of intensity and commitment. Only when this has been shown will the court consider the cohabiting party's financial situation. A few states employ a rebuttable presumption that cohabitation automatically improves a party's financial situation. This presumption shifts the burden of proof to the cohabiting spouse to show that his or her financial situation has not improved as a result of the relationship.

### Change in Financial Circumstances

Parties frequently seek to modify support based on a change in the financial circumstances of one or both of them. As noted above, a court will generally not modify due to foreseeable changes such as an annual cost-of-living salary increase. On the other hand, an increase in salary based on an unexpected promotion may warrant an upward revision of support. However, many jurisdictions will not modify based on this type of event alone and instead also require proof of an increased financial need on the part of the recipient spouse. A mutual change in circumstances is generally required on the theory that the recipient spouse does not have an automatic right to share in this gain as it is unrelated to the marital enterprise. In response, the recipient spouse might argue that she is entitled to a share in this increase to compensate for the fact that the original order did not provide her with adequate income, but it was all that the payor spouse could afford at the time. Here, the modification would serve a compensatory purpose. If the recipient spouse's financial circumstances improve, a downward revision is generally allowed.

## Modifiability of Specific Types of Support

Even where a change in circumstances can be established, spousal support awards other than permanent alimony are generally considered nonmodifiable.

### Lump-Sum Support

The majority rule is that a lump-sum award is not modifiable or terminable by death or remarriage. The support recipient is deemed to have acquired a vested right to the full amount, even if it is payable in installments.

### Rehabilitative Support

The rules regarding modifiability of rehabilitative support are more complex. Because this award is for a designated purpose, most courts — absent extraordinary circumstances — will not modify it for reasons unrelated to the original purpose of the award. For example, whereas a change in circumstance such as a job promotion might warrant an increase in permanent alimony, it would not warrant an increase in rehabilitative support, as this is incidental to the goal of helping the support recipient achieve economic self-sufficiency.

Some courts will not modify a rehabilitative award to extend the durational limit or increase the support amount even where the request is directly related to the goal of achieving economic self-sufficiency.

Although this may be fair where the party has not taken reasonable steps to obtain education or training, it can be a harsh result where the person has made a good-faith effort but the original time estimate was inadequate or where she or he has encountered unanticipated obstacles such as illness or the loss of affordable child care.

### Reimbursement Alimony

The general rule is that reimbursement alimony is not modifiable or terminable by the death of either party or the remarriage of the recipient spouse. This is a logical result because the award is not based on present financial circumstances but rather is designed to repay a spouse for past expenditures. Accordingly, post-divorce changes in circumstances are irrelevant. However, it is hard to imagine a court refusing to make some adjustment, perhaps in the nature of a temporary suspension of payments, in a case of genuine hardship such as serious illness.

## Agreement of the Parties to Prohibit Modification

Sometimes parties include a clause in a separation agreement stating that neither will seek to modify the support award in the future. Such a clause often is insisted upon by the supporting spouse, who wants to limit his or her obligation. Some jurisdictions may refuse to honor such a clause on public policy grounds, especially if enforcement would force a spouse into public assistance. Here, the duty to pay support is regarded as having a public dimension that cannot be abrogated by a private agreement.

## ENFORCEMENT OF SUPPORT AWARDS

As is often the case with child support orders, once spousal support has been ordered, the risk of nonpayment is substantial, and the recipient may need to take action to enforce the order.

## Contempt

In most states, the primary enforcement mechanism is an action for **contempt**. As with child support, the contempt action can be either civil or criminal in nature (see Chapter 6). Most likely, an obligor will not be found in contempt if the inability to pay existed at the time the support payments were due. A more complicated question, which jurisdictions split on, is whether present inability to pay is a valid defense where the defendant had the ability to pay at the time payments were due.

If a defendant is found to be in civil contempt, the court will order him or her to pay the overdue amount, and a payment schedule is usually established. To compel payment, the court may impose a jail sentence, but, in keeping with the remedial purpose of a civil contempt action, the defendant must be given the opportunity to purge the contempt by paying the arrearage and thus avoid jail. The right to purge oneself of the contempt is ongoing, and the jail sentence is imposed for an indefinite time terminable upon payment of the arrearage. Where there is a present inability to pay (and this is not considered a valid defense), a jail sentence will generally not be imposed because the obligor does not have the means to purge the contempt. In contrast, a sentence in a criminal contempt case is imposed for a fixed period of time because the purpose is punitive, and the defendant cannot shorten it by purging the contempt.

## Other Enforcement Measures

In seeking to enforce a spousal support award, a recipient who also has a child support order in place may be able to obtain enforcement assistance from the state's IV-D agency, and many of the same collection tools, such as wage withholding and tax refund intercepts, are available to secure spousal support payments (see Chapter 6). Additionally, many states, in implementing the enforcement procedures required under federal law for child support, extended their availability to spousal support recipients who choose not to go through the IV-D agency or are not eligible for IV-D agency support because they do not also have a child support order in place.

As with child support, spousal support awards can be enforced across state lines under the Uniform Interstate Family Support Act (UIFSA). However, child support collection is the priority of the interstate system and dominates enforcement efforts.

## BANKRUPTCY AND THE SUPPORT OBLIGATION

Filing for **bankruptcy** provides an individual who is overwhelmed by debt with the opportunity to discharge qualified debts, thus enabling him or her to make a "fresh start."[22] What then happens if the individual seeking to be relieved of his or her debts has existing financial obligations to a spouse or child stemming from a divorce or separation? Until recently, the Bankruptcy Code prevented the discharge of debts that were in the nature of "alimony, maintenance or support." The Code allowed, however, the discharge of debts that were in the nature of a property settlement, such as payments being made to a former spouse to effectuate the debtor's buyout of the equity in the marital home (see Chapter 8), unless the payor former spouse could establish some kind of hardship or inability to pay. The distinction between support and property distribution was eliminated, though, by the Bankruptcy Abuse Prevention and Consumer Protection Act of 2005. Thus, now essentially all debts stemming from the dissolution of a marriage are non-dischargeable in bankruptcy.

## TAX CONSEQUENCES

As developed in this section, unlike child support, spousal support payments have tax implications for both the payor and the recipient spouse.

### The Basic Rule of Includibility/Deductibility

The basic tax rule is that spousal support payments are considered income to the recipient and are includible in his or her taxable income; correspondingly, the payor is entitled to a deduction from gross income for spousal support payments he or she has made.[23] To qualify as alimony, payments must be in cash or a cash equivalent, must cease at the death of the recipient, and must be required under a divorce or separation instrument, and the parties may not live in the same household at the time payments are made. If parties wish to avoid this rule of includibility/deductibility, they may specifically state that payments that would otherwise qualify as alimony are not includible in the income of the recipient nor deductible by the payor. In effect, this means that for tax purposes, the payments are no longer considered to be alimony.

The basic rule of includibility/deductibility is straightforward; however, under the following two circumstances, the tax consequences may be other than what the parties intended.

### Unallocated Payments

Where both spousal support and child support are to be paid, it may be better financially for the parties if the payments are characterized as spousal support. This gives the payor a deduction for the entire amount, and the tax savings may be then used to increase the amount of support payments. Although this increases the recipient's taxable income, he or she may nonetheless realize a net gain.

If a separation agreement provides for a support amount without designating how much is for spousal support and how much is for child support, the entire amount will be treated as spousal support. However, as mentioned in Chapter 6, if the agreement provides for reductions in support based on child-related contingencies (such as reaching age 18, marriage, or establishing a separate residence) or at a time that is "clearly associated" with a child-related contingency, a rebuttable presumption arises that the amount of the reduction was in the nature of child, rather than spousal, support. The presumption may be rebutted upon proof that the reduction is attributable to a valid nonchild-related reason. Even if the agreement does not specifically mention the contingency, the Internal Revenue Service may treat a reduction as child-related if it finds that it occurred at a time associated with such a contingency, unless again the parties can establish a valid nonchild-related explanation for the reduction.

Reclassification can have significant tax repercussions, especially for the obligor. If payments are reclassified, it means that the obligor has been taking a deduction that he or she is not entitled to, since child support, unlike alimony, is not deductible from gross income.

## Recapture of Excess Payments

As discussed in Chapter 8, payments made from one spouse to the other as part of a property settlement are neither deductible from the income of the payor spouse nor includible in the income of the recipient spouse. For example, if an agreement calls for a husband to buy out his wife's interest in the marital residence by paying her $300 a month over three years, these payments are "tax-neutral." However, over the years, divorcing couples have often attempted to disguise these payments as alimony, thus allowing the payor to deduct them from gross income.

To deter parties from doing this, the Tax Code now includes "alimony **recapture** provisions." These provisions are triggered when parties engage in the "excess front loading" of support payments in the first years following a divorce. These front-loaded payments serve as a red flag that the parties may be attempting to disguise payments that are in the nature of a property settlement as support payments.

The recapture rules focus on payments that are made in the first three years following divorce. This time frame was chosen because property settlements are usually paid within a relatively short period of time. Excess front-loading of alimony is deemed to occur when payments in year one significantly exceed the average payments in years two and three, and there is more than a $15,000 decrease in payments between years two and three. The excess or disguised payments must then be included in the gross income of the payor, as he or she is deemed to have taken an unwarranted deduction. This amount is thus "recaptured" for tax purposes. The recipient becomes entitled to a corresponding deduction.

## Chapter Summary

Prior to no-fault reform, marriage embodied a clearer notion of permanent commitment and obligation. Upon divorce, if the husband were at fault, the wife had a claim to continued support. After no-fault reform, marriage was often analogized to a partnership, with divorce as the vehicle for making a clean break from the past. In keeping with this partnership model of marriage, property distribution became the preferred approach to adjusting economic rights between spouses. The clean-break approach has been criticized for failing to account for economic disparities between spouses that frequently result from the marital division of labor.

In deciding whether to provide spousal support, judges usually consider multiple factors, with need as a central determinant. In most jurisdictions, fault is no longer a central consideration, and it may not play any role in the support determination; however, marital misconduct continues to operate as a bar to a support award in a few states. This approach promotes flexibility, as judges may assign whatever weight they deem appropriate to individual factors based on the facts of a case; however, such flexibility also contributes to a lack of predictability and coherence. Consequently, a few jurisdictions have implemented numeric guidelines for the computation of amounts, much as in the child support arena, and the ALI recommends shifting to a compensatory focus.

Following no-fault reform, "permanent" alimony fell out of favor, and rehabilitative support, with its emphasis on helping a spouse to become economically self-sufficient, became the preferred approach. However, some courts have reevaluated the appropriateness of rehabilitative support in cases involving long-term marriages where a spouse has little chance of becoming economically self-sufficient. In addition to permanent and rehabilitative support, courts may award lump-sum alimony. Additionally, in professional degree cases, some courts may award reimbursement alimony.

"Permanent" support awards are subject to modification based on changed circumstances and are terminable upon remarriage, death, and (possibly) cohabitation. Some states permit the modification of a rehabilitative award if, despite a good-faith effort, the recipient has not become self-sufficient. Lump-sum payments are generally not modifiable.

The most common enforcement mechanism for failure to pay spousal support is a contempt action. Other enforcement mechanisms—such as wage withholding—are also now available following the expansion of available procedures in the child support arena.

Support payments are not dischargeable in bankruptcy. With respect to taxation, the basic rule is that support payments are includible in the income of the recipient and deductible by the payor, although parties may choose to opt out of this rule. Unallocated payments will be treated as alimony unless reductions correspond to child-related contingencies. Care also must be taken to avoid recapture rules, which may be triggered when property settlement payments are characterized as alimony.

## Key Terms

| | |
|---|---|
| Alimony | Change in Circumstances |
| Spousal Support | Lump-Sum Support |
| Clean Break | Alimony in Gross |
| Economic Self-Sufficiency | Rehabilitative Support |
| Diminished Earning Capacity | Transitional Support |
| Enhanced Earning Capacity | Reimbursement Alimony |
| Permanent Alimony | Modification |
| Opportunity Cost | Contempt |
| Alimony Pendente Lite | Bankruptcy |
| Temporary Alimony | Recapture |

## Review Questions

1. What is the historical origin of our spousal support laws?

2. Historically, what was the relationship between marital fault and alimony?

3. What vision of marriage did the no-fault divorce laws embody?

4. Describe the key way in which the support obligation was reformulated following no-fault reform.

5.  What criticisms have been raised regarding the clean-break approach to spousal support awards?

6.  What kinds of factors do courts consider when making an alimony determination?

7.  What are the advantages of the multifactored approach to support determinations? What are the potential problems?

8.  What approach does the ALI recommend adopting? What other reform has been suggested?

9.  What is permanent alimony? What functions does it serve? Why is permanent alimony not really permanent?

10.  What is lump-sum alimony?

11.  What is rehabilitative alimony? What functions does it serve?

12.  Why have some appeals courts begun to reverse awards of rehabilitative support?

13.  When one spouse earns a professional degree during a marriage, how might this be factored into a spousal support award?

14.  What is the basic rule regarding modification of a permanent support award?

15.  Why is an increase in the cost of living generally not an appropriate ground for a modification?

16.  What are the rules regarding remarriage and the termination of support regarding cohabitation and termination?

17.  What are the rules regarding modification of lump-sum alimony? rehabilitative alimony? reimbursement alimony?

18.  In a civil contempt action, what right does a defendant have if a jail sentence is imposed?

19.  What is the principal defense in a contempt action?

20.  What are the rules regarding the dischargeability of family support obligations in a bankruptcy proceeding?

21. What are the basic rules regarding the taxation of spousal support awards?

22. Explain what happens if reductions in unallocated support payments are tied to child-related contingencies.

23. Explain the concept of recapture.

## **Discussion Questions**

1. If a divorce terminates the marital relationship, should the law recognize any continuing obligations to a former marital partner? Explain your position carefully.

2. If a husband and wife mutually agree that the wife will devote most of her energies to caring for the couple's home and rearing their children, should she be "compensated" for this through a spousal support award if the couple divorces? What kinds of considerations do you think are important here?

3. Despite the gender neutrality of spousal support laws, many people express discomfort at the thought of alimony being awarded to men. Why do you think this is? What is your reaction?

4. Some would argue that we have gone too far in eliminating fault as a consideration in support awards. What role do you think fault should play, if any?

## **Assignments**

1. Locate the statutory provisions that govern the award of spousal support for your state and determine the following:

   • What factors, if any, are enumerated for court consideration?
   • Can marital fault be considered? If yes, under what conditions?
   • Do any of the sections specify what kinds of support can be awarded? If so, identify the available support approaches and describe their statutory features.

2. The lawyer for whom you work has asked you to research and draft an in-house memo regarding the approach that your jurisdiction takes in spousal support cases involving professional degrees.

In approaching this assignment, you should assume that the attorney, al though an expert in family law, has little familiarity with the law in this specific area. Make sure that you find all the relevant cases and analyze them carefully, as the attorney needs this information to prepare for a negotiation session in a pending case. (Note: If your jurisdiction does not have any professional degree cases, rehabilitative alimony cases can be substituted.)

3.  The attorney you are working for does not do much family law and has asked you to help her figure out whether her client, Mary Smith, is likely to be awarded spousal support — and if so, what kind and in what amount. At this point, you do not have all the necessary information about the case, but she wants you to provide her with a reasonable range of options. To do this, you should examine the cases in your jurisdiction and write her an interoffice memo. Try to identify what additional information will be needed in order to determine what, if anything, the client is likely to receive in spousal support.

    Following are the facts as they are presently known: Mary Smith was married to her husband for eight years. They have two minor children, ages six and eight. Ms. Smith is a paralegal with an associate's degree in paralegal studies. She has worked half-time since the birth of her first child. She presently earns $18,000 per year. Her husband, David Smith, is the director of personnel at a large company. He earns $140,000 per year. You can assume that Ms. Smith will have primary physical custody of the children.

4.  Following a lengthy trial, a client of the office you work for was denied spousal support. The attorney on the case is thinking about filing an appeal and has asked you to provide some initial research assessing whether you think the judge made an error of law. He thinks his client is certainly entitled to rehabilitative support and possibly to permanent support. Here are the facts: Tom (your office's client) and his wife Melanie were married for eight years. Melanie was a corporate executive and worked extremely long hours. The couple has no children. They agreed that because Melanie earned so much money, Tom would not work outside of the home, but would maintain their house, pursue his various interests in the arts and music, and serve as a volunteer for various charitable enterprises. In year three of their marriage, Melanie obtained her Ph.D. in Business Administration; she had begun work on this degree the year before the couple married. Tom has an associate's degree in commercial art, although he has never pursued this line of work.

In year five, Tom was diagnosed with multiple sclerosis; so far, the disease has been mild with no impact on his level of functioning.

After locating the cases that you think are relevant, write an informal in-house memorandum to the attorney on the case in which you discuss whether you think the client is entitled to support and why. Be sure to discuss and cite all relevant cases.

5.  Assume you are a legislative aide to a state representative who is considering introducing a bill that would adopt the ALI's compensatory approach to the award of spousal support. The legislator has asked you to read up on this proposal and to prepare a background memo for him in which you explain the ALI approach, including how it differs from your state's present approach to spousal support, and identify at least two key possible advantages and disadvantages of this new approach.

## Cases for Analysis

The following case includes a bit of everything. Among other issues, the court considers the relationship between a division of property and spousal support, the appropriateness of rehabilitative versus permanent support, differential earning capacities, imputed income, and fault. It also pays close attention to the statutory factors for determining spousal support.

### TURNER v. TURNER
**147 Md. App. 350; 809 A.2d 18 (Md. Ct. Spec. App. 2002)**

This appeal arises from two law suits instituted by E. Diane Turner, appellant. . . . One involves the dissolution of the marriage of appellant and Donald Turner, appellee. The other concerns Mr. Turner and the family business, Baltimore Stage Lighting, Inc. ("BSL" or the "Company"), appellee, a close corporation wholly owned by the Turners.

In a sense, the Turners epitomize the rags to riches American dream. At the outset of their lengthy marriage, the Turners were of modest means. Then, they combined their enterprising spirit with creativity and determination to create BSL, a very profitable business.

### I. Factual and Procedural Summary

The divorce case was filed on July 15, 1997, initially on the ground of desertion. It was later amended to allege adultery. The corporate suit . . . contains twelve counts. Ms. Turner alleged . . . that Mr. Turner misappropriated corporate funds to finance his drug habit, for which she sought various remedies in her capacities as stockholder and employee. She also claimed an equitable ownership of a 50% interest in BSL . . .

After thirty-one years of marriage, the couple separated in June 1997. At the time of the trials, they were in their early 50's, and generally in good health.

While working full-time at another job, Mr. Turner devoted his evenings to the development of a lighting business. . . . By 1974, it had grown so much that appellee began to work for it on a full-time basis. The business evolved into BSL . . . Although Mr. Turner became the president of BSL, it is undisputed that Ms. Turner was actively involved in BSL from its inception, and worked full-time in the business for many years. . . .

While both parties devoted considerable time and effort to BSL, appellee was paid a significantly higher salary than appellant. Moreover, Mr. Turner owned 65 shares of BSL stock, while only 10 shares were titled to appellant. Ms. Turner testified that she periodically discussed with appellee her desire to hold title to an amount of BSL stock equal to his. She claimed that appellee assured her that they had an "equal" interest in BSL, and "it didn't make any difference" how the stock was titled. . . .

Ms. Turner recalled that problems in the marriage surfaced in 1995, when she noticed that Mr. Turner was coming home less frequently. By 1996, she suspected that he was involved with drugs and other women. Ms. Turner's concerns were confirmed in January 1997, when she discovered that appellee was using cocaine and had a relationship with another woman. Appellant also learned on June 9, 1997, that appellee had been removing cash from BSL. Soon afterwards, the parties separated . . .

Ms. Turner . . . seeks to review the amount of alimony that was awarded, contending that it is inadequate to meet her needs . . .

Significantly, the court below substantially reduced appellant's alimony from $2000 a week to $2000 per month, expressly because it believed the marital award would generate an income stream for appellant's support; it clearly regarded the marital award as a significant component of appellant's support. . . .

## II. ATTRIBUTION OF INCOME TO APPELLANT

[A]ppellant had "no intention to seek employment, and her only source of revenue has been alimony payments." Moreover, appellant believed she had "paid her dues." Nevertheless, the court imputed earned income to appellant of $35,000. In so doing, Ms. Turner . . . argues that it was grossly unfair for the court "to essentially force [her] to get employment, inevitably as a start-up employee" given the length of the parties' marriage, her age, contributions to BSL, and appellee's egregious conduct.

This contention shall not detain us long. Appellant conflates the court's finding of employability, for which it attributed income to appellant for purposes of the alimony analysis, with the view that the court has forced her to obtain employment outside the home. As we see it, the court's finding that appellant is capable of employment does not mean that she must actually obtain employment. Put another way, appellant has not been driven into the marketplace, as she seems to suggest; whether appellant actually chooses to obtain employment remains entirely up to her. Nevertheless, appellant is clearly employable, given her age, health, work experience, skills, and the absence of minor children in the home. Therefore, the court was more than justified in attributing potential earnings to appellant as a predicate to determining the appropriate amount of alimony.

## III. THE ALIMONY AWARD

Appellant contends that, even if she is capable of earning $35,000 annually . . . [u]nder the circumstances attendant here, she maintains that the alimony award of $2000 a month is "grossly inadequate." Appellant advances several grounds to support her claim. In particular, she suggests that appellee earns substantially more than the court found, and therefore the court erred as to the annual income attributed to him for purposes of making its alimony determination. Further, while recognizing that she received a sizeable marital award, appellant asserts that the award merely "placed [her] long-term assets on a par with that of her husband." Appellant also complains of the inequity in being forced out of BSL, a business that she worked hard to develop, and of having to "start all over," with the attendant difficulty of finding suitable employment, while appellee is allowed to "reap the rewards" of their joint effort. Appellant is particularly disgruntled in light of appellee's conduct, which led to the dissolution of the marriage.

For his part, appellee argues that, in deciding the amount of alimony, the trial court properly considered the division of marital property and the income stream that appellant's share will inevitably generate. Appellee also relies on Blaine v. Blaine, 336 Md. 49, 646 A.2d 413 (1994), for the view that "the formerly dependent spouse ordinarily is not entitled to have his or her standard of living 'keep pace' with that of the other spouse after the divorce, or to share in the other spouse's future accumulations of wealth." Id. at 70. . . .

Thus, our sole focus here concerns the amount of the monthly alimony award. . . . It is well settled that "the 'policy of this State is to limit alimony, where appropriate, to a definite term in order to provide each party with an incentive to become fully self-supporting.'" Digges v. Digges, 126 Md. App. 361, 386, 730 A.2d 202 (quoting Jensen v. Jensen, 103 Md. App. 678, 692, 654 A.2d 914 (1995)), *cert. denied*, 356 Md. 17 (1999); . . . In the seminal case of Tracey v. Tracey, 328 Md. 380, 614 A.2d 590 (1992), the Court of Appeals explained:

> The purpose of alimony is not to provide a lifetime pension, but where practicable to ease the transition for the parties from the joint married state to their new status as single people living apart and independently. Expressed otherwise, alimony's purpose is to provide an opportunity for the recipient spouse to become self-supporting. The concept of alimony as life-long support enabling the dependent spouse to maintain an accustomed standard of living has largely been superseded by the view that the dependent spouse should be required to become self-supporting, even though that might result in a reduced standard of living.

Id. at 391 (citations and quotations omitted).

The party seeking indefinite alimony bears the burden of satisfying the statutory criteria . . . Notably, "self-sufficiency per se does not bar an award of indefinite alimony . . . If a court projects that a party will become self-supporting, subsection (2) provides that, if and when a party makes as much progress toward becoming self-supporting as can reasonably be expected, an award of indefinite alimony may still be justified if the standards of living will be unconscionably disparate. . . .

To the extent that the court found that appellant currently earns $175,000 per year, or even $200,000 a year, the finding was not supported by the evidence. Among other factors, the propriety of the annual alimony award of $24,000 must be measured against the income appellee actually earns . . .

Significantly, in light of the divorce, appellant no longer has to divide or apportion between himself and appellant the salaries previously generated by BSL for the two corporate employees who were also the only owners of the Company . . . Because appellant no longer draws a salary from BSL, that money is now available to appellee, minus any cost of hiring someone to do the work that appellant once performed. Therefore, Mr. Turner can undoubtedly retain for himself a large portion of the $80,000 to $85,000 that appellant, individually, had been paid while the parties were married . . .

[T]he court's finding that appellee earns between $175,000 and $200,000 is between $60,000 and $85,000 less than appellee's actual earnings or earnings capacity over the past several years. Based on the evidence, appellee could reasonably expect to earn about $260,000 annually from BSL. Moreover, as best we can determine, the earnings that the court attributed to appellee did not include the value of the benefits provided to him by BSL, such as a car, insurance, phone, and bonuses. It follows that appellee's current salary of about $260,000 exceeds appellant's imputed income of $35,000 by about $215,000, exclusive of her investment income . . .

Even if we agreed with the court's income calculations for appellee of $175,000 to $200,000, our conclusion as to the court's alimony award would be the same. By the court's own analysis, appellee's income is quite substantial and likely to increase. Whether appellee earns $175,000, $200,000, or $260,000 a year, we believe the court erred and/or abused its discretion with respect to its alimony award. In reaching our conclusion, we rely, in part, on many of the court's own findings. We explain.

As the circuit court found, this was a marriage of considerable length, and it was appellee's "conduct [that] gave rise to the estrangement between the parties." Moreover, the court recognized that during their thirty-one years of marriage, both parties made "significant contributions" and devoted "substantial time and effort" to "the development of BSL from a fledgling company" to a significant corporate entity. The court found that appellant "was equally involved [with appellee] in the development of the business," . . . Nevertheless, . . . Mr. Turner alone retains "the controlling ownership interest" in BSL; only he "remains enmeshed" in BSL, notwithstanding that "BSL has been as much [appellant's] career and a focal point for her interests . . . as it was for her husband." Of particular import, the court expressly found that, as a consequence of the dissolution of the marriage, appellant "lost her career path . . . ," and now has an earning capacity of $35,000 a year.

The parties' lengthy mutual involvement in the lucrative family business distinguishes this case from others that suggest that, after divorce, a dependent spouse cannot expect to "keep pace" with the economic status of the person who was the primary economic provider during the marriage. See, e.g., Blaine, 336 Md. at 70. Although we do not suggest that appellant was necessarily entitled to economic parity upon divorce, we recognize, as did the circuit court, that this is a case in which both parties helped to create BSL, and appellant worked for the Company for almost 25 years. . . . While recognizing the length and value of appellant's efforts, the circuit court noted that Mr. Turner's "career path is set, and will continue to prove lucrative," but appellant has been completely "derailed." In awarding appellant $24,000 a year in alimony, the court was of the view that the "significant assets" with which both parties left the marriage would yield an adequate supplement to appellant's alimony and earned income. As noted, the court awarded appellant 55% of the marital property, which included the value of BSL. Appellee maintains that the marital award is sufficient to rectify any inequity in earnings, despite the fact that he received marital property of almost equal value.

As the trial court found, appellant played a vital role in helping the parties to amass their wealth. Yet, the almost equal division of the value of the Company hardly puts appellant on an equal footing with Mr. Turner. Appellee alone retains control of BSL, not merely 55% of its value, while appellant is no longer employed by the Company. Therefore, appellee alone will continue to benefit from the opportunity to maintain lucrative employment with BSL, annually drawing about a quarter of a million dollars in salary, benefits, and bonuses. In contrast, appellant must now decide whether to confront the uncertainties of the marketplace, in the hope of obtaining new employment that will likely yield an income that is less than half of what appellant earned in her own name while at BSL, and a fraction of what the couple earned collectively. While the parties were married, it was not particularly significant as to how they apportioned their salaries, because both benefited economically from the success of the enterprise that they jointly formed. . . .

As we indicated, [Family Law] § 11-106(b)(3) entitles the court to consider the standard of living that the parties established during the marriage. In order to live as appellant was accustomed during the marriage — a lifestyle that she helped the parties to achieve — the unassailable fact is that appellant must supplement her income by using money generated from investments . . . Recent times have underscored the difficulty of predicting a yield on investments, and the challenges of relying on the stock market as a supplement to support.

Family Law § 11-106(b)(9) provides that, in regard to the alimony determination, the court must consider "the ability of the party from whom alimony is sought to meet" his own needs, along with the needs of appellant. . . . In contrast to appellant, because appellee's career remains intact, and he continues at the helm of a prosperous company, with a salary that far exceeds his expenses, it is unlikely that he will have to use investment income or invade the corpus of investments to meet current expenses. Instead, it appears that Mr. Turner will be in a position to maintain the corpus and reinvest the income generated by his investments, thereby adding to his wealth and widening the disparity in the parties' economic status.

Appellant is the one who has been deprived of an opportunity to continue to enjoy the sizeable economic rewards of working for BSL, while appellee will continue to work there, earning far more than appellant can ever hope to achieve. In light of all the circumstances discussed above, including the length of the marriage, the reasons for and consequences of the parties' estrangement, the wife's contributions to BSL, the couple's respective economic positions and financial resources, the undetermined amount of investment income that appellant can reasonably expect to earn from her share of the marital assets, and the court's reliance on an incorrect amount of earned income for appellee, we conclude that the court erred and abused its discretion in its award of indefinite monthly alimony in the amount of $2000. Therefore, we shall vacate the alimony award and remand for further proceedings.

## QUESTIONS

1. What are the legally significant facts?

2. Why did the lower court reduce the original support amount?

3. Why did this court impute income to the wife?

4. Identify each of the factors that the court considered in making its support award.

5. As identified by the court, what is the purpose of rehabilitative alimony?

6. What statutory factor did the court focus on in deciding to award indefinite support?

7. What factors did the court consider when discussing the gross disparity in the parties' earning capacity?

8. What role do you think considerations of fairness played in the Court's decision?

**Endnotes** ————————————————————————————————————————————

1. *See* Mary O'Connell, Alimony After No-Fault: A Practice in Search of a Theory, 23 N. Eng. L. Rev. 437 (1988).

2. *Id.* at 454-455.

3. *Id.* at 482-491.

4. Doyle v. Doyle, 5 Misc.2d 4, 158 N.Y.S.2d 909, 912 (1957).

5. Lenore J. Weitzman, The Divorce Revolution: The Unexpected Social and Economic Consequences for Women and Children in America 145 (1985).

6. Orr v. Orr, 440 U.S. 268, 288 (1978) (citing United Jewish Orgs. v. Carey, 430 U.S. 144, 173-174 (1977)).

7. *See* Cynthia Lee Starnes, Mothers as Suckers: Pity, Partnership, and Divorce Discourse, 90 Iowa L. Rev. 1513, 1546 (2005).

8. *Id.* at 1520.

9. Robert Kirkman Collins, The Theory of Marital Residues: Applying an Income Adjustment Calculus to the Enigma of Alimony, 24 Harv. Women's L.J. 23, 50 (2001). For a discussion of various reform proposals, *see* Alicia Brokars Kelly, Rehabilitating Partnership Marriage as a Theory of Wealth Distribution at Divorce: In Recognition of a Shared Life, 19 Wis. L.J. 141 (2004); June Carbone, Income Sharing Redefining the Family in Terms of Community, 31 Hous. L. Rev. 359 (1994); Ann L. Estin, Alimony and the Rehabilitation of Family Care, 71 N.C. L. Rev. 721 (1993); Twila L. Perry, Alimony: Race, Privilege, and Dependency in the Search for Theory, 82 Geo. L. Rev. 2481 (1994); Cynthia Starnes, Divorce and the Displaced Homemaker: A Discourse on Playing with Dolls, Partnership Buyouts, and Dissociation Under No-Fault, 60 U. Chi. L. Rev. 67 (1993); Joan Williams, Is Coverture Dead?, 82 Geo. L. Rev. 2227 (1994).

10. *See* Marie Gordon, Spousal Support Guidelines and the American Experience: Moving Beyond Discretion, 19 Can. J. Fam. L. 247 (2002); June Carbone, The Futility of Coherence: The ALI's *Principles of the Law of Family Dissolution*, Compensatory Spousal Payments, 43 J.L. & Fam. Stud. 43 (2002).

11. Gordon, *supra* note 10, at 301 (citing Leslie Herndon Spillane, Spousal Support: The Other Ohio Lottery, 24 Ohio N.U. L. Rev. 281, 318-331 (1998)).

12. Geoffrey C. Hazard, Jr., Forward to the Principles of the Law of Family Dissolution: Analysis and Recommendations, at § 5.02 cmt. a (proposed final draft 1997), *cited in* Carbone, *supra* note 9, at 64-65.

13. Carbone, *supra* note 9, at 65 (citing § 5.05 of the Principles of the Law of Family Dissolution).

14. Gordon, *supra* note 10, at 269.

15. *See* Elizabeth Smith Beninger and Jeanne Wielage Smith, Career Opportunity Cost: A Factor in Spousal Support Determination, 16 Fam. L.Q. 200 (1982); Ralph J. Brown and Linda Lea Viken, Recognition of Homemaker Career Opportunity Costs in Marital Dissolution Cases, 35 S.D. L. Rev. 40 (1990).

16. Avirett v. Avirett, 187 N.J. Super. 380, 383, 454 A.2d 917, 919 (Ch. Div. 1982) (overruled on other grounds). For discussion of this trend, *see* Joan M. Krauskopf, Rehabilitative Alimony: Uses and Abuses of Limited Duration Alimony, 21 Fam. L.Q. 579 (1988).

17. It is worth noting that despite the reluctance of the family courts to engage in this kind of valuation, it is done routinely in personal injury cases when deciding how much to award a plaintiff for lost future earnings.

18. Mahoney v. Mahoney, 91 N.J. 488, 453 A.2d 527, 534-535 (1982).

19. 453 A.2d at 534.

20. *See* Alicia Brokars Kelly, The Marital Partnership Pretense and Career Assets: The Ascendancy of Self over the Marital Community, 81 B.U. L. Rev. 59, 107 (2001).

21. COBRA, Pub. L. No. 99-272, 100 Stat. 82 (29 U.S.C. §§1161 et seq.) (1986). For additional detail, *see* Elizabeth L. Bennett and John W. Goldsborough, Guaranteeing Medical Insurance Coverage After Separation and Divorce, 28 Fam. L.Q. 305 (1994).

22. This section is intended to be a brief, simple introduction to the relationship between support obligations and bankruptcy law. This area of the law, however, is quite complex. For more detail, *see* Shayna M. Steinfeld and Bruce R. Steinfeld, Bankruptcy Strategies, Defensive Moves for Clients and Lawyers, 25 Family Advoc. 43 (2003); Elisa A. Smith, Partial Dischargeability of Property in a Divorce Settlement: A Call for an Equitable Remedy Under Section 523(a)(15) of the Code, 15 Bankr. Dev. J. 87 (1999); Catherine E. Vance, Till Debt Do Us Part: Irreconcilable Differences in the Union of Bankruptcy and Divorce, 45 Buff. L. Rev. 369 (1997).

23. The spousal support rules can be found in §71 of the Internal Revenue Service Code, 26 U.S.C. §71 (1988). Please be aware that these rules are complex and are presented here in a simplified manner. The following sources are a good starting-place for learning more about tax issues that arise in divorce cases: Craig D. Bell, Need-to-Know-Divorce Tax Law for Legal Assistance Officers, 177 Mil. L. Rev. 213 (2003); Duncan A. Peete and William E. Coffee, Tax Consequences of Divorce and Legal Separation, 55 Mont. L. Rev. 359, 366-372 (1994).

# 8 Division of Marital Property

This chapter focuses on the division of **marital property** at divorce. Since no-fault reform, the trend has been to treat the division of property as the primary economic event between divorcing spouses. The rationale for this development is that a division of property, as distinct from an award of alimony, is more in keeping with the modern partnership view of marriage, which seeks to allow both spouses to make a clean break from the past, unencumbered by the failed relationship. In theory, the partnership is fully dissolved after the distribution, leaving the parties free to reconstruct their lives without ongoing financial obligations or entanglements.

Accordingly, in some jurisdictions, spousal support is now an option only where the court determines there is insufficient property to provide for the needs of both spouses. However, as discussed in the previous chapter, this approach has drawn increasing criticism for failing to recognize that a division of property may not account for the fact that spouses may exit from a marriage with very different earning capacities based, at least in part, on the marital allocation of work and family commitments.

## OVERVIEW OF THE TWO MARITAL PROPERTY SYSTEMS

Although the differences have become less pronounced over time, two marital property systems exist in this country. In this section, we compare the community property and the common law approaches to marital property.

### The Community Property Approach

The majority of states looked to English common law when devising rules regarding marital property rights, but eight states, based on patterns of colonial influence and territorial acquisition, looked to Spanish or French civil law and adopted their community property approach. These states are Arizona, California, Idaho, Louisiana, Nevada, New Mexico, Texas, and Washington.[1]

Unlike English common law, civil law did not consider the husband and wife to be a single person (see Chapter 1). A wife's legal existence survived marriage—her identity did not merge into her husband's. Marriage was considered a partnership of two individuals, and married women retained the right to own property. Although recognizing the legal person-hood of married women, civil law did not regard the spouses as equal partners in the marital enterprise. Husbands were given the right of exclusive management and control over community assets, and, in some jurisdictions, they also had this authority over their wives' separate property. This has changed over time, and the rights of management and control are now essentially equal.

Based on this understanding of marriage as a partnership, the **community property approach** assumes that each spouse acts for the benefit of the marital unit rather than for his or her own individual gain. The contribution of each spouse to the marriage, including domestic and child-rearing contributions, is recognized, entitling each spouse to share in the financial gains of the marriage. This is accomplished by giving both parties an immediate, vested interest in one-half of the property acquired during the marriage through the efforts of either spouse or the expenditure of marital funds. Upon divorce, this community property is subject to division based on a theory of co-ownership without regard to financial contribution. Although most community property states initially divided property on an equal basis, many now use an equitable division standard, which (as developed below) allows a court to make an unequal distribution based on considerations of fairness.[2]

Property that is not acquired through the expenditure of marital efforts or funds is considered separate property and belongs to the acquiring spouse rather than to the community. Neither spouse acquires rights in the other's separate property because it stands apart from the marital enterprise. Typically, separate property includes assets brought into the marriage, gifts and inheritances acquired by one spouse during the marriage, and property acquired in exchange for separate property. At divorce, each spouse takes his or her separate property, although in a few states, courts may have limited authority to transfer separate property in cases of extreme hardship. The distinction between separate and community property is easy to state; however, in practice, navigating the boundaries between the two can be difficult (see Classification of Property below).

## The Common Law Approach

### Doctrinal Underpinnings

As discussed in Chapter 1, the common law vision of the marital relationship assumed the loss of a wife's legal identity. She lost the right to own personal property or control any real property to which she had title. The common law approach to marital property rights flowed directly from this understanding of the marital relationship. Here, there was no community — there was simply the husband who owned all of the property except for his wife's realty, which he controlled. Accordingly, there was no notion of a marital enterprise representing the cumulative efforts of both spouses.

Even as married women gradually acquired property rights through the passage of the Married Women's Property Acts, the concept of marital community did not take hold in the common law states. Instead, traditional common law property concepts, which extolled the virtues of individual rights, were extended to married women.[3] Property was his or hers depending on who supplied the purchase funds — which in reality meant that it was mostly his. In contrast to the community property states, the nonfinancial contributions of a homemaker spouse did not give rise to ownership rights.

Until fairly recently, most common law states divided property according to **title**. This meant that the spouse who owned an asset was entitled to it at divorce. Mitigating the potential harshness of this approach, a number of courts developed the **special equity** rule, under which a spouse who had made a financial contribution to property titled in the name of the other could be granted an equitable interest in the asset, thus entitling her or him to a share at divorce. Some courts expanded this rule to provide rights based on the nonfinancial contributions of a homemaker spouse. Begun as an exception, this rule helped pave the way for the shift from a title-based approach to the division of marital property to the equitable distribution rules now in effect in all common law states.

### Equitable Distribution

No-fault divorce also helped to usher in changes in the rules of property distribution. All common law states now divide marital property according to **equitable distribution** principles rather than title. Influenced by the sharing principles long recognized in community property states, the equitable distribution approach acknowledges that the accumulation of marital assets derives from the efforts of both spouses. Accordingly, at divorce, a spouse's nonfinancial contributions to the well-being of a household will give rise to an enforceable property interest in accumulated assets.

Following the community property approach, the majority of equitable distribution jurisdictions classify property at divorce as either marital or separate. This is often referred to as the **dual property** approach because a formal distinction is made between the two categories of assets. The distributive authority of the courts is restricted to the marital estate, although a few states have created a limited exception to this rule and permit distribution of separate property in cases of hardship. The classifying principle is essentially the same as in the community property states. Property acquired during the marriage through the efforts of either spouse or the expenditure of marital funds is considered marital because it derives from the contribution each is credited with making to the partnership. **Separate property** is that which is unrelated to this joint undertaking and generally includes property owned prior to marriage, gifts, inheritances, and property acquired in exchange for separate property.

In contrast to the dual property approach, a minority of states have adopted what is known as an "**all property**" approach. Here, no formal distinction is made between separate and marital property, and courts are empowered to distribute all assets, regardless of when and how they were acquired. This is sometimes referred to as the "hotchpot of assets" approach. It should be noted, however, that the informal practice among attorneys in all-property states when negotiating a settlement may be to disregard property that would be considered separate in a community or dual property state, or to allocate it separately from the balance of the marital estate in order to give greater weight to its "separate" identity.

With the adoption of equitable distribution laws, the difference between common law and community property states has become less pronounced, although the all-property approach is exclusively identified with common law states. Accordingly, this chapter will focus on general legal concepts and will not distinguish between the two approaches unless relevant; however, you should bear in mind that regardless of which approach is followed, each state has its own rules and standards.

Before proceeding, however, one essential difference should be noted. In community property states, the ownership interest of each spouse attaches at the time of property acquisition. Consequently, co-ownership rights come into being during the marriage; at the time of divorce, the court is dividing property that is already jointly owned by the spouses. In contrast, in common law states, each spouse holds the property acquired during the marriage as his or her own, and the ownership interest of the nonacquiring spouse does not attach until the time of divorce. As a result, when property is divided, a spouse may resent that something that "belongs" to him or her is being taken away and given to the other spouse as a consequence of the divorce rather than recognizing that the accumulated assets represent the cumulative efforts of both parties.

## THE PROPERTY DISTRIBUTION PROCESS

The process of dividing property between divorcing spouses can be broken down into four steps:

1. *Defining property.* A preliminary issue in some cases is whether a particular asset falls within the definition of the term "property"; if it falls outside the definition, the asset is not subject to distribution.
2. *Classification.* Except in all-property states, property must be classified as either marital or separate.[4]
3. *Valuation.* The value of each asset must be determined.
4. *Distribution.* The assets must be allocated in accordance with the applicable legal standard.

Before we look at these four steps, a few general points should be considered. First, in many cases, especially where the parties have few assets, the division of property is relatively simple, and couples often figure this out themselves without involving their attorneys or applying formal legal principles. A couple may simply divide their belongings based on need or preference. Of course, an attorney should ensure that a client understands that without a more formal process, there is no way of knowing whether the client is getting the share of assets that he or she may legally be entitled to.

Second, when couples do fight about property, the fight is often rooted in the emotional undertow of divorce. An object may be treasured for its sentimental meaning or it may have tremendous symbolic importance for one or both parties. For example, if your client is fighting fiercely for the old brown sofa, it may have become the symbolic locus of his or her anger and he or she may not really care about the sofa itself. Alternatively, the client may believe it is worth fighting for based on its sentimental worth — perhaps it was the couple's first purchase, thus standing as a reminder of happier times. If you are involved in helping to resolve a property dispute, it is important to be aware of these potential dynamics so you can help a client sort out what is going on so that needless time, money, and emotional energy is not spent pursuing an object for the wrong reason.

Third, when a property dispute does involve legal considerations, such as classification or valuation, the governing rules are often complex and variable; for example, there are multiple approaches to valuing a closely held corporation, which differ from the multiple approaches to valuing pension plans or commodity futures. Expert witnesses are often required to resolve the complex legal and accounting issues.

## Defining Property

Most cases do not involve definitional questions. During the marriage, couples accumulate items such as furniture, jewelry, cars, and household goods, which are so clearly property that this definitional step is bypassed without any thought to the matter. However, there are times when it is not clear whether a particular item, such as the goodwill of a professional practice or an unvested pension, is in fact property.

Since the enactment of equitable distribution laws and increased emphasis on the division of property, these definitional questions have assumed increasing importance, and this is an ever developing and expanding area of the law. When working on a case, you must carefully consider all possible property interests. This means there is much room for creative legal thinking. Who knows? Given the right opportunity, you may "discover" a new form of property!

### The Tangible/Intangible Distinction

Traditionally, property was defined as a tangible item over which an individual could exercise absolute dominion and control. **Tangible property** is easy to identify, as it is what we normally think of as property — it has a physical presence and can be touched, seen, and transferred from one person to another.

Over time, the definition of property has expanded. Moving beyond physical presence, property is now usually described in relational terms as the "bundle of rights" a person has in something. In essence the concept has been "dephysicalized,"[5] and thus, **intangible assets** — assets that lack a physical presence and cannot be ascertained by the senses — may well come within the concept of property. Intangible assets often involve the right to something, such as the future right to participate in a pension plan or, as evidenced by a stock certificate, the right to participate in the management of a corporation and receive a proportional share of earnings.

Common examples of intangible assets include the goodwill of a business, a legal claim, stocks, bonds, and pension plans.

Few property distribution statutes provide a definition of the term *property*, so courts have had to struggle with the concept. Some jurisdictions are expansive and consider a broad array of intangibles to be property. Other jurisdictions are more restrictive and tend to exclude intangibles that lack traditional property attributes. Accordingly, if an intangible asset cannot easily be transferred to another person, is difficult to value, and cannot be owned jointly, a court in a restrictive jurisdiction is likely to determine that it is not property. Thus, for example, in comparing a professional degree (see Chapter 7) with a car, one can see how such a court might refuse to consider it property. Unlike the car, the degree cannot be transferred or left to someone as an inheritance, its worth is much harder to determine, and it cannot be jointly owned. Underlying these distinctions—and potentially significant to the courts—is that many of these intangibles, such as a degree or goodwill, seem personally connected to the efforts of the holder.

Most definitional battles focus on whether or not an intangible interest should be treated as property. The outcome can have significant consequences for the economic future of the divorcing spouses because intangibles, such as a pension or the goodwill of a business, may be very valuable. Before looking at these definitional disputes more closely, however, we turn to a question that has recently received considerable attention: At the time of divorce, how should disputes over the family pet be resolved? Should a pet be treated as an item of property or as a member of the household?

### Divorce and the Family Pet

According to established legal doctrine, pets (now also referred to "companion animals") are considered to be the property of their owners. As such, upon divorce, the determination of a pet's future is controlled by property distribution principles. Thus, for example, a dog might be awarded to the party who came into the marriage with the pet, rather than to the party who had been the pet's primary caretaker over the course of the marriage.

Over the past twenty years or so, there has been an increasing effort to move pets out of the property category and to characterize them more as family members. A corollary of this shift would be a reclassification of the related human from "owner" to "guardian." Proponents argue that the "recharacterization of the relationship from 'owner and pet' to 'guardian and companion animal' honors the fact that" companion animals are sentient and emotional beings "and that these relationships are of a deep and enduring nature.[6] Some commentators have even asserted that" [t]he relationship between an animal guardian and a companion animal is similar to a parent and child."[7] Accordingly, animal rights proponents argue that disputes between divorcing spouses over a pet should be treated as a custody dispute rather than as a disagreement over the allocation of marital assets, and that a standard akin to the" best interest of the companion animal "should be employed to determine custody and visitation rights. To date, this approach has not been widely accepted.

In a 1995 Florida divorce case, the parties were able to agree on all issues, except for what was to happen with their dog. After a hearing, the trial court awarded possession of the dog to the husband and gave the wife visitation rights on alternate weekends and every other Christmas. Both parties filed motions objecting to this decision. The husband contested the award of visitation rights, claiming that the dog was a premarital asset and thus belonged solely to him, and the wife sought a transfer of custody claiming that the husband refused to comply with the visitation order. The appeals court concluded that the trial court had erred in granting visitation rights to the wife because under Florida law, a dog is personal property and "[t]here is no authority which provides for a trial court to grant custody or visitation pertaining to personal property."[8] As a policy matter, the court further stated: "Determinations as to custody and visitation lead to continuing enforcement and supervision problems (as evidenced by the proceedings in the instant case). Our courts are overwhelmed with the supervision of custody, visitation, and support matters related to the protection of our children. We cannot undertake the same responsibility as to animals."[9]

The Pennsylvania appeals court reached a similar result. In this case, a divorcing couple entered into an agreement setting out custody and visitation arrangements for their dog, Barney. Following a dispute over visitation, the husband (appellant) sought to enforce the agreement; however, the court refused to recognize the agreement, stating:

> In seeking "shared custody" and a "visitation" arrangement, Appellant appears to treat Barney, a dog, as a child. Despite the status owners bestow on their pets, Pennsylvania law considers dogs to be personal property . . . Appellant, however, overlooks the fact that any terms set forth in the Agreement are void to the extent that they attempt to award custodial visitation with or shared custody of personal property. . . . As the trial court aptly noted, Appellant is seeking an arrangement analogous, in law, to a visitation schedule for a table or a lamp.[10]

Although the "pet as property" approach remains the unquestioned dominant paradigm in divorce cases, those hoping for a more "animal-centered" approach will take heart from a recent New York decision involving a dispute over a cat between two roommates. Here the original "owner" of the cat "Lovey" moved out of the apartment she had lived in with her cat for four years, leaving her roommate to care for the cat. She later sought the return of the cat, thus triggering a legal battle over who had the right to the cat. Moving away from an owner-ship approach, the court, aware of "the cherished status accorded to pets in our society,"[11] awarded the cat to the roommate based on what one might identify as a "best interests" standard, stating that "we think it best for all concerned that, given his limited life expectancy, Lovey, who is now almost ten years old, remain where he has lived, prospered, loved and been loved for the past four years."[12] It remains to be seen whether or not courts begin to shift from a property to a custody model in the often contentious disputes over beloved family pets/companionship animals.

### Unvested Pensions, Accrued Leave Time, and Professional Goodwill: Are They Property?

In this section, we look at three intangible assets that have posed definitional difficulties for the courts—unvested pensions, accrued vacation and sick leave time, and professional goodwill. These assets have been selected because they raise recurring issues that are central to the defini-tional process. Before proceeding, it should be noted that sometimes the question we are considering here—whether an intangible asset is property or not—is framed as an inquiry into whether the asset should be consid-ered a separate rather than a marital asset because of its special characteristics, such as that it is personal to the holder, and nontransferable. Regardless of which approach is used, the relevant considerations are quite similar—for example, professional goodwill (discussed below) may be deemed not property because it is personal to the holder, or it may be deemed separate property for the same reason.

**Unvested Pensions. Pensions** are an important job-related benefit. They are a form of deferred compensation: An employee earns the right to the benefit in the present, but realization of the benefit is deferred until retirement or some other future date after the employee has left his or her job. Some pension plans are funded solely by employer contributions; others are funded solely by employee contributions; and some are funded by a combination of employer and employee contributions.

An individual's interest in his or her pension is either vested or un-vested.[13] When rights are vested, an employee does not forfeit retirement benefits when he or she leaves the place of employment prior to retirement. Vesting usually occurs after an employee has worked for an employer for a specified number of years. In contrast, if an employee who is not vested leaves the job, he or she forfeits the retirement benefits. The right to retirement benefits is thus contingent on continued employment through the vesting period.

The clear trend is to recognize both vested and unvested pensions as a property interest. However, there has been considerable debate over unvested pensions, and some jurisdictions continue to regard them as an expectancy interest rather than as a form of property because the right to benefits is contingent upon continued employment through the vesting period, which may or may not take place. In general, an expectancy is not considered a form of property because of its uncertain, conditional nature.

Other jurisdictions give greater weight to a spouse's interest in an unvested pension because, although presently uncertain, the right to benefits will become legally enforceable upon the happening of a future contingency—fulfillment of the time requirement. This greater certainty serves to distinguish an interest in an unvested pension from a true expectancy, such as the hope of being named a beneficiary in a will, which is completely speculative, and supports treating unvested pensions as property.

In defining unvested pensions as property, many jurisdictions have been influenced by equitable considerations. A pension is often a couple's most valuable asset, and exclusion based on a technical distinction would downgrade the contribution of a homemaker spouse to the marital enterprise because, although both partners contributed to the marriage, only the employed spouse would enjoy retirement benefits. Another fairness consideration is that the right, although contingent, is acquired during the marriage. (See below regarding distribution of pensions.)

**Accrued Vacation and Sick Leave Time.** Many employers permit their employees to accumulate unused sick and vacation time. Upon retirement, an employee may be paid the value of this accrued time. The question has arisen in a number of cases as to whether this accrued time is a marital asset, capable of valuation and division upon divorce. Although the courts that have considered this issue are divided, the majority approach is toward inclusion.

In seeking to determine whether accrued leave time is an asset, many courts have framed it as a question of whether this time is an alternative form of wages and thus not property, or more akin to deferred compensation, such as a pension, and thus includible as property. In a recent Kentucky Court of Appeals decision, the court concluded that accrued leave time was "less tangible, more difficult to value, and more personal than pension and retirement benefits," and therefore should not be classified as property.[14]

The court found the reasoning of an earlier decision from Maryland to be persuasive:

> We just are not persuaded that accrued holiday and vacation entitlement is the same as a pension or retirement benefit, a form of deferred compensation; since it replaces wages on days when the worker does not work, it is really only an alternative form of wages. . . . It need not be liquidated by the payment of cash; it may be, and often is, dissipated when the person entitled to do so takes vacation or holiday time. Thus, it is far from as tangible as, and much more difficult to value, not to mention and more personal than pension and retirement benefits.[15]

In contrast, the New Mexico appeals court found that the value of accumulated hours comes within the definition of marital property, much like other employee benefits:

> The essence of leave is that it is a benefit of employment and . . . it has independent value. If taken during marriage, leave time devoted to vacation or to recovery from illness benefits the community. If not taken, leave that accumulates will be available to benefit the community in the future. If the community ends, the accumulated leave attaches to the employee. Unless some equitable distribution is made or the asset is divided upon dissolution of marriage, the employees take the full community asset.[16]

Unlike other courts that have considered this issue, the New Mexico court was more concerned with fairness than with deciding if accrued time is more like wages or more like deferred compensation. The court continued on to state that there was no policy reason why the husband should exit the marriage with the full value of the accumulated leave time given that it resulted from marital effort. Thus, as we saw above with respect to unvested pensions, considerations of fairness may influence the definitional process.

**Goodwill of a Professional Practice. Goodwill** is an intangible asset that is most commonly identified with commercial businesses. It can be defined generally as a business's good reputation in the community that generates the expectation of continued future patronage. Put another way, it is the value of a business that "exceeds the combined value of the net assets" of that business.[17] Because it can readily be valued and transferred for consideration if the business is sold, there is little question that the goodwill of a business is an intangible property interest that is subject to distribution upon divorce.

There is less agreement, however, where the goodwill of a professional practice is involved. A minority of jurisdictions do not regard the goodwill of a professional practice as property. Underlying this exclusion is the belief that the goodwill attaches to the individual professionals in the practice rather than to the practice itself. So attached, **professional goodwill** is both nontransferable and hard to value; moreover, even if a value could be assigned, it would be too tied to the vagaries of the individual's career path to have real meaning. Thus lacking these essential attributes of property—transferability and amenability to valuation—this minority of jurisdictions regard professional goodwill more like future earning capacity, which can be considered in calculating child support, rather than as a marital asset. At the other end of the spectrum, a few jurisdictions take the view that professional goodwill attaches to the practice itself rather than to the individual partners, and thus it is fully included in the marital estate.

Most states, however, take an in-between position and seek to distinguish between "enterprise" and "personal" goodwill. Here, goodwill that is attributable to the reputation of an individual is not considered property because, as noted above, it cannot be readily valued or transferred, whereas goodwill that is attributable to the reputation of the business itself is considered part of the marital estate and subject to division at the time of divorce. As with unvested pensions, some courts that treat personal professional goodwill as an intangible asset may also be influenced by the fact that the goodwill, although securing future benefits, is built up during the marriage, thus making exclusion unfair.

## Classification of Property

The classification of property as marital or separate is a crucial step in both common law dual property and community property states because it determines the pool of assets that is subject to division. (Although, in a few states, courts can reach even separate property in cases of hardship.) In theory, classification is not relevant in all-property states; however, in practice, classification principles may influence how attorneys and possibly judges approach the distribution of property.

### Defining Marital and Separate Property

In most states, marital and separate property are defined in relationship to one another: One is what the other is not. Frequently, a statute will define marital property as all property acquired during the marriage, except for that which is considered separate. Separate property is then specifically defined, and almost always includes property owned at the time of marriage, gifts, inheritances, and items received in exchange for separate property. Some statutes also identify specific assets, such as appreciation on separate property, unvested pensions, and professional licenses, as coming within the definition of separate property. Again, the rationale underlying the distinction between marital and separate property is that marital accumulations derive from the overall contribution of both spouses to the marriage, regardless of which spouse actually paid for any particular item, whereas separate assets do not derive from the marital efforts of either spouse and thus stand apart from the marriage. However, as discussed below in the section on transmutation, the initial characterization of an asset may change over time. Classification also can be influenced by presumptions, and in most states it is presumed that all property owned by the spouse at the time of divorce is marital. This places the burden of proof on the party who is claiming that a particular asset is separate property, and he or she must produce sufficient evidence to rebut the presumption, or the asset will be considered marital and subject to division.

### The Significance of Timing

A central characteristic of marital property is that it is acquired during the marriage. As a general rule, **premarital acquisitions**, property that a spouse comes into the marriage with, remain his or her separate property. This distinction usually is straightforward, but a few situations require elaboration.

**Determining the Time of Acquisition.** If a person purchases an asset, such as a car, before getting married and then makes payments on it after the marriage, is the car a premarital or a marital acquisition? One approach known as the **inception of title rule** fixes the time of acquisition at the time of initial purchase because this is when title or the right to title is obtained. Once set, the characterization cannot be changed, and postmarital contributions have no impact on the classification. Here, property is a unitary concept and value cannot be apportioned between the marital and the separate estates, although the nonowner spouse might be entitled to some reimbursement for his or her contribution.

Most jurisdictions have rejected this approach as too formalistic and incompatible with sharing principles because it focuses on title to the exclusion of contribution. The preferred approach to determining the time of acquisition is the **source of funds rule**. Here, acquisition is seen as a dynamic process that unfolds over time as payment is made; one might say that each payment effectuates a partial acquisition. Accordingly, an asset can be both marital and separate, and its value apportioned between the two estates in proportion to contribution.

A brief example will demonstrate the difference between these approaches. Let's say that in 2001, Nekeisha purchases an oil painting for $12,000. She pays $8,000 in cash and takes out a loan to pay the balance.

One month later, she marries Victor, and payments on the loan are made from their newly established joint checking account. In year three, the loan is paid off. Unfortunately, in year four, the couple divorces.

Under the inception of title rule, the entire value of the painting would be the separate property of Nekeisha because she acquired title or the right to title before the marriage, although Victor may be entitled to reimbursement. Under the source of funds rule, the value of the painting would be apportioned between Nekeisha's separate estate and the marital estate in the amounts of $8,000 and $4,000 respectively, thus adding to the total worth of marital assets. (Note that this example assumed the painting did not increase in value during the marriage. Appreciation raises other issues, which are discussed below.)

**Property Acquired in Contemplation of Marriage or During Cohabitation.** Usually there is no doubt that property owned by a person at the time of marriage is separate. However, sometimes purchases may be made in contemplation of marriage. In this situation, some jurisdictions have stretched statutory categories and will treat this property as marital based on the parties' intent to use it as such. Here, intent displaces the timing of acquisition as the controlling factor.

A related question is how property acquired during a period of pre-marital cohabitation will be treated. Reluctant to treat cohabitation as the legal equivalent of marriage, most courts do not consider assets acquired during a period of cohabitation as marital. However, if, while cohabiting, property is purchased in contemplation of marriage, it might come within the above rule and be treated as marital based on the parties' intent rather than on the fact of cohabitation.

**Fixing a Cut-Off Point for Marital Acquisitions.** Timing questions that can influence classification also arise at the other end of the relationship—specifically, at what point in the dissolution process will acquired assets no longer be considered marital? Strictly speaking, a husband and wife remain legally married until a final decree of divorce is entered; thus, property that is acquired up until this moment in time are technically marital. However, motivated by practical and policy considerations, most jurisdictions use an earlier cut-off point after which time property that is acquired is no longer considered marital despite the continuation of the legal relationship.

Signaling the effective end of the marital partnership, common cut-off points include the date of legal separation, the initiation of a permanent separation, or the filing of a dissolution action. Clearly, once spouses have gone their separate ways, the theoretical justification for pooling based on mutual contribution and effort no longer exists.

Practical problems may arise where the cut-off point is the date of permanent separation. Frequently, a separation that is intended to be permanent is followed by a series of contacts, some or all of which may rise to the level of reconciliation. This makes it difficult to fix the date of separation, particularly if the spouses disagree about the meaning and impact of these post-separation contacts, which makes it difficult to classify property accumulated during these intervals of parting and coming together.

### *Looking Beyond Definitions: The Complexities of Classification*

Although the distinction between marital and separate property is easy to state, applying it can be difficult. This section discusses some situations that present difficult classification issues.

**Gifts.** As a general matter, a **gift** is a voluntary transfer of property made with donative intent, meaning that the gift-giver (donor) simply wishes to give the recipient something without requiring anything in exchange. For a gift to be effective, the transfer must be complete — the donor must fully relinquish all vestiges of ownership and control.

In the divorce context, a gift is generally classified as separate property, as it is not acquired through the effort of either spouse. Sometimes, however, a transfer that appears to be a gift is really not, such as when the donor, rather than being motivated by donative intent, is providing compensation for past or future services. Community property jurisdictions have long distinguished between gifts made with true donative intent and those that are really a form of compensation, treating the latter as marital property because the acquisition is tied to the recipient's efforts. This distinction is now also made in some common law dual property jurisdictions.

For example, assume that Bob and Karen are married. One day Karen's great-aunt Ernestine gives her a beautiful oil painting that is worth a lot of money. At first glance, classification appears obvious: The painting is a gift to Karen and is thus her separate property. However, what happens if the next time Bob and Karen visit Ernestine, she mentions that she gave the painting to Karen as a way of thanking her for taking such good care of her during her last illness? Now, arguably, if the couple were to divorce, Bob could argue that the painting should be classified as marital property because it was not given to Karen as a gift but as a form of compensation and thus was acquired through the expenditure of marital efforts.

What if instead of being from a third party, the gift is from one spouse to another? Should these be treated in the same manner? What if the gift was purchased from marital funds — should the source of contribution or the nature of the exchange control the classification?

In some states, interspousal gifts have been exempted from the general characterization of gifts as separate property by either statute or judicial decision, with some of these states limiting the exclusion to gifts that were purchased with marital funds. The underlying rationale here is that unlike third-party gifts, interspousal gifts derive from partnership efforts. In contrast, other jurisdictions focus on the gift aspect of the transaction, rather than on the source of funds. These courts treat completed inter-spousal gifts in the same manner as third-party gifts, even where purchased with marital funds.

**Appreciation of Separate Property.** Difficult classification issues can arise in situations where separate property has increased in value over the course of the marriage. One approach is to tie the classification of the **appreciation** to the classification of the underlying asset. This means that if the asset is characterized as separate, any appreciation in value — even if it occurred during the marriage — will also be classified as separate. This approach is similar to the previously discussed inception of title rule that fixes ownership at the time of acquisition.

Let's return to Nekeisha and the oil painting she purchased for $12,000 one month before her marriage to Victor. If the painting increased in value during the marriage, under this approach the entire increase would be classified as separate based on the classification of the underlying asset. Note that any reimbursement due Victor would not capture the value of this increase.

As with the inception of title rule, most jurisdictions have rejected this approach as too rigid and not in keeping with contemporary sharing principles. The preferred approach is to classify appreciation based on the reason for the increase. If the increase is unrelated to spousal efforts and is due to causes such as inflation or market conditions, it is usually considered the separate property of the spouse who owns the asset. This kind of increase is often referred to as *passive appreciation*. If instead the gain is due to the investment of marital funds or efforts, it is usually considered marital. This kind of increase is often referred to as *active appreciation*. If the gain is attributable to both passive and active forces, it can be apportioned between the separate and marital estates.[18]

**Property Received in Exchange for Separate Property.** What happens if a spouse exchanges or sells separate property during the marriage? Most jurisdictions treat property that is received in exchange for separate property as separate: The exchange is regarded as an alteration in the form of the asset, which leaves its underlying separate nature intact.

Generally, based on the presumption that all property owned at the time of divorce is marital, the party seeking to segregate an asset from the marital estate has the burden of proving its separate identity. Where exchanged property is involved, segregation requires **tracing** the asset directly back to a separate source. Tracing can be simple, such as where one painting has been exchanged for another, or it can be complex, such as where there have been successive exchanges or where funds from an account containing separate and marital funds have been used. If the tracing fails, and the separate identity of the asset cannot be established, it will be treated as marital. As discussed below, this result is transmutation by commingling.[19]

**The Nature of the Asset.** Classification difficulties also may be triggered by specific types of property. As noted above, these inquiries are sometimes framed as definitional questions and sometimes as classification ones. Personal injury awards are a good example of an interest that poses difficult classification issues as well as presenting an underlying definitional question. Similar issues are raised when other damages awards, such as disability or workers' compensation benefits, are involved.[20]

Assuming, for the sake of discussion, that we are in a jurisdiction that considers a personal injury award to be property, the classification trend is to divide the award into component parts and allocate them between the separate and marital estates in accordance with general classification principles. Using this approach, most states will classify the portion of the award attributable to lost wages and medical expenses as marital property because it compensates for economic loss incurred during the marriage.[21] The portion of the award attributable to the pain and suffering of the injured spouse is then classified as separate property because it is so intimately connected to the injured spouse that it is deemed to exist apart from the marriage. If the award also compensates the injured person for future economic losses, this portion of the award usually would be classified as separate because the other spouse has no recognized interest in these future rights.

### Transmutation

Our final classification topic is transmutation. **Transmutation** refers to a post-acquisition change in an asset's classification from separate to marital or from marital to separate, although almost all transmutation cases involve the reclassification of separate assets. Transmutation can occur in four ways: (1) by agreement, (2) by joint titling, (3) by commingling, and (4) by use.

**Transmutation by Agreement.** The simplest way that transmutation can occur is where the parties agree to recharacterize property. Statutes in many community property states and a few common law jurisdictions specifically authorize this result, although the term "transmutation" is usually not used. In the absence of express authority, most courts will uphold an agreement between spouses to recharacterize property. The agreement may need to be in writing and conform to whatever requirements the particular jurisdiction imposes on marital agreements.

**Transmutation by Joint Titling.** Property may be transmuted if a spouse places separate property or property purchased with separate funds in joint name — for example, where one spouse purchases a car with inherited funds and then takes title in both names. In most jurisdictions, joint titling triggers a rebuttable presumption that the separate asset has transmuted into a marital one because the titling demonstrates an intent to bestow a benefit on the marital estate. To rebut the presumption, a spouse may be able to show that the intent of joint titling was not to confer a benefit upon the marital estate but instead was done for estate planning purposes or to satisfy the requirements of a lender or because of pressure from his or her spouse. If the presumption is rebutted, the property will not transmute but rather will retain its original characterization as separate property.

**Transmutation by Commingling.** The most common way for property to transmute is by commingling. When separate property has been mixed with marital property, it will be treated as marital unless the party wishing to segregate the asset can establish its separate identity. Here the failure of a party to keep assets separate may be regarded as evidence of an intent to benefit the marital estate. The party wishing to claim an asset as separate must be able to "uncommingle" the mass of property. As with exchanged property, this is done by tracing. If the separate identity of the asset cannot be established with sufficient certainty, the tracing fails and the property is deemed to have transmuted by commingling.

**Transmutation by Use.** A few jurisdictions allow transmutation by use. For example, if a spouse permits the other to use his or her separately owned car on a regular basis, this use could transmute the car into a marital asset. This approach has been both praised for promoting sharing principles and criticized as an encroachment on individual property rights that effectively punishes a spouse for his or her generosity.[22] Depending on the situation, the same result might also be accomplished by reference to the commingling doctrine.

## Valuation

Before property can be divided between spouses, marital assets need to be valued. Valuation involves determining the worth of the assets so that an appropriate distribution can be effectuated. Where an equitable as distinct from an equal distribution standard is used, separate assets also may need to be valued, as the value and nature of this estate may influence the allocation of marital property. For example, if one spouse has considerable separate assets, it may be fair to give the other spouse a greater share of the marital estate (see Distribution below).

As a practical matter where property issues are resolved by agreement rather than at trial, parties often divide up their belongings without having them valued, as **valuation** can be both expensive and time consuming. Of course, this means that there is no real way of knowing whether the settlement is fair, especially if potentially valuable assets are involved. In this situation, attorneys usually include a provision in the separation agreement in which the parties acknowledge that they have knowingly and willingly dispensed with a valuation and have divided their property without full knowledge of its worth.

When property issues are resolved at trial, it can be a reversible error for the court to divide property without first determining value. Although valuation may be framed as the court's responsibility, in many jurisdictions, a party who fails to present evidence of value is deemed to have waived his or her right of appeal on this issue.

### Valuation Methods

Few statutes specify how assets should be valued, and a wide range of approaches are generally acceptable. When a trial court is presented with competing valuation methods, it has relative freedom to select among the approaches or to combine them to arrive at its own value.

A common valuation approach is to determine an asset's fair market value. **Fair market value** is generally described as the price a willing buyer would pay to a willing seller where neither party is under any compulsion to buy or sell. Establishing this price requires detailed knowledge of the asset as well as the specific market conditions that would influence transferability. Although common, the fair market value approach is far from universal and would not be appropriate where, for example, a closely held corporation or a pension is involved, as neither has a readily determinable market value.[23]

### The Role of Experts

The valuation of assets is generally outside the expertise of lawyers and requires the use of experts. As a general rule, there is no such thing as an all-purpose valuation expert. Instead, an expert must be carefully selected based on his or her specialized knowledge. For example, an accountant may be the most appropriate person to value a professional corporation but would not be the best choice where a rare stamp collection is involved; this would require the services of a rare stamp appraiser. Where real estate is involved, a real estate broker or appraiser would be appropriate, but if the present value of a pension needs to be determined, the services of an actuary would be required as this entails an assessment of how future risks impact the value of the employee spouse's interest.

Clearly, in any single case, the valuation process may require more than one expert. This can greatly increase the time and expense of a divorce proceeding and can significantly disadvantage the spouse with less income, who may lose the battle of the experts. To address this problem, some courts, upon request, may order one spouse to pay the costs of the other's experts or may appoint its own expert and order one party to pay all or most of the costs. The expense and time involved in hiring experts may encourage couples to settle rather than litigate; alternatively, it may encourage the financially more secure spouse to litigate vigorously in order to outdo the other.

### Time of Valuation

An important valuation issue is when value should be determined. Possible dates include time of (1) separation, (2) trial, or (3) entry of the decree of dissolution. Traditionally, most jurisdictions selected a single valuation time and used it in all cases. However, the trend is toward greater flexibility, with a preference for determining value as close to the date of distribution as possible. However, most courts will readily depart from this approach where required by considerations of fairness. For example, if after separation one party dissipates assets, the court may use the date of separation for valuation purposes. This date might also be used if an asset has appreciated in value based on the post-separation efforts of one spouse.

## Distribution

After property has been classified as marital or separate and valued, the actual distribution must be effectuated. This final step is the focus of this section.

### The Standard for Division: Equal or Equitable?

When dividing property, the majority of states use an *equitable distribution standard*, which directs courts to divide the property in a manner that is described as fair, just, or equitable. A minority of states, made up mainly of community property jurisdictions, use an *equal distribution standard.* These courts must divide marital property equally between the spouses — although a few states permit deviations based on equitable considerations, such as where one spouse has no other resources and is otherwise likely to end up on public assistance. A few states use a *hybrid approach.* Here, property is to be divided equitably, but there is a rebuttable presumption that equitable is in fact equal. Accordingly, a party seeking a greater share of the assets would have the burden of proving why this is fair under the particular circumstances.

With the exception of the hybrid states, appellate courts in jurisdictions using an equitable distribution standard have generally made clear that it is inappropriate for trial courts to rely on fixed formulas or presumptions. However, it is generally acceptable for a court to use a 50-50 split as its starting point, as long as this does not result in an overly mechanistic approach to the allocation of assets. Nonetheless, as a practical matter, some judges and lawyers seem to assume that equitable means equal, thus implicitly placing a burden on the party seeking a greater share of the assets to justify why this division is appropriate.

A frequent concern raised by commentators who have examined the economic impact of divorce on women is that a division that appears equal or equitable on its face may have a very different value to each spouse based on differences in earning capacity, as the spouse with higher earnings can more readily replace items that were lost in the distribution.[24] This problem may be exacerbated if the low-earning spouse also has custody of the children, as the custodial parent often has increased household needs. Moreover, as we have seen, these considerations are often linked, because a spouse with greater domestic responsibilities frequently has a diminished earning capacity. One suggested solution is for courts to look beyond ensuring that the distribution appears equitable or equal solely at the time of divorce, and to assess the relative impact of the distribution on each spouse over time in light of earning potential and domestic arrangements as well. When this suggests a diverging value, the allocation could be adjusted to ensure greater fairness over time.

### Consideration of Specific Factors

Most states with an equitable distribution standard have a statute that enumerates the factors that must be considered in determining how property is to be allocated. Some statutes are general in their approach, while others are detailed. Frequently, the factors that must be considered are the same as those that must be considered in making a spousal support award.

The following section from the Illinois law on the disposition of property is a good example of a fairly detailed approach:

(d) In a proceeding for dissolution of marriage or declaration of invalidity of marriage, or in a proceeding for disposition of property following dissolution of marriage by a court which lacked personal jurisdiction over the absent spouse or lacked jurisdiction to dispose of the property, the court shall assign each spouse's non-marital property to that spouse. It also shall divide the marital property without regard to marital misconduct in just proportions considering all relevant factors, including:

(1) the contribution of each party to the acquisition, preservation, or increase or decrease in value of the marital or non-marital property, including the contribution of a spouse as a homemaker or to the family unit;

(2) the dissipation by each party of the marital or non-marital property;

(3) the value of the property assigned to each spouse;

(4) the duration of the marriage;

(5) the relevant economic circumstances of each spouse when the division of property is to become effective, including the desirability of awarding the family home, or the right to live therein for reasonable periods, to the spouse having custody of the children;

(6) any obligations and rights arising from a prior marriage of either party;

(7) any antenuptial agreement of the parties;

(8) the age, health, station, occupation, amount and sources of income, vocational skills, employability, estate, liabilities, and need of each of the parties;

(9) the custodial provisions for any children;

(10) whether the apportionment is in lieu of or in addition to maintenance;

(11) the reasonable opportunity of each spouse for future acquisition of capital assets and income; and

(12) the tax consequences of the property division upon the respective economic circumstances of the parties.[25]

As we have seen in other contexts, most statutes set out the factors that must be considered in dividing property, but do not require that equal weight be given to each one. Accordingly, judges are free to weigh the factors as deemed appropriate in light of the circumstances of the individual case. This approach maximizes the flexibility and discretion of the court and is generally considered to be consistent with the goal of achieving a fair result, but, as we have seen, the potential downside of this flexibility is that it can lead to inconsistent results.

In some jurisdictions, judges must make detailed findings of fact showing the consideration given each statutory factor. In others, a more general statement in support of the result is acceptable. In states using an equal distribution standard or presumption, findings of fact are usually required only when the judge departs from the norm and makes an unequal distribution.

### Effectuating the Distribution

There are many ways that property can be divided between the parties. The simplest and most common way to distribute property is for each spouse to take possession of a designated portion of the assets. For example, the wife might get the living room furniture and the husband the dining room furniture; the wife the computer and the husband the stereo; each might get one-half of the linens, the towels, the kitchen items, and so on until everything is distributed.

If a couple has a significant asset — such as a business, a valuable collection, or (as discussed in greater detail below) a house or pension — with no other comparable assets, a number of options are possible. Probably the simplest alternative is to award one spouse the major asset and give the other a greater share of the remaining assets. However, this may not always be feasible because the remaining property is often not of sufficient offsetting value. Another option is for the asset to be sold and the proceeds divided. Or one spouse could retain the asset and buy out the other's marital interest in it. Where a buyout occurs, a lump-sum payment (where feasible) is generally preferable to installment payments because it provides a clean break and minimizes the risk of nonperformance.

**The Marital Residence.** Many property disputes center on the marital residence, most likely due to the convergence of financial, emotional, and practical considerations. In the event of a dispute, a court may consider the desirability of enabling the children to remain in their home because this provides them with some stability at a time of tremendous change. In fact, some property distribution statutes expressly include this as a factor for judicial consideration. (See, e.g., paragraph (d)(5) of the Illinois statute above.) Dispositional options for the marital residence include the following:

1. Sell the house and divide the proceeds.
2. One spouse keeps the house, buying out the other spouse or exchanging offsetting assets.
3. Keep the house in joint name, with one spouse having the right of exclusive use and occupancy until a future dispositional date.

If neither spouse wishes to retain the house, it can be sold and the proceeds divided equally or in accordance with the overall distribution formula. In some cases, a sale may be the ultimate result because no other option is feasible.

If the parties agree in principle that one spouse can retain the house, the question becomes how this can be accomplished. Often the simplest solution is to give the other spouse an asset or assets of roughly equal value; sometimes a pension will be used as the offsetting asset. Frequently, however, there will not be enough resources to do this, since a house is often the most valuable asset a couple owns. Another option is for the acquiring spouse to buy out the interest of the other spouse. To do this, the acquiring spouse usually takes out a home equity loan or refinances the existing loan. Again, this may not be feasible because he or she may not qualify for the loan or have the ability to make the loan payments.

If neither of the above options is feasible, another possibility is to keep the property in joint name and give one spouse the right of exclusive use and occupancy until a designated time in the future, such as the emancipation of the youngest child or the remarriage of the occupying spouse. Upon the earliest of these to occur, the occupying spouse would be required to effectuate a buyout of the other spouse's interest or to sell the house and allocate the proceeds according to a preexisting formula. The nonoccupying spouse is often given the right of first refusal.

The advantage of this approach is that it enables a spouse to remain in the home, which may be particularly important where children are involved, without having to either give up a share of other assets or go into debt. But there is also a significant drawback: The property continues to be owned by two people with enough relational difficulties that they cannot live together. For this arrangement to have any hope of working, it is best that all necessary details be spelled out in the court's order or in the parties' separation agreement. It may also be advisable for the court to retain jurisdiction in case problems arise after the divorce. Some of the issues that need to be addressed are the following: Who pays for repairs? Who pays for improvements that increase the value of the house? How are these expenses accounted for upon sale? What if the occupying spouse neglects the house and its value declines? How are sale proceeds to be allocated? How is appreciation accounted for? Even when these details are worked out with care, the emotional risk factor involved in this approach remains a wild card.

**Pensions.** The distribution of pensions raises complex issues. This section provides a basic overview of the two principal ways pensions can be divided.[26]

*The Present Value Approach.* One approach is to determine the present value of the pension and then assign the non-employee spouse an offsetting share of property. The primary advantage of this approach is that the matter is resolved at the time of divorce and is not left hanging until some future date. However, it also presents some potential disadvantages. First, it is often difficult and costly to determine the present value of a pension plan because it is not payable until some time in the future and a number of contingencies — such as the salary of the employee spouse — can influence its value or affect whether it is payable at all. Second, there may not be enough offsetting property; even where there is, the non-employee spouse gets the offsetting property immediately, while the employee spouse must wait until a future date to enjoy his or her share of the distribution. Additionally, if the plan is not vested, the employee spouse bears the risk of not receiving a full share of the distribution; however, she or he has some control over this, as a voluntary job change can be postponed until after the pension has vested. Accordingly, this approach is not generally used if a plan is unvested or the employee spouse is years away from retirement.

*The "If, As, and When" Approach.* The other approach is to award the non-employee spouse a share of pension funds "if, as, and when" the employee spouse receives them. At the time of divorce, the court uses a formula for allocating the future payments between the spouses. Most states use a "marital fraction" formula that calculates the non-employee's share based on the ratio that the years of the marriage bear to the total number of years of employment at the time of distribution. The court retains jurisdiction so that it can oversee this future event. Accordingly, this approach is also referred to as the "reserved jurisdiction" approach.

The primary advantages of this distribution method are that it avoids the need to determine the present value of the plan; an offsetting award is not required; and the risk of nonreceipt is not born solely by the employee spouse because the non-employee spouse receives his or her share "if, as, and when" the employee spouse does. If the employee leaves before his or her pension vests, neither spouse gains or loses in a differential fashion. However, a potential disadvantage to the non-employee spouse is the fact that the other spouse has control over this eventuality and thus has the ability to defeat the interest of the non-employee spouse. This could give the employee spouse the upper-hand in the event of postmarital disagreements, as he or she could threaten to quit work if the other spouse did not capitulate to his or her demands.

Where the pension funds are actually reached, distribution is usually made pursuant to a **Qualified Domestic Relations Order** (QDRO), which is served on the administrator of the pension. A QDRO is a judgment or decree of a state court that enables the non-employee spouse to receive all or part of the benefits that are payable to the employee spouse. A QDRO must be carefully drafted so it satisfies the legal requirements of the Employee Retirement Income Security Act (ERISA), as modified by the Retirement Equity Act of 1984 (REA), and contains all of the necessary information, such as the formulas used to determine the amounts of payment, how payments are to be made, and when payments will begin and end.[27]

## TAX CONSEQUENCES OF A PROPERTY DISTRIBUTION _____

For federal tax purposes, property transfers between spouses either during a marriage or after a marriage ends that are incidental to a divorce are not taxable events.[28] To understand the significance of this rule, it is helpful to step outside the divorce context for a moment. Assume that A purchases a painting for $10,000 and five years later sells it to B for $20,000. Upon the sale, A has realized a gain of $10,000, which is subject to taxation. However, if A were married to B, and this transfer were made during the marriage or incident to a divorce, A would not realize any taxable gain even if A receives an asset worth $20,000 in exchange for the painting.

Let us now analyze the transfer from B's perspective. Where A and B are strangers, and B purchases the painting for $20,000, B acquires what is referred to as a **cost basis** in the painting of $20,000. If B subsequently transfers the property, his gain will be computed using this basis as the starting point. Accordingly, if he sells the painting for $35,000, he will realize a gain of $15,000 ($35,000 − $20,000). However, if A and B are spouses, and the transfer is incident to a divorce, the tax consequences for B are quite different. Here, B acquires A's basis of $10,000 — it is literally carried over from A to B (as it would be in the case of a gift). Now, if B sells the painting for $35,000, he will realize a gain of $25,000 ($35,000 − $10,000).

Clearly, this rule impacts the actual value of a property transfer because the recipient of appreciated property may eventually be accountable for a significant gain. These potential tax consequences must be taken into account when effectuating a division; otherwise, parties may not actually receive the value that they believe they have agreed to.

## Chapter Summary

Historically, courts in common law states had limited distributive authority — property followed title. Courts in community property states had much greater authority; marriage was viewed as a partnership, and all property acquired through the expenditure of marital efforts or funds was divisible. Now, title is no longer determinative in common law states. With the passage of equitable distribution laws, these jurisdictions have moved closer to the community property model. Most states, including all community property states, distinguish between separate and marital property, although some permit distribution of all property owned by a couple at the time of divorce. Most of these states employ a rebuttable presumption that all property owned by a couple at the time of divorce is marital.

A division of property entails four critical steps: (1) a determination whether the asset in question is in fact "property"; (2) the classification of property as either marital or separate (this step is not required in all-property states because the courts in these jurisdictions can reach both separate and marital property); (3) the value of each asset must be determined; and (4) the assets must be allocated in accordance with the applicable legal standard, with states employing either an equitable or an equal division rule.

The transfer of property incident to a divorce does not result in a taxable gain or loss to the transferring spouse; however, the recipient acquires a carry-over basis in the transferred asset that may result in a significant gain at the time of a future transfer.

## Key Terms

Marital Property
Community Property
  Approach
Title
Special Equity
Equitable Distribution
Dual Property
Separate Property
All Property
Tangible Property
Intangible Assets
Pensions
Goodwill

Professional Goodwill
Premarital Acquisitions
Inception of Title Rule
Source of Funds Rule
Gift
Appreciation
Tracing
Transmutation
Valuation
Fair Market Value
Qualified Domestic Relations
  Order
Cost Basis

## Review Questions

1. Following no-fault reform, why did property distribution become the preferred way to address the economic interests/needs of divorcing spouses?

2. Describe the partnership view of marriage that underlies the community property approach to the division of marital assets.

3. Prior to the passage of equitable distribution laws, how did common law states divide property? What was the special equity rule?

4. When and why did common law states shift to an equitable distribution model?

5. What is a dual property state? What is an all-property state?

6. What is the key difference between community property and common law equitable distribution states?

7. What steps are involved in the division of property?

8. How has the definition of property changed over time?

9. What is the difference between tangible and intangible property?

10. How does the law characterize family pets (a.k.a. "companion animals")? What implications does this have for divorce cases? What new approach have some suggested the law should take?

11. What is the difference between a vested and an unvested pension?

12. Why do some states exclude unvested pensions from their definition of property?

13. Explain why some jurisdictions include professional goodwill in their definition of property and others exclude it.

14. Why is classification a critical step in dual property and community property states but not in all-property states?

15. How is marital property generally defined?

16. What is generally included within the definition of separate property?

17. Why is it important to determine when property is acquired?

18. What is the inception of title rule? the source of funds rule?

19. How might property acquired in contemplation of marriage be classified? Why? What about property acquired during premari-tal cohabitation? Why?

20. What cut-off dates are commonly used for determining when property will no longer be considered marital?

21. What is a gift? When might a gift be classified as marital rather than separate?

22. What is the difference between passive and active appreciation? Why is this difference important with respect to the appreciation of separate property?

23. What happens to the classification of separate property that is exchanged for other property during the marriage?

24. Explain the concept of tracing.

25. How are personal injury awards classified?

26. What is transmutation? Explain the four different ways by which property can transmute.

27. Why is valuation important?

28. What is meant by the term "fair market value"?

29. At what point in the process is property usually valued?

30. What is the difference between an equal and an equitable distribution standard?

31. How do courts decide what is equitable? What factors are generally considered important?

32. What are basic ways a distribution can be effectuated?

33. Describe the dispositional options for the marital residence.

34. What are the two different approaches to distribution of a pension? What are the relative advantages and disadvantages of each approach?

35. What is a QDRO?

36. What are the basic tax consequences of a property distribution?

## **Discussion Questions**

1. Do you think it is appropriate to treat marriage as a partnership? Is this fair to both spouses? Does it imply an equality that may not exist in all marriages? How might this be problematic?

2. Let's assume that Mr. Jones worked hard at a small company to provide for his family. He never particularly enjoyed his work but took his financial obligations to his family seriously. His wife, Ms. Jones, happily stayed home and raised the children and took care of the house.

   Assume that the Joneses are getting divorced after 15 years of marriage. During this time, Mr. Jones contributed to his pension plan at work, and he is fully vested. Should this asset be subject to division? Is it fair to Mr. Jones to divide this employment asset, which is based on his workplace efforts? Explain your position.

3. Some commentators have argued that what is equal or equitable should be determined, at least in part, by looking at future results. Viewed from this perspective, a division that appears equal or fair on its face may reveal itself as less valuable to a more economically vulnerable spouse who cannot readily replace lost assets.

   In dividing property, should the court seek to ensure that the resulting impact of the award is equal or fair, even if this would require making disproportionate allocations?

4. Assume that for most of an eight-year marriage the husband has been very depressed. As a result, he has bounced from job to job with frequent periods of unemployment and has contributed little by way of caring for the house and the children. The wife has held down a steady job and has done most of the home care and child care.

   There is no question that their contributions are grossly unequal. How should this impact the property division? Does it make any difference to the issue if the wife knew about the husband's depression before the marriage? Does it make any difference if, instead of being depressed, the husband was an alcoholic? drug dependent? physically ill? lazy?

5. In the divorce context, do you think the law should treat pets as personal property, and distribute them like other assets, or more like children, and make a custody and visitation determination based on the needs/interests of the animal?

# Assignments

1. Locate the property distribution statute for your state and try to answer the following questions based on the statutory language. Note that all questions will not be relevant in all jurisdictions.

   a. Are you in a community property or an equitable jurisdiction state?
   b. Does your state use a dual property or an all-property approach?
   c. How is marital/community property defined? How is separate property defined?
   d. Are there any statutory presumptions?
   e. Is there a cut-off date for the acquisition of marital property?
   f. What factors must a court consider when making a distribution?

2. Review the relevant cases in your jurisdiction to determine what factors the courts seem to think are the most important when allocating property. Write a memo analyzing your findings.

3. Interview an attorney or a paralegal who works in the family law field. Ask him or her about the following:

   • In what proportion is property usually divided between the spouses?
   • Under what circumstances does this vary?
   • What factors do lawyers and judges seem to think are the most important?
   • How are the nonfinancial contributions of spouses with regard to domestic responsibilities viewed? Are they respected as much as financial contributions?

4. The attorney you work for has asked you to draft him a memorandum setting out the options in the following situation: His client, Ms. Perez, is getting divorced from Mr. Rivera. The parties have two small children, and Ms. Perez will have physical custody. The couple owns a small house. Ms. Perez wishes to remain there while the children are young. In theory, Mr. Rivera has no problem with this, but he's not going to let her do this without receiving what he is

entitled to. The house is worth about $150,000, and there is an outstanding mortgage of $120,000. Mr. Rivera has a vested pension plan, but its value has not yet been determined.

What are all of the possible ways that a settlement could be structured? Set out the advantages and disadvantages of each possible option.

As part of the memo, he also wants you to draft some preliminary separation agreement language that gives Ms. Perez the right of exclusive use and occupancy of the residence. You should cover as many contingencies as you can.

5. Draft a comprehensive checklist that can be used when working on cases to ensure that all property has been considered.

6. The attorney you work for has asked you to look into how appreciation of premarital property is handled in your state. Her client, Rita Small, came into the marriage with a summer home and a rare stamp collection. Both assets appreciated in value during the course of the marriage. Although she does not yet have accurate or complete information about the increases in value, you can assume that the increase in the value of the stamp collection is attributable to market forces and the increase in the value of the house is attributable to market forces as well as to improvements that were made by the husband. Write an in-house memorandum explaining how the appreciation will be classified. Be sure to consider whether your jurisdiction treats passive and active appreciation differently.

7. The judge you work for has asked you to do some research in preparation for a divorce case that includes a dispute over a much-loved family dog. She wants you to do the following:

   a. Determine if there are any statutes in your state that are relevant to determining the legal status of pets.
   b. Determine if there are any cases in your state that would have bearing on this matter—do not limit yourself to divorce cases.
   c. Locate and read at least three articles on the topic, and provide the judge with a summary of the different arguments that are presented in terms of how pets should be treated in a divorce case.

## Cases for Analysis

The following case focuses on the question of whether the wife is entitled to an equal share of the husband's inheritance proceeds based on the donative intent of the decedent.

## OLESBERG v. OLESBERG
### 206 Ore. App. 496, 136 P.3d 1202 (2006)

Wife appeals from a judgment of dissolution of the parties' 27-year marriage, . . . We . . . conclude that the trial court erred in finding that husband had rebutted the presumption of equal contribution as to the inheritance and we modify the property division to award wife one-half of the account bearing the inheritance proceeds.

The parties were both 47 years old at the time of trial and in good health. They were married in 1976 and separated in 2001. The parties met in high school and married when husband was in his second year of college in Idaho. While husband completed college, wife worked full time and husband worked part time. In 1978, they moved to Portland so that husband could attend dental school. Wife found a job checking groceries at Safeway and became head checker. Husband's parents helped the parties financially in the early part of their marriage, including payment of tuition and a house down payment. Husband graduated from dental school in 1982 and, in December 1982, the parties jointly purchased a dental practice. For the first few years, the dental practice earned little or no income and wife supported the family with her full-time employment. The dental practice began to turn a profit in 1985 and the parties' income from the practice has increased over the years. Wife worked full time at Safeway until 1985, when their third child was born, at which time she began working three days a week. In 1986, wife quit work to stay home with the children. . . .

From 1987 to 1994, wife managed the household. . . . In 1995, wife took a part-time job, but continued to manage the family's finances and do all the dental practice billing and bookkeeping until 2001, when the parties separated. . . .

After husband's father retired, the parties began sending husband's parents money each month, which the parties considered repayment of college tuition and the house down payment. Additionally, husband's parents had a cabin in Coeur d'Alene, Idaho. To help the parents financially, in 1985, husband and wife — together with husband's sister, Janae, and her husband — purchased the cabin and began making monthly payments on a 10-year contract. Husband's brother did not participate in that transaction. Husband's father passed away in 1996, and husband's mother inherited his estate.

Shortly before the parties separated in 2001, husband's mother died. Her estate consisted of her home, the balance due on the Idaho cabin, and some cash. Husband's sister, Janae, was the personal representative of the estate. She set up an account for each beneficiary — Janae, husband, and their brother Mark — and divided the proceeds of the estate equally among them. The estate forgave $45,000 of indebtedness on the cabin. Husband's inheritance from his mother came to approximately $65,000. Husband kept the money in the same account set up by Janae and has never commingled it with the parties' assets. The balance has grown to $87,000. . . .

The . . . question is whether the trial court erred in failing to award wife an equal share of the account bearing the proceeds of husband's inheritance from his mother. Husband concedes that the inheritance is a marital asset because it was acquired during the marriage and that, like any other gift, it is subject to a rebuttable presumption of equal contribution. ORS 107.105(1)(f); Kunze and Kunze, 337 Ore. 122, 133, 92 P.3d 100 (2004). The presumption is rebutted by evidence that the asset was acquired "free of any contributions from the other spouse." Kunze, 337 Ore. at 135.

In Kunze, the court held that a finding that the wife "had been the sole object of her aunt's donative intent" overcame the presumption that the husband had contributed equally to the initial acquisition of the inherited asset. 337 Ore. at 143. Since Kunze, we held in Tsukamaki and Tsukamaki, 199 Ore. App. 577, 583, 112 P.3d 416 (2005), that, when the marital asset is a gift, one spouse may rebut the presumption of equal contribution by evidence that "the other spouse neither contributed to its acquisition nor was the object of the donative intent." 199 Ore. App. at 583. Thus, the evidence necessary to rebut the presumption of equal contribution in this case is that wife did not contribute to the inheritance and was not the object of husband's mother's donative intent.

Wife contends that she contributed to the acquisition of the inheritance because there is evidence that the inheritance is related in part to funds that wife and husband provided to his parents over the years. We find that husband's inheritance did not bear a direct relationship to past financial support that the parties provided to his parents; rather, it was simply the result of an equal division of the mother's estate among her three children, husband and his two siblings. Thus, we find that wife did not contribute financially to the acquisition of the inheritance.

The remaining question is whether husband established that wife was not an object of his mother's donative intent. The trial court, apparently relying on husband's evidence that the estate was simply divided three ways, found that "there was no donative intent from [husband's mother] to [wife]" and held that husband had rebutted the presumption of equal contribution. Wife contends that the trial court erred, because there is no evidence that husband's mother did not intend for her to benefit from the inheritance.

We agree with wife that to rebut the presumption of equal contribution, it is not sufficient to show simply that the inheritance devolved only to husband and his siblings in equal shares. The fact that the mother's estate was divided three ways among her children does not establish that she had no intention to benefit wife, her daughter-in-law of 25 years. If that evidence were sufficient to overcome the presumption of equal contribution, the presumption would not only be rendered meaningless, but it would also incorrectly place the burden on the nonrecipient spouse to rebut it. See Wilson and Wilson, 155 Ore. App. 512, 516-17, 964 P.2d 1052 (1998) (in determining whether a party has rebutted the presumption, "we consider whether the party seeking to rebut the presumption has produced evidence that his or her spouse was not the object of the donor or devisor's intent and did not otherwise contribute to the acquisition of the gift or inheritance. Mere lack of evidence tending to reinforce the presumption is insufficient." (Citation omitted.)). We conclude that, to defeat the presumption, husband must provide affirmative evidence that wife was not an object of her mother-in-law's donative intent. No such evidence was presented here. Cf. Ahearn and Whittaker, 200 Ore. App. 29, 113 P.3d 439 (2005) (evidence that the husband's parents' gift to the husband was intended to replace property that he had received before the marriage and given without consideration to a sibling established that the husband was sole object of his parents' intent). Thus, we conclude that the presumption of equal contribution was not rebutted.

If the presumption of equal contribution is not rebutted, then, in the absence of other considerations, the appropriate "just and proper" division of that asset is an equal division. Kunze, 337 Ore. at 134. We conclude on this record that an equal division of the account bearing the inheritance proceeds is just and proper.

Dissolution judgment modified to award wife . . . an equal share of account bearing proceeds of inheritance; otherwise affirmed.

## QUESTIONS

1. Why, under Oregon law, is there no dispute over the fact that the inheritance proceeds are marital rather than separate?

2. Explain the role that the "rebuttable presumption of equal contribution" plays in this case.

3. What evidence does the husband offer to rebut the presumption?

4. What arguments does the wife offer to show equal contribution?

5. What does the court conclude and why?

---

The following case focuses on classification issues. In deciding if the assets in question are separate or marital, the court focuses on marital effort, the distinction between transmutation and active appreciation, and on the tracing process.

## SCHMITZ v. SCHMITZ
### 88 P.3d 1116 (Alaska 2004)

## II.  FACTS AND PROCEEDINGS

### A.  FACTUAL HISTORY

Michael Schmitz and Christina Schmitz married in Juneau in January 1999. The couple's child, Johnathon, was born in March 1999. While Christina and Michael were married, Christina was Johnathon's primary caregiver. Michael and Christina separated in August 2001.

Michael is a certified public accountant and a partner in the firm of Schmitz & Buck. Michael has owned a fifty percent interest in Schmitz & Buck. . . . In addition to his partnership in Schmitz & Buck, Michael owns a twelve-and-a-half percent share in the Nugget Men's Store . . . Michael's share in the store was purchased with proceeds from a tort settlement resulting from a car accident. . . .

Michael holds two accounts at First National Bank Alaska. He refers to one account as his "checking" or "regular" account and the second as his "investment" or "business" account. Michael deposited income from his accounting business into both of the accounts. . . .

### B.  CHARACTERIZATION OF THE COUPLE'S ASSETS AS SEPARATE OR MARITAL

The first step in equitable division of marital property requires the trial court to determine what property is available for distribution; to accomplish this, the trial court must characterize assets as separate or marital property. . . .

### 1.  Michael's Businesses: Schmitz & Buck and the Nugget Men's Store

The trial court found that Michael's separate property, including his interest in the Nugget Men's Store and Schmitz & Buck, remained his separate property because Michael had no intention to transmute the assets from separate to marital. Christina argues that the trial court made two errors in its characterization of the Nugget Men's Store and Schmitz & Buck as separate property. First, she argues that the court erred in applying a transmutation analysis rather than an active appreciation analysis. Second, . . . Christina asserts that Michael spent significant marital time and energy on both . . . Specifically, Christina argues that Michael worked at Schmitz & Buck seven days a week during tax season . . . and that he worked approximately eleven hours each day during that period. She notes that for the Nugget Men's Store, Michael did the monthly accounting, prepared the monthly financial statements, as well as the business's tax return, and attended the store's annual meeting. . . .

Marital property includes all property acquired during the marriage, "excepting only inherited property and property acquired with separate property which is kept as separate property." We have recognized that a spouse's premarital separate property can become marital through transmutation or active appreciation. Transmutation occurs when a married couple demonstrates an intent, by virtue of their words and actions during marriage, to treat one spouse's separate property as marital property. "Active appreciation occurs when marital funds or marital efforts cause a spouse's separate property to increase in value during the marriage. . . ."

The elements of active appreciation are significantly different from those of transmutation. Transmutation requires intent, as demonstrated through conduct, to change the character of property from separate to marital. To find active appreciation in separate property, the court must make three subsidiary findings: "First, it must find that the separate property in question appreciated during the marriage. Second, it must find that the parties made marital contributions to the property. Finally, the court must find a causal connection between the marital contributions and at least part of the appreciation."

In addressing the question whether the property at issue was separate or marital, the trial court focused only on the theory of transmutation. This focus was overly narrow and should have included an analysis of whether Michael's efforts during the marriage caused the value of his businesses to increase. . . .

As to Schmitz & Buck, Christina proved that Michael spent significant marital time working at the business. . . .

Because the proof of Michael's increased income that Christina was able to present suggests that the business's value may have increased during the marriage, we remand this issue to the superior court, to allow Christina an opportunity to present evidence of the increase in the value of Schmitz & Buck during the marriage.

By contrast, an active appreciation analysis fails on the element of marital contribution when applied to the Nugget Men's Store. The record shows that Michael's involvement with the store was quite limited: He only performed some accounting and tax returns for the store and attended its annual meeting. We cannot say, therefore, that Christina met her burden of proof on the element of marital contribution for the Nugget Men's Store.

Accordingly, we affirm the superior court's determination that the Nugget Men's Store is Michael's separate property.

## 2.  THE FIRST NATIONAL BANK ACCOUNTS

Christina argues that because Michael deposited money he earned during the marriage into both of his First National Bank accounts, the superior court should have characterized the accounts as marital property. Michael counters that the accounts are comprised in part of his separate property and that commingling of separate and marital funds in the accounts does not transmute the accounts into marital property. He argues that these accounts are his separate property. . . .

Some assets might have been acquired . . . from another asset "through exchange, appreciation, or income." These assets are referred to as secondary property because such an asset requires for its classification the classification of another asset.

To classify secondary assets, courts "must first identify the specific asset from which it was derived (the source asset), and then determine the classification of that asset." This process is referred to as tracing . . . The process of tracing can . . . be described as a search of sources backward through time until every asset is linked to primary marital or primary separate property. . . .

The party seeking to establish that the property is separate always bears that burden of proof; thus untraceable assets are marital property.

Both parties concede that the bank accounts included both marital and separate property. . . . The record suggests that Michael deposited earnings from his accounting business into his "business" account. The record also suggests that in addition to marital property, Michael also deposited separate property, for example, proceeds from the Nugget Men's Store.

A spouse's separate property does not become untraceable to its separate source merely because it is mixed with marital property in the same secondary asset. However, placing separate property in joint ownership is rebuttable evidence that the owner intended the property to be marital. If evidence is presented that is sufficient to overcome this presumption, tracing can take place.

If, however, the sources can be proved but their respective amounts cannot, the proper ratio cannot be determined. Thus, even when it is known that a mixed secondary asset derived partly from a separate source, if the amount contributed from that source cannot be determined, then the asset cannot be traced and "the unknown amount contributed from the separate source transmutes by commingling and becomes marital property." [W]e remand to the superior court to make findings as to whether the presumption that commingled property is intended to be marital has been rebutted and if so, to make findings recharacterizing the accounts.

## QUESTIONS

1. What does the court say the basic distinction is between separate and marital property?

2. Why did the trial court hold that the two businesses remained the separate property of the husband?

3. Why does the court discuss the concepts of appreciation and transmutation — why are they relevant?

4. As discussed by the court, what is the key difference between these two concepts?

5. What does the court conclude with respect to Schmitz & Buck? with respect to Nugget's Men's Store? Why is the result different?

6. What is a "secondary" asset?

7. Explain what the court means by "tracing"?

8. What does the court conclude with respect to the bank accounts? Why?

## Endnotes

1. Wisconsin also is now generally regarded as a community property state due to statutory changes initiated in 1986.

2. *See generally* Scott Greene, Comparison of the Community Property Aspects of the Community Property and Common-Law Marital Property Systems and Their Relative Compatibility with the Current View of the Marriage Relationship and the Rights of Women, 13 Creighton L. Rev. 71, 88 (1979); Judith T. Younger, Marital Regimes: A Story of Compromise and Demoralization, Together with Criticism and Suggestions for Reform, 67 Cornell L. Rev. 45 (1981).

3. *See* Younger, *supra* note 2, at 61-64.

4. For the sake of simplicity, the term "marital property" includes what would be referred to as "community property" in community property jurisdictions.

5. This word, coined by Willard H. DaSilva, conveys wonderfully the shift in the meaning of the word "property." Willard H. DaSilva, Property Subject to Equitable Distribution, *in* Valuation and Distribution of Marital Property (John P. McCahey ed., 1985).

6. Elizabeth Paek, Fido Seeks Full Membership in the Family: Dismantling the Property Classification of Companion Animals by Statute, 25 Hawaii L. Rev. 481, 489 (2003). *See also* Rebecca Huss, Separation, Custody and Estate Planning Issues Relating to Companion Animals, 74 U. Colo. L. Rev. 181 (2003). These articles also discuss how "dismantling the property classification" would impact other areas of the law as well; for example, potentially opening up tort claims based on injury to a companion animal.

7. Paek, *supra* note 6, at 484.

8. Bennett v. Bennett, 650 So. 2d 109, 111 (Fla. Dist. Ct. App. 1995).

9. *Id.*

10. Desanctis v. Pritchard, 803 A.2d 230, 233 (Pa. Super. Ct. 2002).

11. Raymond v. Lachmann, 695 N.Y.S.2d 308, 309 (N.Y. App. Div. 1999).

12. *Id.* at 310. *See also* Huss, *supra* note 6, at 224-228.

13. Note that the concept of vesting applies only to the employer's contribution; an employee is always vested with respect to his or her own contribution.

For a good discussion of pension plans, *see* Mary E. O'Connell, On the Fringe: Rethinking the Link Between Wages and Benefits, 67 Tul. L. Rev. 1421 (1993); Susan J. Prather, Characterization, Valuation, and Distribution of Pensions at Divorce, 15 J. Am. Acad. Matrimonial Law. 443 (1998).

14. Bratcher v. Bratcher, 26 S.W.3d 797, 801 (Ky. Ct. App. 2000).

15. *Id.* (citing Thomasian v. Thomasian, 556 A.2d 675, 681 (Md. Ct. Spec. App. 1989)). (Internal citations omitted.)

16. Arnold v. Arnold, Opinion No. 2003-NMCA-114 (N.M. Ct. App. 2003), http://pub.bna.com/fl/22765.htm.

17. *See* Diane Green Smith, 'Til Success Do Us Part: How Illinois Promotes Inequities in Property Distribution Pursuant to Divorce by Excluding Professional Goodwill, 26 J. Marshall L. Rev. 147 (1992).

18. *See generally* Joan M. Krauskopf, Classifying Marital and Separate Property: Combinations and Increase in Value of Separate Property, 89 W. Va. L. Rev.

996, 997 (1987). For discussion of specialized rules developed by some states regarding appreciation, *see* Suzanne Reynolds, Increases in Separate Property and the Evolving Marital Partnership, 24 Wake Forest L. Rev. 239, 291-299 (1989).

19. For a detailed analysis of the complexities of tracing, *see* Thomas J. Oldham, Tracing, Commingling, and Transmutation, 23 Fam. L.Q. 219 (1989).

20. *See* Aloysius A. Leopold, "Loss of Earning Capacity" Benefits in the Community Property Jurisdiction—How Do You Figure? 30 St. Mary's L.J. 367 (1999).

21. For a review of different approaches to the classification of the loss of earning capacity benefits, *see* Leopold, *id.* at 385-397.

22. *See* Krauskopf, *supra* note 18, at 1008. On transmutation generally, *see* Thomas J. Oldham, *supra* note 19, ch. 11.

23. For detail on valuation approaches, *see* The Handbook for Divorce Valuations (Robert E. Kleeman, Jr., R. James Alerding, and Benjamin D. Miller eds., 1999).

24. *See* Joan Williams, Do Wives Own Half? Winning for Wives after *Wendt*, 32 Conn. L. Rev. 249 (2000).

25. Ill. Ann. Stat. ch. 530, para. 5/503(8)(d) (Smith-Hurd 1993).

26. This discussion is very general in nature. It does not address valuation issues, the different kinds of private pensions, or the connection between the two. For further information, *see* Dylan A. Wilde, Obtaining an Equitable Distribution of Retirement Plans in a Divorce Action, 49 S.D. L. Rev. 141 (2003); Elizabeth Barker Brandt, Valuation, Allocation, and Distribution of Retirement Plans at Divorce: Where Are We?, 35 Family L.Q. 237 (2001).

27. Prior to the Retirement Equity Act (REA), pension funds could not be reached in a divorce because of ERISA's general anti-assignment rule, prohibiting the transfer of an employee's pension funds to a third party. The rules governing distribution of pension funds are complex and must be followed with great care in order for the QDRO to be effective. *See* Dodi Walker Gross, How to Ensure That a QDRO Qualifies Under the Detailed Tax and ERISA Requirements, 81 J. Taxn. 346 (1994).

28. I.R.C. § 1041. *See generally*, Craig D. Bell, Need-to-Know Divorce Tax Law for Legal Assistance Officers, 177 Mil. L. Rev. 213 (2003).

# 9 Jurisdiction

This chapter focuses on **jurisdiction**, which, stated broadly, refers to the authority of a court to hear and resolve cases. The question of jurisdiction must be carefully considered before a legal action is commenced because the lack of jurisdiction affects the availability and validity of court orders.

## OVERVIEW OF SUBJECT MATTER AND PERSONAL JURISDICTION

Before looking at the jurisdictional issues that arise in divorce actions, it is important that you understand the basic concepts of subject matter jurisdiction and personal jurisdiction.

## Subject Matter Jurisdiction

**Subject matter jurisdiction** refers to the authority of a court to hear a particular type of dispute. The subject matter jurisdiction of a court is generally established by statute. Some courts, such as a housing court or a juvenile court, are granted limited subject matter jurisdiction and can hear only certain kinds of cases. Other courts, such as a district court, are granted general subject matter jurisdiction and can hear a wide array of criminal and civil matters. In most states, exclusive subject matter jurisdiction over divorce actions — including all collateral issues such as support, property, and custody — is vested in a specialized court commonly known as the family court or the family and probate court.

In contrast to personal jurisdiction, which a party can voluntarily assent to (see below), parties cannot confer subject matter jurisdiction on a court, and judgment that is rendered by a court that lacks subject matter jurisdiction is void.

## Personal Jurisdiction

Personal jurisdiction refers to a court's ability to exercise authority over a defendant. The exercise of jurisdiction must conform to the requirements of the due process clause of the fourteenth amendment, which prohibits a state from "depriving any person of life, liberty or property" without providing fair procedures, such as notice and the opportunity to be heard. The requirement of procedural fairness has also been interpreted to mean that a state may not exercise authority over a defendant who lacks a sufficient relationship with that state. Accordingly, considerations of personal jurisdiction are significant in cases involving parties who live in different states. To ensure that the court has personal jurisdiction over the defendant, the plaintiff can always file the action in the state where the defendant lives, but this is more expensive, time consuming, and inconvenient.

Consistent with the due process clause, states can acquire personal jurisdiction over a defendant based on domicile, minimum contacts, consent, or presence.

1. *Domicile*. States have personal jurisdiction over all persons who are domiciled within its borders. **Domicile** means that the state is someone's permanent home — the place they leave from and return to. It is important to be aware of the distinction between "domicile" and "residence." A person may have several places of residence, such as a college dorm or one's family home, but only one domicile (one's "permanent" home).[1]

2. *Minimum contacts*. A state may exercise personal jurisdiction over a nonresident defendant who has sufficient **minimum contacts** with the state such that it is not unfair to require him or her to return to the state and respond to a lawsuit there.

To implement this minimum contacts rule, most states have enacted what are known as **long-arm statutes**. These statutes generally specify the kinds of contacts that will give rise to personal jurisdiction and typically include the following contacts: transacting business within the state, owning property within the state, or committing a tortious act within the state. A few states have elected not to enumerate the qualifying contacts but instead employ statutory language to the effect that the state will permit the exercise of jurisdiction to the fullest extent possible under the due process clause.

A number of states have also enacted special long-arm provisions for use in family law cases. Here, the assertion of jurisdiction is often premised on the fact that the state was the marital domicile for a period of time preceding the filing of the divorce action. Other provisions are framed more broadly and tie the exercise of jurisdiction to the maintenance of an ongoing relationship with a person located in that state or to the payment of support; however, these contacts must be of a sufficient nature to satisfy the fairness requirements of the due process clause. Additionally, all states have enacted the Uniform Interstate Family Support Act (UIFSA), which contains a broad, long-arm provision for the assertion of jurisdiction over nonresident defendants in support matters.

*3. Consent.* A nonresident may consent to jurisdiction and thereby agree to submit him- or herself to the authority of the court.

*4. Presence.* A state can exercise personal jurisdiction over a non-resident who is physically present and personally served with a summons within that state.

## JURISDICTION AND THE DIVORCE ACTION

Turning to the divorce action, jurisdictional concepts are best understood if examined in relationship to specific aspects of the proceeding, as different considerations come into play at different points in the process. Specifically, we will look at the jurisdictional standards that govern the dissolution of the marital relationship, the award of support, the distribution of property, and the determination of custody.

It thus goes without saying that in the course of your work as a paralegal, you must always be attuned to jurisdictional considerations and any relevant time periods within which jurisdiction must be asserted. If you are responsible for interviewing clients, it is essential that you inquire into the location of all parties as this can have critical consequences for your client.

### Does the Court Have Jurisdiction to Dissolve the Marriage?

Having just set out the importance of personal jurisdiction, we immediately bump up against the well-worn maxim that for every rule, there is an exception. In this instance, divorce provides the exception because in most, if not all, states, a court can dissolve a marriage even if it does not have personal jurisdiction over the defendant, if the plaintiff is domiciled in that state.

Thus, when it comes to divorce, it is the plaintiff's relationship with the "forum" state (the state in which the action is filed) that matters. The rationale for this domicile rule is captured by the following passage from a 1942 United States Supreme Court decision:

Each state as a sovereign has a rightful and legitimate concern in the marital status of persons domiciled within its borders. The marriage relation creates

problems of large social importance. Protection of offspring, property interests, and the enforcement of marital responsibilities are but a few of the
commanding problems in the field of domestic relations with which the
state must deal. Thus it is plain that each state . . . can alter within its own
borders the marriage status of the spouse domiciled there, even though the
other spouse is absent.[2]

According to this reasoning, a relationship with the defendant is not
necessary because states have an overriding interest in the marital status
of persons living within their borders.

Many commentators have suggested that this domicile rule is out of
keeping with the modern jurisdictional emphasis on the relationship of the
defendant to the adjudicating state and recommend that a minimum contacts standard be used in divorce cases, as it is in other civil actions.[3]
However, an important concern is that such a shift could prevent domestic
violence victims from being able to file for divorce in a state that they have
fled to escape abuse because the minimum contacts requirement would not
be satisfied unless the defendant happened to have a qualifying relationship with that state. Accordingly, the victim would be forced to return to
her prior home state (or if the defendant had moved, to his new home state)
in order to file a divorce.

If a spouse is not actually domiciled in a state, but has gone there for
the purpose of obtaining a divorce, the defendant-spouse may be able to
attack the validity of the divorce judgment for lack of jurisdiction. This
right is generally limited to a spouse who did not receive notice of the
action and therefore did not have an opportunity to raise jurisdictional
objections during the divorce proceeding.

## Does the Court Have Jurisdiction to Award Support?

As discussed above, jurisdiction to dissolve a marriage is based on
domicile—personal jurisdiction over the defendant is not required.
However, the jurisdictional rule is different where spousal and child
support is involved; a state must have personal jurisdiction over a
defendant in order to adjudicate support rights. Accordingly, it is possible
that a state would have the authority to dissolve a marriage but lack the
authority to enter a support award. This is sometimes referred to as a
**divisible divorce**.

This, however, is where long-arm statutes come into play. These statutes
permit a state to assert its authority over a nonresident within the fairness
requirements of the due process clause, and many states authorize the assertion of long-arm jurisdiction over a nonresident when that state had been

the marital domicile of the parties. Often, this is a time-limited option, and personal jurisdiction will only continue for a fixed period of time, perhaps for a year or two, after the individual has left the state. Once this time period has run, the state loses its ability to assert personal jurisdiction over the defendant unless there are other independent qualifying bases.

In addition to state long-arm statutes, UIFSA (as noted above) also contains a long-arm provision that a state can use to acquire personal jurisdiction over a nonresident defendant to establish a spousal or child support order. Moreover, this state will retain continuing exclusive jurisdiction to modify the order so long as either the support obligor, the support obligee, or the child for whose benefit support is being paid continues to live in that state. In addition, in states that have adopted the 2001 amended version of UIFSA, the parties may consent to continued jurisdiction in this state even if everyone has moved out.[4] UIFSA sets out the following eight grounds for the exercise of personal jurisdiction over a nonresident defendant:

1. The defendant is personally served within the state.
2. The defendant consents to jurisdiction.
3. The defendant at one time resided with the child in the state.
4. The defendant resided in the state at one time and provided "prenatal expenses or support for the child."
5. The child lives in a state as a result of the parent's "acts or directives."
6. The defendant "engaged in sexual intercourse in the state" that may have led to the child's conception.
7. The defendant "asserted paternity in the putative father registry."
8. Or where there is any other basis for the state's exercise of jurisdiction.[5]

All of these jurisdictional grounds are available in child support cases, but only grounds one, two, and eight are available for the assertion of personal jurisdiction over a nonresident in spousal support cases.

## Does the Court Have Jurisdiction to Divide Property?

The jurisdictional rules regarding property distribution are more complex than they are with respect to support and will be set out as a series of general principles:

1. As a foundational matter, jurisdiction is not premised upon domicile as it is for the divorce itself.

2. If the court has personal jurisdiction over the defendant, it may effectuate a division of all property located within its borders.

3. Even if a court lacks personal jurisdiction over a defendant, it may be able to effectuate a division of property based on its authority over property located within its borders. This is known as **in rem jurisdiction**. As a general rule, to satisfy due process requirements, in rem jurisdiction requires a connection between the underlying cause of action and the claims to the property—a connection that would be satisfied in the divorce context. [Some commentators have questioned the fairness of this rule, and we thus may see a gradual shift to a minimum contacts rule—as always, you should check the status of your state's jurisdictional requirements when it comes to dividing property in a divorce with a nonresident defendant.]

4. Even if it has personal jurisdiction over the defendant, a court cannot directly affect title to property that is located outside the state. However, it may be able to accomplish this result indirectly by ordering the defendant to convey title to the property. In short, based on its authority over the defendant, a court can require him or her to take actions that affect how the property is held, even though the court is unable to affect title directly.

## Does the Court Have Jurisdiction to Determine Custody?

Traditionally, most states exercised jurisdiction over child custody matters based on the physical presence of the child within its borders. Although this rule usually meant that the court that granted the divorce had jurisdiction over the initial custody determination, it also served to encourage a dissatisfied spouse to remove his or her children to a new state in order to relitigate the issue in hope of a more favorable outcome. In addition to encouraging parental removals, this approach often resulted in conflicting decrees, creating an enforcement nightmare.

In 1968, prompted by this jurisdictional morass, the National Conference of Commissioners on Uniform State Laws (NCCUSL) approved the Uniform Child Custody Jurisdiction Act (UCCJA) in the hope that consistent jurisdictional standards would deter the removal or kidnapping of children, eliminate interstate jurisdictional competition, and prevent states from relitigating custody decisions from other states. All states have since adopted the UCCJA, although some states have modified the uniform provisions. In 1980, in the face of continued parental removals and interstate jurisdictional conflicts, Congress passed the Parental Kidnapping Prevention Act (PKPA)[6] to close some of the gaps left open by the UCCJA. In 1997, in light of ongoing jurisdictional complexities and inconsistencies, the

National Conference adopted the Uniform Child Custody Jurisdiction and Enforcement Act (UCCJEA), which revises the UCCJA.[7] The UCCJEA has been adopted by over half the states. Where adopted, it replaces the UCCJA.

Interstate custody cases are among the most complex in the family law field and contain many traps for the unaware. This section will provide you with a basic overview of key jurisdictional rules; however, you should be aware that the Acts contain many other important rules, such as those pertaining to notice and disclosure, that are not addressed here. Moreover, the discussion does not cover the array of differences and potential conflicts between the three Acts, nor does it discuss other laws that might come into play in an interstate custody case, such as the Full Faith and Credit provisions of the Violence Against Women Act.[8] In light of these complexities, it is very important that when conducting a client interview, you elicit detailed information about the present and past locations of both parties and the children as this can have important jurisdictional implications.

### Jurisdictional Requirements Under the UCCJA and the UCCJEA

In this section, we consider the four jurisdictional bases for **initial custody determinations** under the UCCJA and the UCCJEA: (1) home state, (2) significant connection, (3) emergency, and (4) last resort. We then look at when a state may assume modification jurisdiction under these Acts and the full faith and credit requirement of PKPA. An important consideration underlying these Acts is that in contrast to the traditional approach, the mere physical presence of a child in a state is not sufficient to confer jurisdiction; in fact, with the exception of emergency jurisdiction, the physical presence of a child, although preferred, is not an essential prerequisite to a state's assumption of jurisdiction.

### Initial Custody Determinations

**Home State Jurisdiction.**[9] A state that is or has been the child's home may assert **"home state" jurisdiction** over a custody dispute. A home state is the state in which a child has lived for six continuous months or, if younger than six months, has lived in from birth. Temporary absences from the state do not stop the running of the clock but are included in the time computation.

A state may exercise jurisdiction if it is the child's home state at the commencement of the custody proceeding or if it was the child's home state within six months prior to the commencement of the proceeding. Once a state acquires "home state" status, it can retain that status for six months after the departure of the child so long as a parent or a parent substitute remains in that state.

**Significant Connection Jurisdiction.**[10] A state may exercise **"significant connection" jurisdiction** in situations where it has a significant connection with the child and at least one contestant, and substantial evidence is available in that state that is relevant to the merits of the custody determination.

**Comparing the Relationship Between "Home State" and "Significant Connection" Jurisdictions in the UCCJA and the UCCJEA.** "Home state" and "significant connection" jurisdictions are the most important jurisdictional bases. However, because the UCCJA does not expressly prioritize between them, it is possible for two states to claim jurisdiction at the same time. For example, let's assume that a couple who has been living in state $Y$ separates. Dad moves to state $X$ with the couple's daughter, who is ten years old, and Mom remains in state $Y$. Eight months later, Dad files for divorce and seeks custody of the child. At this point, state $Y$ has lost home state status, and state $X$ has become the child's home state because she has lived there for the six months prior to the filing of the action. However, because the child has spent most of her life in state $Y$, it is possible that $Y$ could claim significant connection jurisdiction.[11] The UCCJEA closes this loophole (as does PKPA, which is discussed below) by prioritizing home state jurisdiction. Under the UCCJEA, a state may exercise significant connection jurisdiction only where there is no home state, or the home state declines jurisdiction. Thus, in our above example, state $Y$ could not claim significant connection jurisdiction because $X$ is now the home state, unless state $X$ declines to hear the case.[12]

**Emergency Jurisdiction.**[13] A state may exercise **emergency jurisdiction** where the child is physically present in the state and has been abandoned or needs emergency protection from abuse or neglect. Although the child must be physically present, the endangerment need not have occurred within that state. Courts are generally cautious when proceeding under this section and will generally assume emergency jurisdiction only in "extraordinary circumstances." Also, most courts will assume emergency jurisdiction only on a temporary basis to stabilize the situation and will then refer the case back to the state with either home state or significant connection jurisdiction.

**Comparing Emergency Jurisdiction in the UCCJA and the UCCJEA in Domestic Violence Cases.** Although the UCCJA's emergency jurisdiction provision references harm to children, it is silent when it comes to spousal abuse. Accordingly, most courts have declined to exercise emergency jurisdiction in situations where a parent has fled to escape abuse in the absence of direct harm to the child, even though (as discussed in Chapter 6) bearing witness to violence can be devastating to children. Some states, however, either by statute or judicial decision, do take violence against a parent into account, such as where "one parent has been assaulted or terrorized by an intimate partner in the child's presence."[14] In contrast, under the UCCJEA, emergency jurisdiction has been broadened to include situations in which it is necessary in an emergency "to protect the child because the child, or a sibling or parent of the child, is subjected to or threatened with mistreatment or abuse."[15]

**Last Resort Jurisdiction.**[16] Last, and in this case least, a state that does not meet the requirements of any other section may assume jurisdiction if no other state has or is willing to assume it, and it is in the best interest of the child for it to do so. This section is subsidiary in nature to the others, and is rarely invoked. An example of when it might be used is where a child has moved around so frequently that no state qualifies as the home state or has a significant connection to the child.

### Modification Jurisdiction

An important goal of the UCCJA was to limit the ability of states to modify custody determinations of other states to prevent the proliferation of potentially conflicting orders. Accordingly, under the Act, a state could modify the custody order of another state only if it appeared that the decree state no longer had jurisdiction and the new state could assert jurisdiction in accordance with the UCCJA.[17] This means that the initial decree state should have exclusive **modification jurisdiction**, sometimes referred to as **continuing jurisdiction**, until such time as it no longer can satisfy the jurisdictional requirements of the UCCJA.

However, as with initial determination jurisdiction, it is possible that two states could simultaneously assert modification jurisdiction. For example, let's say that state A makes an initial determination giving custody to Mom, with visitation rights to Dad. Mom then moves to state B with the child, but the child visits Dad regularly in state A. What happens if Dad files a modification action in state A ten months after Mom's departure? At this point in time, home state status has shifted to state B, but state A still has a connection to the child and one parent and could thus claim significant connection jurisdiction. But if Mom then filed a modification action in state B, that court could decide that A's connection is not significant enough to retain authority over the case and that modification jurisdiction had shifted to state B, the child's present home state.

As with the exercise of initial custody jurisdiction, the UCCJEA has addressed this problem (as does PKPA) by providing for continuing, exclusive modification jurisdiction in the initial state (subject to the emergency jurisdiction exception) until one of two determinations are made: (1) the initial state determines that it no longer has jurisdiction because it lacks a significant connection to the case and substantial evidence is no longer available there or (2) it is established that neither the child nor either parent still lives there.[18] Returning to our example, under the UCCJEA, state *B* could not modify the initial order based on its status as the home state, unless state *A* first determined that it no longer had a significant connection to the case. Given the facts, this is unlikely, as the dad still lives there, the child left the state only ten months earlier, and the child still visits there on a regular basis.

### Declining Jurisdiction

In addition to determining when a state may properly assume jurisdiction over a custody dispute, the UCCJA and the UCCJEA also encourage states to decline jurisdiction under certain circumstances. Based on the doctrine of *forum non conveniens*, states are encouraged to decline jurisdiction if it is an inconvenient forum and another state is in a better position to hear the case. Further, based on the "clean hands" doctrine, states are urged to refuse jurisdiction where the petitioner has engaged in wrongful conduct such as improperly removing a child from the home state. However, a parent who has fled a state with a child for good cause, such as to escape from violence, should not be penalized by this provision. Although not explicit in the UCCJA, the UCCJEA makes clear that as long as the emergency jurisdiction requirements are met, a state may not decline jurisdiction based on the conduct of the petitioner.[19]

### Jurisdictional Requirements of PKPA

As we have seen, the UCCJA did not resolve the problem of interstate jurisdictional conflicts. Accordingly, in 1980, Congress enacted the Parental Kidnapping and Prevention Act. PKPA requires states to give full faith and credit to custody decrees of other states if they conform to PKPA's jurisdictional requirements. Thus, states must enforce and cannot modify conforming decrees from other states unless certain conditions (discussed below) are met. Like the UCCJA and the UCCJEA, PKPA has four jurisdictional bases: home state, significant connection, emergency and last resort. However, as with the UCCJEA, PKPA prioritizes home state jurisdiction. Accordingly, for a decree to be enforceable under PKPA, it can assume significant connection jurisdiction only if no other state qualifies as the home state; the two are not alternative jurisdictional bases. If a state does assume jurisdiction based on its connection with the case where another state qualifies as the home state, the decree will not be entitled to interstate recognition in other states.[20] PKPA also vests exclusive, continuing jurisdiction in the initial state so long as a parent or the child remains there, and the state has jurisdiction under its own laws. So long as this state has jurisdiction, no other state may modify its decree. Modification jurisdiction shifts only when everyone has moved away from the decree state (or it declines jurisdiction) and another state can satisfy PKPA's jurisdictional requirement.

To understand how PKPA interacts with the UCCJA, let's return to our modification fact pattern. As set out above, Mom received custody in state *A* and then moved to state *B* with the child, while Dad remained in state *A*. Under the UCCJA, it is almost certain that at some point modification jurisdiction would shift to state *B* as either the new home state or the significant connection state. However, under PKPA, state *A* has continuing jurisdiction so long as Dad continues to live there. This means that if state *B* modified the decree, it would not be entitled to interstate recognition even though the requirements of the UCCJA were met. Again, given that the UCCJEA also vests continuing, exclusive jurisdiction in the home state, this problem is not likely to arise under the UCCJEA.

In sum, the hope is that PKPA (and now also the UCCJEA), by giving priority to the home state and vesting continuing jurisdiction in a single state, will eliminate the final vestiges of interstate competition in the custody arena. However, due to the complex legal and factual nature of these cases, true interstate harmony is unlikely in the foreseeable future.

## Chapter Summary

Broadly stated, jurisdiction refers to the authority of a court to hear a case and render a binding decree. More specifically, subject matter jurisdiction refers to the authority of a court to hear specific types of cases, while personal jurisdiction refers to a court's authority over a defendant. Personal jurisdiction can be based on domicile, minimum contacts, consent, or physical presence. Long-arm statutes allow states to assert personal jurisdiction over nonresident defendants who have sufficient minimum contacts with the forum state. The assertion of personal jurisdiction must satisfy the fairness requirement of the due process clause.

Jurisdiction to dissolve the marriage is usually based on domicile; personal jurisdiction over the defendant is not required. However, a court cannot order a defendant to pay support if it does not have personal jurisdiction over him or her. Personal jurisdiction may be asserted over a nonresident through the long-arm provisions of UIFSA or state jurisdictional statute. Where property is concerned, a distribution can be effectuated based either on personal jurisdiction over the defendant or on the court's in rem authority over property located within its borders.

Jurisdiction over child custody disputes is determined by the UCCJA, the UCCJEA, and PKPA. These Acts respond to the earlier "physical presence" rule, which encouraged parental abductions and created enforcement nightmares. These Acts establish four jurisdictional bases for when a state may assert jurisdiction over a custody dispute: home state, significant connection, emergency, and last resort. The UCCJA does not prioritize between these bases; thus, it is possible for two states to claim authority over a case at the same time; however, both PKPA and the UCCJEA priori-tize home state jurisdiction. The UCCJEA and PKPA vest continuing exclusive jurisdiction in the home state until certain conditions are met; PKPA also requires states to give full faith and credit to conforming custody decrees from other states.

## Key Terms

Jurisdiction
Subject Matter Jurisdiction
Personal Jurisdiction
Domicile
Minimum Contacts
Long-Arm Statutes
Divisible Divorce
In Rem Jurisdiction

Initial Custody Determinations
"Home State" Jurisdiction
"Significant Connection" Jurisdiction
Emergency Jurisdiction
Last Resort Jurisdiction
Modification Jurisdiction
Continuing Jurisdiction

## Review Questions

1. Broadly defined, what is jurisdiction?

2. What is subject matter jurisdiction?

3. Explain the concept of personal jurisdiction. What are the ways in which a court can obtain personal jurisdiction over a defendant?

4. What is a long-arm statute?

5. Why doesn't a state need to have personal jurisdiction over a defendant in order to dissolve a marriage? What is required?

6. Explain the jurisdictional role of UIFSA in support cases.

7. What is meant by the term "divisible divorce"?

8. Explain the jurisdictional concepts that are relevant to the distribution of property.

9. Traditionally, what has been the basis for the exercise of jurisdiction over a child custody dispute? What problems did this create?

10. What is the UCCJA? the UCCJEA? PKPA? Why were these laws enacted?

11. What is a home state? When may a state assert home state jurisdiction?

12. What is significant connection jurisdiction?

13. Explain how two states could assert initial jurisdiction at the same time under the UCCJA.

14. What is emergency jurisdiction?

15. What is last resort jurisdiction?

16. What provision does the UCCJEA make for domestic violence victims?

17. Explain how two states might both seek to assert modification jurisdiction at the same time under the UCCJA. How would this work under the UCCJA and PKPA?

18. Under what circumstances do the UCCJA and the UCCJEA encourage states to decline jurisdiction?

19. Under PKPA, when must a state enforce the decree of another state?

20. Under PKPA, what is the relationship of home state and significant connection jurisdiction? What would be the result if a state asserted significant connection jurisdiction when another state qualified as the home state?

21. Under PKPA, when can a state modify the decree of another state?

22. Under PKPA, at what point does the continuing jurisdiction of the decree state terminate?

23. What would be the result if a new state modified a decree where the decree state had continuing jurisdiction?

## Discussion Questions

1. PKPA's continuing jurisdiction rule has been criticized as favoring stability over the needs of children because it can vest exclusive jurisdiction in a state that has lost any meaningful relationship with the child. Do you think the Act has gone too far? Should a state with no present connection with a child have modification jurisdiction? How do you accommodate the goals of flexibility and predictability?

2. Do you think the emergency jurisdiction provision of the UCCJA and the UCCJEA might encourage parents to flee with children in the absence of a genuine emergency situation in order to try and gain an advantage in a custody dispute? Is there another way to protect the needs of victims of violence?

## Assignments

1. Determine whether your state uses the UCCJA or the UCCJEA in interstate custody cases. Read the applicable statute carefully.

2. Using the appropriate digest, find all the cases from your state that involve an interstate custody dispute. Now choose two of the cases and analyze how the court made its decision. In the course of your analysis, refer back to the UCCJA or the UCCJEA and make sure that you both understand and discuss all provisions relevant to the court's analysis in each case.

3. Locate UIFSA as adopted by your state. Now, locate any additional long-arm statutes that can be used in support cases in your state. Review the circumstances under which long-arm jurisdiction can be asserted and determine if they add anything to the UIFSA grounds.

4. Assume a client has come to your firm's office seeking a divorce. All you know at this point is that she and her husband and their children have moved frequently over the past five years, and she has recently moved to your state with the children. In preparation

for the interview, an attorney in your office has asked you to develop some questions in advance so that all facts bearing on jurisdiction will be covered. In developing the questions, make sure you think about all aspects of the case.

## Cases for Analysis

The following case focuses on personal jurisdiction and service of process.

### GOODIN v. DEPARTMENT OF HUMAN SERVICES
#### 772 So.2d 1051 (Miss. 2000)

STATEMENT OF THE CASE

The Mississippi Department of Human Services ("DHS"), on behalf of Diana Goodin-McKay ("McKay"), sought to enforce an Arizona child support order against John T. Goodin ("Goodin") in the Chancery Court of Winston County. The chancellor granted DHS' petition, and Goodin has appealed, asserting the following assignments of error: . . .
. . . The chancery court lacked personal jurisdiction over Goodin. . . .

STATEMENT OF THE FACTS

Goodin and McKay married in Mississippi and later became residents of Arizona where they eventually divorced. Pursuant to the divorce, the Superior Court of Cochise County, Arizona, ordered Goodin to pay $776 in monthly child support for the two unemancipated children born of this marriage.

After the divorce, McKay and the two children returned to Mississippi to live. . . . Goodin also returned to Mississippi. . . .

Goodin, by his own admission, did not pay child support between February 1998 and July 31, 1999. . . . Because Goodin had not paid child support in that period, DHS, on behalf of McKay, sought to enforce the Arizona order in Mississippi, filing a Petition to Enforce and Give Full Faith and Credit to a Foreign Child Support Judgment ("Petition") in the Chancery Court of Winston County, Mississippi.

Following the filing of the Petition, Goodin appeared before Chancellor Edward Prisock, and with the assistance of counsel opposite, objected to the court's jurisdiction over him [and] . . . to service of process. . . . At the hearing, . . . Goodin again objected to the court's jurisdiction, stating that he was a resident of Arizona, not Mississippi. . . .

Goodin reiterated his previous position as to service of process, testifying that he had never been personally served, that service had been left with his mother at her home, and that he did not reside with her. . . .

## LEGAL ANALYSIS

### I.   DID THE CHANCERY COURT POSSESS PERSONAL JURISDICTION OVER GOODIN?

Goodin contends that he is an Arizona resident as he still owns a house and is still a registered voter there and, therefore, is not subject to the jurisdiction of the Winston County Chancery Court. This Court, however, need not consider whether Goodin is a domiciliary as he was properly served process while physically present in Mississippi.

The United States Supreme Court has held that a nonresident of a State is subject to the jurisdiction of that State's courts if properly served process while physically present in that State. Burnham v. Superior Court, 495 U.S. 604, 628, 110 S. Ct. 2105, 2119, 109 L. Ed. 2d 631, 650 (1990). One may properly serve process to a defendant in Mississippi by having the sheriff or his deputy physically deliver a copy of the summons and complaint to the defendant. . . .

[T]his Court finds Goodin personally subject to the jurisdiction of this State's courts under *Burnham*. DHA properly served Goodin a copy of the summons and complaint as is reflected in the "proof of service" form, signed by Winston County Deputy Sheriff Curtis Austin, indicating he personally served process to Goodin in Mississippi. While Goodin maintained at the hearing that he had not been properly served process by DHS, Goodin fails to raise that issue on appeal. The Court has long held that issues not properly raised on appeal are procedurally barred from consideration. . . . Even were Goodin's contention not procedurally barred, this Court finds substantial, credible evidence in the "proof of service" form to support the chancellor's finding that the trial court had jurisdiction over the parties and affirms the trial court's decision. . . .

## QUESTIONS

1. What was the Mississippi Department of Human Services seeking to do in this case?

2. Why did Goodin argue that the court lacked personal jurisdiction over him?

3. Why did he argue that service had been improper?

4. How did the court respond to his arguments? According to the court, what was the connection between service and jurisdiction? What case did the court rely on in reaching its result?

---

The following case addresses the issue whether, as part of a divorce, a court has the authority to order parties to sell property that is located out of state. To resolve this, the court focuses on the distinction between in rem and personal jurisdiction.

## RUSSO v. RUSSO
### 714 A.2d 466 (Pa. Super. Ct. 1998)

The issue is whether the order of the trial court was an exercise of its in rem or in personam jurisdiction. The order, entered in the context of the parties' divorce action, directed the parties to sell real property outside of the Commonwealth of Pennsylvania and prescribed the distribution of the proceeds from the sale. We conclude the order implicated the court's in personam jurisdiction, and affirm the trial court.

Appellant-husband appeals from that portion of the trial court's final order of equitable distribution which directed the parties to sell their vacation home located in Ohio and prescribed how the proceeds from the sale should be divided between them. . . .

Husband concedes that 23 Pa.C.S. § 3104(a)(1) provides that in cases of divorce the courts shall have original jurisdiction over, inter alia, "the determination and disposition of property rights and interests between spouses." He argues on appeal, however, that such jurisdiction extends only to property located in Pennsylvania because a Pennsylvania court cannot exercise in rem jurisdiction over real or personal property which is located outside the state. Husband contends that the basis of jurisdiction over property is the presence of that property within the territorial jurisdiction of the forum state and that a Pennsylvania court thus lacks jurisdiction over property located in Ohio because such property is not within the territorial jurisdiction of Pennsylvania.

While we agree with husband's assertion that a Pennsylvania court cannot exercise in rem jurisdiction over property outside Pennsylvania . . . , we find that when it ordered the parties to sell the Ohio property, the trial court was not exercising in rem jurisdiction over the property. Instead, we conclude that the court was ordering the parties, over whom it had personal jurisdiction, to sell the property and distribute the proceeds in a particular fashion.

A similar distinction between a court's in rem and in personam jurisdiction was highlighted by this court in Whitmer v. Whitmer, 243 Pa.

Super. 462, 365 A.2d 1316 (Pa. Super. 1976). At issue in that case was the propriety of a Florida court's order awarding the appellant an undivided one-half interest in the assets of Edward H. Whitmer Co., located in Pennsylvania. We held that although the Florida court had personal jurisdiction over the parties, "it was beyond the jurisdiction of the Florida court to make a conveyance to appellant of a one-half interest in appellee's Pennsylvania property." 365 A.2d at 1319. In so holding, however, we noted the difference between a court's exercise of in rem jurisdiction by effectuating a transfer of out-of-state property and the exercise of personal jurisdiction over the parties by ordering them to take some action with regard to such property. In that case, we commented as follows: "having personal jurisdiction over appellee, the Florida court might have ordered appellee to convey a one-half interest in his Pennsylvania property to appellant and, if necessary, enforce its order by contempt proceedings." *Id.*

Unlike the Florida court's order purporting to effectuate a conveyance of the property in *Whitmer*, the trial court's order in the present case does not itself act as a conveyance, but instead directs the parties to take certain action. It is clear, and husband does not contest, that the court had personal jurisdiction over both husband and wife. It also had the authority, under the Divorce Code, to determine their respective rights and interests in marital property. It is thus clear that the trial court had the power to order these parties to sell their marital vacation home, regardless of its location, and to direct them to divide the proceeds in any manner necessary to effectuate economic justice between them.

We conclude that the trial court did not err ordering the parties to sell the Ohio property because we find that the court, in doing so, was exercising personal jurisdiction over the parties, rather than in rem jurisdiction over the property. Order affirmed.

## QUESTIONS

1. What did the Pennsylvania trial court order with respect to the Ohio property?

2. In jurisdictional terms, why did the husband object to this order?

3. The court agreed with the husband's argument—why?

4. Although agreeing with the husband's argument, the court nonetheless concluded that the trial court had jurisdiction to enter the order regarding the out of state property. How did the court reach

this conclusion? What kind of jurisdiction did this court determine the trial court had been exercising when it made this order?

---

This case takes a look at the complicated jurisdictional issues that can arise when a custody cases involves more than one state. Making matters more complicated, the case involves a dispute between parties to a Vermont civil union, a point that prompts arguments that PKPA does not apply in this context due, at least in part, to the Defense of Marriage Act (DOMA).

## MILLER-JENKINS v. MILLER-JENKINS
### 2006 VT 78, 912 A.2d 951 (2006)

J. Lisa Miller-Jenkins appeals a family court decision finding her ex-partner, Janet Miller-Jenkins, to be a parent of their three-year-old child conceived via artificial insemination. . . .

Lisa and Janet lived together in Virginia for several years in the late 1990's. In December 2000, the parties traveled to Vermont and entered into a civil union. In 2001, while Lisa and Janet were still a couple, Lisa began to receive artificial insemination from sperm provided by an anonymous donor. Janet participated in the decision that Lisa become impregnated and helped select the anonymous donor. In April 2002, Lisa gave birth to IMJ, with Janet present in the delivery room. Lisa, Janet, and IMJ lived in Virginia until IMJ was approximately four months old and then moved together to Vermont around August of 2002. The parties lived together with IMJ in Vermont until the fall of 2003, when they decided to separate. After the separation, in September 2003, Lisa moved to Virginia with IMJ.

On November 24, 2003, Lisa filed a petition to dissolve the civil union in the Vermont family court in Rutland. In her complaint, Lisa listed IMJ as the "biological or adoptive child of the civil union." Lisa requested that the court award her custodial rights and award Janet parent-child contact. The family court issued a temporary order on parental rights and responsibilities on June 17, 2004. This order awarded Lisa temporary legal and physical responsibility for IMJ, and awarded Janet parent-child contact for two weekends in June, one weekend in July, and the third full week of each month, beginning in August 2004. The family court also ordered Lisa to permit Janet to have telephone contact with IMJ once daily.

Although Lisa permitted the first court ordered parent-child-contact weekend, she did not allow Janet to have parent-child contact after that date, nor did she allow Janet to have telephone contact with IMJ, as the family court had ordered. In fact, Lisa has not allowed Janet to have any contact with IMJ other than during that first weekend. Meanwhile, on July 1, 2004, after the Vermont court had already filed its temporary custody and visitation order and parentage decision, Lisa filed a petition in the Frederick County Virginia Circuit Court and asked that court to establish IMJ's parentage.

In response, on July 19, 2004, the Vermont court reaffirmed its "jurisdiction over this case including all parent-child contact issues," stated that it would not "defer to a different State that would preclude the parties from a remedy," and made clear that the temporary order for parent-child contact was to be followed. It added that "[f]ailure of the custodial parent to allow contact will result in an immediate hearing on the need to change custody."

Although the Vermont and Virginia courts consulted by telephone, an interstate parental-rights contest ensued. On September 2, 2004, the Vermont court found Lisa in contempt for willful refusal to comply with the temporary visitation order. On September 9, the Virginia court held it had jurisdiction to determine the parentage and parental rights of IMJ and that any claims of Janet to parental status were "based on rights under Vermont's civil union laws that are null and void under Va. Code § 20-45.3." On October 15, the Virginia court followed with a parentage order finding Lisa to be the "sole biological and natural parent" of IMJ and holding that Janet has no "claims of parentage or visitation rights over" IMJ. That order is on appeal to the Virginia Court of Appeals.

On November 17, 2004, the Vermont court found that both Lisa and Janet had parental interests in IMJ and set the case for a final hearing on parental rights, property, and child support. Thereafter, on December 21, 2004, the Vermont court issued a ruling refusing to give full faith and credit to the Virginia parentage decision. Lisa appealed both of these decisions, as well as the decision finding her in contempt.

## I.  INTERSTATE JURISDICTION AND FULL FAITH AND CREDIT

This case is, at base, an interstate jurisdictional dispute over visitation with a child. Lisa argues here that the Vermont family court should have given full faith and credit to the Virginia court's custody and parentage decision, which determined Janet had no parentage or visitation rights with respect to IMJ. The family court rejected this argument because it concluded the Virginia decision did not comport with the PKPA, "which was designed for the very purpose of eliminating jurisdictional battles between states with conflicting jurisdictional provisions in child custody disputes." The Vermont court determined it had exercised jurisdiction consistent with the requirements of the PKPA and had continuing jurisdiction at the time Lisa's action was filed in Virginia. Therefore, it further concluded the Virginia court was prohibited from exercising jurisdiction by the PKPA, §1738A(g), and the Vermont court had no obligation to give full faith and credit to the conflicting Virginia decision.

In analyzing Lisa's arguments, we note that she does not contest that if she and Janet were a validly married heterosexual couple, the family court's PKPA analysis would be correct . . .

The purpose of the PKPA is to determine when one state must give full faith and credit to a child custody determination of another state, such that the new state cannot thereafter act inconsistently with the original custody determination. Thompson v. Thompson, 484 U.S. 174, 181, 108 S. Ct. 513, 98 L. Ed. 2d 512 (1988). The PKPA follows on, and includes many of the provisions of, the Uniform Child Custody Jurisdiction Act (UCCJA), adopted in Vermont as 15 V.S.A. §§ 1031-1051. These acts were adopted to respond to "a growing public concern over the fact that thousands of children are shifted from state to state and from one family to another every year while their parents or other persons battle over their custody in the courts of several states." National Conference of Commissioners on Uniform State Laws, Uniform Child Custody Jurisdiction Act, Prefatory Note (1968). The PKPA embodies preferences "to leave jurisdiction in the state which rendered the original decree[,] . . . to promote the best interests of the child[,] . . . [and to] discourage[] interstate abduction and other unilateral removals of children for the purpose of obtaining a favorable custody decree." Michalik v. Michalik, 172 Wis. 2d 640, 494 N.W.2d 391, 398 (Wis. 1993). . . .

Because the first custody and visitation determination with respect to IMJ was made by the Vermont court, we must first examine whether that court exercised jurisdiction "consistently with the provisions of" the PKPA. Id. If it did, and if it continued to have jurisdiction when Lisa filed her proceeding in the Virginia court, the Virginia court was without jurisdiction to modify the Vermont order. Id. § 1738A(g), (h).

In order for a Vermont court to exercise jurisdiction consistent with the PKPA, it must have jurisdiction under Vermont law, id. § 1738A(c)(1), and meet one of four conditions, id. § 1738A(c)(2)(A)-(D). In this case, it met the condition in subsection (c)(2)(A)(ii) that Vermont "had been the child's home State within six months before the date of the commencement of the proceeding and the child is absent from such State because of his removal or retention by a contestant or for other reasons, and a contestant continues to live in such State." Id. § 1738A(c)(2)(A)(ii). . . . Because Vermont had been IMJ's home state within six months before Lisa filed her dissolution petition in November 2003, Lisa had removed IMJ from Vermont, and Janet lived in Vermont on the date the dissolution proceeding was commenced, the requirements of subsection (A)(ii) were met. . . .

The PKPA also requires that the court have jurisdiction under Vermont law. Whether local jurisdiction is present is determined by the UCCJA. 15 V.S.A. § 1032(a); Matthews, 162 Vt. at 406, 649 A.2d at 235. For the exact reason that the Vermont proceeding met the PKPA condition discussed above, supra, P 13, it met the identically-worded provision of the UCCJA. Compare 15 V.S.A. § 1032(a)(1)(B) with 28 U.S.C. § 1738A(c)(2)(A)(ii). Thus, the family court had jurisdiction under Vermont law as required by 28 U.S.C. § 1738A(c)(1).

Because the Vermont dissolution proceeding was still pending in July 2004, when Lisa filed her action in the Virginia court, and the Vermont proceeding was consistent with the PKPA, the Virginia court lacked jurisdiction pursuant to § 1738A(g) of the PKPA. That section specified that the court could not exercise jurisdiction over a proceeding to determine the custody of, or visitation with, IMJ while the Vermont proceeding was pending. The Virginia court violated this section by exercising jurisdiction over the case filed by Lisa.

Because the Vermont court had issued a temporary custody and visitation order, the Virginia court was also governed by § 1738A(h) of the PKPA. That section prohibited the Virginia court from modifying the Vermont court's order unless the Vermont court "no longer [had] jurisdiction to modify such determination" or had "declined to exercise jurisdiction to modify such determination." Since the Vermont court continued to exercise jurisdiction over the Vermont proceeding, the Virginia court could have modified the order only if the Vermont court had lost its initial jurisdiction. Under the PKPA, a court that had initial jurisdiction to issue a custody or visitation order continues to have jurisdiction as long as it continues to have jurisdiction under state law and one of the contestants remains a resident of the state. Id. § 1738A(d); Matthews, 162 Vt. at 407, 649 A.2d at 236. The latter requirement is met because Janet continues to reside in Vermont.

Again, the former requirement of continuing jurisdiction is met if it is authorized by the UCCJA. . . . At the time the Virginia court acted, the Vermont court had jurisdiction to modify its own visitation order if:

> (2) it is in the best interest of the child that a court of this state assume jurisdiction because:
> (A) the child and his parents, or the child and at least one contestant, have a significant connection with this state; and
> (B) there is available in this state substantial evidence concerning the child's present or future care, protection, training, and personal relationships.

15 V.S.A. § 1032(a)(2). These provisions were met because IMJ had recently resided in Vermont and the evidence of IMJ's relationship with Janet was present in Vermont. . . .

The Vermont court had continuing jurisdiction over the matter of Janet's visitation with IMJ. Therefore, the Virginia order extinguishing Janet's visitation right was issued in violation of § 1738A(h) of the PKPA. The Vermont court was not required to give full faith and credit to the Virginia order issued in violation of the PKPA. . . .

Lisa makes three arguments against applying this analysis in this case. First, she argues that the Virginia proceeding is a parentage action, and the PKPA does not apply to parentage actions. . . .

[W]e reject the argument that the PKPA is inapplicable. The PKPA applies to custody or visitation determinations. 28 U.S.C. § 1738A(a). . . . Lisa's dissolution petition to the Rutland Family Court sought a custody determination, and the court's temporary order included a temporary determination of both custody and visitation. Lisa's parentage petition in the Virginia court sought a determination that Janet had no parental rights, and the Virginia court issued a temporary order requiring Janet's visitation to be supervised and then a permanent order that Janet had no right to visit IMJ. Plainly, the Virginia court decisions included visitation determinations as the term is defined in the PKPA. Just as plainly, the PKPA applied to those decisions.

Lisa's argument, then, is that a custody or visitation determination arising out of one kind of proceeding is covered by the PKPA, and a custody or visitation determination arising out of another is not. All of the decisions interpreting the PKPA in private family disputes conclude that the PKPA draws no such distinction. . . .

For the above reasons, we reject Lisa's argument that the PKPA does not apply to the Virginia parentage decision. We hold that the PKPA applies to this case and does not command the Vermont court to give full faith and credit to the parentage decision of the Virginia court that was issued in violation of the PKPA.

Lisa's second argument is that the PKPA has been superseded by the Defense of Marriage Act (DOMA), 28 U.S.C. § 1738C (2000), and DOMA requires that the Vermont court give full faith and credit to the Virginia decision and order. DOMA reads:

> No State, territory, or possession of the United States, or Indian tribe, shall be required to give effect to any public act, record, or judicial proceeding of any other State, territory, possession, or tribe respecting a relationship between persons of the same sex that is treated as a marriage under the laws of such other State, territory, possession, or tribe, or a right or claim arising from such relationship.

Id. Lisa argues that a Vermont civil union is a relationship between persons of the same sex that is treated as a marriage under Vermont law and that

Janet's right of visitation, if any, arises from that relationship. Thus, she argues that DOMA authorized the Virginia court to reject any right of visitation based on the Vermont court order, and the Vermont court must give full faith and credit to the Virginia order.

The family court concluded that DOMA would not provide Lisa the relief she sought:

> Nor is the application of the PKPA in this case, as Lisa's counsel has suggested, hindered by the more recently enacted Federal Defense of Marriage Act (DOMA). . . . Whether or not a Virginia court may be permitted under DOMA to decline to give effect to the judicial proceedings in Vermont in a Virginia court is not relevant to the essential question before this court, or before the court of Virginia as a prerequisite for exercising its jurisdiction, of whether this Vermont court had jurisdiction under Vermont law over this dispute before it was filed in Virginia. Clearly Vermont has jurisdiction and therefore the Commonwealth of Virginia's judgment is not entitled to full faith and credit. . . .

We affirm on the ground employed by the Vermont court. This case is about whether the Vermont court must give full faith and credit to the decision of the Virginia court, and not the reverse. Unlike the PKPA, in no instance does DOMA require a court in one state to give full faith and credit to the decision of a court in another state. Its sole purpose is to provide an authorization not to give full faith and credit in the circumstances covered by the statute. Thus, DOMA does not aid Lisa's attack on the Vermont order. . . .

Lisa's third ground for arguing the PKPA does not apply is that the civil union was void because both Janet and Lisa were residents of Virginia when they entered the civil union in Vermont, and, as a result, Virginia courts did not have to recognize it. We consider this argument in the next section of the opinion and reject it.

In summary, none of Lisa's arguments change our conclusion that this is a straightforward interstate jurisdictional dispute over custody, and the governing law fully supports the Vermont court's decision to exercise jurisdiction and refuse to follow the conflicting Virginia visitation order.

## QUESTIONS

1. What is the underlying fact pattern that led to the interstate jurisdictional conflict?

2. What are the conflicting state custody/visitation/parentage orders?

3. On what basis does the Vermont court conclude that its family court had jurisdiction to enter the temporary custody and visitation order?

4. On what basis does it conclude that its family court had continuing jurisdiction over the custody and visitation dispute?

5. What three arguments does Lisa make to support her claim that PKPA does not apply in this case? How does the court respond to each of these arguments?

# Endnotes ————————————————————————————————————

1. Although many statutes use the term "residence," virtually all courts have interpreted this to mean domicile. Rhonda Wasserman, Divorce and Domicile: Time to Sever the Note, 39 Wm & Mary L. Rev. 1, 23 (1997)

2. Williams v. North Carolina, 317 U.S. 287, 298-299 (1942).

3. *See* Rhonda Wasserman, Divorce and Domicile: Time to Sever the Note, 39 Wm & Mary L. Rev. 1 (1997); Rhonda Wasserman, Parents, Partners, and Personal Jurisdiction, 1995 U. Ill. L. Rev. 813; E. Roy Hawkins, The Effect of Schaffer v. Heitner on the Jurisdictional Standard in Ex Parte Divorces, 18 Fam. L.Q. 311 (1984). For a somewhat different approach, *see* Walter W. Meiser, A "Minimum Interest" Approach to Personal Jurisdiction, 35 Wake Forest L. Rev. 919 (2000).

4. As discussed in Chapter 7, pursuant to the 1996 welfare reform act, the Personal Responsibility and Work Opportunity Reconciliation Act (PRWORA), all states were required to adopt UIFSA as a condition of receiving federal child support funds. As of 1998, all states had complied. For details on UIFSA, the following two articles are recommended: Patricia Wick Hatamyar, Critical Applications and Proposals for Improvement of the Uniform Interstate Family Support Act and the Full Faith and Credit for Child Support Orders Act, 71 St. John's L. Rev. 1 (1997); Patricia Wick Hatamyar, Interstate Establishment, Enforcement, and Modification of Child Support Orders, 25 Okla. City U. L. Rev. 511 (2000).

In 2000, the child support community asked the National Conference of Commissioners on Uniform State Laws (NCCUSL) to review UIFSA, and in 2001, the NCCUSL approved a number of important amendments to the Act. To date, states are not required to adopt these amendments, although a number of states have done so. For present purposes, the critical amendment is that which clarifies that the long-arm provisions apply only to the establishment and not to the modification of support orders. The revised version of UIFSA along with prefatory notes and comments can be found at http://www.law.upenn.edu/bll/ulc/uifsa/final2001.htm (accessed June 15, 2004).

5. UIFSA § 201(1)-(8) (2001). The text of this Act can be found at http://www.law.upenn.edu/bll/ulc/ulc_frame.htm and clicking on the link to the Uniform Interstate Family Support Act, Final Act 2001 (accessed October 11, 2004).

6. 28 U.S.C. § 1738A (1994).

7. The texts of the UCCJA and the UCCJEA can be found on the University of Pennsylvania's Law School's web site, which is the official site for the NCCUSL. The address is: http://www.law.upenn.edu/bll/ulc/ulc.htm.

The following articles provide more detail and a comparative discussion of the UCCJA and the UCCJEA. *See* Deborah M. Goelman, Shelter from the Storm: Using Jurisdictional Statutes to Protect Victims of Domestic Violence after the Violence Against Women Act of 2000, 13 Colum. J. Gender & L. 101 (2004) (this article also discusses PKPA); Joan Zorza, The UCCJEA: What Is It and How Does It Affect Battered Women in Child-Custody Disputes? 27 Fordham Urb. L.J. 909 (2000); Russell M. Coombs, Child Custody and Visitation by Non-parents Under the New Uniform Child Custody Jurisdiction and Enforcement Act: A Rerun of Seize-and-Run, 16 J. Am. Acad. Matrimonial Law. 1 (1999); Kelly

Gaines Stoner, The Uniform Child Custody Jurisdiction & Enforcement Act (UCCJEA)—A Metamorphosis of the Uniform Child Custody Jurisdiction Act (UCCJA), 75 N.D. L. Rev. 301 (1999) (briefly discusses jurisdictional issues with respect to custody orders issued by Indian tribal courts.); Patricia M. Hoff, The ABC's of the UCCJEA: Interstate Child Custody Practices Under the New Act, 32 Fam. L.Q. 267 (1998).

The following texts provide a thorough comparison of PKPA and the UCCJA. *See* Linda M. DeMelis, Interstate Child Custody and the Parental Kidnapping Prevention Act: The Continuing Search for a National Standard, 45 Hastings L.J. 1329 (1994); Ann B. Goldstein, The Tragedy of the Interstate Child: A Critical Reexamination of the Uniform Child Custody Act and the Parental Kidnapping Prevention Act, 25 U.C. Davis L. Rev. 845 (1992); Russell M. Coombs, Interstate Child Custody: Jurisdiction, Recognition, and Enforcement, 66 Minn. L. Rev. 711 (1982).

8. You should be aware that other laws come into play if the child who is the subject of the custody dispute is an American Indian or if the conflict involves more than one country. In the former situation, reference must also be made to the Indian Child Welfare Act of 1978, 25 U.S.C. §§ 1901 *et seq.,* the Indian Civil Rights Act of 1968, 25 U.S.C. §§ 1301 *et seq.,* and the appropriate Tribal Code. Other laws also may come into play. If the dispute is international, the Hague Convention on the Civil Aspects of International Child Abduction and the Federal Kidnapping Crime Act of 1993, as well as other possible laws, should be consulted. *See* Robert J. Spector, International Child Custody Jurisdiction and the Uniform Child Custody and Jurisdiction Act, 33 N.Y.U. J. Intl. L. & Pol. 651 (2000).

Although the focus here is on custody disputes that arise in the context of divorce actions, the UCCJA, UCCJEA, and PKPA pertain to a whole range of child custody disputes, including adoption and child placement disputes.

9. *See* UCCJA §§ 2 & 3(a)(1).

10. *See id.* § 3(a)(2).

11. The UCCJA contains a mechanism for resolving these conflicts; it prohibits simultaneous proceedings and requires a state to defer to another state if proceedings are pending and that state is exercising jurisdiction in "substantial conformity" with the Act. However, states have been able to avoid these limitations by, for example, deciding that the first state is not exercising jurisdiction in "substantial conformity" with the Act.

12. UCCJEA, § 201.

13. *See* UCCJA § 3(a)(3).

14. Goelman, *supra* note 7, at 122-123.

15. UCCJEA § 204 (a).

16. UCCJA § 3(a)(4).

17. *Id.* § 14.

18. UCCJEA § 201.2.

19. *Id.* § 208(a).

20. Some experts have cautioned, however, that similar kinds of jurisdictional quagmires are still likely under the UCCJEA. *See* Coombs, *supra* note 8, at 54-63.

# 10 The Divorce Process

In this chapter, we look at how a divorce case makes its way through the legal system. We begin with the initial client interview and move through each successive stage of the process from the filing of the action through post-judgment procedures. As we progress, we look at the role paralegals play in the preparation of a case and at the skills they need. We also look at some important ethical considerations.

## THE INITIAL CLIENT INTERVIEW

We begin with the initial client interview. At this meeting, detailed information about the client's situation is obtained; of equal importance, the interview establishes the foundation for the office's relationship with the client. One important goal is to develop a sense of mutual trust and purpose between the interviewer and the client.

Good interviews do not just happen; they require sensitivity and skill. Unfortunately, many legal professionals do not give much thought to client interviewing, perhaps because it does not appear to require specialized legal skills and knowledge. However, a poorly conducted interview can have long-term repercussions. A client who leaves a law office feeling disrespected or unheard may not develop the trust and confidence essential to a good working relationship. As a result, he or she may be reluctant to fully disclose all relevant information, particularly if it is of a sensitive or potentially damaging nature.

It is important to be attuned to the role that culture plays in the communication process, as the failure to do so can lead to misunderstandings with potentially serious consequences. In a powerful example of this dynamic, sociolinguist Diane Eades describes how differences in cultural approaches to seeking information played a major role in the conviction of an Australian Aboriginal woman for killing her abusive husband. Using standard interviewing techniques, which are based on the assumption that

429

direct questions are the best way to elicit information, the woman's attorneys had been unsuccessful in eliciting her story, which included a horrific history of violence, from her. As Eades explains, when "Aboriginal people want to find out what they consider to be significant or . . . personal information, they do not use direct questions. . . . People volunteer some of their own information, hinting about what they are trying to find out. Information is sought out as part of a two-way exchange."[1] Moreover, personal information is not generally shared in the absence of a developed, trusting relationship. Called in as a sociolinguistic expert in the appeal, Eades concluded that it would have been extremely difficult for the defendant to share highly personal information in the context of a formal interview with a stranger. This is a dramatic example of the failure of cultural sensitivity, but it is an important reminder of how cultural differences (as well as other differences, including class and educational backgrounds) can lead to communication difficulties between clients and legal professionals.

Another important consideration in conducting effective interviews is understanding the emotional impact of divorce. Clients going through a divorce frequently enter a law office with intense feelings and emotional needs that cannot be ignored. Before we look at the interview process, we briefly consider the emotional framework within which divorce interviews often take place.

## The Emotional Context

The breakup of a marriage can wreak emotional havoc in a person's life. Profound feelings of jealousy, anger, hopelessness, and despair are often unleashed. The process of divorce has been described as the emotional opposite of falling in love, generating powerful feelings of hate and rage rather than of intense pleasure.[2] A person going through a divorce may feel as if he or she has failed in a central aspect of life, and thus may be struggling with acute feelings of worthlessness. He or she is likely to go through many emotional stages: "Divorce is best conceptualized as a series of transitional life experiences rather than a single discrete event. Therefore . . . the impact of divorce on family members will vary with the point in the transition process."[3]

Many of the clients you interview are thus likely to be experiencing overwhelming and constantly shifting emotions. This can make your task difficult, but it is important to remain sensitive to what the client may be going through. If clients are going to trust you, they need to feel that their well-being matters. The failure to acknowledge a client's emotional needs can also interfere with his or her ability to move onto other topics, whereas the acknowledgment of these feelings can facilitate this process.

Providing emotional support is particularly important in the divorce context where, as noted above, individuals often experience a diminished sense of self-worth. Moreover, divorce often disrupts a person's social support system. Friends and family may disapprove of the marital split, feel loyalty to the other spouse, be uncomfortable with the intensity of feeling, or fear that "another person's divorce will illuminate the cracks in their own relationships."[4]

However, as important as providing support is, you also need to be aware of the limitations of your role. Your job is not to help the client analyze or resolve his or her feelings, although the client may on some level expect you to do this. You are not the client's friend or therapist, and you should be careful not to take on these roles. You should be attuned to when a referral to a mental health professional might be appropriate. Before bringing up the possibility of a referral with a client, be sure that you know what the policy of your office is. It may be that this responsibility is entrusted to the supervising attorney.

## Conducting the Client Interview

### The Role of the Paralegal

In many offices, paralegals are responsible for conducting the initial interview. In other offices, attorneys conduct them; while in others, the two work as a team. Also, within a single office, the practice might vary based on the nature, sensitivity, and complexity of the case. Regardless of who conducts the interview, it is important, if possible, that the client meet both the attorney and paralegal who will be working on the case. This personalizes the process and helps establish rapport and trust.

### Ethical Considerations

When working with clients, it is important to be aware of the ethical rules that define the parameters of the professional relationship.[5] Interviews and all other contact must conform to ethical requirements. Accordingly, before focusing on the client interview, we consider the ethical framework within which paralegals operate. We then focus on the rules regarding the unauthorized practice of law and client confidentiality because these bear most directly on the paralegal-client relationship.

### The Ethical Framework

All states have a code of ethics that is binding on attorneys. These codes are not directly binding on paralegals, but paralegals are expected to adhere to them, and noncompliance may result in a disciplinary action against the attorney for whom the paralegal works. These codes are promulgated by the highest court in each state, and most are modeled after the American Bar Association's (ABA) Model Rules of Professional Conduct.

The codes contain disciplinary sanctions for ethical violations. The most serious sanction is disbarment. In many states, the code of ethics has been supplemented by statutes that impose civil or criminal penalties for certain unethical acts, such as the unauthorized practice of law.

Many states now have guidelines in place to assist attorneys in working effectively with paralegals, and some states specifically require that "attorneys take affirmative steps to educate legal assistants about the attorney's ethical obligations and to ensure their compliance."[6]

The two major national paralegal organizations, the National Federation of Paralegal Associations and the National Association of Legal Assistants, have both promulgated ethical codes that are binding on paralegals, as have some local and regional paralegal associations. Sanctions, including removal from membership, may be imposed for ethical violations. These codes do not carry the same weight as those for attorneys do, both because they are not court-promulgated and because paralegals are not presently state licensed and thus cannot be barred from practice as can an attorney.[7]

Also relevant when considering standards of conduct is the fact that like attorneys, paralegals can be sued for malpractice. Although malpractice actions extend well beyond ethical breaches, the failure to conform to expected standards of behavior can play a role in these suits.

### Specific Practices

**The Unauthorized Practice of Law.**[8] All states limit the practice of law to licensed attorneys, but determining what is meant by the term "practice of law" is not always easy. Certain conduct, such as signing court pleadings, conducting depositions, or representing a client in court, are considered to be the practice of law. But even here, there are some exceptions. For example, some states allow paralegals to appear in court for an attorney on uncontested matters, and many allow paralegals to serve as advocates in domestic violence cases. Paralegals also are allowed to represent clients before many state and federal administrative agencies.

The giving of legal advice is also regarded as the practice of law; however, the definition of this term is imprecise. At a minimum it includes independently advising a client about her or his legal rights, a potential course of action, and the predicting of legal outcomes. Thus, it is clear that advising a client as to what kind of divorce should be filed is the giving of legal advice—but what about explaining basic statutory options such as the difference between a fault and a no-fault divorce? Some would classify this as legal information, which a paralegal could disseminate, while others would classify it as advice. Although a paralegal cannot provide legal advice independently, he or she can serve as a conduit between the attorney and client as long as it is made clear to the client that the advice is from the attorney and not from the paralegal.

Maintaining the appropriate boundaries can be difficult. Clients are often vulnerable and without reliable support, and may implore you to tell them what to do. This can be hard to resist. It is flattering, and you are likely to be moved by the client's situation and want very much to help. But, no matter how difficult, it is important to work within the existing ethical framework and not be pulled into doing more than is appropriate.

**Client Confidentiality.** In working with clients, you must always be aware of your ethical responsibility to maintain strict client **confidentiality**. The duty to maintain client confidences is at the heart of the attorney-client relationship and is also binding on paralegals.[9] Without the assurance of confidentiality, a client may be reluctant to provide all of the information that is needed to thoroughly prepare a case, especially if it is of a sensitive, embarrassing, or potentially damaging nature. The client may worry that it will be disclosed to the opposing side or to other third parties. Accordingly, clients should be told at the outset of the interview that their communications with the office are strictly confidential. If you sense a client is struggling with whether to tell you something, it can be helpful to remind him or her that disclosures are confidential.

You should also be aware that there may be limited exceptions to the confidentiality rule, such as where a client discloses that he or she is planning to commit a serious crime or where there is good cause to believe that the client is harming his or her children.[10] Depending on the situation and the state you are in, disclosure may be discretionary or it may be required, such as where a child protective law requires all persons who believe a child is being abused or neglected to file a report with a state's child protective agency (see Chapter 13). A decision to disclose should never be made lightly, as it is a clear exception to the overriding duty to maintain client confidentiality. As a paralegal, you should never act on your own in this regard. You should review the situation with the supervising attorney who may well be the one who is ultimately responsible for the disclosure decision.

### Developing Good Listening Skills

The manner in which you listen to clients is vital because it signals whether you are simply going through the motions or are really paying attention to what is being said. If a client senses that you are engaged, he or she is likely to open up more because people are generally more comfortable when they sense their listener is responsive to what they are saying.

**Nonverbal Communication.** In thinking about how you listen to someone, it is important to recognize that much is communicated nonver-bally. Direct eye contact signals that you are present and engaged. It also enables you to pick up nonverbal clues from the client that might otherwise be missed.

Likewise, your body position is important. Leaning forward toward the client indicates involvement. A somewhat relaxed posture tends to reduce the distance between the interviewer and interviewee. In contrast, leaning back in a chair with legs up on a desk can signal a lack of focused attention and involvement. This position also can be intimidating to a client because it tends to enhance the status of the interviewer.[11]

**Active Listening.** Through a technique known as **active listening**, you can let a client know that you are really hearing what is being said. Active listening involves the use of verbal responses that reflect back to the client the informational or emotional content of what has been said.

With respect to the reflection of informational content, you should occasionally repeat back to the client some of the key information he or she has given you. This makes it clear that you have heard what has been said and have not been daydreaming about the upcoming weekend. It also helps ensure the accuracy of your information gathering because it gives the client the opportunity to correct any misunderstandings.

This should not become a mechanical process, and you should not break the flow of the story. A good time to reflect back is when the client has come to a logical break in the narrative. Be careful, however, that you do not begin to sound like a parrot, who is mindlessly repeating back what it has heard.

With respect to the reflection of emotional content, you should occasionally respond to what the client says she or he is going through on an emotional level. This acknowledges that you are aware of the client's emotional needs and that it is acceptable for him or her to express them. Although it may be tempting to share your personal experiences as a way of showing the client that you can understand what he or she is going through, these kinds of disclosures should be avoided. Although it is important to be supportive, you should never lose track of the fact that this is a professional relationship.

To illustrate the technique of active listening, let's assume that you are interviewing a client named Carl Johnson and that you are beginning the narrative phase of the interview. (See below for discussion on the narrative phase.) You have asked him, "Why don't you tell me something about your marriage?" and he has responded as follows:

> Well, my wife and I have been married for 15 years. We met in college — she was my first true love, and has remained my only love during all these years. We have had a few rocky patches. My mother died right after our daughter was born. I became depressed. I had been very close to both my parents and had already lost my dad.
>
> My wife felt I withdrew from her and the baby. I denied it at the time, but in retrospect, I realize she was right. In any event, I thought we had a loving marriage.
>
> Well, a few years ago, my wife seemed more remote. She lost interest in sex and, well, things just seemed different. At first I attributed it to the pressure we were under. My business had gone under, I was looking for work, we had our daughter, my wife was working full-time, and I was still struggling with depression.
>
> We were also threatened with foreclosure proceedings, although we were able to save the house by borrowing money from her parents. Since then, they haven't let me forget that if I had been a proper husband, able to hold down a decent job, my family would not have been in that predicament. I also think they blame me for the fact that their daughter works so hard, but they don't understand that she loves her job.
>
> Anyway, I gradually began to get suspicious that something else was going on. My wife began to have more night meetings, a few times when I answered the phone the person at the other end hung up — all the classic signs. For a while she denied that anything was going on, but finally, about a month ago she admitted that she had been seeing someone in her office. I asked her to break it off, but she said she couldn't promise to do that and needed some time to work things out. Well, that was it. I was and still am totally destroyed. It's embarrassing to admit, but she is the only woman I have ever had sex with. As far as I am concerned the marriage is over.

This is probably a logical point to interject briefly. To reflect the emotional content, you might simply say something like: "I can see why you are devastated. This must be a very difficult time for you." You want to avoid statements like, "I know what you are going through, I remember what it was like when my husband walked out on me." This may seem obvious, but, in the intensity of the moment, the temptation to support a client in this manner can be hard to resist.

To reflect the informational content, you might say something like:

> I'd like to take a minute to make sure I understand what you have just told me; please let me know if anything I say is inaccurate.

You and your wife have been married for 15 years, and despite a few rough times, you would characterize your relationship as solid. You have one child.

You've struggled with depression, particularly after the death of your mother. Recently, your wife has acknowledged she is having an affair, and is not sure what she wants to do. As a result, you have decided your marriage is over.

### *The Interview Itself: A Three-Stage Approach*

It is useful to think of the interview as having the following three distinct stages:

1. *Opening stage*: establishes the parameters of the interview and creates an atmosphere of trust
2. *Information-gathering stage*: elicits the client's basic story (narrative phase) and fills in the key details with questions (focused phase)
3. *Wrapping up or disengaging phase*: concludes the interview

This three-stage approach should not be followed mechanistically. Each person you interview is unique, and you need to accommodate a range of expressive styles. Some clients may respond only to focused questions; while others, at least initially, will be so overwhelmed that they will not respond to focused questions. They may need to tell you their story over and over in their own manner and sequence. This human dimension is the great challenge that no book can fully prepare you for.

In the following sections, we will look at each stage of the interview process, using the interview with Mr. Johnson to demonstrate various points. The model presented here assumes that a preprinted form is not being used for anything more than obtaining the basic factual information needed to complete a divorce complaint—such as the place and date of the marriage, the date last lived together, and the names and birthdates of the marital children—although some offices do use forms to obtain comprehensive client information.

**Stage 1: Establishing the Parameters and Creating an Atmosphere of Trust.** When a client first comes in to a law office, it is important to realize that he or she is probably nervous. Engaging in some preliminary chit-chat can help put a client at ease. For example, you might inquire whether he or she found the office without difficulty, whether it is still snowing, or the like. It is also a nice gesture to offer a cup of coffee or tea.

At the beginning, you should explain who you are and what role you will play. Let's assume that Mr. Johnson has just entered your office. To begin the interview, you might say something like the following:

> Hi, Mr. Johnson, my name is Elaine Chin. I am the family law paralegal who will be working on your case with Attorney Jane Martin. I am going to be interviewing you today. Afterward, Attorney Martin and I will meet to review the information and begin preparing your case. If Ms. Martin returns from court before we are finished with the interview, I will introduce you to her.

You should then inform the client that everything he or she tells you will be held in strict confidence, and explain what will take place during the interview. Following is an example of what this might sound like:

> Mr. Johnson, I am going to begin by asking you some very basic questions so I'm sure to get all the information that is asked for on the court forms. I will use our standard questionnaire for this.
>
> Afterward, I'll ask you to tell me about your situation and what you are thinking about doing at this stage. During the course of the interview, I will take some notes so I'm sure to remember everything you tell me.
>
> Also, you should know that everything you tell me is strictly confidential within this office. You do not need to worry that somehow your wife or her attorney will find out about what you tell us.
>
> Once I have a complete picture of your situation, we'll be through for the day. But, before you go, I'll tell you what you can expect and what you need to begin doing, such as collecting necessary papers.
>
> Do you have any questions before we begin?

At this point, the client knows who you are, what to expect, and that communications are confidential. This establishes a solid foundation for the interview itself.

**Stage 2: Obtaining Information.** Where possible, it is best to gather information in two phases. In the first phase, the client should be encouraged to tell his or her story. In the second phase, the interviewer can complete the inquiry by asking focused questions. This is sometimes referred to as a "funneling" process because the questions begin broadly and then gradually become narrower.

*Eliciting the Client Narrative.* In the first phase of information gathering, the emphasis is on having the client tell his or her story. This is done by asking open-ended questions that elicit a narrative rather than a focused response. In using open-ended questions, the interviewer loses some control over the process because the client shapes the telling of the story. However, this approach respects the fact that it is the client's problem and acknowledges that "the client is an important, essential resource in the information gathering process."[12] Open-ended questions can be either general or topic-specific. By asking topic-specific questions, the interviewer focuses the field of inquiry while still calling for a narrative response.

By way of example, let's return to Mr. Johnson. As set out above, the initial question to him was, "Why don't you tell me something about your marriage?" and in answering, he mentioned he has a child. A logical follow-up question might be, "Why don't you tell me about your child?" This question is topic-specific but is still open-ended because it asks for a narrative response. Let's assume that he gives the following answer:

> Well, Sara is our only child. She's seven and is in the second grade. She's a terrific kid, I know all parents say that, but she really is special. She does real well in school, has a lot of friends, and loves sports.
>
> Lately, though, she seems to be having a bit of a hard time. I've tried to talk to her about it, but sometimes she just doesn't seem to want to talk much to me. My wife says it's because I didn't bond with her as a baby, but I think she's going through something now, maybe with all this marriage stuff. I'm sure it's nothing serious.
>
> Her last report card was real good, but her teacher says that Sara has been kind of withdrawn at school. I am very worried about how she'll react to the divorce. I guess she's kind of a sensitive kid.

As he completes talking about his daughter, you could direct him to other topic areas by asking similar questions, such as, "You mentioned earlier that a few years ago your wife started seeming remote. Why don't you describe this period to me?"

It is during this narrative phase that the technique of active listening is particularly important. If possible, it is best to take a minimum of notes during this phase because note taking can interfere with your ability to remain focused and engaged.

*Focusing in: Following up with Closed-Inquiry Questions.* After the narrative phase, you should proceed with more focused questions to elicit more complete information. At this point, you will probably want to take detailed notes. As you shift to the closed-inquiry phase, you gain greater control over the process; however, where possible, your inquiry should be informed by and responsive to what the client tells you.

To begin this phase, you might say something like this to the client:

> Mr. Johnson, you've given me a good picture of your situation. Now, what I would like to do is go back over what you have told me and ask you some specific questions so I am sure my information is complete. Also, I will now be taking notes so I have a good record of what you tell me.

You can then go back over the information in a focused manner. Here is what some follow-up questions to Mr. Johnson about his daughter might sound like:

*Q:* You used the word "special" in describing your daughter; why don't you tell me what you mean by that?

*A:* Well like I said, she does well in school, has a lot of friends, and loves sports. But, I guess beyond that, she is just a very kind and thoughtful child. She seems to have a sensitivity beyond her years. She understands a lot about the world, and really wants to help people.

*Q:* Does she understand what is happening at home?

*A:* To some extent. We've told her that Mommy and Daddy don't love each other anymore and that Daddy will be moving to a new home, but that I still love her very much. I don't think she really understands why I've been sleeping in the guest room or why Mommy and Daddy aren't speaking to each other much.

*Q:* Why don't you tell me more about your relationship with Sara?

*A:* As I said, I was somewhat depressed when she was first born, and maybe I wasn't really that involved with her care, but I think I've made up for that in the past five or so years. During this time, I've been very involved in her care.

*Q:* Can you describe your caretaking role?

*A:* Well, sometimes I bring her to school in the morning, but I usually have to be at the office pretty early and I try to pick her up from her after-school program a few times a week. I share putting her to bed at night, and on weekends I try to do a special activity with her — just the two of us.

*Q:* How would you characterize the division of child-care responsibilities between you and your wife?

*A:* Well, I think it's pretty equal. I'm a pretty involved dad — I mean maybe it's not fifty-fifty, but I'm not one of those dads who doesn't even know the names of his child's friends.

*Q:* At some point, I'll probably want to get more detail on the caretaking arrangements, but let me ask you a few other things first. You mentioned that your daughter has been having a hard time, and hasn't wanted to speak with you about what's going on. Can you elaborate on this?

*A:* Let me start with our relationship. We've been pretty close. I don't spend as much time with her as I would like, but when we're together we have a lot of fun. Sometimes I get impatient with her and then I feel badly. I guess she usually confides more in her mother; I try not to get jealous, but sometimes I feel left out. I can't express my feelings as well as my wife can — we didn't do any of that in my family, and maybe it's a male thing also—so maybe Sara feels somewhat closer with her mom. But I love my daughter and would do anything for her.

*Q:* Who does your daughter turn to for comfort when she is sick or doesn't feel well?

*A:* Both of us, but my wife is usually the one to stay home with her when she is sick. Her job is more flexible than mine is, and when I was self-employed, I couldn't afford to take the time off. Also, sometimes, I think my wife overindulges her, and keeps her home if she just has a sniffle. I don't think it's good to treat kids like babies. . . . With respect to what Sara has been going through, she's been kind of moody and withdrawn. I don't know if it's in response to what has been going on at home, or if it's just one of those things that kids go through.

*Q:* Have you consulted anyone about this?

*A:* No—it hasn't seemed like that big a deal. But, maybe with the divorce we should have her talk to someone. I don't really know.

Here, the interviewer is clearly trying to elicit specific information, but the questions flow from the client's answers, and there is a nice sense of give and take. This is not always possible. Where the client is less focused, the interviewer cannot be as responsive and will need to impose more of a structure in order to obtain the necessary information. Also, in reviewing these questions, you should note the constant pattern of moving from broader to narrower questions; this funneling process is also valuable within this closed-inquiry phase.

**Stage 3: Wrapping Up the Interview.** Once you have obtained the necessary information, it is time to wrap up the interview. At this point, you need to tell the client what will happen next and explain what he or she needs to do, if anything. You should remind the client to feel free to call you with any questions.

To conclude the interview, you might say something like this:

Mr. Johnson, I think I have gotten all of the information that I need today. Let me explain what will happen next. I will write up the results of our interview and will go over them with Attorney Martin. She will evaluate your options, and we will then set up a meeting so she can go over things with you in detail. At that time she will also review our office's fee structure and if you wish to proceed she will work out a fee agreement with you.

In the meantime, I am going to give you a financial statement to fill out. I'll give you some written instructions, but feel free to call me if you have any questions. It would be very helpful if you could complete this before our next meeting.

I will call you by the end of the week to set up the next meeting. But please don't hesitate to call me if anything at all comes up before then. You can also call Attorney Martin directly, but it is likely easier to reach me because she is often in court. You should also be aware that as a paralegal, I cannot give you legal advice. I can answer some questions for you, but others I will need to convey to Ms. Martin, and then she can call you back, or I can communicate her response to you.

## THE DIVORCE ACTION: INITIAL STEPS AND DISCOVERY

In this and subsequent sections, we trace the stages of a divorce case from the drafting of the complaint through post-judgment procedures. This discussion is intended to give you an overview of this process, but it is important to recognize that each state has its own procedural rules. In some states, these rules are found in the code of civil procedure, which applies generally to all civil actions;[13] other states have specialized rules of domestic procedure; and other states use a combination of general and specialized procedural rules. When working on a case, it is essential that the applicable rules be ascertained and followed so that a client's rights are safeguarded.

Please note a couple of points about terminology. First, this chapter uses the terms *complaint, plaintiff,* and *defendant*; but other terms such as *petition, petitioner,* and *respondent* (respectively) may be used in some states. Also, in most instances where a phrase such as "the plaintiff files the complaint" or "the defendant must answer in a timely fashion" is used, the task is actually performed by that party's attorney. The language denotes which side is responsible for the task, not the allocation of responsibility between a party and his or her attorney.

### The Initial Steps

The following steps in the divorce process will be discussed in this section:

1. Drafting/filing the complaint
2. Service of process
3. Defendant's response

#### The Complaint

The first official step in the divorce process is the filing of the **complaint** (or **petition**); until the complaint is filed, the court has no authority over the parties. Divorce complaints tend to be fairly straightforward, and, in many states, preprinted forms are available from the court. (See Exhibit 10.1 for an example of a preprinted petition from the state of Connecticut.) Despite this relative simplicity, the complaint is a crucial document that must be drafted with care because it frames the plaintiff's case to both the court and the defendant.

**The Functions of a Complaint.** Like any other complaint, the divorce complaint serves a number of purposes. It identifies the parties to the action and, through a recitation of the parties' addresses and the length of time that the plaintiff has lived in the state, establishes whether the court is the proper one with respect to both jurisdiction (see Chapter 10) and venue (see below).

The complaint also sets out the facts that underlie the action. At a minimum, these would include the following basic allegations:

- when and where the parties were married
- the names and birthdates of any children of the marriage
- the location where the parties last lived together
- the date and cause of marital separation

Beyond this, states vary with respect to how much factual detail is required, but at a minimum, the complaint must include sufficient information to establish the basis for the divorce. For instance, if a plaintiff filed a divorce for cruel and abusive treatment, in some states it would be sufficient to state that the defendant treated him or her in a cruel and abusive manner on a particular occasion or occasions; while in other jurisdictions, greater detail about the acts constituting the cruel and abusive behavior would need to be set out.

The complaint also includes a **request for relief** (sometimes known as a **prayer for relief**), in which the plaintiff sets out the relief he or she is seeking. In addition to asking the court to dissolve the marriage, the plaintiff sets out what she or he is seeking with respect to collateral matters such as custody, support, and the division of property. These are usually stated in general terms; for example, the plaintiff may request a reasonable amount of support or a fair and equitable division of property. However, local rules or customs might call for greater detail. States' rules differ with respect to whether a plaintiff can ask for something at trial that was not requested in the complaint. Some states strictly limit a plaintiff to the relief requested in the complaint, while others are more liberal. To avoid potential problems, many complaints are drafted to include a "catch-all" phrase, asking the court to award any and all further relief that is deemed fair and equitable.

**Amending the Complaint.** After filing, a plaintiff may wish to change something on the complaint. For example, a plaintiff who files a fault

## Exhibit 10.1 Divorce Complaint

| DIVORCE COMPLAINT (DISSOLUTION OF MARRIAGE) | STATE OF CONNECTICUT | CROSS COMPLAINT CODE ONLY |
| --- | --- | --- |
| JD-FM-159 Rev. 6-03 C.G.S. § 46b-40, et seq., P.B. § 25-2, et seq. | SUPERIOR COURT www.jud.state.ct.us | CRSCMP |

☐ **Complaint:** Complete this form. Attach a completed Summons (JD-FM-3) and Notice of Automatic Court Orders (JD-FM-158).
☐ **Amended Complaint.**
☐ **Cross Complaint:** Complete this form and attach to the Answer (JD-FM-160) unless it is already filed.

| JUDICIAL DISTRICT OF | AT *(Town)* | RETURN DATE *(Month, day, year)* | DOCKET NO. |
| --- | --- | --- | --- |

| PLAINTIFF'S NAME *(Last, First, Middle Initial)* | DEFENDANT'S NAME *(Last, First, Middle Initial)* |
| --- | --- |

1. WIFE'S BIRTH NAME *(First, Middle Initial, Last)*

| 2. DATE OF MARRIAGE | 3. TOWN AND STATE, OR COUNTRY WHERE MARRIAGE TOOK PLACE |
| --- | --- |

4. *(Check all that apply)*

☐ The husband or the wife has lived in Connecticut for at least twelve months before the filing of this divorce complaint or before the divorce will become final.
☐ The husband or the wife lived in Connecticut at the time of the marriage, moved away, and then returned to Connecticut, planning to live here permanently.
☐ The marriage broke down after the wife or the husband moved to Connecticut.

5. A divorce is being sought because: *(Check all that apply)*

☐ This marriage has broken down irretrievably and there is no possibility of getting back together. **(No fault divorce)**
☐ Other *(must be reason(s) listed in Connecticut General Statute § 46b-40(c)):*

_____
_____
_____

*Check and complete all that apply for items 6-13. Attach additional sheets if needed.*

6. ☐ No children were born to the wife after the date of this marriage.
7. ☐ There are no minor children of this marriage.
8. ☐ The following children have been born to the wife or have been adopted before, on or after the date of this marriage and the husband is the father/adoptive father. *(List only children who have not yet reached the age of 23.)*

| NAME OF CHILD *(First, Middle Initial, Last)* | DATE OF BIRTH *(Month, day, year)* |
| --- | --- |
| | |
| | |
| | |
| | |
| | |
| | |

9. ☐ The following children were born to the wife **after** the date of the marriage and the husband **is not the father.** *(List only children who have not yet reached the age of 23.)*

| NAME OF CHILD *(First, Middle Initial, Last)* | DATE OF BIRTH *(Month, day, year)* |
| --- | --- |
| | |
| | |
| | |

*(Continued...)*

## Exhibit 10.1   Continued

10. ☐ The wife is pregnant with a child due to be born on *(date)* _____

    The father of this unborn child is *(check one)* ☐ the husband    ☐ not the husband    ☐ unknown.

11. If there is a court order about any child listed above, name the child(ren) below and the person or agency awarded custody or providing support:

| CHILD'S NAME | NAME OF PERSON OR AGENCY |
|---|---|
| CHILD'S NAME | NAME OF PERSON OR AGENCY |
| CHILD'S NAME | NAME OF PERSON OR AGENCY |

12. The husband, the wife, or any of the child(ren) listed above has received financial support from the State of Connecticut. *(Check one)*   ☐ Yes   ☐ No   ☐ Do not know
    If yes, send a copy of the Summons, Complaint, Notice of Automatic Court Orders and any other documents filed with this Complaint to the Assistant Attorney General, 55 Elm Street, Hartford, CT 06106, and file the Certification of Notice *(JD-FM-175)* with the court clerk.

13. The husband, the wife, or any of the child(ren) listed above has received financial support from a city or town in Connecticut. *(Check one)*   ☐ Yes *(State city or town:* _____ *)*   ☐ No   ☐ Do not know
    If yes, send a copy of the Summons, Complaint, Notice of Automatic Court Orders and any other documents filed with this Complaint to the City Clerk of the town providing assistance and file the Certification of Notice *(JD-FM-175)* with the court clerk.

**The Court is asked to order:** *(Check all that apply)*

☐ A divorce (dissolution of marriage).

☐ A fair division of property and debts.

☐ Alimony.

☐ Child Support.

☐ An order for the post-majority educational support of the child(ren) pursuant to C.G.S. § 46b-56c.

☐ Visitation.

☐ Name change to:

_____

☐ Sole custody.

☐ Joint legal custody, Primary residence with:

_____

**And anything else the Court thinks is fair.**

| SIGNATURE | PRINT NAME OF PERSON SIGNING | | DATE SIGNED |
|---|---|---|---|
| ADDRESS | | JURIS NO. *(If applicable)* | TELEPHONE (Area code first) |

> • *If this is a Complaint, attach a copy of the Automatic Court Orders before serving a copy on the Defendant.*
>
> • *If this is an Amended Complaint or a Cross Complaint, you must mail or deliver a copy to anyone who has filed an appearance and you must complete the certification below.*

I certify that a copy of the above was mailed/delivered to all counsel and pro se parties of record on:

| .DATE MAILED OR DELIVERED | SIGNED *(Attorney or pro se party)* |
|---|---|
| NAME OF EACH PERSON SERVED* | ADDRESS WHERE SERVICE WAS MADE *(No., street, town, zip code)** |

*If necessary, attach additional sheet with name of each party served and the address at which service was made.

JD-FM-159 *(Back)* Rev. 6-03

divorce may subsequently agree to amend to a no-fault divorce. In most states, a plaintiff is permitted to amend the complaint within a specified time period, such as before the defendant files the answer, without seeking permission from the court or the defendant. After this time, the plaintiff must seek the permission of either the defendant or the court. Most courts are fairly liberal in allowing amendments unless the rights of the defendant would be prejudiced.

**Joint Petitions.** In some states, spouses may have the option of filing a no-fault petition for divorce jointly. Here, the parties are considered co-petitioners; neither is the plaintiff or the defendant. Joint petitions may entail special procedures or requirements. For example, in Massachusetts, parties who file a **joint petition** also must file an affidavit of irretrievable breakdown of the marriage, attesting to the fact that the marriage is over. A signed separation agreement also must be filed at this time or shortly thereafter. In California, couples without children who have been married a short time and have few assets may be eligible to file a Joint Petition for Summary Dissolution, which enables them to get divorced without a court hearing. (See Exhibit 10.2 for a sample joint petition and supporting affidavit.)

### Filing the Complaint

Once the complaint is drafted, it is filed in the appropriate court together with any other required documents, such as a certified copy of the parties' marriage certificate. Before the complaint and any accompanying documents are accepted for filing, they are usually reviewed by a clerk to ensure that everything is in order. Upon acceptance, the case is assigned a **docket number**, which is then used on all subsequent case documents. In most states, filing can be done either in person or by mail. The advantage of filing in person is that any problems with the paperwork can be taken care of at the time. Also, as this responsibility is frequently delegated to paralegals, it provides a good opportunity to become familiar with the courts and court personnel.

**Venue. Venue** is a geographical concept that determines the specific court in which an action must be filed. Thus, for example, once it is ascertained that the probate and family court has subject matter jurisdiction over divorce actions, venue rules would tell you which probate and family court the action should be filed in. As a general rule, an action is filed where either the plaintiff or the defendant lives or where the cause of action arose. In divorce cases, other factors, such as where the parties last lived together as spouses, may be relevant to determining venue.

## Exhibit 10.2   Joint Petition and Affidavit

**Commonwealth of Massachusetts**
**The Trial Court**

Middlesex Division          Probate and Family Court Department          Docket No. _____

### Joint Petition For Divorce Under M.G.L. Ch. 208, Sec. 1A

_____ and _____
                 Petitioner                                              Petitioner

of _____          of _____
         (Street and No.)                                       (Street and No.)

_____          _____
(City or Town)      (State)        (zip)            (City or Town)      (State)        (ZIP)

1. Now come the Husband and Wife in a joint petition for divorce pursuant to Massachusetts General Laws, Chapter 208, Sec. 1 A.

2. The parties were lawfully married at_____
   on _____ and last lived together at_____
   on _____,20_____

3. The minor child _____ of this marriage and date(s) of birth is/are:

   _____          _____

   _____          _____

4. The parties certify that no previous action for divorce, annulment, affirmation of marriage, separate support, desertion, living apart for justifiable cause, or custody of child _____ has been brought by either party against the other except _____

5. On or about_____,20_____, an irretrievable breakdown of the marriage under M.G.L. Ch. 208, Sec. 1A occurred and continues to exist.

6. Wherefore, the parties pray that the Court:
   ☐ grant a divorce on the ground of irretrievable breakdown
   ☐ approve the separation agreement executed by the parties
   ☐ incorporate and merge said agreement executed by the parties
   ☐ incorporate but not merge said agreement, which shall survive and remain as an independent contract
   ☐ allow Wife to resume her former name of  _____
   ☐ _____

Date_____

_____          _____
SIGNATURE OF WIFE OR ATTORNEY                    SIGNATURE OF HUSBAND OR ATTORNEY

_____          _____
(Print address if not pro so)                              (Print address if not pro so)

_____          _____

Tel. No.  (___) _____          Tel. No.  (___) _____

B.B.O. #_____          B.B.O. #_____

CJ-D 101A (6190)

mcpfc. - c.g.f.

## Exhibit 10.2   Continued

### Joint Petition for Divorce
### Under M.G.L. c. 208, Sec. 1A

For Wife:

_____

Address _____

_____

Tel No.  (___)_____


For Husband:

_____

Address _____

_____

Tel. No.  (___)_____

Docket No. _____

Filed _____ ,20 _____

Agreement Approved _____ ,20 _____

Judgment _____ ,20 _____


Documents filed:

Marriage Certificate                                    ☐

Wife's Financial Statement                         ☐

Husband's Financial Statement                  ☐

Separation Agreement                                ☐

Affidavit of Irretrievable Breakdown         ☐

Affidavit Disclosing Care                           ☐
or Custody Proceedings

Child Support Guidelines                           ☐
Worksheet

**Filing Fees and Fee Waivers.** Most states charge a **filing fee** for the entry of a civil action. Filing fees are imposed to help defray administrative costs and possibly to deter frivolous actions. This fee, together with the related costs of service of process, can impose a serious financial hardship on low-income persons. So that these costs do not impose a barrier to court access, states must allow low-income divorce plaintiffs to seek a waiver of the filing fee. Plaintiffs also may be able to request that the state pay for costs related to the service of process and, less commonly, for those related to discovery (e.g., the hiring of a stenographer for a deposition). Although ensuring access to the court, the waiver of these fees does not, of course, resolve the greater problem of obtaining access to affordable legal representation. (See Exhibit 10.3 for Affidavit of Indigency.)

## Exhibit 10.3   Affidavit of Indigency

INSTRUCTIONS FOR FLORIDA SUPREME COURT APPROVED FAMILY LAW FORM
12.902(a),
AFFIDAVIT OF INDIGENCY

### When should this form be used?

This form should be used by anyone in a family law case who is unable to pay court fees and costs and is requesting a waiver of those fees and costs.

This form should be typed or printed in black ink. After completing this form, you should sign the form before a **notary public** or **deputy clerk**. You should **file** the original with the **clerk of the circuit court** in the county where the **petition** was filed and keep a copy for your records. In addition, you must attach a **Family Law Financial Affidavit,** ✎❏ Florida Family Law Rules of Procedure Form 12.902(b), to this form.

### What should I do next?

A copy of this form, along with all of the other necessary forms, must be mailed or hand delivered to your spouse in your case.

### Where can I look for more information?

**Before proceeding, you should read "General Information for Self-Represented Litigants" found at the beginning of these forms.** The words that are in **"bold underline"** in these instructions are defined there.

### Special notes...

If this is a domestic violence case and you want to keep your address confidential for safety reasons, do not enter the address, telephone, and fax information at the bottom of this form. Instead, file **Petitioner's Request for Confidential Filing of Address,** ✎❏ Florida Supreme Court Approved Family Law Form 12.980(i).

Remember, a person who is NOT an attorney is called a nonlawyer. If a nonlawyer helps you fill out these forms, that person must give you a copy of a **Disclosure from Nonlawyer,** ✎❏ Florida Family Law Rules of Procedure Form 12.900(a), before he or she helps you. A nonlawyer helping you fill out these forms also **must** put his or her name, address, and telephone number on the bottom of the last page of every form he or she helps you complete.

## Exhibit 10.3 Continued

IN THE CIRCUIT COURT OF THE _____ JUDICIAL CIRCUIT,
IN AND FOR _____ COUNTY, FLORIDA

Case No.: _____
Division: _____

_____,
Petitioner,

and

_____,
Respondent.

### AFFIDAVIT OF INDIGENCY

I, *{full legal name}* _____, being sworn, certify that the following statements are true:

I am financially insolvent and unable to pay the charges, costs, or fees otherwise payable by law to the clerk of the circuit court or sheriff in this civil action. I make this claim because:

[ √ **one** only]

____    a. I am currently receiving public assistance in the amount of: $_____ per ( ) week ( ) month. My public assistance case number is:_____. My financial affidavit, ✎❒ Florida Family Law Rules of Procedure Form 12.902(b), is attached.

____    b. I am unable to pay those clerk's fees and costs because of indigency, based on facts contained in my Family Law Financial Affidavit, ✎❒ Florida Family Law Rules of Procedure Form 12.902(b), which is attached.

**I CERTIFY THAT NO PERSON HAS BEEN PAID OR PROMISED ANY PAYMENT OF ANY REMUNERATION BY ME FOR SERVICES PERFORMED ON MY BEHALF IN CONNECTION WITH THIS ACTION OR PROCEEDING.**

I certify that a copy of this document was [ √ **one** only] ( ) mailed ( ) faxed and mailed ( ) hand delivered to the person(s) listed below on *{date}* _____.

**Other party or his/her attorney:**
Name: _____
Address: _____
City, State, Zip: _____
Fax Number: _____

**I understand that I am swearing or affirming under oath to the truthfulness of the claims made in this affidavit and that the punishment for knowingly making a false statement includes fines and/or imprisonment.**

Dated: _____     _____

Signature of Party
Printed Name: _____
Address: _____
City, State, Zip: _____

## Exhibit 10.3   Continued

Telephone Number: _____

Fax Number: _____

STATE OF FLORIDA

COUNTY OF _____

Sworn to or affirmed and signed before me on _____ by _____.

_____

NOTARY PUBLIC or DEPUTY CLERK

_____

[Print, type, or stamp commissioned name of notary or clerk.]

____    Personally known

____    Produced identification

      Type of identification produced _____

**IF A NONLAWYER HELPED YOU FILL OUT THIS FORM, HE/SHE MUST FILL IN THE BLANKS BELOW:** [ ✍ fill in **all** blanks]

I, {full legal name and trade name of nonlawyer} _____,

a nonlawyer, located at {street} _____, {city} _____,

{state} _____, {phone} _____, helped {name} _____,

who is the [ √ **one** only] ___ petitioner **or** ___ respondent, fill out this form.

**Accompanying Documents.** Other documents may need to be filed with the complaint. The requirements vary from state to state and may vary within a state depending on the nature of the divorce action. For example, as noted above, in Massachusetts, an affidavit of irretrievable breakdown must accompany a joint petition or the petition will not be accepted for filing. The most common requirement is that the complaint be accompanied by a certified copy of the parties' marriage certificate; if the marriage took place in a foreign country, a qualified translation of the certificate may also need to be filed. Also, if there are minor children, an affidavit, or like document, may need to be filed disclosing any prior or pending custody actions involving the children.

### Service of Process

After the complaint is filed, it must be served on the defendant so that he or she is provided with notice of the action. The right to notice is grounded in the due process clause, which, as discussed in Chapter 10, requires states to provide individuals with procedural rights.

**The Summons.** Upon the filing of the complaint, the court issues a summons to the plaintiff (see Exhibit 10.4). A **summons** is a document that informs the defendant that he or she has been sued and that the failure to respond within a certain time period may result in a default judgment. The plaintiff is responsible for completing the summons and serving it on the defendant with a copy of the complaint. This is referred to as **service of process**.

**Methods of Making Service.** Service must be made in strict accordance with the applicable rules of procedure. Improper service may result in dismissal of the action. Although procedural requirements vary from state to state, making familiarity with local rules critical, some general principles can be identified. In discussing service, it is useful to distinguish between resident and nonresident defendants.

*Serving a Resident Defendant.* The most common method of service is by personal service of the papers on the defendant or, where allowed, by leaving them at his or her usual place of residence. In the latter situation, most states require that the papers be left with a competent adult. Traditionally, most states have required that **personal service** be made by a sheriff, a marshal, or other person specially designated to serve process, but the modern trend is to allow personal service to be made by any disinterested person over the age of 18.

Most states also allow service to be made by mail. Here, the summons and complaint are mailed to the defendant, usually by certified mail requesting acknowledgment of receipt. For the service to be considered

## Exhibit 10.4   Summons

IN THE CIRCUIT COURT OF THE _____ JUDICIAL CIRCUIT,
IN AND FOR _____ COUNTY, FLORIDA

> Case No.: _____
> Division: _____

_____,
                    Petitioner,

and

_____,
                    Respondent.

SUMMONS: PERSONAL SERVICE ON AN INDIVIDUAL
ORDEN DE COMPARECENCIA: SERVICIO PERSONAL EN UN INDIVIDUO
CITATION: L'ASSIGNATION PERSONAL SUR UN INDIVIDUEL

TO/PARA/A: *{enter other party's full legal name}* _____,
*{address(including city and state)/location for service}* _____.

### IMPORTANT

A lawsuit has been filed against you. You have **20 calendar days** after this summons is served on you to file a written response to the attached complaint/petition with the clerk of this circuit court, located at: *{street address}* _____.
A phone call will not protect you. Your written response, including the case number given above and the names of the parties, must be **filed** if you want the Court to hear your side of the case.

**If you do not file your written response on time, you may lose the case, and your wages, money, and property may be taken thereafter without further warning from the Court.** There are other legal requirements. You may want to call an attorney right away. If you do not know an attorney, you may call an attorney referral service or a legal aid office (listed in the phone book).

If you choose to file a written response yourself, at the same time you file your written response to the Court, you must also mail or take a copy of your written response to the party serving this summons at:

*{Name and address of party serving summons}* _____

_____.

**Copies of all court documents in this case, including orders, are available at the Clerk of the Circuit Court's office. You may review these documents, upon request.**

**You must keep the Clerk of the Circuit Court's office notified of your current address. (You may file Notice of Current Address, ✎❑ Florida Supreme Court Approved Family Law Form 12.915.) Future papers in this lawsuit will be mailed to the address on record at the clerk's office.**

Florida Family Law Rules of Procedure Form 12.910(a), Summons: Personal Service on an Individual (9/00)          C-193

## Exhibit 10.4 Continued

**WARNING:** Rule 12.285, Florida Family Law Rules of Procedure, requires certain automatic disclosure of documents and information. Failure to comply can result in sanctions, including dismissal or striking of pleadings.

THE STATE OF FLORIDA
TO EACH SHERIFF OF THE STATE: You are commanded to serve this summons and a copy of the complaint in this lawsuit on the above-named person.

DATED: _____

CLERK OF THE CIRCUIT COURT

(SEAL)

By: _____
Deputy Clerk

good, the defendant must sign and return the acknowledgment card, which is returned to the plaintiff by the postal service. This can be a simple and inexpensive way to obtain service, but if the defendant does not acknowledge service, it does not qualify as personal service.

If the defendant is "of parts unknown" or is avoiding service, most states permit service to be made by publication and mailing. Service by this method usually involves two discrete steps. First, the summons is published in a newspaper for a specific number of weeks; second, the plaintiff sends a copy of the summons and complaint to the defendant at his or her last known usual place of residence. Again, this would be sent by certified mail with acknowledgment requested so the plaintiff would know whether it was actually received.

Service by publication and mailing is often referred to as **constructive service** because — unless the defendant signs the acknowledgment card — there is no way of knowing whether he or she received notice of the action. This has potentially serious ramifications because it most likely means that even if the jurisdictional requirements are met, the court will not be able to assert personal jurisdiction over the defendant (see Chapter 10).

In some states, the plaintiff may be able to avoid the potential difficulties of trying to obtain service on the defendant by arranging for the defendant to accept service of the complaint. If the defendant is cooperative, the plaintiff can simply provide him or her with a copy of the complaint and the original summons, which the defendant signs to acknowledge **acceptance of service**.

If the plaintiff's attorney arranges for the acceptance of service and the defendant is unrepresented, he or she must be careful not to provide the defendant with any legal advice about the divorce and should encourage the defendant to seek representation. Of course, this applies to paralegals as well.

*Serving an Out-of-State Defendant.* Most states authorize service to be made on a nonresident by the same methods that are available for serving residents or by any manner authorized by the defendant's home state. There are practical difficulties in serving a nonresident; however, where the state can exercise personal jurisdiction over the defendant, it is important to make the effort to actually serve the defendant because, as mentioned above, it is usually a necessary precondition to the court's ability to exercise personal jurisdiction over the defendant where the jurisdictional requirements of the long-arm statute are otherwise satisfied.

**Return of Service.** The person who serves the defendant must certify when, where, and how service was made. This is usually done on the back of the original summons under the caption Proof of Service (see Exhibit 10.5). The summons is then filed in court. This is known as the **return of service**. Depending on the method of service used, additional

## Exhibit 10.5  Proof of Service

INSTRUCTIONS FOR FLORIDA SUPREME COURT APPROVED FAMILY LAW FORM 12.914, CERTIFICATE OF SERVICE

### When should this form be used?

After the petition has been properly served (through either a **personal service** or **constructive service**), both parties **must** send copies of all additional documents or papers they **file** with the clerk to the other **party** or his or her attorney, if he or she has one. Each time you file a document, you must certify that you provided the other party with a copy. Many of the Florida Family Law Forms already have a place above the signature line for this certification. It looks like this:

> I certify that a copy of this document was [ √ **one** only] ( ) mailed ( ) faxed and mailed ( )
> hand-delivered to the person(s) listed below on *[date]* _____
>
> **Other party or his/her attorney:**
> Name: _____
> Address: _____
> City, State, Zip: _____
> Fax Number: _____

If a form you are filing has a certificate, you do not need to file a separate **Certificate of Service**, ✎☐ Florida Supreme Court Approved Family Law Form 12.914. However, **each time** you file a document that does not have a certificate like the one above, you must file a **Certificate of Service**, ✎☐ Florida Supreme Court Approved Family Law Form 12.914, and send a copy of the document to the other party. This includes letters to the **judge**.

This form should be typed or printed in black ink. After completing this form (giving the name of each form, document, or paper filed), you should sign the form before a **notary public** or **deputy clerk**. You should file the original with the **clerk of the circuit court** in the county where your case was filed and keep a copy for your records.

**The copy you are providing to the other party must be mailed (postmarked) or delivered to the opposing party or his or her attorney on the same day indicated on the certificate of service.**

### Where can I look for more information?

**Before proceeding, you should read "General Information for Self-Represented Litigants" found at the beginning of these forms.** For more information, see rule 1.080, Florida Rules of Civil Procedure and rule 12.080, Florida Family Law Rules of Procedure.

### Special notes...

Remember, a person who is NOT an attorney is called a nonlawyer. If a nonlawyer helps you fill out these forms, that person must give you a copy of **Disclosure from Nonlawyer**, ✎☐ Florida Family Law Rules of Procedure Form 12.900 (a), before he or she helps you. A nonlawyer helping you fill out these forms also **must** put his or her name, address, and telephone number on the bottom of the last page of every form he or she helps you complete.

Instructions for Florida Supreme Court Approved Family Law Form 12.914, Certificate of Service (9/00)

## Exhibit 10.5    Continued

IN THE CIRCUIT COURT OF THE _____ JUDICIAL CIRCUIT,
IN AND FOR _____ COUNTY, FLORIDA

Case No.: _____

Division: _____

_____,

Petitioner,

and

_____,

Respondent.

### CERTIFICATE OF SERVICE

I certify that a copy of {name of document(s)} _____

was [ √ one only] ( ) mailed ( ) faxed and mailed ( ) hand delivered to the person listed below on {date} _____.

**Other party or his/her attorney:**

Name: _____

Address: _____

City, State, Zip: _____

Fax Number: _____

_____

Signature of Party

Printed Name: _____

Address: _____

City, State, Zip: _____

Telephone Number: _____

Fax Number: _____

**IF A NONLAWYER HELPED YOU FILL OUT THIS FORM, HE/SHE MUST FILL IN THE BLANKS BELOW:** [ ✍ fill in all blanks]

I, {full legal name and trade name of nonlawyer} _____,

a nonlawyer, located at {street} _____, {city} _____,

{state} _____, {phone} _____, helped {name} _____,

who is the [ √ one only] ____ petitioner or ____ respondent, fill out this form.

Florida Supreme Court Approved Family Law Form 12.914, Certificate of Service (9/00) papers may need to be filed for the return of service to be complete. For example, if service was by publication, the pages from the newspaper usually must be submitted to the court.

### The Defendant's Response

Once the defendant is served, he or she is allowed a certain time period within which to file a response to the complaint; this responsive document is the **answer** (see Exhibit 10.6). This response period is usually significantly longer when service is made by publication.

What happens if a defendant fails to respond? In the typical civil action, a defendant who fails to answer in a timely manner is in default. This has two consequences: (1) the plaintiff is relieved of the obligation of providing the defendant with notice about subsequent case proceedings, and (2) the plaintiff may seek to have a judgment entered in his or her favor without a hearing on the merits. This is known as a **default judgment**.

The practice is somewhat different in the divorce context. Because of the importance of the rights at stake, courts tend to be reluctant to consider a divorce defendant in default and will generally not do so where the defendant has made any effort to preserve his or her rights. Even where the defendant has not responded at all, courts may not consider a divorce defendant to be in default. Accordingly, the plaintiff will not be relieved of the obligation of providing the defendant with notice of all related case proceedings and the court will not enter a judgment by default without a hearing.

As a result of the more relaxed rules about defaults in the divorce context, the local practice custom may be to forgo the filing of an answer. However, this failure may serve to preclude the defendant from contesting matters raised by the plaintiff or from seeking certain kinds of relief. Accordingly, given the unpredictable nature of divorce litigation, the better practice is to file an answer in all cases to ensure that a client's rights are safeguarded.

**The Component Parts of an Answer.** *Admissions/Denials.* In the first portion of an answer, the defendant responds to the factual allegations in the complaint by either admitting or denying them. For example, a defendant might deny the validity of the parties' marriage, that a child named on the complaint was in fact born of the marriage, or that the plaintiff is entitled to the requested relief. Denials thus serve to delineate areas of potential controversy. If the defendant lacks knowledge about an allegation, the defendant can state that he or she is without sufficient information to either admit or deny the matter. If the defendant fails to respond to an allegation, it is usually treated as an admission of that fact.

## Exhibit 10.6    Answer

FL-120

| ATTORNEY OR PARTY WITHOUT ATTORNEY *(Name, state bar number, and address):* | FOR COURT USE ONLY |
|---|---|

TELEPHONE NO. *(Optional):*          FAX NO. *(Optional):*

E–MAIL ADDRESS *(Optional):*

ATTORNEY FOR *(Name):*

**SUPERIOR COURT OF CALIFORNIA, COUNTY OF**

STREET ADDRESS:

MAILING ADDRESS:

CITY AND ZIP CODE:

BRANCH NAME:

**MARRIAGE OF**

PETITIONER:

RESPONDENT:

**RESPONSE** ☐ **and REQUEST FOR**
☐ **Dissolution of Marriage**
☐ **Legal Separation**
☐ **Nullity of Marriage**          ☐ **AMENDED**

CASE NUMBER:

1. RESIDENCE (Dissolution only) ☐ Petitioner ☐ Respondent   has been a resident of this state for at least six months and of this county for at least three months immediately preceding the filing of the *Petition for Dissolution of Marriage.*

2. STATISTICAL FACTS
   a. Date of marriage:                                   c.  Period between marriage and separation
   b. Date of separation:                                      Years:               Months:

3. DECLARATION REGARDING MINOR CHILDREN *(include children of this relationship born prior to or during the marriage or adopted during the marriage):*
   a. ☐  There are no minor children.
   b. ☐  The minor children are:
   
   | Child's name | Birth date | Age | Sex |
   |---|---|---|---|

   ☐  Continued on Attachment 3b.
   c.  If there are minor children of the Petitioner and Respondent, a completed *Declaration Under Uniform Child Custody Jurisdiction and Enforcement Act (UCCJEA)* (form FL-105) must be attached.
   d. ☐  A completed voluntary declaration of paternity regarding minor children born to the Petitioner and Respondent prior to the marriage is attached.

4. ☐  **Respondent requests** confirmation as separate property assets and debts the items listed
   ☐ in Attachment 4   ☐ below:
   
   | Item | Confirm to |
   |---|---|

**NOTICE: Any party required to pay child support must pay interest on overdue amounts at the "legal" rate, which is currently 10 percent.**

Page 1 of 2

Form Adopted for Mandatory Use
Judicial Council of California
FL-120 [Rev. January 1, 2003]

**RESPONSE**
(Family Law)

Family Code, § 2020
www.courtinfo.ca.gov.

## Exhibit 10.6  Continued

| MARRIAGE OF *(last name, first name of parties):* | CASE NUMBER: |
|---|---|
| | |

5. DECLARATION REGARDING COMMUNITY AND QUASI-COMMUNITY ASSETS AND DEBTS AS CURRENTLY KNOWN
    a. ☐ There are no such assets or debts subject to disposition by the court in this proceeding.
    b. ☐ All such assets and debts have been disposed of by written agreement.
    c. ☐ All such assets and debts are listed    ☐ in Attachment 5c    ☐ below *(specify):*

6. ☐ **Respondent contends** that there is a reasonable possibility of reconciliation.

7. ☐ **Respondent denies** the grounds set forth in item 6 of the petition.

8. **Respondent requests**
    a. ☐ Dissolution of the marriage based on
        (1) ☐ irreconcilable differences. Fam. Code, § 2310(a)
        (2) ☐ incurable insanity. Fam. Code, § 2310(b)
    b. ☐ Legal separation of the parties based on
        (1) ☐ irreconcilable differences. Fam. Code, § 2310(a)
        (2) ☐ incurable insanity. Fam. Code, § 2310(b)
    c. ☐ Nullity of void marriage based on
        (1) ☐ incestuous marriage. Fam. Code, § 2200
        (2) ☐ bigamous marriage. Fam. Code, § 2201

    d. ☐ Nullity of voidable marriage based on
        (1) ☐ Respondent's age at time of marriage. Fam. Code, § 2210(a)
        (2) ☐ prior existing marriage. Fam. Code, § 2210(b)
        (3) ☐ unsound mind. Fam. Code, § 2210(c)
        (4) ☐ fraud. Fam. Code, § 2210(d)
        (5) ☐ force. Fam. Code, § 2210(e)
        (6) ☐ physical incapacity. Fam. Code, § 2210(f)

9. **Respondent requests** that the court grant the above relief and make injunctive (including restraining) and other orders as follows:

| | Petitioner | Respondent | Joint | Other |
|---|---|---|---|---|
| a. Legal custody of children to | ☐ | ☐ | ☐ | ☐ |
| b. Physical custody of children to | ☐ | ☐ | ☐ | ☐ |
| c. Child visitation be granted to | ☐ | ☐ | | ☐ |
|   (1) ☐ Supervised for: | ☐ | ☐ | | |
|   (2) ☐ No visitation for: | ☐ | ☐ | | |
|   (3) ☐ Continued on Attachment 9c(3). | | | | |

    d. ☐ Determination of parentage of any children born to the Petitioner and Respondent
        prior to the marriage.

| | Petitioner | Respondent |
|---|---|---|
| e. Spousal support payable to (wage assignment will be issued) | ☐ | ☐ |
| f. Attorney fees and costs payable by | ☐ | ☐ |

    g. ☐ Terminate the court's jurisdiction (ability) to award spousal support to Petitioner.
    h ☐ Property rights be determined.
    i. ☐ Respondent's former name be restored *(specify):*
    j. ☐ Other *(specify):*

        ☐ Continued on Attachment 9j.

10. If there are minor children born to or adopted by the Petitioner and Respondent before or during this marriage, the court will make orders for the support of the children. An earnings assignment will be issued without further notice.

I declare under penalty of perjury under the laws of the State of California that the foregoing is true and correct.
Date:

▶

| _____ | _____ |
|---|---|
| (TYPE OR PRINT NAME) | (SIGNATURE OF RESPONDENT) |

Date:

▶

| _____ | _____ |
|---|---|
| (TYPE OR PRINT NAME) | (SIGNATURE OF ATTORNEY FOR RESPONDENT) |

> **The original response must be filed in the court
> with proof of service of a copy on Petitioner.**

*Affirmative Defenses.* In an **affirmative defense**, a defendant seeks to establish that the plaintiff is not entitled to prevail even if his or her allegations are established. Thus, for example, a defendant might assert that by continued cohabitation, the plaintiff forgave the defendant's marital trespasses. Since no-fault divorce, however, as discussed in Chapter 5, affirmative defenses are far less significant. Because it is virtually impossible for one spouse to prevent the other from obtaining a divorce, parties are much less likely to fight about the legal significance of marital fault.

*Counterclaims.* A defendant can also assert claims for relief against the plaintiff in his or her answer by way of a **counterclaim**. Where a counterclaim is asserted, roles are reversed: The defendant functions as a plaintiff, and the plaintiff functions as a defendant and has a right to respond to the counterclaim.

In a divorce case, a defendant might counterclaim for a divorce from the plaintiff and set out the relief he or she is seeking, such as custody of the children or a spousal support award. Depending on local rules, a defendant might also be able to set out claims for relief even if he or she is not actually counterclaiming for divorce.

**The Motion to Dismiss.** A defendant may also respond to a complaint by filing a **motion to dismiss** the divorce action. Common grounds for seeking a dismissal are lack of jurisdiction, inadequate service, or improper venue. If the action is dismissed, the defendant does not need to file an answer. If the motion is denied, the defendant will need to answer, although the time period for responding will be extended. Of course, the plaintiff will most likely refile, making sure to correct the error that led to the dismissal.

# Discovery

**Discovery** is a pretrial process for obtaining information from the other side. Most states have modeled their discovery rules after the federal discovery rules contained in the Federal Rules of Civil Procedure, so these rules will serve as the basis for our discussion. Of course, the rules of your state should always be consulted when working on a case.

## General Purpose

Discovery serves a number of important purposes, including the following:

1. It facilitates trial preparation because both parties can use the obtained information to help develop their respective cases.

2. It reduces the possibility of surprise during trial, since information is obtained in advance.
3. It enables both sides to assess the relative strengths and weaknesses of the case and can thus facilitate the settlement process.

Despite these benefits, there is a potentially troubling aspect to discovery. Given how open-ended the process is, it is possible for the spouse with greater resources to "out-discover" the other. This can push the spouse with fewer resources into a premature and potentially disadvantageous settlement. It can also result in different levels of trial preparedness. Either outcome may be the result of a well-crafted strategy or simply a byproduct of thorough preparation. Although courts can impose some limitations, they generally will not interfere with discovery absent egregious behavior.

### Scope of Discovery

In most states, the permissible scope of discovery is broad. In keeping with the federal standard, discovery can be had of any unprivileged matter that is *relevant* to the case. The information sought does not need to be admissible at trial so long as it is "reasonably calculated to lead to the discovery of admissible evidence."[14] State rules may or may not define what is considered *privileged* and beyond the scope of discovery. In most states, communications between an attorney and client, a doctor and patient, and a priest and penitent are privileged; communications between spouses and between a psychotherapist and patient may also be considered privileged. Additionally, states generally recognize the privilege against self-incrimination. Many states now also recognize a privilege based on rights of privacy; thus certain very personal information may be off limits. However, the parameters of this privilege are not always clear, and a party may be deemed to have waived it if she or he has put a particular matter in issue.

In the divorce context, an enormous range of information is commonly sought through the discovery process. For instance, where property or support is at issue, discovery will focus on the other party's financial situation. He or she will be asked for detailed information about income, expenditures, assets, and liabilities in accordance with the applicable statutory factors. For example, a stay-at-home spouse might be asked to detail all of the nonfinancial contributions he or she has made to the marriage by way of household and child-care responsibilities. Where conduct is a permissible factor, a spouse might be asked to detail all of his or her "bad acts." Where custody is at issue, a party may be asked to provide detailed information about his or her relationship with the children, including caretaking functions performed. Discovery can also be used to explore potential areas of concern. A party may be asked about whether he or she has ever struck the child or used drugs or alcohol in the child's presence. Pertinent information can also be discovered from other persons with knowledge about the child, such as neighbors, teachers, and therapists.

### Discovery Methods

There are five basic methods of discovery:

1. Depositions
2. Interrogatories
3. Request for production of documents
4. Request for a physical or mental examination
5. Request for admissions

In any given case, a single method may be used, or they may be used in combination with one another. Before considering these different methods, it is important to be aware that some cases are completed without any or with only a minimum of discovery. This may be because the case is simple or is uncontested. It also may be because the parties have the information they need in order to proceed. Cost may also be an important consideration, which, as noted earlier, can be particularly problematic if the weight of this concern falls more heavily on one spouse than the other.

Paralegals often play a major role in the discovery process. Thus, the discussion of each method of discovery includes the responsibilities that a paralegal might be asked to assume. Although not the focus of our discussion, keep in mind that paralegals also often play a significant role in coordinating the logistical aspects of discovery, such as arranging deposition dates. Of course, each office is different, and in any workplace you will need to establish exactly what is expected of you. Also, in setting out these responsibilities, it is assumed that the paralegal's work is subject to an attorney's direction and review.

**Depositions.** One common method of discovery is the **deposition**. A deposition can be taken of a party or any potential witness, including an expert witness such as a real estate appraiser or a psychiatrist. If the **deponent** is a party, the deposition can be taken upon sending the party a notice naming the date, time, and location of the deposition and listing any documents he or she should bring. If the deponent is a nonparty witness, his or her presence must be secured by a **subpoena**; if the nonparty witness is to bring documents, he or she must be served with a **subpoena duces tecum**, which specifically designates the documents to be produced.

At the deposition, the deponent is placed under oath and is questioned by the attorney taking the deposition. The other attorney is in the role of "defending the deposition" and may also ask questions. Usually these questions are limited to clearing up confusion or eliciting information that the deponent forgot to provide.

A court reporter or certified shorthand reporter is usually present at a deposition. He or she records the proceeding and prepares a verbatim transcript. Due to the cost involved, some states may permit depositions to be audio- or videotaped. Where this is done, all of the procedural requirements must be carefully adhered to so the validity of the deposition is not subject to challenge.

The primary advantages of depositions are their flexibility and spontaneity. Although most attorneys prepare their witnesses in advance, it is virtually impossible to anticipate and prepare for all possible questions. Even when prepared, the witness must answer the questions on his or her own; unlike answering interrogatories, the defending attorney cannot help craft the answers. Additionally, the deponent's answers can be immediately followed up with additional questions, and the attorney conducting the deposition can pursue a line of inquiry to its logical conclusion. This spontaneous interchange can lead to valuable information. An additional benefit is that witness credibility can be assessed and a determination made about how well he or she is likely to do in court.

The primary disadvantages of depositions are that they are expensive and time-consuming. To minimize these burdens, an attorney might choose to wait to do depositions until he or she has established a baseline of information through the use of interrogatories and requests for documents, and then use the depositions to focus on matters already determined to be significant.

---

### THE ROLE OF THE PARALEGAL

**Taking Depositions**

If your office is taking the depositions:

- Determine who should be deposed.
- Prepare the notice of intent to take deposition if a party deponent; prepare the summons or the summons duces tecum if a nonparty deponent.
- Organize the information that will be useful in preparing the deposition questions, such as financial documents, bank statements already in your possession, and school records.
- Draft the deposition questions.

- Listen carefully at the deposition and take detailed notes. Provide the attorney with possible additional questions that you think will be useful. Also, help to evaluate the witnesses' credibility—be prepared to discuss how well you think each witness will do in court.
- Review any documents that have been brought to the deposition to ensure that the production request has been fully complied with.
- After the depositions, carefully review the transcript of the deposition and prepare a summary in accordance with your office's summary procedure.

If your office is defending the deposition:

- Develop questions that you anticipate the other side will ask and conduct a mock deposition.
- Organize the documents that your witness is asked to bring. If the attorney is objecting to a production request, draft a motion for a protective order.
- At the deposition, listen carefully and suggest questions that the defending attorney might want to ask the deponent to clarify responses or elicit missing information. Also, evaluate the witness's credibility—be prepared to discuss how well you think the witness will do in court.
- Obtain a copy of the deposition transcript and review it with the witness for accuracy. Correct any mistakes in accordance with local rules.
- Prepare a summary of the deposition transcript in accordance with your office's summary procedures.

**Interrogatories. Interrogatories** are written questions that must be answered in writing within a certain time period, usually 30 days. Unlike depositions, interrogatories can only be served on parties—they cannot be served on nonparty witnesses. Interrogatories are answered under oath, and in many states the respondent has a duty to supplement answers if additional information becomes available.

Many states limit the number of questions that can be asked, although courts usually have the authority to allow additional questions. Attorneys can also agree to allow additional questions, and some have been known to employ creative numbering techniques in an effort to squeeze in as many questions as possible! Some states have developed standard interrogatory forms for use in appropriate circumstances.

In responding to interrogatories, a party must base his or her answers on all available information. Unlike a deposition, a party cannot respond based solely on what he or she knows personally but instead has an obligation to consult resources in his or her custody or control. For example, if a husband is asked about how much money he spent on clothing in the past five years, he would be obligated to review relevant financial records, such as canceled checks and credit card statements, whereas no such obligation would exist if this question were asked during a deposition. As a result of this duty to investigate, interrogatory answers may be more complete than answers given in a deposition; however, this method lacks the spontaneity and flexibility that characterize the deposition process.

When interrogatories are received by an office, the usual approach is to have the client provide the requested information to the legal team, which then drafts the responses. Clearly, although honesty is required, good drafting skills can help to shape the answers in a light most favorable to the client. Even if follow-up interrogatories are generated by the answers, the second round of responses are again subject to scrutiny. There is no opportunity for the open-ended give-and-take that characterizes the deposition process.

---

### THE ROLE OF THE PARALEGAL

**Interrogatories**

If your office is preparing the interrogatories:

- Analyze what information is needed from the other side.
- Draft the interrogatory questions.
- When the answers are returned, review them carefully to determine if all requested information has been provided. If not, discuss strategies and then draft a letter to the other side seeking supplemental information or draft a motion to compel.
- Summarize the responses and determine what information still needs to be obtained.

If your office is responding to the interrogatories:

- Enter the return date on your office's tickler system, and keep track of it.
- Remind the attorney to contact the other side if additional time is needed; if necessary, prepare a motion requesting additional time.
- Determine if any questions are objectionable and should not be answered; if necessary, prepare a motion for a protective order.

- Contact the client immediately and provide him or her with a copy of the interrogatories and instructions for preparing a response.
- Meet with the client, and review the information and relevant documentation.
- Draft answers. When complete, have client come in to review, make appropriate adjustments, and obtain client signature.
- Make sure that if required by state law, the client understands the obligation to supplement answers.

**Request for Production of Documents.** As part of the discovery process, a party may seek to review documents in the possession or under the control of the other side. To access the documents, a party serves a **request for production of documents** that details what is to be made available for inspection. The term "document" is usually defined in the request, and liberal, all-encompassing definitions are the norm. The request also specifies the time, place, and manner of production. Commonly, production is made at the office of the requesting attorney. The requesting party then has the right to make copies of the documents that he or she wishes to retain. A party may also enter onto land or other property in the possession or control of the other side for the purpose of inspection, although court permission may be needed for this. This is not done routinely in divorce cases, but could be important where, for example, the value of a professional practice or a closely held corporation is at issue.

In a divorce case, parties often make very liberal use of the production process, especially when seeking financial information. Among other things, a spouse may be asked to produce all of his or her pay stubs, canceled checks, credit card and bank statements, receipts for purchases over a specified amount, and loan payments over a specific time period, which could well be the length of the marriage. Clearly, these requests can be burdensome to the party who must locate the requested documents as well as to the person, most commonly a paralegal, who must review them!

Interesting issues arise when one spouse requests access to books and records from a professional practice. Access to these documents may be necessary for property distribution purposes in order to establish the value and the nature of the spouse's interest in the practice. The request may be objected to, however, where production could compromise confidentiality through disclosure of information about clients, patients, or work associates. In this situation, a judge is likely to order production but structure it in such a way that confidentiality is preserved by, for example, ordering the deletion of names and identifying information.

## THE ROLE OF THE PARALEGAL

**Requesting the Production of Documents**

If your office is requesting the documents:

- Determine what documents are needed.
- Draft the request with the requisite specificity so you get what is needed without being flooded with extraneous documents.
- When the documents are received, match them against the request to ensure it has been compiled with. If information is missing or objected to, develop a strategy for obtaining it — draft a letter to the other side requesting the information or draft a motion to compel for court.
- Determine what documents are needed and make copies of them. In the event of uncertainty, err on the side of copying more than is needed rather than less.
- Organize and label the documents so they are immediately accessible.

If your office is responding to a request for documents:

- Upon receiving the request for production, immediately contact the client and set up a time to review the request with him or her. Make sure the client understands the time frame.
- Keep track of the production deadline. If it cannot be met, remind the attorney to contact the other side to arrange an extension; if necessary, draft a motion for an extension of time.
- Determine if any of the requests are objectionable.
- When the documents are provided by the client, review them to see if the request has been complied with and if any documents should be held back based on privilege.
- Organize the documents for production, indicating any objections, and note all instances where documents are unavailable.[15]

**Request for a Physical or Mental Examination.** If a party's mental or physical condition is at issue, such as in a contested custody case, the other side may request that he or she submit to a mental or physical examination. Given the inherently invasive nature of this request, court permission usually must be obtained before a party can be required to submit to such an exam. Courts generally will approve such a request upon proof of "good cause."

---

**THE ROLE OF THE PARALEGAL**

**Physical and Mental Examinations**

If your office is requesting the examination:

- Draft the motion asking for court permission and, if necessary, draft an accompanying memorandum or affidavit to support the request.
- If in accordance with local practice, develop a short list of proposed examiners for presentation to the court.
- Review the report and, if needed, prepare a summary. If incomplete, prepare a list of possible follow-up questions to ask the examiner.

If your office is responding to the request for an examination:

- If the request is contested, prepare a memorandum or affidavit setting out the grounds for opposition to the request.
- If in accordance with local practice, prepare a short list of proposed examiners for presentation to the court.
- If the request is allowed, help prepare the client for what to expect.
- View the report and, if needed, prepare a summary.

---

**Request for Admissions.** The final discovery device is the **request for admissions**, in which one side asks the other party to admit to specific legal or factual allegations, to the authenticity of documents, or to the qualifications of an expert witness. Thus, for example, the husband might be asked to admit to the fact that he is taking medication for depression, or that he has twice been married and divorced, or that all documents relating to his business are authentic. This is done primarily to simplify the issues for trial because once something has been admitted to, it does not need to be proved. The request for admission thus differs from other discovery devices because it is used to confirm rather than to obtain information.

In responding to a request for admission, a party can either admit or deny an allegation, state that he or she is without sufficient information to admit or deny, or object to the propriety of the request. However, before responding that he or she is without sufficient information, a party has a duty to conduct a limited inquiry into the matter. In most states a party has 30 days in which to reply to a request for admission.

---

**THE ROLE OF THE PARALEGAL**

---

**Requests for Admissions**

If your office is making the request:

- Determine which documents are likely to be introduced at trial, and what factual or legal assertions may possibly be reduced to an admission.
- Draft the request for admission.
- Review the response, and prepare a summary of what has been admitted to. If the response is incomplete or objections made, draft a letter to the other side or prepare a motion to compel.

If your office is responding to the request:

- Promptly review the document and set up a time to meet with the client. Make sure the client knows about the time limit for responding.
- Keep track of the time limit, and remind the attorney to contact the other side if it cannot be complied with; if necessary, draft a motion for an extension of time.
- Carefully prepare a response, making sure that each and every request is properly addressed.

---

### Discovery Difficulties

In most cases discovery proceeds without too many wrinkles; however, occasionally problems do arise that may require court intervention. Following is a brief discussion about the ways in which the court may be pulled into the discovery process.

**Limiting Discovery.** A party who believes that discovery has become excessive may seek to limit it by bringing a motion for a **protective order**. A protective order can also be sought when irrelevant or privileged information is requested, but the more common response in this situation is to object to the request. In evaluating the motion, the court looks to determine if the discovery request would produce "annoyance, embarrassment, oppression, or undue burden or expense."[16] If the answer is yes, the court may impose limits even if the information is otherwise discoverable. Courts tend, however, to hold the moving party to a fairly high standard and do not impose limitations lightly.

A party who is concerned about discovery can also file a motion requesting that the court convene a **discovery conference**; in most states, a discovery conference can also be initiated by a judge. At the conference, the court may develop a discovery plan, which typically clarifies the issues for discovery, the methods by which it will proceed, and a time frame for the completion of each phase.

**The Motion to Compel and the Imposition of Sanctions.** Where discovery requests are not complied with, attorneys usually try to resolve the matter informally. If this fails, a party can file a **motion to compel**, asking the court to order a response and, possibly to impose the cost of bringing the motion on the noncomplying party.

Where the motion is allowed, the noncomplying party is then under court order to respond according to the terms and conditions set by the court. Thereafter, the failure to respond will subject this party to **sanctions**. Possible sanctions include imposing costs, treating certain matters in contention as established, preventing the sanctioned party from introducing certain evidence, and in extreme cases entering a default judgment or a dismissal of the action. In some jurisdictions, a judge may have the discretion to impose sanctions without having first entered a motion to compel.

# THE MIDDLE PHASE: MOVING TOWARD RESOLUTION OR TRIAL

In addition to discovery, other important events take place between the time of filing of the divorce and the divorce hearing. During this time, the parties generally seek to resolve outstanding issues and protect their respective interests. If matters are resolved, the parties will reduce their agreement to writing and proceed to a relatively simple, uncontested divorce hearing. If matters remain unresolved, they will proceed to trial. This discussion assumes that both parties are participating in the process. If the defendant cannot be located or refuses to participate, an uncontested hearing will eventually be held, but it will be uncontested due to lack of participation — rather than because of agreement.

In this section, we look at what takes place during this middle phase of the divorce process. We begin by looking at court motion practice, followed by a discussion of other dispute resolution mechanisms, specifically negotiation, mediation, and arbitration. We then discuss separation agreements, taking a close look at a sample agreement.

Although this chapter treats each of these topics separately, you should be aware that in the unfolding of an actual divorce case, parties may utilize some or all approaches in various combinations and in various sequences in the process. For example, in one case, a party might first seek temporary orders and then enter into negotiations; in another, the parties might work out an informal interim agreement and then proceed directly to a settlement conference, or they might then turn to the court for temporary orders if an impasse is reached and then resume negotiations. Another couple might reach their final agreement through mediation before the divorce is even filed. In short, there is no prescribed pattern, and the flow of this phase is determined by the circumstances of the individual case.

## Motions for Temporary Relief

### Overview of Motion Practice

During the pendency of a divorce action, issues may arise that require immediate attention. In this situation, either side can file a motion asking the court to enter an order resolving the matter. Any order entered in response to the motion is temporary and will eventually be superseded by the divorce judgment. The fact that the relief is temporary does not lessen its importance; significant rights may be at stake. Moreover, **temporary orders** frequently shape the final result. As a basic rule, a court's ruling on a motion cannot be appealed because the right of appeal generally attaches to final judgments. However, this rule is not absolute. Thus, for example, a ruling on a motion that would bring a case to an end, such as where a court allows a motion to dismiss, can usually be appealed. Depending on the applicable rules of procedure, appeals may be allowed in other limited situations as well, such as where particularly significant interests are at stake.

**Preparation and Service.** Motions are prepared in writing and served on the other party, together with notice as to when and where the motion is to be heard. (For an exception to the advance notice requirements, see "Ex Parte Relief" below.) Service requirements are usually less formal than at the complaint stage. Most commonly, service is made by the attorney for the moving party either in hand or by mail within the requisite number of days, as determined by the applicable rules of procedure, before the motion is scheduled to be heard.

Frequently, a party will submit an affidavit to the court in support of the motion. An **affidavit** is a first-person, sworn statement that, in this instance, sets out the underlying facts showing why the moving party is entitled to the requested relief. A motion may also be accompanied by a legal memorandum that provides legal support for the moving party's position. The opposing party may also submit an affidavit or a legal memorandum (or both) to show why the requested relief should be denied. In some jurisdictions, either or both of these documents may be required.

**Ex Parte Relief.** In certain situations, a party may be harmed if he or she gives the other side advance notice of the motion and hearing date.

For example, let's say that a father is threatening to take the children out of the country and the mother wants to get a court order prohibiting him from doing this. If she gives him advance notice, he might disappear before the hearing takes place. In this situation, the court could hear her motion on an **ex parte** basis, meaning without notice, enter an order, and then provide the father with the opportunity to come to court and present his side of the story. Other examples of when ex parte relief may be appropriate include situations where a party is seeking protection from abuse or seeking to prevent a spouse from dissipating marital assets, as again, advance notice could trigger the very result the party is trying to avoid.

Grounded in considerations of procedural fairness, as required by the due process clause, most courts will grant ex parte relief only if the moving party can show that giving notice poses a substantial risk of harm. In deciding whether to allow the requested relief, a court must balance the right of an individual to be heard before his or her interests are affected with the need to protect the moving party from the risk of injury or loss. Only where the risk is substantial will it outweigh the procedural rights of the other side. If an order is entered, notice will be provided and the other side will have an opportunity to be heard within a short period of time following the ex parte hearing.

**Presentation to the Court.** Following service, the motion is presented to the court. The procedure for scheduling motions varies from state to state, and within a state may vary from court to court. If you are responsible for scheduling a motion, you should always call the particular court to find out how to get the motion heard.

In some states, the hearing on a motion is conducted like a mini-trial. The rules of evidence are in effect, and the parties take the witness stand and give testimony in response to questions by counsel. In most states, however, the presentation is less formal. The parties are not sworn in as witnesses; instead, they stand before the judge with their attorneys, who present and oppose the motion through oral argument. The parties may then be asked some questions by the judge. Here, formal rules of evidence or procedure are not in effect. After hearing the matter, the judge can enter an order on the spot or can take the matter under advisement. A judge is likely to postpone making the decision when the issue is especially complex or controverted. In some states, judges may be able to make decisions based solely on written submissions, thus eliminating the need for a hearing.

**Diversion to Court Conciliation or Mediation Services.** In some states, the parties must sit down with a court worker to see if they can resolve matters before the motion can be heard by the judge. Typically, this worker is from the court's family service office or a court-based mediation program. In some states, an exception to the diversion requirement will be made in cases where there is a history of domestic violence. This exception is based on the recognition that it can be unfair and potentially unsafe to require a victim of violence to mediate with an abusive spouse.

If an agreement is reached through this process, it is reduced to writing and presented to the judge for approval. If approved, it becomes the temporary order of the court. If agreement is not reached, the motion is then argued before the judge. In many states, the court worker participates in this court hearing. He or she may report back to the judge on what took place during their session and make recommendations. In other states, the meeting with the court worker is considered confidential, and the worker thus does not participate in the motion session.

While this diversion to a court-based mediation or conciliation program can help couples reach mutually satisfactory agreements, a number of concerns, including the following, have been raised about this process:

1. Especially where they are unrepresented, parties, in locales that do not protect these communications, may not realize that what they tell the court worker is not confidential and will be reported back to the judge.
2. Court workers may pressure the parties to settle, and the failure by a party to agree to a settlement proposal may result in an unfavorable report or recommendation to the court.
3. This process is inappropriate where there has been domestic violence because it requires a victim to sit down, in a spirit of cooperation and conciliation, with someone who has been abusive. In this regard, it should be noted that some diversion programs have domestic violence exemption.

### Specific Divorce Motions

Motion practice in the divorce context is extremely varied. Many motions, such as those for temporary custody or support, are fairly standard, but much creativity can be used to fashion motions to deal with specific problems. For example, let's say that a couple has temporary joint legal custody of their daughter, and the mother has physical custody. The mother gives the daughter a haircut that substantially alters the length and style of her hair. The father objects to her having done this without his consent, and seeks to prevent it from recurring. He could design a motion to address this situation with a caption such as: "Motion to Prevent Wife from Altering Daughter's Hair without the Husband's Prior Consent. Many attorneys enjoy this creative aspect of family law practice, while it drives others to distraction, particularly when they are on the receiving end of a highly original motion.

Following is a brief description of some of the commonly filed motions, followed by a sample motion and supporting affidavit.

**Motion for Temporary Custody and Visitation.** After a divorce is filed, many couples work out an informal, temporary arrangement regarding the children. Where this is not possible, one party will usually file a motion asking the court to award him or her temporary custody. After a hearing, the court will enter an order for custody and visitation, which will then be in effect until the divorce judgment is entered unless problems arise and a change is sought via another motion.

The importance of a temporary arrangement—whether through agreement or by a court order—should not be underestimated. Because courts are reluctant to disrupt children once they are settled into a satisfactory routine, temporary arrangements often ripen into permanent ones. The longer the interim stage, the more likely it is that the parent with temporary custody will end up as the custodial parent.

Temporary custody orders are also important where there is any risk that one parent might flee with the children. If an order is in place, a parent who interferes with the custodial or visitation rights of the other parent can be held in contempt of court. Moreover, a temporary custody order may be a necessary prerequisite to the initiation of parental kidnapping charges in the event a parent disappears with the children. Accordingly, even where parties are able to work things out informally, a temporary custody order may be prudent.

**Motion for the Appointment of an Investigator or Evaluator.** Where custody is contested, a party may ask to have someone appointed to perform a custody evaluation or investigation. An investigation is usually done by a **guardian ad litem** (G.A.L.). Typically, a guardian ad litem interviews the parents and other involved adults, such as teachers and neighbors, and spends time with the children. He or she may also visit the homes of both parents. The guardian ad litem then files a written report with the court containing his or her recommendations about custodial and visitation arrangements.

In some cases, such as where there are concerns about the mental or emotional well-being of a parent or child, it may make more sense to have an evaluation done by a mental health professional. Here, the evaluation most likely would consist of a series of interviews and observations. Typically, each parent and each child is interviewed separately, and the children are observed alone and with each parent. Again, a written report and recommendations are filed with the court.

In either situation, the parties are entitled to a copy of the report and to an opportunity to question the guardian ad litem or the evaluator in court. This right is important because these reports tend to carry a lot of weight with judges, and parties must be given the chance to question the findings where they disagree with them.

**Motion for Temporary Support.** During the pendency of a divorce, a party may be in immediate need of child or spousal support and unable to wait until a permanent financial arrangement is in place. Accordingly, all states permit an interim award of child support and most permit an interim award of spousal support. Again, because this interim order often ripens into the permanent one, it is vital that all supporting financial documentation be carefully prepared and presented to the court.

**Motion for Payment of Fees and Costs.** As a general rule, each party is responsible for paying his or her own **attorney's fees**. However, in most states, a spouse who lacks the resources to secure ongoing representation can ask the court to order the other spouse to pay his or her fees. This request can be made at trial or during the pendency of the action.

In evaluating the request, the court will compare the financial status of both parties. Where there is a significant disparity, the court may award fees. However, there is no right to a fee award, and the decision is generally within the sound discretion of the trial judge. In many states, judges tend to award fees only in cases of extreme hardship.

**Motions Relating to the Protection of Assets.** A frequent concern during the pendency of a divorce is that a party will dissipate marital assets. To protect against this, the other spouse can seek a variety of protective court orders.

A party can ask the court to issue a restraining order enjoining the other spouse from disposing of or encumbering the asset in question. He or she can also ask the court to attach property, which serves to put the world on notice that the asset is subject to an unresolved claim and makes the asset difficult to sell. The court can also freeze assets that belong to a spouse but are under the control of a third party, such as a bank. Here, the order would command the bank not to allow the spouse to withdraw or transfer funds. These motions need to be drafted with particular care, as they may need to satisfy the technical requirements of nondivorce statutes that govern interests in property.

As mentioned earlier, if a party has a well-grounded fear that upon receiving notice of a motion to protect assets, his or her spouse is likely to dispose of the assets in question, he or she can appear before the court on an ex parte basis. If the court agrees that the danger is real, it will secure the asset first and then provide the other side with notice and the opportunity to be heard.

**Motion for Protection from Abuse.** During the pendency of the divorce, most states allow either party to seek protection from abuse by way of a motion. A spouse can ask that the other party be ordered to leave him or her alone and, if they are still living together, that the abusive spouse be vacated from the marital premises. In most states, this approach is not exclusive; a divorcing spouse may bring a motion within the framework of the divorce, file a separate petition under the state's abuse protection act, or both. However, these approaches may yield different results. The order entered in response to a divorce motion may have less clout than one entered pursuant to the state's abuse prevention law; it is less likely to be criminally enforceable and it may not enhance the arrest powers of the police (see Chapter 4). Of course, these differences should be assessed before action is taken, so the most appropriate course can be pursued.

### Sample Motion and Supporting Affidavit

Exhibit 10.7 is a sample motion for temporary custody with a supporting affidavit. The body of the motion contains the following three parts:

1. The relief desired
2. Supporting reasons
3. A prayer for relief

As a general rule, motions are written in simple, straightforward language so the judge, who in all likelihood has countless motions before him or her, can quickly determine what is being requested.

### The Role of the Paralegal

As with discovery, paralegals play an important and varied role in motion practice. Paralegals may be responsible for drafting the necessary court papers — such as the motion, supporting affidavit, and legal memorandum. Drafting the affidavit requires careful interviewing of the affiant to get his or her story, putting it into a cohesive, first-person narrative, and reviewing it with the affiant for accuracy. Preparation of the memorandum requires good research and writing skills, as the appropriate legal authority must be identified and presented in a persuasive manner.

Paralegals can also play a vital role in preparing for the court hearing. Supporting documents such as financial statements may need to be gathered, and clients need to be prepared so they can respond to questions from counsel or the judge. Some attorneys also like to have the paralegal who is working on the case accompany him or her to court. In court, the paralegal can perform a variety of important tasks. For instance, she or he can continue to prepare the client, offer the client emotional support, assist in the preparation of an updated financial statement if requested by the court, or assist the attorney in handling the flow of paperwork. In some jurisdictions, paralegals are allowed to present uncontested motions to the court.

## Exhibit 10.7 Motion for Temporary Custody and Supporting Affidavit

STATE OF ANYWHERE

Middlesex County

Family Court,
Civil No. 2245

JERRY FREEMAN,
        Plaintiff

v.                              PLAINTIFF'S MOTION FOR
                                TEMPORARY CUSTODY

CARRIE GREEN,
        Defendant

NOW COMES the plaintiff in the above-captioned action and asks that this Honorable Court award him temporary physical and legal custody of the party's minor daughter, Melissa, age seven years old.

In support of his Motion, Plaintiff states as follows, and also incorporates by reference the attached Affidavit, which more fully sets out the facts in support of his request:

1. That the plaintiff has been the primary caretaker of Melissa for the past three years. Before this time, the parties shared child-care responsibilities on a more or less equal basis.

2. That over the past three years, as a result of depression and increased alcohol consumption, the wife has provided little attention or care to Melissa, and has been emotionally abusive toward her.

3. That the wife moved out of the family home approximately six months ago, and since then has had infrequent and irregular contact with Melissa.

4. That the best interest of Melissa would be served by awarding temporary legal and physical custody to the father so that continuity of care and nurturing is maintained.

WHEREFORE, the Plaintiff requests that this Honorable Court grant this Motion and award him temporary custody of Melissa.

Respectfully Submitted,
Jerry Freeman
By his Attorney

_____

Ellen Jones
Jones & Hernandez
11 Court Street
Freeport, Any State 02167

## Exhibit 10.7   Continued

**STATE OF ANYWHERE**

| | |
|---|---|
| Middlesex County | Family Court, |
| | Civil No. 2245 |

JERRY FREEMAN,
    Plaintiff

v.             AFFIDAVIT OF PLAINTIFF IN SUPPORT OF
                HIS MOTION FOR TEMPORARY CUSTODY

CARRIE GREEN,
    Defendant

I, Jerry Freeman, do depose and say:

1.  I am married to the defendant Carrie Green, and I filed a divorce complaint with this Court on June 18, 2004.

2.  We have one child. Her name is Melissa and she was born on March 15, 1997.

3.  During the first four years of Melissa's life, my wife and I shared child-care responsibilities, although Carrie was the primary caretaker of Melissa during her first six months. After this time, we both fully participated in all aspects of Melissa's life, including making child-care arrangements for her while we were at work.

4.  Three years ago, Carrie lost both of her parents in a tragic accident. As a result, she became depressed and began to drink heavily. She has refused to get any help for either the depression or the drinking.

5.  Since then, our family life has been torn apart. Carrie has been unable to hold down a job and has essentially withdrawn from the family. She has been unable to care for Melissa in any predictable manner. For example, she forgot to pick Melissa up from her after-school program on several occasions due to the fact that she was drinking. Needless to say, this was extremely upsetting for Melissa. After this occurred several times, I took over the responsibility for picking up Melissa. I also took her to school, except on those rare occasions when Carrie was able to get out of bed on time to take her.

6.  Although she has not been physically abusive, Carrie has become emotionally abusive, especially when she has been drinking. She yells at Melissa for no reason, and also belittles her. But even more upsetting to Melissa has been her mother's withdrawal of love and affection.

7.  I feel that I tried desperately to help my wife, but nothing worked, and about six months ago, she moved out.

8.  During all of this time, I have been the primary caretaker of Melissa in addition to working full-time. I may not be a perfect parent, but I provide her with love and stability. I also am able to take care of all her daily needs.

**Exhibit 10.7   Continued**

9.   Melissa and I are attempting to rebuild a life. She is in counseling to try to resolve some of her pain and confusion. On a few occasions, in order to help Melissa, the counselor has arranged to have all of us attend a family counseling session. Carrie has failed to attend all but one of these sessions. The one time she showed up she was intoxicated, and the counselor had to ask her to leave.

10.   I fully believe that it is in Melissa's best interest that I be awarded sole custody and I am fully prepared to continue as her primary caretaker.

Signed under pains and penalties of perjury, this 20th day of June, 2004.

Jerry Freeman

## Alternative Approaches to Dispute Resolution

Ultimately, the overwhelming majority of divorce cases are settled before trial, most commonly through the process of negotiation. In recent years, increasing numbers of divorcing couples also have used two alternative approaches to resolving their differences: mediation and, although far less common, arbitration. In this section, we compare these three dispute resolution approaches. Please note that the discussion is general in nature and does not address the more formal principles and theories of each approach. We also consider two new approaches to the practice of law — the provision of **"unbundled" legal services** and the **collaborative law model**.

### Negotiation

Through **negotiation**, each attorney acts on behalf of his or her client to see if a settlement can be reached. In contrast to mediation and arbitration, no neutral third party is involved.

Negotiations can take place on the telephone, but it is also common for one side to contact the other at some point in the divorce process to see if a settlement conference can be arranged. This conference can be either two-way, involving just the attorneys, or four-way, involving the attorneys as well as the clients. A four-way conference is generally more productive because the clients can play an active role in initiating and responding to settlement proposals. However, in some situations, such as where there is tremendous animosity between the parties or there is a history of abuse, it may make more sense to have the attorneys meet, at least initially, without the clients present.

Ideally, each attorney will have met with his or her client before the conference to explore what the client wants and where he or she is willing to compromise. The attorney should also help the client to anticipate what the other side is likely to request so he or she can think about possible responses. If this advance work is done, both attorneys will begin the negotiations with a good understanding of their clients' positions.

At the conference, ground rules are usually established. An important consideration is whether each issue will be negotiated separately until impasse or agreement or whether everything will be placed on the table at the same time. The advantage of the former approach is that it minimizes the possibility of inappropriate linkage of issues; for example, the husband offering to give the wife sole custody if she drops her request for spousal support. If the parties decide to negotiate each issue separately, any agreement reached on a single issue is usually not considered final until all other issues have been resolved. By conditioning finality of each issue on reaching a comprehensive settlement, the parties do not risk the loss of potential bargaining chips. For example, if the parties agree on a division of property, a spouse could reopen this matter if unable to get what he or she wants with respect to spousal support. Thus, a husband might back away from his agreement to allow a wife to remain in the home if, later in the negotiations, she insists on spousal support.

Once the basic framework is established, one side will open with its offer. This offer rarely represents the party's bottom line because this would leave no room for the give-and-take that characterizes the negotiation process. However, if the proposal is too outrageous, the party may not appear to be negotiating in good faith, which can jeopardize the integrity of the process. When the other side responds, they too will leave room for concessions but again should avoid unreasonable counterproposals.

As the negotiations proceed, it is common for each party to confer privately with his or her attorney. At this time, responses and new proposals can be formulated. These meetings can also serve as valuable cooling-off periods because these conferences tend to get heated.

The negotiating session can conclude in a number of ways. One party may unilaterally declare it over and may even storm out, perhaps because of frustration with the process or as a deliberate "bullying" tactic designed to exact concessions. The parties may also mutually recognize that they can go no further. At this point, they may decide that the case should be marked for trial or that they should reconvene at a future date and give settlement another chance.

If the negotiations end in agreement, one side usually offers to prepare an initial draft of a separation agreement and then send it to the other side for review. This is possible even where the parties have not ironed out all of the details; here, one side offers to see if they can work out the missing details in a mutually satisfactory manner. Although drafting the agreement is time-consuming and potentially more expensive for the client, it is usually advantageous to be the drafter because once something is in writing, it seems to acquire a presumptive validity and suggesting changes has a bit of an uphill quality to it.

Although paralegals do not, as a rule, participate in the negotiations themselves, they can serve a number of very useful functions at a settlement conference. Because the paralegal is not directly involved in the negotiations, he or she may be able to make observations that the attorney is too engaged to notice, such as subtle shifts in tone of voice or body language that may indicate that the other side is altering its position. An attending paralegal who is able to take in the whole process may also be in a good position to help formulate proposals and counterproposals. Note taking can also make an important contribution; good notes can lay the foundation for a subsequent settlement agreement and are essential if disputes arise over what was agreed on. Before the conference, the paralegal can, of course, play a crucial role in helping to prepare the client for what is often a nerve-wracking experience.

### *Mediation*

**Mediation** is a nonadversarial approach to dispute resolution. It has become a popular option for divorcing couples who wish to resolve their differences without going to trial. Through mediation, a neutral third party — the mediator — helps couples reach their own agreement. The mediator is not an advocate for either side but rather guides the parties through the process of reaching agreement by helping them to identify important issues, consider options, and structure a realistic settlement.

Divorce mediators come from a range of professional backgrounds,[17] although most are either mental health professionals or attorneys. Mediators may work in interdisciplinary teams. Thus, for example, a social worker and an attorney might work together, as each brings a distinct but complementary body of knowledge and set of skills to the process.

Although there has been a marked increase in the use of mediation as an alternative dispute resolution method, some experts in the field have raised the concern that the field lacks an "articulated theoretical framework" to guide practitioners,[18] and there is therefore a lack of awareness that "very different goals and values among mediators . . . could shape competent performance in fundamentally different ways."[19] In an effort to bring a coherent theoretical framework to the field, some scholars have identified two primary mediation models: the problem-solving model and the transformative model.

According to the *problem-solving model*, the goal of mediation is to arrive at a solution that "solves tangible problems on fair and realistic terms, and good mediator practice is a matter of issue identification, option creation, and effective persuasion to 'close the deal.'"[20] This model is rooted in an "individualist ideology" that presumes that people act in a contained, self-directed way in "pursuit of satisfaction of his or her own separate self interests."[21] Presently, this model is the dominant mediation paradigm.

In contrast, the *transformative model* sees the conflict as "first and foremost a crisis in some human interaction,"[22] as a result of which "the interaction between the parties quickly degenerates and assumes a mutually destructive, alienating, and dehumanizing character."[23] Here, the primary goal of mediation is not problem solving, but changing the interactional patterns between the parties:

> [S]uccess is measured not by settlement per se but by party shifts toward personal strength, interpersonal responsiveness and constructive interaction. . . . The transformative framework is based on and reflects relational ideology, in which human beings are assumed to be fundamentally social — formed in and through their relations with other human beings, essentially connected to others, and motivated by a desire for both personal autonomy and constructive social interaction.[24]

Significantly, the role of the mediator is quite different in each model. In the problem-solving model, the mediator structures the process to help the parties reach a settlement. In the transformative model, the mediator's role is less outcome oriented and geared more toward empowering the parties to transform their interactional patterns so that they can reengage in a more positive way.[25]

**The Mediation Process.** Mediation is usually conceptualized as occurring in distinct stages, although the progression is not always linear. Couples often move back and forth between stages as new issues, conflicts, and emotions surface. The following presentation is intended to give you a sense of the stages involved in mediation. Keep in mind that there is no single fixed or correct model and that each mediator develops his or her own style.[26]

*Stage One: Building Trust and Establishing Parameters.* During the initial session, parties are encouraged to articulate why they have come to mediation and what their expectations, concerns, and goals are. The mediator explains the process, including the nature of his or her role, the responsibilities of the participants, and the applicable ground rules, such as those relating to confidentiality. By the end of this meeting, the parties should have a clear understanding of the process and be able to make an informed decision as to whether they wish to proceed. If the mediation is to continue, a contract to mediate, which sets out the operative framework, is usually signed by the couple and the mediator.

For many mediators, this initial session also serves a screening purpose. As discussed below, some mediators do not believe mediation is appropriate where there has been a history of domestic violence. At this initial meeting, the mediator might ask about abuse or look for clues suggesting a history of abuse. If reasonably certain that abuse has taken place, the mediator might not accept the case. Other mediators, while acknowledging the importance of screening for abuse, would not reject a couple for this reason but instead would set specific ground rules, such as that physical safety is nonnegotiable.

*Stage Two: Fact-Finding.* To be effective, mediation requires the voluntary disclosure of all relevant information. Generally, as part of the mediation agreement, parties commit to complete disclosure and to provide copies of documents that would ordinarily be requested in the course of discovery, such as tax returns, bank statements, and asset inventories. Formal discovery is not available in mediation, and the mediator has no authority to compel disclosure. To some, this raises troubling questions about the potential fairness of the process. Of primary concern is the risk that a spouse who has less knowledge of and control over economic resources might unknowingly give up rights to income or assets. Where the mediator knows or suspects that a party is concealing assets, he or she can break off mediation and refuse to resume unless the parties confer with counsel. However, some mediators believe this would be overstepping their bounds, reasoning that the parties assumed this risk when they entered mediation.[27]

*Stage Three: Identification/Creation of Options and Alternatives.* After everyone is satisfied that all relevant information has been provided, the mediator helps the parties identify what they see as the various options and assists them in expanding the range of acceptable alternatives. The mediator also seeks to prevent the parties from getting locked into fixed positions before all options have been considered. Thus, a mediator is likely to take an active role in this stage of the process.

*Stage Four: Negotiating and Drafting the Agreement.* Once the acceptable options have been identified, the parties are faced with the task of sorting through the possibilities. At this point, the mediator generally steps back so that the parties themselves can reach the agreement, although he or she may play a critical facilitative role.

As the parties seek to reach an agreement, it is not uncommon for one or both of them to ask the mediator whether he or she thinks a certain provision is fair. This raises interesting questions about the mediator's role. Some mediators hold the view that answering such a question would compromise their stance as a neutral third party. Rather than responding, the mediator might direct the party to think about how that option would play out in his or her life and might also suggest that he or she confer with counsel. Other mediators take a more activist stance and will provide the parties with an assessment of what the likely outcome would be if the matter went to court, thus providing them a framework within which to make their decision.

A further potential complication is where the mediator realizes that the agreement is unfair and that one spouse would fare considerably better in court. Here, some mediators simply encourage each party to review the final agreement with an attorney before signing it, reasoning that when the parties agreed to the process they assumed the risk of operating outside formal legal rules. Other mediators take a more active role, especially where the unfavorable result stems from an underlying power imbalance. They might raise pointed questions to push the parties to confront the unfairness of the bargain or strongly urge consultation with counsel during the process rather than waiting until the end.

---

### Consideration

What should the role of the mediator be where there is an imbalance of power between the parties?

---

Once a settlement is reached, the mediator usually drafts an agreement embodying the parties' understanding. Most, if not all, mediators will strongly encourage each person to review the agreement with his or her lawyer before signing it.[28] The mediated agreement may be redrafted into a formal separation agreement, which includes the standard separation agreement provisions, or it may serve as the document presented to the court for approval at the divorce hearing.

**The Controversy: The Appropriateness of Mediation in Cases Involving Domestic Violence.** People working in the family law field have responded to the increased use of divorce mediation with both enthusiasm and trepidation. According to enthusiasts, a primary advantage of mediation is that it stresses cooperation and encourages parties to work out long-term solutions that make sense for them. As a client-centered process, it stresses individual responsibility for decision making, and by not abdicating responsibility to judges or lawyers, participants gain a sense of control over their future. Moreover, it is hoped that by stressing cooperation and communication, mediation will give couples the tools they will need to resolve future disputes, thus promoting greater post-divorce stability and satisfaction.

Despite these potential benefits, many persons who work with battered women, including some mediators, have raised serious concerns about the appropriateness of mediation where violence is a factor.[29] Of primary concern is that mediation emphasizes conciliation and cooperation, which assumes some degree of mutual respect and equality of status within the relationship. Where violence is present, however, there is no equality or mutuality; goals are not achieved through cooperation but rather through coercion and fear. Accordingly, a battered woman may respond based on fear and the overriding desire to remain safe. A further concern is that even a highly skilled mediator will not be able to redress this imbalance of power because it is so deeply embedded in the relationship. The requirement of neutrality, while facilitative in other contexts, will be insufficient to overcome a legacy of fear and lack of mutuality.

Prompted by these concerns, some mediators now attempt to screen out cases with a history of domestic violence as inappropriate for mediation; while others have adopted specific protocols, such as separate interviews, in an effort to ensure a safe process and fair results. However, critics fear that many cases will not be screened out because violence victims often downplay the seriousness of the abuse, and that although well-intentioned, "violence-sensitive" procedures are simply not enough to redress the enduring impact of violence such that a victim can participate in mediation without a sense of fear and disempowerment.

### Arbitration

Long identified with labor, commercial, and international disputes, arbitration has not traditionally been used by divorcing couples to reach a settlement agreement. Where utilized in the divorce context, it has typically been pursuant to a clause in a separation agreement in which the parties agree to submit certain post-divorce disputes to arbitration. However, there has been a notable increase in the use of predivorce arbitration as an alternative to litigation.

**Arbitration** is similar to the judicial process in that the parties present their case to a neutral, third-party decision maker (or panel of decision makers), but the process is considerably more flexible, and the parties retain a greater degree of control than they have in court. A dispute can be submitted to arbitration only if the parties so agree; one side cannot force the other to arbitrate unless specifically required by prior agreement. The arbitrator's authority derives from the parties' agreement — the arbitrator cannot make decisions about matters not directly entrusted to him or her by the parties. Although, as discussed below, an arbitrator's decision is usually entitled to great deference, some courts will not enforce an agreement to submit custody and visitation disputes to arbitration. Other courts have been willing to enforce these agreements, with "the caveat that any decision rendered by the arbitrator is subject to de novo judicial review."[30]

The arbitrator is selected by the parties. Where this is contentious, the attorneys will usually assist in the selection process. In a post-divorce dispute, a selection mechanism may be provided for in the separation agreement. The arbitrator may be a professional working under the auspices of the American Arbitration Association or any other mutually acceptable individual, such as a clergyperson, accountant, therapist, or lawyer. The choice of arbitrator often turns on the nature of the dispute and whether a particular expertise is required.

Arbitration hearings are fairly informal. They are held in a private setting and generally take less time to complete than a trial. In most instances, the arbitrator's decision is binding, subject to very limited rights of court review. As a general rule, there is a presumption in favor of the validity of the arbitral award, and a court will modify or vacate an award only under limited circumstances, such as where there has been fraud or bias, or where the arbitrator exceeded the scope of his or her authority. However, many courts review arbitral decisions more carefully when they are made in the family law context, especially when the rights of children are at stake, and some courts will not enforce provisions relating to custody and visitation. Expressing this perspective, the Supreme Court of Ohio recently stated, "The process of arbitration, useful when the mundane matter of the amount of support is in issue, is less so when the delicate balancing of the factors composing the best interests of a child is at issue," thus concluding that these decisions must remain with the court.[31]

## The Collaborative Law Model

In addition to these three established dispute resolution alternatives, some lawyers are now offering their clients the option of a "collaborative" divorce, which is a non-adversarial approach to lawyering that uses "cooperative negotiation and problem-solving techniques" and "values collaboration, compromise, and direct communication among disputing parties combined with an explicit commitment to settlement" at the outset of the case.[32] The commitment to settle the case is the hallmark of this approach. Reflecting this commitment, the attorneys in a collaborative divorce agree in advance to disqualify themselves from representing their clients in court should the process break down before all issues are fully resolved.

The collaborative divorce process bears some resemblance to both mediation and negotiation. Like mediation, the focus is on helping the parties work through their differences in a nonconfrontational manner. The parties also are encouraged to speak directly to one another in the course of the settlement process. However, in contrast to mediation, no neutral third party guides the process; rather, each spouse is simply represented by his or her own attorney. Individual representation aligns the process with negotiation; in contrast, though, and in addition to the emphasis on cooperation, the threat that a party will break off negotiations in favor of litigation if they do not get what they want is considerably less immediate, as the party would have to hire a new lawyer to represent him or her in court. Thus, there is a built-in incentive to settle the case. Collaborative divorce also can be characterized as a type of unbundled legal services (see below), as an attorney is hired for the limited purpose of settling the case, agreeing in advance not to take the matter to court.

## Unbundled Legal Services

Although not quite an alternative mode of dispute resolution, an innovative approach to the practice of law that has gained popularity over the past twenty years also merits our attention, particularly since it has become more popular in the family law arena. In what is referred to as "unbundled" legal services, or limited task representation, an attorney agrees to provide a client with limited assistance from a menu of options instead of providing the client with comprehensive representation. Typically, rather than entering into a retainer agreement, the client pays for each separate service at the time it is rendered. Unbundled services include the giving of legal advice, coaching on how to handle the case, assistance with drafting pleadings, and representation in court.

Clearly cost-effective, this approach has emerged as a way to provide legal assistance to low- and middle-income litigants who lack the resources to retain a lawyer for full-service representation—and who therefore would otherwise try to navigate the legal system on their own. Another potential benefit of limited service representation is that it can give clients greater control over their cases.

Some concerns have also been raised about this innovative approach to the practice of law. One problem is that a client may not fully understand the allocation of responsibilities between him- or herself and the lawyer, particularly if the case turns out to be more complex or contested than originally anticipated, which is not uncommon in the divorce arena. Supporters of the unbundled approach stress that potential confusion can be avoided through the drafting of clear contracts for services; others worry that a party who is confronting the emotional strain of divorce may not have a clear understanding of an agreement for limited assistance, and the party therefore may come to expect more from the attorney, especially if the case becomes more complex or contested than initially anticipated.[33]

## Reaching Resolution: The Separation Agreement

As discussed in the above section, divorce cases may proceed along many different pathways, but the vast majority of cases are ultimately settled before trial. Where the parties are able to resolve all outstanding issues, their understanding is embodied in a **separation agreement**. The usual process is for one side to offer to draft an initial agreement, which is then reviewed by the other side. Comments are made, and the agreement usually goes through several revisions before the parties sign it. Once the agreement is executed, the case is considered uncontested, and a simple divorce hearing rather than a trial on the merits can be scheduled. (See "The Uncontested Case" below.)

Technically, a separation agreement is a contract in which the parties structure their post-divorce rights and responsibilities. However, because of the state's interest in the marital relationship, separation agreements are not treated like ordinary contracts. In most states, they are subject to careful review at the divorce hearing, and a judge can set aside an agreement or any provisions that he or she determines to be unfair or to have been agreed on without adequate disclosure.

### Drafting the Agreement

In drafting agreements, most offices rely to some extent on standard forms. For routine clauses, such as those regarding waivers, severability, and the governing law, this usually presents no problem, although each provision should nonetheless be reviewed to make certain it is appropriate in the particular case. (See sample separation agreement below.) Beyond routine clauses, great care must be taken to tailor the separation agreement to the case at hand. Each situation should be carefully reviewed and the agreement drafted with all of the particulars in mind. Unfortunately, this is not always done, and the drafting process can be reduced to a filling in of names and dates on a standardized form. This is unfair to clients because it minimizes the importance of this document that, especially where children are involved, regulates critical aspects of a couple's post-divorce lives for many years into the future.

## The Role of the Paralegal

As a paralegal, an important part of your work may be to assist in the drafting of separation agreements. Before you begin drafting, it is essential that you have a clear understanding of what has been decided on so the agreement is both complete and accurate. Despite the care with which you approach the task, issues sometimes do not become apparent until the drafting is under way. For example, as you are drafting the visitation provisions, you may realize that in the complexity of the arrangements, the parties neglected to spell out arrangements for the children's birthdays. It can be helpful to the attorney handling the case if you keep track of all possible omissions and bring them to the attorney's attention. It can also be useful for you to draft the missing provisions, but you must make it clear that these are proposed as distinct from agreed-upon provisions.

After the attorney reviews the agreement, he or she may go over it with the client or ask you to do so before mailing it to the other side. Reviewing the agreement with the client ensures that it accurately reflects what your client believes he or she has settled on. In the event your client changes his or her mind about anything — a not infrequent occurrence — it is better to know about it before the agreement is sent to the other side.

If your office is reviewing rather than drafting an agreement, you may be asked to assist in this process. The agreement should be read carefully to make sure that it conforms with what has been decided on. After reviewing it, you should draft a memorandum to the attorney in charge of the case, setting out any potential discrepancies. Also, during your review, you may notice issues that have not been addressed; these should be noted in your memo, making clear that to the best of your knowledge, these are omissions as distinct from inaccuracies. Most offices will also have the client review the agreement to ensure that it conforms with his or her understanding of what was agreed upon. Again, in the event your client has changed his or her mind about anything, it is always better to know about it before the other side is told that the agreement as drafted looks fine.

## Sample Separation Agreement and Comments

The sample separation agreement (Exhibit 10.8), with its explanatory comments, will give you an understanding of how to construct a well-drafted agreement.[34] Keep in mind that this agreement covers one couple's situation; it is not universal in its reach and does not contain all possible provisions.

## Exhibit 10.8　Separation Agreement

### SEPARATION AGREEMENT BY AND BETWEEN
### MARIE SMITH AND DAVID SMITH

This Separation Agreement is entered into this 10th day of May, 2007, by David Smith (the "husband" or the "father") and Marie Smith (the "wife" or the "mother"). All of the references to "parties" shall be to the husband and wife.

**Statement of Facts**

1. The parties were married at Chicago, Illinois, on July 6th, 1996, and last lived together at 129 Cherry Lane in Newtowne, Any State, on or about September 15, 2006.

2. Two children were born to the marriage. John was born on October 17, 1998, and Carla was born on May 11, 2001. All of the references to "children" shall be to John and Carla.

3. The husband and wife have separated, are living apart, and the wife has filed a Complaint for Divorce on the grounds of irretrievable breakdown of the marriage in the Any County Probate and Family Court.

The husband and wife desire by this Agreement to confirm their separation and to settle between themselves all of the questions pertaining to their respective property and estate rights, spousal support, care and custody of their children, and all other rights and obligations arising from their marital relationship that should be settled in view of the pending Complaint for Divorce.

NOW THEREFORE, in consideration of the foregoing and of the mutual covenants and agreements hereinafter contained, the parties mutually agree as follows:

*Comment:* These introductory clauses, sometimes referred to as recitals, set out basic factual information about the parties. If the divorce has not been filed at the time the agreement is signed, language should be included to make clear that the subsequent filing of the divorce will not affect the validity of the agreement.

Most commonly the parties are referred to as "husband" and "wife." To avoid confusion, it is best not to refer to them as the plaintiff and defendant, since in a future action the designations could be reversed. Some agreements refer to the parties by their first names. This imparts a friendlier, less formal tone, and may not be appropriate in many cases.

The "NOW THEREFORE," clause sets out that the agreement is supported by consideration in that both parties are relinquishing certain rights in exchange for promises from the other.

## Exhibit 10.8  Continued

### Article One—Custody and Visitation

#### A. Custody

The wife shall have physical custody of the children subject to the husband's right of visitation. Her home shall be their primary residence, and subject to the below exception for when the children are with the husband, the wife shall be responsible for making the day-to-day decisions regarding the children. However, when the children are with their father, he may make the day-to-day decisions necessary in order for him to care for them.

The parties shall have joint legal custody of the children and shall make all major decisions regarding the children together. Major decisions include, but are not limited to, decisions about education, medical care, mental health treatment, camps, and significant after-school activities, such as participation in Little League baseball.

In the event of a medical emergency, either parent may act without obtaining the prior consent of the other parent if consent cannot be secured in a timely fashion. The other parent shall be notified of the emergency at the first possible moment.

***Comment:*** *It is always a good idea to define the custodial terms used in the agreement. If the applicable statute contains a definition, this language can be incorporated into the agreement.*

*As can be gleaned from the above clause, a fertile ground for post-divorce disputes is whether a certain decision is major or minor. This, of course, is relevant to the allocation of decision-making authority between the parties. One approach to this potential problem is to include a list identifying possible areas of future decision making as either major or minor, but it is virtually impossible to anticipate all contingencies.*

#### B. Visitation

The parties agree that the husband may spend time with the children in accordance with the following schedule:

1. The father shall pick both children up from school on Wednesdays and return them to the mother's house by 7:30 P.M. It is understood that he will usually pick them up from their extended day program by 5:00 P.M., but he may pick them up anytime following the end of their regular school day. If the children have homework, he will make sure it is completed before he returns them to the mother's house.

2. So that the father can enjoy separate time with each child, he shall pick John up on Tuesdays, and Carla up on Thursdays in accordance with the arrangement described in paragraph 1 above. The inability of one child to visit in a given week due to illness or other commitments will not affect the father's right to spend separate time with the other child. Also, the parties agree to try to arrange another

**Exhibit 10.8    Continued**

visit to replace the missed one; if this is not practical, the father will forgo the visit for that week.

3. The arrangement described above in paragraphs 1 and 2 shall continue during the summer without alteration, except during designated vacation times, and the father will pick the children up from whatever activity they are enrolled in instead of from school.

4. The arrangement described above in paragraphs 1 and 2 shall be suspended during Christmas, February, and spring vacations. The children will spend February vacation with their father, and he shall be responsible for arranging for child care while he is at work. The children shall remain with their mother for Christmas and spring vacations, but the father agrees to take two days off during each of these weeks, excluding Christmas, New Year's Day, or any other legal holiday that falls during either week, in order to be with the children. These days may be consecutive, and the children can sleep at the father's house on the intervening night.

5. The children will visit with their father every Saturday. On alternate weeks, they may sleep at his house on Saturday night. He will pick them up from their mother's at 9:00 A.M. on Saturday. If it is not an overnight week, he will return them on Saturday at 5:00 P.M. If it is an overnight week, he shall return them by 11:00 A.M. on Sunday.

6. In addition to the above, the parties agree to the following with respect to the summer and holidays:

(a) Every summer, each parent may spend an uninterrupted two weeks with the children. In selecting vacation weeks, the parties will confer so that vacation schedules can be coordinated with the children's summer activities. Each agrees to provide the other with information about where they will be during this vacation time, and will provide a telephone number and allow the other reasonable telephone access to the children.

(b) With respect to holidays, time shall be allocated in accordance with the below schedule. The parties agree that this schedule supersedes the regular visitation schedule.

(i) The children shall be with the mother on Mother's day and her birthday.

(ii) The children shall be with the father on Father's day and his birthday. The children may stay over at the father's house on both of these occasions.

(iii) The children shall be with the father on the first two nights of Passover and on the first and last nights of Hanukkah. The children may stay over at the father's house on these occasions. The parties further agree that at the request of the father, the children may visit with him on any other major Jewish holiday. However, these will not be overnight visits.

(iv) The children shall be with the mother on Christmas eve and Christmas day and on Easter.

(v) The children shall be with their mother on Halloween. However, the parties agree that the father may come to the mother's home before the children go out trick-or-treating so he can see them in their costumes.

## Exhibit 10.8  Continued

(vi) The parties will rotate Thanksgiving day on a yearly basis. The children shall be with their mother in 2001, their father in 2002, and shall continue to alternate yearly. The parent who does not have the children with him/her on Thanksgiving day may spend that Friday with them.

(vii) The parties will rotate spending New Year's Eve and New Year's Day with the children. In 2001, the children shall spend New Year's Eve with their father and New Year's Day with their mother, and shall alternate on a yearly basis.

(viii) With respect to the children's birthdays, the parties agree that they both shall have the right to spend time with the children on their birthdays. At present, the parties believe they can work out the details on their own. If this does not work, they agree to consult with their attorneys to develop a more structured arrangement.

(ix) The parties agree that there will be no special schedule for the rest of the holidays, and the regular schedule will be followed on these occasions.

7. The parties recognize that from time to time something may come up that requires an adjustment in this visitation schedule. For example, the mother occasionally has meetings on Monday evenings; when this occurs, she shall notify the father, and he shall make every effort to arrange his schedule so he can visit with the children on Monday instead of Wednesday. The parties agree they will make every effort to accommodate reasonable requests of the other parent. If such adjustment results in a loss of visitation time by the father, the parties will try to make up this time.

**Comment:** This is a very detailed visitation arrangement. Many agreements do not include this level of detail, and some simply provide for the right of reasonable visitation. However, unless the parties get along well, detail can be crucial to the success of visitation arrangements. Parents often underestimate how painful the coordination of custody and visitation arrangements can be, and how easily things can fall apart. A set schedule reduces the amount of negotiation that must take place, and thus reduces the potential for conflict, although, as this agreement does, parties can certainly include language that permits schedule changes based on mutual agreement.

Moreover, even where parents are reasonably friendly, holidays can trigger strong emotional reactions. Without a structure in place, parents may be unable to work out arrangements that permit both of them to spend holiday time with the children. As any family law attorney can attest to, the holiday season is likely to be one of their busiest and most stressful times of year.

Another matter that suggests caution when contemplating an unstructured visitation clause is the new relationship factor. Parents often fail to anticipate how painful it can be when their former spouse begins dating, especially if a relationship becomes serious. At this juncture, even parents who have been flexible and accommodating may find themselves caught up in conflict about arrangements. Mom might be less willing to let the children go to Dad's house when she suspects his new romantic interest is present, and Dad might seek increased time with the children to keep them away from Mom's new romantic interest. In short, parental jealousy and hurt may result in a distortion of previous arrangements.

**Exhibit 10.8    Continued**

This agreement makes a clear distinction between physical custody and visitation rights — there is no doubt that the children live with their mother and visit with their father. However, there may be situations where this distinction is blurred. For example, let's assume that at the four-way settlement conference, Mom asks for sole physical custody, and Dad asks for joint physical custody, but, in fact they have similar views about how much time the children should spend with each parent and that the allocation is essentially sole physical custody with liberal visitation rights. But what if Dad objects to being characterized as a visiting parent because it connotes a lack of involvement? Here, creative drafting might save the agreement. Instead of using the terms "sole physical custody" and "visiting parent," Mom could be identified as the primary caretaker parent with her home as the children's primary residence, and Dad could be identified as the secondary care parent. Sometimes when parents are fighting about how they are to be identified, rather than how time is actually to be spent with the children, these kinds of creative compromises can prevent negotiations from collapsing (see Chapter 6).

### C. Parental Cooperation

Each party agrees to foster a feeling of affection between the children and the other party, and each agrees not to do anything to estrange the children from the other party or to hamper the free and natural development of either child's love and respect for the other party. The parties agree not to discuss the other's personal life with the children.

**Comment:** Although it is fairly standard to include a parental cooperation clause, these clauses are probably not enforceable. It is unlikely that a court would hold someone in contempt for failing to foster a feeling of affection for the other parent, although a court might alter custody or visitation arrangements if one parent was actively seeking to alienate the children from the other.

### D. Right of Each Parent to Full Medical and School Information

Each parent is entitled access to the health and educational records of the children to the extent permitted by law. Neither parent shall interfere with the other parent's right of access.

**Comment:** Language to this effect is pretty standard in most separation agreements. However, when abuse is an issue, access may need to be restricted in order to protect the safety of a spouse or child. Where a right of access to records is provided by statute, a parent may need some kind of court order in order to limit the rights of the other parent.

## Exhibit 10.8   Continued

### Article Two — Child Support

#### A. Base Amount and Applicability of the Guidelines

1. The husband shall pay to the wife the sum of $175.00 per week for the support of the children in accordance with the Child Support Guidelines ("Guidelines"). The parties agree that the payments shall be by wage assignment, and the husband agrees to promptly notify the court of any changes in his employment and to complete any necessary paperwork so delays will not be occasioned by the change. He shall also maintain group health insurance for the benefit of the children until they reach the age of 23.

2. The parties agree to review the support amount on a yearly basis to determine if it remains in conformity with the Guidelines, and to exchange all documentation necessary for completion of this review no later than ten days before the review date.

If the amount no longer conforms with the Guidelines, it shall be adjusted so that it is in conformity. If the parties cannot reach agreement, they will consult with their attorneys who shall attempt to reach agreement. Any adjustment shall be reduced to writing as a modification of this agreement, and presented to the court for approval. If the parties acting alone or with the assistance of counsel cannot reach agreement, either party can petition the court for a modification.

In addition to the above, the parties agree to the following support obligations. In no event shall payments made pursuant to this paragraph affect the husband's weekly support obligation.

(a) The wife shall be responsible for the first $500.00 of uninsured medical expenses for each child in each calendar year. As used in this paragraph, the term "uninsured medical expenses" shall include, but not be limited to, any deductibles and co-payments, dental expenses, and the cost of mental health therapy so long as both parties have consented to the particular course of therapeutic treatment. Once this amount is reached, the husband will pay half of the uninsured expenses for that child or both children if the limit is reached for both.

(b) The parties agree that the children are entitled to a post-secondary education, and that they both will contribute to this education in proportion to their taxable income. The parties further agree that at a minimum their contribution should enable each child to attend a four-year state university, and that contributions should cover the cost of applications and tests, tuition, fees, room and board, and books. The parents' obligation to make educational contributions shall terminate upon the child's reaching his/her 23rd birthday, or upon graduation, whichever occurs first.

4. Upon emancipation of John, the husband's support obligation shall be adjusted downward so it conforms with the guideline amount for one child.

Upon emancipation of Carla, the husband's support obligation shall cease, subject to his obligations set out above in paragraph 3(b).

## Exhibit 10.8   Continued

For purposes of this agreement, emancipation shall be defined as:

(a) the child's achieving the age of 18, graduation from high school, or marriage, whichever is later.

**Comment:** In addition to establishing the support amount, it is useful to build in a review process tied to the guidelines. Some agreements also contain language defining what constitutes a change in circumstances that would warrant a modification. This can eliminate an area of possible contention, although again, it is virtually impossible to cover all possible contingencies.

Note that with respect to college education, the agreement does not bind the parents to a specific dollar amount. Instead, it provides for proportional contributions and establishes a minimal level of commitment. Often parents are reluctant to commit themselves to paying for college in an agreement. However, without such a commitment, it can be difficult to get the noncustodial parent to contribute, especially if over the years he or she has become less involved with the children, and in many states, the court has no statutory authority to order contribution in the absence of an agreement. Where parents have sufficient income, the option of setting up an educational trust whereby parents are obligated to set aside money on a yearly basis should be explored.

### Article Three — Spousal Support

The husband acknowledges that he is fully self-supporting, and he hereby waives any right he may have to seek past, present, or future alimony from the wife.

The wife acknowledges that she is fully self-supporting, and she hereby waives any right she may have to seek past, present, or future alimony from the husband.

**Comment:** Here, each spouse is waiving the right to seek alimony from the other. Sometimes, based on the assumption that only the wife might seek alimony, attorneys fail to make these waiver provisions reciprocal, but if the true intent is that neither party shall have a claim, reciprocal waivers are appropriate.

It is important to be aware that some judges will not accept a clause calling for a permanent waiver of support rights. Even where such a waiver is accepted, a court might later override it on public policy grounds if support becomes necessary to prevent a former spouse from going on public assistance.

If spousal support is to be paid, the precise nature and extent of the obligation should be spelled out. For example, if the husband is to make rehabilitative alimony payments, the agreement should define the circumstances under which the obligation can be extended, such as where the wife has been unable to complete her course of training due to no fault of her own.

## Exhibit 10.8   Continued

Also, as discussed in Chapter 8, alimony payments are normally deductible by the payor spouse and includible in the income of the payee spouse. If the parties wish to alter this so that the payments are neither deductible nor includible, they can do so, but the agreement must specifically set out their intent.

Last, in this case, each party is employed and has health insurance. If one spouse has been covered on the other's plan, language regarding continued coverage should be included, unless other arrangements for coverage have been made.

### Article Four — Life Insurance

Until the youngest child has reached the age of 23, the husband shall pay for and maintain in full force and effect a life insurance policy on his life having death benefits of no less than $600,000, and he shall name the wife as beneficiary. If the husband dies while the policy is in effect, the wife shall use the funds for the benefit of the children.

Until the youngest child has reached the age of 23, the wife shall pay for and maintain in full force and effect a life insurance policy on her life having death benefits of no less than $400,000, and she shall name the husband as beneficiary. If the wife dies while the policy is in effect, the husband shall use the funds for the benefit of the children.

***Comment:*** It is common to require a support obligor to maintain life insurance for the duration of the support obligation. In the event of death, the insurance would serve as a support replacement. If the custodial parent is also employed, it makes sense to have him or her maintain insurance as well.

In this agreement, the other spouse is named as the beneficiary. This is the simplest way to set things up, but it requires a degree of trust that many parties do not have in one another. Another option is to name the children as direct beneficiaries, but if they are young, this is impractical. Also, where proceeds are left to minors, many states require that management of the funds be placed under court control, which can be inconvenient. Alternatively, the money could be left to the children in trust, with the surviving spouse or a third party named as trustee. This would place the spouse under a formal legal obligation to spend the money on behalf of the children; there is thus greater accountability than if he or she is simply named as the beneficiary with a contractual obligation to use the money for the children.

### Article Five — Real Property

1. The parties presently own as tenants by the entirety a house and land located at 129 Cherry Lane, Newtowne ("house").

2. The parties agree that the fair market value of the house is $260,000, as determined by the appraisal done by Best Real Estate Company on April 15, 2004.

**Exhibit 10.8    Continued**

The parties have placed the house on the market at this price and have listed it with Best Real Estate Company.

3. The parties agree that they will both fully cooperate with all matters related to the sale, including the execution of all necessary documents.

4. Until the house is sold, the wife shall have the right of exclusive use and occupancy and agrees to maintain the house in its present condition. The husband agrees that the wife is entitled to be reimbursed for all expenses related to maintaining the house, including the cost of a weekly cleaning so the house is presentable during this sale period. The wife shall make the monthly mortgage payments to Evergreen Mortgage Company, including principal, interest, and the tax escrow. The husband shall be responsible for paying the water and sewer bills and the homeowner's insurance.

5. Upon sale, after the payment of the mortgage, the broker's commission, and all related costs, the wife shall be reimbursed for all expenditures during the sale period related to maintaining the house; thereafter, sale proceeds shall be divided equally between the parties.

6. If the house is not sold by July 15, 2004, the parties agree to reconsider the asking price. If they cannot agree on a new price, they agree to be bound by the price recommendation of Best Real Estate Company. This process shall be repeated every three months until the house is sold.

**Comment:** As discussed in Chapter 9, there are many ways to dispose of real estate in a divorce. Here, the sale option was most likely selected because neither spouse could buy out the interest of the other and there were no significant offsetting assets that could be used to lower the buyout price. Another option would have been to give the wife, as the custodial parent, the right of use and occupancy until some future date, but, as discussed in Chapter 9, the downside of this arrangement is that it keeps the parties enmeshed and frequently leads to unanticipated problems. Here, the parties must continue to interact, but only until the house is sold. If the parties are uncooperative, additional safeguards might be included relative to this time period, such as specifying what happens if the wife does not maintain the property or if a party fails to make a required payment.

### Article Six — Personal Property

The parties state that they have divided all of their personal property to their mutual satisfaction. Hereafter, each shall own, have, and enjoy all items of personal property of every kind now or hereafter acquired free of any claim or right of the other with full power to dispose of the same as fully and effectively, in all respects and for all purposes as if he or she were unmarried.

## Exhibit 10.8 Continued

*Comment:* It is generally advisable for the parties to divide their assets before the agreement is executed, as this avoids potential enforcement problems. If this is not feasible, the details of any post-execution transfer should be spelled out.

### Article Seven—Debts

1. The wife agrees that she will be solely responsible for payment of the following debts:
    (a) Mastercard (joint account)
        Account number: 66793021
        Amount due: $1,500
    (b) Sears (wife's account)
        Account number: 3390
        Amount due: $479.56
    (c) Evergreen Mortgage Company
        Account number: 73796
        Amount due: $140,000

2. The husband agrees that he will be solely responsible for payment of the following debts:
    (a) American Express (joint account)
        Account number: 440902881
        Amount due: $5,600
    (b) Student Loan Service (husband's student loan)
        Account number: 4490
        Amount due: $4,500

3. Each party represents and warrants to the other that exclusive of the debts identified in this agreement he or she has not incurred any obligations for which the other shall or may be liable. If either party is called upon to pay an obligation that the other is responsible for, the responsible party shall indemnify and hold the other harmless therefrom, including attorney's fees and related expenses. Each, or the estate of each, promises to notify the other if any claim is made against him or her or his or her estate as a result of any debt charge or liability incurred by the other, and to give the other an opportunity to defend against the claim.

*Comment:* It is important to recognize that although parties may spell out who is responsible for payment of joint debts, their arrangement is not binding on creditors, as they are not parties to the agreement. Accordingly, notwithstanding the agreement, each party remains obligated to joint creditors. It is extremely important that this be pointed out to clients; otherwise, they may not be getting what they think they agreed to.

As in the above provision, an indemnification clause should always be included whereby each spouse agrees to reimburse the other if called upon to pay a debt

## Exhibit 10.8  Continued

allocated to the other. However, this clause may be of limited utility because the non-payment probably stems from a lack of funds.

### Article Eight — General Provisions

**General Comment:** In all states, boilerplate provisions such as those that follow are routinely included in agreements. However, they should not be included without review because adjustments may need to be made in individual circumstances.

#### A. Separation

The husband and wife shall continue to live apart. Each shall be free from interference, molestation, or restraint by the other. Neither shall seek to force the other to live with him or her, or to otherwise interfere with the other's personal liberty.

**Comment:** Despite the language establishing that neither party shall molest or restrain the other, this clause does not take the place of a protective order and should not be relied on as a substitute for one. In most states, it is not placed on record with the police and is not criminally enforceable.

#### B. General Release

Each party releases and forever discharges the other from all causes of action, claims, rights, or demands whatsoever, at law or in equity, he or she ever had or now has or can hereafter have against the other, by reason of any matter, cause, or thing from the beginning of the world to the date of this Agreement, except any causes of action for divorce and except further that nothing contained in this Article shall release or discharge either party from such party's covenants, promises, agreements, representations, warranties, or other undertakings or obligations as contained in this Agreement.

**Comment:** As drafted, this is a very broad release. Each spouse is giving up all rights against the other except for filing for divorce and securing rights pursuant to the agreement. This should be carefully explained to the client, as there may be situations where such a broad waiver is not appropriate.

#### C. Waiver of Estate Claim

Except as otherwise provided in this Agreement, each party waives, releases, and relinquishes any and all rights that he or she may now have in the property of the other (such as the right of election, dower, curtesy, and inheritance) and all

## Exhibit 10.8   Continued

rights he or she may now have or hereafter acquire under the laws of this state or any other jurisdiction:

(a) To share, as a result of the marital relationship, in the other party's property or estate upon the latter's death; or

(b) To act as executor or administrator of the other's estate, or to participate in the administration thereof.

This Agreement shall and does constitute a mutual waiver by the parties of their respective rights of election to take against each other's last will and testament now or hereafter in force under the laws of any jurisdiction.

It is the intention of the parties that their respective estates shall be administered and distributed in all respects as though no marriage had been solemnized between them. The consideration for each party's waiver and release is the other party's reciprocal waiver and release.[35]

*Comment:* The primary importance of this clause is to protect each spouse's estate in the event of death before divorce. It serves to shift the statutory consequences of divorce, which is a divestiture of estate rights based on marital status, to the time the agreement is executed.

### D. Entire Understanding

The husband and wife have incorporated into this Agreement their entire understanding. No oral statement or prior written matter, extrinsic to this Agreement, shall have any force or effect.

*Comment:* This relatively simple clause is important because it prevents either party from enforcing any side agreements. For example, let's say that the wife promises the husband that he can have a certain painting in her possession, but this promise is not reflected in the agreement. After execution, the husband cannot enforce this promise because it is not included in this agreement.

### E. Voluntary Execution

The husband and wife acknowledge that they are entering into this Agreement freely and voluntarily and that they have each obtained independent legal advice; that they have ascertained all the relevant facts and circumstances; that they understand their legal rights; that each is satisfied that he or she has received full disclosure as to the other's finances, assets, income, expectancies, and other economic matters; and that they clearly understand and assent to all of the provisions of this Agreement.

**Exhibit 10.8    Continued**

### F. Modification

Any modification of this Agreement shall be in writing and shall be duly signed and acknowledged by each party in the same manner as this Agreement. No oral representation or statement shall constitute an amendment, waiver, or modification of the terms of this agreement.

**Comment:** This language requiring that all modifications be in writing precludes either party's establishing new rights based on oral representations.

### G. Waiver

A waiver by either party of any provision of this Agreement shall not prevent or stop such party from enforcing such provision in the future. The failure of either party to insist upon the strict performance of any of the terms and provisions of this Agreement by the other party shall not be a waiver or relinquishment of such term or provision; the same shall continue in full force and effect.

**Comment:** This language should be read in conjunction with paragraph F above. Here, it is made clear that failure to insist on performance of any term will not modify the agreement and is not a waiver of that party's right to subsequently insist on strict performance. For example, if the wife agreed to take a reduced amount of child support for a few weeks because the husband was having financial difficulties, this would not modify the original agreement and at any point she could again insist on full payment.

### H. Consent to Jurisdiction

The parties acknowledge that this Agreement is to be construed and governed by the laws of *State X*. Both parties consent to the continuing jurisdiction of this State in any subsequent action to modify or enforce this Agreement.

**Comment:** Generally, the term "continuing jurisdiction" as used here is understood to refer to jurisdiction over the persons of both parties and is not intended to deal with jurisdiction over subsequent custody disputes.

### I. Agreement to Mediate

In the event a dispute arises between the parties concerning any of the terms or provisions of this Agreement, which they are unable to resolve on their own or with the assistance of their attorneys, they agree that before filing any action in court, they will try to resolve the dispute through mediation at the Family Mediation Service or other similar agency. However, nothing in this

**Exhibit 10.8 Continued**

paragraph shall prevent the wife from going directly to court or pursuing any other legal remedy if the husband defaults on any of his financial obligations under this Agreement.

### J. Severability

If any provision of this Agreement shall be held invalid or unlawful by any court of competent jurisdiction, the remainder of this Agreement shall nevertheless remain valid and enforceable according to its terms.

**Comment:** This clause protects the validity of the agreement in the event any provision is found to be invalid or illegal. A clause found to be invalid or illegal would thus be dropped from the agreement without affecting any other clause.

### K. Article Headings — No Effect

The headings at the beginning of each article of this Agreement and the titles of the same are included for reference purposes only. They are not terms or conditions of this Agreement.

### L. Execution in Counterpart

This Agreement may be executed in two or more counterparts, each of which shall be deemed as original.

### M. Incorporation and Merger with Spousal Support Exception

At any hearing on the Divorce Complaint, a copy of this Agreement shall be submitted to the court and shall be incorporated and, subject to the below exception, merged into the judgment of divorce and shall not retain any independent legal significance. However, Article Three shall not be merged into the judgment of divorce, but instead shall survive and retain its independent legal significance.

**Comment:** At the divorce hearing, the parties' separation agreement is presented to the court for approval. If it is approved, the court incorporates the agreement into the divorce judgment. In effect, through the process of incorporation, the agreement becomes an enforceable order of the court.

Beyond this, the agreement either merges with the court decree and loses any significance as an independent contract, or it survives the incorporation and retains its significance as an independent contract. Whether the agreement merges or survives has important future consequences. If the agreement merges, it ceases to exist as a separate document and is fully modifiable and enforceable as the court's own judgment would be. If the agreement survives, it continues to exist as a contract. This

**Exhibit 10.8   Continued**

makes modification more difficult because choosing survival over merger usually indicates that the parties intended for the agreement to be permanent. Moreover, if the agreement survives, it is, at least in theory, an independent contract, which may still be enforceable as such.

Frequently, as in the present agreement, some provisions merge and others survive the incorporation. Here, as is commonly done, the spousal support provisions survive, making modification much more difficult.

Signed this 10th day of May, 2007.

_____    _____
David Smith                                          Marie Smith

### STATE OF X

Then personally appeared the above-named David Smith and acknowledged the foregoing instrument to be his free act and deed for the purposes therein set forth before me.

_____
Notary Public
My Commission Expires: _____

### STATE OF X

Then personally appeared the above-named Marie Smith and acknowledged the foregoing instrument to be her free act and deed for the purposes therein set forth before me.

_____
Notary Public
My Commission Expires: _____

## THE DIVORCE HEARING

Once the parties have worked out their differences and reduced their agreement to writing, or it has become clear that a settlement is not possible, a **divorce hearing** is requested. Where the parties have reached an agreement, an uncontested hearing is requested; where they have not reached agreement, the request would be for a contested hearing, more commonly referred to as a trial. Most courts retain separate scheduling calendars for contested and uncontested cases. Uncontested hearings are brief and easily scheduled, whereas contested cases usually must be pre-tried, and the trial itself can easily last a week or longer.

## The Uncontested Case

In most jurisdictions, the uncontested hearing is a relatively simple matter and may last only for five or ten minutes. The typical hearing occurs in two phases: First is the dissolution phase and second is the separation agreement review phase. Our focus is on cases that are uncontested because the parties have reached an agreement, but a case can also be uncontested because the defendant fails to appear. In the latter situation, the plaintiff must comply with the requirements of the Soldiers and Sailors Relief Act of 1940, which protects members of the military from default judgments.[36] The plaintiff must attest to the fact that the defendant's nonappearance is not because he or she is serving in the military. If uncertain, the plaintiff may need to determine this before the divorce can proceed.

### Dissolving the Marriage

During the marital dissolution phase, the plaintiff must establish that the parties have a validly contracted marriage and that the divorce grounds set forth in the complaint actually exist. Where a joint petition has been filed, either or both of the parties would testify to these matters. Establishing grounds is usually little more than a formality, but the court must be satisfied that the requisite elements are present. Also, keep in mind that "uncontested" is not synonymous with "no-fault." Parties can reach agreement regardless of the underlying grounds; thus, one could have an uncontested divorce that is premised on cruel and abusive treatment. However, once agreement is reached, the plaintiff frequently amends the complaint from fault to no-fault grounds.

Generally, the plaintiff's attorney or the judge will ask the plaintiff a series of questions to elicit the necessary information. Since the case is uncontested, there is no cross-examination. Usually the defendant does not testify; however, in a no-fault case, the judge may ask the defendant if he or she agrees with the plaintiff that the marriage is truly over.

*Approving the Separation Agreement*

In the second phase of the typical no-fault hearing, the judge reviews the separation agreement. If it is accepted, the judge will approve it for **incorporation** into the divorce judgment, and the agreement will either **survive** or **merge** in accordance with its terms (see paragraph M of Sample Separation Agreement).

In some states, the primary focus of the review is on procedural fairness. The judge will inquire into whether the parties entered into the agreement freely and voluntarily and whether they understand it. Even where the focus is on procedural rather than substantive fairness, the judge will usually check to see if the child support amount conforms to the guidelines, and if not, will evaluate whether the deviation is justifiable; some judges will also review spousal support arrangements. In other states, there is an additional focus on substantive fairness, and a judge will scrutinize the agreement in its entirety. In some states, judges will reject a term only if it is unconscionable; in others, judges may reject a term that is unfair or significantly favors one side over the other.

Where the judge believes the agreement is unfair, he or she will usually give the parties a chance to correct the problems and resubmit it for approval. If the necessary changes are minor, they can usually be made on the spot, and the hearing can proceed to completion. However, if the unfairness permeates the agreement, such as where one spouse was forced into signing it, the hearing will probably be suspended until the agreement is reworked or the case recast as a contested one.

Assuming the separation agreement is approved, the judge will enter the **divorce judgment**. The judgment both dissolves the marriage and incorporates the separation agreement, making it an enforceable order of the court. The timing of the entry of judgment varies from state to state. In some states, the judgment enters at the conclusion of the hearing; in others, it does not enter until a certain amount of time has elapsed. In some states, the initial judgment is in the form of a **decree nisi**. This is an interim judgment, which automatically ripens into a final one unless the parties seek to revoke it. This interim judgment gives the parties a chance to be absolutely certain that they do not wish to reconcile.

## The Contested Case

When a divorce case is contested, a trial, rather than a simple hearing, becomes necessary. It is important to keep in mind that when a case is contested, it is almost never because the parties are fighting the divorce grounds; most cases are contested because the parties cannot reach agreement on one or more of the collateral issues, such as support or custody.

### The Pretrial Conference

In most jurisdictions, a case cannot proceed to trial until there has been a **pretrial conference** with a judge. This conference generally serves two primary purposes. First, it may be used to explore settlement. In some instances, a judge may actively encourage settlement by indicating the likely outcome if the case were to go to trial. Second, it can be used to simplify matters for trial. The judge can help the parties identify the issues in dispute, and uncontested matters can then be admitted. Additionally, documents can be authenticated and witness lists established.

In preparation for this conference, each party must submit a **pretrial statement**. This document provides the judge with information about the parties and the procedural history of the case. Each party identifies the facts and issues in dispute and his or her position relative to the matters in contention.

### The Trial

Throughout this chapter, references have been made to the fact that procedural rules tend to be applied in a more relaxed fashion in the divorce context. However, once a divorce is at the trial stage, this is no longer true; a divorce trial proceeds much like any other civil trial, except it is not tried before a jury. The rules of evidence are in effect, and all testimony and submissions must conform to these rules. Each side has the opportunity to present an opening and closing statement, introduce evidence, call witnesses, and cross-examine the other side's witnesses, and the entire proceeding is recorded by a court stenographer.[37]

Following the trial, the judge reviews all of the evidence and makes a decision on the merits. The divorce decree is then entered, which both dissolves the marriage and contains the court's order regarding the issues before it. As in uncontested cases, the judgment may enter as a decree *nisi*. In many jurisdictions, the order must contain detailed findings of fact and conclusions of law. These details can be crucial because this order, much like a separation agreement, structures the postmarital relationship between the parties.

### Trial Preparation and the Role of the Paralegal

Trials require intensive preparation, and paralegals are often involved in this process.[38] They may be responsible for setting up the **trial notebook**, which is a binder containing everything needed to present the case in court, such as pleadings and motions, witness lists, deposition summaries, and a description of all exhibits. Paralegals may also be responsible for gathering and organizing all potential exhibits and assisting with witness preparation, including preparation of the client. This is an important task, which usually includes the following steps:

1. Reviewing all relevant information with the client to ensure that it is complete and accurate.
2. Reviewing the direct examination questions—the questions that each side asks of its witnesses—with each witness so he or she knows what to expect at trial. Although witnesses cannot be told what to say, they can be helped with how to present their answers to the court so they are delivered in the most effective or, depending on the circumstances, least damaging manner.
3. Reviewing with the client and other witnesses what the other side is likely to ask of them during cross-examination and explaining how best to respond to these questions, which are usually designed to undermine credibility.

## POST-DIVORCE PROCEEDINGS

A case is not necessarily over once a judgment has been entered. A party who is dissatisfied with the result can file a post-trial motion for relief or an appeal. Further on down the line, either party can file a modification action (if there has been a change in circumstances) or a contempt action (if the other side has violated an order).

## Post-Trial Motions

The two most common post-trial motions are the **motion for a new trial** and a **motion for relief from judgment**, although other motions may be available in some jurisdictions. In permitting these forms of relief, most states have looked to the cognate provisions of the Federal Rules of Civil Procedure and have adopted similar, if not identical, rules.[39]

*Motion for a New Trial*

After judgment has been entered, the losing party can bring a motion asking the court to set aside the judgment and order a new trial. The essential basis for this motion is that prejudicial errors were made during the course of trial that affected the outcome. The motion is usually presented to the judge who presided over the trial. It must be brought within a short time after entry of judgment, usually within ten days.

*Motion for Relief from Judgment*

Most states also allow a party to seek relief from judgment for a variety of reasons, including, but not limited to, mistake, inadvertence, excusable neglect, fraud, newly discovered evidence, or for "any other reason justifying relief from judgment."[40] A party usually has longer to file this motion than a motion for a new trial. Under the Federal Rules of Civil Procedure, a party must file the motion within a "reasonable time," which in most instances is not later than a year after judgment was entered. The year time limit does not apply if the underlying reason for the motion falls into the catchall category.

The motion for relief from judgment is generally regarded as a request for extraordinary relief and will be granted only in exceptional circumstances. For example, when a party seeks to set aside a judgment for newly discovered evidence, the party must show that even with due diligence, it could not have been discovered either during the trial or within the period for bringing a motion for a new trial, and that it would likely have led to a different outcome. Where allowed, the court may vacate and modify its judgment, or order a retrial.

# Appeals

*Overview of Appellate Practice*

The losing party can **appeal** from the court's final judgment, or that portion of the judgment that is adverse to him or her. The general rule is that a party can appeal only from a final judgment. For appeal purposes, a decree *nisi* is considered the final judgment—and if a party waits until the *nisi* decree ripens into a final decree, the appeal is likely to be untimely. Usually, the appeal goes from the trial court to the intermediate **appellate court**, but, in states without an intermediate level court, the appeal goes directly to the state's supreme court. The decision of an intermediate court can usually be appealed to the supreme court.

An appeal is not a retrial. The appellate court reviews what took place at the trial level to determine if any errors were made that might have affected the outcome of the case. This review is based on the record, and new evidence cannot be introduced. In reviewing for errors, the court is primarily concerned with errors of law. Findings of fact cannot be upset unless the court determines that they are unsupported by the evidence. The appeals court cannot substitute its view of what took place for the findings of the trial judge, who actually sees and hears the witnesses and is in the best position to evaluate their credibility.

The appeals court can affirm or reverse the decision of the trial court, or remand the case for a new trial. A remand is likely if additional information is needed, such as if the court improperly excluded evidence or allowed evidence that should have been excluded, as either may have altered the outcome of the case.

### Appellate Procedure

Each state has its own rules governing the particulars of appellate procedure. These rules tend to be very detailed and contain multiple time limits that must be met at each step of the process to preserve the right of review. Nonetheless, some basic steps common to most, if not all, states can be identified.

An appeal is commenced by the filing of a notice of appeal. This notice is usually filed in the court that heard the case. After it is commenced, the record on appeal must be prepared. Typically, the appealing party (appellant) is responsible for designating those portions of the trial court materials that he or she wishes to include in the record. In addition to pleadings and documents, the record also includes the transcript of the proceedings or relevant portions of it. The appellant is responsible for contacting the stenographer and making arrangements to have the transcript prepared and filed. If the appellant does not need to have all of the documents or the entire transcript included in the record, the appellant must inform the other side (appellee) what he or she has designated for inclusion, and the appellee then has the right to cross-designate documents or portions of the transcript for inclusion. The actual assembly of the record is done by a trial court clerk. Once it is assembled, the case is docketed with the appeals court.

The parties then submit briefs to the court. The appellant submits the first brief within a certain amount of time after docketing, and the appellee then has a specified number of days after this within which to file his or her brief. The appellant can then file a reply brief responding to the points made in the appellee's brief. After the briefs are submitted, the court can decide the case based on the written submissions alone, or it can schedule oral arguments, which give the attorneys a chance to argue the case before the court. Many states impose strict limits on the time allotted for oral argument.

### The Role of the Paralegal

A paralegal may be asked to oversee the appeals process. This is a daunting task that requires making sure each step is taken at the right time and that all rules are complied with. There is very little give here — an omitted detail or a missed deadline can lead to the dismissal of the appeal. Another important role a paralegal can play is in researching and writing the appellate brief. These briefs are painstaking to write. They require fine-tuned analytical skills and must conform to all of the particulars governing the submission of appellate briefs; accordingly, this task is usually assigned only to senior paralegals.

## The Complaint for Modification

Modification of judgments has been discussed at various points in this book. Here, some general points are made, and this action is distinguished from other post-judgment procedures.

The basis for a modification action is that circumstances have changed since the entry of the divorce order, making enforcement of certain provisions unfair. A modification is thus different from the post-judgment remedies discussed above because it does not challenge the validity of the order as originally entered; rather, it focuses on subsequent events that have since made it unworkable. Accordingly, a modification action can be filed in a case that was initially settled by the parties.

In principle, a modification is considered a continuation of the original action. In some jurisdictions, it is initiated by the filing of a motion, while in others, a new complaint must be filed and served (see Exhibit 10.9). As with the divorce, a court can enter temporary orders during the pendency of the modification proceeding, and the resulting judgment is itself subject to modification if there is a subsequent change in circumstances. Unlike other post-judgment remedies, there are generally no time limits within which a party may file a modification complaint.

**Exhibit 10.9**   *Motion for Modification*

**Form Number 2**

STATE OF INDIANA                )                IN THE _____ SUPERIOR/CIRCUIT COURT

                              ) SS:

COUNTY OF _____        )                CASE NO. _____

IN RE THE _____ OF: _____

_____

Petitioner,

and

_____

Respondent.

**VERIFIED PETITION FOR MODIFICATION OF CHILD SUPPORT**

    Comes now _____, pro se, and hereby files a Verified Petition for Modification of Child Support, and states as follows:

    1.    That parties have _____ minor child (ren), namely:

        NAME                                    DATE OF BIRTH

        _____        _____

        _____        _____

        _____        _____

        _____        _____

    2.    On _____, this Court ordered that _____ pay child support to

_____ in the weekly amount of $_____ to the above named child(ren) effective on _____.

    3.    Since that time, there has been a change in circumstances, so substantial and continuing as to make the terms of the current support order unreasonable for the following reasons: _____
_____
_____
_____.

    4.    Child support should be modified to reflect the substantial change in circumstances as outlined above.

    5.    A hearing should be set to determine if child support should be changed.

    WHEREFORE, _____ requests that this Court set this matter for hearing, and upon hearing, modify the existing child support as is appropriate, and order all other further relief that is just and proper in the premises.

    I affirm under the penalties of perjury that the foregoing representations are true.

                                    _____

                                    Signature

                                    _____

                                    Print your name

**Exhibit 10.9   Continued**

---

Mailing address

Town, State and Zip Code

Telephone number, with area code

### CERTIFICATE OF SERVICE

I hereby certify that I sent a copy of this Petition by first class mail to the opposing attorney, or the opposing party if the opposing party is not represented by an attorney, on _____.

Signature

Print your name

## The Complaint for Contempt

Contempt actions also have been discussed at various points throughout the book; the primary purpose of this section is to contrast this action with other post-judgment remedies.

A contempt action is brought to enforce an existing order where a party is in noncompliance. Like a modification action, a complaint for contempt can be brought following a case that was settled by the parties (see Exhibit 10.10). The action, by seeking enforcement, affirms the ongoing validity of the existing order. It is not uncommon for a defendant in a contempt hearing to argue that as entered, the underlying order is unfair or that circumstances have changed, which makes its current enforcement unfair. Given the range of available corrective procedures, courts are not very sympathetic to these arguments. Most judges will inform a contempt defendant that if he or she wishes to challenge the order, he or she must take the appropriate steps to do so and that until that time, the plaintiff has a right to rely on the order as it exists.

## Exhibit 10.10    *Complaint for Contempt*

**MOTION FOR CONTEMPT**
JD-FM-173 Rev. 2-2001
C.G.S. § 46b-87 § 46b-220 P.B. § 25-27

STATE OF CONNECTICUT
**SUPERIOR COURT**

COURT USE ONLY
**MFCONTP**

(Check one) ☐ Before Judgment (pendente lite) ☐ After Judgment

| JUDICIAL DISTRICT OF | AT (Town) | DOCKET NO. |
|---|---|---|

| PLAINTIFF'S NAME (Last, First, Middle Initial) | DEFENDANT'S NAME (Last, First, Middle Initial) |
|---|---|

| PLAINTIFF'S ADDRESS (No.,street, city, state, zip code) | DEFENDANT'S ADDRESS (No.,street, city, state, zip code) |
|---|---|

I, the ☐ PLAINTIFF ☐ DEFENDANT, respectfully represent that this Court issued an order on _____
(month, day, year)

directing the ☐ plaintiff ☐ defendant to *(complete only the information below that applies to the order(s) you claim was/were disobeyed):*

| PAY CHILD SUPPORT IN THE AMOUNT OF | PAY ALIMONY IN THE AMOUNT OF | TOTAL BALANCE OWED | AS OF (Date) |
|---|---|---|---|
| per | per | | |

| HAVE VISITATION OR PARENTING TIME AS FOLLOWS: (Attach a copy of the visitation schedule if available) |
|---|

| PAY MEDICAL BILLS OR PROVIDE HEALTH INSURANCE AS FOLLOWS |
|---|

| OTHER: |
|---|

The ☐ plaintiff or ☐ defendant has disobeyed the court order in the following ways: *(Please be specific. Include the amount of any arrears claimed due as of the date of this motion or a date specifically identified.)*

I ask the Court to find the ☐ plaintiff ☐ defendant in contempt. I certify that the above information is true to the best of my knowledge.

| SIGNATURE* | DATE | TELEPHONE (Area Code first) |
|---|---|---|

**CERTIFICATION (Complete if motion is filed before judgment (pendente lite))**

| I certify that I mailed/delivered a copy of this motion to: | NAME** | DATE MAILED/DELIVERED |
|---|---|---|
| ADDRESS (No., street, city, state, zip code) | | |

| SIGNATURE | PRINT NAME | DATE SIGNED |
|---|---|---|

**If necessary, attach additional sheet with name of each party served and the address at which service was made.

**ORDER TO ATTEND HEARING AND NOTICE *(TO BE COMPLETED BY THE COURT)***

The court orders ☐ the plaintiff ☐ the defendant to attend a hearing at the time and place shown below to show why you are not in contempt. The Court also orders the ☐ plaintiff ☐ the defendant to give notice to the opposing party of the Motion and of the time and place where the Court will hear it, by having a true and attested copy of the Motion and this Order served on the opposing party by any proper officer at least **12 days** before the date of the hearing. Proof of service shall be made to this Court at least **six days** before the hearing.

| BY THE COURT (Judge/Assistant Clerk) | DATE SIGNED |
|---|---|

| **HEARING TO BE HELD AT** → | SUPERIOR COURT, JUDICIAL DISTRICT OF | DATE | TIME |
|---|---|---|---|
| | COURT ADDRESS | ROOM NO. (If known) | TELEPHONE (Area code first) |

**If you do not attend the court hearing, a civil arrest order (capias) may be issued against you.**

*(Continued on back/page 2)*    *Check appropriate court: ☐ Superior Court    ☐ Family Support Magistrate Division

## Exhibit 10.10 *Continued*

---

### SUMMONS

**TO ANY PROPER OFFICER:**
By the Authority of the State of Connecticut, you must serve a true and attested copy of the above Motion and Order to Attend Hearing on the below named person in one of the ways required by law at least **12 days** before the date of the hearing, and file proof of service with this Court at least **six days** before the hearing.

| PERSON TO BE SERVED | ADDRESS | |
|---|---|---|
| ASSISTANT CLERK | | DATE SIGNED |

---

### ORDER

The Court has heard the above Motion and finds that the ☐ plaintiff ☐ defendant:

☐ **is not in contempt.** ☐ **is in contempt in the following way(s):**

☐ owes arrears as of _____ in the amount of _____

☐ other *(specify):* _____

_____

**IT IS ORDERED:**

☐ payment in the amount of _____ for current support and _____ on arrears by *(date)* _____ .

☐ income withholding in the amount of _____

☐ suspension of professional, occupational, recreational, or driver's license with a 30-day stay (attach "License Suspension Order," Form JD-FM-153)

☐ posting of a surety bond

☐ incarceration

☐ attorney's fees

☐ marshal's fees

☐ this matter is continued to _____ at _____
　　　　　　　　　　　　　　 *(date)* 　　　 *(time)*

☐ other *(specify):* _____

| BY THE COURT *(Judge/FSM)* | SIGNED *(Assistant Clerk)* | DATE OF ORDER |
|---|---|---|

---

### RETURN OF SERVICE

I left a true and attested copy of the Motion for Contempt ☐ personally with the defendant ☐ personally with the plaintiff

☐ at the current home of the ☐ defendant or ☐ plaintiff at _____
　　　　　　　　　　　　　　　　　　　　　　　　　　　　 *(Number, street, town or city)*

The original Motion is attached.

| NAME AND TITLE | COUNTY | DATE OF SERVICE |
|---|---|---|

**MARSHAL'S USE ONLY**
**FEE INFORMATION:**

COPY _____

ENDORSEMENT _____

SERVICE _____

TRAVEL _____

TOTAL _____

JD-FM-173 *(Back)* Rev. 2-2001

# Chapter Summary

Good case preparation begins with a well-organized client interview. At this interview, essential information is obtained and a foundation of trust is established. Active listening and respect for the client's emotional concerns are important in establishing an effective relationship.

The first formal step in a divorce case is the filing of the complaint (or a joint petition). The complaint and summons are then served on the defendant, who must answer within a certain period of time. In theory, failure to respond will result in a default judgment, but most courts are reluctant to default a defendant in a divorce case. Once the case has been initiated, both sides usually engage in the process of discovery, which is used to acquire information about the other side in order to help prepare for trial and/or structure the settlement.

Frequently, during the period between filing and the final hearing, motions for temporary orders will be filed asking the court to provide interim relief. The general rule is that advance notice must be given to the other side; however, ex parte relief may be allowed where such notice poses a substantial risk of harm. Notice and an opportunity to be heard must subsequently be provided. Common motions include those for support, custody, the protection of assets, and protection from abuse.

Most parties wish to settle their case and avoid a trial on the merits. The most common approach to dispute resolution is negotiation, where each attorney acts in a representational capacity and seeks to obtain the best possible settlement for his or her client. Another approach, which is growing in popularity, is mediation. Here, a neutral third party assists the parties to reach agreement on their own. A primary advantage of this approach is that it is client-centered; however, concerns have been raised about its appropriateness where there is a history of domestic violence or a significant power imbalance between the parties. Arbitration is another alternative, but it is not used frequently in divorce cases. Here, the dispute is presented to a decision maker who renders a binding decision. The process is more flexible than a court hearing, and the parties retain a greater degree of control.

If all issues are resolved through any of these methods, the parties reduce their understanding to a written separation agreement. This agreement is comprehensive and must be drafted carefully because it governs the post-divorce relationship between the parties. With the execution of the agreement, the case becomes uncontested, and a relatively simple hearing can be scheduled at which the marriage is dissolved and the agreement reviewed and approved by the court.

If the parties cannot reach resolution, the case is contested and a trial on the merits is scheduled. Here, a judge resolves the dispute and enters an order reflecting his or her decision. The losing party can challenge this decision by way of motion or appeal. Further down the line, parties may seek to modify or enforce the existing order by filing a modification or contempt action.

## Key Terms

Confidentiality

Active Listening

Complaint/Petition

Request for Relief/Prayer

Joint Petition

Docket Number

Venue

Filing Fee

Summons

Service of Process

Personal Service

Constructive Service

Acceptance of Service

Return of Service

Answer

Default Judgment

Affirmative Defense

Counterclaim

Motion to Dismiss

Discovery

Deposition

Deponent

Subpoena

Subpoena Duces Tecum

Interrogatories

Request for Production of
    Documents

Request for a Physical or Mental
    Examination

Request for Admissions

Protective Order

Discovery Conference

Motion to Compel

Sanctions

Temporary Orders

Affidavit

Ex Parte

Guardian ad Litem

Attorney's Fees

Negotiation

Mediation

Arbitration

Unbundled Legal Services

Collaborative Law

Separation Agreement

Divorce Hearing

Incorporation

Survival

Merger

Divorce Judgment

Decree *Nisi*

Pretrial Conference

Pretrial Statement

Trial Notebook

Motion for a New Trial

Motion for Relief from
    Judgment

Appeal

Appellate Court

# Review Questions

1. Why is it important to pay attention to cultural differences when interviewing a client?

2. Why is it important to acknowledge how a client is feeling at the initial interview?

3. What does the term "unauthorized practice of law" mean, and how does it limit your relationship with a client?

4. Why is maintaining client confidentiality so important?

5. What is meant by the term "active listening"?

6. What are the three stages of a client interview?

7. What are the benefits of asking open-ended questions during an interview?

8. What is the funneling process?

9. What purposes are served by the divorce complaint?

10. What are the basic component parts of a divorce complaint?

11. What are the possible consequences of failing to include something in a complaint?

12. What is a joint petition?

13. Explain what is meant by the term "venue."

14. What is a summons?

15. What is meant by the term "service of process"?

16. Why is it important to try to personally serve a defendant?

17. What are the ways in which service can be accomplished?

18. What is "return of service"?

19. What happens if a divorce defendant does not respond to the complaint in a timely fashion? How is this different from other civil actions?

20. What are the component parts of an answer?

21. Why is it generally advisable to file an answer?

22. What is a motion to dismiss, and when might a defendant file one?

23. What is the purpose of discovery?

24. Describe the five available discovery procedures.

25. Describe some of the key ways in which paralegals can assist with discovery.

26. What is a protective order, and when may a party seek one?

27. What can a party do when the other side fails to respond to discovery requests?

28. What is a motion? Why would a party file one?

29. When would a party file a motion ex parte?

30. What happens to temporary orders once a divorce judgment is entered?

31. Can a temporary order be appealed? Why or why not?

32. What is an affidavit?

33. Describe each of the three dispute resolution approaches, and explain what the key differences are among them.

34. Why do some people argue that mediation is not appropriate in cases where there has been domestic violence?

35. Explain the differences between the two important approaches to mediation, the problem-solving model and the transformative model.

36. Describe the four stages of mediation (using the problem-solving model).

37. What is a collaborative divorce? How is it similar to and different from other alternative dispute resolution approaches?

38. Explain what is meant by the term "unbundled" legal services.

39. What is a separation agreement?

40. What are the benefits of spelling out the custody and visitation arrangements?

41. What are the most common ways for real estate to be disposed of?

42. With respect to the allocation of joint debts, why might a spouse be called on to pay a debt allocated to the other party in a separation agreement?

43. What are meant by the terms "incorporation," "merger," and "survival as an independent contract" as used in separation agreements?

44. What takes place at an uncontested hearing?

45. What does a judge look at when reviewing an agreement for procedural fairness? for substantive fairness?

46. How does a trial in a contested case differ from an uncontested hearing?

47. What purpose is served by a pretrial conference?

48. What is a motion for a new trial?

49. What is a motion for relief from judgment?

50. What is the primary focus of an appeals court when reviewing a lower court decision?

51. Outline the steps involved in bringing an appeal.

52. How do modification and contempt actions differ from other post-judgment procedures?

# Discussion Questions

1. Assume that you are conducting an initial client interview with a client who is involved in a custody dispute with her husband, and that you become fairly certain the client is lying to you. What do you think you should do at this stage of the process? Do you confront the client? Do you ignore your concerns? Are there any techniques you might use for eliciting the truth? Is it your responsibility to elicit the truth?

   Assume that you continue working with this client and, despite your concern, have established a good relationship with her. One day she comes into your office and tells you that she has been lying to you and that she is a drug addict and is frequently high when she is with her children.

   What do you do at this point? In thinking about it, assume that you are the only paralegal in a busy office and that although you could ask to be taken off the case, this would make matters difficult for the supervising attorney.

2. Do you think the discovery process should be as open-ended as it currently is? Why or why not? Are there ways it could be limited without interfering with a party's ability to prepare a case?

3. Is it fair to require one party to pay the other side's attorney where there is a disparity of income? Why or why not?

4. Do you think mediation is appropriate in cases involving domestic violence? What about cases not involving violence, but where there is a significant power imbalance between the spouses?

5. Under what circumstances, if any, do you think that paralegals should be able to provide clients with legal advice?

# Assignments

1. Draft the custody provisions of a separation agreement in accordance with the following instructions:

   To: Polly Paralegal
   From: Anita Attorney
   Re: Ramirez divorce

As you know, we represent Ms. Ramirez in her current divorce action. I just completed a round of settlement negotiations, and I would like you to try to draft the custody and visitation provisions of the separation agreement. Following are the things you need to know in order to do this:

a. The parties have one child, a daughter named Lucinda, who is eight.
b. Both parents work outside the home, with the mother working about 35 hours per week and the father working about 50.
c. Both parents have a good relationship with Lucinda, although Mom is clearly the primary parent.
d. Ms. Ramirez and her husband, Mr. Lewis, cannot stand each other, although they think they can handle joint legal custody.
e. The real issue is physical custody. We have more or less reached agreement as to when each parent will spend time with Lucinda, but we are stuck with how to define the arrangement. Dad is adamant that he not be called the visiting parent, and Mom is adamant that the arrangement not be called joint physical custody.
f. Your job is to try to come up with a creative solution! At this point, just worry about the regular weekly schedule; we will deal with holidays, etc., later.
g. Here are the agreed-on time allocations: (1) Lucinda will stay at Mom's house during the school week, with the exception of Wednesday nights, when Dad will pick her up and she will stay with him. (2) Every other week, Lucinda will stay with Dad from 10:00 A.M. on Saturday until school-time on Monday, and he will take her to school. On the other weekends he will spend Saturdays from 10:00 A.M. until 8:00 P.M. with her.
h. As you can see, Mom has the bulk of time, and there is no doubt in anyone's mind that she will do most of the general parenting stuff, such as schedule doctor's appointments, buy clothes, etc., but it's also clear that Dad has some real time with her. So, good luck with the drafting.

2. This assignment requires you to go to your local family court. Observe at least two different types of court procedures, such as a motion session and part of a trial, and then write a paper detailing what you have observed. In your paper you should do the following:

a. identify all participants in the proceeding, including court personnel, making sure that you use the correct titles

    b. identify the nature of the proceeding, such as a motion for temporary support

    c. identify what each side was trying to accomplish and how they were seeking to do this

    d. discuss what was most effective, and discuss any weaknesses you identified in either side's presentation of their case

3.  With respect to motion practice in your area, determine the following:

    a. how motions are served

    b. what the time requirements for service are

    c. how motions are marked up

    d. when, if ever, accompanying affidavits are required

    e. whether parties are ever diverted to some kind of settlement process, and if so, under what circumstances

4.  Assume you are working in an office and a divorce client has just frantically called to inform the attorney handling the case that her husband has just threatened to take the kids out of the country so she will never receive custody of them. The attorney has asked you to draft an ex parte motion with a supporting affidavit seeking to prevent the father from doing this. Please draft these documents in accordance with the governing standards in your jurisdiction.

5.  Your office is representing the husband in a divorce case. The parties have three children and are involved in a bitter custody dispute. The husband strongly suspects that the wife has begun dating a local drug dealer and may have begun using drugs herself. He also worries that she is neglecting the children. The children live with their mom but see their dad fairly regularly. Their ages are two, four, and five. The mom is not employed outside the home. The attorney you work for has asked you to draft a set of interrogatories relevant to custody. He wants useful information but would like to proceed with tact so things do not blow up. He would also like the interrogatories to inquire into the wife's financial situation, as child and spousal support are likely to become contested.

# Endnotes

1. Diane Eades, Lawyer-Client Communication: " 'I Don't Think the Lawyers Were Communicating with Me': Misunderstanding Cultural Differences in Communicative Style," 52 Emory L.J. 1109, 1118 (2003). This discussion about cultural differences in communication is based on Eades' outstanding article that should be required reading for anyone engaged in client interviewing. It should be pointed out that the defendant's conviction was reversed on appeal, at least in part due to the author's testimony. The article also provides a fascinating description of how the appeal came about.

In addition to the Eades article and those cited in notes 11 and 12, *see* the following for thoughtful approaches to the client interview: Robert Dinerstein, Stephen Ellmann, Isabelle Gunning, and Ann Shalleck, Connection, Capacity, and Morality in Lawyer-Client Relationships: Dialogues and Commentary, 10 Clinical L. Rev. 755 (2004); V. Pualani Enos and Lois H. Kanter "Problem Solving in Clinical Education: Who's Listening? Introducing Students to Client-Centered, Client-Empowering, and Multidisciplinary Problem-Solving in a Clinical Setting, 9 Clinical L. Rev. 83 (2003); Laurel E. Fletcher and Harvey M. Weinstein, Problem Solving in Clinical Education: When Students Lose Perspective: Clinical Supervision and the Management of Empathy, 9 Clinical L. Rev. 135 (2002).

2. *See* Judith S. Wallerstein and Sandra Blakeslee, Second Chances — Men, Women and Children a Decade After Divorce: Who Wins, Who Loses — and Why 6 (1990).

3. Mavis E. Hetherington and Kathleen A. Camara, Families in Transition: The Process of Dissolution and Reconstitution, *in* The Review of Child Development Research 406 (Ross Park ed., 1984).

4. Wallerstein and Blakeslee, *supra* note 2, at 8.

5. This section on ethics is based on Therese A. Cannon, Ethics and Professional Responsibility for Legal Assistants (1999). This book is written for both students and working paralegals and is an invaluable guide to legal ethics. For more detail on the topics covered in this section, as well as other ethical considerations, please refer to this book.

6. Cannon, *supra* note 5, at 28.

7. However, a number of states are actively considering licensing paralegals, and some states, such as California, have enacted laws regulating the paralegal profession. Regarding California's law, *see* http://www.calbar.ca.gov/calbar/2cbj/01feb/mclestdy.htm (accessed June 16, 2004). For more information on the licensure debate, you can visit the Web sites of the two major national paralegal organizations at http://www.paralegal.org and http://www.nala.org.

8. *See* Cannon, *supra* note 5, ch. 3. *See also* Debra Levy Martinelli, Are You Riding a Fine Line? Learn to Identify and Avoid Issues Involving the Unauthorized Practice of Law, 15 Utah Bar J. 18 (2002); Marilu Peterson, Do You UPL? 15 Utah Bar J. 44 (2002).

9. *See* Cannon, *supra* note 5, ch. 4. See also, Clark D. Cunningham How to Explain Confidentiality?, 9 Clinical L. Rev. 579 (2003).

10. *See* Cannon, *supra* note 5, at 87-115.

11. *See* Robert M. Bastress and Joseph D. Harbaugh, Interviewing, Counseling, and Negotiating: Skills for Effective Representation (1990).

12. *See* Don Peters, You Can't Always Get What You Want: Organizing Matrimonial Interviews to Get What You Need, 26 Cal. W. L. Rev. 256, 268 (1990).

13. For a good basic book on civil procedure, *see* Joseph W. Glannon, Civil Procedure: Examples and Explanations (4th ed. 2001).

14. Fed. R. Civ. P. 26(b)(1). In addition to the protection of privileged materials, an attorney's work product (e.g., notes) is generally not subject to discovery.

15. *See* Peggy N. Kerley, Civil Litigation 285-291 (3d ed. 2001).

16. Fed. R. Civ. P. 26(c).

17. At present, most states do not have formal training and licensing requirements for mediators, although a number of professional organizations have developed practice standards.

18. Dorothy J. Della Noce, Robert A. Baruch Bush, and Joseph P. Folger, Clarifying the Theoretical Underpinnings of Mediation: Implications for Practice and Policy, 3 Pepp. Disp. Resol. L.J. 39, 41 (2002). It should be noted that this article draws from and builds on the following work: Robert A. Baruch Bush and Joseph P. Folger, The Promise of Mediation: Responding to Conflict Through Empowerment and Recognition (1994).

19. *Id.* at 47.

20. *Id.* at 50.

21. *Id.*

22. *Id.* at 51.

23. *Id.*

24. *Id.* at 52.

25. *Id.* at 50-52.

26. This discussion of the mediation process is consistent with "problem-solving" model; it is based in part on the approach set out by Alison Taylor, A General Theory of Divorce Mediation, *in* Divorce Mediation, Theory and Practice (Milne and Folberg eds., 1988).

27. I wish to thank my colleague, Professor David Matz, Director of Graduate Programs in Dispute Resolution at the University of Massachusetts, Boston, for sharing many of his thoughtful insights into this and other complexities inherent in the mediation process. For a critical look at some of the complexities posed by mediation, *see* Marsha B. Freeman, Divorce Mediation: Sweeping Conflicts Under the Rug, Time to Clean House, 780 U. Det. Mercy L. Rev. 67 (2000).

28. For an interesting argument that this review comes too late in the process to be meaningful, *see* Kevin M. Mazza, Divorce Mediation: Perhaps Not the Remedy It Was Once Considered, 14 Fam. Advoc. 40 (1992).

29. For further discussion of the issues discussed in this section, *see* Joyce, *supra* note 17. *See also* Lydia Belzer, Domestic Abuse and Divorce Mediation: Suggestions for a Safer Process, 5 Loy. J. Pub. Int. L. 37 (2002); Sarah Krieger, The Dangers of Mediation in Domestic Violence Cases, 8 Cardozo Women's L.J. 235 (2002); Penelope E. Bryan, Killing Us Softly: Divorce Mediation and the Politics of Power, 40 Buff. L. Rev. 441 (1992); Peter Salem and Kristin Koeffler, When Domestic Abuse Is an Issue, 14 Fam. Advoc. 34 (1992); Barbara J. Hart, Gentle

Jeopardy: The Further Endangerment of Battered Women and Children in Custody Mediation, 7 Mediation Q. 317 (1990).

30. Andre R. Imbrogno, Arbitration as an Alternative to Divorce Litigation: Redefining the Judicial Role, 31 Cap. U.L. Rev. 413, 417 (2003). *See also* Allan R. Koritzinsky, Robert M. Welch, and Stephen W. Schlissel, The Benefits of Arbitration, 14 Fam. Advoc. 45 (1992); David Hoffman and David Matz, Massachusetts Alternative Dispute Resolution (1994).

31. Kelm v. Kelm, 623 N.E.2d 39, 42 (Ohio 1993). For a discussion of this case as well as others pertaining to arbitration in the divorce context, *see* Imbrogno, *supra* note 30.

32. Larry R. Spain, Collaborative Law: A Critical Reflection on Whether a Collaborative Orientation Can Be Ethically Incorporated into the Practice of Law, 56 Baylor L. Rev. 141, 143 (2004). *See also* Susan Daicoff, The Law as a Healing Profession" The "Comprehensive Law Movement," 6 Pepp. Disp. Resol. L.J.1 (2006).

33. For further reading, *see* The Changing Face of Legal Practice: Twenty-Six Recommendations for the Baltimore Conference: A National Conference on 'Unbundled' Legal Services, 40 Fam Ct. Rev. 26 (2002). Mary Helen McNeal, Having One Oar or Being without a Boat: Reflections on the Fordham Recommendations on Limited Legal Assistance, 67 Fordham L. Rev. 2617 (1999).

34. For an excellent book on separation agreements that includes the applicable law, drafting checklists, and sample provisions, *see* Stephen W. Schlissel, Elena Karabatos, and Ronald F. Poepplein, Separation Agreements and Marital Contracts (2d ed. 1997).

35. This language is taken from Stephen W. Schlissel, Separation Agreements and Marital Contracts 617-618 (1986).

36. 50 U.S.C. § 520.

37. A detailed look at the trial process is beyond the scope of this book and is likely to be covered in other courses.

38. A number of good books discuss the skills that paralegals need to develop if they are to effectively assist with case preparation. For example, *see* Peggy N. Kerley, Civil Litigation (3d ed. 2001).

39. Fed. R. Civ. P. 59 & 60(b).

40. Fed. R. Civ. P. 60(b).

# 11 Determining Paternity

Historically, the legal relationship between parent and child was determined by the marital status of the parents. Simply put, children were considered **"legitimate"** if born to married parents and **"illegitimate"** if born to unwed parents. Gradually, the law has moved away from strict reliance on marital status as the legal determinant of the parent-child relationship, and the traditional distinction between children of married parents and those of unmarried parents has been virtually eliminated. However, some differences remain; most notably, unwed fathers do not always have the same rights and status that both unwed mothers and married fathers have.

We begin this chapter by tracing the evolution of the legal status of children of unmarried parents. We then consider the constitutional rights of unwed fathers, followed by a discussion of paternity establishment and a look at the relatively new topic of paternity disestablishment. We conclude with a discussion about sperm donation and paternal rights. With the exception of the discussion on sperm donors, the focus of this chapter is on heterosexual couples because this is the context within which the law related to paternity has developed. For a discussion regarding children of unmarried same-sex couples, see Chapter 5.

## THE EMERGING LEGAL STATUS OF CHILDREN OF UNMARRIED PARENTS

### Common Law Status: A Child of No One

English common law drew a sharp distinction between children born to married parents and those born to unmarried parents. A child of unmarried parents was considered a "filius nullius"—a child of no one, a bastard. "Bastardy" rules were designed to deter sexual promiscuity, reinforce the institution of marriage, and protect family lineage by ensuring that a father's property, name, and status passed to his legitimate sons in an orderly manner.[1] As a child had no recognizable legal bond with either parent, neither parent had right to custody or a duty of support, although a limited support obligation was imposed by the English Poor Laws, which sought to protect towns from having to maintain these children. Nonetheless, children of unmarried parents often ended up as wards of the parish in which they were born, especially if a parent died, as they had no rights of inheritance.

Some children were saved from the harsh consequences of the bastardy rules by the common law **presumption of paternity**. Based on this presumption, all children born to a married woman were considered offspring of the marriage, even if they were the result of an extramarital relationship. Rebuttal was difficult, and at times could be accomplished only by proof of the husband's impotence or his extended absence from England. Although the presumption of paternity aided children by enfolding them into a family unit, its primary purpose was to shield the family from the taint of immorality. Significantly, this presumption, which remains operative today, allows for the creation of a father-child relationship based upon a legal rule rather than a biological connection.

## Early American Reform Efforts

### *The Roots of Reform*

Following the English tradition, our early laws also placed children of unmarried parents outside the connective threads of family relations. As explained by one commentator: "I apprehend this rule to be partly founded in that anxiety which the law everywhere exhibits, to secure domestic tranquility, and partly, in policy, to discourage illicit commerce betwixt the sexes. If a bastard might inherit either to his father or his mother, where they had married, and had a family of children, it might be a real source of domestic uneasiness."[2]

By the beginning of the nineteenth century, attitudes toward these children had begun to soften, resulting in some legal reforms. This shift in views reflected two broader trends. First, as discussed in Chapter 6, attitudes toward children changed as we moved from an agrarian to an early industrial nation. Children were no longer seen as embodiments of original sin in need of harsh corrective measures but as innocent creatures in need of love and nurturance.[3] Second, the post-Revolutionary emphasis on individual rights and responsibilities raised questions about the fairness of the bastardy rules, which stigmatized children based on the conduct of their parents.

Yet we should keep in mind that these legal reforms were not extended to all segments of the U.S. population. For those bound in slavery, family ties continued to be disregarded despite the strength and endurance of the bonds. Slave unions were not accorded legal status, and children continued to be forcibly taken from their parents without regard for the affective ties that linked them together.

### Creating Limited Family Rights

A central reform was the extension of legal recognition to the mother-child unit. No longer a child of no one, nonmarital children were now formally recognized as the children of their mothers; as a result, mothers were entitled to custody and obligated to provide support. Mothers were favored over fathers both because, unlike paternal identity, maternal identity was readily established, and because a maternal preference was consistent with the prevailing emphasis on female domesticity and the belief in women's superior nurturing capabilities. Thus, by the middle of the nineteenth century, children were considered "legitimate" in relationship to their mothers regardless of their mothers' marital status, although, as discussed below, states maintained clear legal distinctions between children of married parents and those of unmarried parents.[4]

### Legitimation

A second significant reform was the gradual rejection of the harsh common law rule that a child's status was fixed permanently at birth. Beginning with Virginia in 1823, most states amended their laws to allow for **legitimation** where parents married each other after the birth of a child. A few states went further than this and were willing to recognize a father-child relationship based on an acknowledgment of paternity. Although seemingly mild by today's standards, many criticized these innovations for rewarding immorality and destroying the integrity of marriage.[5]

### The End of Legal Innovation

For many, these reforms were profoundly disturbing. By focusing on the child as a separate person, they threatened to erode the unity of the marital family in favor of individual recognition and rights. By the end of the nineteenth century, the period of innovation drew to a close, and further change of this magnitude would have to wait until the constitutional challenges of the next century.[6]

## Constitutional Developments ————————————————————————

Although these nineteenth-century reforms mitigated some of the harsh common law rules, children of unmarried parents remained a distinct legal category of persons. Referred to as "bastards" or "illegitimates," they suffered a variety of legal disabilities, particularly in relationship to their fathers. For example, they were frequently excluded as beneficiaries under statutory benefit programs, such as workers' compensation; they lacked inheritance rights under state intestacy laws; and they were denied standing in wrongful death actions for the loss of a parent. Additionally, unwed fathers had few legal rights in relationship to their children. Beginning in the 1960s, a number of lawsuits were brought challenging this differential treatment of children of unmarried parents and the denial of rights to unwed fathers. In the following sections, we will look at the Supreme Court's response to these challenges.

### The Equal Protection Challenge to Differential Treatment

In 1968, in the landmark case of Levy v. Louisiana, the Supreme Court held that the state of Louisiana had violated the **equal protection clause** by denying a child the right to recover for the death of his mother under the state's wrongful death law because he was "illegitimate." As explained by the Court:

> Legitimacy or illegitimacy of birth has no relation to the nature of the wrong allegedly inflicted on the mother. These children, though illegitimate, were dependent on her; she cared for them and nurtured them; they were indeed hers in the biological and spiritual sense; in her death they suffered wrong in the sense that any dependent would.[7]

The Court thus recognized that the significance of the parent-child relationship does not depend on the marital status of the parents and further that children should not be discriminated against based on parental conduct over which they had no control.

Since *Levy*, the Court has decided a number of cases involving similar equal protection challenges to laws that discriminated against children born to unmarried parents by, for example, denying or limiting their ability to obtain statutory benefits or to inherit under state intestacy laws. Unfortunately, these decisions are not always clear and consistent with one another; nonetheless, some general principles do emerge from them.[8]

First, a court must carefully review any law that classifies children based on the marital status of their parents. Central to this review, the court must evaluate the reason for the statutory classification. If its purpose is to deter nonmarital sexual relations or promote the state's interest in marriage, the classification is invalid because these goals do not justify the discriminatory treatment of children. Children may not be disadvantaged based on circumstances over which they have no control. Moreover, states may not deprive children of benefits based on the assumption that there can be no meaningful parent-child relationship outside the marital family unit.

Second, although a law may not discriminate against children of unmarried parents in order to promote marriage or regulate sexual behavior, all legal distinctions between children of unmarried parents and children of married parents are not necessarily unconstitutional. Most important, if a distinction is carefully drawn for the purpose of preventing fraudulent claims, it is likely to withstand constitutional scrutiny. For example, although a state may not deprive nonmarital children of paternal inheritance rights under its intestacy statute in order to encourage marriage, it probably can condition these rights upon a prior adjudication of paternity in order to prevent fraudulent claims. Thus, a state may be able to exclude a child from receiving a statutory share of benefits where the father-child relationship had not been formally established prior to the father's death.

By limiting the differential legal treatment of children based on the marital status of their parents, the long shadow of the common law has all but been erased. The potential for establishing fully developed legal relationships with both parents now exists. All is not crystal clear, however, and the Supreme Court continues to struggle with the weight and meaning of the father-child bond where it exists outside the marital relationship.

### The Legal Status of the Unwed Father

As developed above, the differential treatment of children of unmarried parents is impermissible for the purpose of discouraging nonmarital sexual relations or promoting marriage. Let's look at the issue from a different perspective: What if it is the unwed father rather than the child who is singled out for differential treatment? Should the law treat him in the same manner that it treats an unwed mother or a married father, or does he occupy a distinct legal position in relationship to his child? Are the cases involving the interests of unwed fathers the flip side of the cases involving children, or are different considerations at stake? To consider these questions, we turn to a series of landmark United States Supreme Court cases focusing on the rights of unwed fathers. These cases give us a different lens through which to view the unfolding and uncertain legal construction of nonmarital family relations.

**Challenging the Exclusion of Unwed Fathers: Stanley v. Illinois.** In 1972, in the case of Stanley v. Illinois,[9] the Supreme Court considered whether it was unconstitutional for a state to presume that all unwed fathers were unfit parents. Peter and Joan Stanley had lived together on an intermittent basis for 18 years. During this time, they had three children. When Joan Stanley died, the state of Illinois initiated a dependency proceeding. The children were declared wards of the state for lack of a surviving parent and placed in the care of a court-appointed guardian. Peter Stanley was not provided with an opportunity to challenge the removal of his children because the state of Illinois presumed that all unwed fathers were unfit to raise their children. In contrast, married parents and unwed mothers could not be deprived of their children without a hearing on the issue of fitness.

Stanley challenged the presumption of unfitness, which effectively severed his tie with his children without inquiry into their actual circumstances, and argued that, like other parents, he too was entitled to a hearing on the question of fitness. Although acknowledging, as argued by the state, that most unwed fathers may in fact be "unsuitable and neglectful" parents, the Court nonetheless agreed with Stanley that he could not be deprived of custody without a hearing. In supporting Stanley's claim, the Court recognized the potential for meaningful relationships between unwed fathers and their children and made clear that paternal rights do not merit protection only when developed within a marital family unit.

Following *Stanley*, it appeared as if the Court might be moving in the direction of eliminating all distinctions between unwed fathers and other parents. However, the Court did not make clear why it was protecting Stanley's rights. Would a mere biological connection to these children have entitled him to a hearing, or was he entitled because he had both "sired and raised" them?

**What Makes an Unwed Father a Father?** After *Stanley*, a number of unwed fathers brought lawsuits challenging state laws that permitted the adoption of nonmarital children based solely on the consent of the mother. Building on *Stanley*, they argued (1) that an unwed father has a constitutionally protected liberty interest in maintaining a parental relationship with his child that cannot be abrogated without his consent absent proof of unfitness and (2) that differential treatment of unwed fathers and unwed mothers violates the equal protection clause.

In responding to these challenges, the Court answered the question left open in *Stanley*. In the 1983 case of Lehr v. Robertson, the Court clarified that the rights of unwed fathers do not spring into being based solely on the biological link between father and child. According to the Court, the significance of the biological connection is that it provides a father with the unique opportunity to develop a relationship with his offspring. If he grasps that opportunity and assumes some responsibility for the child, he may be entitled to some of the benefits and rights that attach to the parent-child relationship; however, if he fails to grasp this opportunity, he cannot claim a constitutionally protected right to participate in the adoption decision.[10] (Note: We return to the adoption rights of unmarried fathers in Chapter 13.) In short, outside of the marital context, biology alone does not a father make. Instead, a man must act like a father to be legally recognized as one and thus entitled to an equal say regarding adoption. This "biology-plus" approach drew harsh criticism from the dissent, who argued that the biological tie itself merits protection because it is the nature rather than the weight of the interest that is important.

In the 2001 case of Nguyen v. Immigration & Naturalization Services (*Nguyen*),[11] the Court reaffirmed its support of the "biology-plus" approach. In *Nguyen*, the Court upheld the constitutionality of a provision of the Immigration and Naturalization Act that treated unwed fathers and mothers differently with respect to the citizenship of children born outside the United States where only one parent was a citizen. Under the Act, if the citizen parent was the mother, the child was automatically considered a U.S citizen (assuming the mother met very liberal residency requirements); however, if the father was the citizen parent, citizenship was not automatic. Among other requirements, the father had to formally establish paternity and agree in writing to support the child. The Court reasoned that this differential treatment was justifiable because motherhood is established by birth, whereas fatherhood, in both its biological and relational dimensions, is not. As expressed by the Court: "Fathers and mothers are not similarly situated with respect to biological parenthood . . . Given the proof of motherhood that is inherent in birth itself, it is unremarkable that Congress did not require the same affirmative steps of mothers. . . . In the case of a citizen mother and a child born overseas, the opportunity for a meaningful relationship between citizen parent and child inheres in the very event of birth . . . [T]he same opportunity does not result from the event of birth, as a matter of biological inevitability, in the case of the unwed father."[12] Again, the dissent was critical, chastising the majority for relying "on the generalization that mothers are significantly more likely than fathers . . . to develop caring relations with their children,"[13] and called for the use of gender-neutral criteria.

Thus, as it presently stands, the legal treatment of unmarried fathers differs from the treatment of unmarried mothers, as women are not required to demonstrate that they have "grasped the opportunity" provided by the biological relationship in order to be legally recognized as a mother. For women, the parental relationship is thought to flow directly from the fact that she "carries and bears" the child. Here, biology is central — while men must become fathers, women are mothers. For men, biology provides the opportunity to become a legally recognized father; for women, motherhood is embedded in biology.[14] An unmarried father is also treated differently from a married father, who, because of marriage, is presumed to have a developed relationship with his children.

Unfortunately, the matter is a bit more complex than presented so far. In 1989, after *Lehr* but before *Nguyen*, the Court rendered a very important decision, which appears to limit the scope of the biology-plus approach — at least where it bumps up against the presumption of paternity. We now turn to the case of Michael H. v. Gerald D.

**The Biology-Plus Approach Confronts the Presumption of Paternity.** The following facts will set the stage for our analysis of the Court's decision in Michael H. v. Gerald D. (*Michael H.*).[15] In 1981, a girl named Victoria was born to a woman named Carol. At the time, Carol was married to Gerald, who was listed as the father on the birth certificate. However, subsequent blood tests showed a 98.7 percent probability that a man named Michael was actually Victoria's father. During Victoria's early years, three men moved in and out of her life. At times, Victoria, Carol, and Gerald made up a household; at other times, Victoria, Carol, and Michael made up a household. (We'll ignore the third man, Scott, who for our purposes is irrelevant, as he did not seek to assert paternal rights.)

To secure his relationship with Victoria, Michael filed a paternity action seeking formal legal recognition as her father. Not surprisingly, Gerald opposed his quest for recognition, arguing that under California law he was Victoria's presumed father based on his marriage to Carol and that Michael lacked standing to assert paternal rights. In response, Michael argued that the presumption was unconstitutional because it deprived him of his interest in maintaining a relationship with his daughter. Drawing on the unwed father cases, Michael argued that since he satisfied both prongs of the *Lehr* test — biological fatherhood plus a developed relationship — he was entitled to recognition as Victoria's father. Having grasped the opportunity afforded him by his biological connection to Victoria, he maintained that California could not bar his assertion of paternal rights based on the marital presumption.

Although there was little doubt that Michael met the biology-plus standard, the Court chose to focus its attention elsewhere. Zooming in on the adulterous relationship between Michael and Carol, the Court determined that the bond between Michael and Victoria was not deserving of recognition because it did not take root within the sanctity of a "unitary family." The Court thus concluded that when faced with a choice between an "adulterous natural father" and a marital father who parents within "the integrity of the traditional family unit," the Constitution does not compel recognition of the "irregular" relationship over one that conforms to traditional standards.[16]

In a biting dissent, it was argued that the unwed father cases had nothing to do with protecting "unitary families" and everything to do with protecting unwed fathers who, like Michael, had developed a relationship with their children. From the dissenter's perspective, the relevant inquiry should have been whether the "relationship under consideration is sufficiently substantial to qualify as a liberty interest under our prior cases," without reference to the constellation of household arrangements.[17] In short, according to the dissent, the goal of protecting the marital unit does not justify overriding the interests of a biological father who seeks to maintain a relationship with his child.

According to the *Michael H.* decision, the federal constitution does not require states to provide unwed fathers with the opportunity to challenge the marital presumption; however, they are not prohibited from doing so. Accordingly, a number of states permit unwed fathers to challenge the presumption and assert their own claim to fatherhood, although many of these states impose a threshold requirement that a father must meet before he can proceed. Typically, he may be required to show that rebuttal of the presumption would be in the child's best interest and/or that he has a substantial relationship with the child. A few states do not impose these limitations and permit a challenge in almost all situations; here, the interests of unwed fathers may be given heightened protection under the state constitution.

> ### *Consideration*
>
> Do you think unwed fathers should be afforded legal protections based on biology alone, or should more be required?

## ESTABLISHING PATERNITY

When parents are unmarried, paternity must be established in order for a man to be recognized as the legal father of a child. The two primary approaches to establishing paternity are **adjudication** and **acknowledgment**. In some instances, as we have seen, it may also be established by presumption, such as when a child is born to a married woman.

In 1973, when Congress entered the child support arena, it also sought to upgrade state procedures for paternity establishment so that more support awards could be established for the benefit of children of unmarried parents. Accordingly, the aptly named Child Support Enforcement and Establishment of Paternity Act (see Chapter 6) directed states to conform their paternity laws to the new federal requirements or risk loss of federal funding. These federal requirements (which have since been strengthened by subsequent federal laws) apply to both the adjudication and the acknowledgment of paternity.

## The Adjudication of Paternity

The modern-day paternity action evolved from the colonial era bastardy proceeding, which was criminal in nature and intended to punish the "fornicator." The goal of punishing sexual misconduct has dropped by the historical wayside, and today, paternity actions (see Exhibit 11.1) are brought to identify a man as the legal father of a child based on his biological connection.

Most paternity actions are initiated by mothers or an IV-D agency (recall from Chapter 6 that in order to receive TANF benefits, a mother must assign her child support rights to the state and cooperate in establishing paternity, unless she can show good cause for noncooperation) so that the child can receive support as well as other potential benefits that flow from an established parent-child relationship. Although far less common, men may also initiate paternity proceedings in order to secure custody and visitation rights. Here, in a historical shift, the father seeks to affirm rather than to deny his paternity. However, as discussed above, if the mother is married to someone else, the presumption of paternity may bar the action, or a man may first have to satisfy a threshold requirement, such as that he has a substantial relationship with the child.

When paternity is contested, states must, under federal law, have procedures in place that require the parties and the child submit to **genetic testing** if requested by either party. If the case is being handled by the IV-D agency, the agency must pay for the testing; however, it is entitled to recoup the funds from the father if paternity is established. Unlike in years past, when testing required the drawing of blood and was unreliable, DNA-based identity testing today can be done through a cheek swab and can prove or disprove paternity with virtual certainty. Unless an objection is made, the tests must be admissible without foundation testimony or proof of authenticity.

Under federal law, states must have rules in place that create a rebuttable presumption of paternity if the tests indicate that the man is the father of the child within a threshold degree of probability. Once the presumption is triggered, the burden shifts to the man in question to prove nonpaternity by, for example, establishing "nonaccess" or that he is sterile. States also have the option of making the presumption conclusive, in which case it would operate like a court judgment and could be challenged only under very limited circumstances.

## Exhibit 11.1 *Complaint for Paternity*

F. C. A. §§ 522, 523                                    Form 5-1
S.S.L. § 111-g                                              (Paternity)
                                                                  12/97

FAMILY COURT OF THE STATE OF NEW YORK
COUNTY OF
........................................................................................
In the Matter of a Paternity Proceeding            Docket No.

                                        Petitioner,     PATERNITY
S.S.#                                                        PETITION
                  -against-                                (Parent)
                                        Respondent
S.S.#

........................................................................................

TO THE FAMILY COURT:

The undersigned petitioner respectfully shows that:

1.  a. Petitioner resides at

    b. Respondent resides at

2.  Petitioner had sexual intercourse with the above-named Respondent during a period of time beginning on or about the        day of        ,
19      , ending on or about the        day of        , 19      , and as a result thereof (Petitioner) (Respondent) became pregnant.

[Alternative allegations; delete inapplicable provisions]:

3.  (a) (Petitioner) (Respondent) gave birth to a (male) (female) child out of wedlock on the day of.

    (b) (Petitioner) (Respondent) is now pregnant with a child who is likely to be born out of wedlock.

4.  (Petitioner) (Respondent) is the father of the child.

5.  At the time of conception of the child, the mother (was not married).

**Exhibit 11.1    Continued**

(was married to [name]                                    , whose last known address
is                                                                                   ).

6.   (Petitioner) (Respondent) (has acknowledged) (acknowledges) paternity
of the child (in writing) (and) (by furnishing support).

7.   The name, date of birth and social security number of the child involved is:

Name                              Date of birth                        Social Security #


8.   No previous application has been made to any court or judge for the relief
herein requested (except

).

9.   Petitioner: [alternative allegations, delete inapplicable clauses]

(a. has made application for child support services with the local Department of Social Services).

(b. hereby makes application for child support enforcement services by
the filing of this petition).

(c. does not wish to make application for child support services).

(d. is the non-custodial parent of the subject child).

10.   The subject child (is) (is not) a Native American child subject to the
Indian Child Welfare Act of 1978 (25 U.S.C. §§ 1901-1963).

11.   Pursuant to F.C.A. § 545, upon the entry of an Order of Filiation, the
Court shall, upon application of either party, enter an order of support for the
subject child.

WHEREFORE, Petitioner requests that this Court issue a summons or
warrant requiring the Respondent to show cause why the Court should not
enter a declaration of paternity, an order of support and such other and further
relief as may be appropriate under the circumstances.

_____
Petitioner

_____
Print or type name

**Exhibit 11.1 Continued**

---

_____

Signature of Attorney, if any

_____

Attorney's Name (Print or Type)

_____

_____

Attorney's Address and Telephone Number

Dated:            , 19      .

VERIFICATION

STATE OF NEW YORK      )
                                  :ss.:
COUNTY OF                  )

being duly sworn, says that (s)he is the Petitioner in the above-entitled proceeding and that the foregoing petition is true to (his) (her) own knowledge, except as to matters herein stated to be alleged on information and belief and as to those matters (s)he believes it to be true.

_____

Petitioner

Sworn to before me this
        day of              , 19      .

_____

(Deputy) Clerk of the Court
    Notary Public

## Voluntary Acknowledgment of Paternity

Paternity can also be established voluntarily. This approach has gained favor, and under federal law all states must have a simple procedure in place that enable parents to acknowledge paternity by completing a notarized paternity affidavit (Exhibit 11.2). States must offer paternity

## Exhibit 11.2   *Voluntary Acknowledgment of Paternity*

| STATE OF NORTH CAROLINA | | | | **File No.** | |
|---|---|---|---|---|---|
| _____ County | | | | In the General Court of Justice<br>District Court Division | |
| Name Of Plaintiff | | | | **AFFIRMATION** | |
| | | | | **ACKNOWLEDGMENT** | |
| | | V E R S U S | | **AND** | |
| Name Of Defendant | | | | **ORDER OF PATERNITY** | |
| | | | | G.S. 110-132 | |
| Name And Address Of Natural Father | | | | Name And Address of Natural Mother (Name As Shown On Birth Certificate) | |
| Date of Birth | Race | Social Security No. | | Social Security No. | |

| Name Of Child(ren) | Date<br>I.  Of<br>Bi<br>rt<br>h | Birthplace<br>(County and State) | Social<br>Security No. | Address |
|---|---|---|---|---|
| | | | | |
| | | | | |
| | | | | |
| | | | | |
| | | | | |
| | | | | |

### MOTHER'S AFFIRMATION

I, the undersigned. being duly sworn. declare and affirm that (1) I am the natural mother of the above-named child(ren), (2) the above-named father is the natural father of the above-named child(ren), and (3) the above information regarding myself, the father, and the minor child(ren) is true and correct to the best of my knowledge, information, and belief. I also declare and affirm that I [ ] was unmarried at the time I became pregnant [ ] was married to someone other than the above-named father at the time I became pregnant with the above-named child(ren) or when the above-named child(ren) was born.

**N O T E:** *If you were married to someone other than the defendant at the time you became pregnant or when the child(ren) was born, you must provide additional evidence (eg., affidavit from your husband or a court order) that your husband is not the child(ren)'s father.*

| **SWORN AND SUBSCRIBED TO BEFORE ME** | CAUTION: *Providing false or inaccurate information may result in sanctions against you.* |
|---|---|
| Date | |
| Signature | Date |
| Title Of Person To Administer Oaths | Signature Of Natural Mother |
| Date Commission Expires<br><br>**S E A L** | Name Of Natural Mother (As Shown On Birth Certificate) |

AOC-CV-604 (Combines CV-604/605/606))   Figure 3<br>Rev. 5/93   (Over)

## Exhibit 11.2 Continued

---

**FATHER'S ACKNOWLEDGMENT**

CAUTION: *You have the right to consult a lawyer at your expense before signing this paper. If signed, this paper may impose substantial legal obligations upon you, and you should be sure to fully understand those obligations before signing.*

I, the undersigned, being duly sworn, freely and voluntarily declare and acknowledge that I am the natural father of the child(ren) named herein, and that the information regarding myself, the natural mother, and the minor child(ren) is true and correct to the best of my knowledge, information and belief.

I understand that this sworn, written Acknowledgment of Paternity which I am signing shall have the same force and effect as a judgment of the district court establishing my paternity of the child(ren) named herein when accompanied by the sworn, written Affirmation of Paternity signed by the child(ren)'s natural mother and when filed with the Clerk of Superior Court and approved by the district court judge. I also understand that the determination of my paternity of the child(ren) named herein shall be binding on me and shall not be reconsidered by the court in any subsequent legal proceedings regarding my obligation to support my child(ren) named herein.

| SWORN AND SUBSCRIBED TO BEFORE ME | Date |
|---|---|
| Date    II.   *Signature* | *Signature of Natural Father* |
| *Title Of Person Authorized to Administer Oaths* | *Name Of Natural Father (Type Or Print)* |
| *Date Commission Expires* | |
| **S E A L** | |

**O R D E R**

The court finds that the sworn, written Acknowledgment of Paternity executed by the natural father of the child(ren) named herein, and the sworn, written Affirmation of Paternity executed by the natural mother of the child(ren) have been executed in accordance with G.S. 110-132(a) and hereby approves the Affirmation and Acknowledgment of Paternity pursuant to G.S. 110-132(a). This Affirmation/Acknowledgment and Order of Paternity shall have the same force and effect as a judgment of the court establishing the named father's paternity of the child(ren) named herein and shall be res judicata as to the issue of paternity and shall not be reconsidered by the court.

| *Date Entered* | *Signature of District Court Judge* |
|---|---|
| | *Name of District Court Judge (Type Or Print)* |

NOTE: *Upon entry of this Order Of Paternity, the Clerk must provide certain information to the State Registrar of Vital Statistics pursuant to G.S. 130A-119. The State Registrar requires that said information be reported on form AOC-CV-611/DEHNR 1054 (Vital Records).*

AOC-CV-604 (Combines CV-604/605/606), Side Two
Rev. 5/93

establishment services at hospitals and at the state agency responsible for maintaining birth records. States may also offer paternity establishment services at other locations where children and parents receive services or care, such as at pediatricians' offices and Head Start programs.

Before signing the paternity acknowledgment form, a parent must be provided with information regarding the legal consequences of establishing paternity. Some states have developed separate materials for mothers and fathers in recognition of the different concerns that each may have regarding, for example, child support obligations and custody and visitation rights. Although most state materials emphasize the benefits of acknowledging paternity, some address the concerns that victims of violence may have and may recommend against signing if the mother fears for her own safety or the safety of the child.[18] Typically, the parties are told about the availability of genetic testing; such notification is not required, however, thus creating the possibility that the acknowledged father, either knowingly or unknowingly, may not necessarily be the biological father. (See Paternity Disestablishment below.)

The parties have a sixty-day period within which to rescind the acknowledgment and thereby disestablish paternity. After this window of opportunity, if paternity is not rescinded, the acknowledgement operates as a legal finding of paternity and is entitled to full faith and credit in other states. After the sixty-day period has elapsed, the acknowledgment can be challenged only in a court proceeding on the limited grounds of fraud, duress, or mistake of fact.

## Following the Determination of Paternity

Once paternity is established, the formerly putative father is now the legal father of the child with the rights and responsibilities that this status entails. He can be required to pay child support and can seek court-ordered custody and visitation rights.

If paternity is established in court, a child support order can usually be established at the same time. The fact that the parties are not married should not impact the support amount. As far as custody and visitation are concerned, if the court is one of limited jurisdiction without broad authority over family matters, the father may need to bring a separate action in family court. Moreover, unlike with child support, some states use different substantive standards where parents of unmarried children, as distinct from divorcing parents, are involved. Although the focus remains the best interest of the child, some states employ a rebuttable presumption that it is in the child's best interest to remain with the parent who has been the child's primary caretaker or with whom the child has lived continuously for a certain period of time. This standard often favors the mother, who, especially where parents are unmarried, is likely to be the primary care parent.

## PATERNITY DISESTABLISHMENT ————————————————

One of the hottest issues in family law today is whether a father should be permitted to "disestablish" his paternity — that is, to undo a determination that he is the child's biological father. In large part, the ready availability of reliable genetic testing has prompted this push for biological certainty, even if the quest threatens to disrupt a well-established father-child relationship.

Like joint custody, **paternity disestablishment** is closely identified with the fathers' rights movement, which as noted in Chapter 5, emerged in the 1970s to address a perceived anti-male bias in the family courts. In this context, the ability to disavow fatherhood is seen as necessary to vindicate the rights of men who have been "duped" by women, often with the aid of the legal system. Proponents of "paternity fraud reform" often compare the situation of fathers who learn that they are not a child's biological parent to a criminal who has been wrongly convicted, and argue that "just as DNA evidence has revolutionized criminal laws, it should . . . lead to a revolution in family law . . . in the sense that evidence admissible to 'convict' should also be available to 'exonerate.'"[19] However, "exoneration" in the family law domain does not simply undo a mistake; it also serves to dismantle an established parent-child relationship with potentially devastating emotional or financial consequences for an innocent child. Another potentially troubling distinction is that rather than simply seeking to right a grievous wrong, men seeking to disestablish paternity may well be motivated by "anger and a desire to strike back at ex-wives and girlfriends."[20]

Paternity disestablishment cases once again present us with important questions regarding the weight and meaning of fatherhood. Is it a genetic link that makes a man a father? Is it grasping the opportunity presented by a genetic link to develop a relationship with a child, or can fatherhood be achieved in the absence of a biological link by assuming the role of a father in a child's life? How should the competing interests of a father who wishes to disavow his misidentified status be balanced with the needs of the child? As noted in a leading monograph on the subject, other critical questions include the following:

> At what point should the truth about genetic parentage outweigh the consequences of leaving a child fatherless? Is a child better off knowing his/her

genetic heritage or maintaining a relationship with his/her father and his family that provides both emotional and financial support? Should it matter who brings the action or should the rules be the same for men trying to disestablish paternity, women seeking to oust a father from the child's life, and third parties trying to assert their paternity of a child who already has a legal father?[21]

Broadly speaking, paternity disestablishment cases fall into one of two categories. First, following the establishment of paternity through either a voluntary acknowledgment or a court action, an unmarried father begins to doubt whether he is the biological father and thus seeks to disestablish his paternity. Depending on the state, it may also be possible for the action to be initiated by a mother who seeks to limit or end the involvement of this man in her child's life or by another man who believes that he is the child's biological father. The second category of cases involves an attempt to disestablish the paternity of a man who is the presumed father of a child based on his marriage to the child's mother. The presumed father may seek to disestablish paternity based on doubts about his biological relationship to the child; a man who believes he might be a child's biological father might wish to challenge the paternity of the husband; and the mother herself, often in connection with a pending divorce action, may seek the disestablishment in order to end her husband's formal relationship with the child.[22]

If disestablishment is allowed, a question arises as to what impact this has on the child support obligation. As a general matter, disestablishment ends the father's obligation to pay present and future child support. However, courts have been less willing to forgive support arrearages for a number of reasons, including the hardship that this would impose on children, and that forgiveness would reward the father who had been remiss in making support payments. Likewise, most courts do not permit a father to recoup payments made prior to the disestablishment of paternity, although this is not an absolute rule, and some statutes permit recoupment under carefully delineated circumstances.[23]

States have begun addressing the issue of when to allow paternity disestablishment through both statutory enactments and judicial decisions. For example, some states have passed laws allowing men who have been adjudicated fathers to reopen the court decision to disprove their paternity through the introduction of genetic evidence. In other states, either the mother or the father can seek judicial relief where paternity has been adjudicated or acknowledged. Courts have expressed a dizzying array of opinions on the matter. In part, this reflects differences in underlying fact patterns; however, it also reflects deeply divided views on how the competing interests should be accommodated. We turn now to two paternity disestablishment decisions that weigh the best interest of the child in the decisional calculus very differently.

## Considering Best Interest: Conflicting Approaches

In the case of Paternity of Cheryl,[24] the Massachusetts Supreme Judicial Court (SJC) refused to permit an unmarried father to disestablish paternity. Briefly, the facts are as follows. Cheryl was born in 1993. Shortly thereafter, the parents, who were not married, signed a voluntary acknowledgment, which was entered as a court judgment. The father participated in Cheryl's life as a father, and she referred to him as "daddy." When Cheryl was six, the state's IV-D agency sought an increase in child support. Five days later, the father raised doubts about his paternity, and genetic tests revealed that he was not the girl's biological father. In rejecting his request to vacate the paternity judgment, the SJC focused on the impact this would have on Cheryl:

> Where a father challenges a paternity judgment, courts have pointed to the special needs of children that must be protected, noting that consideration of what is in a child's best interest will often weigh more heavily than the genetic link between parent and child. . . . [C]hildren benefit psychologically, socially, educationally and in other ways from stable and predictable parental relationships. . . . [W]here a father and child have a substantial parent-child relationship, an attempt to undo a determination of paternity is "potentially devastating to a child who has considered the man to be the father."[25]

In contrast to this child-centered focus, the Court of Appeals of Maryland in Langston v. Riffe[26] concluded that the best interest of the child has no place in a paternity disestablishment action. In this consolidated action, three men were seeking to set aside a paternity judgment based on new evidence indicating in each case that another man might be the child's biological father. At issue was whether, in seeking reconsideration of a paternity judgment, the fathers had an automatic statutory right to blood or genetic testing as they would at the time of paternity establishment or, as argued by the state on behalf of the mothers, whether in this context, the court must first consider the best interest of the children. In reviewing the legislative history, the court concluded that the "'best interests of the child' standard generally has no place in a proceeding to reconsider a paternity declaration. . . . To not allow testing now would violate . . . the Legislature's intent . . . to provide relief to putative fathers seeking review of potentially false paternity declarations entered against them."[27]

## What Makes a Man a Father?

Underlying these decisions is the familiar struggle to arrive at an understanding of what makes a man a father. The two cases embody different understandings of the role that biology plays in determining fatherhood. By focusing on the developed relationship between Cheryl and her father, the SJC downgraded the importance of the biological link between a father and child in favor of relational considerations. However, it is possible that the court would have paid less attention to this connection if Cheryl's biological father had been standing in the wings, ready, willing, and able to assume a role in her life. In contrast, the Maryland court, in focusing on the vindication of the father's interest without regard to the impact of disestablishment on the children of these men, elevated the biological dimension of fatherhood over relational considerations.

## WHAT IF THE GENETIC "FATHER" IS A SPERM DONOR?

Before concluding this chapter, we will take a brief look at how questions of paternity, or perhaps better parentage, are resolved in situations where conception has been accomplished through **donor insemination**.

## Sperm Donation and the Married Heterosexual Couple

Where a married woman and her husband are unable to conceive due to his infertility (or possibly the risk of passing down a genetic disease), one possibility is for her to be inseminated with the sperm of another man. Here, although she is married, the child is actually the biological offspring of two persons who are not married to each other. Under these circumstances, who is entitled to legal recognition as the father?

The previously discussed presumption of paternity, which operates to identify a woman's husband as the legal father of all children born during the marriage, provides a partial answer. This presumption, however, is not absolute, and it can be rebutted by proof of infertility. To address this situation, most states have enacted sperm donor laws that operate to make a husband who consents to the insemination of his wife the legal father of the resulting child with all the attendant parental rights and responsibilities.[28] In effect, his consent to the insemination serves as a substitute for sexual intercourse. Most of these statutes also cut off any potential rights of the sperm donor.

Even in the absence of a statute, a court is likely to hold that a consenting husband is the legal father. For instance, in the case of People v. Sorenson,[29] one of the earliest and still influential decisions on this issue, a husband who had consented to the insemination of his wife and had held himself out as the child's father argued upon divorce that he should not have to pay child support because the sperm donor, not he, was the child's legal father. In rejecting this position, the court stated:

> [W]here a reasonable man who because of his inability to procreate, actively participates and consents to his wife's artificial insemination in the hope that a child will be produced whom they will treat as their own, knows that such behavior carries with it the legal responsibilities of fatherhood. . . . One who consents to the production of a child cannot create a temporary relation to be assumed and disclaimed at will . . . [I]t is safe to assume that without defendant's active participation and consent, the child would not have been procreated.[30]

Accordingly, the father's consent bound him to the child, and he was not permitted to disavow the relationship.

## Sperm Donation and the Lesbian Couple

As discussed in Chapter 5, many lesbian couples use donor insemination to become parents. In most jurisdictions, the nonbiological co-parent does not have a legally enforceable right to maintain a continuing relationship with the child if the adult relationship should end. In contrast, a small but growing number of jurisdictions have embraced the concept of "de facto parenthood," which gives a co-parent the right to maintain an ongoing relationship with the child she has helped to raise based on a best interest standard.[31]

Adding another layer of complexity to this discussion, we now consider two issues that bear on the determination of parenting ties in the context of a committed lesbian relationship where one woman bears a child conceived through donor insemination. The first issue is whether she or her partner can avail herself of any of the rules that are used to identify a man as the legal parent of a child in the absence of a biological link to secure her formal status as a parent.[32] The other issue concerns the potential legal status of the sperm donor.

As we have seen, based on the presumption of paternity and sperm donor rules, the husband of a woman who has a child during the marriage will be recognized as the legal father based on the marriage itself and his consent to the insemination. By logical extension, the question that arises is whether a same-sex partner in a committed relationship can use these legal rules to secure her status as the other parent of the child born to her partner.

Although most states are not likely to take this step because it indicates an acceptance of the integrity of same-sex relationships, in those states that either allow same-sex marriage (presently only Massachusetts) or require that the benefits and obligations of marriage be equally extended to same-sex couples through civil union or domestic partnership laws (see Chapter 1), this approach is likely to be extended to lesbian co-parents. (However, see the discussion below regarding known donors.) In 2005, for example, a New Jersey trial court concluded that the state's sperm donor law, which treats a husband who consents to his wife's insemination as the child's legal father, should be applied equally to a committed same-sex couple, thus allowing the names of both women to be placed on the birth certificate.[33]

The other consideration is the potential status of the sperm donor. If a couple uses an unknown donor, the chances of future legal conflicts over the assertion of parental rights are minimal as most facilities promise the parties anonymity and maintain their records in such a way as to make the subsequent matching of sperm donor and birth mother virtually impossible. There is, however, a growing push for greater openness, and many programs now provide sperm donors with an identity-release option that allows children conceived with their sperm to obtain certain information about their biological fathers when they reach adulthood. This small step, though, is far from establishing the donors as legal parents.[34]

However, sometimes a couple (or an individual) prefers to use a known donor. This choice gives them more control over the process and greater knowledge of the child's origins and allows for the possibility that the donor can play a continuing role in the child's life. A potential downside of using a known donor is that the parties may not be able to control the legal outcome should a dispute arise.

Where a known donor is used, the parties may agree for him to play an ongoing role in the child's life, or they may enter into an agreement in which the donor relinquishes parental rights and the woman agrees not to seek child support or any other potential benefits for the child. What then happens if the donor later regrets his decision and wishes to assume a parental role in the child's life? Based on the view that they have an independent obligation to assess what is in a child's best interest, judges are generally reluctant to enforce these agreements, which make advance determinations about how to structure parenting, custodial, and visitation rights. Further, in actually determining the child's best interest, judges are prone to conclude that, despite his prior disavowal of paternity, the donor should be recognized as the legal father and entitled to some relationship with the child. The law in this area is in tremendous flux, however, and the growing willingness of courts to recognize the rights of co-parents may compel a reassessment of this traditional best interest outcome because it might mean that a child would have three legal parents—a result most courts would probably seek to avoid.

## Chapter Summary

Once considered children of no one, the legal status of children of unmarried parents has improved greatly since the colonial era. Today, laws that differentiate children based on the marital status of their parents are unconstitutional if the underlying purpose is deterrence of nonmarital sexual relations or the promotion of an idealized family type. However, laws that differentiate for the narrow purpose of preventing fraud are generally allowed.

The rights of unwed fathers have also been expanded. Although biology alone does not give a man a protected interest in maintaining a relationship with his child, his rights cannot be unilaterally terminated where he has sought to develop a relationship with his child. However, where the mother is married to another man, the presumption of paternity may preclude the unwed father from seeking paternal rights.

Paternity cannot simply be assumed. It must be established either through a court proceeding (i.e., adjudication) or a voluntary acknowledgment of paternity. To improve paternity establishment procedures, states must now comply with federal requirements or risk the loss of federal funds. A court must order genetic testing if requested by one party, and states must have rules that create a rebuttable presumption of paternity if the tests establish that the man is the father of the child within a threshold degree of probability. States must also have simplified procedures in place, such as the availability of paternity affidavits, for the voluntary acknowledgment of paternity.

A highly contested issue is whether a man should be allowed to disestablish paternity based on scientific evidence that he is not the biological father. States are divided on how to approach this issue. Some focus on the effect that disestablishment will have on the child and take best interest into account in determining whether a father can disavow his legal relationship with the child. Other states take the position that best interest is irrelevant, and the focus should be solely on the rights and status of the man who is contesting his paternal status.

Where conception is accomplished through sperm donation, the presumption of paternity and sperm donor laws operate to make the husband of a married woman who consents to the insemination the legal father of the child despite the lack of a biological connection, and the rights of the sperm donor are terminated. These same rules are likely to be extended to a lesbian co-parent in states that provide equal rights to committed same-sex couples. However, this outcome may be less clear where a known donor is used.

## Key Terms

Legitimate

Illegitimate

Presumption of Paternity

Legitimation

Equal Protection Clause

Adjudication of Paternity

Acknowledgment of Paternity

Genetic Testing

Paternity Disestablishment

Donor Insemination

## Review Questions

1. What was the common law status of children of unmarried parents? Why were these children treated so harshly?

2. What is the presumption of paternity?

3. Describe the early U.S. reform efforts.

4. What underlying statutory purposes will invalidate a law that treats children of married parents and children of unmarried parents differently? What purpose will sustain differential treatment?

5. In the case of Stanley v. Illinois, how was the father treated differently from unwed mothers or married fathers? How did the Court respond to Stanley's challenge?

6. Based on the case of Lehr v. Robinson, when must an unwed father be given a voice in the adoption process?

7. Why did the dissent in *Lehr* disagree with the majority position? What did they think should be controlling?

8. On what basis did the *Nguyen* Court justify the differential treatment of mothers and fathers in the immigration context?

9. Why was the biological father barred from pursuing his paternity claim in the case of Michael H. v. Gerald D.?

10. Explain current state approaches with respect to allowing a father to pursue a paternity claim where the mother is married to another man.

11. What is the significance of establishing paternity?

12. What are the two ways that paternity can be established?

13. What federal requirements are imposed on states in contested paternity actions?

14. What is a voluntary acknowledgment of paternity? What legal effect does an acknowledgment have?

15. What information must a state provide to persons who are thinking about acknowledging paternity?

16. What are the legal consequences of establishing paternity?

17. What does it mean to disestablish paternity? In what situations do these cases arise? What are the two basic approaches that courts use in these cases?

18. Where a married woman becomes pregnant through donor insemination with the consent of her husband, who is the legal father? Why?

19. Focusing on states that either allow same-sex marriage or extend marital rights to same-sex couples, what would the likely outcome be where a woman seeks to be recognized as the legal parent of a child born to her partner?

20. Discuss the benefits and risks of using a known sperm donor.

## Discussion Questions

1. Thinking back to the case of Michael H. v. Gerald D., do you think the biological father should have been permitted to establish his paternal rights, or do you think the Court was right to bar his claim? What competing rights and interests are at stake here?

2.  Assume that a man and woman who know each other casually have sexual intercourse one time. As a result, she becomes pregnant and decides to have the baby. Based on this fleeting moment of intimacy, is it fair that the father be responsible for 18 years of child support? What if he offers to pay for an abortion? What if he already has a family? What if the woman lied and said she was using birth control when she was not?

3.  If a woman who is not married becomes pregnant, do you think she and the father should have equal rights with respect to the child? Is your thinking influenced by the circumstances? For example, does it matter if they were in a long-term serious relationship or if the pregnancy resulted from a casual fling? Should the law take circumstances such as these into consideration?

4.  Assume that upon separation from his wife or partner, a man who has believed himself to be the father of the child he has been raising suddenly has doubts and wishes to have genetic testing done to determine if he is in fact the biological father. Do you think he should be allowed to do this and, if the tests show he is not the father, to disestablish paternity? What considerations do you think are important here?

5.  Assume that a lesbian couple has chosen to use a known donor, and they enter into an agreement in which the donor agrees not to seek any parental rights or to see the child, and the women agree not to hold him responsible for child support. If he later changes his mind and wants to establish his paternity and see the child, should he be allowed to do so, or should he be held to his agreement?

## Assignments

1.  For your state, locate the applicable paternity statute (and custody statute, if separate) and determine the following:

    a.  What court are the proceedings held in?
    b.  With respect to the use of genetic tests, at what percentage of probability of paternity is a man presumed to be the father?
    c.  Does your state employ a rebuttable or a conclusive presumption of paternity?
    d.  What is the legal standard for determining custody? Are there any difference in the treatment of married and unmarried parents?

2. Go to the appropriate court or other local agency and obtain the form your state uses for voluntary paternity acknowledgments. If explanatory information is not contained on the form, make sure that you obtain any supplementary documents.

Now, assume that your office has a client who is contemplating executing the acknowledgment. You have been asked to send him the relevant documents with a cover letter explaining the process and its significance. In writing the letter, assume the client is young and has no familiarity with legal concepts.

3. Assume your office is representing an unmarried woman who is planning to be inseminated with the sperm of a known donor. You have been asked to draft an agreement between the parties to memorialize their intent. They have agreed on the following:

- The donor waives all potential parental rights.
- The donee agrees not to pursue any child support or other claims.
- The donor may see the child as a friend of the family but agrees not to disclose his true relationship to the child or to anyone else.
- The child is to have no established relationship with the donor's extended family.

After drafting the agreement, draft a cover letter to the client explaining the legal significance of the agreement.

## Cases for Analysis

In the following case, the court relies on the marital presumption and the "equitable" parent doctrine to vest legal fatherhood in the husband, although genetic tests established that another man was the biological father.

### A. J. v. I. J.
**259 Wis.2d 120, 655 N.W.2d 195 (Wis. Ct. App. 2002)**

This divorce case presents an unusual factual scenario. Randy A. J. is willing to continue supporting and providing care for a child that is not biologically his own. He seeks to maintain the parent-child relationship he established with a child born during his marriage to the natural mother, Norma I. J., despite the fact that genetic tests have established to a 99.99% degree of certainty that Brendan B. is the child's father. Norma and Brendan argue that because the genetic tests showed that Brendan is the biological father of the child, the trial court had no authority to determine that establishing Randy as the legal father and awarding him custody were in the best interests of the child. . . .

In 1997, during her marriage to Randy, Norma began a relationship with Brendan . . . , while she was still married to Randy, Norma gave birth to a child. In May 1999, Norma was sentenced to eight years in prison. For the fifteen months prior to Norma's incarceration, Norma and the child would visit Brendan on a weekly basis. Since Norma's incarceration, the child has resided with Randy . . .

. . . Randy filed a petition for divorce and obtained a temporary order prohibiting Brendan from having any contact with the child . . . In December, Norma filed a counterclaim in the divorce action alleging that Brendan was the biological father of the child.

. . . Brendan filed a motion to intervene in the divorce action. Brendan sought to be adjudicated the natural father and requested legal custody and primary physical placement of the child.

In an action to establish the paternity of a child who was born to a woman while she was married, where a man other than the woman's husband alleges that he, not the husband, is the child's father, a party may allege that a judicial determination that a man other than the husband is the father is not in the best interest of the child. . . .

The statute is specific. It is clearly intended to grant the court the authority to prevent the parties from taking genetic tests where a child would be harmed by a determination that someone other than the husband is his or her father. If the court determines that it is not in the marital child's best interests to have a judicial determination of paternity, genetic tests may not be performed under court order and the court is authorized to dismiss the paternity action. But once the parties have submitted to genetic tests . . . the trial court cannot dismiss the action on these grounds.

We therefore hold that . . . the trial court erred when it concluded that it had the authority to dismiss Brendan's motion to intervene based upon a best interests of the child determination . . .

The trial court next concluded that despite the fact that the genetic tests had established Brendan's parentage to a 99.99% degree of certainty, Brendan had not rebutted the marital presumption contained in Wis. Stat. § 891.41(1)[, which] provides that a man is presumed to be the natural father of a child if he and the child's natural mother have been married to each other and the child is born during the marriage. . . .

Norma gave birth to the child while married to Randy and thus by statute Randy was the child's presumptive father. However, once the genetic tests demonstrated that Brendan was the father to a 99.99% degree of certainty, Brendan had rebutted this marital presumption according to the plain language of the statute and is rebuttably presumed to be the child's father according to Wis. Stat. §767.48(lm). We, therefore, conclude the trial court erred when it determined that Brendan had not rebutted the presumption of paternity set forth in Wis. Stat. §891.41(1) with the genetic tests establishing his parentage to the requisite degree of certainty.

While the trial court may have used the incorrect vehicle in the law, the court clearly felt compelled by the evidence to declare that Randy, not Brendan, should be the child's father . . .

[I]t is evident from the law that even if a test shows a man to be the natural father, his legal fatherhood is only presumed. Next, we must consider "how" such a presumption may be overcome. In our view, the presumption may be overcome by evidence that the marital father has so bonded with the child as to be considered the "equitable parent." Therefore, we see the real issue in this case to be whether the evidence supports affirmance on grounds that Randy is the equitable parent, thus overcoming Brendan's rebuttable presumption that he, as the natural parent, is the legal parent. We begin our analysis with a discussion of what the "equitable parent" doctrine is and where it came from . . .

The equitable parent doctrine extends the rights and responsibilities of a natural parent to a nonbiological parent seeking custody or visitation. Once a court determines that a party is an equitable parent, there is no distinction between the equitable parent and any other parent. . . .

During the pregnancy and up until Norma's incarceration, Randy, Norma and the child lived together. After Norma's incarceration, Randy became the sole custodian of the minor child and has continued to assume responsibility for her. The child considers Randy to be her only father and, up until the divorce proceedings, Randy believed her to be his biological daughter . . . The trial court found that "he has been her only parent from the standpoint of regular and daily contact and custodial care since May of 1999."

. . . Prior to the divorce proceeding, and with Norma's cooperation, Randy believed he held the status of a natural parent and assumed the rights and responsibilities of fatherhood. Norma and Brendan never took any steps to change Randy's belief despite the fact that they had suspected Brendan was the father of the child.

. . . The trial court also found that Brendan had the opportunity and ability to assume parental responsibility for the child and chose not to do so. The court determined that while Brendan saw the child on a weekly basis prior to Norma's incarceration, the relationship established between the two was not that of father and daughter . . .

Prior to the divorce proceedings, Randy believed he was the child's natural parent. Indeed, he is the only father the child has ever known. Randy has established that he is willing to continue assuming responsibility for support obligations and further desires the rights accorded to parenthood. Brendan and Norma chose not to take any action regarding Brendan's paternity until long after they suspected he was the father of the child, and as a result, Randy formed a bond with the child and Brendan has no relationship with the child. We therefore conclude that Randy is the child's equitable father.

The question remaining is whether Norma still may assert the child's parentage . . . As the trial court noted, and as we have just stated, Norma chose not to take any action regarding Brendan's paternity until well after she and Brendan suspected that Randy was not the father of the child. Norma's actions allowed Randy and the child to form a close bond. We affirm the trial court's determination that it was in the child's best interests that the court estop Norma from asserting the child's parentage. We hold that Randy is the legal father and affirm the trial court in that regard. We also hold that Randy is entitled to custody and affirm the trial court's determination on that issue.

## QUESTIONS

1. Why did this court hold that the trial court should not have dismissed the best interest hearing?

2. Why did this court conclude that the trial court was in error when it concluded that Brendan had rebutted the marital presumption?

3. What vehicle did the court use to establish Randy as the child's legal father?

4. What evidence did it rely on in making this determination?

―――――――――

The following case raises an important issue — whether a man who has voluntarily acknowledged paternity and participated in a child's life as her father can thereafter seek to revoke the acknowledgment based on tests showing that he in fact is not the biological father.

### PATERNITY OF CHERYL
**434 Mass. 23, 746 N.E.2d 488 (2001)**

We consider in this case whether a father may move to set aside a judgment of paternity when, more than five years after he voluntarily acknowledged paternity, genetic tests established that he was not the child's biological father. . . .

. . . The mother gave birth to the child (Cheryl) on August 29, 1993. In November, 1993, the [Department of Revenue (department)] filed a complaint in the Probate and Family Court against the father on behalf of the mother and the Department of Public Welfare (now the Department of Transitional Assistance), seeking to establish his paternity. . . .

On December 16, 1993, the mother and the father executed an acknowledgment of parentage in which the father acknowledged that he was the father of Cheryl, that he understood his acknowledgment would have the effect of a judgment against him, and that the acknowledgment would obligate him to support Cheryl. . . . The mother, in turn, acknowledged and affirmed that he was the father of Cheryl. That same day, a judge in the Probate and Family Court entered a judgment of paternity. The father, who was not represented by counsel at the time, did not submit to genetic marker testing prior to the entry of the paternity judgment. Nothing in the record explains why. . . .

The mother and the father apparently were never married. In the years following the entry of the paternity judgment, the father behaved as though he were Cheryl's father. He and his family visited and bonded with Cheryl. In 1995 and again in 1996, the father, acting pro se, sought successfully to expand and enforce his visitation rights with his daughter. According to the mother, Cheryl, now seven years old, has always called the father "Daddy" and "is bonded to and loves him as her father." . . .

In April, 1999, the department filed a complaint seeking to increase the father's child support obligation, and on May 27, 1999, a Probate Court judge ordered the father to pay $90 per week, an increase of $33.50 each week. Five days later, on June 1, 1999, the father filed for the first time a motion requesting an order for genetic marker testing, and an amendment to the 1993 paternity judgment should the test results warrant it. The motion contained a number of unsworn statements, tending to suggest that he believed he was not Cheryl's biological father. More particularly, and of relevance to this appeal, the father's motion suggested that, as early as Cheryl's birth, he may have had reason to suspect that he might not be Cheryl's biological father. . . .

With his 1999 motion, the father submitted a doctor's letter stating that laboratory testing of the father's semen conducted in June, 1996, had revealed that he has a low sperm count . . . The motion also stated that, in 1993, the father had acknowledged his paternity "based on misleading information and without the benefit of a paternity test of any kind."

On July 21, 1999, a judge, "after careful review," denied the father's motion for genetic marker testing. . . .

On November 12, 1999, . . . the father took Cheryl for genetic testing, without the knowledge of the mother. The test report, contained in the record, concluded that he was not the biological father of Cheryl. Relying on the report, on January 27, 2000, the father moved for a second time to amend or to vacate the paternity judgment. He also requested reimbursement for all of the child support that he had paid since the 1993 judgment of paternity. The department and the mother opposed the motion.

On May 30, 2000, . . . a judge in the Probate & Family Court filed a memorandum and order in which he ordered the mother, the father, and Cheryl to participate forthwith in blood or genetic marker testing . . . [T]he judge said that if the tests established that the father was not the biological parent of Cheryl, he would be entitled to relief from the prospective application of the 1993 paternity judgment . . . The judge explained that the father's "interests in no longer being obligated to support a child not his own" outweighed Cheryl's interests "in maintaining a relationship with someone she believed to be her biological father." He said that a contrary conclusion would prolong "an apparent fraud and falsehood."

[The father] argues that, because he now knows with "scientific certainty" that he is not Cheryl's biological father, the prospective application of the 1993 paternity judgment is no longer equitable. His motion is timely, he says, because he did not discover the mother's "deceit" until he received the results of the genetic marker tests in late 1999.

There is a compelling public interest in the finality of paternity judgments. . . . Where a father challenges a paternity judgment, courts have pointed to the special needs of children that must be protected, noting that consideration of what is in a child's best interests will often weigh more heavily than the genetic link between parent and child. . . . Like those courts, we have recognized that stability and continuity of support, both emotional and financial, are essential to a child's welfare. . . .

Social science data and literature overwhelmingly establish that children benefit psychologically, socially, educationally and in other ways from stable and predictable parental relationships. . . .

Where a father and child have a substantial parent-child relationship, as the father and Cheryl apparently have, and the father has provided the child with consistent emotional and financial support, an attempt to undo a determination of paternity "is potentially devastating to a child who has considered the man to be the father." Hackley v. Hackley, 426 Mich. 582, 598 n.11, 395 N.W.2d 906 (1986).

We assess the reasonableness of the five and one-half year interval between the entry of the paternity judgment in 1993, and the father's first motion for relief filed in 1999 . . . In 1993, the father had an opportunity to, but did not seek, genetic testing . . . He never claimed, and the record, such as it is, does not establish that his decision to acknowledge paternity voluntarily at that time was conditioned solely on his understanding that he was Cheryl's biological father. A man may acknowledge paternity for a variety of reasons, and we cannot assume that biology is the sole impetus in every case. . . .

Moreover, the father failed to challenge the paternity judgment at the earliest reasonable opportunity, in the face of what he acknowledges was mounting evidence that he might not be Cheryl's biological father. He took no action in 1995 after he was informed, he says, by friends of the mother that he was not Cheryl's biological father. He took no action after the mother "unequivocally" confirmed, he says, that he was not Cheryl's biological father. He took no action after he observed that Cheryl did not share his, his parents', the mother's, or the mothers' parents' physical attributes. He took no action in 1996 when he discovered that his low sperm count could explain his and his wife's fertility problems. During all those years, Cheryl knew and relied on him as her father, and he enjoyed her love and companionship. . . .

[W]e conclude that, as a consequence of the father's long delay before he challenged the paternity judgment, Cheryl's interests now outweigh any interest of his. . . . Our conclusion is consistent with our prior jurisprudence, and the decisions of numerous other courts, that a father's challenge to a paternity judgment may be untimely even though he may establish conclusively that he is not a child's genetic parent. . . .

. . . We harbor no illusion that our decision will protect Cheryl from the consequences of her father's decision to seek genetic testing and to challenge his paternity. We cannot protect Cheryl from learning about her genetic parentage: If Cheryl does not yet know of her father's challenge, he (or others) may disclose it to her. No judgment can force him to continue to nurture his relationship with Cheryl, or to protect her from whatever assumptions she may have about her father. But we can protect her financial security and other legal rights. . . . Relieving him of child support obligations might itself unravel the parental ties, as the payment of child support "is a strand tightly interwoven with other forms of connection between father and child," and often forms a critical bond between them. Bowen v. Gilliard, 483 U.S. 587, 617, 97 L. Ed. 2d 485, 107 S. Ct. 3008 (1986) (Brennan, J., dissenting). We can ensure that Cheryl, who may be deprived of her father's affection and long held assumptions about her paternity, is not also deprived of the legal rights and financial benefits of a parental relationship. . . .

Our rejection of the father's claim for relief . . . is consistent with the Legislature's clear intention to limit the ability of a voluntary signatory to a paternity agreement to challenge the validity of that agreement at some later time. . . .

## QUESTIONS

1. What was the nature of the relationship between the "father" and Cheryl?

2. Why did the father seek to set aside the paternity judgment? Why do you think he waited so long to act?

3. What role did genetic marker tests play in this case?

4. What did the trial court say the result should be if the tests showed the father was not Cheryl's biological father?

5. Why did this court decide that the father could not set aside the paternity judgment?

6. Do you think the result would have been different if the father had not delayed as long as he had?

7. What role does biology play in the outcome of this case?

———————————

The court in the following case concludes that the husband is the legal father of the child of the marriage—without resorting to the marital presumption—because his name is on the birth certificate and because of his relationship with the child in question. Note that the biological father has no interest in the child.

### J.P.M. v. T.D.M.
932 So.2d 760 (Miss. 2006)

Husband (Tom) and wife (Jane) were married, and a child (Catherine) was born to the marriage five months later. The couple separated, and the husband sued for divorce years later, after he had assumed the primary child-rearing responsibilities at the wife's request. Husband sought custody of the child because of the wife's drug use. . . .

Jane initially apprised the chancellor that Tom may not be Catherine's natural father on October 28, 2002, the morning their divorce trial was to begin. Tom and Jane subsequently agreed to have a paternity test conducted, the results of which showed that Tom was not Catherine's biological father. The chancellor later held a hearing on Jane's petition to terminate Tom's parental rights. At the end of the hearing, the chancellor ruled it was in Catherine's best interests to "remain the child of these two parents forever and ever" and declared Tom to be Catherine's father despite the fact that he is not her biological father, stating "my ruling is going to be that Mr. [Morgan] is the father in fact—either equitably through judicial adoption of some sort, or through judicial estoppel on the part of anyone complaining about it." . . .

In the revised decree, the chancellor noted that Catherine was born on June 21, 1996, while Tom and Jane were legally married, Tom was listed as Catherine's father on her birth certificate, Tom's paternity was never called into question until October 28, 2002, and Catherine has been in Tom's custody by court order since July of 2002. The chancellor also noted that the man whom Jane has alleged to be Catherine's natural father, Nick Harrison, testified before the court that he was unaware if he were Catherine's father but that even if he were adjudicated to be her father, he was not interested in custody, visitation or any relationship with her. Additionally, the chancellor found that Tom was the only father Catherine had ever known, Jane had encouraged the relationship between Tom and Catherine, and Jane had failed to raise the issue of Catherine's paternity in earlier court hearings on temporary custody. . . .

[T]he chancellor relied most heavily on an Iowa case, Gallagher v. Gallagher, 539 N.W.2d 479 (Iowa 1995), as the basis for his ruling. . . . In Gallagher, the husband filed for divorce, and the wife sought an adjudication that the husband was not the father of a child conceived and born during the marriage and to have the husband's parental rights terminated. Gallagher, 539 N.W.2d at 480. The trial court ruled that because the husband was neither the biological nor adoptive father of the child at issue, he had no parental rights. The Supreme Court of Iowa granted the husband's interlocutory appeal and ruled that Iowa would now recognize equitable fatherhood, finding:

> we believe equitable parenthood may be established in a proper case by a father who establishes all the following: (1) he was married to the mother when the child is conceived and born; (2) he reasonably believes he is the child's father; (3) he establishes a parental relationship with the child; and (4) shows that judicial recognition of the relationship is in the child's best interest.

Id. at 481. . . . The chancellor specifically adopted the reasoning in Gallagher as the basis for his decision to establish Tom as the equitable father of Catherine, stating:

> This Court adopts the view of the Gallagher Court that, if a Husband were married to the wife when the child was conceived and born; Husband

believes that he is Child's father; a parent/child relationship is fostered; and shows that it is in the child's best interest for a judicial determination of the relationship, then the courts should recognize an equitable parenthood.

The chancellor conceded that, unlike the child in Gallagher, Catherine was not conceived during her parents' marriage but held this factual difference to be of no consequence since Catherine was born after her parents were married.

In finding that the law of Gallagher should be extended to Mississippi to establish equitable fatherhood, the chancellor distinguished the instant factual situation from the scenarios in two prior Mississippi cases which he found were not controlling here. The chancellor invoked the cases of W.H.W. v. J.J., 735 So.2d 990 (Miss. 2000) and Rafferty v. Perkins, 757 So.2d 992 (Miss. 2000). In each of those cases, this Court ruled that a "putative father 'has the legal right to attempt to overcome the rebuttable presumption' that the [presumed father] is the father of the child in question." Rafferty, 757 So.2d at 995 (quoting W.H.W., 735 So.2d at 992). The chancellor reasoned that because there is no putative father seeking to have his paternity established in the instant case, as there was in W.H.W. and Rafferty, and because Tom has maintained a parent-child relationship with Catherine for her entire life, and wishes to continue that relationship, Jane should not be allowed to pursue a course of action that would disestablish Tom's paternity and essentially bastardize Catherine.

Jane argues that the chancellor's decision completely ignores Mississippi law, as this Court has established that the doctrine of "in loco parentis" controls in child custody actions where a third party seeks to gain custody over a natural parent. As support for her argument, Jane cites to Sellers v. Sellers, 638 So.2d 481, 484 (Miss. 1994), where this Court articulated the standard for making a custody determination in situations involving a natural parent and a third party. In Sellers, this Court stated as follows:

> In custody battles involving a natural parent and a third party, it is presumed that a child's best interest will be served by placement in the custody of his or her natural parent, as against any third party. In order to overcome this presumption there must be a clear showing that the natural parent has 1) abandoned the child; 2) the conduct of the parent is so immoral as to be detrimental to the child; or 3) that the parent is unfit mentally or otherwise to have custody.

Sellers, 638 So.2d at 484 (citing Keely v. Keely, 495 So.2d 452, 453 (Miss. 1986)). . . . In Sellers, this Court reversed a chancellor who had awarded custody of a child to a maternal aunt over the natural father without making a finding that the father was clearly unfit to assume custody of the child. . . .

Because the chancellor found that Tom is not Catherine's natural father based on genetic testing, Jane would have us declare Tom to be a third party to the custody dispute under Sellers and find that Tom can only obtain custody of Catherine upon a specific finding that Jane has either abandoned Catherine, her conduct is so immoral as to be detrimental to Catherine, or she is mentally or otherwise unfit for custody. We find the instant situation distinguishable from the cases on which Jane relies and note that the third parties seeking custody in Sellers and Keely were an aunt and a grandfather, respectively, whereas Tom has been Catherine's "legal father" since her birth. Thus, he has existing legal rights and obligations that the third parties in Sellers and Keely did not. . . .

In the instant case, Tom was established as Catherine Morgan's legal father at the time of her birth (as his name appears on her birth certificate) and has supported her under that assumption without challenge for several years. Because Tom is Catherine's legal father, he has legal rights and obligations which cannot be compromised without sufficient cause. Also, Catherine and Jane have continually relied on the support that Tom has provided for Catherine, and the record reflects that Tom and Catherine have established a strong father-daughter relationship. . . .

[W]e, therefore find the chancellor did not abuse his discretion in awarding custody to Tom, despite his reliance on an equitable fatherhood doctrine. Furthermore, we note that there is no putative father in this case seeking to be recognized as Catherine's father, as there was in Rafferty. Because Catherine's biological father has not been conclusively established and no man is seeking to fill Tom's role as Catherine's father, disestablishing Tom as Catherine's father would require Jane, DHS, and the court system to expend additional time and resources in an effort to establish another man as Catherine's father, without any guarantee that such an individual would pay child support or attempt to establish a father-daughter relationship with Catherine. Such a result is not likely to be in Catherine's best interests.

We decline to adopt the "equitable fatherhood" doctrine upon which the chancellor based his custody ruling in favor of Tom. We do, however, uphold the chancellor's finding that Tom is Catherine's "father in fact" and is thus entitled to rights of custody, visitation, and the like, as this finding comports with our decision in Pell. Therefore, we affirm the chancellor as to this issue.

## QUESTIONS

1. Why does Jane believe the court has misapplied Mississippi law? What standard does she think should be applied here?

2. Why does the court distinguish the cases that Jane relies upon?

3. What factors does the court consider in determining that Tom is the "father in fact?"

4. What standard does it use in resolving the dispute?

5. How significant do you think it is to the court that the biological father was not also asserting rights to the child?

# Endnotes

1. Michael Grossberg, Governing the Hearth—Law and the Family in Nineteenth-Century America 196-198 (1985). This text was extremely helpful in the development of this historical section.

2. Tapping Reeve, Law of Baron and Femme 274 (1816) (cited in Grossberg, *supra* note 1, at 200).

3. For a discussion of changing attitudes toward children, *see* John Demos, Past, Present and Personal: The Family and the Life Course in American History chs. 1-3 (1986); Steven Mintz and Susan Kellog, Domestic Revolutions: A Social History of American Family Life ch. 3 (1968). *See also* Chapter 6.

4. Grossberg, *supra* note 1, at 207-215.

5. *Id.* at 201-207.

6. *Id.* at 228-233.

7. Levy v. Louisiana, 391 U.S. 68, 72 (1968).

8. For further detail, *see* Laurence C. Nolan, "Unwed Children" and Their Parents Before the United States Supreme Court from *Levy* to *Michael H.*: Unlikely Participants in Constitutional Jurisprudence, 28 Cap. U. L. Rev. 1 (1999).

9. 405 U.S. 645 (1972).

10. Lehr v. Robinson, 463 U.S. 248, 262 (1983). *See also* Quillion v. Walcott, 434 U.S. 246 (1977) (challenge to Georgia law denying an unwed father the right to prevent the adoption of his child unless the child had been legitimated); Caban v. Mohammed, 441 U.S. 380 (1979) (challenge to New York law allowing adoption of a nonmarital child upon the consent of the mother only).

11. Nguyen v. Immigration & Naturalization Servs., 533 U.S. 53 (2001).

12. 533 U.S. at 64-66. Interestingly, the Court did not require proof of an actual relationship but was satisfied that the establishment of paternity created the opportunity for the development of a relationship.

13. *Id.* at 90 (citing Miller v. Albright, 523 U.S. 420, 482-483 (1998), dissenting opinion of Justice O'Connor, joined by Justices Souter, Ginsburg, and Breyer). For a discussion of an earlier decision that raises similar issues, see Kif Augestine-Adams, Gendered States—A Comparative Construction of Citizenship and Nation, 41 Va. J. Intl. L. 93 (2000).

14. *See Lehr*, 463 U.S. at 260 n.16. *See also* Janet L. Dolgin, Just a Gene: Judicial Assumptions About Parenthood, 40 UCLA L. Rev. 637 (1993) (a fascinating analysis of the unwed father adoption cases in which the author argues that the Court is principally concerned with the relationship of the unwed father to the mother, and is more comfortable recognizing fathers where the bond with the child is effectuated through an established relationship with the mother).

15. 491 U.S. 110 (1989).

16. *Id.* at 130.

17. *Id.* at 142 (dissenting opinion of Justice Brennan with Justices Marshall and Blackmun).

18. For detail on these efforts, including concerns about the potential for coercion, *see* Paula Roberts, Paternity Establishment: An Issue for the 1990s,

26 Clearinghouse Rev. 1019 (1993). *See also* Paula Roberts, The Family Law Implications of the 1996 Welfare Legislation, 30 Clearinghouse Rev. 988 (1997).

19. Mary R. Anderlik and Mark A. Rothstein, DNA-Based Identity Testing and the Future of the Family: A Research Agenda, 28 Am. J. L. and Med. 215, 221 (2002). *See also* Melanie B. Jacobs, When Daddy Doesn't Want to Be Daddy Anymore: An Argument Against Paternity Fraud Cases, 16 Yale J. L. & Feminism 193 (2004).

20. Anderlik and Rothstein, *supra* note 19, at 221. *See also* Jacobs, *supra* note 19.

21. Paula Roberts, Truth and Consequences: Part I — Disestablishing the Paternity of Non-Marital Children 2 (2003), http://www.clasp.org/DMS/ Documents/1046817229.69/truth_and_consequences1.pdf (accessed October 21, 2004). This is the first of a three-monograph series on paternity disestablishment, which is supplemented by a 2004 case update. This series provides outstanding coverage of the topic.

22. As Roberts' monographs series makes clear, this is a very complex area of the law. The legal rules vary from state to state and may also vary within a jurisdiction based on a number of considerations, including who is bringing the action, whether the parties are married, and whether paternity has been adjudicated or acknowledged. *See also* Jana Singer, Marriage, Biology, and Paternity: The Case for Revitalizing the Marital Presumption, 65 Md. L. Rev. 246 (2006). In her article, Singer argues against a narrow biological definition of fatherhood and calls for the reinvigoration of the marital presumption such that marriage would "ordinarily constitute a legally sufficient basis . . . for ascribing paternal rights and responsibilities." *Id.* at 267. Rather than permitting presumed fathers to disestablish their paternity, Singer suggests acceptance of "dual paternity" to reconcile "a revitalized marital presumption with the interests of a nonmarital biological father who has established a relationship with a marital child." This approach, as Singer recognizes, runs directly counter to the thinking of the United States Supreme Court in the *Michael H.* case. Dual paternity is also discussed in Melanie B. Jacobs, My Two Dads: Disaggregating Biological and Social Paternity, 38 Ariz. L. J. 809 (2006).

23. *See* Paula Roberts, Truth and Consequences: Part III — Who Pays When Paternity Is Disestablished? (2003), http://www.clasp.org/DMS/Documents/ 1049829469.17/truth_and_consequences3.pdf (accessed October 21, 2004).

24. 746 N.E.2d 488 (Mass. 2001).

25. *Id.* at 496-497, quoting Hackley v. Hackley, 426 Mich. 582, 598 n.11, 395 N.W.2d 906 (1986).

26. 754 A.2D 389 (Md. 2000).

27. *Id.* at 405 & 428.

28. Many of these statutes appear to require that the insemination be done by a physician. Thus, it is possible that the result would be different if the woman inseminated herself — a distinct possibility given the ease by which insemination can be accomplished. *See* Jhordan C. v. Mary K., 224 Cal. Rptr. 530 (Ct. App. 1986) (finding that the sperm donor law did not apply to non-physician-assisted insemination).

29. 437 P.2d 495 (Cal. 1968).

30. *Id.* at 499. Again, contrast this result with the result in the co-mother cases.

31. As in Chapter 5, we are not focusing on gay male couples here because such an emphasis would require a discussion of surrogacy, which is beyond the scope of this book. Note, however, that the discussion of gay parent adoption in Chapter 13 is equally applicable to lesbian and gay male couples.

Also, although this book's discussion focuses on couples, many of the same issues come up when a single woman chooses to have a child through donor insemination.

32. For purpose of the present discussion, assume that only the woman who bears the child has a biological link to that child. However, it is certainly possible for both women to have a biological connection to the child, such as where sperm is donated to one woman by a relative of the other, or where the egg of one woman is fertilized outside of the body and implanted in the other, thus making one the "genetic" mother and the other the "gestational" mother.

33. *See* Lisa Brennan, Judge Rules Lesbian Partner Can Be Second Mother on Birth Certificate, 180 N.J. L. J., May 30, 2005 at 11. *See also* Susan Frelich Appleton, Presuming Women: Revisiting the Presumption of Legitimacy in the Same-Sex Couple Era, 86 B.U. L. Rev. 227 (2006); Maggie Manternach, Where Is My Other Mommy?: Applying the Presumed Father Provision of the Uniform Parentage Act to Recognize the Rights of Lesbian Mothers and Their Children, 9 J. Gender, Race & Justice 385 (2005).

34. *See* Ethics Committee of the American Society for Reproductive Medicine, American Society for Reproductive Medicine, Informing Offspring of Their Conception by Gamete Donation, 81 Fertility and Sterility 527 (2004); Jenna H. Bauman, Discovering Donor's Legal Rights to Access Information About Anonymous Sperm Donors Given to Children of Artificial Insemination in Johnson v. Superior Court of Los Angeles County, 31 Golden Gate U. L. Rev. 193 (2001).

# 12 Child Abuse and Neglect

In this chapter, we look at the difficult topic of child abuse and neglect. The enormity of the problem is overwhelming. Each year, countless parents inflict devastating injuries upon their children. The newspapers are filled with lurid stories of children who have been burned, beaten, suffocated, and locked in filthy apartments with no heat, food, or water.

In thinking about how the legal system should respond to these situations, one must confront the tension that exists between respecting family autonomy and protecting children from harm. Respect for family privacy is enshrined in our legal system. The due process clause of the fourteenth amendment protects the fundamental right of parents to the care and custody of their children based on the assumption that parents are in the best position to love and nurture their children. However, this right is not absolute, and at some point, the state may step in to shield children from maltreatment.[1]

Although it is clear that protection of children is an important social goal, how do we determine the point at which parental claims of autonomy can be overridden? How do we define "bad" parenting, and how do we compare the impact of bad parenting with the impact of disruption and dislocation, which may also result in lasting harm? How do we respect the multiplicity of views about appropriate ways to parent without abdicating responsibility to children? And how do we respond to the fact that many parents who harm their children are themselves victims of violence or other traumas and may be struggling desperately to care for their children in a way that is not hurtful to them?

To help frame the discussion, I would like to share a troubling incident that I witnessed a number of years ago. I was ice-skating at an outdoor rink in what could generally be described as a middle-class community. Two parents were skating with their child who looked about ten years old. The child was miserable. He was cold, tired, and wanted to get off the ice. When the child would ask to leave the rink, the father would insist that he continue skating—that he must master the basics before sitting down. Eventually, he began stumbling from fatigue and begged to leave the ice, but the father would still not permit him to stop skating. The father did not raise his voice or strike the child, but it was clear that the child felt he had no choice but to continue. During this time, the mother must have been aware of what was going on, but she continued to skate as if all was fine.

At one point, I cast a hostile glance at the father, who told me to mind my own business. When I left, the child was still on the ice despite his exhaustion and abject misery. This scenario raises troubling questions about how we evaluate parental behavior. Was this abuse? Alternatively, was this possibly an effective parenting technique — teaching a child how to push beyond obstacles and strive for perfection? It also raises difficult questions about what response is called for. Should I have said something to the father? to the mother? Should I have reported the situation to the rink manager? to the state child protection agency? Would outside intervention have been helpful? intrusive? destructive? By whose standards are these determinations to be made?

Defining an appropriate social and legal response to child abuse and neglect is not a new task, and so we begin with a historical overview. We then consider the kinds of behaviors that may constitute abuse or neglect. Finally, we focus on how states respond to families where child abuse or neglect is suspected.

## HISTORICAL OVERVIEW

### The Colonial Period

The role of the family in early America was well-defined. It was the essential building block of a well-ordered society and was responsible for the moral character, education, discipline, religious training, and economic well-being of its members. The family was presided over by the husband, who, as the household governor, was vested with broad authority over both his wife and children; as legal subordinates, they were expected to defer to his authority.[2]

Judged by today's standards, punishment of children was harsh, but according to the then-prevailing view, children required strict correction to stamp out the stain of sin that marked each child at birth. Parental authority was not absolute; theoretically, the community could step in where a parent either engaged in excess cruelty or failed to properly discharge his or her child-rearing responsibilities. In practice, however, intervention was rare due to deference to parental authority. When it did occur, the primary goal was the preservation of social order rather than the protection of the child. Most interventions were triggered by parental neglect (e.g., exposing children to drunkenness or immorality or failing to provide them with basic necessities)[3] rather than by physical cruelty because neglect was thought to pose a greater risk of harm to the social fabric.[4]

## The Emergence of the Privatized Family

As we have seen, industrialization helped to usher in a new family ideal. No longer the locus of production, the family became less integral to community life; home became a refuge — a place of escape from the harshness of the external, rapidly changing world, a private realm associated with maternal nurture. Influenced by the Enlightenment and the ideals of the Revolution, the view that children were stamped with original sin and needed to have their spirits broken lost hold. Childhood was reconceived as a time of innocence when individual potential could flourish under the watchful and gentle guidance of the newly sentimentalized maternal figure.

As the home came to be viewed as a sanctuary from the public realm, family relations were sealed off from community scrutiny. Family privacy was enshrined as a cherished value, and future generations of reformers would have to struggle against this ideal as they sought to protect children from parental harm. This retreat into privacy was a middle-class family ideal that was unattainable for many families, notably the poor, especially in the newly emerging cities, and the enslaved, whose family life was subject to external scrutiny and control.[5]

## Child Rescue: Preventing Cruelty to Children

In the late 1800s, the plight of one small child, Mary Ellen Wilson, drew public attention to the horrors of child abuse and led to the formation of the first Society for the Prevention of Cruelty to Children. This case penetrated the barrier of domestic privacy and ushered in an era of intense concern for the maltreated child.

### The Rescue of Mary Ellen

In 1874, a New York charitable worker's attention was drawn to the plight of Mary Ellen, a ten-year-old who was being brutalized by her foster mother, Mrs. Connolly. Not knowing where to turn, the worker appealed to the American Society for the Prevention of Cruelty to Animals (ASPCA), in the belief that the society had the authority to intercede on behalf of maltreated children as well as maltreated animals. Moved by Mary Ellen's plight, the ASPCA decided to help. Lacking an obvious legal approach, the ASPCA's attorney petitioned to have Mary Ellen brought before the court under the authority of an old English writ that permitted a magistrate to remove a person from the custody of another. In court, Mary Ellen recounted the horrors she had suffered, including being gashed on the face with a large pair of scissors and almost daily beatings. Mrs. Connolly was convicted of assault and battery, and Mary Ellen was committed to an orphanage and subsequently entrusted to a new family.[6]

Mary Ellen's case built on reforms that had taken place in the early part of the century when a number of states had expanded their neglect laws to encompass grounds beyond parental poverty. Motivated by fear that children would become public charges or turn to a life of crime, removal became sanctioned in cases of parental immorality, drunkenness, or where a child was living in idleness. In upholding the constitutionality of these laws against claims that they abrogated family rights, the courts relied on the English common law doctrine of *parens patriae*, literally "parent of the country," which gives the state, as the sovereign power, the authority to protect those unable to care for themselves.

### The Emergence of Societies for the Prevention of Cruelty to Children

Mary Ellen's case triggered a public outcry and generated an awareness that although many societies existed to help mistreated animals, none existed for child victims. Within a year of Mrs. Connolly's conviction, the ASPCA's attorney, who had helped Mary Ellen, founded the New York Society for the Prevention of Cruelty to Children (NYSPCC), the first organization dedicated to child cruelty work. Similar societies soon emerged in other cities and towns.[7]

In general, these child protection agencies regarded themselves as an arm of the police and were committed to seeing that existing laws were vigorously enforced. Agents could arrest offending parents, search homes for evidence of abuse or neglect, remove children, and initiate prosecutions. The focus of the agents was on the offending parent rather than on the child, and punishment rather than assistance was the likely result.

The societies reached the peak of their influence in the 1920s. The Depression brought a loss of funding and a shift in societal emphasis from concern about family violence to family economic survival. Protection of children from parental harm would not surface again as a significant social issue until the 1960s.[8]

### The Rediscovery of Child Abuse and the Initial Legislative Response

In the late 1950s, child abuse was "rediscovered" as a social problem. Based mainly on advances in x-ray technology, doctors came to identify patterns of injuries in children that were inconsistent with parental explanations of accidental occurrences. Doctors were also faced with parents who disclaimed a history of past injuries, yet x-rays revealed old fractures in various stages of healing. In 1962, a major study entitled The Battered Child Syndrome was published; based on medical findings, the study detailed the harms that children suffer at the hands of their caretakers.[9] As with the case of Mary Ellen Wilson nearly a century earlier, this study triggered a public outcry and paved the way for a major reworking of abuse and neglect laws.

Within about five years after publication of The Battered Child Syndrome, all states had enacted **abuse reporting laws**. Initially narrow in scope, these laws focused on physical abuse and generally imposed reporting requirements only on doctors. A variety of agencies — including the police, juvenile courts, and child protective agencies — were designated to receive reports, but, unfortunately, most of the reporting laws did not specify who was to assume responsibility once a report had been made. As a result, reports often fell into a void and were passed from agency to agency without any clear lines of accountability. This fragmentary approach resulted in the loss of vital information and a gross inattention to the children who had been identified as possible abuse victims.[10]

Frustrated by this fragmentation, reformers pushed for greater coordination of protective services, and in 1974, Congress responded by passing the Child Abuse Prevention and Treatment Act (CAPTA). Since 1974, CAPTA has been reauthorized and amended multiple times in order to refine and expand the scope of the law, and it remains at the center of the child protective system.[11]

Under CAPTA, states that developed a coordinated child protective system, in accordance with federal requirements, would become eligible for federal funding. In response, all states revised their existing laws and centralized responsibility in a single **child protection agency**. These agencies now stand at the forefront of what is intended to be a coordinated system to protect children from harm by parents or other caretakers. They are charged with responsibility for receiving and investigating reports of abuse or neglect, providing services to families, taking children into emergency custody, and initiating court dependency and termination proceedings. In some states, protection agencies may also be obligated to refer certain cases, such as those in which a child has been raped, has suffered serious physical injury, or has died, to the district attorney's office for investigation of possible criminal charges.[12]

## THE CHILD PROTECTIVE SYSTEM ─────────────────────────

In most cases, a family comes to the attention of a child protection agency when a report of suspected abuse or neglect is filed. The reporting triggers a complex responsive process that, in extreme cases, may ultimately result in a termination of parental rights. This section provides a general overview of this process

## Defining Abuse and Neglect ──────────────────────

CAPTA provides a foundational definition of **abuse** and **neglect** as follows:

- Any recent act or failure to act on the part of a parent or caretaker which results in death, serious physical or emotional harm, sexual abuse or exploitation; or
- An act or failure which presents an imminent risk of serious harm.[13]

With these minimal definitions as the operative floor, states are responsible for developing their own definition of abuse and neglect. Some statutes provide broad definitions and speak generally about conduct that poses a threat to a child's well-being, while others provide considerable definitional detail regarding the behaviors that come within the scope of the law.

Determining which behaviors meet the statutory definitions of "abuse" and "neglect" is a powerful act as it mediates the boundary between family autonomy and permissible intervention. Once parental behavior is defined as coming within the statute, the door is opened to ongoing state involvement. Accepting the premise that family autonomy is worth protecting, how do we decide when it must yield in order to protect children? What if one family's notion of acceptable punishment is a social worker's idea of abuse? What if the family's view is shaped by cultural values that differ from the social worker's? What if lack of food or inappropriate clothing is due to poverty rather than lack of parental concern? These are delicate questions that highlight the pervasive tension between the need to protect children and the privacy rights of families.[14]

### Physical Abuse

Physical abuse is generally defined as conduct that causes physical injury or endangers the health of a child. This definition clearly leaves room for some physical "correction." For example, slapping a child's hand would not support a finding of abuse, but submerging the hand in boiling water would. Between these acts, however, lies a range of behaviors that are more difficult to categorize, and a determination whether a child is being abused may involve multiple factors such as the frequency of punishment and the state of mind of the parent. For example, a parent who occasionally spanks a child in accordance with his or her understanding of the appropriate boundaries of parental authority is not likely to be considered abusive, whereas a parent who frequently spanks a child, especially if an instrument is used, may well be considered abusive.

Physical abuse can be difficult to prove. Often there are no witnesses, and parents may be able to provide a plausible explanation for their child's injuries. For example, a cigarette burn on an arm may be the result of an intentional act or an accidental occurrence. Complicating matters in cases of intentional injuries, the victim may be too young or too afraid to tell anyone what really happened. If a case reaches court, testimony from persons such as doctors, social workers, and teachers who observed the condition of the child as well as expert witness testimony on the battered child syndrome can be helpful in establishing that injuries were intentionally inflicted rather than accidental.

### Sexual Abuse

Child sexual abuse encompasses a range of actions from inappropriate touching to penetration. Unlike sexual assaults by strangers, incest by a family member often begins with nonspecific sexualized touching and gradually evolves into more overt sexual acts. The child is usually sworn to secrecy and may be threatened with great harm if disclosure is made.

Because sexual abuse is cloaked in secrecy and obvious physical manifestations are often lacking, it can be difficult to detect. At some point, a child may reveal what has been happening or may inadvertently say something that suggests abuse has occurred. Sexual abuse may also come to light when a child complains about physical problems such as vaginal soreness; when physical manifestations such as vaginal scarring or a venereal disease are noticed during a physical examination; or when an adult becomes concerned about unusual or developmentally inappropriate behavior.

### Emotional Abuse and Neglect

Emotional abuse and emotional neglect are more recently recognized forms of child maltreatment, and many statutes now include them as distinct categories of behavior that can trigger state intervention. These terms are difficult to define, and many statutes refer generally to parental conduct that is causally linked to mental or emotional injuries in a child, such as depression, self-destructive impulses, acute anxiety, withdrawal, and uncontrollable aggression.

*Emotional abuse* frequently involves subjecting a child to intense and recurring anger or hostility. The child may constantly be belittled, scapegoated, threatened, insulted, and verbally assaulted. Prolonged isolation or acts such as locking a child in a closet can also constitute emotional abuse. *Emotional neglect* usually refers to the withdrawal of love and affection. The boundary between emotional abuse and neglect is often blurry, and both may be present simultaneously.

State intervention is rarely based solely on emotional maltreatment for a number of reasons: (1) it usually co-exists with other kinds of abuse or neglect; (2) the symptoms identified with emotional harm are difficult to identify and tend to emerge gradually over time; (3) it is difficult to establish a causal link between the parent's conduct and the child's emotional suffering; and (4) it is difficult to determine the standard that parents should be held to. How do we decide what is good enough parenting and when a parent's failure to provide a secure, loving environment slides into destructive behavior? These determinations require tremendous sensitivity and respect for a diversity of parenting styles so that an idealized vision of the "good" parent is not imposed on nonconforming families.

### Neglect

Neglect is the failure to provide for a child's basic needs. It is a broad concept that encompasses a range of acts, including the failure to provide food, the provision of unsanitary or unsafe housing, the failure to obtain adequate medical care and related services, lack of supervision, neglect of personal hygiene, and educational neglect.[15] According to congressional findings, more children suffer from neglect than from any other form of parental maltreatment; for instance, in 2004, 62.4 percent of child maltreatment cases involved neglect.[16]

To support a finding of neglect, most states require some degree of parental willfulness; thus, a parent's inability to meet a child's needs because of poverty should not be considered neglect. Nonetheless, advocates for the poor have raised serious concerns about whether poverty is too readily equated with neglect, as the overt manifestations may be similar. Thus, for example, if a parent sends a young child to school without breakfast because the parent has spent the last of her or his income on heating, that is not neglect, whereas, if a parent does so because she or he stays up late partying and cannot get out of bed in the morning, that may be considered neglectful. An additional concern is that if a child is removed from the home, a family's poverty may influence a social worker's decision not to return the child, particularly if the family lacks adequate shelter.[17]

Establishing neglect usually requires evidence that the child has been harmed or faces a risk of serious harm due to the deprivation. In making this determination, the frequency of the neglectful act may be relevant. An occasional parental slipup, such as occasionally sending a child to school without his or her lunch, is not neglect, whereas a consistent failure to provide a child with adequate clothing in the winter might be (unless this is due to poverty). Also, where the risk of injury is great, such as where a child is left alone in an apartment with exposed wires, a single incident may constitute neglect.

A parent may also be considered neglectful for the failure to protect a child in his or her care from abuse; most commonly, in these situations, the abuse is committed by the parent's partner or the other parent. Thus, although the parent is not directly harming the child, the parent's failure to prevent maltreatment of a child may support a finding of neglect. It is not uncommon in these situations for the "passive" parent to also be a victim of abuse; in these cases, some courts are less likely to find that the parent was neglectful, recognizing that her ability to take action may be impaired by the abuse she is experiencing. Moreover, it would hold the wrong person accountable for the harms rendered to the family.[18]

Taking this rationale a step further, a recent trend has been to consider it neglect when a battered woman "exposes" her children to acts of domestic violence against her. In these situations, the neglect lies, not in failing to protect a child from actual physical injury, but rather in failing to protect the child from witnessing acts of violence. The characterization of failing to protect children from witnessing abuse as neglect, which can lead to the removal of children from their mothers, has emerged as the serious consequences of witnessing domestic violence have become better understood (see Chapter 5).

The practice of removing children from their mothers for neglect based on their failure to shield their children from exposure to domestic violence is quite controversial. Some argue that this approach is necessary to push women to leave their abusers. Others believe that this approach serves to punish the victim, by holding her, rather than the abuser, responsible for the impact of the abuse. It also ignores the fact that a woman may be at greater risk when she leaves. Moreover, the punitive nature of this approach may deter a woman from seeking the services she needs to safely extricate herself from an abusive environment.[19]

This approach has come under increased scrutiny following a 2004 decision by New York's high court concluding that it is not appropriate to remove children on the sole ground that they were exposed to domestic abuse. Although recognizing that witnessing violence can have a negative impact on children, the Court ruled that a parent's failure to protect her children from exposure to such violence is not enough to establish, as required under New York law, that she failed to exercise a "minimum degree of care" and thus neglected her children.[20]

### Drug Use by Pregnant Women

In the mid-1980s, the plight of babies born to women who used drugs, most notably crack cocaine, while pregnant attracted much public attention. Frequently born at low birth weights, these infants may exhibit painful withdrawal symptoms and suffer from a host of serious medical and developmental complications.[21] In response, a number of states expanded the concept of abuse and neglect to include prenatal drug exposure—based on either the actual physical impairment caused by the exposure or the risk of future harm the mother was thought to pose to the child.[22]

Some states now require toxicology screenings of all newborns to determine if there is evidence of prenatal drug exposure; other states require screening in cases where there are indications that the woman has used drugs during pregnancy.[23] Positive results must be reported to the child protection agency. In states that do not have a screening requirement, health care professionals may still be obligated to report suspected prenatal drug exposure. The consequences of determined drug use during pregnancy varies from state to state: "in some states [it] is supposed to trigger only an evaluation of parenting ability and the provisions of services, whereas in others it provides the basis for presuming neglect or qualifies as a factor to be considered in terminating parental rights."[24] However, regardless of approach, a common result is the separation of mother and child and the placement of the infant into foster care.

Treating prenatal drug exposure as a form of child abuse or neglect is controversial. Supporters of this approach point to the potentially devastating effect of prenatal drug exposure and to the need to hold women accountable for their conduct during pregnancy. Many speak of a duty of care that a woman owes to her unborn child once she elects to carry a pregnancy to term, rejecting the idea that a woman's right of privacy bars the state from scrutinizing her conduct in order to protect the unborn.

Critics argue that this approach is unduly punitive and ignores the complex, underlying social reality of drug addiction. Rather than recognizing the often desperate situation of these women, this approach portrays them as the purposeful destroyers of their children. By blaming the individual, it avoids social responsibility for ensuring that pregnant women have access to adequate educational, prenatal, and drug treatment services. In this regard, it is noted that many pregnant drug users cannot get help in fighting their addiction during pregnancy because most drug treatment programs do not serve pregnant women. Critics fear that, beyond shifting attention away from the need to provide essential services, reporting laws will deter women from utilizing whatever services are available for fear that this will result in the loss of their children.

## The Reporting of Suspected Abuse or Neglect

Most families come to the attention of a child protection agency following a report of suspected child abuse or neglect. Far less frequently, a parent who is struggling to care for his or her children will contact a protective agency directly for assistance.

The reporting laws in most states distinguish between mandatory and permissive reporters. **Mandatory reporters** are specifically designated by statute and are usually professionals who are likely to encounter children in the course of their work, such as dentists, social workers, therapists, teachers, and physicians. Mandatory reporters are legally obligated to report suspected instances of abuse or neglect and may be subject to criminal sanctions for the failure to do so, although prosecutions are rare. Generally, these statutes abrogate professional privileges so that a reporter can disclose information without violating any duty of confidentiality. Most, if not all, also protect a reporter from liability for making the report, so long as it was made in good faith.

Any person not specifically identified as a mandatory reporter is considered a permissive reporter. **Permissive reporters** can, but are not obligated to, report suspected cases of abuse or neglect. To encourage these reports, most states permit them to be made on an anonymous basis. Because permissive reporters have no duty to report, the failure to act will not result in sanctions. However, as discussed above, parents may be legally responsible for failing to protect their children from harm inflicted by the other parent or caretaker. Accordingly, even where not required by statute, the duty to protect may effectively impose a reporting obligation on a parent.

Other states do not distinguish between mandatory and permissive reporters. In these states, a reporting duty is imposed on any person who has reasonable grounds to believe a child is being harmed.

Reports are generally made directly to the child protection agency, although in some locales, the reporter may have the option of filing with the police. Also, in specific circumstances such as where a child has been killed, the reporter may be required to contact both the protective agency and another party such as the police or the district attorney's office. As a rule, reports must be made immediately or as soon as practicable after the harm comes to the reporter's attention. Due to this timeliness requirement, reports are usually made by telephone and then followed up on in writing.

In the course of your work as a paralegal, you may face a situation where a client either tells you about abuse that is taking place or you become suspicious that his or her children are being abused or neglected. If this happens, you face the question of whether you must or should file a report. Attorneys and paralegals are almost never included in the list of mandated reporters, although they may be under a general duty to report in states that do not distinguish between mandatory and permissive reporters. Of course, even if not legally required, a report can always be made on a permissive basis. However, reporting raises difficult ethical questions regarding the duty to preserve client confidentiality, as most states do not abrogate the attorney-client privilege for this purpose. It is thus possible that reporting would breach the duty of confidentiality owed to a client. In short, regardless of any impulse you may have, under no circumstances should you take any action without consulting the attorney on the case, as he or she is most likely the appropriate person to make the decision about what should be done.

## Screening and Investigation

When a report is received, it is either screened in for investigation or screened out (i.e., not accepted for investigation). Cases are screened out where:

- the facts do not suggest abuse or neglect,
- the matter falls outside the agency's authority, such as where the perpetrator is not a parent or caretaker,
- there is not enough information to identify or locate the child in question,
- the report was made in bad faith, or
- the agency is already involved with the family.

If a case is screened in, a social worker will promptly conduct an investigation to determine if the allegations can be substantiated. The investigation typically includes a home visit so the investigator can speak with all involved parties and evaluate the child's living situation; where the parents refuse access, the investigator may need to enlist the assistance of the police and/or the courts. Other persons, such as neighbors, teachers, and health care providers may be interviewed as well. In an emergency situation, the investigation must be completed within a very short time period.

If the investigator cannot substantiate the allegations contained in the report, the case is closed, and no further action is taken, although voluntary services such as parenting classes or day-care referrals may be offered to the family. If, however, the investigator has reasonable cause to believe that the child is being abused or neglected, the case will remain open and under the authority of the protective agency.

If the social worker has cause to believe that a child is in immediate danger of serious harm, he or she may remove the child without a court order or prior notice to the parents. Emergency removal is supposed to be limited to situations where there is no other way to ensure a child's safety while the investigation is pending. Following removal, the agency must immediately initiate court proceedings. The parents are entitled to a hearing (usually within 72 hours of removal), at which time they can challenge the state's actions. The court may decide the removal was in error and return the child to the home, or it may decide to keep temporary custody in the agency.

## Substantiated Cases: Federal Law and the "Reasonable Efforts" Requirement

If the allegations of abuse or neglect are substantiated, the child protection agency must, in most cases, make **"reasonable efforts"** to keep the family together before it can seek to remove a child from the home and place him or her in **foster care**. If a child is removed, the agency must again, in most cases, make a reasonable effort to reunite the child with his or her family.

The reasonable efforts requirement has been a cornerstone of the child protective system since the passage of the federal Adoption Assistance and Child Welfare Act of 1980 (CWA).[25] CWA was enacted in response to concerns about children who spent much of their youth adrift in the foster care system. By emphasizing **family preservation,** the Act sought to "replace the costly and disruptive out-of-home placements that had dominated child welfare practice with preventative and reunification programs."[26] Accordingly, a child protective agency could not remove children from their parents unless "reasonable efforts" had been made to keep the family together; if removal did become necessary, the rights of the parents could not be terminated until reasonable efforts had been made to reunify the family.

The focus on family preservation soon came under increasing criticism on two levels. First, it became apparent that, in some instances, children were being left with or returned to abusive parents; notably, several high-profile cases focused public attention on the plight of children who had been killed by a parent following an agency decision to either leave a child with or return a child to his or her parents.[27] The second concern was the lack of permanency in children's lives, as many were spending extended periods of time in the foster care system while child protective agencies attempted to "rehabilitate" their parents, even in situations where family reunification was highly unlikely. Thus, although foster care was supposed to be a short-term intervention strategy, children were "languishing for years in a child welfare system that moved at a 'glacial pace.'"[28]

In 1997, in response to these mounting concerns, Congress passed the Adoption and Safe Families Act (ASFA)[29] which shifts the emphasis of the child protective system from family preservation to child safety. AFSA provides the operative legal framework within which states must operate to receive federal funding for their child protection and adoption programs; however, the Act leaves considerable discretion to the states to determine how best to implement AFSA's requirements, thus resulting in a variety of protective approaches. For example, when it comes to determining what constitutes "reasonable effort":

> Some statutes refer to 'available' services when discussing reasonable efforts, thus limiting the reach of the reasonable efforts requirement. . . . Other state statutes require agencies to use 'every reasonable opportunity' for reunification. Still others detail the type of efforts agencies must provide or the quality of services the courts should consider when assessing reunification efforts for reasonableness.[30]

Although AFSA preserves the reasonable efforts requirement, by making the "health and safety" of the child the paramount consideration, the Act also potentially limits what an agency is required to do and establishes important exceptions to the rule. AFSA also prioritizes permanency and seeks to avoid having children spend much of their youth adrift in the foster care system. It thus "fast-tracks" the permanency planning process so that either children are returned home or parental rights are terminated within a much tighter time frame. As a result, parents now have considerably less time in which to try to remedy the difficulties that brought them into the child protective system in the first place. This change has created considerable debate over whether AFSA unduly penalizes parents who need more time to resolve an often complex myriad of issues, such as drug addiction and mental illness, which impair their ability to care for their children.[31]

### Reasonable Efforts Prior to Removal

When allegations of abuse or neglect have been substantiated, under ASFA a state must make reasonable efforts to work with the family so the child can remain safely at home. However, because "reasonable efforts" under CWA was often understood to mean keeping a family together at all costs, reasonable efforts are no longer permitted to jeopardize a child's safety. Accordingly, in determining whether reasonable efforts have been made, a child's health and safety must be the dominant consideration.

ASFA also includes a number of exceptions to the reasonable efforts requirement. For example, a protective agency is not required to make reasonable efforts to keep a family together if a court has determined that a "parent has subjected the child to aggravated abuse such as torture," or "committed murder or voluntary man slaughter of another of his or her children (or aided in the commission of the same)."[32] A number of states have gone beyond the requirements of AFSA to eliminate the reasonable efforts requirement in a greater range of circumstances, such as where a parent has been convicted of a sexual offense that resulted in the child's conception or convicted of killing the child's other parent.

To meet the "reasonable efforts" requirement, the protective agency (assuming no risk to the child) must offer supportive services to help parents care for their children more successfully. Services may include day care, parenting education classes, counseling, and respite care. A **service plan** outlining the services to be offered is usually developed. The service plan may also impose certain obligations on the parents; for example, they may be required to get the children to school on time or to attend Alcoholics Anonymous meetings on a regular basis. Plans must take the special needs of parents with disabilities into consideration and tailor services to meet those needs.

Although entry into a service plan is voluntary in the sense that a caseworker cannot force a family to accept services, an agency can initiate court proceedings against parents it considers noncooperative, thus subjecting them to the risk that their children will be removed and possibly their parental rights terminated. While the plan is in effect, the family is subject to ongoing monitoring and review until the agency decides either that the situation has improved and the case can be closed or that it has deteriorated and court intervention is necessary.

## Removal of a Child

### The Dependency Proceeding

At some point after the substantiation of abuse or neglect, the protective agency may decide that a child should be removed from his or her home and placed in foster care. In situations where the agency is not required to use reasonable efforts to keep the family together (see above), this decision follows on the heels of substantiation; otherwise, it is made at a point where the agency determines that despite having made such efforts, it appears that the child cannot remain safely at home.

To remove the child, the agency files a court action, commonly referred to as a **dependency proceeding**, in which it seeks to have the child adjudicated dependent or in need of care and protection.[33] Essentially, the state is asking the court to find that the parents are currently unable to care for their child and that alternative arrangements for the child must be made. If the court agrees that the parents cannot presently care for the child, the child is adjudicated dependent. With this determination, custody is usually transferred to the agency, which then assumes primary responsibility for making decisions involving the child, and the child is placed in foster care.

### The Reasonable Efforts Requirement

Following removal, the child protection agency must make reasonable efforts, subject to the exceptions that exempted the agency from having to make reasonable efforts to keep the family together in the first instance. Reasonableness is again determined in light of the child's health and safety needs. A reunification case plan — which usually includes services to help the parents address the problems that led to the removal in the first place — is developed, along with a visitation plan, which helps preserve family connections and may increase the likelihood of reunification.

### Permanency Planning

Under ASFA, a **permanency planning hearing** must be held no later than 12 months after a child has been placed in foster care (or within 30 days if no reasonable effort to reunite the family is required). In addition to assessing both the safety and appropriateness of the child's placement and the services that are being offered to help the family work towards unification, the primary purpose of the hearing is to develop a "**permanency plan,**" which includes a determination of whether the child can return home safely or whether the rights of the parents should be terminated so the child can be freed for adoption.[34] Under the plan, both options can be pursued concurrently so the child is not left hanging if the goal of reunification fails, as the state can only offer "time-limited" **reunification services**.

This fast-track process, referred to by one scholar as a "fish or cut bait" approach,[35] may be the most significant change that ASFA has made to the child protective system. Under CWA, a hearing was also required whenever a child was in the foster care system; however, it was held later in the process, and served as more of a status review than the ultimate determinant of whether the child should go home or be freed for adoption. What this means is that parents now have significantly less time in which to "get their act together" before facing the possibility of the permanent loss of their child.[36]

To appreciate the significance of this change, it is important to understand what is at stake here. **Termination of parental** rights is a drastic measure because it permanently severs the parent-child relationship. Upon termination, the child is freed up for adoption and can thus be permanently incorporated into a new family. Because termination results in an irrevocable change in parental status, it must be based on clear and convincing proof of **parental unfitness**. Unlike in a custody dispute between two parents, a court cannot extinguish the rights of a parent because it believes the child would be better off with a different parent, as this would give the state enormous discretion to reconfigure familial relationships in pursuit of idealized arrangements.

In moving away from the emphasis on family preservation, ASFA sought (1) to protect children from being left with or sent back to abusive parents and (2) to limit the amount of time children spend languishing in the foster care system. Although these are admirable goals, important concerns have been raised that ASFA has gone too far the other way and does not provide parents with a meaningful opportunity to resolve serious problems, such as a drug or alcohol addiction — that in the rush to protect children, the commonality of interest between parent and child has been devalued. As one commentator explains in expressing concern about this new fast-track approach: "Typically, furthering a family's interests will also benefit the children who belong to that family. Children have an interest in maintaining a bond with their parents and other family members and are terribly injured when this bond is disrupted."[37] Of course, on the other side, the argument is that the safety of children should not be subordinated to an idealized vision of family connection and integrity.

---

### Consideration

It is hard not to demonize a parent who inflicts injury on an innocent child. However, can we dismiss such a parent as an evil person who does not deserve assistance? Many parents love their children and are trying desperately to care for them, but are overwhelmed by their own circumstances; for example, there is a growing awareness that battered women are more likely to neglect and possibly harm their children than are other women. How should a parent's life experience be factored into the course of action to be taken by a protective agency?

# Chapter Summary

Child abuse and neglect are not recent phenomena, but a systematic legal response to these problems did not emerge until the latter half of the twentieth century following medical evidence revealing the seriousness and scope of the problem. Following the enactment of the federal Child Abuse Prevention and Treatment Act in 1974, all states enacted abuse reporting laws and established a coordinated child protective system under the authority of a single state agency.

A family usually comes to the attention of a protective agency when a report of suspected abuse or neglect is filed. If, after an investigation, the allegations are substantiated, the family remains under the authority of the agency. Subject to limited exceptions, reasonable efforts must be made to prevent the need to remove the child from the home; reasonableness is determined in light of the child's health and safety needs. If removal becomes necessary, a dependency proceeding is initiated, in which the state seeks a determination that the parents are presently unable to care for the child and that the child should be removed and placed in foster care. Following removal, reasonable efforts at reunification must be made, subject, again, to limited exceptions.

In most cases, a permanency hearing must be held within 12 months of the time the child enters foster care to decide if the child can return home or whether the rights of the parents should be terminated. The termination of parental rights is the most drastic form of intervention because it permanently severs the parent-child relationship. Once parental rights have been terminated, the child can be adopted by another family.

# Key Terms

*Parens Patriae*
Abuse Reporting Laws
Child Protection Agency
Abuse
Neglect
Mandatory Reporters
Permissive Reporters
Reasonable Efforts

Foster Care
Family Preservation
Service Plan
Dependency Proceeding
Permanency Planning
Reunification Services
Termination of Parental Rights
Parental Unfitness

# Review Questions

1.  What role did the family play in colonial America?

2.  Why was harsh discipline of children encouraged?

3.  What was the justification for community intervention?

4.  How did industrialization reshape family norms?

5.  Who was Mary Ellen Wilson, and how did her situation lead to the birth of societies for the prevention of cruelty to children? How did these societies aim to protect children?

6.  What is the doctrine of *parens patriae*?

7.  What role did x-rays play in the rediscovery of child abuse in the 1960s?

8.  Describe the first generation of reporting laws and explain their primary shortcoming.

9.  How did the federal government first become involved in the child protection field?

10. Speaking generally, what is meant by the term "child protective system"? What role does a child protection agency play in this system?

11. What is the core meaning of physical abuse?

12. Why does sexual abuse often remain hidden?

13. What is emotional abuse and neglect?

14. What is neglect? Why is willfulness an important factor?

15. Explain the concept of failure to protect.

16. What is the relationship between the child protective system and partner abuse?

588    Chapter 12    •    Child Abuse and Neglect

17. How have states responded to concerns about babies born to women who use drugs while pregnant?

18. What are the main arguments for and against treating prenatal drug exposure as a kind of child abuse or neglect?

19. How do reporting laws work?

20. Explain the difference between a mandatory and a permissive reporter.

21. Why might a report of suspected abuse or neglect be screened out?

22. What happens after a case is screened in?

23. Explain the concept of reasonable efforts. When is this obligation triggered?

24. What is a dependency proceeding?

25. What is a permanency hearing? When must such a hearing be held?

26. Generally speaking, how did ASFA change the approach to cases of substantiated child abuse or neglect?

27. What does it mean to terminate parental rights? What must the state prove at a termination hearing?

## Discussion Questions

1. Some would argue that the current protective system is over interventionist and tends to disrupt families in pursuit of an idealized vision of family life. In particular, critics argue that the poor are most likely to suffer because their lives fall short of the middle-class norms that pervade protective agencies.

   Others argue that the protective system does not do enough to help children out of deference to parental authority and thus perpetuates the idea that children are a form of parental property.

   Which position do you favor? What kind of deference do you think parents are entitled to? How would you decide when intervention is appropriate? How do you account for different class and cultural styles?

2. Assume that the following report has been made regarding the Smith family: A neighbor knocked on the door of the Smith residence to see if anyone there had seen her missing cat. Upon being admitted to the home, she observed that the house was filthy. Garbage was piled all over, and rotten food was covering the counters. Both the mother and her four-year-old child were dirty, although no symptoms of illness or injury were apparent. The neighbor departed after about five minutes and promptly called the state protective service agency to report what she had seen.

    Based on the above facts, what do you think the agency should do? Is this neglect? Is intervention warranted? If so, what action is appropriate?

3. Do you think a parent should be held accountable for failing to protect his or her child from being abused by the other parent? What if the parent did not know what was going on? Does a parent have an obligation to know? If a parent has knowledge of the abuse, should he or she be obligated to report his or her partner to a protective agency?

4. Do you think parents who have been extremely abusive deserve a second chance at parenting?

5. The Adoption and Safe Families Act has shifted the focus away from family reunification in favor of fast-tracking permanency planning for children in the foster care system. As a result of this shift in emphasis, parents may have less time to address the problems that brought the family into the protective system in the first place. Do you think this shift makes sense in order to protect children, or does it fail to account for the importance of family ties?

## Assignments

1. Locate the statute in your state that governs child abuse and neglect cases as well as the applicable regulations. Answer the following questions:

    a. Who are mandated reporters?
    b. What are the sanctions for failing to report suspected abuse or neglect?
    c. What kinds of services must be offered to families?

2. Develop a set of questions and interview a person who is involved with child protection work, such as an attorney, a judge, or a

protective service worker. Ask them to describe their role in the system. Ask them about some of the most difficult situations they have encountered and their perceptions of the major strengths and weaknesses of the protective system.

3.  Assume you are representing a child who was removed from her home at age three because of extreme neglect. At the time, the parents had serious drug and alcohol problems. The child has been in foster care for 12 months. During this time, the parents have tried to get their act together, but until recently their efforts had fallen short. However, they have recently both completed intensive treatment programs. The father has been at a new, steady job for about 3 months, and the mother is working hard toward her high school degree. Both have completed a parenting class. The agency is pushing termination so the child can be adopted by her foster parents. The child has bonded with them and is thriving.

    The judge has asked you to submit a memorandum outlining your position on behalf of the child. In doing do, you should research relevant case law to determine how your state approaches this kind of case and incorporate the results of your research into the memo.

## Cases for Analysis

The following case addresses the difficult question of determining what constitutes physical abuse of a child and when state intervention into a family is warranted in order to protect a child.

### COBBLE v. COMM'R OF DEP'T OF SOC. SERV.
#### 430 Mass. 385, 719 N.E.2d 500 (1999)

The plaintiff appeals from a judgment of a Superior Court judge affirming an administrative determination by the Department of Social Services (department), that his hitting or spanking his minor child constituted "abuse," as that term is defined by statute and regulation. . . . He argues that the department's decision to support a report of abuse was not adequately supported by the factual record. He further contends that the department's action amounts to an unjustifiable interference by the Commonwealth with his fundamental rights, under both the United States and Massachusetts Constitutions, to the free exercise of his religious beliefs and privacy in child rearing. . . .

## 1.  FACTS

We begin with a summary of relevant facts.

## A.  ....

On March 19, 1997, the department received a report from a mandated reporter, a school teacher, made pursuant to G. L. c. 119, § 51A (51A report), regarding possible abuse and neglect of a nine year old student, the plaintiff's son.[2] An investigation was conducted by a department social worker, Rena L. Ugol, who separately interviewed the reporter, the plaintiff, the boy, the boy's mother, and two of the boy's physicians. . . .

In his interview with Ugol, the plaintiff admitted to striking the boy on his buttocks with a leather belt on five or six occasions during the preceding school year. He denied being a "spontaneous spanker," explaining that he only spanked the boy as punishment for reports of misbehavior at school. He described the punishment as follows: The plaintiff would have the boy stand next to him and place his hands on the plaintiff's outstretched left hand (this latter measure to ensure that the boy would not suffer injury to his hands by attempting to shield his buttocks from the spanking); the plaintiff would grasp the belt buckle in his palm and wrap the belt, which was approximately one and one-half inches wide, around his right hand, leaving approximately one foot of leather strap exposed; he would then hit him on his clothed buttocks once or twice with the strap, explaining to him that it was punishment for bad behavior and that such discipline is required by the Bible. . . .

Both the boy and his mother confirmed much of the plaintiff's account. The mother described the plaintiff as nonviolent and controlled, and stated that his disciplining of the boy was never done in anger and "doesn't escalate" beyond spanking. She reported that, when administering a spanking, the plaintiff would hug the boy, tell him that he loved him, and explain that it was punishment for his misconduct. The boy, although expressing his fear and dislike of the spanking, told Ugol that

---

[2] Persons belonging to a statutorily defined class of mandated reporters have an affirmative obligation to the department when they have reason to believe that a minor "is suffering physical or emotional injury resulting from abuse inflicted upon him which causes harm or substantial risk of harm to the child's health or welfare." G. L. c. 119, § 51A. Regulations promulgated by the department pursuant to its enforcement authority, G. L. c. 119, § 51B(8), define "abuse," in pertinent part, as "the non-accidental commission of any act by a caretaker upon a child under age 18 which causes, or creates a substantial risk of physical or emotional injury. . . ." 110 Code Mass. Regs. § 2.00. "Physical injury" is further defined as, inter alia, "soft tissue swelling or skin bruising depending on such factors as the child's age, circumstances under which the injury occurred, and the number and location of bruises." *Id.*

the plaintiff "wouldn't hurt me but would spank me." . . . The boy variously described the physical effects of the spankings as "red marks" on the skin of his buttocks, as marks that were "not red red red" but more like "pink," and as "a teeny thing of red . . . not really red." . . .

The boy's pediatrician, Dr. Joel Solomon, informed Ugol that the boy suffers from arthrogryposis, a congenital muscle condition which requires him to wear braces on his back and legs and to undergo regular physical therapy. When asked by Ugol whether, given the boy's condition, he would have any special concerns about his being disciplined with a belt, he replied that he "sure would" and that it "wouldn't help the condition," but he did not specify any particular harmful effects. He reported never having seen bruising or other signs of physical abuse on the boy.

Dr. Michael Erlich, the boy's pediatric orthopedist, who examined his "whole body" every three to four months, also reported never having seen bruising or other marks on the boy. . . .

On the basis of this investigation, Ugol supported the 51A report of abuse and neglect against the plaintiff and the boy's mother, concluding that the plaintiff's use of corporal punishment put the boy "at risk of physical hurt/harm, and is not acceptable." . . . Furthermore, although noting the boy's medical condition, Ugol stated that it was "unclear" whether this condition created any heightened risk of physical harm from the spankings. . . .

## B.   ADMINISTRATIVE AND JUDICIAL REVIEW

Pursuant to its regulations, the department held an administrative hearing at the plaintiff's request to review Ugol's decision. . . . At this hearing, Ugol testified that she had not found that the boy had actually suffered any bruising or swelling as a result of this punishment, but agreed that her decision to support the abuse report was based on her conclusion that "hitting a child with an object, in this case a belt, puts a child at substantial risk of serious physical injury" or creates the potential for soft tissue swelling and skin bruising. She further testified that her decision was not predicated on any heightened risk of injury created by the boy's medical condition, which was uncertain, but on her assessment of the risk of injury arising from the nature of the corporal punishment itself.

The hearing officer . . . concluded that Ugol's decision was in conformity with the department's policies and regulations, stating, "It is reasonable to believe that hitting a child with an object in the manner described puts him at substantial risk of physical injury, such as skin bruising or soft tissue swelling. This constitutes physical abuse as defined by Department regulations." The department's decision was subsequently affirmed on appeal by a Superior Court judge . . . The judge concluded that any inter-ference with the plaintiff's religious and parental rights resulting from the department's decision was justified by the Commonwealth's interest in protecting a minor child from harm.

### 2.  DISCUSSION . . .

We do not judge this present case to be a close one. The record contains no affirmative evidence that the boy ever suffered actual "soft tissue swell-ing or skin bruising" as a result of the plaintiff's spankings.[7] The depart-ment argues, however, that its decision to support the 51A report was predicated on there being reasonable cause to believe that the plaintiff's method of disciplining the boy with a belt created a "substantial risk" that the boy would suffer "soft-tissue injury or swelling," which "substantial risk" of injury is encompassed by the statutory and regulatory definition of "abuse." . . .

We are not persuaded that the factual record lends the weight of prob-ability to the department's conclusion that a substantial risk of harm was present. The department's investigator did not observe any physical inju-ries or marks attributable to the plaintiff's spankings, nor did the boy's treating physicians — one of whom, Dr. Erlich, had examined the boy every three to four months from birth — report ever having seen any indi-cia or inflicted harm. The only evidence pertinent to the physical effects of the punishment are the boy's own statements that the spankings left temporary red or pink marks on his buttocks that would fade after ten minutes or so. Such effects do not by themselves justify a conclusion that the boy is at substantial risk of suffering the sort of injury which the reg-ulations denote as "abuse." 110 Code Mass. Regs. § 2.00 (1996).

The department argues, however, that its decision to support the 51A report is rendered reasonable by the totality of the circumstances in this case. It cites the following factors as supportive of its conclusion that a substantial risk of harm was present: the regularity of the corporal punishment; the boy's age and special medical condition; the statement by the boy's pediatrician, Dr. Solomon, that the use of a belt "wouldn't help" the boy's muscular con-dition; the force the plaintiff used in striking the boy; the plaintiff's disregard

---

[7]The department states in its brief that the temporary marks left on the boy's buttocks were "indicative of soft tissue injury" and that the investigating social worker, Rena Ugol, con-cluded that these marks indicated "the possible presence" of soft tissue damage or swelling. These statements exaggerate the record, however. At the hearing, Ugol testified that she was unable to determine whether there was any physical injury to the boy and that her decision to support was, therefore, based on her judgment that, being hit with a belt "can cause such harm," creates the "potential" for such harm, and "gives the possibility that there will be the risk of this kind of injury". . . .

of the boy's physical well-being, as evidenced by his never having checked to see whether he caused any marks; and the lack of any indication by the plaintiff that he would discontinue his practice of disciplining the boy with a belt.

However, the evidence concerning each of these cited factors is at best inconclusive, and its cumulative weight falls short of the threshold of substantiality required to affirm the department's decision. We have already noted that the department's investigator stated in her report, and testified at the hearing, that her decision to support the 51A report was not predicated on any additional risk of harm arising from the boy's medical condition, as the import of this condition was unclear. We note, further, that Dr. Solomon, although he expressed concern about potential harmful effects of the punishment on the boy's medical condition, claimed never to have observed any overt signs of abuse on the boy's body [and] never identified precisely what sort of harmful effects he had in mind . . . Moreover, Dr. Solomon's concerns were not corroborated by Dr. Erlich, the boy's orthopedist . . . Dr. Erlich further remarked on the plaintiff's "devotion" to ensuring that the boy received proper medical treatment and physical therapy, which we view as evidence of the plaintiff's genuine concern for his son's physical well-being.

As to the allegation that the plaintiff spanked the boy with great frequency and excessive force, the only pertinent evidence in the record is the plaintiff's uncontroverted statements that he had spanked the boy five or six times during the preceding seven-month period, the investigator's report that the plaintiff's demonstration on a sofa cushion of the force he used on the boy made "a solid smack," and the boy's own report of temporary red or pink marks on his buttocks. This evidence, without more, does not make reasonably probable the department's conclusion that "soft tissue swelling or skin bruising" was substantially likely to result from the plaintiff's method of corporal punishment. . . .

. . . We conclude that the record does not support a rational inference that a substantial risk of physical injury, as defined by regulation, was present and, therefore, that the department lacked reasonable cause to believe that it was.

### 3.  Conclusion

The department's regulations . . . clearly draw a line between permissible physical discipline and prohibited abuse . . . Today, we conclude only that, on the totality of the record presented in this case, the effects of the plaintiff's physical discipline on his minor child did not satisfy the department's own regulatory definitions of physical injury and abuse. However, a method of corporal punishment similar to the plaintiff's could, in different circumstances, rise to a level of severity that would result in the actual infliction of impermissible injuries or, alternatively, warrant a rational inference that it posed a substantial risk that such injuries would result. In these circumstances, this conduct would, at the least, justify the department to support a 51A report of abuse. . . .

So ordered.

## QUESTIONS

1. Why did the Department of Social Services (the department) decide to support the report of abuse? How do the applicable regulations define "abuse"? "physical injury"?

2. On what basis did the department affirm the support decision?

3. On what basis did the father challenge the support decision?

4. Why did this court decide that his father had not abused the child? What role did the regulatory definitions play in the court's decision? Do you think the court should have considered the risk of "emotional injury" to the child as allowed by the regulations? (See case footnote 2.)

5. Do you agree with the court's decision in this case? Why or why not?

---

The following case involves the termination of parental rights. Note that a major concern with respect to the mother was her failure to protect her daughters from sexual abuse. Also note, as will be discussed in the next chapter under the heading "Open Adoption," that the court allows post-termination visitation with the mother.

## IN RE CHARITY H., COURTNEY H., AND VICTORIA H.
### 215 W.Va. 208, 599 S.E.2d 631 (2004)

I.  FACTUAL AND PROCEDURAL HISTORY

[T]he Department of Health and Human Resources (hereinafter "DHHR"), through its Child Protective Services worker Cary Waybright, filed an abuse and neglect petition against the Appellant, Henry H., and John S., the Appellant's husband at that time. The petition alleged sexual abuse by Henry H. and further alleged that the Appellant was aware of the abuse but continued to permit the children to visit Henry H. The petition also alleged that the Appellant allowed the children to maintain contact with another known sexual offender, Jackie W., the Appellant's own father. Further, physical abuse, parental abuse of alcohol, and domestic violence were included in the petition.

The children were removed from their mother's custody and placed in foster care in Randolph County . . . The DHHR amended the petition on July 24, 2002, to include allegations that John S. physically abused the children, that the Appellant failed to protect the children from that abuse; that the Appellant refused to pay for eye glasses for Courtney; that the Appellant threatened to commit suicide in front of the children; that the Appellant refused to treat the children's head lice; that there were fleas in the carpeting of the Appellant's place of residence; that John S. forced the children to sit on their hands for several hours as punishment for routine offenses; that Henry H. forced the children to watch pornographic movies; that Henry H. engaged in sexual intercourse with the children; and that both Henry H. and Jackie W. are registered sexual offenders with whom the children have regular contact.

In a July 3, 2002, psychological report, Dr. Thomas Stein observed that his examination revealed that the Appellant suffered from post-traumatic stress originating from the sexual abuse she endured in her early adolescence. . . . Dr. Stein opined that the Appellant's inability to protect her children originated in her underlying personality which developed from the sexual abuse she suffered as a child. Dr. Stein further explained that the Appellant had sufficient intellectual capacity to benefit from appropriate psychotherapeutic intervention and that the "in-home services related to child management would do nothing to address the issues of [the Appellant's] own previous sexual abuse and concomitant personality tendencies. . . ."

An adjudicatory hearing was held . . . and the lower court issued an adjudicatory order . . . finding that each of the children had been neglected and abused by the Appellant, Henry H., and John S. Specifically, the lower court found that Henry H. had sexually abused the children; that John S. had repeatedly physically abused the children; that the Appellant had consistently failed to take protective safety measures by exposing the children to sex offenders, by failing to timely submit the children for medical examinations, and by failing to seek appropriate psychological treatment for the children after the sexual abuse was revealed. The lower court further found that the Appellant had failed to protect the children from the harsh discipline and physical and emotional abuse inflicted by John S., their step-father. The court further emphasized that the Appellant had failed to acknowledge the extent of the abuse or its impact on the children. . . .

On October 24, 2002, the Appellant divorced John S., and he was thereafter dismissed from these proceedings. On November 6, 2002, the lower court conducted a hearing on the Appellant's motion for a post-adjudicatory improvement period. Upon conclusion of the evidence on November 6, 2002, the lower court denied the motion for the post-adjudicatory improvement period, finding that the Appellant had received services for several years to little avail. . . .

Specifically, the lower court found that the Appellant failed to keep the children away from their grandfather, a registered sexual offender; failed to keep the children away from their father, a registered sexual offender; and failed to protect the children from the severe physical discipline imposed by John S., even after a "safety agreement" was entered into with the DHHR in August 1999 as a result of John S.'s unreasonable punishment of the children.

A dispositional hearing was conducted on December 9, 2002, and the lower court considered and denied the Appellant's motion for a dispositional improvement period based upon the absence of evidence that she could comply with the requirements of an improvement plan. On January 6, 2003, the lower court entered a dispositional order, finding that the Appellant was unwilling or unable to provide for the children's needs and that she had failed to protect the children from abuse. The court further found that continuation in the home was contrary to the welfare of the children, that the DHHR had made numerous reasonable efforts to preserve the family, and that there was no reasonable likelihood that the conditions of neglect and abuse could be substantially corrected in the near future. The lower court consequently terminated the parental rights of both the Appellant and Henry H.

## III. Discussion

During the pendency of an abuse and neglect proceeding, an individual facing potential termination of parental rights may move the presiding court for an improvement period . . . [E]ntitlement to an improvement period is conditioned upon the ability of the parent/respondent to demonstrate "by clear and convincing evidence, that the respondent is likely to fully participate in the improvement period. . . ." The lower court in the present case specifically stated that "I don't believe that her submissiveness or failure to be assertive can be corrected in any period of time that an . . . improvement period might allow us." . . .

Based upon the above precedent, as well as our review of the entire record in this case, it is clear that the Appellant failed to present evidence to demonstrate that there was a reasonable likelihood that the conditions of abuse and neglect suffered by her children could be substantially corrected in the near future. Given the Appellant's refusal to acknowledge the seriousness of the continuous abuse her children have suffered, we uphold the lower court's conclusion that there is no reasonable likelihood that the conditions of abuse and neglect can be substantially corrected in the near future. The Appellant has simply failed to demonstrate any ability to protect her children from further abuse.

We further conclude that the lower court did not abuse its discretion by denying the requested improvement periods. The lower court's termination of the Appellant's parental rights was supported by clear and convincing evidence and was not clearly erroneous. Finally, we find that the lower court acted in the best interest of the children throughout the underlying proceedings.

## IV.  RELEVANT CONCERNS

While the evidence before the lower court undoubtedly justified its conclusions, and we consequently affirm, there are troubling components of this case that should not elude inquiry. One such issue is the apparent absence of any services directly aimed at remedying the Appellant's underlying personality characteristics which apparently led to her inability to protect her children. An extensive array of in-home parenting services were provided and are documented in the record. Yet, these services were not specifically devised to address the Appellant's real deficiencies. It is fundamentally unfair to castigate the Appellant for failure to improve when the services offered to her were not designed to promote improvement in the specific target area in which she was most deficient. Dr. Stein's opinion indicated that the Appellant could quite possibly, at some unknown point in the future, gain enough confidence and mastery over her own abusive past to become an adequate parent to her daughters. While we are concerned with this situation, the record compels the conclusion, as stated above, that there is no reasonable manner in which to calculate when or if the Appellant would attain that ability. Thus, the lower court's determinations cannot be deemed erroneous.

## V.  RIGHT TO CONTINUED ASSOCIATION

The record clearly reveals that an emotional bond exists between the Appellant and her children. Throughout the proceedings, the visitations have progressed well, and the children have expressed interest in continuing to maintain a relationship with their mother. Based upon this emotional bond, as well as the efforts demonstrated by the Appellant with regard to counseling, divorcing her husband, and actively seeking a relationship with her children, the lower court, upon remand, shall examine the emotional bond between the Appellant and her children. The lower court may grant the Appellant post-termination visitation with the children, provided that such continued relationship is in the children's best interests and "would not unreasonably interfere with their permanent placement." In re Katie S., 198 W. Va. 79, 82, 479 S.E.2d 589, 592 (1996).

## QUESTIONS

1. Why were the mother's parental rights terminated?

2. Why was her request for an "improvement period" denied?

3. What actions had the mother taken to try and improve her situation/parenting abilities?

4. What concern did the court express with respect to the provision of services? Why didn't this effect the outcome in terms of the termination decision?

5. What post-termination rights was the mother granted and why?

## Endnotes

1. *See* Prince v. Massachusetts, 321 U.S. 158 (1944); Pierce v. Society of Sisters, 268 U.S. 510 (1925); Meyer v. Nebraska, 262 U.S. 390 (1923); Wisconsin v. Yoder, 406 U.S. 205 (1972); Stanley v. Illinois, 405 U.S. 645 (1972).

2. Mary Beth Norton, Liberty's Daughters: The Revolutionary Experience of American Women 1750-1800, at 3-9 (1980).

3. Poverty was readily equated with neglect, and local authorities had the statutory authority to remove poor children from their parents and place them in almshouses or bind them out as apprentices. *See* Michael Grossberg, Governing the Hearth: Law and the Family in Nineteenth-Century America 263-268 (1985); Judith Areen, Intervention Between Parent and Child: A Reappraisal of the State's Role in Child Neglect and Abuse Cases, 63 Geo. L.J. 887, 899-902 (1975).

4. *See* Elizabeth Pleck, Domestic Tyranny: The Making of American Social Policy Against Family Violence from Colonial Times to the Present, ch. 1 (1987); Mason P. Thomas, Jr., Child Abuse and Neglect, Part 1: Historical Overview, Legal Matrix, and Social Perspectives, 50 N.C. L. Rev. 293, 300-301 (1972).

5. Pleck, *supra* note 4, at 47-48. *See also* John Demos, Past, Present, and Personal: The Family and the Life Course in American History 41-64 (1986).

6. For more on this case, *see* Pleck, *supra* note 4, ch. 4, and Thomas, *supra* note 4, at 307-313.

7. For the most part, the anti-cruelty societies were founded by upper-class, native-born reformers, while the families who became involved with the societies were generally poor and often immigrants. For an analysis of the tensions caused by the clash of these two worlds, including a discussion of the social control aspects of the child protection movement, *see* Linda Gordon, Heroes of Their Own Lives: The Politics and History of Family Violence (1988). *See also* Pleck, *supra* note 4, ch. 4.

8. Pleck, *supra* note 4, at 72-87.

9. C. Henry Kempe et al., The Battered Child Syndrome, 181 JAMA 17 (1962).

10. Douglas J. Besharov, "Doing Something" About Child Abuse: The Need to Narrow the Grounds for State Intervention, 8 Harv. J.L. & Pub. Poly. 539, 546-547 (1985); Brian G. Frasier, A Glance at the Past, A Gaze at the Present, A Glimpse at the Future: A Critical Analysis of the Development of Child Abuse Reporting Statutes, 54 Chi.-Kent L. Rev. 650, 661 (1978).

11. *See* Pub. L. No. 93-247, 88 Stat. 4 (codified as amended in scattered sections of 42 U.S.C.).

12. Although beyond the scope of this chapter, it is important to be aware that parents may also be criminally prosecuted for abusing or neglecting their children, and that most states have a specific criminal abuse statute.

13. CAPTA, 42 U.S.C.A. sec. 5106g, *as amended by* the Keeping Families Safe Act of 2003.

14. For further discussion of some of these issues, *see* William Y. Chen, Blue Spots, Coining and Cupping: How Ethnic Minority Parents Can Be Misreported as Child Abusers, 7 J.L. Soc'y 88 (2005); Catherine J. Ross, The Tyranny of Time: Vulnerable Children, "Bad" Mothers, and Statutory Deadlines in Parental

Termination Proceedings, 11 Va. J. Soc. Poly. & L. 176 (2004); Michael Futterman, Seeking a Standard: Reconciling Child Abuse and Condoned Child Rearing Practices Among Different Cultures, 34 U. Miami Inter.-Am. L. Rev. 491 (2003); Sandra Bullock, Low-Income Parents Victimized by Child Protective Services, 11 Am. U. J. Gender Soc. Poly. & L. 1023 (2003); Dorothy Roberts, Shattered Bonds: The Color of Child Welfare (2002).

15. With respect to medical neglect, most statutes include a religious exemption for parents who rely on spiritual means to cure their child. However, this exemption does not necessarily mean that a court is prohibited from ordering medical treatment if the child is in imminent danger, and, if the child dies, it may not shield the parent from criminal prosecution. For further detail and references, *see* Jennifer Stanfield, Current Public Law and Policy Issues: Faith Healing and Religious Treatment Exemptions to Child-Endangerment Laws: Should Parents Be Allowed to Refuse Necessary Medical Treatment for Their Children Based on Medical Beliefs?, 22 Hamline J. Pub. L. & Poly. 45 (2000). Religious-based exemptions may also exist for what might otherwise be considered educational neglect. *See* Wisconsin v. Yoder, 406 U.S. 205 (1972) (allowing Amish parents to remove their children from the public schools at age 14 for religious reasons).

16. Child Maltreatment 2004, Administration for Children and Families, Health and Human Services, http://www.acf.hhs.gov/programs/cb/stats_research/index.htm#canc (accessed February 23, 2007).

17. *See generally* Bullock, *supra* note 14.

18. Parents may also be held criminally responsible for failing to protect a child from abuse. This is sometimes referred to as passive abuse. *See* Jeanne A. Fugate, Note: Who's Failing Whom? A Critical Look at Failure-to-Protect Laws, 76 N.Y.U. L. Rev. 272 (2001).

19. For a discussion of these issues, *see* Heidi A. White, Refusing to Blame the Victim for the Aftermath of Domestic Violence: *Nicholson v. Williams* Is a Step in the Right Direction, 41 Fam. Ct. Rev. 527 (2003); Ricki Rhein, Assessing Criminal Liability of the Passive Parent: Why New York Should Hold the Passive Parent Criminally Liable, 9 Cardozo Women's L.J. 627 (2003); Melissa A. Trepiccione, Note: At the Crossroads of Law and Social Science: Is Charging a Battered Mother with Failure to Protect Her Child an Acceptable Solution When Her Child Witnesses Domestic Violence?, 69 Fordham L. Rev. 1487 (2001).

20. Nicholson, et al. v. Scopetta, 820 N.E.2d 840 (N.Y. 2004).

21. Complicating the picture, a number of scientific studies now suggest that other factors, such as poverty, may be to blame for the results previously assumed to be caused by a pregnant woman's cocaine use. *See* Lynn M. Paltrow, Governmental Response to Pregnant Women who Use Alcohol or Other Drugs, 8 DePaul J. Health Care L. 461 (2005).

The topic of women who use drugs while has generated extensive literature. *See* Michael T. Flannery, Court-Ordered Prenatal Intervention: A Final Means to the End of Gestational Substance Abuse, 30 J. Fam. L. 519 (1992); Dorothy E. Roberts, Punishing Drug Addicts Who Have Babies: Women of Color, Equality, and the Right of Privacy, 104 Harv. L. Rev. 1419 (1991); Lynn M. Paltrow, Pregnant Drug Users, Fetal Persons, and the Threat to Roe v. Wade, 62 Alb. L. Rev. 999 (1999).

22. Prenatal drug exposure may also expose a woman to criminal liability.

23. However, the ability of states to conduct nonconsensual drug screens may be limited following the Supreme Court's decision in Ferguson v. City of Charleston, 532 U.S. 67 (2001), which held that consistent with the fourth amendment, states could not perform drug screens without the knowledge of their patients in order to obtain evidence of a patient's criminal conduct for drug enforcement purposes.

24. Paltrow, *supra* note 21, at 456.

25. Pub. L. No. 96-272, 94 Stat. 500 (codified in scattered sections of 42 U.S.C.).

26. Dorothy E. Roberts, Is There Justice in Children's Rights?: The Critique of Federal Family Preservation Policy, 2 U. Pa. J. Const. L. 112, 113 (1999).

27. *See* Ross, *supra* note 14, at 195-196. *See also* Will L. Crossley, Defining Reasonable Efforts: Demystifying the State's Burden Under Federal Child Protection Legislation, 12 B.U. Pub. Int. L.J. 259, 274 (2003).

28. Ross, *supra* note 14, at 195-196.

29. Pub. L. No. 105-89, 111 Stat. 2115 (1997) (codified in scattered sections of 42 U.S.C.).

30. Kathleen S. Bean, Reasonable Efforts: What State Courts Think, 36 U. Tol. L. Rev. 321, 330-331 (2005).

31. Much has been written about these Acts in terms of their requirements and the different philosophies that they embody. In addition to the Roberts article cited *supra* note 26, the Ross article cited *supra* note 14, and the Crossley article cited *supra* note 27, *see also* Kathleen S. Bean, Reasonable Efforts: What State Courts Think, 36 U. Tol. L. Rev. 321 (2005); Libby S. Adler, The Meaning of Permanence: A Critical Analysis of the Adoption and Safe Families Act of 1997, 38 Harv. J. on Legis. 1 (2001); Stephanie Jill Gendell, In Search of Permanency: A Reflection on the First 3 Years of the Adoption and Safe Families Act Implementation, 39 Fam. Ct. Rev. 25 (2001); Rachael Venier, Parental Rights and the Best Interests of the Child: Implications of the Adoption and Safe Families Act of 1997 on Domestic Violence Victims' Rights, 8 Am. U. J. Gender Soc. Poly. & L. 517 (2000).

32. *See* 42 U.S.C.A. § 671(a)(15)(D).

33. This discussion is intended to provide a very general overview of the process, which is quite complex. If you are working on a case, applicable state and federal rules governing both the substance and the procedures of these cases must be carefully reviewed.

34. ASFA includes other options as well, but reunification and adoption are the primary dispositional choices. *See* Adler, *supra* note 31, at 9-10.

35. Adler, *supra* note 31, at 10.

36. States also must seek a termination of parental rights under other circumstances, such as where a child has been in foster care for 15 of the last 22 months, or the parents have been convicted of the murder or the involuntary manslaughter of another child.

37. Roberts, *supra* note 26, at 118.

# 13 Adoption

**Adoption** allows for the creation of family relationships along nonbiological lines. Through adoption, the legal bond between a child and his or her birth parents is terminated, and a new relationship is established between the child and the adoptive parent(s). In effect, the legal bond substitutes for the biological connection as the child is enfolded into a new family. (For exceptions to this general rule regarding termination of the biological parent's rights, see below on stepparent and co-parent adoptions.) After a brief historical overview, we examine the two major methods of adoption — agency adoption and independent or private placement adoption — and consider the adoption process. We then look at some of the issues that can arise in particular contexts, such as when a stepparent or a same-sex couple wishes to adopt a baby. Finally, we consider what happens when adoptive parents are unhappy with the child they have adopted and wish to abrogate or undo the adoption. Note that the terms adoptive parents and adoptive parent are used interchangeably, since both single persons and couples can adopt.

## HISTORICAL OVERVIEW

In ancient Rome, adoptions were for the benefit of the adopting family rather than the adopted child. A family approaching the end of its blood line might adopt a male child or adult who could perform the sacred rites of ancestor worship as well as save the family from extinction. Or, as with Julius Caesar, who adopted his nephew, adoption could be used for political ends by enabling rulers to handpick their successors. With the emergence of Christianity, adoption fell into disrepute due to its association with pagan religious practices and its utilitarian nature.[1]

Unlike many other Roman legal practices, adoption did not find its way into English common law. Beyond being associated with paganism, adoption was regarded as incompatible with the English emphasis on blood lineage in establishing family ties and ensuring the orderly succession of property. Many English children, however, spent portions of their childhood living with families other than their family of origin. Most lived

603

as servants or apprentices, although some lived more as members of the host family.[2]

As in England, the children of many American colonists were sent to live with other families, most commonly as servants or apprentices. Apprentice-ships were formal arrangements by which a child was indentured to a person who was supposed to teach the child a trade and provide him or her with a place to live in exchange for the child's labor. This person stood *in loco parentis* and assumed the rights and responsibilities of a parent for the duration of the apprenticeship. These arrangements were found in all social classes, with children from middle and upper classes being indentured to persons from similar backgrounds in which they could "complete their social and professional training . . . while multiplying their connections and possibili-ties for advancement."[3] However, for the poor, these arrangements were born more from necessity and represented less of an opportunity for advancement; moreover, indenture was frequently imposed by officials in order to reduce the cost to towns of caring for the poor. By the end of the eighteenth century, middle- and upper-class parents no longer indentured their children; however, indenture continued to be a reality for many poor children, including those who were placed in orphanages, which often placed out children in their care.[4] Additionally, children often joined families through less formal arrangements, such as where they were taken in by a friend or relative following the death of one or both parents.

Thus, in the early part of our nation's history, it was not uncommon for children to spend part, or even most, of their youth living apart from their family of origin. Historians generally believe that the widespread accep-tance of this practice, particularly that of apprenticeship, helped pave the way for the more modern practice of adoption.[5]

Adoption was accepted earlier in this country than in England perhaps because there was less historical emphasis on blood lineage, class distinc-tion, and the orderly succession of property. In 1851, Massachusetts passed the nation's first general adoption statute. It quickly became a model, and similar laws were enacted in a majority of states. Although a break with centuries of tradition, these statutes were passed with little fanfare. Scholars speculate that the lack of fanfare reflects the fact that these laws simply formalized the existing practice of incorporating nonbiological chil-dren into a household.

The Massachusetts law, which framed the modern approach, placed adoption under judicial control and made clear that adoption was intended to benefit the child in need of a home rather than the parents in search of an heir. Under the law, each prospective adoptive family was to be scrutinized to ensure they were "of sufficient ability to bring up the child . . . and that it is fit and proper that such adoption should take effect." Upon approval by the court, the child would "to all intents and purposes" become the legal child of the adoptive parents, and the bond with the natural parents would be forever severed.[6]

These newly enacted adoption laws were prompted by a number of considerations. First, the laws were passed to ensure that children living in de facto adoptive relationships would be able to receive a share of the parental estate if the parents died intestate. Second, related to child welfare reforms, these statutes responded to a growing criticism of the common practice of placing poor and orphaned children in institutions and perhaps indenturing them. Corresponding to the emphasis on domestic nurture, placement in homes became the preferred alternative for children not in the care of their parents. Moreover, with the development of a market economy, apprenticeship as a form of employment relationship was becoming obsolete. Accordingly, adoption represented a way for a child to become part of a new family as a member rather than as a quasi-servant.[7]

Although placement in a family was generally a humane alternative to institutionalization, many children were initially "put out" by their parents because of desperate poverty or taken from them because the family did not conform to the emerging middle-class view of the proper family. Moreover, families sometimes lost control of the process, and what was initially intended as a temporary arrangement would evolve into a permanent separation.

## THE DISTINCTION BETWEEN AGENCY AND INDEPENDENT ADOPTIONS

Adoption usually takes place in one of two ways. It can be accomplished either by an agency (**agency adoption**) or by the parents themselves acting with or without the assistance of a third-party intermediary (**independent** or **private placement adoption**). Agency adoptions are permitted in all states; a few states, however, prohibit nonagency adoptions except where a stepparent or a close relative is the adopting parent. To explain the difference between these types of adoption, this discussion will touch on some of the steps in the adoption process; these steps will then be discussed in greater detail in the following section. In addition to the below described role of the birth parents in the each kind of adoption, you should be aware that almost all states require the consent of older children. In some states, the age of consent is set at 10, while in others, consent rights do not attach until the age of 12 or 14. Before proceeding, however, let us first briefly consider "safe haven" laws, which are a new approach to the adoption of abandoned infants.

## Safe Haven Laws

Starting with Texas in 1999, most states have enacted "**safe haven**" laws in response to several highly publicized cases involving newborn babies who had been abandoned in dumpsters, garbage cans, and toilets. These laws allow a birth parent, or an agent of the parent, to leave a baby at a safe location, such as a hospital or fire station, without fear of being prosecuted for child abandonment or neglect. Although these laws permit a parent to relinquish a child anonymously, many states require the provider to whom the baby is relinquished to ask the birth parent for medical and family information and to provide the parent with information about adoption and referral sources. However, the parent is not required to either provide or accept any information. Although not without controversy, including that these laws encourage baby "dumping," and that a better approach would be to ensure that teens have meaningful access to a full range of confidential family planning services, including abortion, safe havens do potentially provide mothers in crisis who might otherwise harm or abandon their newborns with a safe and confidential alternative.[8]

Following relinquishment, the safe haven provider turns the infant over to the appropriate child protective agency, which then presumably proceeds with an adoption plan; however, the parent may be given a certain amount of time to change his or her mind and reclaim the child. Sometimes a complicating factor is that it is not always clear what steps must be taken by the agency in order to terminate the rights of the parents — the safe haven law may have specialized provisions, or it might reference the applicable provisions of the child protection law — and a number of cases have arisen over whether the agency had done enough to provide notice to the birth parents regarding the termination of their rights. (See below regarding unmarried father.)

## Agency Adoptions

In an agency adoption, a state-licensed agency arranges the adoption and oversees the process. The precise contours of an agency's responsibilities are determined by the applicable state statutes, regulations, and licensing laws. An adoption agency can be either public, in that it is part of the state's child protective system, or private. In either instance an agency can obtain custody of a child for purposes of adoption in one of two ways. First, an agency may obtain custody where a child has been freed for adoption following the involuntary termination of parental rights (see Chapter 12). Second, parents who wish to give up a child for adoption can surrender their child to an agency. Before accepting a

**voluntary surrender**, an agency will usually provide the parents with counseling to help them understand their options and make sure their decision is fully informed. A range of other services, such as legal referrals and financial assistance for basic legal and medical services, may also be available. The agency is then responsible for finding a suitable adoptive home for the child.

Before placing a child with prospective adoptive parents, the agency will conduct a home study to determine the appropriateness of the placement. Once a placement has been made, the agency maintains some degree of supervisory responsibility to ensure the placement meets the needs of the child. State rules often require an agency to make a certain number of home visits at specified intervals and to take remedial action, including removal, if the child is not adjusting well. In some states, the agency remains legally responsible for the child until the adoption is finalized.

## Independent Adoptions

Independent adoptions (also known as private or direct placement adoptions) take place without the involvement of an agency. Here, birth parents place their child directly with the prospective adoptive parents; alternatively, prospective adoptive parents may use an intermediary such as a doctor, lawyer, or clergy person to help them find an available child and arrange the placement. As a general rule, unlike in an agency adoption, the child is not actually relinquished to the intermediary—this person simply acts as a conduit between the birth and the adoptive parents.

The role of intermediaries has attracted considerable concern; a primary worry is that because intermediaries stand to gain financially from facilitating adoptions, they may resort to unscrupulous means to procure adoptable children. In response, many states have enacted laws imposing restrictions on intermediaries, such as by limiting the fees they can charge and requiring a strict accounting to the court. A few states have gone further and prohibit the use of intermediaries. Most independent adoptions involve white, healthy newborns. Arrangements are typically made during pregnancy, often after an extensive search for a baby by the prospective adoptive parents. If state law permits, searching parents may well launch an "ad" campaign, which can include advertising in the classified section of a local paper, to help them locate a potential birth mother and demonstrate their qualifications as parents. Once a match is made, the baby is usually placed with the adoptive parents immediately upon release from the hospital.

In contrast to agency adoptions, birth parents who place their children independently are not provided with counseling, and preplacement home studies are not required, although some states now require adoptive parents to be certified before they can accept a child into their home. In further contrast, once a baby is placed, the placement is not supervised, although a postplacement home study must be done before a court can approve the adoption. (Note: As discussed below, virtually all, if not all, adoptions must be approved by a court.)

## THE ADOPTION PROCESS

In this section, we will look at the stages of the adoption process.[9] In the following section, we consider particular issues or exceptions to general principles that may arise in specific circumstances, such as where a same-sex couple wishes to adopt a child, or the birth parents are unwed.

### Adoption Based on Parental Consent or Relinquishment

Unless the rights of parents have been involuntarily terminated, an adoption cannot proceed without their consent. (See, however, below regarding unwed fathers.) In some states, the consent of the child also becomes necessary once he or she reaches a certain age, commonly 14. Although this section generally speaks in terms of the birth parents, it is important to recognize that the parents may not be participating in the adoption as a unit and that each may play a different role in the process.

#### Parental Consent to a Private Placement Adoption

Parental **consent** is an essential requirement in a private placement adoption. To be valid, consent must be fully informed and free from duress, fraud, or undue influence and given in a manner that conforms with all applicable state regulations, such as that it be in writing and signed before a public official.

In some situations, it can be difficult to determine if the consent was truly voluntary. For example, a young birth mother who is under pressure from her parents and friends to give up the child may be ambivalent but feel as if she has no choice but to give up her baby to a married couple who appears to be in a better position to raise the child. Although there may not be undue influence or duress in a strictly legal sense, it is hard to characterize her decision as a purely voluntary one.

In most states, a mother's prebirth consent is not binding, and a legally valid consent cannot be obtained until some time after the birth of the child; a typical waiting period is 48 or 72 hours after birth. This rule recognizes the impact of giving birth and the fact that it may be impossible to fully comprehend the import of a decision to give up a child until the child is actually born. Interestingly, in many states, a father's prebirth consent is binding. This differential treatment reflects both conventional views about fathers as less impacted by the birth process and thus less likely to regret a prior decision to give up a child, as well as the practical concern that a father might not be around to give consent at the time of birth.

By itself, the consent does not actually terminate the rights of the birth parents or transfer them to the adoptive parents. In effect, by executing a consent, the birth parents are authorizing the court to proceed with the adoption.[10]

### Relinquishment to an Agency

In an agency adoption, the operative legal act is the **relinquishment** of the child to the agency, rather than the giving of consent to the adoption itself. By relinquishing their child, parents are effectively transferring their right to consent to the adoption to the agency. In many states, the act of relinquishment automatically terminates the rights of the birth parents. In other states, this result is not automatic, but relinquishment enables an agency to seek an immediate court order terminating parental rights. (Note: Keep in mind that these adoptions begin with a voluntary act and are thus different from adoptions that result from an involuntary termination of parental rights — these adoptions are discussed below.)

### What If a Parent Changes His or Her Mind?

What happens if, after either consenting to an adoption or relinquishing a child to an agency, a parent changes his or her mind about going forward with the adoption? Although this occurs only in a small number of cases, it can result in bitter litigation that pits the birth parents against the prospective adoptive parents.

**Private Placement Adoptions.** Most states allow parents to revoke their consent within a specified time period, such as up until the time the adoption is approved by the court. Thereafter, consent is deemed irrevocable. In some jurisdictions, however, irrevocability is limited to validly obtained consents. This leaves open the possibility that even after the adoption has been finalized, a birth parent could seek to revoke his or her consent by establishing that it was improperly obtained.

In most states, the **revocation of consent** (including those within the applicable time period) requires court approval. The standards for determining whether to allow a revocation vary widely from state to state. Some states are fairly tolerant of parental changes of heart, and judges have considerable discretion. In other states, judges can approve revocations based only on specific statutory factors, which typically address the validity of the consent and do not allow for changes of heart that are not bound up with considerations of duress and the like. In these states, a birth mother who experiences profound regret about her decision would not be permitted to revoke her consent even if requested within the statutory time frame. But a young birth mother who could establish that the prospective adoptive parents in concert with her own parents repeatedly pressured her to give up the child might be allowed to revoke her consent.

Where a parent seeks to revoke his or her consent, the prospective adoptive parents may respond by asking the court to **dispense with the parental consent requirement**. In effect, the adoptive parents are asking the court to terminate the parental rights of the birth parents so the adoption can proceed without their consent. In evaluating this request, the court may treat the consent as evidence of an intent to abandon the child and count it against the biological parents in evaluating their fitness. Thus, what began as a voluntary process may result in litigation and a possible involuntary termination of parental rights. (See below for greater detail on involuntary termination.)

**Agency Adoptions.** Most states are stricter about revocations where a relinquishment has been made to an agency, and in many states the relinquishment becomes irrevocable once the child has been placed with the prospective adoptive parents for a specified period of time. This stricter standard reflects the fact that greater safeguards, such as pre-relinquishment counseling for the birth parents, are built into the agency process.

## Adoption Based on the Involuntary Termination of Parental Rights

If the rights of parents have been involuntarily terminated because of abuse or neglect, an adoption can proceed without their consent because the termination frees the child for adoption. Following termination, custody is generally transferred to the state or, more specifically, to a public adoption agency, which must then try to find an appropriate adoptive home for the child.

If the rights of both parents have been terminated, the placement is virtually risk-free because they have been divested of any say in the matter.[11] If, however, the rights of both parents have not been terminated, such as where one parent has vanished, the agency may not be able to proceed with the adoption until that parent's status is resolved. However, if allowed by state law, an agency may choose to make an **at-risk placement**. These placements are subject to the risk of disruption if a parent whose rights have not been terminated subsequently seeks to assert his or her right to the child.

Many children who are available for adoption following the termination of parental rights have been in the protective services system for considerable periods of time. Few are infants, and many have experienced severe abuse or neglect and have lived in a variety of foster homes and institutional settings.[12] Although desperate for homes, these children are often passed over in favor of infants who are generally more available through the independent or private agency adoption route.

In most states, parental rights can also be terminated within the context of the adoption proceeding itself. Unlike a separate termination proceeding, which is almost always initiated by the state, here the request, generally referred to as "a request to dispense with parental consent," is usually initiated by a private party. These requests are made under a variety of circumstances. For example, a child may be living with relatives who then decide they want to adopt him or her, but the parents are opposed. The relatives would file an adoption petition and ask the court to dispense with the need for parental consent. Or an unmarried mother who places her newborn with prospective adoptive parents might seek to have the court dispense with the father's right of consent. Similarly, if a child was relinquished to an agency by one birth parent, the agency might seek to dispense with the consent of the other parent. In order to prevail, it must be shown that the parent is unfit, otherwise his or her consent is legally required.

## The Adoption Placement

Before an adoption can be finalized, a child must live with the prospective parents in a **pre-adoption placement**; however, many states exempt close relative, stepparent, and co-parent adoptions from this requirement. The pre-adoption placement requirement applies to both agency and independent adoptions; however, as discussed below, important differences exist in the placement process.

### The Home Study

Perhaps the most significant distinction in the placement process between agency and independent adoptions is the **home study**. Home studies, which are intended to weed out potentially unsuitable parents, are generally not required in independent adoptions, whereas an agency cannot place a child until a home study has been completed. During the home study, prospective parents are usually asked about the following:

- religious beliefs and practices
- approaches to child rearing and discipline
- child-rearing skills
- the nature of relationships with extended family members
- history of prior intimate relationships
- career plans and how the child will be cared for
- ability to provide for the child financially
- history of criminal convictions
- emotional stability and maturity

Most adoption professionals regard the home study as essential to protect the well-being of adoptive children. While recognizing its potential intrusiveness, it is widely believed that in the absence of a biological connection from which affective bonds are thought to naturally flow, prospective parents must be evaluated to determine their capacity for developing a loving relationship with an adoptive child.

However, the home study process has also been subject to two major criticisms. First, that the process often serves as a thinly disguised effort to rank prospective parents based on how closely they conform to an idealized vision of the perfect family. Through the use of highly subjective evaluative criteria, "nonconforming" adults, including single parents, same-sex couples, and low-income parents are placed at the bottom of waiting lists or are offered only children no one else wishes to adopt.[13]

The other major criticism is that the process exemplifies the cultural bias that exists against adoptive families, as individuals who choose to become parents through biological reproduction are not subject to an evaluative process. As stated by Professor Elizabeth Bartholet, a leading proponent of this view and an adoptive parent herself:

> [T]hose seeking to reproduce retain the sense that they are normal rights-bearing citizens. No one asks them to prove that they are fit to parent. They are perceived as having a God-given right to reproduce if they are capable of doing so . . .

[R]egulation also sends a powerful message about the essential inferiority of adoption as a form of parenting. By subjecting adoptive but not biologic parents to regulation, society suggests that it trusts what goes on when people give birth and raise a child but profoundly distrusts what goes on when a child is transferred from a birth to an adoptive parent. The specific nature of adoption regulation constantly reinforces the notion that biologic parenting is the ideal, adoption a poor second best.[14]

### Configuration of Relationships During the Placement

**Private Placement Adoptions.** As noted above, in these adoptions, parental rights are usually not terminated until the adoption is approved by the court. This makes these placements somewhat riskier than agency placements because the possibility exists that a biological parent will change his or her mind and seek the return of the child. As discussed earlier, states vary in their approach to post-placement revocations — some are very strict, while others are more flexible and may permit a change of mind unless harm to the child can be shown.

Because the rights of the biological parents are not terminated until the adoption is approved, the authority of the prospective adoptive parents to make decisions on behalf of the child during the placement needs to be established. This is usually done through a voluntary transfer of temporary custody from the birth parents to the adoptive parents.

**Agency Adoptions.** Unless it is an at-risk placement, the rights of both parents will have been terminated by the time the placement is made; accordingly, the agency usually has legal custody of the child, although it may delegate some decision-making authority to the prospective parents. As the repository of legal authority, the agency retains supervisory control over the placement, and a social worker will make periodic visits to evaluate how the placement is working out. The agency has the right to remove the child if it determines that the placement is not in the child's best interest. Most states place some limits on the authority of an agency to revoke a placement, and aggrieved adoptive parents may have a form of redress, such as the right to an administrative hearing.

### The Social Study

Although preplacement home studies are characteristic of agency adoptions, a **post-placement social study** must be completed in both private placement and agency adoptions before an adoption can be finalized, although the requirement may be waived in certain situations, such as where a close relative or a stepparent is the adopting parent. These studies are intended to provide the judge with information to help him or her decide whether or not to approve the adoption. In some states, the evaluator must also make a specific recommendation in favor of or against the adoption. Although important, these studies tend to be less comprehensive than the initial preplacement home study.

## The Adoption

### *Judicial Review and Approval*

All adoptions must be approved by a judge, and proper notice of the proceeding must be given to all persons with an interest in the child, including, for example, foster parents, pre-adoptive parents, and relatives who have been caring for the child.[15] To protect the validity of the adoption, it is critical that notice rules be carefully followed.

The rights of the parents must be terminated before the adoption can be approved. As has been discussed elsewhere in this chapter, parental rights may already have been terminated in a separate proceeding, such as where the child has been in foster care, or termination may occur as part of the adoption proceeding itself. In a private placement adoption, termination is usually a formality, as the court is simply being asked to approve what the parties have agreed to; however, when a party is requesting that the court dispense with the parental consent requirement, the termination phase of the hearing may well be contested.

Once parental rights are terminated, the court determines whether the adoption is in the best interest of the child. If approved, the court may also at the same time approve an **open adoption** agreement, allowing for post-adoption contact between the birth parents, the child, and the adoptive parents (see below). If the court concludes the adoption is not in the child's best interest, it is not approved. If it is an agency adoption, the underlying relinquishment remains in effect, and the agency can attempt a subsequent placement. However, in a private placement adoption, parents usually consent to an adoption by a specific person or couple, and if the adoption fails, the consent is nontransferable. This is a difficult situation, as the prospective adoptive parents lose the child they were hoping to adopt, and the birth parents may find themselves with custody of a child they were planning to relinquish.

## MAKING ADOPTION MORE OPEN

Once the adoption is approved (subject to any rights of appeal or post-judgment challenges), a child's legal ties with his or her family of origin are severed, and the child is now legally incorporated into a new family. Completing this transformation, the records of the proceeding are sealed along with the original birth certificate, and a new birth certificate is issued, naming the adoptive parents as the child's parents. The sealing of the records and the issuance of the new birth certificate exemplify the secrecy in which adoptions have typically been shrouded. As a rule, no information was shared either before or after an adoption, and adoptive parents were counseled not to disclose the fact of adoption to the child. This secrecy was thought necessary to protect the interests of all participants; birth mothers would be protected from the taint of immorality or shame, adopted children could grow up with unquestioned ties to their adoptive parents, and adoptive parents would not be threatened with the lurking presence of a child's "true parents."[16]

However, this began to change in the 1960s in large part because secrecy was no longer thought to be in an adoptive child's best interest: "Social scientists accumulated evidence that attempts by adoptive parents to supplant the biological parents by pretending that the child had no biological ancestry could be damaging to the child's orderly, normal development as well as to the adoption family's stability."[17] Supporting these findings, adult adoptees began to speak out about how damaging and confusing the silence about their origins had been and of their deep longing to know of their past. Other considerations, such as the lessening of the stigma of unwed motherhood, also contributed to a lifting of the shroud of secrecy, and today, many states facilitate open adoption and increased access to adoption records.

## Open Adoption

The central feature of an open adoption is that it anticipates some degree of continued contact between the birth parents and the adopted child, despite the severance of their legal bond. Open adoptions are generally associated with private placement adoptions and those in which parents voluntarily relinquish a child to an agency; however, open adoption is also a possibility when the rights of a parent have been involuntarily terminated, if continued contact is determined to be in the best interest of the children.[18]

Open adoption offers a wide range of post-adoption contact arrangements. For example, contact might simply consist of a yearly exchange of letters and photographs with no direct interaction between the child and his or her birth parents. On the other hand, it might consist of regular telephone calls or even regular visits. Where visits are involved, they are often arranged through an intermediary so there is no direct contact between the birth and the adoptive parents.

Although no state expressly prohibits open adoption, most states do not expressly permit it. This means that if parties choose to enter into a post-adoption agreement, it will probably not be judicially enforceable in the event a party violates its terms. A minority of states expressly allow open adoptions, and courts are authorized to approve and enforce agreements for post-adoption contact between the adopted child and his or her birth parents and possibly also between other members of the child's birth family, most commonly siblings and grandparents. Where allowed, the failure of either the birth parent or the adoptive parent to comply with the agreement will not effect the validity of the underlying adoption. (Note: Many states also allow grandparents to seek visitation rights if a child is adopted by a stepparent or possibly by another relative.)

Open adoption remains controversial. Many believe that children will feel a greater sense of security and wholeness if they are permitted to retain a connection with their birth parents and that this will obviate the longing and loss that some adopted children experience. But others believe that this continued contact will interfere with the ability of children to fully integrate into their new families; as a result, they may feel caught between two worlds and never wholly part of either.[19]

## Access to Adoption Records

Beginning in the 1970s, adult adoptees began to call for the opening of sealed birth adoption records, both so that they could fill in the missing pieces of their past and possibly also search for their birth parents. Asserting a right to know about their past, adult adoptees brought several class action suits challenging the constitutionality of state laws requiring the sealing of adoption records. They argued that these laws violated their right to privacy, including a right to know one's identity, and their right to equal protection of the law by conditioning access to birth information upon one's adoptive status. Courts weighed these claims against the interests of the other parties in the "adoption triangle," namely the privacy rights of birth parents and the interest of adoptive parents in safeguarding the integrity of their newly constituted families, and generally concluded that the sealed record laws served valid state interests.

Thereafter, reform efforts shifted to the legislative arena, with considerably more success. Today, almost all states allow the release of nonidentifying information about the birth parents to both adopted children and adoptive parents. Typically, a child who has been adopted cannot access this information directly until she or he is eighteen. Depending on the state, nonidentifying information may include medical information;

information about the birth parents, such as their age, race, and religion; and information about the birth and the adoption process.

The pattern is considerably more complex when it comes to identifying information, which is commonly defined as "data which may lead to the positive identification of an adopted adult, birth mother, or birth father."[20] This information is typically contained in the sealed birth records.

States differ in the ease with which they permit adoptees to access their adoption records. At one end of the spectrum, a handful of states allow children who have been adopted to access their birth records once they reach adulthood, without needing either the consent of the birth parents or proof of good cause or best interest. Most of these states give birth parents who do not want to be contacted the option of filing a "contact veto," and states providing this option also subject adoptees who violate the veto to civil or criminal penalities.[21] At the other end of the spectrum, many states do not allow individuals who have been adopted to access their birth records without a court order, which typically must be premised upon proof of good cause or that disclosure is in the adoptee's best interest. In the middle of the spectrum, many states have created various kinds of registry systems through which adult adoptees and birth parents (and sometimes birth siblings and adoptive parents) may be able to access identifying information. Some states use a "passive" registry system, which requires that both parties register their consent to the release of information before a match can be attempted. In other states, search efforts can be initiated based on the request of one party. If the other party is located and gives his or her consent, identifying information can be released to the person initiating the search.

## ADOPTION IN SPECIFIC SITUATIONS

The section above traced the general stages of the adoption process. However, given the myriad of family arrangements, certain situations involve more specialized rules or raise unique issues. In this section, we consider some, although certainly not all, of these situations.

### Stepparent Adoptions

Many of the adoptions that take place each year involve stepparents. Typically, this occurs when a divorced custodial parent remarries, and the couple wishes to establish a formal parent-child relationship between the new spouse and the children from the previous marriage. Most states have a "streamlined" procedure which allows a judge to waive the home study requirement; however, in some states, the adoption cannot be approved until the parties have been married for at least a year.

The custodial parent must consent to the adoption, as must the non-custodial parent. If the noncustodial parent refuses to consent, the adoption can proceed only if there are grounds for dispensing with his or her consent (see above). Some states have relaxed the requirements for the dispensing of consent in the stepparent adoption context by either statute or judicial decision. Thus, for example, the failure of a parent to maintain communication with his or her children, although not usually by itself considered unfitness, may be enough here to allow the adoption to proceed over the objection of the noncustodial parent.

As you are now aware, adoption typically severs the legal rights of the birth parents. Thus, in a "regular" adoption situation, the custodial parent, by consenting to the adoption, is agreeing to a termination of his or her legal status. However, given that the entire point of a stepparent adoption is to create a new parental unit consisting of the custodial parent and his or her new spouse, it would make no sense to apply the **"cut-off" rule** in this situation. In recognition of the absurdity of this potential outcome, most statutes include an explicit exception to the cut-off rule for stepparent adoptions, making it clear that the parental rights of the biological spouse continue in full force and effect following the adoption.

As far as the noncustodial parent is concerned, adoption by a stepparent does result in the termination of that parent's rights. However, questions have been raised as to whether severing all ties with this parent makes sense in every situation, and courts appear increasingly willing to grant post-adoption rights to the noncustodial parent even though legal parenthood now resides in the adopting parent. These rights can range from a yearly exchange of letters and photographs to regularly scheduled visitation.

In support of this open adoption model, many experts believe that it is important for a child's sense of well-being to provide the child with a continued connection to a parent with whom he or she previously enjoyed a relationship, and that severing this relationship cuts the child off from a vital sense of continuity with the past. In contrast, other experts fear that this more flexible, open arrangement will jeopardize the ability of the new family to develop a coherent identity and will subject the child to competing loyalty claims and uncertainty about the stability of the family.

## Adoption by Gay Men and Lesbians

As discussed in earlier chapters, over the past few decades, gay men and lesbians have struggled to secure legal recognition of their family relationships. As parents, they have fought to eliminate sexual orientation as a negative factor in custody disputes and to secure the parental status of co-parents (see Chapter 5). Additionally, as discussed in this section, gay men and lesbians have sought the right to become parents through adoption both as individuals and as couples.

### Single-Parent Adoption

As a general rule, a single person is eligible to adopt a child, although such adoptions were almost unheard of as recently as thirty years ago; in some states, single-person adoption was prohibited by law. What if the single person happens to be a gay man or a lesbian? Currently, only Florida has an express statutory ban on such adoptions, although other states may have statutory provisions making these adoptions more difficult, by, for example, including sexual orientation as a factor that can be taken into account in the adoption placement process.

However, many agencies and birth parents prefer to place a child with a married couple, thus making it more difficult for unmarried individuals in general to become adoptive parents. Many adoption agencies have an often unstated ranking system that places white, middle-, or upper-class couples at the top. Individuals or couples who are lower in the preference hierarchy may never be offered a child to adopt or may be offered only children who are considered harder to place, such as children with serious special needs.

These barriers are likely to be even more daunting if the single person seeking to adopt is a gay man or lesbian. As the former director of an adoption agency bluntly puts it: "Often gay parents will get harder children because it's the last resort. . . . A lot of social workers will say 'Well, no one is going to take this kid except gay people.' Being homosexual is not usually seen as a positive factor."[22] According to one expert in the field, the irony in this is that "the same bureaucracies that believe that lesbians and gay men are not suitable parents will place children who require the most highly skilled parenting with them."[23]

### Co-Parent Adoption

In a typical **co-parent adoption** situation, a couple is raising a child together, but only one is recognized as the child's legal parent (through birth or adoption). Accordingly, the couple seeks to have the second-parent (or co-parent) adopt the child so both partners are fully recognized as his or her legal parents.

In seeking adoptive rights for co-parents, the stepparent adoption cases have been drawn on as analogous since, as with a stepparent, legal recognition is being sought for an established parent-child relationship that exists within the framework of a committed relationship with the child's legal parent. Recognizing this structural similarity, a number of courts have recently approved co-parent adoptions as being in a child's best interest. As explained by a New York court in one of the first cases to allow a second-parent adoption:

> It seems clear that the proposed adoption is in Evan's best interest. He is part of a family unit that has been functioning successfully . . . The adoption would bring no change or trauma to his daily life; it would serve only to provide him with important legal rights which he does not presently possess. It would afford him additional economic security because Diane would become legally obligated to support him. . . . He would also be entitled to inherit from Diane and her family under the law of intestate succession and be eligible for Social Security benefits in the event of her disability or death. He would also be able to participate in the medical and educational benefits provided by her employment . . .
>
> Even if, as anticipated, the petitioners remain together, there is a significant emotional benefit to Evan from adoption which is perhaps even more crucial than the financial.[24]

Courts have also been influenced by the fact that adoption ensures the survival of the parent-child relationship in the event the couple splits up or one partner dies. This is important because many jurisdictions do not grant custodial or visitation rights to co-parents (see Chapter 5). As with stepparent adoptions, in approving these adoptions, courts have agreed that it would be absurd to apply the cut-off provisions to terminate the rights of the legal parent. To avoid this result, courts have either read in a statutory exception based on the absurdity of the result or extended the stepparent exception to the cut-off rule by analogy.

Despite the similarity to stepparent adoptions, many jurisdictions are unlikely to approve co-parent adoptions. Here, structural similarities are likely to be disregarded in favor of a critical difference between the two — namely, that while a stepparent adoption is premised on a marital relationship and results in a family unit that resembles the traditional nuclear family, a co-parent adoption recognizes the validity of nonmarital families and results in a legally sanctioned parenting unit composed of two same-sex partners. Thus, recognition is likely to turn, at least in part, on a jurisdiction's willingness to expand the traditional notions of family to encompass the reality of two-mother or two-father households.

Another potential issue is that some jurisdictions may be reluctant to recognize the validity of co-parent adoptions that were entered into in other states. Exemplifying this approach, in 2004 Oklahoma passed a law declaring that the state would not recognize any adoptions by same-sex couples; following suit, the Attorney General of Michigan subsequently declared that "since gay adoption is against state law . . . as a matter of public policy, Michigan will not recognize adoptions performed in other states."[25] However, casting doubt upon the validity of this approach, a federal district court recently invalidated Oklahoma's law holding that recognition of out-of-state adoptions is required under the full faith and credit clause of the United States constitution. The court also concluded that by singling out gay parents and breaking up their families based on sexual orientation, the law violated their equal protection and due process rights.[26] Of course, this decision is not binding beyond this judicial district, which means that adoption recognition is yet another area of uncertainty for same-sex families.

### Joint Adoption

In a joint adoption, a couple, whether same-sex or heterosexual, seeks to adopt a child who is not related to either party. It is here that gay men and lesbians are likely to face the greatest barrier, although most states allow unmarried individuals to adopt a child, they do not permit adoption by unmarried couples, regardless of sexual orientation. Of course, this means that in states where same-sex couples are either allowed to marry or entitled to all of the rights and benefits of marriage, this traditional barrier should not be a problem.

## Unwed Fathers

Historically, many jurisdictions permitted the adoption of a child born to unmarried parents based solely on the consent of the mother. Although the legal status of unwed fathers has improved, they do not have the same adoption consent rights as unmarried mothers. For women, consent rights vest automatically at the time of birth, whereas, as we saw in Chapter 11, under the "biology-plus" rule, men must take some step to demonstrate their parental commitment to the child. This differential treatment reflects a number of considerations:

- Because the mother is always present at birth, maternal identity is readily determined and a maternal consent requirement does not introduce delays into the process. In contrast, if the consent of the father were always required, many adoptions would be delayed until the father could be located and his paternity established.

- The automatic vesting of rights in women may also reflect the asymmetrical involvement of men and women during pregnancy. Since only women are directly involved in the gestational process, social motherhood is seen as taking root during this time; at birth, the mother may be regarded as already having demonstrated a commitment to being a parent, thus making her consent essential. This difference may be less significant where the father is involved with the pregnancy; on the other hand, the difference may be even more pronounced where the pregnancy resulted from a casual sexual encounter. A related consideration is the generally operative assumption that the mother is most likely to be the one to care for the infant, thus giving her a more direct and immediate stake in the decision-making process.
- Third, this differential treatment is also rooted in the recognition that women may become pregnant in the context of an abusive relationship or as a result of rape and that exclusive consent rights may be necessary to protect her safety and ensure that paternal rights do not automatically spring forth from an act of coerced sexual intercourse.[27]

---

### Consideration

Do you think unwed fathers should have the same rights as unwed mothers where adoption is concerned?

---

Within these parameters, states have been sorting out, with inconsistent results, how to provide a meaningful role for unwed fathers in light of potentially competing maternal interests and the goal of providing children who are to be adopted with immediate homes. At the simplest level, all states now provide consent rights to unwed fathers who have taken steps to actualize a relationship with their children. Once the right to consent attaches, an adoption cannot proceed over the father's objection unless he is proved unfit — at this point, he is legally indistinguishable from either an unmarried mother or a married father. Note that even if an unwed father has not demonstrated enough of a parental commitment to become a consenting party, he may still be entitled to receive notice of the adoption hearing as an interested party. As an interested party, although he lacks authority to approve or veto the adoption, he most likely will be permitted to give testimony on the issue of whether the adoption is in the best interest of the child.

States take a variety of approaches with respect to what an unwed father must do to acquire consent rights. Over half of the states have established what are known as **putative father registries** that enable men who are or believe they may be the father of a child to register with the state in order to protect their potential interest in the child. Registration must usually be accomplished within a statutorily prescribed time period following a child's birth; once registered, a man is entitled, at a minimum, to notice of any adoption proceeding involving the child. In some states, the failure to register cuts off the father's rights. Exceptions may be included, though (see Exhibit 13.1), for situations in which a man did not have a reasonable opportunity to comply with the statutory requirements, such as where the mother moved to another state before he knew she was pregnant, or where he did not know about the birth of the child under circumstances that do not suggest abandonment.[28]

Some states employ a more open-ended approach and look to see whether an unwed father has demonstrated a substantial commitment to developing a relationship with his child. Just what is meant by a substantial commitment, however, is far from clear. In some states, a minimal level of involvement seems to be enough, while in others, the father must demonstrate that he participates in his child's life in a consistent, meaningful manner.

When the child is a newborn, there is considerable confusion over what constitutes a substantial commitment. Some states will evaluate the father's conduct during pregnancy to determine if he demonstrated a commitment to becoming a parent through the financial and emotional support of the mother. A lack of involvement during the pregnancy may deprive him of consent rights, while an active, involved role may serve as the basis for finding a demonstrated commitment to the assumption of parental responsibilities. In other jurisdictions, the father's conduct during pregnancy appears to be irrelevant, and consent rights seem to turn more on the overall weight that the particular jurisdiction gives to the rights of unwed fathers.

What happens if the father has not been able to take advantage of the **"opportunity interest"** in developing a relationship with his child either because he does not know about the pregnancy or because the mother has prevented him from developing a relationship with the child? If he somehow learns about the proposed adoption, will he be given the opportunity to consent or object to it going forward? Most courts have permitted a father to participate in the adoption proceeding in the absence of an established relationship with the child where he can show that he sought to establish a relationship in a timely manner, even if his efforts failed. Thus, his rights will generally not be defeated in situations where the mother prevented the relationship from developing. However, even less

## Exhibit 13.1    Intent to Claim Parental Rights

**State of Minnesota**                                          **District Court**

| County | | Judicial District: | |
| --- | --- | --- | --- |
| | | Court File Number: | |
| | | Case Type | Family Court |

In the Matter of:

Petitioner

vs.                                              **INTENT TO CLAIM**
                                                 **PARENTAL RIGHTS**

Respondent

I, _____ , state as follows:

1.  I am _____ years of age; and reside at _____
                                            (Street Address)    (City)    (State)    (County).

2.  I have been advised _____ is the mother of a _____ child
                                                                    (Male/Female)

    named _____ born or expected to be born on _____

3.  I declare I am the father.

4.  I understand the mother wishes to consent to the adoption of this child. I do not consent to the adoption of this child, and I understand I must return this form to the court administrator within 30 days of receiving the adoption registry notice.

5.  I further understand I must bring a paternity action under the Parentage Act (Minn. Stat. §§ 257.51 to 257.85) within 30 days of receiving the adoption registry notice, or, if the child is not yet born, within 30 days after the birth of the child, unless I am unable to do so. I understand a paternity action is separate from the mailing of this form. In the paternity action, I must state I am the father of the child for one or more of the reasons stated in Minn. Stat. § 257.55, subd. 1. I intend to retain my legal rights with respect to the child, and request to be notified of any further proceedings with respect to custody or adoption of the child.

6.  I enter my appearance in this case.

**DO NOT SIGN UNTIL YOU ARE BEFORE A NOTARY PUBLIC OR COURT ADMINISTRATOR.**

**OATH**

I have been sworn and say under oath I have read and understand this form. The facts it contains are true and correct to the best of my knowledge, and I understand that by signing this document I admit paternity. I have signed this document freely and voluntarily.

Signature: _____
            Sign only in presence of notary or court clerk

Print Name: _____

Street Address: _____

City/State/Zip: _____

Telephone: (_____) _____

## Exhibit 13.1    Continued

Sworn/affirmed before me this

_____ of _____, _____

Notary Public/Court Deputy

### ACKNOWLEDGMENT

Pursuant to Minn. Stat. §549.21, the undersigned acknowledges that costs, disbursements, and reasonable attorney and witness fees may be awarded to the opposing party or parties for actions in bad faith; the assertion of a claim or a defense that is frivolous and that is costly to the other party; the assertion of an unfounded position solely to delay the ordinary course of the proceedings or to harass; or the commission of a fraud upon the Court.

Signature: _____
Sign only in presence of notary or court clerk
Print Name: _____

Street Address: _____

City/State/Zip: _____

Telephone: (_____)

Sworn/affirmed before me this

_____ of _____, _____

Notary Public/Court Deputy

clear is what the result will be where the mother can show good cause, such as a history of abuse, for preventing the father from "seizing the opportunity" to develop a relationship with the child, or where the putative father has no knowledge of the pregnancy and thus made no attempt to establish a relationship with the child. If he has no idea, should that be regarded as evidence of a lack of interest in or commitment to parenting? On the other hand, is it fair to expect someone to grasp an opportunity that he knows nothing about—should the court focus on protecting the option itself?

These kinds of questions can also arise in the context of the safe haven laws (discussed above) if the father does not know either of the pregnancy or of the mother's decision to avail herself of this option. Many safe haven laws do not have clear notice provisions, and as a result, some courts have refused to terminate the father's rights. Others do include specific notice provisions, such as that a search be made for the father using any information that might be available; that service be made through publication in the paper, which includes any possible identifying information about the baby; and that a search be done of the putative father registry.[29]

Last, and perhaps raising the most difficult questions, what should happen in a situation where an unwed father does not learn about the child until after an adoption has been approved by a court? Should the adoption be set aside in order to vindicate a father's right to develop a relationship with his child? Does this approach elevate the biological claims of fatherhood over the best interests of the child? What weight should be given to the adoptive parents? Should the outcome turn on the conduct of the mother, in terms of whether or not she lied to the father about the existence of the child? Is her conduct relevant from the perspective of the child's needs? Should the outcome turn on the conduct of the father—whether he did what he could to learn about and connect with the child?

These are agonizing questions to which there are no simple answers, and these cases highlight the tension between the long cherished rights of biological parenthood and the need to secure stable adoptive homes for children where there does not appear to be a birth parent who is ready and able to assume the responsibilities of parenthood. Some courts have focused on the harm to the father and have been willing to set an adoption aside to vindicate his right to develop a relationship with his child. Here, his underlying biological connection to the child is given priority in determining which parenting relationships will be permitted to continue. In contrast, other courts have refused to set aside an adoption in this situation if it determines that it is in the best interest of the child to maintain the continuity of the adoptive relationships.

The much publicized 1993 *"Baby Richard"* case exemplifies both judicial approaches.[30] In this case, an unwed mother placed her newborn for adoption without informing the father. During her pregnancy, the father had returned to Czechoslovakia to care for his dying grandmother. While he was away, the mother received a call from his aunt informing her that he had resumed a former romantic relationship with another woman. As a result of this news, the mother moved out of their shared home and gave birth in a different hospital than the couple had decided on.

Upon the father's return, the mother informed him that the child had died. He did not believe this and made a number of attempts to find out what had happened to the child, including checking with the hospital they had planned to use, checking birth and death certificates, and going through the garbage at the mother's house for signs that a baby was living there. About six months later, the parties married and subsequently sought the return of the child based on the fact that the father had not consented to the adoption.

The trial court held that the father was unfit because he had failed to demonstrate a reasonable degree of interest, concern, or responsibility during the first 30 days of the child's life as required by state law, and his consent to the adoption was therefore not required. The appeals court was similarly unimpressed with the father's efforts to determine what had happened to the baby and agreed that he had failed to demonstrate a reasonable degree of interest, concern, or responsibility for the child. However, in upholding the adoption, the court's primary focus was on the best interest of the child rather on the rights of the father, as it powerfully explained:

> Fortunately, the time has long past when children in our society were considered the property of their parents. Slowly, but finally, when it comes to children even the law has rid itself of the *Dred Scott* mentality that a human being can be considered a piece of property "belonging" to another human being. To hold that a child is the property of his parents is to deny the humanity of the child. Thus, in the present case we start with the premise that Richard is not a piece of property with property rights belonging to either his biological or adoptive parents. Richard "belongs" to no one but himself . . .
>
> . . . A child's best interest is not part of an equation. It is not to be balanced against any other interest.[31]

In evaluating Richard's best interest, the court found that he should remain with his adoptive parents with whom he had lived since four days after his birth.

The Illinois Supreme Court had a radically different view of the situation. It disagreed that the father's actions to discover what had happened to the child had been inadequate in light of the mother's dishonesty, which was compounded by the fact that the lawyer for the adoptive parents had also encouraged concealment of the truth. Finding that the father had been wrongfully deprived of an opportunity to express his interest in the child, the court focused on the "preemptive rights" of a natural parent in his own children. It held that these rights had to be considered apart from the best interest of the child:

> If it were otherwise, few parents would be secure in the custody of their own children. If best interests of the child were a sufficient qualification to determine child custody, anyone with superior income, intelligence, education, etc., might challenge and deprive the parents of their right to their own children.[32]

Accordingly, wholly apart from any considerations of best interest, the adoption was overturned, and the child returned to his birth parents based on the primacy of the biological link and the potentiality it embodies.

---

### Consideration

Do you think a child should be returned to his or her biological father where the father was deprived of his right to have a say in adoption proceedings?

---

## Transracial Adoption

Significant controversy surrounds the issue of the role that race should or should not play in the creation of families by adoption.[33] Until the 1950s many states had laws prohibiting the placement of children across racial lines, and, even where not expressly prohibited, most agencies had explicit policies against such placements. Similar to laws banning interracial marriage, this prohibition reflected racial animus and a belief in the desirability of maintaining white racial purity. As courts began to strike down racial classifications in the late 1950s, these laws were eventually declared unconstitutional.

This constitutional direction, combined with other factors — including the increased numbers of children in the foster care system, the decline in the number of white infants available for adoption, and a greater societal acceptance of interracial relationships — led to an upsurge in the number of **transracial adoptions** during the late 1950s and 1960s. Another contributing factor was that social workers had also begun to question their generally held assumption that children should be placed in families that most closely matched their families of origin. Matching had long been a goal of adoptive placements based on the belief that children would do best if they blended into their adoptive families.[34]

Most of these transracial adoptions involved the adoption of black children by white families.[35] In 1972, this trend was denounced by the National Association of Black Social Workers, and in an influential position paper they took an unequivocal stand against the adoption of black children by white families:

> The National Association of Black Social Workers has taken a vehement stand against the placement of Black children in white homes for any reason. We affirm the inviolable position of Black children in Black families where they belong physically, psychologically and culturally in order that they receive the total sense of themselves and develop a sound projection of their future . . .
>
> Black children in white homes are cut off from the healthy development of themselves as Black people, which development is the normal expectation and only true humanistic goal . . .
>
> In our society, the developmental needs of Black children are significantly different from those of white children. Black children are taught, from an early age, highly sophisticated coping techniques to deal with racist practices . . . Only a Black family can transmit the emotional and sensitive subtleties of perception and reaction essential for a Black child's survival in a racist society.[36]

In short, a primary concern was the believed inability of white parents to foster a healthy sense of racial identity and pride in their adopted children and to equip them with the skills they would need to cope with a racist dominant culture.

In response to these concerns, the role of race in adoption placements was reconsidered and in-racial placements were again preferred. However, in contrast to the earlier policies that embodied notions of white racial supremacy, racial matching was now based on positive concerns for the well-being of black children. Regulations and agency policies were amended to reflect this preference for in-racial placements, which often meant that a child would not be placed with white families unless it was clear that no black adoptive home was available.

However, this shift in favor of in-racial placements also generated significant concern because children often remained waiting in foster care or institutional settings until a particular type of home became available. Additionally, a number of studies indicated that where adoptive parents are sensitive to the issue, transracially adopted children can develop a clear sense of racial identity and may be particularly adept at functioning in a world that is gradually coming to embrace the benefits of diversity.

Accordingly, in 1994, Congress passed the Multiethnic Placement Law (MEPA), which was amended in 1996 by the Interethnic Placement Provisions.[37] Together, these enactments are intended to prevent agencies that receive federal funding from denying or delaying adoption (or foster care) placements based on considerations of race, color, or national origin. In short, MEPA is intended to eliminate the practice of race-matching. However, in considering the best interests of an individual child, an agency may take race or ethnicity into account based on an individualized determination that this consideration will advance the needs of that particular child, so long as the individualized determination does not delay the adoption process.

Although strictly limiting the role of race in the placement process, MEPA does recognize the importance of having a diverse pool of prospective foster and adoptive parents. Accordingly, the Act imposes a duty on states to make a diligent effort to recruit foster and adoptive parents who reflect the ethnic and racial diversity of the children in their state for whom homes are needed.

## ADOPTION ABROGATION AND THE TORT OF WRONGFUL ADOPTION

Like any other parent, most adoptive parents are prepared to handle the daily vicissitudes that come with raising children, but what happens if an adopted child develops unforeseen problems that make life far more difficult to manage than originally anticipated—can the parents abrogate or undo the adoption? The difficult question of **adoption abrogation** has arisen in a number of cases, where, for example, unbeknownst to the adoptive parents, the child had previously experienced severe physical and sexual abuse or is genetically predisposed to a debilitating disease.

The majority view is that children cannot be sent back—that once finalized, adoptions cannot be undone. Underlying this position is the recognition that children are not goods who can be returned if they later are viewed as "damaged." However, this position is not universal. A few states, either by statute or judicial decision, permit parents to undo an adoption in what are deemed extraordinary circumstances, such as where a child is facing a lifetime of institutional care; however, most judges are wary of these actions because they effectively orphan the child. Note, however, that as with any parent, if adoptive parents cannot care for their child, they may eventually lose their parental rights due to abuse or neglect.

Taking another approach, a number of jurisdictions permit parents to bring an action against an adoption agency for the tort of **wrongful adoption** where the agency deliberately misrepresented facts about the child, such as where it told the prospective parents that a child had no history of mental disorders when it knew the child had been institutionalized for mental illness or failed to disclose information it was legally obligated to provide. In allowing these suits, the courts have been careful to make clear that adoption agencies cannot be expected to guarantee that adopted children develop as happy and healthy children. Nonetheless, adoptive parents are entitled to rely on the accuracy of the information they obtain from an agency when seeking to make an informed choice about whether to proceed with an adoption.

## Chapter Summary

Through adoption, a child acquires new parents who assume all of the rights and responsibilities previously vested in the biological parents, and the child's legal relationship with his or her birth parents is extinguished. This cut-off rule is subject to limited exceptions, most commonly in step-parent and co-parent adoptions. Adoptions can be accomplished through an agency or by the parents themselves acting with or without the assistance of a third-party intermediary. In addition, most states now have safe haven laws, which permit birth parents to anonymously drop a newborn off at a designated location without fear of being prosecuted for abandonment.

An adoption cannot proceed without the consent of the birth parents, subject to a limited exception for some unwed fathers, unless parental rights have been terminated or the court has approved a request to dispense with parental consent. In private placement adoptions, the consent attaches to the adoption itself; in an agency adoption, the consent attaches to the relinquishment of the child to the agency, which in turn acquires the right of consent. Most states allow a birth parent to revoke consent under specific circumstances; some states give birth parents considerable latitude, while others are quite strict; however, in all jurisdictions, it is harder to revoke a relinquishment to an agency.

In most situations, the child must live with the prospective adoptive parents in a pre-adoption placement before the adoption can be finalized. In an agency adoption, placement will not be made until a home study has been completed, and the placement is supervised by the agency. Post-placement social studies are done in both agency and private placement adoptions in order to assist the judge in deciding whether to approve the adoption. This decision is based on the best interest standard.

A developing trend is to provide for greater openness in adoption. Many states now allow open adoptions, which permit post-adoption contact between the adopted child and the birth parent. Additionally, most states now permit the release of non-identifying information to adopted children, and many now permit the release of identifying information in accordance with specific procedures, which may result in communication between an adult adoptee and his or her birth parents.

Stepparent adoptions account for a considerable number of yearly adoptions. Here, in a significant exception to the cut-off rule, the parental rights of the custodial spouse survive the adoption. This same exception has been made in co-parent adoptions involving gay and lesbian couples, however, all states do not permit these adoptions. Most states prohibit joint adoption by same-sex couples; however, in some states, gay men and lesbians can adopt a child as a single parent.

Unwed fathers now have considerably more rights in the adoption arena than they had in the past and may be entitled to consent rights based on a substantial parenting commitment or an acknowledgment of paternity or the filing of notice in a putative father registry. If a father comes forward after an adoption has been finalized, some courts may allow the adoption to be disrupted, while other courts refuse to do this based on the best interests of the child.

There has been considerable controversy over the role that race should play in adoption placements. Presently, federal law prohibits delays in or denials of adoption placements based on considerations of race, color, or national origin.

When an adoption does not live up to parental expectations, most courts will not permit the parents to abrogate or undo the adoption, although abrogation has been permitted by some courts under extraordinary circumstances. Where the agency has breached its obligation to properly disclose information, parents may be able to sue the agency in tort for wrongful adoption.

## Key Terms

Adoption

Agency Adoption

Independent Adoption

Private Placement Adoption

Safe Haven

Voluntary Surrender

Consent

Relinquishment

Revocation of Consent

Dispensing with Parental Consent

At-Risk Placement

Pre-Adoption Placement

Home Study

Post-Placement Social Study

Open Adoption

"Cut-Off" Rule

Co-Parent Adoption

Putative Father Registry

Opportunity Interest

Transracial Adoptions

Adoption Abrogation

Wrongful Adoption

# Review Questions

1. What purpose did adoptions serve in ancient Rome?

2. Why were adoptions not recognized under English common law?

3. When was the first adoption statute in this country passed? What factors prompted its passage?

4. What is an agency adoption?

5. What is an independent or private placement adoption?

6. What is meant by the term "direct placement"?

7. Detail the differences between private placement and agency adoptions.

8. Explain how safe haven laws work.

9. Discuss the parental consent requirements. Why might it be difficult to determine if consent is truly voluntary?

10. What is meant by the term "voluntary surrender"?

11. Under what circumstances may a parent revoke his or her consent?

12. Why is it more difficult to revoke a relinquishment made to an agency?

13. How might prospective adoptive parents respond to a parental attempt to revoke consent?

14. What is the purpose of the home study? When are they usually done? What is usually inquired into?

15. Why has the home study process been subject to criticism?

16. During an agency placement, who usually has legal custody of the children?

17. Does the execution of the consent document effectively transfer parental rights over to the adoptive parents?

18. During the placement in an independent adoption, who has authority to make decisions regarding the child?

19. What is the purpose of a post-placement social study?

20. What standard does the court use in deciding whether to approve an adoption?

21. Why have adoptions traditionally been cloaked in secrecy? Why has this been challenged?

22. What is an open adoption?

23. What approaches do states take with respect to open adoption?

24. What typically happens to the original birth records and the adoption records once an adoption is approved? Why has this traditional approach been challenged?

25. What approaches do states take to provide children who have been adopted access to their birth records?

26. Following a stepparent adoption, what is the status of the custodial parent?

27. In what ways are co-parent adoptions similar to stepparent adoptions? In what ways are they different?

28. Explain the adoption rights of gay men and lesbians in each of the discussed types of adoption.

29. Historically, what rights did an unwed father have relative to the adoption of his child and why?

30. How are unwed mothers and unwed fathers treated differently with respect to consent rights? What accounts for this differential treatment?

31. Under what circumstances will an unmarried father be entitled to consent rights?

32. What did the Illinois appeals court decide in the *Baby Richard* case? What did the Illinois Supreme Court decide?

33. Historically, what accounted for the policy against transracial placements? When and why did this policy begin to change?

34. What was the response of the National Association of Black Social Workers to increasing numbers of transracial adoptions? How did agencies respond to their concerns? What concerns have since been raised?

35. Under federal law, what role, if any, can race play in the adoption placement process?

36. What is meant by the concept "adoption abrogation"?

37. What is the tort of wrongful adoption?

## Discussion Questions

1. Should persons who wish to become adoptive parents be screened and subject to either pre- or post-placement studies? Should we subject persons who wish to reproduce biologically to similar requirements? Do you agree with the argument that this differential treatment relegates adoptive families to a second-class status? Do the two situations warrant this differential treatment? Why or why not?

2. The *Baby Richard* case raises difficult questions about the meaning of biological parenthood and the weight that should be given to this connection. Do you think Baby Richard should have been returned to his birth parents, or would you have allowed him to remain with his adoptive parents? Assuming both that the father was wrongfully deprived of his opportunity to develop a relationship with his child and that removing the child from his adoptive family would be harmful to him, how do you go about resolving this case? What factors take precedence? Can a child's best interest and a parent's rights be balanced against each other in order to arrive at a solution?

3. If you were an adoptive parent, how would you feel about an open adoption plan that allowed the child to visit regularly with his or her birth parents? How would you feel about this if you were a birth parent?

4. What role do you think race should play in the formation of adoptive families? What about the sexual orientation of the parents?

5. Do you think safe haven laws make sense? What arguments can you think of in favor of and against this approach?

# **Assignments**

1. Determine whether private placement adoptions are permitted in your jurisdiction. If they are, determine the following by consulting the relevant statutory and/or regulatory provisions:

   a. Are prospective adoptive parents subject to a certification requirement?
   b. Is the use of intermediaries allowed?
   c. If so, are they subject to any legal requirements, such as limitations of fees and costs or accounting requirements?

2. Determine what the rules are in your jurisdiction governing when a parent can revoke his or her consent to an adoption. In developing your answer, please detail both the substantive standards as well as the procedural requirements. To do this, you may need to consult both the relevant statutory and regulatory provisions as well as case law.

3. Locate an adoption agency in your area and interview someone who works there. In your interview, see if you can determine the following:

   a. Does the agency specialize in a particular type of adoption?
   b. How does it screen parents who want to adopt?
   c. What is the cost of a typical adoption?
   d. How long does the typical adoption take?
   e. What areas of inquiry are of particular importance when conducting a home study?
   f. Does the agency ever revoke placements? Under what circumstances?

4. Assume that you are the judge in a *Baby Richard* situation. Please write your opinion setting out how you would decide the case and why.

5. Assume the attorney you work for has asked you to do some research on co-parent adoptions, as he is seeking to file a petition on behalf of one of his clients. As there is no law in your jurisdiction on co-parent

adoptions, he has asked you to locate rulings from other jurisdictions that both permit and deny second-parent adoptions. Carefully read and analyze the cases you have located, and prepare a memorandum setting out the essential reasons behind the court decisions.

## Cases for Analysis

The following case is an important decision involving the constitutionality of a sealed records law. The case highlights the difficulty of sorting out the potentially conflicting interests of parties in what is often referred to as the "adoption triangle."

### ALMA SOCIETY, INC. v. MELLON
**601 F.2d 1225 (2d Cir. 1979)**

This appeal presents the question whether adopted persons upon reaching adulthood ("adult adoptees") are constitutionally entitled, irrespective of a showing of cause, to obtain their sealed adoption records, including the names of their natural parents. Appellants are adult adoptees and an association of such persons; and they urge that the New York statutes that require the sealing of adoption records are . . . invalid on Fourteenth Amendment Due Process and Equal Protection grounds and on further basis that those statutes impose upon them badges or incidents of slavery in violation of the Thirteenth Amendment. The . . . District Court . . . dismissed appellants' complaint. We affirm.

Appellants argue that adult adoptees should be given access to the records of their adoptions with no showing of cause whatsoever. Their supporting affidavits . . . indicate that lack of access to such records causes some of them serious psychological trauma and pain and suffering, may cause in them or their children medical problems or misdiagnoses for lack of history, may create in some persons a consciousness of danger of unwitting incest, and in others a "crisis" of religious identity or what they feel is an impairment of religious freedom because they are unable to be reared in the religion of their natural parents. . . .

The attack upon the New York statutes is three-fold. Appellants first argue that the interests of an adult adoptee in learning from the State (or from agencies acting under compulsion of state law) the identity of his natural family is a fundamental right under the Due Process clause of the Fourteenth Amendment. . . .

Second, appellants argue that adult adoptees constitute a suspect or "quasi-suspect" classification under the Equal Protection clause of the Fourteenth Amendment. Under this view semi-strict or intermediate scrutiny of the New York statutes would be appropriate, and appellants maintain that such a review does not indicate that the statutes are based on sufficiently important state interests.

Finally, appellants argue that the Thirteenth Amendment also applies to this case because the statutes that require sealing of the adoption records as to adults constitute the second of the five incidents of slavery namely, the abolition of the parental relation . . . Under appellants' view, the rights that the Thirteenth Amendment guarantees are not subject to balancing but are instead protected absolutely. We will discuss each of appellants' three arguments in turn.

### SUBSTANTIVE DUE PROCESS

What appellants assert is a right to "personhood." They rely on a series of Supreme Court cases involving familial relationships, rights of family privacy, and freedom to marry and reproduce. As they put it, "an adoptee is someone upon whom the State has, by sealing his records, imposed lifelong familial amnesia . . . injuring the adoptee in regard to his personal identity when he was too young to consent to, or even know, what was happening." . . .

[W]e must look to the nature of the relationships and [recognize] that choices made by those other than the adopted child are involved. . . . [T]he State may take these choices into consideration and protect the natural mother's choice of privacy which not all have forsaken even if appellants are correct, as we are told, that many mothers would be willing in this day and age to have their adult adopted children to contact them. So, too, a state may take into account the relationship of the adopting parents, even if, as appellants assert, many of them would not object to or would even encourage the adopted child's seeking out the identity of or relationship with a natural parent. The New York statutes in providing for release of the information on a "showing of good cause" do no more than to take these other relationships into account. As such they do not unconstitutionally infringe upon or arbitrarily remove appellants' rights of identity, privacy, or personhood. Upon an appropriate showing of psychological trauma, medical need, or of a religious identity crisis though it might be doubted upon a showing of "fear of unconscious incest" the New York courts would appear required under their own statute to grant permission to release all or part of the sealed adoption records.

### EQUAL PROTECTION

Appellants begin their equal protection analysis with the argument that adult adoptees are a suspect classification (and the correlative argument that the State has no compelling interests to support the validity of the sealed records laws). Appellants refer us to Trimble v. Gordon, 430 U.S. 762, 766 (1977), where the Court stated that classifications based on illegitimacy fall in a "realm of less than strictest scrutiny" although the scrutiny "is not a toothless one." By the citation of *Trimble,* appellants suggest that they are at least entitled to the same level of constitutional scrutiny as illegitimates who have been termed a "sensitive" or quasi-suspect category for which the appropriate level of scrutiny is "intermediate," not "strict," . . .

Even assuming that the classification here were subject to intermediate scrutiny, it would not violate equal protection; for we conclude that it is substantially related to an important state interest. . . .

[T]he New York sealed record statutes do not want constitutional validity. The statutes, we think, serve important interests. New York Domestic Relations Law § 114 and its related statutes represent a considered legislative judgment that the confidentiality statutes promote the social policy underlying adoption laws. . . . Moreover, the purpose of a related statute, Section 4138 of the Public Health Laws, was to erase the stigma of illegitimacy from the adopted child's life by sealing his original birth certificate and issuing a new one under his new surname. And the major purpose of adoption legislation is to encourage natural parents to use the process when they are unwilling or unable to care for their offspring. . . . These significant legislative goals clearly justify the State's decision to keep the natural parents' names secret from adopted persons but not from non-adopted persons.

To be sure, once an adopted child reaches adulthood, some of the considerations that apply at the time of adoption and throughout the child's tender years no longer apply or apply with less force. Illegitimacy might stigmatize an adult less than a child, and the goal of encouraging adoption of unwanted and uncared for children might not be significantly affected if adult adoptees could discover their natural parents' identities. But the state does have an interest that does not wane as the adopted child grows to adulthood, namely, the interest in protecting the privacy of the natural parents. . . .

### THIRTEENTH AMENDMENT

Appellants make the novel argument . . . that the Thirteenth Amendment's prohibition of slavery and involuntary servitude gives them an Absolute right to release of their adoption records. . . . The argument is that in abolishing slavery and involuntary servitude the Framers also intended to abolish five "necessary incidents of slavery." We address only the second point because we find that the Amendment is entirely inapplicable to this case.

Appellants refer us particularly to the speech of Senator James Harlan of Iowa of April 6, 1864, in which he set forth a number of such incidents. The second named was

> the abolition practically of the parental relation, robbing the offspring of the care and attention of his parents, severing a relation which is universally cited as the emblem of the relation sustained by the Creator to the human family. And yet, according to the matured judgment of these slave States, this guardianship of the parent over his own children must be abrogated to secure the perpetuity of slavery.

1 B. Schwartz, *supra*, at 72. . . . Appellants liken their situation . . . to that of the antebellum South where a slave child was "sold off" while too young to remember his parents and grew up separated from them by inability to communicate as well as by distance. The analogy according to appellants is that however literate they may be, they cannot write to their natural parents, cannot visit them, and thereby wear a "badge or incident" of slavery. . . .

. . . Although it is doubtless true that an "incident" of slavery (in the original sense) was the abolition of the parental relation, i.e., the offspring of a slave was deprived of the care and attention of parents, . . . the New York sealed records laws do not deprive appellants of their parental relation. It is the New York adoption laws themselves and not the sealed records laws that recognize the divestment by natural parents of their guardianship because of formal surrender, abandonment, or forfeiture by unfitness or jeopardy of the child's best interests; and it is the adoption laws that create a new parent-child relationship between appellants and their adoptive parents. Appellants do not challenge the constitutionality of the adoption laws; thus their challenge to the sealed records laws, even if cognizable under the Thirteenth Amendment in the absence of congressional legislation, is misdirected. Appellants are left to their remedies under the New York statute or with the New York legislature.

## QUESTIONS

1. What statute did the plaintiffs challenge in this case? What harms did the plaintiffs say were caused by this law? What were they seeking?

2. What constitutional arguments did the plaintiffs make in challenging this statute?

3. How did the court respond to each one of the constitutional arguments? What themes run through the court's analysis? What competing interests does the court identify? How does the court balance these considerations?

4. In cases involving important policy issues, courts sometimes suggest possible legislative alternatives. Do you think it would be possible to craft a law that strikes a different balance between the competing interests, or do you think the balance struck by the New York law is the appropriate one?

---

The following leading case is one of the first to permit a same-sex couple to jointly adopt a child, thus giving her two legal mothers.

## ADOPTION OF TAMMY
### 416 Mass. 205, 619 N.E.2d 315 (1993)

In this case, two unmarried women, Susan and Helen, filed a joint petition . . . to adopt as their child Tammy, a minor, who is Susan's biological daughter. . . . Based on her finding that Helen and Susan "are each functioning, separately and together, as the custodial and psychological parents of [Tammy]," and that "it is the best interest of said [Tammy] that she be adopted by both," the judge entered a decree allowing the adoption. . . .

. . . Helen and Susan have lived together in a committed relationship, which they consider to be permanent, for more than ten years. In June, 1983, they jointly purchased a home in Cambridge. Both women are physicians specializing in surgery. . . .

For several years prior to the birth of Tammy, Helen and Susan planned to have a child, biologically related to both of them, whom they would jointly parent. . . . Susan successfully conceived a child through artificial insemination by Helen's biological cousin, Francis. . . .

Since her birth, Tammy has lived with, and been raised and supported by, Helen and Susan. Tammy views both women as her parents, calling Helen "mama" and Susan "mommy." Tammy has strong emotional and psychological bonds with both Helen and Susan. Together, Helen and Susan have provided Tammy with a comfortable home, and have created a warm and stable environment which is supportive of Tammy's growth and over-all well-being. Both women jointly and equally participate in parenting Tammy, and both have a strong financial commitment to her. . . . Francis does not participate in parenting Tammy and does not support her. His intention was to assist Helen and Susan in having a child, and he does not intend to be involved with Tammy, except as a distant relative. Francis signed an adoption surrender and supports the joint adoption by both women.

Helen and Susan, recognizing that the laws of the Commonwealth do not permit them to enter into a legally cognizable marriage, believe that the best interests of Tammy require legal recognition of her identical emotional relationship to both women. Susan expressed her understanding that it may not be in her own best interest to permit Helen to adopt Tammy because, in the event that Helen and Susan separate, Helen would have equal rights to primary custody. Susan indicated, however, that she has no reservation about allowing Helen to adopt. Apart from the emotional security and current practical ramifications which legal recognition of the reality of her parental relationships will provide Tammy, Susan indicated that the adoption is important for Tammy in terms of potential inheritance from Helen. . . .

Over a dozen witnesses, including mental health professionals, teachers, colleagues, neighbors, blood relatives and a priest and nun, testified to the fact that Helen and Susan participate equally in raising Tammy, that Tammy relates to both women as her parents, and that the three form a healthy, happy, and stable family unit. . . .

The Department of Social Services (department) conducted a home study in connection with the adoption petition which recommended the adoption, concluding that "the petitioners and their home are suitable for the proper rearing of this child." . . . A court-appointed guardian ad litem, Dr. Steven Nickman, assistant clinical professor of psychiatry at Harvard Medical School, conducted a clinical assessment of Tammy and her family with a view toward determining whether or not it would be in Tammy's best interests to be adopted by Helen and Susan. . . . Dr. Nickman concluded that "there is every reason for [Helen] to become a legal parent to Tammy just as [Susan] is," and he recommended that the court so order. An attorney appointed to represent Tammy's interests also strongly recommended that the joint petition be granted.

Despite the overwhelming support for the joint adoption and the judge's conclusion that joint adoption is clearly in Tammy's best interests, the question remains whether there is anything in the law of the Commonwealth that would prevent this adoption. . . . The primary purpose of the adoption statute, particularly with regard to children under the age of fourteen, is undoubtedly the advancement of the best interests of the subject child. . . .

1. The initial question is whether the Probate Court judge had jurisdiction under G. L. c. 210 to enter a judgment on a joint petition for adoption brought by two unmarried cohabitants in the petitioner's circumstances. We answer this question in the affirmative.

There is nothing on the face of the statute which precludes the joint adoption of a child by two unmarried cohabitants such as the petitioners. Chapter 210, §1, provides that "[a] person of full age may petition the probate court in the county where he resides for leave to adopt as his child another person younger than himself . . . Other than requiring that a spouse join in the petition, if the petitioner is married and the spouse is competent to join therein, the statute does not expressly prohibit or require joinder by any person. Although the singular "a person" is used, it is a legislatively mandated rule of statutory construction that "words importing the singular number may extend and be applied to several persons" unless the resulting construction is "inconsistent with the manifest intent of the law-making body or repugnant to the context of the same statute." G. L. c. 4, §6 (1992 ed.). In the context of adoption, where the legislative intent to promote the best interests of the child is evidenced throughout the governing statute, and the adoption of a child by two unmarried individuals accomplishes that goal, construing the term "person" as "persons" clearly enhances, rather than defeats, the purpose of the statute. . . .

. . . Adoption will not result in any tangible change in Tammy's daily life; it will, however, serve to provide her with a significant legal relationship which may be important in her future. At the most practical level, adoption will entitle Tammy to inherit from Helen's family trusts and from Helen and her family under the law of intestate succession . . . , to receive support from Helen, who will be legally obligated to provide such support . . . , to be eligible for coverage under Helen's health insurance policies, and to be eligible for social security benefits in the event of Helen's disability or death. . . .

Of equal, if not greater significance, adoption will enable Tammy to preserve her unique filial ties to Helen in the event that Helen and Susan separate, or Susan predeceases Helen.[8] As the case law and commentary on the subject illustrate, when the functional parents of children born in circumstances similar to Tammy separate or one dies, the children often remain in legal limbo for years while their future is disputed in the courts. . . . In some cases, children have been denied the affection of a functional parent who has been with them since birth, even when it is apparent at [sic] this outcome is contrary to the children's best interests. Adoption serves to establish legal rights and responsibilities so that, in the

---

[8] Although Susan has designated Helen guardian of Tammy in her will, Helen's custody of Tammy could conceivably be contested in the event of Susan's death, particularly by Francis, members of his family or members of Susan's family. Absent adoption, Helen would have a dispositive legal right to retain custody of Tammy, because she would be a "legal stranger" to the child.

event that problems arise in the future, issues of custody and visitation may be promptly resolved by reference to the best interests of the child within the recognized framework of the law. . . .

2. The judge also posed the question whether, pursuant to G. L. c. 210, § 6 (1992 ed.), Susan's legal relationship to Tammy must be terminated if Tammy is adopted. Section 6 provides that, on entry of an adoption decree, "all rights, duties and other legal consequences of the natural relation of child and parent shall . . . except as regards marriage, incest or cohabitation, terminate between the child so adopted and his natural parents and kindred." Although G. L. c. 210, § 2, clearly permits a child's natural parent to be an adoptive parent, § 6 does not contain any express exceptions to its termination provision. The Legislature obviously did not intend that a natural parent's legal relationship to its child be terminated when the natural parent is a party to the adoption petition.

Section 6 clearly is directed to the more usual circumstances of adoption, where the child is adopted by persons who are not the child's natural parents (either because the natural parents have elected to relinquish the child for adoption or their parental rights have been involuntarily terminated). The purpose of the termination provision is to protect the security of the child's newly-created family unit by eliminating involvement with the child's natural parents. Although it is not uncommon for a natural parent to join in the adoption petition of a spouse who is not the child's natural parent, . . . the statute has never been construed to require the termination of the natural parent's legal relationship to the child in these circumstances. . . .

3. We conclude that the Probate Court has jurisdiction to enter a decree on a joint adoption petition brought by the two petitioners when the judge has found that joint adoption is in the subject child's best interests. We further conclude that, when a natural parent is[,] a party to a joint adoption petition, that parent's legal relationship to the child does not terminate on entry of the adoption decree. . . .

## QUESTIONS

1. Explain what the court means by the term "joint adoption."

2. Why does the court decide that a joint adoption is in Tammy's best interest?

3. The court looks at whether the Massachusetts adoption law would prohibit this adoption. On what basis does the court determine that

the adoption is permissible? How does the court interpret the term "person" as it is used in the adoption statute?

4. What is the legal significance of permitting the adoption to take place?

5. What question does the court consider with respect to Susan's relationship with Tammy? How does this court resolve this question?

---

This well-publicized case highlights the heartbreaking complexity of cases involving children caught between disputing families. It also reveals the potential vulnerability of immigrant parents who may not fully understand the consequences of their actions because of language barriers or unfamiliarity with local laws and customs.

## IN RE ADOPTION OF A.M.H.
### 215 S.W.3d 793 (Tenn. 2007)

The parents of A.M.H. are citizens of China. Prior to the child's birth, her father, Shao-Qiang ("Jack") was a tenured college professor in China. He moved to the United States on a student visa. . . . In 1997, he enrolled in an economics doctorate program at the University of Memphis and was awarded a scholarship and a graduate assistant position with a stipend. The mother of A.M.H., Qin ("Casey") Luo, although unmarried, obtained a visa as the father's wife. The mother arrived in the United States on June 30, 1998; the parents did not marry immediately. The mother speaks little English and has used an interpreter throughout these proceedings.

The mother became pregnant in July of 1998. Soon after, a student at the University of Memphis filed a complaint with the university alleging that the father had attempted to rape her. Although the father . . . was eventually acquitted by a jury, this charge had severe consequences. Because of the charge, the father was terminated from his graduate assistant position in October of 1998. With no job or stipend, the parents had very little income and no health insurance; in late 1998, they decided to meet with a birth-parent counselor at Mid-South Christian Services (hereinafter "Mid-South"). . . .

On January 28, 1999, A.M.H. was born. Shortly after the birth, the mother told the Mid-South counselor that A.M.H. was not to be placed for adoption. . . . Instead, the parents desired help with the care of their child for six to twelve months while they tried to regain financial stability. Consequently . . . when A.M.H. was four weeks old, the parents went to juvenile court and explained that they could not afford to care for A.M.H. and wanted temporary foster care. . . . [T]he juvenile court officer telephoned Mid-South, which agreed to provide three months of foster care for A.M.H. That same day, the parents entered into an "interim care agreement" with Mid-South that specifically stated that the agreement did not terminate parental rights. A.M.H. was placed in the foster care home of the appellees, Jerry L. Baker and Louise K. Baker, the couple now seeking the termination of parental rights and the adoption of A.M.H. . . .

After placing A.M.H. with the Bakers, the parents visited her regularly in the Bakers' home, consistently bringing food and gifts and taking photographs at every visit. . . .

Because their financial condition was not improving, the parents decided to send A.M.H. to China to have relatives care for her temporarily. The father testified that in May of 1999, Mr. Baker told the father that it was a bad idea to send A.M.H. to China and that the Bakers would keep A.M.H. until the father graduated from the university. . . . According to the Bakers' testimony, because the parents of A.M.H. would not agree to an adoption, they entered into an oral agreement after the father of A.M.H. led them in prayer and the parties discussed the issue. Under the oral agreement, the Bakers would raise A.M.H. until she was eighteen, and the parents of A.M.H. would retain their parental rights. . . .

On June 4, 1999, Mid-South's attorney went with the Bakers and the parents of A.M.H. to the Juvenile Court of Shelby County to obtain a consent order transferring custody of A.M.H. to the Bakers. A juvenile court officer drafted the "Petition for Custody" and a "Consent Order Awarding Custody." . . . The juvenile court officer who drafted the consent order testified that the mother was very concerned that the arrangement be temporary and that the parents would continue to have "open visitation" with A.M.H. through the duration of the Bakers' custody.

Despite the mother's concerns that the arrangement be temporary, the juvenile court officer added a guardianship provision to the consent order so that the Bakers could obtain medical insurance for A.M.H. . . .

The Bakers testified that as part of the custody agreement, the parents agreed that the Bakers would raise A.M.H. until she was eighteen years old and that the child would refer to the Bakers as "mommy" and "daddy." Contrary to the Bakers' testimony, the juvenile court officer testified that the parents were not agreeing that the Bakers could raise A.M.H. until she was eighteen years old. Indeed, the juvenile court officer testified that the mother "was fairly adamant that at some point she wanted her child back." The mother testified as follows: "I was told I can get my daughter back at any time. I asked him three or four times about that." Finally, the juvenile court interpreter, Pastor Kenny Yao, testified that the mother understood the agreement to be temporary and for the purpose of obtaining medical insurance for A.M.H. An order transferring custody and awarding guardianship was entered by consent; there was no court hearing on the matter. . . .

In November of 1999, when A.M.H. was ten months old, the father of A.M.H. asked Mr. Baker to return A.M.H. to the parents' custody. Mr. Baker responded that he and Mrs. Baker did not want to return A.M.H. and told the father not to mention his request to Mrs. Baker because she was pregnant. Mr. Baker also stated that he would hold the father responsible if Mrs. Baker had a miscarriage because she was worried about the custody situation. The father testified that he felt threatened and intimidated. The parents decided to wait for the Bakers' child to be born before pursuing the return of their daughter. The relationship between the parties continued to deteriorate; nevertheless, the parents continued to visit consistently and bring gifts. . . .

On May 3, 2000, the parents went to the Juvenile Court of Shelby County and signed a petition alleging a change in circumstances and seeking custody of A.M.H. . . . At the hearing on June 28, 2000, the Court Appointed Special Advocate submitted a report recommending that the Bakers retain custody and the parents be allowed supervised visitation twice a week for four hours each visit. . . .

The parents did not appeal the custody order. However, they continued to visit their daughter at the Bakers' home despite the increase in animosity between the parties. . . .

Prior to January 28, 2001, A.M.H.'s second birthday, the parents requested to take their daughter for a family picture; they invited the Bakers to go with them and made an appointment at a photography studio. When the parents arrived with their son at the Bakers' home, they were told A.M.H. could not go because she was sick. The father testified to the following:

> Number one that was our child — our first daughter's birthday — second birthday. That was a special day. Number two, according to Chinese culture, on birthday, family picture together is of much significance — whole family. . . . That was such a special day for us. We made appointment. If she was sick . . . why didn't you call me and tell me in advance, one day or two days, so that we made a rescheduled appointment. . . . They knew my phone number. . . . Jerry Baker was so — he was, oh, so upset. He was not very happy. . . . I said, "Today, we cannot accept any more excuses. We want the — we want to take our daughter to the studio for family to get a picture made, period." That's what I said, "Period," and he noticed that I was very pushy, very insistent, and he said, "you've got to leave here. You've got to leave here." I said, "I won't — not today, I won't leave here. Until we have picture made, I won't leave here." And then he said, "I'm going to call the police." I said, "Call the police. I won't leave here."

The police were called, and the officer told the parents not to return to the Bakers' house or they would be arrested. The Bakers' answers to interrogatories state that the parents were instructed by the police "not to return to the home of the Bakers." The police officer testified at trial that, even though it was late afternoon when he arrived at the Bakers' home, he would have told the parents not to return "that day." There were no further visits. On June 20, 2001, four months and five days later, the Bakers filed a petition to terminate parental rights to A.M.H. This four-month lapse in visitation is the ground upon which the chancery court found abandonment of A.M.H. and terminated the parents' rights to their daughter.

Although the parents no longer pursued a relationship with A.M.H. through visits in the Bakers' home, they soon contacted the juvenile court and asked for assistance in regaining custody of A.M.H. . . .

On June 6, 2001, the parents appeared in juvenile court for the hearing on their custody petition. Had the matter been heard that day . . . the four-month period required for statutory abandonment would not have run. The hearing was rescheduled, however, to accommodate the Bakers' attorney. . . . However, two days previously (which was four months and five days after the parents' last visit with A.M.H.), the Bakers had filed a petition for adoption and termination of parental rights in chancery court. Consequently, rather than hear the modification of the custody petition, the juvenile court transferred the custody case to chancery court. . . .

The filing of the petition for adoption and termination of parental rights by the Bakers began chancery court proceedings that would span thirty-two months and generate a technical record containing eleven volumes of motions, responses, and orders. . . . The grounds alleged in the original petition seeking termination of the parents' rights were the parents' abandonment of A.M.H. by willfully failing to visit and the parents' abandonment of A.M.H. by willfully failing to support the child financially. The petition was later amended to assert grounds of termination based on the father's lack of legal status as a parent, the parents' mental incompetence, and the persistence of conditions preventing the child's reunification with the parents. . . .

On February 7, 2002, upon the guardian ad litem's motion, the chancery court ordered the parents to surrender A.M.H.'s passport to the court. The order also appointed the Bakers as A.M.H.'s guardians as defined in section 36-1-102(24) and (25) of the Tennessee Code Annotated and ordered that the parents have no contact with their daughter.

None of the witnesses could explain why the court ordered that the parents have no contact with their daughter. It may have been intended as a means of forcing the parents to surrender A.M.H.'s passport; however, it is also possible that the court ordered no contact upon the advice of the guardian ad litem. The guardian ad litem testified that she did not recommend visitation because "the status quo was that the child had not seen her biological parents in a number of months, I didn't believe that throwing the child into something different than the status quo was necessarily in her best interest." The guardian ad litem continued to oppose visitation and reunification with the parents throughout the proceedings. She believed that A.M.H. was attached to the Bakers and considered them to be her parents, although the guardian ad litem had never seen A.M.H. with her biological parents. She further stated that she had read a book about Chinese girls being placed in orphanages and consequently was concerned that the parents wanted to return to China.

From the very beginning of the case, it was very clear to me that [the parents'] intention was that if the child were returned to them, they wanted to go back to China. They have never said anything different than that. They have always said that when this case is over they would like to take her back. . . . I honestly can't tell the Court today I know to an absolute certainty what kind of life she would have there. This book that I read caused me some concerns. . . .

In July of 2002, Dr. Goldstein submitted a report that found that A.M.H., who by this time was three years old and had not seen her parents in over a year, considered the Bakers her psychological parents and concluded that a child who experiences loss in early childhood is at a greater risk of developing serious psychological disorders. . . .

At the trial, the parents of A.M.H. introduced evidence from . . . a Chinese culture expert. . . .

The Chinese culture expert testified to the importance of "family" to the Chinese and the practice among Chinese students of allowing family members to care for their children temporarily. The chancery court found that the Chinese expert lacked credibility, despite similar testimony given by Pastor Kenny Yao, who the court found to be honest and without bias. Pastor Yao, who served as the mother's interpreter on several occasions (including in juvenile court when the petition to transfer temporary custody to the Bakers was drafted) testified as follows: "There is substantial difference between temporary custody and adoption in the Chinese culture. Adoption is you're giving the parental rights of the baby . . . to someone else . . . . But temporary custody is someone is helping to take care of the baby while you are unable to take care of the baby." He also testified that when the consent order was signed by the mother in juvenile court, he understood and translated the term "temporary custody" to the parents as follows: "[C]ustody means taking care. Temporary means not permanent."

Additionally, the parents introduced expert testimony from Dr. Yih-Jia Chang, who spoke fluent Mandarin Chinese. Dr. Chang performed a psychological evaluation (based on Chinese norms) on A.M.H.'s parents.

She testified that they were both within the normal range. . . . Dr. Chang's report also states that it is a common practice in China for a child to be placed temporarily in the care of extended family. Dr. Chang testified that she believed the evaluations were valid because the answers were consistent with her determinations while meeting with each parent. . . .

After considering this evidence, the chancery court concluded that the parents are manipulative and dishonest people who appeared to have no intent to raise A.M.H. but have used the child from birth for financial gain and to avoid deportation. The chancery court found that the parents willfully abandoned A.M.H. by failing to visit or provide support for the four months immediately preceding the filing of the Bakers' petition to terminate parental rights. The court concluded that it would be in A.M.H.'s best interest to terminate parental rights and allow her to remain with the Bakers. . . .

The Court of Appeals reversed the chancery court's ruling that the parents had abandoned A.M.H. in willfully failing to support her. . . . However, the Court of Appeals affirmed the termination based on the parents' willful failure to visit their daughter for four months and held that termination was in the best interest of A.M.H. . . . Consequently, the sole ground for termination presented in this Court is abandonment grounded on the parents' willful failure to visit A.M.H. for a period of four consecutive months immediately preceding the filing of the petition to terminate parental rights.

### ANALYSIS

Parties seeking to terminate parental rights must prove two elements. First, they have the burden of proving that there exists a statutory ground for termination. Tenn. Code Ann. §36-1-113(c)(1) (2005); Jones v. Garrett, 92 S.W.3d 835, 838 (Tenn. 2002). Second, they must prove that termination of parental rights is in the child's best interest. Tenn. Code Ann. §36-1-113(c)(2) (2005); In re F.R.R., III, 193 S.W.3d 528, 530 (Tenn. 2006). . . .

### TERMINATION OF PARENTAL RIGHTS

The sole ground for termination presented in this appeal is the parents' willful abandonment of A.M.H. by failing to visit her for four months preceding the filing of the termination petition. It is well established that both the United States and Tennessee Constitutions protect parents' rights to the custody and care of their children. See Hawk v. Hawk, 855 S.W.2d 573, 578-79 (Tenn. 1993) ("[P]arental rights constitute a fundamental liberty interest."). Therefore, before a parent's rights to a child may be terminated by a court, "there must be a showing that the parent is unfit or that substantial harm to the child will result if parental rights are not terminated." In re Swanson, 2 S.W.3d 180, 188 (Tenn. 1999). By statute, the legislature has designated "abandonment" as a valid ground for the termination of parental rights. . . .

A parent who has abandoned a child by "willfully" failing to visit is "unfit" under constitutional standards. In re Swanson, 2 S.W.3d at 188. Therefore, under those circumstances, termination of parental rights is appropriate. See, e.g., In re F.R.R., 193 S.W.3d at 530. Where the failure to visit is not willful, however, a failure to visit a child for four months does not constitute abandonment. We have held that a parent who attempted to visit and maintain relations with his child, but was thwarted by the acts of others and circumstances beyond his control, did not willfully abandon his child. See In re Swanson, 2 S.W.3d at 189.

Here, we are presented with a situation in which the parents of A.M.H. actively pursued legal proceedings to regain custody of A.M.H. during the "abandonment" period but failed to visit for a period of four consecutive months immediately prior to the filing of a petition for termination of parental rights. . . . We hold that the evidence in this case does not support a finding that the parents intentionally abandoned A.M.H.

Disregarding the witnesses that the trial court found to lack credibility, the record clearly shows the following undisputed facts:

(1) On January 28, 2001, the parents visited A.M.H. in the home of the Bakers;

(2) The parents became upset when they could not take A.M.H. with them to sit for a family portrait;

(3) The parents refused to leave A.M.H. until a police officer arrived and told them to leave;

(4) During the subsequent four months and five days prior to the filing of the petition for termination, the parents pursued help in regaining the custody of their child by contacting the juvenile court and the local media;

(5) During this time, the parents initiated two juvenile court hearings on a petition to regain custody of A.M.H.;

(6) The first hearing was thwarted by the Bakers' request for a continuance; and

(7) The second hearing was thwarted by the Bakers' initiation of proceedings in chancery court.

This undisputed evidence does not support a finding that the parents' failure to visit A.M.H. was willful. Where, as here, the parents' visits with their child have resulted in enmity between the parties and where the parents redirect their efforts at maintaining a parent-child relationship to the courts the evidence does not support a "willful failure to visit" as a ground for abandonment. . . . Therefore, we hold that there has been no willful abandonment and reverse the termination of parental rights. Accordingly, the Petition for Adoption and Termination of Parental Rights is dismissed. . . .

When this Court reverses a lower court's termination of parental rights in a contest between parents and non-parents for custody, we usually remand the case to the trial court for the preparation and implementation of a plan to return custody of the child to the parent. In this case, however, we must first address the consent order entered by the juvenile court in June of 1999 that transferred the custody and guardianship of A.M.H. to the Bakers. Unless we conclude that the consent order is unenforceable, the parents of A.M.H. have no superior rights to the custody of A.M.H. The parents argue that the consent order is unenforceable and ask that they be granted custody. . . .

The evidence establishes that the parents were misled as to the consequences of a change in custody and uninformed about the guardianship provision and, therefore, did not enter into the agreement with knowledge of the consequences of the transfer of custody and guardianship. . . .

This evidence overwhelmingly shows that the parents' voluntary relinquishment of custody was entered as a temporary measure to provide health insurance for A.M.H. with the full intent that custody would be returned. Therefore, we hold that the parents of A.M.H. did not voluntarily transfer custody and guardianship of A.M.H. to the Bakers with knowledge of the consequences and, therefore, are entitled to superior rights to custody. . . .

Accordingly, we hereby revoke the parental consent to the change of custody and guardianship, and consider the competing claims of the parties, giving due deference to the parents' superior rights to the care and custody of A.M.H.

Under the superior rights doctrine, "a natural parent may only be deprived of custody of a child upon a showing of substantial harm to the child." In re Askew, 993 S.W.2d 1, 4 (Tenn. 1999). Therefore, the determination of a custodial dispute between a parent and a non-parent rests on a determination of whether there is substantial harm threatening a child's welfare if the child returns to the parents. Only then may a court find a sufficiently compelling justification for the infringement of the parents' fundamental right to raise a child as they see fit. See id. at 3.

Here, the only evidence of substantial harm arises from the delay caused by the protracted litigation and the failure of the court system to protect the parent-child relationship throughout the proceedings. Evidence that A.M.H. will be harmed from a change in custody because she has lived and bonded with the Bakers cannot constitute the substantial harm required to prevent the parents from regaining custody. . . .

Additionally, we note that the testimony concerning the general conditions in China is not relevant to a finding of substantial harm. Financial advantage and affluent surroundings simply may not be a consideration in determining a custody dispute between a parent and a non-parent. . . . "[M]ere improvement in quality of life is not a compelling state interest and is insufficient to justify invasion of Constitutional rights." (internal quotation marks and citation omitted). The evidence at trial showed that the parents have overcome many obstacles to achieve financial stability and are ably taking care of their other two children. Given the lack of evidence of a threat of substantial harm to A.M.H. if she is returned to her parents, we conclude that physical custody of A.M.H. must be returned to the parents. . . .

The Juvenile Court of Shelby County is directed to consider, prepare, and implement a plan to resolve the pending custody matter with a view toward reunification of A.M.H. with her natural parents, Shao-Qiang ("Jack") He and Qin ("Casey") Luo, in a manner that minimizes trauma to the child.

## QUESTIONS

1. Explain the various stages in this case.

2. What was the issue before the appeals court?

3. What legal standard did the court use in deciding to return A.M.H. to her biological parents? Why?

4. What role do you think cultural differences played in this case?

**Endnotes** ——————————————————————————————

1. C. M. A. McCauliff, The First English Adoption Law and Its American Precursors, 16 Seton Hall L. Rev. 656, 657-659 (1986); Stephen B. Presser, The Historical Background of the American Law of Adoption, 11 J. Fam. L. 443, 445-448 (1971).

2. McCauliff, *supra* note 1, at 659-665; Presser, *supra* note 1, at 448-456.

3. Catherine J. Ross, Welfare Reform and Juvenile Courts: Families Without Paradigms: Child Poverty and Out-of-House Placements in Historical Perspective, 60 Ohio St. L.J. 1249, 1257-1258 (1999).

4. *Id.* at 1258-1259.

5. McCauliff, *supra* note 1, at 659-665; Presser, *supra* note 1, at 448-456.

6. Presser, *supra* note 1, at 465 (citing Act of 1851, ch. 324).

7. Presser, *supra* note 1, at 465-480. *See also* Michael Grossberg, Governing the Hearth — Law and the Family in Nineteenth-Century America 259-269 (1985).

8. For a discussion of some of the complexities of safe haven laws, *see* Jeffrey A. Parness, Deserting Mothers, Abandoned Babies, Lost Fathers: Dangers in Safe Havens, 24 Quinnipiac L. Rev. 335 (2006); Carol Sanger, Infant Safe Haven Laws: Legislating in the Culture of Life, 106 Colum. L. Rev. 753 (2006); Dayna R. Cooper, Fathers Are Parents Too: Challenging Safe Haven Laws with Procedural Due Process, 31 Hofstra L. Rev. 877 (2003); Michael S. Raum and Jeffrey L. Skaare, Encouraging Abandonment: The Trend Towards Allowing Parents to Drop Off Unwanted Newborns, 76 N.D. L. Rev. 511 (2000).

9. For further detail on the process, *see* Joan Heifetz Hollinger ed., Adoption Law and Practice (2000).

10. For a thoughtful discussion of some the complexities inherent in the consent process, *see* Elizabeth J. Samuels, Time to Decide? The Laws Governing Mothers' Consents to the Adoption of Their Newborn Infants, 72 Tenn. L. Rev. 509 (2005).

11. Courts in several states have recently grappled with the complex interplay between termination and adoption proceedings in situations where the adoption of a child was approved while a parent's appeal of the termination of her parental rights was under review. For a discussion of these cases, *see* Kate M. Heideman, Avoiding the Need to "Unscramble the Egg:" A Proposal for the Automatic Stay of Subsequent Adoption Proceedings When Parents Appeal a Judgment Terminating Their Parental Rights, 24 St. Louis U. Pub. L. Rev. 445 (2005).

12. Many of these children may be classified as having "special needs," thus making prospective adoptive parents eligible for financial assistance under the federal Adoption Assistance and Child Welfare Assistance Act, as well as under various state adoption assistance programs.

13. *See* Elizabeth Bartholet, Family Bonds Adoption and the Politics of Parenting ch. 5 (1993).

14. *Id.* at 33-34.

15. In interstate cases, the applicable jurisdictional requirements of PKPA, the UCCJA, and the UCCJEA must be complied with. For a general discussion of

these Acts, see Chapter 9 of this book; for adoption specifics, *see* Hollinger, *supra* note 10, ch. 4.

16. It should, however, be pointed out that the adoption process was initially more open, and that the emphasis on secrecy emerged over the course of the twentieth century as adoption became a more regulated practice. For further detail on both this history and some of the debates over open adoption, *see* Amanda C. Pustinik, Private Ordering, Legal Ordering, and the Getting of Children: A Counterhistory of Adoption Law, 20 Yale L. & Policy Rev. 263 (2002); Jennifer R. Racine, A Fundamental Rights Debate: Should Wisconsin Allow Adult Adoptees Unconditional Access to Adoption Records and Original Birth Certificates?, 2002 Wis. L. Rev. 1453; Heidi Hildebrand, Because They Want to Know: An Examination of the Legal Rights of Adoptees and Their Parents, 24 S. Ill. U. L.J. 515 (2000); Naomi Cahn and Jana Singer, Adoption, Identity, and the Constitution: The Case for Opening Closed Records, 2 U. Pa. J. Const. L. 150 (1999); Lucy S. McGough and Annette Peltier-Falahahwazi, Secrets and Lies: A Model for Cooperative Adoption, 60 La. L. Rev. 13 (1999).

17. McGough and Peltier-Falahahwazi, *supra* note 16, at 41.

18. Although the term "open adoption" is usually identified with post-adoption arrangements, in a broader sense the term also applies to pre-adoption processes in situations where the birth parents and the prospective adoptive parents meet, share information, and, if the placement is agreed upon, determine how the post-adoption contact is to be structured.

19. *See* McCough and Peltier-Falahahwaze, *supra* note 16 at 56-71.

20. Access to Adoption Records, Child Welfare Information Gateway, http://www.childwelfare.gov (accessed March 3, 2007).

21. *See* Rosemary Cabellero, Open Records Adoption: Finding the Missing Piece, 30 S. Ill. U.L.J. 291 (2006); Caroline B. Fleming, The Open-Records Debate: Balancing the Interests of Birth Parents and Adult Adoptees, 11 Wm. & Mary J. of Women & L. 461 (2005).

22. Child Welfare Information Gateway, Gay and Lesbian Adoptive Parents: Resources for Professionals and Parents, p. 9 (2000), quoting Bob Diamond, a former Executive Director of Aid to Adoption of Special Kids, of Northern California, available on: http://www.childwelfare.gov/adoption/types/families/gay.cfm (accessed May 16, 2007).

23. *Id.* (citing psychologist April Martin, author of the Lesbian and Gay Parenting Handbook (1993)).

24. In re Adoption of Evan, 153 Misc.2d 844, 583 N.Y.S.2d 997, 998-999 (Sur. Ct. 1992). *See also* Adoption of Tammy, 416 Mass. 205, 619 N.E.2d 315 (Mass. 1993); B.L.U.B. & E.L.V.B., 628 A.2d 1271 (Vt. 1993); In re Jacob, 660 N.E.2d 397 (N.Y. 1995).

25. As quoted in: Lisa S. Chen, Second-Parent Adoptions: Are They Entitled to Full Faith and Credit?, 46 Santa Clara L. Rev. 171, 173 (2005).

26. Finstuen v. Edmondson, Civ.04-1152-C (W.D. Oklahoma 2004).

27. For an excellent analysis of these issues, *see* Mary L. Shanley, Unwed Fathers' Rights, Adoption, and Sex Equality: Gender-Neutrality and the Perpetuation of Patriarchy, 95 Colum. L. Rev. 60 (1995) (contains comprehensive citations

to other related articles); Deborah L. Forman, Unwed Fathers and Adoption: A Theoretical Analysis in Context, 72 Tex. L. Rev. 967 (1994).

28. *See* Robbin Pott Gonzalez, The Rights of Putative Fathers to Their Infant Children in Contested Adoptions: Strengthening State Laws that Currently Deny Adequate Protection, 13 Mich. J. Gender & L. 39 (2006); Kimberly Barton, Who's Your Daddy?: State Adoption Statutes and the Unknown Biological Father, 32 Cap. U. L. Rev. 113 (2003); Mary Beck, Towards a National Putative Father Registry, 25 Harv. J.L. & Pub. Poly. 1031 (2002); Rebecca Aizporu, Protecting the Unwed Father's Opportunity to Parent: A Survey of Paternity Registry Statutes, 18 Rev. Litig. 703 (1999).

29. *See* Cooper, *supra* note 8, at 896-901.

30. The name of the case is actually In re Doe. The citation for the appeals court decision is 254 Ill. App. 3d 405, 627 N.E.2d 648 (1993). The citation for the Illinois Supreme Court decision is 159 Ill. 2d 347, 638 N.E.2d 181 (1994).

31. In re Doe, 627 N.E.2d at 651-652.

32. In re Doe, 638 N.E.2d at 182-183.

33. Most of the debate has focused on the adoption of black children by white families, and this chapter's discussion is based on the literature on this subject. Many of the same considerations will be present, though, whenever an adoption crosses racial or ethnic lines. *See* Stephanie R. Richardson, Strict Scrutiny, Biracial Children and Adoption, 12 B.U. Pub. Int. L.J. 203 (2002); Kim Forde-Mazrui, Black Identity and Child Placement: The Best Interests of Black and Biracial Children, 92 Mich. L. Rev. 925 (1994) (discusses placement issues relative to biracial children); Margaret Howard, Transracial Adoption: Analysis of the Best Interest Standard, 59 Notre Dame L. Rev. 503 (1984) (examines concerns relative to the placement of Native American children).

34. For detail, *see* Howard, *supra* note 33, at 505-516; Cynthia G. Hawkins-Leon and Carla Bradley, Mid-Atlantic People of Color Legal Scholarship Conference: Race and Transracial Adoption: The Answer Is Neither Simply Black Nor White or Wrong, 51 Cath. U. L. Rev. 1227 (2002); Valerie Phillips Herman, Transracial Adoption: "Child-Saving" or "Child-Snatching," 13 Natl. Black L.J. 147 (1993).

35. The gap between the number of black children needing homes and available black adoptive parents has been attributed in part to the failure of agencies to recruit black parents and to the use of screening criteria that are weighted in favor of white families. *See* Hawkins-Leon and Bradley, *supra* note 34, at 1233-1238; Howard, *supra* note 33, at 513-514; Herman, *supra* note 34, at 157-158.

36. National Association of Black Social Workers, Position Paper (Summer 1972), *reprinted in* Forde-Mazrui, *supra* note 33, at 926.

37. *See* the Multiethnic Placement Act of 1994, Pub. L. No. 103-382, 108 Stat. 405, *as amended by* the Removal of Barriers to Interethnic Adoption Provisions of the Small Business Job Protection Act of 1996, Pub. L. No. 104-188, 110 Stat. 1755, § 1808. For detail on these laws, *see* Elizabeth Bartholet, Taking Adoption Seriously: Radical Revolution or Modest Revisionism?, 28 Cap. U. L. Rev. 77 (1999).

# Glossary

**Abuse.** Usually refers to the causing of physical harm within the context of familial or other intimate relationships; may also refer to inappropriate sexual contact (sexual abuse) or emotionally destructive conduct (emotional abuse).

**Abuse prevention laws.** Laws that enable domestic violence victims to obtain emergency protective orders.

**Abuse reporting laws.** Laws that establish a mechanism for the reporting of suspected cases of child abuse and/or neglect to a state protective agency. *See also* Mandatory reporter; Permissive reporter.

**Acceptance of service.** Assent by a defendant to being presented with the summons and complaint, and the defendant's willing acknowledgment of the receipt of the same.

**Acknowledgment of paternity.** Voluntary acknowledgment by the parents of the paternity of the father. This is accomplished through the completion of a notarized paternity affidavit.

**Active listening.** An engaged way of listening, involving reflection back of informational and emotional content.

**Adjudication of paternity.** Paternity determined through a court action.

**Adoption.** The legal process by which someone becomes a parent to a child with whom he or she does not have a biological relationship and assumes all the rights and responsibilities of parenthood. Adoption is premised on the termination of rights in the biological parents unless a co-parent or a stepparent is adopting the child, in which case the parental rights of that party's partner will remain in effect. *See also* Adult adoption; Agency adoption; Independent adoption; Open adoption; Transracial adoption.

**Adoption abrogation.** The undoing of an adoption by the adoptive parent(s).

**Adoption placement.** *See* Preadoptive placement.

**Adult adoption.** The adoption of one adult by another.

**Adultery.** Voluntary sexual intercourse between a married person and someone who is not his or her spouse; a fault divorce ground.

**Affidavit.** A factual statement that is signed under the penalties of perjury; often submitted to a court in support of a motion.

**Affirmative defense for relief.** A response to an allegation in a complaint in which the defendant seeks to establish that the plaintiff is not entitled to recover on his or her claim.

**Age of capacity.** The minimum age below which a young person may not marry — commonly set at age 14.

657

**Age of consent.** The age at which a young person becomes eligible to consent to his or her own marriage — usually set at the age of majority.

**Agency adoption.** As distinct from an independent adoption, an adoption that is handled by a state or private agency. A key component of these adoptions is that a home study is done prior to the placement of a child with a prospective adoptive family.

**Alimony.** *See* Spousal support.

**Alimony in Gross.** Sometimes referred to as a lump-sum support payment. Unlike permanent alimony, it involves the payment of a sum certain; it is generally paid in a single installment, although it can also be made payable in periodic installments until the full amount of the order is reached.

**Alimony pendente lite.** Temporary support paid to one spouse by the other during the pendency of a divorce.

**All property.** States that allow a couple's accumulated assets to be distributed at divorce without a formal distinction between separate property and marital property.

**Annulment.** A decree establishing that a husband and wife were never actually married because an impediment existed at the time the marriage was celebrated.

**Answer.** The pleading filed by a defendant in response to a plaintiff's complaint, in which he or she seeks to avoid liability; component parts include responses to the plaintiff's factual allegations, affirmative defenses, and counterclaims.

**Appeal.** Resort to an appellate court for review of a lower court decision; usually involves questions of law rather than of fact.

**Appellate court.** A court with jurisdiction to review lower-court decisions.

**Appreciation.** The increase in value of an asset.

**Arbitration.** A dispute resolution mechanism whereby parties agree to submit their disagreement to a neutral decision maker. The arbitrator's authority derives from the party's agreement, and his or her decision is usually binding subject to a limited right of court review.

**Arrearage.** Money that is overdue or unpaid; in this context, an outstanding support obligation.

**At-risk placement.** An adoption placement that is made before the rights of both parents have been terminated.

**Attorney's fees.** An order of the court requiring one side to pay all or a portion of the other side's legal fees where one party lacks the resources to retain an attorney or as a punitive measure, often pursuant to a contempt proceeding.

**Attributed income.** *See* Imputed income.

**Bankruptcy.** The filing of a court action in which a party seeks to be discharged from responsibility for paying his or her debts.

**Batterer Intervention Program.** A treatment or counseling program that works specifically with batterers.

**Best interest.** The predominant legal standard for resolving custody disputes between parents; the standard is child-centered, focusing on the needs of the child rather than on the rights of the parents.

**Bigamy.** The unlawful act of contracting a second marriage while one or both of the partners is already married to someone else.

**Change in circumstances.** A future event that arguably makes an existing order unfair and serves as the basis for a request for modification.

**Child protection agency.** Usually a state agency with responsibility for handling cases of child abuse and neglect.

**Child support.** The duty of financial support owed by a noncustodial parent to his or her minor children and to children over the age of majority in limited situations, such as in cases of disability.

**Child support guidelines.** Mandated by federal law, guidelines employing numeric criteria used to calculate the amount of child support to be paid by the non-custodial parent; under certain circumstances, deviations from the resulting amount may be allowed.

**Child Tax Credit.** Credit against tax liability provided to parents. Available to the parent with the dependency exemption.

**Civil union.** A formal status that provides same-sex couples with the rights, benefits, protections, and responsibilities that are available to married heterosexual couples under state (but not federal) law.

**Clean break.** Refers to the view that upon divorce, obligations stemming from the marriage should be kept to a minimum, leaving each partner free to start life anew unencumbered by claims from the past.

**Cohabitation.** Two unmarried persons living together in an intimate relationship. The term applies to both same-sex and heterosexual couples.

**Collaborative Law Model.** An approach to the practice of law that stresses cooperation and the avoidance of litigation.

**Collusion.** Agreement by a couple to obtain a divorce in avoidance of the fault principle that requires a guilty and an innocent spouse.

**Common law.** The law of England as accepted by the colonies prior to the American Revolution; also refers to judge-made law.

**Common law marriage.** A marriage created by the conduct of the parties rather than through a formal ceremony. Creation usually requires agreement, cohabitation, and a reputation in the community as husband and wife.

**Community property.** A system of property ownership between husband and wife in civil law jurisdictions in which each spouse has a vested one-half ownership interest in all marital property regardless of title; excluded is all property classified as separate property.

**Comparative rectitude.** A doctrine that ameliorates the harsh effects of the traditional divorce defense of recrimination by allowing a divorce when one party's marital fault is regarded as less serious than the other party's.

**Compelling state interest.** A governmental interest of sufficient magnitude that it may justify limitations on fundamental rights.

**Complaint.** In a civil case, the pleading filed by the plaintiff to initiate a lawsuit; includes factual allegations, a statement of legal claims against the defendant, and a request for relief; called **petition** in some states.

**Complaint for Contempt.** A parent's return to court following a divorce, to enforce existing arrangements about custody or visitation arrangements after a dispute.

**Complaint for Modification.** A parent's return to court following a divorce, to change existing arrangements about custody or visitation arrangements after a dispute.

**Condonation.** A divorce defense, the essence of which is that the plaintiff has forgiven the acts of marital misconduct upon which his or her complaint for divorce is based.

**Confidentiality.** An ethical rule prohibiting attorneys and persons working with them from disclosing client information, except under limited circumstances such as to prevent the commission of a serious crime.

**Connivance.** A divorce defense, the essence of which is that the plaintiff consented to the wrongdoing upon which his or her complaint for divorce is based.

**Consent.** Relative to adoption law, the requirement that a biological parent must assent to the adoption of his or her child, unless his or her parental rights have been terminated.

**Consideration.** The bargained-for exchange that underlies the formation of an enforceable contract; consideration serves to distinguish a contract from a promise.

**Constructive desertion.** Imputes the act of desertion to the spouse responsible for the other's departure.

**Constructive service.** Service of a summons and complaint on a defendant in a manner other than by delivering it to him or her in person, usually by publication and/or mailing.

**Contempt proceeding.** A proceeding against a party who is in violation of a court order; contempt proceedings can be either civil or criminal in nature. The purpose of a civil contempt action is to obtain compliance with a court order, while the purpose of a criminal contempt action is to punish a party for his or her noncompliance.

**Continuing jurisdiction.** In the custody context, the continuation of the initial decree state's authority to modify a decree to the exclusion of other states.

**Contract.** A legally enforceable agreement between two or more parties. *See also* Express contract; Implied-in-fact contract; Implied-in-law contract; Quasi-contract.

**Co-parent.** A parent who shares the raising of a child with his or her partner in the absence of a formally recognized parent-child relationship.

**Co-parent adoption.** Adoption by a co-parent (*see above*); here, the adoption does not extinguish the rights of the biological parent.

**Cost basis.** The cost of an asset, used to calculate the amount of appreciation from the time of purchase.

**Counterclaim.** A claim made by the defendant against the plaintiff; in effect, roles are reversed: the defendant assumes the role of plaintiff, and vice versa.

**Covenant marriage.** Developed in response to concerns about the prevalence and impact of divorce, convenant marriage law emphasize the permanency of marriage and limit the availability of divorce.

**Credit reporting.** In the child support context, the provision of information to a credit agency about a party's failure to make child support payments.

**Criminal nonsupport.** The willful failure to pay child support when one has the ability to do so; may also apply to the willful failure to pay spousal support.

**Cruelty.** A fault ground for divorce based on mistreatment of a relatively serious nature; cruelty generally can include either physical or emotional wrongdoing.

**Custody.** Broadly, the care of and responsibility for a child. *See also* Joint custody; Legal custody; Physical custody; Sole custody.

**Cut-off rule.** Principle that operates to extinguish the parental rights of the biological parents at the time of adoption; may not be applied when a step-parent or a co-parent is adopting the child.

**Cyberstalking.** The use of the internet or other mode of electronic communication to threaten or harass someone.

**De Facto parent.** An individual who has no biological relation to a child, but who has functioned as a family member; must show that they resided with the child and shared caretaking responsibilities with the consent and cooperation of the legal parent.

**Decree *nisi*.** A provisional judgment of divorce that automatically ripens into the final divorce decree absent a challenge or decision by the parties to vacate the divorce.

**Default judgment.** A judgment entered against a defendant who fails to respond to a complaint or otherwise defend the action.

**Defense of Marriage Act (DOMA).** A federal statute that allows states to deny recognition to marriages between same-sex partners that were validly entered into in a sister state. Additionally, DOMA, for purposes of federal law, restricts the definition of marriage to heterosexual couples.

**Dependency exemption.** Deduction that a taxpayer can take from gross income for a person who is principally dependent on the taxpayer for support.

**Dependency proceeding.** A court process to determine if a child's parents lack the present ability to care for him or her, may result in a transfer of custody to the state.

**Deponent.** The person whose deposition is being taken.

**Deposition.** A method of discovery in which the oral testimony of a witness is obtained through questions that are answered under oath.

**Desertion.** A fault ground for divorce; involves the voluntary, nonconsensual departure of one spouse without justification for a period of time defined by statute.

**Diminished earning capacity.** A decrease in a spouse's earning potential due to a lack of a sustained connection with the paid workplace, usually because of domestic responsibilities.

**Discovery.** The process by which each side is able to acquire information from the other side in advance of trial. *See also* Deposition; Interrogatories; Request for admissions; Request for physical and mental examination; Request for production of documents.

**Discovery conference.** A meeting at which the court develops a plan for how discovery will proceed in a case.

**Dispensing with parental consent.** In the course of an adoption proceeding, a decision by the court to proceed with the adoption without the consent of the parents based on a finding of parental unfitness.

**Divisible divorce.** A divorce in which the court has jurisdiction to dissolve the marriage based on a party's domicile but cannot resolve support and property matters because it lacks personal jurisdiction over the defendant.

**Divorce.** The legal dissolution of a marital relationship, such that the parties are no longer husband and wife. *See also* Divisible divorce; *Divorce a mensa et thoro*; Fault divorce; No-fault divorce.

*Divorce a mensa et thoro.* A common law term meaning a "divorce from board and bed"; this is a decree of separation that permits a husband and wife to live apart without dissolving the marital relationship.

**Divorce hearing.** The court hearing at which a marriage is dissolved and collateral issues resolved; results in a divorce judgment. If the case is uncontested, the hearing is usually simple; the judge will inquire into the circumstances underlying the request for divorce and review the parties' separation agreement. If the case is contested, a trial on the merits will be conducted.

**Divorce judgment.** The court decree that dissolves the marriage; a decree *nisi* may be entered initially.

**Docket number.** The number assigned to each case by the court; the number is used for organizational and reference purposes and is included on all papers filed in a case.

**Domestic partnership.** Usually refers to a municipal ordinance enabling unmarried couples to register as domestic partners; provides some legal recognition and possible eligibility for benefits. Domestic partnerships are also recognized by some private employers.

**Domestic violence.** Abusive behavior toward someone with whom one is in a dating, familial, household, or intimate relationship. *See also* Intimate Partner Violence.

**Domicile.** A person's permanent home; the place to which the person intends to return when away.

**Donor insemination.** The process by which a woman is inseminated with or inseminates herself with sperm contributed by a donor, who may be known or unknown.

**Dual property.** States that distinguish between marital property and separate property for distribution purposes.

**Due process clause.** A clause found in both the fifth and fourteenth amendments to the U.S. Constitution that protects persons from arbitrary or intrusive governmental actions. The clause provides both procedural protections and substantive rights.

**Economic self-sufficiency.** The idea that after a divorce, both spouses should become self-supporting as quickly as possible.

**Emancipation.** The point at which a child is no longer considered a dependent of his or her parents; generally occurs at the age of majority or upon the occurrence of certain acts, such as marriage of the child.

**Emergency jurisdiction.** A jurisdictional ground that permits a court to assert jurisdiction over a custody dispute when a child is physically present in the state and has been abandoned or needs immediate protection from abuse or neglect.

**Enhanced earning capacity.** An increase in a spouse's earning ability attributable to a marital division of labor which enabled that spouse to concentrate on career development without major domestic responsibilities.

**Equal protection clause.** A clause in the fourteenth amendment to the U.S. Constitution that prevents states from imposing arbitrary and discriminatory legislative classifications.

**Equitable distribution.** The division of property at divorce based principally on considerations of fairness and contribution rather than title.

**Equitable parenthood.** A doctrine used to extend parenting rights to a stepparent when there is a developed, consensual relationship between the child and the stepparent, and he or she wishes to assume the rights and responsibilities of parenthood; may also be applicable when a co-parent is seeking custodial or visitation rights.

**Ex parte.** A hearing that is held without prior notice to the other side due to the urgent nature of the proceeding or the harm that such notice would cause.

**Express contract.** A contract that is created by the actual, articulated agreement of the parties. *See also* Implied-in-fact contract.

**Extraordinary expenses.** Large, discrete expenditures that do not recur on a regular basis, as distinct from the day-to-day expenses of raising a child.


**Fair market value.** The price that a willing buyer would pay to a willing seller when neither party is under compulsion to buy or sell.

**Family Preservation.** "Reasonable efforts" to keep a family together before removing a child from the home and placing him or her in foster care and reasonable efforts to reunite the child with his or her family.

**Fault divorce.** A divorce that is premised on the marital fault of one spouse.

**Federal Marriage Amendment (FMA).** An amendment first introduced in Congress in 2003, stating that "[m]arriage in the United States shall consist only of the union of a man and a woman," and the FMA would prevent either the federal or any state constitution from being construed to require that "marriage or the legal incidents thereof be conferred upon any union other than the union of a man and a woman."

**Filing fee.** The administrative fee charged by a court for the filing of an action.

**Financial affidavit.** A document that discloses income and assets, which parties must complete in family court proceedings where property or support is at issue.

**Foster care.** The taking in and caring for a child who is unable to live at home, usually because of parental abuse and/or neglect.

**IV-D agency.** Under Title IV-D, the agency in each state responsible for administering that state's child support program.

**Freedom of contract.** The right of each individual to freely structure his or her own affairs.

**Genetic testing.** Performed when paternity is contested; can be done through a cheek swab and can prove or disprove paternity with virtual certainty. Unless an objection is made, the tests must be admissible without foundation testimony or proof of authenticity.

**Gift.** A voluntary transfer of property made with donative intent, meaning that the gift-giver (donor) simply wishes to give the recipient something without requiring anything in exchange. For a gift to be effective, the transfer must be complete — the donor must fully relinquish all vestiges of ownership and control.

**Goodwill.** An intangible asset, the good reputation of a business in the community that generates future patronage.

**Guardian ad litem.** A person who is appointed by a court to conduct a custody investigation; may also refer to a person appointed to provide legal representation to a child.

**Home state jurisdiction.** A jurisdictional ground that enables a state to assert jurisdiction over a custody dispute based on the fact that the child lives or had lived in that state for the six months prior to the initiation of the action.

**Home study.** An evaluation of a person or couple seeking to adopt a child to determine potential suitability, usually done only in agency adoptions.

**Illegitimate.** An outdated term for a child born to unmarried parents.

**Implied-in-fact contract.** A contract that is inferred from the conduct of the parties. *See also* Express contract.

**Imputed/attributed income.** The attribution of income to a party who is deliberately un- or underemployed, based on earning capacity, for the purpose of establishing the amount of his or her support obligation.

**Inception of title rule.** A rule fixing title at the time an asset is acquired.

**Incest.** Unlawful sexual relations between persons who are closely related to each other; marriages contracted in violation of incest provisions are invalid.

**Incorporation.** In the divorce context, upon approval of a separation agreement, the inclusion of its terms into the divorce judgment such that those terms become part of the judgment. *See also* Merger; Survival.

**Independent adoption.** An adoption that is accomplished without an agency; parents can either place the child directly or utilize an intermediary.

**Indissoluble.** In reference to marriage, the belief that the legal relationship between a husband and wife is permanent and can never be terminated.

**Initial custody determination.** The first custody decision in a case, as distinct from subsequent modifications.

**In loco parentis.** Common law doctrine conferring parental rights and responsibilities on someone who voluntarily assumes a parenting role.

**Innocent spouse.** Pertaining to fault divorce, the requirement that the petitioning spouse not have engaged in marital misconduct.

**In rem jurisdiction.** The authority of a court to resolve a case based on the presence of property within its borders.

**Intangible assets.** Property that lacks a physical presence and cannot be ascertained by the senses.

**Interrogatories.** A discovery method involving written questions to a party, which must be answered under oath.

**Intimate partner violence.** Violence between partners who are in a same-sex or heter-sexual relationship, including dating relationships. *See also* domestic violence.

**Irreconcilable differences.** A no-fault divorce ground, the essence of which is that the parties are no longer compatible and there is no hope of reconciliation.

**Joint custody.** As distinct from sole custody, the sharing of parental rights and responsibilities — can apply to legal or physical custody, or both.

**Joint petition.** A pleading filed in a no-fault divorce action by co-petitioners to initiate the divorce.

**Judgment.**

**Jurisdiction.** Broadly speaking, the authority of a court to hear and resolve a case before it. *See also* Emergency jurisdiction; In rem jurisdiction; Personal jurisdiction; Subject matter jurisdiction.

**Lack of capacity.** Lack of ability of a party to enter into legally enforceable agreements.

**Last resort jurisdiction.** A relatively insignificant jurisdictional ground that enables a state to assert jurisdiction over a custody dispute when no other state has or is willing to assume jurisdiction, and it is in the best interest of the child for the state to do so.

**Legal custody.** As distinct from physical custody, legal custody confers on a parent the authority to make major decisions related to his or her child's life; legal custody can be sole or joint.

**Legal separation.** A judicial decree permitting parties to live apart, usually for cause, without dissolving the legal relationship of husband and wife. *See also* Separate maintenance.

**Legitimate.** In contrast to the term "illegitimate," refers to a child born to married parents.

**Legitimation.** The process of altering the status of a child born to unmarried parents so that he or she is the legal equivalent of a child born to married parents.

**Lien.** A nonpossessory interest in the property of another that operates as a cloud against title.

**Living separate and apart.** A no-fault divorce ground that requires the parties to have lived apart for a statutory period of time, with the separation serving as proof of marital breakdown.

**Long-arm statute.** A statute that spells out when a state may assert personal jurisdiction over a nonresident.

**Lump-sum support.** A support award of a specific amount of money, usually payable in a single installment.

**Mandatory reporter.** In contrast to a permissive reporter, a person, usually a professional who comes into contact with children in the course of his or her work, who is legally obligated to report suspected cases of child abuse or neglect pursuant to an abuse reporting law.

**Marital breakdown.** *See* Irreconcilable differences.

**Marital fault.** Acts of wrongdoing by one spouse toward the other that serve as the basis of a fault divorce. *See* Adultery; Cruelty; Desertion.

**Marital property.** As distinct from separate property, assets acquired during the marriage as a result of marital efforts or funds, which are subject to division at divorce.

**Marital unity.** A common law principle espousing that upon marriage a husband and wife become one, resulting in the suspension of the wife's legal identity.

**Marriage restriction laws.** Laws that prevent certain people, such as close relatives, from marrying each other.

**Married Women's Property Acts.** The series of statutory reforms that gradually improved the legal status of married women, principally through extending rights of property ownership and control that had been denied at common law.

**Mediation.** A nonadversarial approach to dispute resolution in which a neutral third party—the mediator—helps parties reach a mutually satisfactory resolution to a conflict; an increasingly popular option in divorce cases.

**Merger.** Going beyond incorporation, merger refers to when a separation agreement, once approved by the court, loses its separate identity and thereafter exists only as part of the court's judgment; this contrasts with the concept of survival.

**Minimum contacts.** A jurisdictional concept enabling a state to assert personal jurisdiction over a nonresident when he or she has a sufficiently developed relationship with that state.

**Modification.** The alteration of an existing order based on a change in circumstances.

**Modification jurisdiction.** The authority of a court to modify a custody or support decree.

**Motion.** In general, a request made to a court for some kind of relief during the pendency of an action.

**Motion for a new trial.** A post-trial request that the court set aside the judgment and order a new trial because of prejudicial errors during the trial.

**Motion for relief from judgment.** A post-trial request that the court vacate or modify its judgment, usually because of an error, unfairness, or newly discovered evidence.

**Motion to compel.** A request to the court that it order the other side to comply with a discovery request.

**Motion to dismiss.** A request to the court that it dismiss the plaintiff's case for lack of jurisdiction, improper service, or the plaintiff's failure to state a valid claim entitling him or her to relief.

**Mutual orders of protection.** Orders of protection granted by some courts to both parties where only one party has sought court intervention.

**Neglect.** Usually a parent's willful failure to provide for a child's basic needs; may also be to the extreme withdrawal of emotional support and affection (emotional neglect).

**Negotiation.** The process through which attorneys seek to resolve a case outside court; often done at a settlement conference at which the clients are present.

**Nexus approach.** As distinct from the per se approach, this approach requires that parental conduct have a demonstrated detrimental impact on a child before it will be taken into account in a custody determination.

**No-contact order.** A protective order that prohibits someone from having any contact with the party he or she has abused.

**No-fault divorce.** A divorce that is based on the breakdown of the marital relationship rather than on the marital fault of one spouse. *See also* Irreconcilable differences.

**Noncustodial parent.** A parent who has been divested of both legal and physical custody, but is still a legal parent with enforceable rights, such as visitation.

**Open adoption.** An adoption that permits some degree of contact with the biological parent(s).

**Opportunity cost.** The loss of earning potential attributable to a lack of a sustained relationship with the labor force, often due to a spouse's primary investment in the domestic realm.

**Opportunity interest.** The opportunity that the biological link provides to an unmarried father to develop a meaningful relationship with his child.

**Order (QMCSO).** A qualified medical child support order; requires every employer group health plan to provide coverage to the children named by the court or a qualified administrative agency to facilitate coverage of children.

*Parens patriae.* The authority of the state, as a sovereign power, to protect those who cannot protect themselves, most notably children.

**Parent locator service.** A federal or state agency that is responsible for locating absent parents in order to establish or enforce a child support award.

**Parental unfitness.** Parental abuse or neglect that is severe enough to warrant a termination of rights.

**Parenting Plan.** A written agreement in which the parents detail how they intend to care for their children following a divorce.

**Paternal preference.** The common law doctrine that vested fathers with the absolute right to care and custody of their children.

**Paternity disestablishment.** The undoing/revocation of a determination that a man is a child's legal father.

**Pension.** Retirement benefits paid regularly, based on length of service and salary amount.

**Permanency Plan.** A plan which either calls for the return of a child home following removal for abuse or neglect or for the termination of parental rights.

**Permanency hearing.** A hearing to determine if a child who has been removed from the home due to abuse or neglect can safely return home or whether parental rights should be terminated and the child freed for adoption.

**Permanent alimony.** An ongoing support award to a spouse who is unlikely to become economically self-sufficient; the award is subject to modification and is generally terminable upon death of either spouse or remarriage of the recipient.

**Permissive reporter.** In contrast to a mandatory reporter, a person who may report suspected cases of child abuse or neglect to a child protective agency but is not legally obligated to do so.

**Per se approach.** As distinct from the nexus approach, the idea that some behaviors are so inherently harmful that they should be the basis for denying custody to a parent without proof of actual harm.

**Personal jurisdiction.** The authority of a court over the person of a defendant.

**Personal property.** Broadly, all property owned by an individual other than real property; includes both tangible and intangible assets.

**Personal service.** In contrast to constructive service, delivering the summons and complaint by hand to the defendant.

**Petition.** *See* Complaint.

**Physical custody.** As distinct from legal custody, physical custody refers to where a child lives; a parent with physical custody usually maintains a home for the child and is responsible for the child's day-to-day care. Physical custody can be either sole or joint.

**Polygamy.** The situation where an individual (most commonly a man) has multiple spouses at the same time.

**Post-placement social study.** An assessment of an adoption placement done to provide information to the judge who will be deciding if the adoption should be approved.

**Prayer for relief.** *See* Request for relief.

**Pre-adoptive placement.** The specified period of time a child must live with his or her prospective adoptive parents before the adoption can be approved.

**Premarital acquisitions.** Property owned by a spouse prior to marriage.

**Premarital agreement.** A contract entered into by prospective spouses in which they seek to establish their respective rights in the event the marriage fails; most commonly, provisions address spousal support and the allocation of property.

**Presumption of paternity.** The legal assumption that the father of a child born to a married woman is the woman's husband.

**Pretrial conference.** A meeting held by a judge with counsel prior to trial, mainly to streamline issues and determine the possibility of settlement.

**Pretrial statement.** A memorandum prepared by each side in advance of a pretrial conference; a key purpose is the delineation of issues still in contention.

**Primary caretaker.** The parent who has been primarily responsible for the day-today care and nurture of a child. *See also* Psychological parent.

**Primary caretaker presumption.** A legal rule that gives preference to the primary caretaker parent in the event of a custody dispute.

**Private placement adoption.** *See* Independent adoption.

**Procedural fairness.** Fairness of the parties in their treatment of one another in the process of negotiating an agreement, as distinct from fairness in the resulting terms (substantive fairness).

**Professional goodwill.** The reputation of a professional practice in the community that generates future patronage.

**Protective order.** 1. In domestic violence cases, a court order to protect the victim from harm; although civil in nature, violation of these orders is a criminal offense in many states. *See also* No-contact order; Restraining order; Stay-away order; Vacate order. 2. A court order limiting discovery that is unreasonable or oppressive.

**Qualified Domestic Relations Order (QDRO).** A court order that allows the distribution of pension benefits to a non-employee spouse.

**Qualified Medical Child Support Order (QMCSO).** A court order requiring that a child be covered by the noncustodial parent's group health insurance plan.

**Real property.** As distinct from personal property, real property refers to land and that which is growing upon or affixed to it.

**Reasonable efforts.** The effort a child protective agency must make (in most situations) to prevent removal of a child from his or her home, or if the child has been removed, the effort the agency must put toward reunification.

**Recapture.** The recomputation of a support obligor's gross income to include amounts that had been improperly deducted as spousal support payments, and the readjustment of his or her tax obligation.

**Recrimination.** A divorce defense that prevents a divorce from being granted on the basis that both parties are guilty of marital misconduct; may be ameliorated by the doctrine of comparative rectitude.

**Rehabilitative support.** Time-limited support intended to enable a spouse to obtain the education or training necessary to become economically self-sufficient.

**Reimbursement alimony.** A support award intended to reimburse a spouse for contributions to the professional education of the other spouse; in addition to reimbursing the financial contribution, it may also compensate for the loss of future income.

**Relinquishment.** The surrender by a parent of a child to an adoption agency.

**Relocation disputes.** A disagreement arising during or after a divorce in which the custodial parent seeks to move to another state with the children, and the noncustodial parent seeks to prevent the move.

**Request for admissions.** A discovery method in which a party asks the other side to admit to the truth of certain facts or to the authenticity of certain documents; done mainly to simplify matters for trial.

**Request for mental or physical examination.** A discovery method in which a party asks the court to order the other side to submit to a medical or mental evaluation, used when such information is arguably relevant to the outcome of the case.

**Request for production of documents.** A discovery method in which a party can obtain documents from the other side that are needed to prepare the case.

**Request for relief.** The portion of a complaint in which the plaintiff sets out the relief he or she is seeking from the court.

**Restraining order.** A court order directing a perpetrator to refrain from committing further acts of domestic violence against the party seeking protection from abuse; may also protect the children.

**Return of service.** The acknowledgment to the court by the person serving the defendant that service was made; usually includes a notation of how and when the service was made.

**Reunification services.** Services that a child protection agency provides to a family following the removal of a child for the purpose of enabling the child to return home.

**Review and adjustment procedure.** The periodic assessment and potential revision of a child support order by a IV-D agency.

**Revival.** The restoration of certain rights deriving from a prior marriage following the annulment of a subsequent marriage.

**Revocation of consent.** A parent's seeking to take back his or her consent to an adoption.


**Safe Haven.** These laws allow a birth parent, or an agent of the parent, to leave a baby at a safe location, such as a hospital or fire station, without fear of being prosecuted for child abandonment or neglect.

**Sanctions.** The penalties imposed by a court when a party fails to comply with discovery requests.

**Second glance doctrine.** Review by a court of the terms of a premarital agreement to determine whether they are fair as of the time of enforcement.

**Separate maintenance.** Similar to a legal separation, but here the essence of the action is a request for support. *See also* Legal separation.

**Separate property.** As distinct from marital property, property that belongs to the acquiring spouse and is not subject to distribution at divorce. It usually consists of gifts, inheritances, and premarital acquisitions.

**Separation agreement.** A contract between divorcing spouses in which they set out the terms of their agreement relative to all collateral matters, such as custody, support, and the distribution of property.

**Service of process.** Delivery of a summons and complaint to a defendant; provides the defendant with notice of the action and informs him or her that a default judgment may be entered unless an answer is filed within a specified time. *See also* Constructive service; Personal service.

**Service plan.** A plan developed by the child protection agency in cases of substantiated abuse that sets out the services to be provided to the parents to help them care for their children; may also impose certain obligations on the parents.

**Significant connection jurisdiction.** A jurisdictional ground that permits a court to assert jurisdiction over a custody dispute based on the fact that a child and at least one contestant has a meaningful relationship with that state, and relevant evidence is available there; only available under PKPA when no state qualifies as the home state.

**Sole custody.** The vesting of custodial rights in one parent — can apply to legal or physical custody, or both.

**Source of funds rule.** As distinct from the inception of title rule, an approach that ties the time of acquisition of an asset to the contribution of funds and permits the dual characterization of an asset as both marital and separate in proportion to contribution.

**Special equity.** A rule giving a spouse who contributed purchase funds to an asset titled in the name of the other an interest in the asset, which is reachable at divorce; was relevant in jurisdictions that divided property according to title.

**Spousal support.** An allowance paid to one spouse by the other for support pending or after legal separation or divorce. *See also* Alimony pendente lite; Lump-sum support; Permanent alimony; Rehabilitative support; Reimbursement alimony.

**Stalking.** The malicious, willful, and repeated tracking down and following of another person; stalking is often a precursor to acts of serious bodily harm.

**Standing.** A jurisdictional concept requiring a person to have a sufficient stake in the outcome of a controversy in order to maintain a legal action.

**Statute of frauds.** A rule requiring that certain kinds of contracts be in writing in order to be enforceable.

**Stay-away order.** A court order, pursuant to an abuse prevention law, requiring the perpetrator to keep away from the victim's home or from other places where the victim regularly goes (e.g., work).

**Stepparent.** The legal relationship of a new spouse to the children of a prior marriage.

**Subject matter jurisdiction.** The authority of a court to hear a particular kind of case.

**Subpoena.** A writ commanding a witness to appear at a particular time and place to give testimony.

**Subpoena duces tecum.** A writ commanding a witness to produce books, papers, or other items, usually at a deposition or trial.

**Substantive fairness.** Fairness of the actual terms of an agreement, as distinct from procedural fairness.

**Summons.** Issued by the court at the commencement of an action for service on the defendant, informs the defendant of the action and that he or she is required to respond within a certain period of time or risk entry of a default judgment.

**Support worksheet.** A worksheet that is tied to child support guidelines and is used in calculating a support award.

**Survival.** In contrast to a merger, the incorporation of a separation agreement into the divorce judgment but the retention of its significance as an independent agreement.

**Tangible property.** Property with a physical presence, which is capable of being felt and seen.

**Tax refund intercept.** A support enforcement mechanism that allows for the taking of a tax refund to pay off a support arrearage.

**Temporary alimony.** Support awarded during the pendency of the divorce action intended to assist a spouse during this interim period.

**Temporary order.** An order made during the pendency of a legal proceeding; temporary orders are superseded by the judgment.

**Tender years presumption.** The traditional custodial assumption that children of a young age should be raised by their mothers.

**Termination of parental rights.** The permanent severance of the parent-child relationship based on parental unfitness.

**Testamentary capacity.** The legal ability to dispose of one's property at death through the execution of a will.

**Title.** The right of exclusive ownership and control of an asset.

**Title IV-D.** Law that amends the Social Security Act to establish a cooperative federal-state program for the obtaining and enforcement of child support orders.

**Tracing.** The process by which a party seeks to establish the separate identity of an asset owned at the time of divorce so that it is not subject to distribution.

**Transitional support.** *See* Rehabilitative support.

**Transmutation.** The post-acquisition change in the classification of an asset from marital to separate or vice versa. Transmutation can occur through agreement, commingling, the taking of title in joint name, or use.

**Transracial adoption.** Adoption across racial lines.

**Trial notebook.** A binder containing everything needed to present a case in court.

**Unallocated support.** Child and spousal support awards combined in a single support amount without designation.

**Unbundled legal services.** Also referred to as limited task representation. An attorney agrees to provide a client with limited assistance from a menu of options instead of providing the client with comprehensive representation. Typically, rather than entering into a retainer agreement, the client pays for each separate service at the time it is rendered. Unbundled services include the giving of legal advice, coaching on how to handle the case, assistance with drafting pleadings, and representation in court.

**Unconscionability.** When a contract is grossly unfair to one side, usually involves parties with a significant disparity in bargaining power.

**Vacate order.** A court order requiring a perpetrator of domestic violence to move out of the home he or she shares with the party who has been abused; vacate orders do not affect title to property.

**Valuation.** The determination of what an asset is worth, most commonly by ascertaining its fair market value; usually done by an expert.

**Venue.** A geographical concept designating which locale an action is to be filed in.

**Violence Against Women Act (VAWA).** Federal law providing protection to victims of domestic violence, and funding for anti-violence programs.

**Virtual Visitation.** The use of e-mail and the Internet as a way to supplement communication between a child and a noncustodial parent.

**Visitation.** The time that a noncustodial parent spends with his or her child.

**Void.** A marriage that is without any legal effect from its inception; a void marriage does not require a decree of annulment to invalidate it. *See also* Voidable.

**Voidable.** A marriage that is considered valid unless and until it is declared invalid by a decree of annulment. *See also* Void.

**Void as against public policy.** The invalidation of a contract on the basis that it violates deeply held community beliefs.

**Voluntary surrender.** *See* Relinquishment.


**Wage withholding.** An order directing a support obligor's employer to take support payments directly out of that party's paycheck.

**Wrongful adoption.** An action that an adoptive parent can bring against an adoption agency if the agency failed to tell the parents the truth about the child they adopted.

# Index

# Buck

No Marital: $50,000
(cabin)

Cottage worth at marriage: $80,000

Skunk figurines: $10,000 to "My daughter Bambi" - probably non-marital

Bambi's retirement account at Marriage $20,000

Bambi's googlesoft stock 60 shares at ($20) $1200
+ bought 60 more w/ dividends   120 shares x $20
- ($2400)

## At divorce

Cabin = $100,000

Bambi's retirement: $120,000

Googlesoft stock $18,000 total

figurines: $25,000

Bank account: $45,000

# Bambi:

$1200 (20 shares) Googlesoft stock